INTEGRATION
OF THE ARMED FORCES
1940-1965
by Morris J. MacGregor, Jr.

Foreword

The integration of the armed forces was a momentous event in our military and national history; it represented a milestone in the development of the armed forces and the fulfillment of the democratic ideal. The existence of integrated rather than segregated armed forces is an important factor in our military establishment today. The experiences in World War II and the postwar pressures generated by the civil rights movement compelled all the services—Army, Navy, Air Force, and Marine Corps—to reexamine their traditional practices of segregation. While there were differences in the ways that the services moved toward integration, all were subject to the same demands, fears, and prejudices and had the same need to use their resources in a more rational and economical way. All of them reached the same conclusion: traditional attitudes toward minorities must give way to democratic concepts of civil rights.

If the integration of the armed services now seems to have been inevitable in a democratic society, it nevertheless faced opposition that had to be overcome and problems that had to be solved through the combined efforts of political and civil rights leaders and civil and military officials. In many ways the military services were at the cutting edge in the struggle for racial equality. This volume sets forth the successive measures they and the Office of the Secretary of Defense took to meet the challenges of a new era in a critically important area of human relationships, during a period of transition that saw the advance of blacks in the social and economic order as well as in the military. It is fitting that this story should be told in the first volume of a new Defense Studies Series.

The Defense Historical Studies Program was authorized by the then Deputy Secretary of Defense, Cyrus Vance, in April 1965. It is conducted under the auspices of the Defense Historical Studies Group, an *ad hoc* body chaired by the Historian of the Office of the Secretary of Defense and consisting of the senior officials in the historical offices of the services and of the Joint Chiefs of Staff. Volumes produced under its sponsorship will be interservice histories, covering matters of mutual interest to the Army, Navy, Air Force, Marine Corps, and the Joint Chiefs of Staff. The preparation of each volume is entrusted to one of the service historical sections, in this case the Army's Center of Military History. Although the book was written by an Army historian, he was generously given access to the pertinent records of the other services and the Office of the Secretary of Defense, and this initial volume in the Defense Studies Series covers the experiences of all components of the Department of Defense in achieving integration.

Washington, D.C.
14 March 1980

The Author

Morris J. MacGregor, Jr., received the A.B. and M.A. degrees in history from the Catholic University of America. He continued his graduate studies at the Johns Hopkins University and the University of Paris on a Fulbright grant. Before joining the staff of the U.S. Army Center of Military History in 1968 he served for ten years in the Historical Division of the Joint Chiefs of Staff. He has written several studies for military publications including "Armed Forces Integration—Forced or Free?" in *The Military and Society: Proceedings of the Fifth Military Symposium of the U.S. Air Force Academy.* He is the coeditor with Bernard C. Nalty of the thirteen-volume *Blacks in the United States Armed Forces: Basic Documents* and with Ronald Spector of *Voices of History: Interpretations in American Military History.* He is currently working on a sequel to *Integration of the Armed Forces* which will also appear in the Defense Studies Series.

Preface

This book describes the fall of the legal, administrative, and social barriers to the black American's full participation in the military service of his country. It follows the changing status of the black serviceman from the eve of World War II, when he was excluded from many military activities and rigidly segregated in the rest, to that period a quarter of a century later when the Department of Defense extended its protection of his rights and privileges even to the civilian community. To round out the story of open housing for members of the military, I briefly overstep the closing date given in the title.

The work is essentially an administrative history that attempts to measure the influence of several forces, most notably the civil rights movement, the tradition of segregated service, and the changing concept of military efficiency, on the development of racial policies in the armed forces. It is not a history of all minorities in the services. Nor is it an account of how the black American responded to discrimination. A study of racial attitudes, both black and white, in the military services would be a valuable addition to human knowledge, but practically impossible of accomplishment in the absence of sufficient autobiographical accounts, oral history interviews, and detailed sociological measurements. How did the serviceman view his condition, how did he convey his desire for redress, and what was his reaction to social change? Even now the answers to these questions are blurred by time and distorted by emotions engendered by the civil rights revolution. Few citizens, black or white, who witnessed it can claim immunity to the influence of that paramount social phenomenon of our times.

At times I do generalize on the attitudes of both black and white servicemen and the black and white communities at large as well. But I have permitted myself to do so only when these attitudes were clearly pertinent to changes in the services' racial policies and only when the written record supported, or at least did not contradict, the memory of those participants who had been interviewed. In any case this study is largely history written from the top down and is based primarily on the written records left by the administrations of five presidents and by civil rights leaders, service officials, and the press.

Many of the attitudes and expressions voiced by the participants in the story are now out of fashion. The reader must be constantly on guard against viewing the beliefs and statements of many civilian and military officials out of context of the times in which they were expressed. Neither bigotry nor stupidity was the monopoly of some of the people quoted; their statements are important for what they tell us about certain attitudes of our society rather than for what they reveal about any individual. If the methods or attitudes of some of the black spokesmen appear excessively tame to those who have lived through the 1960's, they too should be gauged in the context of the times. If their statements and actions shunned what now seems the more desirable, albeit radical, course, it should be given them that the style they adopted appeared in those days to be the most promising for racial progress.

The words *black* and *Negro* have been used interchangeably in the book, with Negro generally as a noun and black as an adjective. Aware of differing preferences in the black community for usage of these words, the author was interested in comments from early readers of the manuscript. Some of the participants in the story strongly objected to one word or the other. "Do me one favor in return for my help," Lt. Comdr. Dennis D. Nelson said, "never call me a black." Rear Adm. Gerald E. Thomas, on the other hand, suggested that the use of the term Negro might repel readers with much to learn about their recent past. Still others thought that the historian should respect the usage of the various periods covered in the story, a solution that would have left the volume with the term *colored* for most of the earlier chapters and Negro for much of the rest. With rare exception, the term black does not appear in twentieth century military records before the late 1960's. Fashions in words change, and it is only for the time being perhaps that black and Negro symbolize different attitudes. The author has used the words as synonyms and trusts that the reader will accept them as such. Professor John Hope Franklin, Mrs. Sara Jackson of the National Archives, and the historians and officials that constituted the review panel went along with this approach.

The second question of usage concerns the words *integration* and *desegregation*. In recent years many historians have come to distinguish between these like-sounding words. Desegregation they see as a direct action against segregation; that is, it signifies the act of removing legal barriers to the equal treatment of black citizens as guaranteed by the Constitution. The movement toward desegregation, breaking down the nation's Jim Crow system, became increasingly popular in the decade after World War II. Integration, on the other hand, Professor Oscar Handlin maintains, implies several things not yet necessarily accepted in all areas of American society. In one sense it refers to the "leveling of all barriers to association other than those based on ability, taste, and personal preference";[1] in other words, providing equal opportunity. But in another sense integration calls for the random distribution of a minority throughout society. Here, according to Handlin, the emphasis is on racial balance in areas of occupation, education, residency, and the like.

From the beginning the military establishment rightly understood that the breakup of the all-black unit would in a closed society necessarily mean more than mere desegregation. It constantly used the terms integration and equal treatment and opportunity to describe its racial goals. Rarely, if ever, does one find the word desegregation in military files that include much correspondence from the various civil rights organizations. That the military made the right choice, this study seems to demonstrate, for the racial goals of the Defense Department, as they slowly took form over a quarter of a century, fulfilled both of Professor Handlin's definitions of integration.

The mid-1960's saw the end of a long and important era in the racial history of the armed forces. Although the services continued to encounter racial problems, these problems differed radically in several essentials from those of the integration period considered in this volume. Yet there is a continuity to the story of race relations, and one can hope that the story of how an earlier generation struggled so that black men and women might serve their country in freedom inspires those in the services who continue to fight discrimination.

2

This study benefited greatly from the assistance of a large number of persons during its long years of preparation. Stetson Conn, chief historian of the Army, proposed the book as an interservice project. His successor, Maurice Matloff, forced to deal with the complexities of an interservice project, successfully guided the manuscript through to publication. The work was carried out under the general supervision of Robert R. Smith, chief of the General History Branch. He and Robert W. Coakley, deputy chief historian of the Army, were the primary reviewers of the manuscript, and its final form owes much to their advice and attention. The author also profited from the advice of the official review panel, which, under the chairmanship of Alfred Goldberg, historian, Office of the Secretary of Defense, included Martin Blumenson; General J. Lawton Collins (USA Ret.); Lt. Gen. Benjamin O. Davis, Jr. (USAF Ret.); Roy K. Davenport, former Deputy Assistant Secretary of the Army; Stanley L. Falk, chief historian of the Air Force; Vice Adm. E. B. Hooper, Chief of Naval History; Professor Benjamin Quarles; Paul J. Scheips, historian, Center of Military History; Henry I. Shaw, chief historian of the U.S. Marine Corps; Loretto C. Stevens, senior editor of the Center of Military History; Robert J. Watson, chief historian of the Joint Chiefs of Staff; and Adam Yarmolinsky, former assistant to the Secretary of Defense.

Many of the participants in this story generously shared their knowledge with me and kindly reviewed my efforts. My footnotes acknowledge my debt to them. Nevertheless, two are singled out here for special mention. James C. Evans, former counselor to the Secretary of Defense for racial affairs, has been an endless source of information on race relations in the military. If I sometimes disagreed with his interpretations and assessments, I never doubted his total dedication to the cause of the black serviceman. I owe a similar debt to Lt. Comdr. Dennis D. Nelson (USN Ret.) for sharing his intimate understanding of race relations in the Navy. A resourceful man with a sure social touch, he must have been one hell of a sailor.

I want to note the special contribution of several historians. Martin Blumenson was first assigned to this project, and before leaving the Center of Military History he assembled research material that proved most helpful. My former colleague John Bernard Corr prepared a study on the National Guard upon which my account of the guard is based. In addition, he patiently reviewed many pages of the draft manuscript. His keen insights and sensitive understanding were invaluable to me. Professors Jack D. Foner and Marie Carolyn Klinkhammer provided particularly helpful suggestions in conjunction with their reviews of the manuscript. Samuel B. Warner, who before his untimely death was a historian in the Joint Chiefs of Staff as well as a colleague of Lee Nichols on some of that reporter's civil rights investigations, also contributed generously of his talents and lent his support in the early days of my work. Finally, I am grateful for the advice of my colleague Ronald H. Spector at several key points in the preparation of this history.

I have received much help from archivists and librarians, especially the resourceful William H. Cunliffe and Lois Aldridge (now retired) of the National Archives and Dean C. Allard of the Naval Historical Center. Although the fruits of their scholarship appear often in my footnotes, three fellow researchers in the field deserve special mention: Maj. Alan M. Osur and Lt. Col. Alan L. Gropman of the U.S. Air Force and Ralph W. Donnelly, former member of the U.S. Marine Corps Historical Center. I have benefited from our exchange of ideas and have had the advantage of their reviews of the manuscript.

I am especially grateful for the generous assistance of my editors, Loretto C. Stevens and Barbara H. Gilbert. They have been both friends and teachers. In the same vein, I wish to thank John Elsberg for his editorial counsel. I also appreciate the help given by William G. Bell in the selection of the illustrations, including the loan of two rare items from his personal collection, and Arthur S. Hardyman for preparing the pictures for publication. I would like to thank Mary Lee Treadway and Wyvetra B. Yeldell for preparing the manuscript for panel review and Terrence J. Gough for his helpful pre-publication review.

Finally, while no friend or relative was spared in the long years I worked on this book, three colleagues especially bore with me through days of doubts and frustrations and shared my small triumphs: Alfred M. Beck, Ernest F. Fisher, Jr., and Paul J. Scheips. I also want particularly to thank Col. James W. Dunn. I only hope that some of their good sense and sunny optimism show through these pages.

Washington, D.C.
14 March 1980

INTEGRATION OF THE ARMED FORCES 1940-1965
CHAPTER 1

3

Introduction

In the quarter century that followed American entry into World War II, the nation's armed forces moved from the reluctant inclusion of a few segregated Negroes to their routine acceptance in a racially integrated military establishment. Nor was this change confined to military installations. By the time it was over, the armed forces had redefined their traditional obligation for the welfare of their members to include a promise of equal treatment for black servicemen wherever they might be. In the name of equality of treatment and opportunity, the Department of Defense began to challenge racial injustices deeply rooted in American society.

For all its sweeping implications, equality in the armed forces obviously had its pragmatic aspects. In one sense it was a practical answer to pressing political problems that had plagued several national administrations. In another, it was the services' expression of those liberalizing tendencies that were permeating American society during the era of civil rights activism. But to a considerable extent the policy of racial equality that evolved in this quarter century was also a response to the need for military efficiency. So easy did it become to demonstrate the connection between inefficiency and discrimination that, even when other reasons existed, military efficiency was the one most often evoked by defense officials to justify a change in racial policy.

The Armed Forces Before 1940

Progress toward equal treatment and opportunity in the armed forces was an uneven process, the result of sporadic and sometimes conflicting pressures derived from such constants in American society as prejudice and idealism and spurred by a chronic shortage of military manpower. In his pioneering study of race relations, Gunnar Myrdal observes that ideals have always played a dominant role in the social dynamics of America.[1-1] By extension, the ideals that helped involve the nation in many of its wars also helped produce important changes in the treatment of Negroes by the armed forces. The democratic spirit embodied in the Declaration of Independence, for example, opened the Continental Army to many Negroes, holding out to them the promise of eventual freedom.[1-2]

Yet the fact that the British themselves were taking large numbers of Negroes into their ranks proved more important than revolutionary idealism in creating a place for Negroes in the American forces. Above all, the participation of both slaves and freedmen in the Continental Army and the Navy was a pragmatic response to a pressing need for fighting men and laborers. Despite the fear of slave insurrection shared by many colonists, some 5,000 Negroes, the majority from New England, served with the American forces in the Revolution, often in integrated units, some as artillerymen and musicians, the majority as infantrymen or as unarmed pioneers detailed to repair roads and bridges.

Again, General Jackson's need for manpower at New Orleans explains the presence of the Louisiana Free Men of Color in the last great battle of the War of 1812. In the Civil War the practical needs of the Union Army overcame the Lincoln administration's fear of alienating the border states. When the call for volunteers failed to produce the necessary men, Negroes were recruited, generally as laborers at first but later for combat. In all, 186,000 Negroes served in the Union Army. In addition to those in the sixteen segregated combat regiments and the labor units, thousands also served unofficially as laborers, teamsters, and cooks. Some 30,000 Negroes served in the Navy, about 25 percent of its total Civil War strength.

The influence of the idealism fostered by the abolitionist crusade should not be overlooked. It made itself felt during the early months of the war in the demands of Radical Republicans and some Union generals for black enrollment, and it brought about the postwar establishment of black units in the Regular Army. In 1866 Congress authorized the creation of permanent, all-black units, which in 1869 were designated the 9th and 10th Cavalry and the 24th and 25th Infantry.

CREWMEN OF THE USS MIAMI DURING THE CIVIL WAR

Military needs and idealistic impulses were not enough to guarantee uninterrupted racial progress; in fact, the status of black servicemen tended to reflect the changing patterns in American race relations. During most of the nineteenth century, for example, Negroes served in an integrated U.S. Navy, in the latter half of the century averaging between 20 and 30 percent of the enlisted strength.[1-3] But the employment of Negroes in the Navy was abruptly curtailed after 1900. Paralleling the rise of Jim Crow and legalized segregation in much of America was the cutback in the number of black sailors, who by 1909 were mostly in the galley and the engine room. In contrast to their high percentage of the ranks in the Civil War and Spanish-American War, only 6,750 black sailors, including twenty-four women reservists (yeomanettes), served in World War I; they constituted 1.2 percent of the Navy's total enlistment.[1-4] Their service was limited chiefly to mess duty and coal passing, the latter becoming increasingly rare as the fleet changed from coal to oil.

4

When postwar enlistment was resumed in 1923, the Navy recruited Filipino stewards instead of Negroes, although a decade later it reopened the branch to black enlistment. Negroes quickly took advantage of this limited opportunity, their numbers rising from 441 in 1932 to 4,007 in June 1940, when they constituted 2.3 percent of the Navy's 170,000 total.[1-5]Curiously enough, because black reenlistment in combat or technical specialties had never been barred, a few black gunner's mates, torpedomen, machinist mates, and the like continued to serve in the 1930's.

Although the Army's racial policy differed from the Navy's, the resulting limited, separate service for Negroes proved similar. The laws of 1866 and 1869 that guaranteed the existence of four black Regular Army regiments also institutionalized segregation, granting federal recognition to a system racially separate and theoretically equal in treatment and opportunity a generation before the Supreme Court sanctioned such a distinction in *Plessy* v. *Ferguson*.[1-6] So important to many in the black community was this guaranteed existence of the four regiments that had served with distinction against the frontier Indians that few complained about segregation. In fact, as historian Jack Foner has pointed out, black leaders sometimes interpreted demands for integration as attempts to eliminate black soldiers altogether.[1-7]

The Spanish-American War marked a break with the post-Civil War tradition of limited recruitment. Besides the 3,339 black regulars, approximately 10,000 black volunteers served in the Army during the conflict. World War I was another exception, for Negroes made up nearly 11 percent of the Army's total strength, some 404,000 officers and men.[1-8] The acceptance of Negroes during wartime stemmed from the Army's pressing need for additional manpower. Yet it was no means certain in the early months of World War I that this need for men would prevail over the reluctance of many leaders to arm large groups of Negroes. Still remembered were the 1906 Brownsville affair, in which men of the 25th Infantry had fired on Texan civilians, and the August 1917 riot involving members of the 24th Infantry at Houston, Texas.[1-9] Ironically, those idealistic impulses that had operated in earlier wars were operating again in this most Jim Crow of administrations.[1-10] Woodrow Wilson's promise to make the world safe for democracy was forcing his administration to admit Negroes to the Army. Although it carefully maintained racially separate draft calls, the National Army conscripted some 368,000 Negroes, 13.08 percent of all those drafted in World War I.[1-11]

Black assignments reflected the opinion, expressed repeatedly in Army staff studies throughout the war, that when properly led by whites, blacks could perform reasonably well in segregated units. Once again Negroes were called on to perform a number of vital though unskilled jobs, such as construction work, most notably in sixteen specially formed pioneer infantry regiments. But they also served as frontline combat troops in the all-black 92d and 93d Infantry Divisions, the latter serving with distinction among the French forces.

Established by law and tradition and reinforced by the Army staff's conviction that black troops had not performed well in combat, segregation survived to flourish in the postwar era.[1-12] The familiar practice of maintaining a few black units was resumed in the Regular Army, with the added restriction that Negroes were totally excluded from the Air Corps. The postwar manpower retrenchments common to all Regular Army units further reduced the size of the remaining black units. By June 1940 the number of Negroes on active duty stood at approximately 4,000 men, 1.5 percent of the Army's total, about the same proportion as Negroes in the Navy.[1-13]

Civil Rights and the Law in 1940

The same constants in American society that helped decide the status of black servicemen in the nineteenth century remained influential between the world wars, but with a significant change.[1-14] Where once the advancing fortunes of Negroes in the services depended almost exclusively on the good will of white progressives, their welfare now became the concern of a new generation of black leaders and emerging civil rights organizations. Skilled journalists in the black press and counselors and lobbyists presenting such groups as the National Association for the Advancement of Colored People (NAACP), the National Urban League, and the National Negro Congress took the lead in the fight for racial justice in the United States. They represented a black community that for the most part lacked the cohesion, political awareness, and economic strength which would characterize it in the decades to come. Nevertheless, Negroes had already become a recognizable political force in some parts of the country. Both the New Deal politicians and their opponents openly courted the black vote in the 1940 presidential election.

These politicians realized that the United States was beginning to outgrow its old racial relationships over which Jim Crow had reigned, either by law or custom, for more than fifty years. In large areas of the country where lynchings and beatings were commonplace, white supremacy had existed as a literal fact of life and death.[1-15] More insidious than the Jim Crow laws were the economic deprivation and dearth of educational opportunity associated with racial discrimination. Traditionally the last hired, first fired, Negroes suffered all the handicaps that came from unemployment and poor jobs, a condition further aggravated by the Great Depression. The "separate but equal" educational system dictated by law and the realities of black life in both urban and rural areas, north and south, had proved anything but equal and thus closed to Negroes a traditional avenue to advancement in American society.

In these circumstances, the economic and humanitarian programs of the New Deal had a special appeal for black America. Encouraged by these programs and heartened by Eleanor Roosevelt's public support of civil rights, black voters defected from their traditional allegiance to the Republican Party in overwhelming numbers. But the civil rights leaders were already aware, if the average black citizen was not, that despite having made some considerable improvements Franklin Roosevelt never, in one biographer's words, "sufficiently challenged Southern traditions of white supremacy to create problems for himself."[1-16] Negroes, in short, might benefit materially from the New Deal, but they would have to look elsewhere for advancement of their civil rights.

Men like Walter F. White of the NAACP and the National Urban League's T. Arnold Hill sought to use World War II to expand opportunities for the black American. From the start they tried to translate the idealistic sentiment for democracy stimulated by the war and expressed in the Atlantic Charter into widespread support for civil rights in the United States. At the same time, in sharp contrast to many of their World War I predecessors, they placed a price on black support for the war effort: no longer could the White House expect this sizable minority to submit to injustice and yet close ranks with other Americans to defeat a common enemy. It was readily apparent to the Negro, if not to his white supporter or his enemy, that winning equality at home was just as important as advancing the cause of freedom abroad. As George S. Schuyler, a widely quoted black columnist, put it: "If nothing more comes out of this emergency than the widespread understanding among white leaders that the Negro's loyalty is conditional, we shall not have suffered in vain."[1-17] The NAACP spelled out the challenge even more clearly in its monthly publication, *The Crisis*, which declared itself "sorry for brutality, blood, and death among the peoples of Europe, just as we were sorry for China and Ethiopia. But the hysterical cries of the preachers of democracy for Europe leave us cold. We want democracy in Alabama, Arkansas, in Mississippi and Michigan, in the District of Columbia—in the *Senate of the United States*."[1-18]

This sentiment crystallized in the black press's Double V campaign, a call for simultaneous victories over Jim Crow at home and fascism abroad. Nor was the Double V campaign limited to a small group of civil rights spokesmen; rather, it reflected a new mood that, as Myrdal pointed out, was permeating all classes of black society.[1-19] The quickening of the black masses in the cause of equal treatment and opportunity in the pre-World War II period and the willingness of Negroes to adopt a more militant course to achieve this end might well mark the beginning of the modern civil rights movement.

INTEGRATION IN THE ARMY OF 1888.
The Army Band at Fort Duchesne, Utah, composed of soldiers from the black 9th Cavalry and the white 21st Infantry.

Historian Lee Finkle has suggested that the militancy advocated by most of the civil rights leaders in the World War II era was merely a rhetorical device; that for the most part they sought to avoid violence over segregation, concentrating as before on traditional methods of protest.[1-20] This reliance on traditional methods was apparent when the leaders tried to focus the new sentiment among Negroes on two war-related goals: equality of treatment in the armed forces and equality of job opportunity in the expanding defense industries. In 1938 the Pittsburgh *Courier*, the largest and one of the most influential of the nation's black papers, called upon the President to open the services to Negroes and organized the Committee for Negro Participation in the National Defense Program. These moves led to an extensive lobbying effort that in time spread to many other newspapers and local civil rights groups. The black press and its satellites also attracted the support of several national organizations that were promoting preparedness for war, and these groups, in turn, began to demand equal treatment and opportunity in the armed forces.[1-21]

The government began to respond to these pressures before the United States entered World War II. At the urging of the White House the Army announced plans for the mobilization of Negroes, and Congress amended several mobilization measures to define and increase the military training opportunities for Negroes.[1-22] The most important of these legislative amendments in terms of influence on future race relations in the United States were made to the

6

Selective Service Act of 1940. The matter of race played only a small part in the debate on this highly controversial legislation, but during congressional hearings on the bill black spokesmen testified on discrimination against Negroes in the services.[1-23] These witnesses concluded that if the draft law did not provide specific guarantees against it, discrimination would prevail.

GUNNER'S GANG ON THE USS MAINE.

A majority in both houses of Congress seemed to agree. During floor debate on the Selective Service Act, Senator Robert F. Wagner of New York proposed an amendment to guarantee to Negroes and other racial minorities the privilege of voluntary enlistment in the armed forces. He sought in this fashion to correct evils described some ten days earlier by Rayford W. Logan, chairman of the Committee for Negro Participation in the National Defense, in testimony before the House Committee on Military Affairs. The Wagner proposal triggered critical comments and questions. Senators John H. Overton and Allen J. Ellender of Louisiana viewed the Wagner amendment as a step toward "mixed" units. Overton, Ellender, and Senator Lister Hill of Alabama proposed that the matter should be "left to the Army." Hill also attacked the amendment because it would allow the enlistment of Japanese-Americans, some of whom he claimed were not loyal to the United States.[1-24]

GENERAL PERSHING, AEF COMMANDER, INSPECTS TROOPS
of the 802d (Colored) Pioneer Regiment in France, 1918.

No filibuster was attempted, and the Wagner amendment passed the Senate easily, 53 to 21. It provided

that any person between the ages of eighteen and thirty-five regardless of race or color shall be afforded an opportunity voluntarily to enlist and be inducted into the land and naval forces (including aviation units) of the United States for the training and service prescribed in subsection (b), if he is acceptable to the land or naval forces for such training and service.[1-25]

The Wagner amendment was aimed at *volunteers* for military service. Congressman Hamilton Fish, also of New York, later introduced a similar measure in the House aimed at *draftees*. The Fish amendment passed the House by a margin of 121 to 99 and emerged intact from the House-Senate conference. The law finally read that in the selection and training of men and execution of the law "there shall be no discrimination against any person on account of race or color."[1-26]

HEROES OF THE 369TH INFANTRY.
Winners of the Croix de Guerre arrive in New York Harbor, February 1919.

The Fish amendment had little immediate impact upon the services' racial patterns. As long as official policy permitted separate draft calls for blacks and whites and the officially held definition of discrimination neatly excluded segregation—and both went unchallenged in the courts—segregation would remain entrenched in the armed forces. Indeed, the rigidly segregated services, their ranks swollen by the draft, were a particular frustration to the civil rights forces because they were introducing some black citizens to racial discrimination more pervasive than any they had ever endured in civilian life. Moreover, as the services continued to open bases throughout the country, they actually spread federally sponsored segregation into areas where it had never before existed with the force of law. In the long run, however, the 1940 draft law and subsequent draft legislation had a strong influence on the armed forces' racial policies. They created a climate in which progress could be made toward integration within the services. Although not apparent in 1940, the pressure of a draft-induced flood of black conscripts was to be a principal factor in the separate decisions of the Army, Navy, and Marine Corps to integrate their units.

To Segregate Is To Discriminate

As with all the administration's prewar efforts to increase opportunities for Negroes in the armed forces, the Selective Service Act failed to excite black enthusiasm because it missed the point of black demands. Guarantees of black participation were no longer enough. By 1940 most responsible black leaders shared the goal of an integrated armed forces as a step toward full participation in the benefits and responsibilities of American citizenship.

The White House may well have thought that Walter White of the NAACP singlehandedly organized the demand for integration in 1939, but he was merely applying a concept of race relations that had been evolving since World War I. In the face of ever-worsening discrimination, White's generation of civil rights advocates had rejected the idea of the preeminent black leader Booker T. Washington that hope for the future lay in the development of a separate and strong black community. Instead, they gradually came to accept the argument of one of the founders of the National Association for the Advancement of Colored People,

7

William E. B. DuBois, that progress was possible only when Negroes abandoned their segregated community to work toward a society open to both black and white. By the end of the 1930's this concept had produced a fundamental change in civil rights tactics and created the new mood of assertiveness that Myrdal found in the black community. The work of White and others marked the beginning of a systematic attack against Jim Crow. As the most obvious practitioner of Jim Crow in the federal government, the services were the logical target for the first battle in a conflict that would last some thirty years.

This evolution in black attitudes was clearly demonstrated in correspondence in the 1930's between officials of the NAACP and the Roosevelt administration over equal treatment in the armed forces. The discussion began in 1934 with a series of exchanges between Chief of Staff Douglas MacArthur and NAACP Counsel Charles H. Houston and continued through the correspondence between White and the administration in 1937. The NAACP representatives rejected MacArthur's defense of Army policy and held out for a quota guaranteeing that Negroes would form at least 10 percent of the nation's military strength. Their emphasis throughout was on numbers; during these first exchanges, at least, they fought against disbandment of the existing black regiments and argued for similar units throughout the service.[1-27]

Yet the idea of integration was already strongly implied in Houston's 1934 call for "a more united nation of free citizens,"[1-28] and in February 1937 the organization emphasized the idea in an editorial in *The Crisis*, asking why black and white men could not fight side by side as they had in the Continental Army.[1-29] And when the Army informed the NAACP in September 1939 that more black units were projected for mobilization, White found this solution unsatisfactory because the proposed units would be segregated.[1-30] If democracy was to be defended, he told the President, discrimination must be eliminated from the armed forces. To this end, the NAACP urged Roosevelt to appoint a commission of black and white citizens to investigate discrimination in the Army and Navy and to recommend the removal of racial barriers.[1-31]

The White House ignored these demands, and on 17 October the secretary to the President, Col. Edwin M. Watson, referred White to a War Department report outlining the new black units being created under presidential authorization. But the NAACP leaders were not to be diverted from the main chance. Thurgood Marshall, then the head of the organization's legal department, recommended that White tell the President "that the NAACP is opposed to the separate units existing in the armed forces at the present time."[1-32]

When his associates failed to agree on a reply to the administration, White decided on a face-to-face meeting with the President.[1-33] Roosevelt agreed to confer with White, Hill of the Urban League, and A. Philip Randolph, head of the Brotherhood of Sleeping Car Porters, the session finally taking place on 27 September 1940. At that time the civil rights officials outlined for the President and his defense assistants what they called the "important phases of the integration of the Negro into military aspects of the national defense program." Central to their argument was the view that the Army and Navy should accept men without regard to race. According to White, the President had apparently never considered the use of integrated units, but after some discussion he seemed to accept the suggestion that the Army could assign black regiments or batteries alongside white units and from there "the Army could 'back into' the formation of units without segregation."[1-34]

Nothing came of these suggestions. Although the policy announced by the White House subsequent to the meeting contained concessions regarding the employment and distribution of Negroes in the services, it did not provide for integrated units. The wording of the press release on the conference implied, moreover, that the administration's entire program had been approved by White and the others. To have their names associated with any endorsement of segregation was particularly infuriating to these civil rights leaders, who immediately protested to the President.[1-35] The White House later publicly absolved the leaders of any such endorsement, and Press Secretary Early was forced to retract the "damaging impression" that the leaders had in any way endorsed segregation. The President later assured White, Randolph, and Hill that further policy changes would be made to insure fair treatment for Negroes.[1-36]

Presidential promises notwithstanding, the NAACP set out to make integration of the services a matter of overriding interest to the black community during the war. The organization encountered opposition at first when some black leaders were willing to accept segregated units as the price for obtaining the formation of more all-black divisions. The NAACP stood firm, however, and demanded at its annual convention in 1941 an immediate end to segregation.

In a related move symbolizing the growing unity behind the campaign to integrate the military, the leaders of the March on Washington Movement, a group of black activists under A. Philip Randolph, specifically demanded the end of segregation in the Army and Navy. The movement was the first since the days of Marcus Garvey to involve the black masses; in fact

8

Negroes from every social and economic class rallied behind Randolph, ready to demonstrate for equal treatment and opportunity. Although some black papers objected to the movement's militancy, the major civil rights organization showed no such hesitancy. Roy Wilkins, a leader of the NAACP, later claimed that Randolph could supply only about 9,000 potential demonstrators and that the NAACP had provided the bulk of the movement's participants.[1-37]

Although Randolph was primarily interested in fair employment practices, the NAACP had been concerned with the status of black servicemen since World War I. Reflecting the degree of NAACP support, march organizers included a discussion of segregation in the services when they talked with President Roosevelt in June 1941. Randolph and the others proposed ways to abolish the separate racial units in each service, charging that integration was being frustrated by prejudiced senior military officials.[1-38]

The President's meeting with the march leaders won the administration a reprieve from the threat of a mass civil rights demonstration in the nation's capital, but at the price of promising substantial reform in minority hiring for defense industries and the creation of a federal body, the Fair Employment Practices Committee, to coordinate the reform. While it prompted no similar reform in the racial policies of the armed forces, the March on Washington Movement was nevertheless a significant milestone in the services' racial history.[1-39]It signaled the beginning of a popularly based campaign against segregation in the armed forces in which all the major civil rights organizations, their allies in Congress and the press, and many in the black community would hammer away on a single theme: segregation is unacceptable in a democratic society and hypocritical during a war fought in defense of the four freedoms.

CHAPTER 2

World War II: The Army

Civil rights leaders adopted the "Double V" slogan as their rallying cry during World War II. Demanding victory against fascism abroad and discrimination at home, they exhorted black citizens to support the war effort and to fight for equal treatment and opportunity for Negroes everywhere. Although segregation was their main target, their campaign was directed against all forms of discrimination, especially in the armed forces. They flooded the services with appeals for a redress of black grievances and levied similar demands on the White House, Congress, and the courts.

Black leaders concentrated on the services because they were public institutions, their officials sworn to uphold the Constitution. The leaders understood, too, that disciplinary powers peculiar to the services enabled them to make changes that might not be possible for other organizations; the armed forces could command where others could only persuade. The Army bore the brunt of this attention, but not because its policies were so benighted. In 1941 the Army was a fairly progressive organization, and few institutions in America could match its record. Rather, the civil rights leaders concentrated on the Army because the draft law had made it the nation's largest employer of minority groups.

For its part, the Army resisted the demands, its spokesmen contending that the service's enormous size and power should not be used for social experiment, especially during a war. Further justifying their position, Army officials pointed out that their service had to avoid conflict with prevailing social attitudes, particularly when such attitudes were jealously guarded by Congress. In this period of continuous demand and response, the Army developed a racial policy that remained in effect throughout the war with only superficial modifications sporadically adopted to meet changing conditions.

A War Policy: Reaffirming Segregation

The experience of World War I cast a shadow over the formation of the Army's racial policy in World War II.[2-1] The chief architects of the new policy, and many of its opponents, were veterans of the first war and reflected in their judgments the passions and prejudices of that era.[2-2] Civil rights activists were determined to eliminate the segregationist practices of the 1917 mobilization and to win a fair representation for Negroes in the Army. The traditionalists of the Army staff, on the other hand, were determined to resist any radical change in policy. Basing their arguments on their evaluation of the performance of the 92d Division and some other black units in World War I, they had made, but not publicized, mobilization plans that recognized the Army's obligation to employ black soldiers yet rigidly maintained the segregationist policy of World War I.[2-3] These plans increased the number of types of black units to be formed and even provided for a wide distribution of the units among all the arms and services except the Army Air Forces and Signal Corps, but they did not explain how the skilled Negro, whose numbers had greatly increased since World War I, could be efficiently used within the limitations of black units. In the name of military efficiency the Army staff had, in effect, devised a social rather than a military policy for the employment of black troops.

9

The White House tried to adjust the conflicting demands of the civil rights leaders and the Army traditionalists. Eager to placate and willing to compromise, President Franklin D. Roosevelt sought an accommodation by directing the War Department to provide jobs for Negroes in all parts of the Army. The controversy over integration soon became more public, the opponents less reconcilable; in the weeks following the President's meeting with black representatives on 27 September 1940 the Army countered black demands for integration with a statement released by the White House on 9 October. To provide "a fair and equitable basis" for the use of Negroes in its expansion program, the Army planned to accept Negroes in numbers approximate to their proportion in the national population, about 10 percent. Black officers and enlisted men were to serve, as was then customary, only in black units that were to be formed in each major branch, both combatant and noncombatant, including air units to be created as soon as pilots, mechanics, and technical specialists were trained. There would be no racial intermingling in regimental organizations because the practice of separating white and black troops had, the Army staff said, proved satisfactory over a long period of time. To change would destroy morale and impair preparations for national defense. Since black units in the Army were already "going concerns, accustomed through many years to the present system" of segregation, "no experiments should be tried ... at this critical time."[2-4]

The President's "OK, F.D.R." on the War Department statement transformed what had been a routine prewar mobilization plan into a racial policy that would remain in effect throughout the war. In fact, quickly elevated in importance by War Department spokesmen who made constant reference to the "Presidential Directive," the statement would be used by some Army officials as a presidential sanction for introducing segregation in new situations, as, for example, in the pilot training of black officers in the Army Air Corps. Just as quickly, the civil rights leaders, who had expected more from the tone of the President's own comments and more also from the egalitarian implications of the new draft law, bitterly attacked the Army's policy.

Black criticism came at an awkward moment for President Roosevelt, who was entering a heated campaign for an unprecedented third term and whose New Deal coalition included the urban black vote. His opponent, the articulate Wendell L. Willkie, was an unabashed champion of civil rights and was reportedly attracting a wide following among black voters. In the weeks preceding the election the President tried to soften the effect of the Army's announcement. He promoted Col. Benjamin O. Davis, Sr., to brigadier general, thereby making Davis the first Negro to hold this rank in the Regular Army. He appointed the commander of reserve officers' training at Howard University, Col. Campbell C. Johnson, Special Aide to the Director of Selective Service. And, finally, he named Judge William H. Hastie, dean of the Howard University Law School, Civilian Aide to the Secretary of War.

A successful lawyer, Judge Hastie entered upon his new assignment with several handicaps. Because of his long association with black causes, some civil rights organizations assumed that Hastie would be their man in Washington and regarded his duties as an extension of their crusade against discrimination. Hastie's War Department superiors, on the other hand, assumed that his was a public relations job and expected him to handle all complaints and mobilization problems as had his World War I predecessor, Emmett J. Scott. Both assumptions proved false. Hastie was evidently determined to break the racial logjam in the War Department, yet unlike many civil rights advocates he seemed willing to pay the price of slow progress to obtain lasting improvement. According to those who knew him, Hastie was confident that he could demonstrate to War Department officials that the Army's racial policies were both inefficient and unpatriotic.[2-5]

Judge Hastie spent his first ten months in office observing what was happening to the Negro in the Army. He did not like what he saw. To him, separating black soldiers from white soldiers was a fundamental error. First, the effect on black morale was devastating. "Beneath the surface," he wrote, "is widespread discontent. Most white persons are unable to appreciate the rancor and bitterness which the Negro, as a matter of self-preservation, has learned to hide beneath a smile, a joke, or merely an impassive face." The inherent paradox of trying to inculcate pride, dignity, and aggressiveness in a black soldier while inflicting on him the segregationist's concept of the Negro's place in society created in him an insupportable tension. Second, segregation wasted black manpower, a valuable military asset. It was impossible, Hastie charged, to employ skilled Negroes at maximum efficiency within the traditionally narrow limitations of black units. Third, to insist on an inflexible separation of white and black soldiers was "the most dramatic evidence of hypocrisy" in America's professed concern for preserving democracy.

Although he appreciated the impossibility of making drastic changes overnight, Judge Hastie was disturbed because he found "no apparent disposition to make a beginning or a trial of any different plan." He looked for some form of progressive integration by which qualified

10

Negroes could be classified and assigned, not by race, but as individuals, according to their capacities and abilities.[2-6]

JUDGE HASTIE

Judge Hastie gained little support from the Secretary of War, Henry L. Stimson, or the Chief of Staff, General George C. Marshall, when he called for progressive integration. Both considered the Army's segregated units to be in accord with prevailing public sentiment against mixing the races in the intimate association of military life. More to the point, both Stimson and Marshall were sensitive to military tradition, and segregated units had been a part of the Army since 1863. Stimson embraced segregation readily. While conveying to the President that he was "sensitive to the individual tragedy which went with it to the colored man himself," he nevertheless urged Roosevelt not to place "too much responsibility on a race which was not showing initiative in battle."[2-7] Stimson's attitude was not unusual for the times. He professed to believe in civil rights for every citizen, but he opposed social integration. He never tried to reconcile these seemingly inconsistent views; in fact, he probably did not consider them inconsistent. Stimson blamed what he termed Eleanor Roosevelt's "intrusive and impulsive folly" for some of the criticism visited upon the Army's racial policy, just as he inveighed against the "foolish leaders of the colored race" who were seeking "at bottom social equality," which, he concluded, was out of the question "because of the impossibility of race mixture by marriage."[2-8] Influenced by Under Secretary Robert P. Patterson, Assistant Secretary John J. McCloy, and Truman K. Gibson, Jr., who was Judge Hastie's successor, but most of all impressed by the performance of black soldiers themselves, Stimson belatedly modified his defense of segregation. But throughout the war he adhered to the traditional arguments of the Army's professional staff.

GENERAL MARSHALL AND SECRETARY STIMSON

General Marshall was a powerful advocate of the views of the Army staff. He lived up to the letter of the Army's regulations, consistently supporting measures to eliminate overt discrimination in the wartime Army. At the same time, he rejected the idea that the Army should take the lead in altering the racial mores of the nation. Asked for his views on Hastie's "carefully prepared memo,"[2-9] General Marshall admitted that many of the recommendations were sound but said that Judge Hastie's proposals

would be tantamount to solving a social problem which has perplexed the American people throughout the history of this nation. The Army cannot accomplish such a solution and should not be charged with the undertaking. The settlement of vexing racial problems cannot be permitted to complicate the tremendous task of the War Department and thereby jeopardize discipline and morale.[2-10]

As Chief of Staff, Marshall faced the tremendous task of creating in haste a large Army to deal with the Axis menace. Since for several practical reasons the bulk of that Army would be trained in the south where its conscripts would be subject to southern laws, Marshall saw no alternative but to postpone reform. The War Department, he said, could not ignore the social relationship between blacks and whites, established by custom and habit. Nor could it ignore the fact that the "level of intelligence and occupational skill" of the black population was considerably below that of whites. Though he agreed that the Army would reach maximum strength only if individuals were placed according to their abilities, he concluded that experiments to solve social problems would be "fraught with danger to efficiency, discipline, and morale." In sum, Marshall saw no reason to change the policy approved by the President less than a year before.[2-11]

The Army's leaders and the secretary's civilian aide had reached an impasse on the question of policy even before the country entered the war. And though the use of black troops in World War I was not entirely satisfactory even to its defenders,[2-12] there appeared to be no time now, in view of the larger urgency of winning the war, to plan other approaches, try other solutions, or tamper with an institution that had won victory in the past. Further ordering the thoughts of some senior Army officials was their conviction that wide-scale mixing of the races in the services might, as Under Secretary Patterson phrased it, foment social revolution.[2-13]

These opinions were clearly evident on 8 December 1941, the day the United States entered World War II, when the Army's leaders met with a group of black publishers and editors. Although General Marshall admitted that he was not satisfied with the department's progress in racial matters and promised further changes, the conference concluded with a speech by a representative of The Adjutant General who delivered what many considered the final word on integration during the war.

The Army is made up of individual citizens of the United States who have pronounced views with respect to the Negro just as they have individual ideas with respect to other matters in

11

their daily walk of life. Military orders, fiat, or dicta, will not change their viewpoints. The Army then cannot be made the means of engendering conflict among the mass of people because of a stand with respect to Negroes which is not compatible with the position attained by the Negro in civil life.... The Army is not a sociological laboratory; to be effective it must be organized and trained according to the principles which will insure success. Experiments to meet the wishes and demands of the champions of every race and creed for the solution of their problems are a danger to efficiency, discipline and morale and would result in ultimate defeat.[2-14]

The civil rights advocates refused to concede that the discussion was over. Judge Hastie, along with a sizable segment of the black press, believed that the beginning of a world war was the time to improve military effectiveness by increasing black participation in that war.[2-15] They argued that eliminating segregation was part of the struggle to preserve democracy, the transcendent issue of the war, and they viewed the unvarying pattern of separate black units as consonant with the racial theories of Nazi Germany.[2-16] Their continuing efforts to eliminate segregation and discrimination eventually brought Hastie a sharp reminder from John J. McCloy. "Frankly, I do not think that the basic issues of this war are involved in the question of whether colored troops serve in segregated units or in mixed units and I doubt whether you can convince people of the United States that the basic issues of freedom are involved in such a question." For Negroes, he warned sternly, the basic issue was that if the United States lost the war, the lot of the black community would be far worse off, and some Negroes "do not seem to be vitally concerned about winning the war." What all Negroes ought. to do, he counseled, was to give unstinting support to the war effort in anticipation of benefits certain to come after victory.[2-17]

Thus very early in World War II, even before the United States was actively engaged, the issues surrounding the use of Negroes in the Army were well defined and the lines sharply drawn. Was segregation, a practice in conflict with the democratic aims of the country, also a wasteful use of manpower? How would modifications of policy come—through external pressure or internal reform? Could traditional organizational and social patterns in the military services be changed during a war without disrupting combat readiness?

Segregation and Efficiency

In the years before World War II, Army planners never had to consider segregation in terms of manpower efficiency. Conditioned by the experiences of World War I, when the nation had enjoyed a surplus of untapped manpower even at the height of the war, and aware of the overwhelming manpower surplus of the depression years, the staff formulated its mobilization plans with little regard for the economical use of the nation's black manpower. Its decision to use Negroes in proportion to their percentage of the population was the result of political pressures rather than military necessity. Black combat units were considered a luxury that existed to indulge black demands. When the Army began to mobilize in 1940 it proceeded to honor its pledge, and one year after Pearl Harbor there were 399,454 Negroes in the Army, 7.4 percent of the total and 7.95 percent of all enlisted troops.[2-18]

The effect of segregation on manpower efficiency became apparent only as the Army tried to translate policy into practice. In the face of rising black protest and with direct orders from the White House, the Army had announced that Negroes would be assigned to all arms and branches in the same ratio as whites. Several forces, however, worked against this equitable distribution. During the early months of mobilization the chiefs of those arms and services that had traditionally been all white accepted less than their share of black recruits and thus obliged some organizations, the Quartermaster Corps and the Engineer Corps in particular, to absorb a large percentage of black inductees. The imbalance worsened in 1941. In December of that year Negroes accounted for 5 percent of the Infantry and less than 2 percent each of the Air Corps, Medical Corps, and Signal Corps. The Quartermaster Corps was 15 percent black, the Engineer Corps 25 percent, and unassigned and miscellaneous detachments were 27 percent black.

The rejection of black units could not always be ascribed to racism alone. With some justification the arms and services tried to restrict the number and distribution of Negroes because black units measured far below their white counterparts in educational achievement and ability to absorb training, according to the Army General Classification Test (AGCT). The Army had introduced this test system in March 1941 as its principal instrument for the measurement of a soldier's learning ability. Five categories, with the most gifted in category I, were used in classifying the scores made by the soldiers taking the test (*Table 1*). The Army planned to take officers and enlisted specialists from the top three categories and the semiskilled soldiers and laborers from the two lowest.

TABLE 1—CLASSIFICATION OF ALL MEN TESTED
FROM MARCH 1941 THROUGH DECEMBER 1942

AGCT Category	White

12

	Number
I	273,626
II	1,154,700
III	1,327,164
IV	1,021,818
V	351,951
Total	4,129,259

Source: Tab A, Memo, G-3 for CofS, 10 Apr 43, AG 201.2 (19 Mar 43) (1).

Although there was considerable confusion on the subject, basically the Army's mental tests measured educational achievement rather than native intelligence, and in 1941 educational achievement in the United States hinged more on geography and economics than color. Though black and white recruits of comparable educations made comparable scores, the majority of Negroes came from areas of the country where inferior schools combined with economic and cultural poverty to put them at a significant disadvantage.[2-19] Many whites suffered similar disadvantages, and in absolute numbers more whites than blacks appeared in the lower categories. But whereas the Army could distribute the low-scoring white soldiers throughout the service so that an individual unit could easily absorb its few illiterate and semiliterate white men, the Army was obliged to assign an almost equal number of low-scoring Negroes to the relatively few black units where they could neither be absorbed nor easily trained. By the same token, segregation penalized the educated Negro whose talents were likely to be wasted when he was assigned to service units along with the unskilled.

Segregation further hindered the efficient use of black manpower by complicating the training of black soldiers. Although training facilities were at a premium, the Army was forced to provide its training and replacement centers with separate housing and other facilities. With an extremely limited number of Regular Army Negroes to draw from, the service had to create cadres for the new units and find officers to lead them. Black recruits destined for most arms and services were assured neither units, billets, nor training cadres. The Army's solution to the problem: lower the quotas for black inductees.

The use of quotas to regulate inductees by race was itself a source of tension between the Army and the Bureau of Selective Service.[2-20] Selective Service questioned the legality of the whole procedure whereby white and black selectees were delivered on the basis of separate calls; in many areas of the country draft boards were under attack for passing over large numbers of Negroes in order to fill these racial quotas. With the Navy depending exclusively on volunteers, Selective Service had by early 1943 a backlog of 300,000 black registrants who, according to their order numbers, should have been called to service but had been passed over. Selective Service wanted to eliminate the quota system altogether. At the very least it demanded that the Army accept more Negroes to adjust the racial imbalance of the draft rolls. The Army, determined to preserve the quota system, tried to satisfy the Selective Service's minimum demands, making room for more black inductees by forcing its arms and services to create more black units. Again the cost to efficiency was high.

Under the pressure of providing sufficient units for Negroes, the organization of units for the sake of guaranteeing vacancies became a major goal. In some cases, careful examination of the usefulness of the types of units provided was subordinated to the need to create units which could receive Negroes. As a result, several types of units with limited military value were formed in some branches for the specific purpose of absorbing otherwise unwanted Negroes. Conversely, certain types of units with legitimate and important military functions were filled with Negroes who could not function efficiently in the tasks to which they were assigned.[2-21]

ENGINEER CONSTRUCTION TROOPS IN LIBERIA, JULY 1942

The practice of creating units for the specific purpose of absorbing Negroes was particularly evident in the Army Air Forces.[2-22] Long considered the most recalcitrant of branches in accepting Negroes, the Air Corps had successfully exempted itself from the allotment of black troops in the 1940 mobilization plans. Black pilots could not be used, Maj. Gen. Henry H. Arnold, Chief of the Air Corps, explained, "since this would result in having Negro officers serving over white enlisted men. This would create an impossible social problem."[2-23] And this situation could not be avoided, since it would take several years to train black mechanics; meanwhile black pilots would have to work with white ground crews, often at distant bases outside their regular chain of command. The Air Corps faced strong opposition when both the civil rights advocates and the rest of the Army attacked this exclusion. The civil rights organizations wanted a place for Negroes in the glamorous Air Corps, but even more to the point the other arms and services wanted this large branch of the Army to absorb its fair share of black recruits, thus relieving the rest of a disproportionate burden.

LABOR BATTALION TROOPS IN THE ALEUTIAN ISLANDS, MAY 1943.
Stevedores pause for a hot meal at Massacre Bay.

SERGEANT ADDRESSING THE LINE.
Aviation squadron standing inspection, 1943.

When the War Department supported these demands the Army Air Forces capitulated. Its 1941 mobilization plans provided for the formation of nine separate black aviation squadrons which would perform the miscellaneous tasks associated with the upkeep of airfields. During the next year the Chief of Staff set the allotment of black recruits for the air arm at a rate that brought over 77,500 Negroes into the Air Corps by 1943. On 16 January 1941 Under Secretary Patterson announced the formation of a black pursuit squadron, but the Army Air Forces, bowing to the opposition typified by General Arnold's comments of the previous year, trained the black pilots in separate facilities at Tuskegee, Alabama, where the Army tried to duplicate the expensive training center established for white officers at Maxwell Field, just forty miles away.[2-24] Black pilots were at first trained exclusively for pursuit flying, a very difficult kind of combat for which a Negro had to qualify both physically and technically or else, in Judge Hastie's words, "not fly at all."[2-25] The 99th Fighter Squadron was organized at Tuskegee in 1941 and sent to the Mediterranean theater in April 1943. By then the all-black 332d Fighter Group with three additional fighter squadrons had been organized, and in 1944 it too was deployed to the Mediterranean.

PILOTS OF THE 332D FIGHTER GROUP BEING BRIEFED
for combat mission in Italy.

These squadrons could use only a limited number of pilots, far fewer than those black cadets qualified for such training. All applicants in excess of requirements were placed on an indefinite waiting list where many became overage or were requisitioned for other military and civilian duties. Yet when the Army Air Forces finally decided to organize a black bomber unit, the 477th Bombardment Group, in late 1943, it encountered a scarcity of black pilots and crewmen. Because of the lack of technical and educational opportunities for Negroes in America, fewer blacks than whites were included in the manpower pool, and Tuskegee, already overburdened with its manifold training functions and lacking the means to train bomber crews, was unable to fill the training gap. Sending black cadets to white training schools was one obvious solution; the Army Air Forces chose instead to postpone the operational date of the 477th until its pilots could be trained at Tuskegee. In the end, the 477th was not declared operational until after the war. Even then some compromise with the Army Air Forces' segregation principles was necessary, since Tuskegee could not accommodate B-25 pilot transition and navigator-bombardier training. In 1944 black officers were therefore temporarily assigned to formerly all-white schools for such training. Tuskegee's position as the sole and separate training center for black pilots remained inviolate until its closing in 1946, however, and its graduates, the "Tuskegee Airmen," continued to serve as a powerful symbol of armed forces segregation.[2-26]

Training for black officer candidates other than flyers, like that of most officer candidates throughout the Army, was integrated. At first the possibility of integrated training seemed unlikely, for even though Assistant Secretary of War for Air Robert A. Lovett had assured Hastie that officer candidate training would be integrated, the Technical Training Command announced plans in 1942 for a segregated facility. Although the plans were quickly canceled the command's announcement was the immediate cause for Hastie's resignation from the War Department. The Air staff assured the Assistant Secretary of War in January of 1943 that qualified Negroes were being sent to officer candidate schools and to training courses "throughout the school system of the Technical Training Command."[2-27] In fact, Negroes did attend the Air Forces' officer candidate school at Miami Beach, although not in great numbers. In spite of their integrated training, however, most of these black officers were assigned to the predominantly black units at Tuskegee and Godman fields.

The Army Air Forces found it easier to absorb the thousands of black enlisted men than to handle the black flying squadrons. For the enlisted men it created a series of units with vaguely defined duties, usually common labor jobs operating for the most part under a bulk allotment system that allowed the Air Forces to absorb great numbers of new men. Through 1943

14

hundreds of these aviation training squadrons, quartermaster truck companies, and engineer aviation and air base security battalions were added to the Air Forces' organization tables. Practically every American air base in the world had its contingent of black troops performing the service duties connected with air operations.

The Air Corps, like the Armor and the Artillery branches, was able to form separate squadrons or battalions for black troops, but the Infantry and Cavalry found it difficult to organize the growing number of separate black battalions and regiments. The creation of black divisions was the obvious solution, although this arrangement would run counter to current practice, which was based in part on the Army's experience with the 92d Division in World War I. Convinced of the poor performance of that unit in 1918, the War Department had decided in the 1920's not to form any more black divisions. The regiment would serve as the basic black unit, and from time to time these regiments would be employed as organic elements of divisions whose other regiments and units would be white. In keeping with this decision, the black 9th and 10th Cavalry regiments were combined in October 1940 with white regiments to form the 2d Cavalry Division.

Before World War II most black leaders had agreed with the Army's opposition to all-black divisions, but for different reasons. They considered that such divisions only served to strengthen the segregation pattern they so opposed. In the early weeks of the war a conference of black editors, including Walter White, pressed for the creation of an experimental integrated division of volunteers. White argued that such a unit would lift black morale, "have a tremendous psychological effect upon white America," and refute the enemy's charge that "the United States talks about democracy but practices racial discrimination and segregation."[2-28] The NAACP organized a popular movement in support of the idea, which was endorsed by many important individuals and organizations.[2-29] Yet this experiment was unacceptable to the Army. Ignoring its experience with all-volunteer paratroopers and other special units, the War Department declared that the volunteer system was "an ineffective and dangerous" method of raising combat units. Admitting that the integrated division might be an encouraging gesture toward certain minorities, General Marshall added that "the urgency of the present military situation necessitates our using tested and proved methods of procedure, and using them with all haste."[2-30]

Even though it rejected the idea of a volunteer, integrated division, the Army staff reviewed in the fall of 1942 a proposal for the assignment of some black recruits to white units. The Organization-Mobilization Group of G-3, headed by Col. Edwin W. Chamberlain, argued that the Army General Classification Test scores proved that black soldiers in groups were less useful to the Army than white soldiers in groups. It was a waste of manpower, funds, and equipment, therefore, to organize the increasingly large numbers of black recruits into segregated units. Not only was such organization wasteful, but segregation "aggravated if not caused in its entirety" the racial friction that was already plaguing the Army. To avoid both the waste and the strife, Chamberlain recommended that the Army halt the activation of additional black units and integrate black recruits in the low-score categories, IV and V, into white units in the ratio of one black to nine whites. The black recruits would be used as cooks, orderlies, and drivers, and in other jobs which required only the minimum basic training and which made up 10 to 20 percent of those in the average unit. Negroes in the higher categories, I through III, would be assigned to existing black units where they could be expected to improve the performance of those units. Chamberlain defended his plan against possible charges of discrimination by pointing out that the Negroes would be assigned wholly on the basis of native capacity, not race, and that this plan would increase the opportunities for Negroes to participate in the war effort. To those who objected on the grounds that the proposal meant racial integration, Chamberlain replied that there was no more integration involved than in "the employment of Negroes as servants in a white household."[2-31]

The Chamberlain Plan and a variant proposed the following spring prompted discussion in the Army staff that clearly revealed general dissatisfaction with the current policy. Nonetheless, in the face of opposition from the service and ground forces, the plan was abandoned. Yet because something had to be done with the mounting numbers of black draftees, the Army staff reversed the decision made in its prewar mobilization plans and turned once more to the concept of the all-black division. The 93d Infantry Division was reactivated in the spring of 1942 and the 92d the following fall. The 2d Cavalry Division was reconstituted as an all-black unit and reactivated in February 1943. These units were capable of absorbing 15,000 or more men each and could use men trained in the skills of practically every arm and service.

This absorbency potential became increasingly important in 1943 when the chairman of the War Manpower Commission, Paul V. McNutt, began to attack the use of racial quotas in selecting inductees. He considered the practice of questionable legality, and the commission faced mounting public criticism as white husbands and fathers were drafted while single healthy

15

Negroes were not called.[2-32] Secretary Stimson defended the legality of the quota system. He did not consider the current practice "discriminatory in any way" so long as the Army accepted its fair percentage of Negroes. He pointed out that the Selective Service Act provided that no man would be inducted "*unless and until*" he was acceptable to the services, and Negroes were acceptable "only at a rate at which they can be properly assimilated."[2-33] Stimson later elaborated on this theme, arguing that the quota system would be necessary even after the Army reached full strength because inductions would be limited to replacement of losses. Since there were few Negroes in combat, their losses would be considerably less than those of whites. McNutt disagreed with Stimson's interpretation of the law and announced plans to abandon it as soon as the current backlog of uninducted Negroes was absorbed, a date later set for January 1944.[2-34]

A crisis over the quota system was averted when, beginning in the spring of 1943, the Army's monthly manpower demands outran the ability of the Bureau of Selective Service to provide black inductees. So long as the Army requested more Negroes than the bureau could supply, little danger existed that McNutt would carry out his threat.[2-35] But it was no victory for the Army. The question of the quota's legality remained unanswered, and it appeared that the Army might be forced to abandon the system at some future time when there was a black surplus.

There were many reasons for the sudden shortage of black inductees in the spring of 1943. Since more Negroes were leaving the service for health or other reasons, the number of calls for black draftees had increased. In addition, local draft boards were rejecting more Negroes. But the basic reason for the shortage was that the magnitude of the war had finally turned the manpower surpluses of the 1930's into manpower shortages, and the shortages were appearing in black as well as white levies for the armed forces. The Negro was no longer a manpower luxury. The quota calls for Negroes rose in 1944, and black strength stood at 701,678 men in September, approximately 9.6 percent of the whole Army. [2-36]The percentage of black women in the Army stayed at less than 6 percent of the Women's Army Auxiliary Corps—after July 1943 the Women's Army Corps—throughout the war. Training and serving under the same racial policy that governed the employment of men, the women's corps also had a black recruitment goal of 10 percent, but despite the active efforts of recruiters and generally favorable publicity from civil rights groups, the volunteer organization was unable to overcome the attitude among young black women that they would not be well received at Army posts.[2-37]

Faced with manpower shortages, the Army began to reassess its plan to distribute Negroes proportionately throughout the arms and services. The demand for new service units had soared as the size of the overseas armies grew, while black combat units, unwanted by overseas commanders, had remained stationed in the United States. The War Department hoped to ease the strain on manpower resources by converting black combat troops into service troops. A notable example of the wholesale conversion of such combat troops and one that received considerable notice in the press was the inactivation of the 2d Cavalry Division upon its arrival in North Africa in March 1944. Victims of the change included the 9th and 10th Cavalry regiments, historic combat units that had fought with distinction in the Indian wars, with Teddy Roosevelt in Cuba, and in the Philippine Insurrection.[2-38]

By trying to justify the conversion, Secretary Stimson only aggravated the controversy. In the face of congressional questions and criticism in the black press, Stimson declared that the decision stemmed from a study of the relative abilities and status of training of the troops in the units available for conversion. If black units were particularly affected, it was because "many of the Negro units have been unable to master efficiently the techniques of modern weapons."[2-39] Thus, by the end of 1944, the Army had abandoned its attempt to maintain a balance between black combat and service units, and during the rest of the war most Negroes were assigned to service units.

According to the War Department, the relationship between Negroes and the Army was a mutual obligation. Negroes had the right and duty to serve their country to the best of their abilities; the Army had the right and the duty to see that they did so. True, the use of black troops was made difficult because their schooling had been largely inferior and their work therefore chiefly unskilled. Nevertheless, the Army staff concluded, all races were equally endowed for war and most of the less mentally alert could fight if properly led.[2-40] A manual on leadership observed:

War Department concern with the Negro is focused directly and solely on the problem of the most effective use of colored troops ... the Army has no authority or intention to participate in social reform as such but does view the problem as a matter of efficient troop utilization. With an imposed ceiling on the maximum strength of the Army it is the responsibility of all officers to assure the most efficient use of the manpower assigned.[2-41]

16

But the best efforts of good officers could not avail against poor policy. Although the Army maintained that Negroes had to bear a proportionate share of the casualties, by policy it assigned the majority to noncombat units and thus withheld the chance for them to assume an equal risk. Subscribing to the advantage of making full use of individual abilities, the Army nevertheless continued to consider Negroes as a group and to insist that military efficiency required racially segregated units. Segregation in turn burdened the service with the costly provision of separate facilities for the races. Although a large number of Negroes served in World War II, their employment was limited in opportunity and expensive for the service.

The Need for Change

If segregation weakened the Army's organization for global war, it had even more serious effects on every tenth soldier, for as it deepened the Negro's sense of inferiority it devastated his morale. It was a major cause of the poor performance and the disciplinary problems that plagued so many black units. And it made black soldiers blame their personal difficulties and misfortunes, many the common lot of any soldier, on racial discrimination.[2-42]

Deteriorating morale in black units and pressure from a critical audience of articulate Negroes and their sympathizers led the War Department to focus special attention on its race problem. Early in the war Secretary Stimson had agreed with a General Staff recommendation that a permanent committee be formed to evaluate racial incidents, propose special reforms, and answer questions involving the training and assignment of Negroes.[2-43] On 27 August 1942 he established the Advisory Committee on Negro Troop Policies, with Assistant Secretary McCloy as chairman.[2-44] Caught in the cross fire of black demands and Army traditions, the committee contented itself at first with collecting information on the racial situation and acting as a clearinghouse for recommendations on the employment of black troops.[2-45]

SERVICE CLUB, FORT HUACHUCA

Serious racial trouble was developing by the end of the first year of the war. The trouble was a product of many factors, including the psychological effects of segregation which may not have been so obvious to the committee or even to the black soldier. Other factors, however, were visible to all and begged for remedial action. For example, the practice of using racially separated facilities on military posts, which was not sanctioned in the Army's basic plan for black troops, took hold early in the war. Many black units were located at camps in the south, where commanders insisted on applying local laws and customs inside the military reservations. This practice spread rapidly, and soon in widely separated sections of the country commanders were separating the races in theaters, post exchanges, service clubs, and buses operating on posts. The accommodations provided Negroes were separate but rarely equal, and substandard recreational and housing facilities assigned to black troops were a constant source of irritation. In fact the Army, through the actions of local commanders, actually introduced Jim Crow in some places at home and abroad. Negroes considered such practices in violation of military regulations and inconsistent with the announced principles for which the United States was fighting. Many believed themselves the victims of the personal prejudices of the local commander. Judge Hastie reported their feelings: "The traditional mores of the South have been widely accepted and adopted by the Army as the basis of policy and practice affecting the Negro soldier.... In tactical organization, in physical location, in human contacts, the Negro soldier is separated from the white soldier as completely as possible."[2-46]

In November 1941 another controversy erupted over the discovery that the Red Cross had established racially segregated blood banks. The Red Cross readily admitted that it had no scientific justification for the racial separation of blood and blamed the armed services for the decision. Despite the evidence of science and at risk of demoralizing the black community, the Army's Surgeon General defended the controversial practice as necessary to insure the acceptance of a potentially unpopular program. Ignoring constant criticism from the NAACP and elements of the black press, the armed forces continued to demand segregated blood banks throughout the war. Negroes appreciated the irony of the situation, for they were well aware that a black doctor, Charles R. Drew, had been a pioneer researcher in the plasma extraction process and had directed the first Red Cross blood bank.[2-47]

Black morale suffered further in the leadership crisis that developed in black units early in the war. The logic of segregated units demanded a black officer corps, but there were never enough black officers to command all the black units. In 1942 only 0.35 percent of the Negroes in the Army were officers, a shortcoming that could not be explained by poor education alone.[2-48] But when the number of black officers did begin to increase, obstacles to their employment appeared: some white commanders, assuming that Negroes did not possess leadership ability and that black troops preferred white officers, demanded white officers for their units. Limited segregated recreational and living facilities for black officers prevented their assignment to some

17

bases, while the active opposition of civilian communities forced the Army to exclude them from others. The Army staff practice of forbidding Negroes to outrank or command white officers serving in the same unit not only limited the employment and restricted the rank of black officers but also created invidious distinctions between white and black officers in the same unit. It tended to convince enlisted men that their black leaders were not full-fledged officers. Thus restricted in assignment and segregated socially and professionally, his ability and status in question, the black officer was often an object of scorn to himself and to his men.

The attitude and caliber of white officers assigned to black units hardly compensated for the lack of black officers. In general, white officers resented their assignment to black units and were quick to seek transfer. Worse still, black units, where sensitive and patient leaders were needed to create an effective military force, often became, as they had in earlier wars, dumping grounds for officers unwanted in white units.[2-49] The Army staff further aggravated black sensibilities by showing a preference for officers of southern birth and training, believing them to be generally more competent to exercise command over Negroes. In reality many Negroes, especially those from the urban centers, particularly resented southern officers. At best these officers appeared paternalistic, and Negroes disliked being treated as a separate and distinct group that needed special handling and protection. As General Davis later circumspectly reported, "many colored people of today expect only a certain line of treatment from white officers born and reared in the South, namely, that which follows the southern pattern, which is most distasteful to them."[2-50]

Some of these humiliations might have been less demeaning had the black soldier been convinced that he was a full partner in the crusade against fascism. As news of the conversion of black units from combat to service duties and the word that no new black combat units were being organized became a matter of public knowledge, the black press asked: Will any black combat units be left? Will any of those left be allowed to fight? In fact, would black units ever get overseas?

Actually, the Army had a clear-cut plan for the overseas employment of both black service and combat units. In May 1942 the War Department directed the Army Air Forces, Ground Forces, and Service Forces to make sure that black troops were ordered overseas in numbers not less than their percentage in each of these commands. Theater commanders would be informed of orders moving black troops to their commands, but they would not be asked to agree to their shipment beforehand. Since troop shipments to the British Isles were the chief concern at that time, the order added that "there will be no positive restrictions on the use of colored troops in the British Isles, but shipment of colored units to the British Isles will be limited, initially, to those in the service categories."[2-51]

The problem here was not the Army's policy but the fact that certain foreign governments and even some commanders in American territories wanted to exclude Negroes. Some countries objected to black soldiers because they feared race riots and miscegenation. Others with large black populations of their own felt that black soldiers with their higher rates of pay might create unrest. Still other countries had national exclusion laws. In the case of Alaska and Trinidad, Secretary Stimson ordered, "Don't yield." Speaking of Iceland, Greenland, and Labrador, he commented, "Pretty cold for blacks." To the request of Panamanian officials that a black signal construction unit be withdrawn from their country he replied, "Tell them [the black unit] they must complete their work—it is ridiculous to raise such objections when the Panama Canal itself was built with black labor." As for Chile and Venezuela's exclusion of Negroes he ruled that "As we are the petitioners here we probably must comply."[2-52] Stimson's rulings led to a new War Department policy: henceforth black soldiers would be assigned without regard to color except that they would not be sent to extreme northern areas or to any country against its will when the United States had requested the right to station troops in that country.[2-53]

Ultimately, theater commanders decided which troops would be committed to action and which units would be needed overseas; their decisions were usually respected by the War Department where few believed that Washington should dictate such matters. Unwilling to add racial problems to their administrative burdens, some commanders had been known to cancel their request for troops rather than accept black units. Consequently, very few Negroes were sent overseas in the early years of the war.

Black soldiers were often the victims of gross discrimination that transcended their difficulties with the Army's administration. For instance, black soldiers, particularly those from more integrated regions of the country, resented local ordinances governing transportation and recreation facilities that put them at a great disadvantage in the important matters of leave and amusement. Infractions of local rules were inevitable and led to heightened racial tension and recurring violence.[2-54] At times black soldiers themselves, reflecting the low morale and lack of discipline in their units, instigated the violence. Whoever the culprits, the Army's files are replete

18

with cases of discrimination charged, investigations launched, and exonerations issued or reforms ordered.[2-55] An incredible amount of time and effort went into handling these cases during the darkest days of the war—cases growing out of a policy created in the name of military efficiency.

Nor was the violence limited to the United States. Racial friction also developed in Great Britain where some American troops, resenting their black countrymen's social acceptance by the British, tried to export Jim Crow by forcing the segregation of recreational facilities. Appreciating the treatment they were receiving from the British, the black soldiers fought back, and the clashes grew at times to riot proportions. General Davis considered discrimination and prejudice the cause of trouble, but he placed the immediate blame on local commanders. Many commanders, convinced that they had little jurisdiction over racial disputes in the civilian community or simply refusing to accept responsibility, delegated the task of keeping order to their noncommissioned officers and military police.[2-56] These men, rarely experienced in handling racial disturbances and often prejudiced against black soldiers, usually managed to exacerbate the situation.

In an atmosphere charged with rumors and counterrumors, personal incidents involving two men might quickly blow up into riots involving hundreds. In the summer of 1943 the Army began to reap what Ulysses Lee called the "harvest of disorder." Race riots occurred at military reservations in Mississippi, Georgia, California, Texas, and Kentucky. At other stations, the Advisory Committee on Negro Troop Policies somberly warned, there were indications of unrest ready to erupt into violence.[2-57] By the middle of the war, violence over racial issues at home and abroad had become a source of constant concern for the War Department.

Internal Reform: Amending Racial Practices

Concern over troop morale and discipline and the attendant problem of racial violence did not lead to a substantial revision of the Army's racial policy. On the contrary, the Army staff continued to insist that segregation was a national issue and that the Army's task was to defend the country, not alter its social customs. Until the nation changed its racial practices or until Congress ordered such changes for the armed forces, racially separated units would remain.[2-58] In 1941 the Army had insisted that debate on the subject was closed,[2-59] and, in fact, except for discussion of the Chamberlain Plan there was no serious thought of revising racial policy in the Army staff until after the war.

Had the debate been reopened in 1943, the traditionalists on the Army staff would have found new support for their views in a series of surveys made of white and black soldiers in 1942 and 1943. These surveys supported the theory that the Army, a national institution composed of individual citizens with pronounced views on race, would meet massive disobedience and internal disorder as well as national resistance to any substantial change in policy. One extensive survey, covering 13,000 soldiers in ninety-two units, revealed that 88 percent of the whites and 38 percent of the Negroes preferred segregated units. Among the whites, 85 percent preferred separate service clubs and 81 percent preferred separate post exchanges. Almost half of the Negroes thought separate service clubs and post exchanges were a good idea.[2-60] These attitudes merely reflected widely held national views as suggested in a 1943 survey of five key cities by the Office of War Information.[2-61] The survey showed that 90 percent of the whites and 25 percent of the blacks questioned supported segregation.

Some Army officials considered justification by statistics alone a risky business. Reviewing the support for segregation revealed in the surveys, for example, the Special Services Division commented: "Many of the Negroes and some of the whites who favor separation in the Army indicate by their comments that they are opposed to segregation in principle. They favor separation in the Army to avoid trouble or unpleasantness." Its report added that the longer a Negro remained in the Army, the less likely he was to support segregation.[2-62] Nor did it follow from the overwhelming support for segregation that a policy of integration would result in massive resistance. As critics later pointed out, the same surveys revealed that almost half the respondents expressed a strong preference for civilian life, but the Army did not infer that serious disorders would result if these men were forced to remain in uniform.[2-63]

By 1943 Negroes within and without the War Department had just about exhausted arguments for a policy change. After two years of trying, Judge Hastie came to believe that change was possible only in response to "strong and manifest public opinion." He concluded that he would be far more useful as a private citizen who could express his views freely and publicly than he was as a War Department employee, bound to conform to official policy. Quitting the department, Hastie joined the increasingly vocal black organizations in a sustained attack on the Army's segregation policy, an attack that was also being translated into political action by the major civil rights organizations. In 1943, a full year before the national elections, representatives of twenty-five civil rights groups met and formulated the demands they would make of the presidential candidates: full integration (some groups tempered this demand by calling for integrated units of volunteers); abolition of racial quotas; abolition of segregation in recreational

19

and other Army facilities; abolition of blood plasma segregation; development of an educational program in race relations in the Army; greater black participation in combat forces; and the progressive removal of black troops from areas where they were subject to disrespect, abuse, and even violence.[2-64]

The Army could not afford to ignore these demands completely, as Truman K. Gibson, Jr., Judge Hastie's successor, pointed out.[2-65] The political situation indicated that the racial policy of the armed forces would be an issue in the next national election. Recalling the changes forced on the Army as a result of political pressures applied before the 1940 election, Gibson predicted that actions that might now seem impolitic to the Army and the White House might not seem so during the next campaign when the black vote could influence the outcome in several important states, including New York, Pennsylvania, Illinois, and Michigan. Already the Chicago *Tribune* and other anti-administration groups were trying to encourage black protest in terms not always accurate but nonetheless believable to the black voter. Gibson suggested that the Army act before the political pressure became even more intense.[2-66]

Caught between the black demands and War Department traditions, the Advisory Committee on Negro Troop Policies launched an attack—much too late and too weak, its critics agreed—on what it perceived as the causes of the Army's racial disorders. Some of the credit for this attack must go to Truman Gibson. No less dedicated to abolition of racial segregation than Hastie, Gibson eschewed the grand gesture and emphasized those practical changes that could be effected one step at a time. For all his zeal, Gibson was admirably detached.[2-67] He knew that his willingness to recognize that years of oppression and injustice had marred the black soldier's performance would earn for him the scorn of many civil rights activists, but he also knew that his fairness made him an effective advocate in the War Department. He worked closely with McCloy's committee, always describing with his alternatives for action their probable effect upon the Army, the public, and the developing military situation. As a result of the close cooperation between the Advisory Committee and Gibson, the Army for the first time began to agree on practical if not policy changes.

The Advisory Committee's first campaign was directed at local commanders. After a long review of the evidence, the committee was convinced that the major cause of racial disorder was the failure of commanders in some echelons to appreciate the seriousness of racial unrest and their own responsibility for dealing with the discipline, morale, and welfare of their men. Since it found that most disturbances began with real or fancied incidents of discrimination, the committee concluded that there should be no discrimination against Negroes in the matter of privileges and accommodations and none in favor of Negroes that compromised disciplinary standards. The committee wanted local commanders to be reminded that maintaining proper discipline and good order among soldiers, and between soldiers and civilians, was a definite command responsibility.[2-68]

General Marshall incorporated the committee's recommendations in a letter to the field. He concluded by saying that "failure on the part of any commander to concern himself personally and vigorously with this problem will be considered as evidence of lack of capacity and cause for reclassification and removal from assignment."[2-69] At the same time, the Chief of Staff did not adopt several of the committee's specific recommendations. He did not require local commanders to recommend changes in War Department policy on the treatment of Negroes and the organization and employment of black units. Nor did he require them to report on steps taken by them to follow the committee's recommendations. Moreover, he did not order the dispatch of black combat units to active theaters although the committee had pointed to this course as "the most effective means of reducing tension among Negro troops."

Next, the Advisory Committee turned its attention to the black press. Judge Hastie and the representatives of the senior civil rights organizations were judicious in their criticism and accurate in their charges, but this statement could not be made for much of the black press. Along with deserving credit for spotlighting racial injustices and giving a very real impetus to racial progress, a segment of the black press had to share the blame for fomenting racial disorder by the frequent publication of inaccurate and inflammatory war stories. Some field commanders charged that the constant criticism was detrimental to troop morale and demanded that the War Department investigate and even censor particular black newspapers. In July 1943 the Army Service Forces recommended that General Marshall officially warn the editors against printing inciting and untrue stories and suggested that if this caution failed sedition proceedings be instituted against the culprits.[2-70] General Marshall followed a more moderate course suggested by Assistant Secretary McCloy.[2-71] The Army staff amplified and improved the services of the Bureau of Public Relations by appointing Negroes to the bureau and by releasing more news items of special interest to black journalists. The result was a considerable increase in constructive

20

and accurate stories on black participation in the war, although articles and editorials continued to be severely critical of the Army's segregation policy.

The proposal to send black units into combat, rejected by Marshall when raised by the Advisory Committee in 1943, became the preeminent racial issue in the Army during the next year.[2-72] It was vitally necessary, the Advisory Committee reasoned, that black troops not be wasted by leaving them to train endlessly in camps around the country, and that the War Department begin making them a "military asset." In March 1944 it recommended to Secretary Stimson that black units be introduced into combat and that units and training schedules be reorganized if necessary to insure that this deployment be carried out as promptly as possible. Elaborating on the committee's recommendation, Chairman McCloy added:

There has been a tendency to allow the situation to develop where selections are made on the basis of efficiency with the result that the colored units are discarded for combat service, but little is done by way of studying new means to put them in shape for combat service.

With so large a portion of our population colored, with the example of the effective use of colored troops (of a much lower order of intelligence) by other nations, and with the many imponderables that are connected with the situation, we must, I think, be more affirmative about the use of our Negro troops. If present methods do not bring them to combat efficiency, we should change those methods. That is what this resolution purports to recommend.[2-73]

Stimson agreed, and on 4 March 1944 the Advisory Committee met with members of the Army staff to decide on combat assignments for regimental combat teams from the 92d and 93d Divisions. In order that both handpicked soldiers and normal units might be tested, the team from the 93d would come from existing units of that division, and the one from the 92d would be a specially selected group of volunteers. General Marshall and his associates continued to view the commitment of black combat troops as an experiment that might provide documentation for the future employment of Negroes in combat.[2-74] In keeping with this experiment, the Army staff suggested to field commanders how Negroes might be employed and requested continuing reports on the units' progress.

The belated introduction of major black units into combat helped alleviate the Army's racial problems. After elements of the 93d Division were committed on Bougainville in March 1944 and an advanced group of the 92d landed in Italy in July, the Army staff found it easier to ship smaller supporting units to combat theaters, either as separate units or as support for larger units, a course that reduced the glut of black soldiers stationed in the United States. Recognizing that many of these units had poor leaders, Lt. Gen. Lesley J. McNair, head of the Army Ground Forces, ordered that, "if practicable," all leaders of black units who had not received "excellent" or higher in their efficiency ratings would be replaced before the units were scheduled for overseas deployment.[2-75] Given the "if practicable" loophole, there was little chance that all the units would go overseas with "excellent" commanders.

93D DIVISION TROOPS IN BOUGAINVILLE, APRIL 1944.
Men, packing mortar shells, cross the West Branch Texas River.

A source of pride to the black community, the troop commitments also helped to reduce national racial tensions, but they did little for the average black soldier who remained stationed in the United States. He continued to suffer discrimination within and without the gates of the camp. The committee attributed that discrimination to the fact that War Department policy was not being carried out in all commands. In some instances local commanders were unaware of the policy; in others they refused to pay sufficient attention to the seriousness of what was, after all, but one of many problems facing them. For some time committee members had been urging the War Department to write special instructions, and finally in February 1944 the department issued a pamphlet designed to acquaint local commanders with an official definition of Army racial policy and to improve methods of developing leaders in black units. *Command of Negro Troops* was a landmark publication.[2-76] Its frank statement of the Army's racial problems, its scholarly and objective discussion of the disadvantages that burdened the black soldier, and its outline of black rights and responsibilities clearly revealed the committee's intention to foster racial harmony by promoting greater command responsibility. The pamphlet represented a major departure from previous practice and served as a model for later Army and Navy statements on race.[2-77]

But pamphlets alone would not put an end to racial discrimination; the committee had to go beyond its role of instructor. Although the War Department had issued a directive on 10 March 1943 forbidding the assignment of any recreational facility, "including theaters and post exchanges," by race and requiring the removal of signs labeling facilities for "white" and "colored" soldiers, there had been little alteration in the recreational situation. The directive had allowed the separate use of existing facilities by designated units and camp areas, so that in many places segregation by unit had replaced separation by race, and inspectors and commanders

21

reported that considerable confusion existed over the War Department's intentions. On other posts the order to remove the racial labels from facilities was simply disregarded. On 8 July 1944 the committee persuaded the War Department to issue another directive clearly informing commanders that facilities could be allocated to specific areas or units, but that all post exchanges and theaters must be opened to all soldiers regardless of race. All government transportation, moreover, was to be available to all troops regardless of race. Nor could soldiers be restricted to certain sections of government vehicles on or off base, regardless of local customs.[2-78]

Little dramatic change ensued in day-to-day life on base. Some commanders, emphasizing that part of the directive which allowed the designation of facilities for units and areas, limited the degree of the directive's application to post exchanges and theaters and ignored those provisions concerned with individual rights. This interpretation only added to the racial unrest that culminated in several incidents, of which the one at the officers' club at Freeman Field, Indiana, was the most widely publicized.[2-79] After this incident the committee promptly asked for a revision of WD Pamphlet 20-6 on the command of black troops that would clearly spell out the intention of the authors of the directive to apply its integration provisions explicitly to "officers' clubs, messes, or similar social organizations."[2-80] In effect the War Department was declaring that racial separation applied to units only. For the first time it made a clear distinction between Army race policy to be applied on federal military reservations and local civilian laws and customs to be observed by members of the armed forces when off post. In Acting Secretary Patterson's words:

The War Department has maintained throughout the emergency and present war that it is not an appropriate medium for effecting social readjustments but has insisted that all soldiers, regardless of race, be afforded equal opportunity to enjoy the recreational facilities which are provided at posts, camps and stations. The thought has been that men who are fulfilling the same obligation, suffering the same dislocation of their private lives, and wearing the identical uniform should, within the confines of the military establishment, have the same privileges for rest and relaxation.[2-81]

Widely disseminated by the black press as the "anti-Jim Crow law," the directive and its interpretation by senior officials produced the desired result. Although soldiers most often continued to frequent the facilities in their own base areas, in effect maintaining racial separation, they were free to use any facilities, and this knowledge gradually dispelled some of the tensions on posts where restrictions of movement had been a constant threat to good order.

With some pride, Assistant Secretary McCloy claimed on his Advisory Committee's first birthday that the Army had "largely eliminated discrimination against the Negroes within its ranks, going further in this direction than the country itself."[2-82] He was a little premature. Not until the end of 1944 did the Advisory Committee succeed in eliminating the most glaring examples of discrimination within the Army. Even then race remained an issue, and isolated racial incidents continued to occur.

Two Exceptions

Departmental policy notwithstanding, a certain amount of racial integration was inevitable during a war that mobilized a biracial army of eight million men. Through administrative error or necessity, segregation was ignored on many occasions, and black and white soldiers often worked and lived together in hospitals,[2-83] rest camps, schools, and, more rarely, units. But these were isolated cases, touching relatively few men, and they had no discernible effect on racial policy. Of much more importance was the deliberate integration in officer training schools and in the divisions fighting in the European theater in 1945. McCloy referred to these deviations from policy as experiments "too limited to afford general conclusions."[2-84] But if they set no precedents, they at least challenged the Army's cherished assumptions on segregation and strengthened the postwar demands for change.

The Army integrated its officer candidate training in an effort to avoid the mistakes of the World War I program. In 1917 Secretary of War Newton D. Baker had established a separate training school for black officer candidates at Fort Des Moines, Iowa, with disappointing results. To fill its quotas the school had been forced to lower its entrance standards, and each month an arbitrary number of black officer candidates were selected and graduated with little regard for their qualifications. Many World War I commanders agreed that the black officers produced by the school proved inadequate as troop commanders, and postwar staff studies generally opposed the future use of black officers. Should the Army be forced to accept black officers in the future, these commanders generally agreed, they should be trained along with whites.[2-85]

GUN CREW OF BATTERY B, 598TH FIELD ARTILLERY,
moving into position near the Arno River, Italy, September 1944.

22

Despite these criticisms, mobilization plans between the wars all assumed that black officers would be trained and commissioned, although, as the 1937 mobilization plan put it, their numbers would be limited to those required to provide officers for organizations authorized to have black officers.[2-86] No detailed plans were drawn up on the nature of this training, but by the eve of World War II a policy had become fixed: Negroes were to be chosen and trained according to the same standards as white officers, preferably in the same schools.[2-87] The War Department ignored the subject of race when it established the officer candidate schools in 1941. "The basic and predominating consideration governing selections to OCS," The Adjutant General announced, would be "outstanding qualities of leadership as demonstrated by actual services in the Army."[2-88] General Davis, who participated in the planning conferences, reasoned that integrated training would be vital for the cooperation that would be necessary in battle. He agreed with the War Department's silence on race, adding, "you can't have Negro, white, or Jewish officers, you've got to have American officers."[2-89]

The Army's policy failed to consider one practical problem: if race was ignored in War Department directives, would black candidates ever be nominated and selected for officer training? Early enrollment figures suggested they would not. Between July 1941, when the schools opened, and October 1941, only seventeen out of the 1,997 students enrolled in candidate schools were Negroes. Only six more Negroes entered during the next two months.[2-90]

Some civil rights spokesmen argued for the establishment of a quota system, and a few Negroes even asked for a return to segregated schools to insure a more plentiful supply of black officers. Even before the schools opened, Judge Hastie warned Secretary Stimson that any effective integration plan "required a directive to Corps Area Commanders indicating that Negroes are to be selected in numbers exactly or approximately indicated for particular schools."[2-91] But the planners had recommended the integrated schools precisely to avoid a quota system. They were haunted by the Army's 1917 experience, although the chief of the Army staff's Organizations Division did not allude to these misgivings when he answered Judge Hastie. He argued that a quota could not be defended on any grounds "except those of a political nature" and would be "race discrimination against the whites."[2-92]

General Marshall agreed that racial parity could not be achieved at the expense of commissioning unqualified men, but he was equally adamant about providing equal opportunity for all qualified candidates, black and white. He won support for his position from some of the civil rights advocates.[2-93] These arguments may not have swayed Hastie, but in the end he dropped the idea of a regular quota system, judging it unworkable in the case of the officer candidate schools. He concluded that many commanders approached the selection of officer candidates with a bias against the Negro, and he recommended that a directive or confidential memorandum be sent to commanders charged with the selection of officer candidates informing them that a certain minimum percentage of black candidates was to be chosen. Hastie's recommendation was ignored, but the widespread refusal of local commanders to approve or transmit applications of Negroes, or even to give them access to appropriate forms, halted when Secretary Stimson and the Army staff made it plain that they expected substantial numbers of Negroes to be sent to the schools.[2-94]

The National Association for the Advancement of Colored People meanwhile moved quickly to prove that the demand for a return to segregated schools, made by Edgar G. Brown, president of the United States Government Employees, and broadcaster Fulton Lewis, Jr., enjoyed little backing in the black community. "We respectfully submit," Walter White informed Stimson and Roosevelt, "that no leader considered responsible by intelligent Negro or white Americans would make such a request."[2-95] In support of its stand the NAACP issued a statement signed by many influential black leaders.

The segregationists attacked integration of the officer candidate schools for the obvious reasons. A group of Florida congressmen, for example, protested to the Army against the establishment of an integrated Air Corps school at Miami Beach. The War Department received numerous complaints when living quarters at the schools were integrated. The president of the White Supremacy League complained that young white candidates at Fort Benning "have to eat and sleep with Negro candidates," calling it "the most damnable outrage that was ever

23

perpetrated on the youth of the South." To all such complaints the War Department answered that separation was not always possible because of the small number of Negroes involved.[2-96]

In answering these complaints the Army developed its ultimate justification for integrated officer schools: integration was necessary on the grounds of efficiency and economy. As one Army spokesman put it, "our objection to separate schools is based primarily on the fact that black officer candidates are eligible from every branch of the Army, including the Armored Force and tank destroyer battalions, and it would be decidedly uneconomical to attempt to gather in one school the materiel and instructor personnel necessary to give training in all these branches."[2-97]

Officer candidate training was the Army's first formal experiment with integration. Many blacks and whites lived together with a minimum of friction, and, except in flight school, all candidates trained together.[2-98] Yet in some schools the number of black officer candidates made racially separate rooms feasible, and Negroes were usually billeted and messed together. In other instances Army organizations were slow to integrate their officer training. The Women's Army Auxiliary Corps, for example, segregated black candidates until late 1942 when Judge Hastie brought the matter to McCloy's attention.[2-99] Nevertheless, the Army's experiment was far more important than its immediate results indicated. It proved that even in the face of considerable opposition the Army was willing to abandon its segregation policy when the issues of economy and efficiency were made sufficiently clear and compelling.

The Army's second experiment with integration came in part from the need for infantry replacements during the Allied advance across Western Europe in the summer and fall of 1944.[2-100] The Ground Force Replacement Command had been for some time converting soldiers from service units to infantry, and even as the Germans launched their counterattack in the Ardennes the command was drawing up plans to release thousands of soldiers in Lt. Gen. John C. H. Lee's Communications Zone and train them as infantrymen. These plans left the large reservoir of black manpower in the theater untapped until General Lee suggested that General Dwight D. Eisenhower permit black service troops to volunteer for infantry training and eventual employment as individual replacements. General Eisenhower agreed, and on 26 December Lee issued a call to the black troops for volunteers to share "the privilege of joining our veteran units at the front to deliver the knockout blow." The call was limited to privates in the upper four categories of the Army General Classification Test who had had some infantry training. If noncommissioned officers wanted to apply, they had to accept a reduction in grade. Although patronizing in tone, the plan was a bold departure from War Department policy: "It is planned to assign you without regard to color or race to the units where assistance is most needed, and give you the opportunity of fighting shoulder to shoulder to bring about victory.... Your relatives and friends everywhere have been urging that you be granted this privilege."[2-101]

The revolutionary nature of General Lee's plan was not lost on Supreme Headquarters, Allied Expeditionary Force. Arguing that the circular promising integrated service would embarrass the Army, Lt. Gen. Walter Bedell Smith, the chief of staff, recommended that General Eisenhower warn the War Department that civil rights spokesmen might seize on this example to demand wider integration. To avoid future moves that might compromise Army policy, Smith wanted permission to review any Communications Zone statements on Negroes before they were released.

General Eisenhower compromised. Washington was not consulted, and Eisenhower himself revised the circular, eliminating the special call for black volunteers and the promise of integration on an individual basis. He substituted instead a general appeal for volunteers, adding the further qualification that "in the event that the number of suitable negro volunteers exceeds the replacement needs of negro combat units, these men will be suitably incorporated in other organizations so that their service and their fighting spirit may be efficiently utilized."[2-102] This statement was disseminated throughout the European theater.

The Eisenhower revision needed considerable clarification. It mentioned the replacement needs of black combat units, but there were no black infantry units in the theater;[2-103] and the replacement command was not equipped to retrain men for artillery, tank, and tank destroyer units, the types of combat units that did employ Negroes in Europe. The revision also called for volunteers in excess of these needs to be "suitably incorporated in other organizations," but it did not indicate how they would be organized. Eisenhower later made it clear that he preferred to organize the volunteers in groups that could replace white units in the line, but again the replacement command was geared to train individual, not unit, replacements. After considerable discussion and compromise, Eisenhower agreed to have Negroes trained "as members of Infantry rifle platoons familiar with the Infantry rifle platoon weapons." The platoons would be sent for assignment to Army commanders who would provide them with platoon leaders, platoon sergeants, and, if needed, squad leaders.

24

Unaware of how close they had come to being integrated as individuals, so many Negroes volunteered for combat training and duty that the operations of some service units were threatened. To prevent disrupting these vital operations, the theater limited the number to 2,500, turning down about 3,000 men. Early in January 1945 the volunteers assembled for six weeks of standard infantry conversion training. After training, the new black infantrymen were organized into fifty-three platoons, each under a white platoon leader and sergeant, and were dispatched to the field, two to work with armored divisions and the rest with infantry divisions. Sixteen were shipped to the 6th Army Group, the rest to the 12th Army Group, and all saw action with a total of eleven divisions in the First and Seventh Armies.

VOLUNTEERS FOR COMBAT IN TRAINING,
47th Reinforcement Depot, February 1945.

In the First Army the black platoons were usually assigned on the basis of three to a division, and the division receiving them normally placed one platoon in each regiment. At the company level, the black platoon generally served to augment the standard organization of three rifle platoons and one heavy weapons platoon. In the Seventh Army, the platoons were organized into provisional companies and attached to infantry battalions in armored divisions. General Davis warned the Seventh Army commander, Lt. Gen. Alexander M. Patch, that the men had not been trained for employment as company units and were not being properly used. The performance of the provisional companies failed to match the performance of the platoons integrated into white companies and their morale was lower.[2-104] At the end of the war the theater made clear to the black volunteers that integration was over. Although a large group was sent to the 69th Infantry Division to be returned home, most were reassigned to black combat or service units in the occupation army.

The experiment with integration of platoons was carefully scrutinized. In May and June 1945, the Research Branch of the Information and Education Division of Eisenhower's theater headquarters made a survey solely to discover what white company-grade officers and platoon sergeants thought of the combat performance of the black rifle platoons. Trained interviewers visited seven infantry divisions and asked the same question of 250 men—all the available company officers and a representative sample of platoon sergeants in twenty-four companies that had had black platoons. In addition, a questionnaire, not to be signed, was submitted to approximately 1,700 white enlisted men in other field forces for the purpose of discovering what their attitudes were toward the use of black riflemen. No Negro was asked his opinion.

More than 80 percent of the white officers and noncommissioned officers who were interviewed reported that the Negroes had performed "very well" in combat; 69 percent of the officers and 83 percent of the noncommissioned officers saw no reason why black infantrymen should not perform as well as white infantrymen if both had the same training and experience. Most reported getting along "very well" with the black volunteers; the heavier the combat shared, the closer and better the relationships. Nearly all the officers questioned admitted that the camaraderie between white and black troops was far better than they had expected. Most enlisted men reported that they had at first disliked and even been apprehensive at the prospect of having black troops in their companies, but three-quarters of them had changed their minds after serving with Negroes in combat, their distrust turning into respect and friendliness. Of the officers and noncommissioned officers, 77 percent had more favorable feelings toward Negroes after serving in close proximity to them, the others reported no change in attitude; not a single individual stated that he had developed a less favorable attitude. A majority of officers approved the idea of organizing Negroes in platoons to serve in white companies; the practice, they said, would stimulate the spirit of competition between races, avoid friction with prejudiced whites, eliminate discrimination, and promote interracial understanding. Familiarity with Negroes dispersed fear of the unknown and bred respect for them among white troops; only those lacking experience with black soldiers were inclined to be suspicious and hostile.[2-105]

General Brehon B. Somervell, commanding general of the Army Service Forces, questioned the advisability of releasing the report. An experiment involving 1,000 volunteers—his figure was inaccurate, actually 2,500 were involved—was hardly, he believed, a conclusive test. Furthermore, organizations such as the NAACP might be encouraged to exert pressure for similar experiments among troops in training in the United States and even in the midst of active operations in the Pacific theater—pressure, he believed, that might hamper training and operations. What mainly concerned Somervell were the political implications. Many members of Congress, newspaper editors, and others who had given strong support to the War Department were, he contended, "vigorously opposed" to integration under any conditions. A strong adverse reaction from this influential segment of the nation's opinion-makers might alienate public support for a postwar program of universal military training.[2-106]

General Omar N. Bradley, the senior American field commander in Europe, took a different tack. Writing for the theater headquarters and drawing upon such sources of information as the personal observations of some officers, General Bradley disparaged the significance of the experiment. Most of the black platoons, he observed, had participated mainly in mopping-up operations or combat against a disorganized enemy. Nor could the soldiers involved in the experiment be considered typical, in Bradley's opinion. They were volunteers of above average intelligence according to their commanders.[2-107] Finally, Bradley contended that, while no racial trouble emerged during combat, the mutual friendship fostered by fighting a common enemy was threatened when the two races were closely associated in rest and recreational areas. Nevertheless, he agreed that the performance of the platoons was satisfactory enough to warrant continuing the experiment but recommended the use of draftees with average qualifications. At the same time, he drew away from further integration by suggesting that the experiment be expanded to include employment of entire black rifle companies in white regiments to avoid some of the social difficulties encountered in rest areas.[2-108]

General Marshall, the Chief of Staff, agreed with both Somervell and Bradley. Although he thought that the possibility of integrating black units into white units should be "followed up," he believed that the survey should not be made public because "the conditions under which the [black] platoons were organized and employed were most unusual."[2-109] Too many of the circumstances of the experiment were special—the voluntary recruitment of men for frontline duty, the relatively high number of noncommissioned officers among the volunteers, and the fact that the volunteers were slightly older and scored higher in achievement tests than the average black soldier. Moreover, throughout the experiment some degree of segregation, with all its attendant psychological and morale problems, had been maintained.

The platoon experiment was illuminating in several respects. The fact that so late in the war thousands of Negroes volunteered to trade the safety of the rear for duty at the front said something about black patriotism and perhaps something about the Negro's passion for equality. It also demonstrated that, when properly trained and motivated and treated with fairness, blacks, like whites, performed with bravery and distinction in combat. Finally, the experiment successfully attacked one of the traditionalists' shibboleths, that close association of the races in Army units would cause social dissension.

ROAD REPAIRMEN,
Company A, 279th Engineer Battalion, near Rimberg, Germany, December 1944.

It is now apparent that World War II had little immediate effect on the quest for racial equality in the Army. The Double V campaign against fascism abroad and racism at home achieved considerably less than the activists had hoped. Although Negroes shared in the prosperity brought by war industries and some 800,000 of them served in uniform, segregation remained the policy of the Army throughout the war, just as Jim Crow still ruled in large areas of the country. Probably the campaign's most important achievement was that during the war the civil rights groups, in organizing for the fight against discrimination, began to gather strength and develop techniques that would be useful in the decades to come. The Army's experience with black units also convinced many that segregation was a questionable policy when the country needed to mobilize fully.

For its part the Army defended the separation of the races in the name of military efficiency and claimed that it had achieved a victory over racial discrimination by providing equal treatment and job opportunity for black soldiers. But the Army's campaign had also been less than completely successful. True, the Army had provided specialist training and opened job opportunities heretofore denied to thousands of Negroes, and it had a cadre of potential leaders in the hundreds of experienced black officers. For the times, the Army was a progressive minority employer. Even so, as an institution it had defended the separate but equal doctrine and had failed to come to grips with segregation. Under segregation the Army was compelled to combine large numbers of undereducated and undertrained black soldiers in units that were often inefficient and sometimes surplus to its needs. This system in turn robbed the Army of the full services of the educated and able black soldier, who had every reason to feel restless and rebellious.

The Army received no end of advice on its manpower policy during the war. Civil rights spokesmen continually pointed out that segregation itself was discriminatory, and Judge Hastie in particular hammered on this proposition before the highest officials of the War Department. In fact Hastie's recommendations, criticisms, and arguments crystallized the demands of civil rights leaders. The Army successfully resisted the proposition when its Advisory Committee on Negro Troop Policies under John McCloy modified but did not appreciably alter the segregation policy. It was a predictable course. The Army's racial policy was more than a century old, and leaders

26

considered it dangerous if not impossible to revise traditional ways during a global war involving so many citizens with pronounced and different views on race.

What both the civil rights activists and the Army's leaders tended to ignore during the war was that segregation was inefficient. The myriad problems associated with segregated units, in contrast to the efficient operation of the integrated officer candidate schools and the integrated infantry platoons in Europe, were overlooked in the atmosphere of charges and denials concerning segregation and discrimination. John McCloy was an exception. He had clearly become dissatisfied with the inefficiency of the Army's policy, and in the week following the Japanese surrender he questioned Navy Secretary James V. Forrestal on the Navy's experiments with integration. "It has always seemed to me," he concluded, "that we never put enough thought into the matter of making a real military asset out of the very large cadre of Negro personnel we received from the country."[2-110] Although segregation persisted, the fact that it hampered military efficiency was the hope of those who looked for a change in the Army's policy.

CHAPTER 3
World War II: The Navy

The period between the world wars marked the nadir of the Navy's relations with black America. Although the exclusion of Negroes that began with a clause introduced in enlistment regulations in 1922 lasted but a decade, black participation in the Navy remained severely restricted during the rest of the inter-war period. In June 1940 the Navy had 4,007 black personnel, 2.3 percent of its nearly 170,000-man total.[3-1] All were enlisted men, and with the exception of six regular rated seamen, lone survivors of the exclusion clause, all were steward's mates, labeled by the black press "seagoing bellhops."

The Steward's Branch, composed entirely of enlisted Negroes and oriental aliens, mostly Filipinos, was organized outside the Navy's general service. Its members carried ratings up to chief petty officer, but wore distinctive uniforms and insignia, and even chief stewards never exercised authority over men rated in the general naval service. Stewards manned the officers' mess and maintained the officers' billets on board ship, and, in some instances, took care of the quarters of high officials in the shore establishment. Some were also engaged in mess management, menu planning, and the purchase of supplies. Despite the fact that their enlistment contracts restricted their training and duties, stewards, like everyone else aboard ship, were assigned battle stations, including positions at the guns and on the bridge. One of these stewards, Dorie (Doris) Miller, became a hero on the first day of the war when he manned a machine gun on the burning deck of the USS *Arizona* and destroyed two enemy planes.[3-2]

By the end of December 1941 the number of Negroes in the Navy had increased by slightly more than a thousand men to 5,026, or 2.4 percent of the whole, but they continued to be excluded from all positions except that of steward.[3-3] It was not surprising that civil rights organizations and their supporters in Congress demanded a change in policy.

Development of a Wartime Policy

At first the new secretary, Frank Knox, and the Navy's professional leaders resisted demands for a change. Together with Secretary of War Stimson, Knox had joined the cabinet in July 1940 when Roosevelt was attempting to defuse a foreign policy debate that threatened to explode during the presidential campaign.[3-4] For a major cabinet officer, Knox's powers were severely circumscribed. He had little knowledge of naval affairs, and the President, himself once an Assistant Secretary of the Navy, often went over his head to deal directly with the naval bureaus on shipbuilding programs and manpower problems as well as the disposition of the fleet. But Knox was a personable man and a forceful speaker, and he was particularly useful to the President in congressional liaison and public relations. Roosevelt preferred to work through the secretary in dealing with the delicate question of black participation in the Navy. Knox himself was fortunate in his immediate official family. James V. Forrestal became under secretary in August 1940; during the next year Ralph A. Bard, a Chicago investment banker, joined the department as assistant secretary, and Adlai E. Stevenson became special assistant.

Able as these men were, Frank Knox, like most new secretaries unfamiliar with the operations and traditions of the vast department, was from the beginning heavily dependent on his naval advisers. These were the chiefs of the powerful bureaus and the prominent senior admirals of the General Board, the Navy's highest advisory body.[3-5] Generally these men were ardent military traditionalists, and, despite the progressive attitude of the secretary's highest civilian advisers, changes in the racial policy of the Navy were to be glacially slow.

DORIE MILLER

The Bureau of Navigation, which was charged with primary responsibility for all personnel matters, was opposed to change in the racial composition of the Navy. Less than two weeks after Knox's appointment, it prepared for his signature a letter to Lieutenant Governor Charles Poletti of New York defending the Navy's policy. The bureau reasoned that since segregation was impractical, exclusion was necessary. Experience had proved, the bureau claimed, that when given supervisory responsibility the Negro was unable to maintain discipline among white subordinates with the result that teamwork, harmony, and ship's efficiency suffered. The Negro, therefore, had to be segregated from the white sailor. All-black units were impossible, the bureau argued, because the service's training and distribution system demanded that a man in any particular rating be available for any duty required of that rating in any ship or activity in the Navy. The Navy had experimented with segregated crews after World War I, manning one ship with an all-Filipino crew and another with an all-Samoan crew, but the bureau was not satisfied with the result and reasoned that ships with black crews would be no more satisfactory.[3-6]

During the next weeks Secretary Knox warmed to the subject, speaking of the difficulty faced by the Navy when men had to live aboard ship together. He was convinced that "it is no kindness to Negroes to thrust them upon men of the white race," and he suggested that the Negro might make his major contribution to the armed forces in the Army's black regimental organizations.[3-7] Confronted with widespread criticism of this policy, however, Knox asked the Navy's General Board in September 1940 to give him "some reasons why colored persons should not be enlisted for general service."[3-8] He accepted the board's reasons for continued exclusion of Negroes—generally an extension of the ones advanced in the Poletti letter—and during the next eighteen months these reasons, endorsed by the Chief of Naval Operations and the Bureau of Navigation, were used as the department's standard answer to questions on race.[3-9] They were used at the White House conference on 18 June 1941 when, in the presence of black leaders, Knox told President Roosevelt that the Navy could do nothing about taking Negroes into the general service "because men live in such intimacy aboard ship that we simply can't enlist Negroes above the rank of messman."[3-10]

ADMIRAL KING AND SECRETARY KNOX
on the USS Augusta.

The White House conference revealed an interesting contrast between Roosevelt and Knox. Whatever his personal feelings, Roosevelt agreed with Knox that integration of the Navy was an impractical step in wartime, but where Knox saw exclusion from general service as the alternative to integration Roosevelt sought a compromise. He suggested that the Navy "make a beginning" by putting some "good Negro bands" aboard battleships. Under such intimate living conditions white and black would learn to know and respect each other, and "then we can move on from there."[3-11] In effect the President was trying to lead the Navy toward a policy similar to that announced by the Army in 1940. While his suggestion about musicians was ignored by Secretary Knox, the search for a middle way between exclusion and integration had begun.

The general public knew nothing of this search, and in the heightened atmosphere of early war days, charged with unending propaganda about the four freedoms and the forces of democracy against fascism, the administration's racial attitudes were being questioned daily by civil rights spokesmen and by some Democratic politicians.[3-12] As protest against the Navy's racial policy mounted, Secretary Knox turned once again to his staff for reassurance. In July 1941 he appointed a committee consisting of Navy and Marine Corps personnel officers and including Addison Walker, a special assistant to Assistant Secretary Bard, to conduct a general investigation of that policy. The committee took six months to complete its study and submitted both a majority and minority report.

The majority report marshaled a long list of arguments to prove that exclusion of the Negro was not discriminatory, but "a means of promoting efficiency, dependability, and flexibility of the Navy as a whole." It concluded that no change in policy was necessary since "within the limitations of the characteristics of members of certain races, the enlisted personnel of the Naval Establishment is representative of all the citizens of the United States."[3-13] The majority invoked past experience, efficiency, and patriotism to support the *status quo*, but its chorus of reasons for excluding Negroes sounded incongruous amid the patriotic din and call to colors that followed Pearl Harbor.

CREW MEMBERS OF USS ARGONAUT
relax and read mail, Pearl Harbor, 1942.

Demonstrating changing social attitudes and also reflecting the compromise solution suggested by the President in June, Addison Walker's minority report recommended that a limited number of Negroes be enlisted for general duty "on some type of patrol or other small vessel assigned to a particular yard or station." While the enlistments could frankly be labeled experiments, Walker argued that such a step would mute black criticism by promoting Negroes out of the servant class. The program would also provide valuable data in case the Navy was later

28

directed to accept Negroes through Selective Service. Reasoning that a man's right to fight for his country was probably more fundamental than his right to vote, Walker insisted that the drive for the rights and privileges of black citizens was a social force that could not be ignored by the Navy. Indeed, he added, "the reconciliation of social friction within our own country" should be a special concern of the armed forces in wartime.[3-14]

Although the committee's majority won the day, its arguments were overtaken by events that followed Pearl Harbor. The NAACP, viewing the Navy's rejection of black volunteers in the midst of the intensive recruiting campaign, again took the issue to the White House. The President, in turn, asked the Fair Employment Practices Committee to consider the case.[3-15] Committee chairman Mark Ethridge conferred with Assistant Secretary Bard, pointing out that since Negroes had been eligible for general duty in World War I, the Navy had actually taken a step backward when it restricted them to the Messman's Branch. The committee was even willing to pay the price of segregation to insure the Negro's return to general duty. Ethridge recommended that the Navy amend its policy and accept Negroes for use at Caribbean stations or on harbor craft.[3-16] Criticism of Navy policy, hitherto emanating almost exclusively from the civil rights organizations and a few congressmen, now broadened to include another government agency. As President Roosevelt no doubt expected, the Fair Employment Practices Committee had come out in support of his compromise solution for the Navy.

But the committee had no jurisdiction over the armed services, and Secretary Knox continued to assert that with a war to win he could not risk "crews that are impaired in efficiency because of racial prejudice." He admitted to his friend, conservationist Gifford Pinchot, that the problem would have to be faced someday, but not during a war. Seemingly in response to Walker and Ethridge, he declared that segregated general service was impossible since enough men with the skills necessary to operate a war vessel were unavailable even "if you had the entire Negro population of the United States to choose from." As for limiting Negroes to steward duties, he explained that this policy avoided the chance that Negroes might rise to command whites, "a thing which instantly provokes serious trouble."[3-17] Faced in wartime with these arguments for efficiency, Assistant Secretary Bard could only promise Ethridge that black enlistment would be taken under consideration.

At this point the President again stepped in. On 15 January 1942 he asked his beleaguered secretary to consider the whole problem once more and suggested a course of action: "I think that with all the Navy activities, BuNav might invent something that colored enlistees could do in addition to the rating of messman."[3-18] The secretary passed the task on to the General Board, asking that it develop a plan for recruiting 5,000 Negroes in the general service.[3-19]

When the General Board met on 23 January to consider the secretary's request, it became apparent that the minority report on the role of Negroes in the Navy had gained at least one convert among the senior officers. One board member, the Inspector General of the Navy, Rear Adm. Charles P. Snyder, repeated the arguments lately advanced by Addison Walker. He suggested that the board consider employing Negroes in some areas outside the servant class: in the Musician's Branch, for example, because "the colored race is very musical and they are versed in all forms of rhythm," in the Aviation Branch where the Army had reported some success in employing Negroes, and on auxiliaries and minor vessels, especially transports. Snyder noted that these schemes would involve the creation of training schools, rigidly segregated at first, and that the whole program would be "troublesome and require tact, patience, and tolerance" on the part of those in charge. But, he added, "we have so many difficulties to surmount anyhow that one more possibly wouldn't swell the total very much." Foreseeing that segregation would become the focal point of black protest, he argued that the Navy had to begin accepting Negroes somewhere, and it might as well begin with a segregated general service.

Adamant in its opposition to any change in the Navy's policy, the Bureau of Navigation ignored Admiral Snyder's suggestions. The spokesman for the bureau warned that the 5,000 Negroes under consideration were just an opening wedge. "The sponsors of the program," Capt. Kenneth Whiting contended, "desire full equality on the part of the Negro and will not rest content until they obtain it." In the end, he predicted, Negroes would be on every man-of-war in direct proportion to their percentage of the population. The Commandant of the Marine Corps, Maj. Gen. Thomas Holcomb, echoed the bureau's sentiments. He viewed the issue of black enlistments as crucial.

If we are defeated we must not close our eyes to the fact that once in they [Negroes] will be strengthened in their effort to force themselves into every activity we have. If they are not satisfied to be messmen, they will not be satisfied to go into the construction or labor battalions. Don't forget the colleges are turning out a large number of well-educated Negroes. I don't know how long we will be able to keep them out of the V-7 class. I think not very long.

The commandant called the enlistment of Negroes "absolutely tragic"; Negroes had every opportunity, he added, "to satisfy their aspiration to serve in the Army," and their desire to enter the naval service was largely an effort "to break into a club that doesn't want them."

The board heard similar sentiments from representatives of the Bureau of Aeronautics, the Bureau of Yards and Docks, and, with reservations, from the Coast Guard. Confronted with such united opposition from the powerful bureaus, the General Board capitulated. On 3 February it reported to the secretary that it was unable to submit a plan and strongly recommended that the current policy be allowed to stand. The board stated that "if, in the opinion of higher authority, political pressure is such as to require the enlistment of these people for general service, let it be for that." If restriction of Negroes to the Messman's Branch was discrimination, the board added, "it was but part and parcel of a similar discrimination throughout the United States."[3-20]

Secretary Knox was certainly not one to dispute the board's findings, but it was a different story in the White House. President Roosevelt refused to accept the argument that the only choice lay between exclusion in the Messman's Branch and total integration in the general service. His desire to avoid the race issue was understandable; the war was in its darkest days, and whatever his aspirations for American society, the President was convinced that, while some change was necessary, "to go the whole way at one fell swoop would seriously impair the general average efficiency of the Navy."[3-21] He wanted the board to study the question further, noting that there were some additional tasks and some special assignments that could be worked out for the Negro that "would not inject into the whole personnel of the Navy the race question."[3-22]

MESSMEN VOLUNTEER AS GUNNERS,
Pacific task force, July 1942.

The Navy got the message. Armed with these instructions from the White House, the General Board called on the bureaus and other agencies to furnish lists of stations or assignments where Negroes could be used in other than the Messman's Branch, adding that it was "unnecessary and inadvisable" to emphasize further the undesirability of recruiting Negroes. Freely interpreting the President's directive, the board decided that its proposals had to provide for segregation in order to prevent the injection of the race issue into the Navy. It rejected the idea of enlisting Negroes in such selected ratings as musician and carpenter's mate or designating a branch for Negroes (the possibility of an all-black aviation department for a carrier was discussed). Basing its decision on the plans quickly submitted by the bureaus, the General Board recommended a course that it felt offered "least disadvantages and the least difficulty of accomplishment as a war measure": the formation of black units in the shore establishment, black crews for naval district local defense craft and selected Coast Guard cutters, black regiments in the Seabees, and composite battalions in the Marine Corps. The board asked that the Navy Department be granted wide latitude in deciding the number of Negroes to be accepted as well as their rate of enlistment and the method of recruiting, training, and assignment.[3-23] The President agreed to the plan, but balked at the board's last request. "I think this is a matter," he told Secretary Knox, "to be determined by you and me."[3-24]

The two-year debate over the admission of Negroes ended just in time, for the opposition to the Navy's policy was enlisting new allies daily. The national press made the expected invidious comparisons when Joe Louis turned over his share of the purse from the Louis-Baer fight to Navy Relief, and Wendell Willkie in a well-publicized speech at New York's Freedom House excoriated the Navy's racial practices as a "mockery" of democracy.[3-25] But these were the last shots fired. On 7 April 1942 Secretary Knox announced the Navy's capitulation. The Navy would accept 277 black volunteers per week—it was not yet drafting anyone—for enlistment in all ratings of the general service of the reserve components of the Navy, Marine Corps, and Coast Guard. Their actual entry would have to await the construction of suitable, meaning segregated, facilities, but the Navy's goal for the first year was 14,000 Negroes in the general service.[3-26]

Members of the black community received the news with mixed emotions. Some reluctantly accepted the plan as a first step; the NAACP's *Crisis* called it "progress toward a more enlightened point of view." Others, like the National Negro Congress, complimented Knox for his "bold, patriotic action."[3-27] But almost all were quick to point out that the black sailor would be segregated, limited to the rank of petty officer, and, except as a steward, barred from sea duty.[3-28] The Navy's plan offered all the disadvantages of the Army's system with none of the corresponding advantages for participation and advancement. The NAACP hammered away at the segregation angle, informing its public that the old system, which had fathered inequalities and humiliations in the Army and in civilian life, was now being followed by the Navy. A. Philip Randolph complained that the change in Navy policy merely "accepts and extends and consolidates the policy of Jim-Crowism in the Navy as well as proclaims it as an accepted,

30

recognized government ideology that the Negro is inferior to the white man."[3-29] The editors of the National Urban League's *Opportunity* concluded that, "faced with the great opportunity to strengthen the forces of Democracy, the Navy Department chose to affirm the charge that Japan is making against America to the brown people ... that the so-called Four Freedoms enunciated in the great 'Atlantic Charter' were for white men only."[3-30]

A Segregated Navy

With considerable alacrity the Navy set a practical course for the employment of its black volunteers. On 21 April 1942 Secretary Knox approved a plan for training Negroes at Camp Barry, an isolated section of the Great Lakes Training Center. Later renamed Camp Robert Smalls after a black naval hero of the Civil War, the camp not only offered the possibility of practically unlimited expansion but, as the Bureau of Navigation put it, made segregation "less obvious" to recruits. The secretary also approved the use of facilities at Hampton Institute, the well-known black school in Virginia, as an advanced training school for black recruits.[3-31]

Black enlistments began on 1 June 1942, and black volunteers started entering Great Lakes later that month in classes of 277 men. At the same time the Navy opened enlistments for an unlimited number of black Seabees and messmen. Lt. Comdr. Daniel Armstrong commanded the recruit program at Camp Smalls. An Annapolis graduate, son of the founder of Hampton Institute, Armstrong first came to the attention of Knox in March 1942 when he submitted a plan for the employment of black sailors that the secretary considered practical.[3-32] Under Armstrong's energetic leadership, black recruits received training that was in some respects superior to that afforded whites. For all his success, however, Armstrong was strongly criticized, especially by educated Negroes who resented his theories of education. Imbued with the paternalistic attitude of Tuskegee and Hampton, Armstrong saw the Negro as possessing a separate culture more attuned to vocational training. He believed that Negroes needed special treatment and discipline in a totally segregated environment free from white competition. Educated Negroes, on the other hand, saw in this special treatment another form of discrimination.[3-33]

ELECTRICIAN MATES
string power lines in the Central Pacific.

During the first six months of the new segregated training program, before the great influx of Negroes from the draft, the Navy set the training period at twelve weeks. Later, when it had reluctantly abandoned the longer period, the Navy discovered that the regular eight-week course was sufficient. Approximately 31 percent of those graduating from the recruit course were qualified for Class A schools and entered advanced classes to receive training that would normally lead to petty officer rating for the top graduates and prepare men for assignment to naval stations and local defense and district craft. There they would serve in such class "A" specialties as radioman, signalman, and yeoman and the other occupational specialties such as machinist, mechanic, carpenter, electrician, cook, and baker.[3-34] Some of these classes were held at Hampton, but, as the number of black recruits increased, the majority remained at Camp Smalls for advanced training.

The rest of the recruit graduates, those unqualified for advanced schooling, were divided. Some went directly to naval stations and local defense and district craft where they relieved whites as seaman, second class, and fireman, third class, and as trainees in specialties that required no advanced schooling; the rest, approximately eighty men per week, went to naval ammunition depots as unskilled laborers.[3-35]

The Navy proceeded to assimilate the black volunteers along these lines, suffering few of the personnel problems that plagued the Army in the first months of the war. In contrast to the Army's chaotic situation, caused by the thousands of black recruits streaming in from Selective Service, the Navy's plans for its volunteers were disrupted only because qualified Negroes showed little inclination to flock to the Navy standard, and more than half of those who did were rejected. The Bureau of Naval Personnel[3-36] reported that during the first three weeks of recruitment only 1,261 Negroes volunteered for general service, and 58 percent of these had to be rejected for physical and other reasons. The Chief of Naval Personnel, Rear Adm. Randall Jacobs, was surprised at the small number of volunteers, a figure far below the planners' expectations, and his surprise turned to concern in the next months as the seventeen-year-old volunteer inductees, the primary target of the armed forces recruiters, continued to choose the Army over the Navy at a ratio of 10 to 1.[3-37] The Navy's personnel officials agreed that they had to attract their proper share of intelligent and able Negroes but seemed unable to isolate the cause of the disinterest. Admiral Jacobs blamed it on a lack of publicity; the bureau's historians, perhaps unaware of the Navy's nineteenth century experience with black seamen, later attributed

31

it to Negroes' "relative unfamiliarity with the sea or the large inland waters and their consequent fear of the water."[3-38]

The fact was, of course, that Negroes shunned the Navy because of its recent reputation as the exclusive preserve of white America. Only when the Navy began assigning black recruiting specialists to the numerous naval districts and using black chief petty officers, reservists from World War I general service, at recruiting centers to explain the new opportunities for Negroes in the Navy was the bureau able to overcome some of the young men's natural reluctance to volunteer. By 1 February 1943 the Navy had 26,909 Negroes (still 2 percent of the total enlisted): 6,662 in the general service; 2,020 in the Seabees; and 19,227, over two-thirds of the total, in the Steward's Branch.[3-39]

The smooth and efficient distribution of black recruits was short-lived. Under pressure from the Army, the War Manpower Commission, and in particular the White House, the Navy was forced into a sudden and significant expansion of its black recruit program. The Army had long objected to the Navy's recruitment method, and as early as February 1942 Secretary Stimson was calling the volunteer recruitment system a waste of manpower.[3-40] He was even more direct when he complained to President Roosevelt that through voluntary recruiting the Navy had avoided acceptance of any considerable number of Negroes. Consequently, the Army was now faced with the possibility of having to accept an even greater proportion of Negroes "with adverse effect on its combat efficiency." The solution to this problem, as Stimson saw it, was for the Navy to take its recruits from Selective Service.[3-41] Stimson failed to win his point. The President accepted the Navy's argument that segregation would be difficult to maintain on board ship. "If the Navy living conditions on board ship were similar to the Army living conditions on land," he wrote Stimson, "the problem would be easier but the circumstances ... being such as they are, I feel that it is best to continue the present system at this time."[3-42]

But the battle over racial quotas was only beginning. The question of the number of Negroes in the Navy was only part of the much broader considerations and conflicts over manpower policy that finally led the President, on 5 December 1942, to direct the discontinuance in all services of volunteer enlistment of men between the ages of eighteen and thirty-eight.[3-43] Beginning in February 1943 all men in this age group would be obtained through Selective Service. The order also placed Selective Service under the War Manpower Commission.

The Navy issued its first call for inductees from Selective Service in February 1943, adopting the Army's policy of placing its requisition on a racial basis and specifying the number of whites and blacks needed for the Navy, Marine Corps, and Coast Guard. The Bureau of Naval Personnel planned to continue its old monthly quota of about 1,200 Negroes for general service and 1,500 for the Messman's Branch. Secretary Knox explained to the President that it would be impossible for the Navy to take more Negroes without resorting to mixed crews in the fleet, which, Knox reminded Roosevelt, was a policy "contrary to the President's program." The President agreed with Knox and told him so to advise Maj. Gen. Lewis B. Hershey, Director of Selective Service.[3-44]

The problem of drafting men by race was a major concern of the Bureau of Selective Service and its parent organization, the War Manpower Commission. At a time when a general shortage of manpower was developing and industry was beginning to feel the effects of the draft, Negroes still made up only 6 percent of the armed forces, a little over half their percentage of the population, and almost all of these were in the Army. The chairman of the War Manpower Commission, Paul V. McNutt, explained to Secretary Knox as he had to Secretary Stimson that the practice of placing separate calls for white and black registrants could not be justified. Not only were there serious social and legal implications in the existing draft practices, he pointed out, but the Selective Service Act itself prohibited racial discrimination. It was necessary, therefore, to draft men by order number and not by color.[3-45]

On top of this blow, the Navy came under fire from another quarter. The President was evidently still thinking about Negroes in the Navy. He wrote to the secretary on 22 February:

I guess you were dreaming or maybe I was dreaming if Randall Jacobs is right in regard to what I am supposed to have said about employment of negroes in the Navy. If I did say that such employment should be stopped, I must have been talking in my sleep. Most decidedly we must continue the employment of negroes in the Navy, and I do not think it the least bit necessary to put mixed crews on the ships. I can find a thousand ways of employing them without doing so.

The point or the thing is this. There is going to be a great deal of feeling if the Government in winning this war does not employ approximately 10% of negroes—their actual percentage to the total population. The Army is nearly up to this percentage but the Navy is so far below it that it will be deeply criticized by anybody who wants to check into the details.

Perhaps a check by you showing exactly where all white enlisted men are serving and where all colored enlisted men are serving will show you the great number of places where

32

colored men could serve, where they are not serving now—shore duty of all kinds, together with the handling of many kinds of yard craft.

You know the headache we have had about this and the reluctance of the Navy to have any negroes. You and I have had to veto that Navy reluctance and I think we have to do it again.[3-46]

In an effort to save the quota concept, the Bureau of Naval Personnel ground out new figures that would raise the current call of 2,700 Negroes per month to 5,000 in April and 7,350 for each of the remaining months of 1943. Armed with these figures, Secretary Knox was able to promise Commissioner McNutt that 10 percent of the men inducted for the rest of 1943 would be Negroes, although separate calls had to be continued for the time being to permit adjusting the flow of Negroes to the expansion of facilities.[3-47] In other words, the secretary promised to accept 71,900 black draftees in 1943; he did not promise to increase the black strength of the Navy to 10 percent of the total.

Commissioner McNutt understood the distinction and found the Navy's offer wanting for two reasons. The proposed schedule was inadequate to absorb the backlog of black registrants who should have been inducted into the armed services, and it did not raise the percentage of Negroes in the Navy to a figure comparable to their strength in the national population. McNutt wanted the Navy to draft at least 125,000 Negroes before January 1944, and he insisted that the practice of placing separate calls be terminated "as soon as feasible."[3-48] The Navy finally struck a compromise with the commission, agreeing that up to 14,150 Negroes a month would be inducted for the rest of 1943 to reach the 125,000 figure by January 1944.[3-49] The issue of separate draft calls for Negroes and whites remained in abeyance while the services made common cause against the commission by insisting that the orderly absorption of Negroes demanded a regular program that could only be met by maintaining the quota system.

Total black enlistments never reached 10 percent of the Navy's wartime enlisted strength but remained nearer the 5 percent mark. But this figure masks the Navy's racial picture in the later years of the war after it became dependent on Selective Service. The Navy drafted 150,955 Negroes during the war, 11.1 percent of all the men it drafted. In 1943 alone the Navy placed calls with Selective Service for 116,000 black draftees. Although Selective Service was unable to fill the monthly request completely, the Navy received 77,854 black draftees (versus 672,437 whites) that year, a 240 percent rise over the 1942 black enlistment rate.[3-50]

Although it wrestled for several months with the problem of distributing the increased number of black draftees, the Bureau of Naval Personnel could invent nothing new. The Navy, Knox told President Roosevelt, would continue to segregate Negroes and restrict their service to certain occupations. Its increased black strength would be absorbed in twenty-seven new black Seabee battalions, in which Negroes would serve overseas as stevedores; in black crews for harbor craft and local defense forces; and in billets for cooks and port hands. The rest would be sent to shore stations for guard and miscellaneous duties in concentrations up to about 50 percent of the total station strength. The President approved the Navy's proposals, and the distribution of Negroes followed these lines.[3-51]

To smooth the racial adjustments implicit in these plans, the Bureau of Naval Personnel developed two operating rules: Negroes would be assigned only where need existed, and, whenever possible, those from northern communities would not be used in the south. These rules caused some peculiar adjustments in administration. Negroes were not assigned to naval districts for distribution according to the discretion of the commander, as were white recruits. Rather, after conferring with local commanders, the bureau decided on the number of Negroes to be included in station complements and the types of jobs they would fill. It then assigned the men to duty accordingly, and the districts were instructed not to change the orders without consulting the bureau. Subsequently the bureau reinforced this rule by enjoining the commanders to use Negroes in the ratings for which they had been trained and by sending bureau representatives to the various commands to check on compliance.

Some planners feared that the concentration of Negroes at shore stations might prove detrimental to efficiency and morale. Proposals were circulated in the Bureau of Naval Personnel for the inclusion of Negroes in small numbers in the crews of large combat ships—for example, they might be used as firemen and ordinary seamen on the new aircraft carriers—but Admiral Jacobs rejected the recommendations.[3-52] The Navy was not yet ready to try integration, it seemed, even though racial disturbances were becoming a distinct possibility in 1943. For as Negroes became a larger part of the Navy, they also became a greater source of tension. The reasons for the tension were readily apparent. Negroes were restricted for the most part to shore duty, concentrated in large groups and assigned to jobs with little prestige and few chances of promotion. They were excluded from the WAVES (Women Accepted for Volunteer Emergency Service), the Nurse Corps, and the commissioned ranks. And they were rigidly segregated.

Although the Navy boasted that Negroes served in every rating and at every task, in fact almost all were used in a limited range of occupations. Denied general service assignments on warships, trained Negroes were restricted to the relatively few billets open in the harbor defense, district, and small craft service. Although assigning Negroes to these duties met the President's request for variety of opportunity, the small craft could employ only 7,700 men at most, a minuscule part of the Navy's black strength.

Most Negroes performed humbler duties. By mid-1944 over 38,000 black sailors were serving as mess stewards, cooks, and bakers. These jobs remained in the Negro's eyes a symbol of his second-class citizenship in the naval establishment. Under pressure to provide more stewards to serve the officers whose number multiplied in the early months of the war, recruiters had netted all the men they could for that separate duty. Often recruiters took in many as stewards who were equipped by education and training for better jobs, and when these men were immediately put into uniforms and trained on the job at local naval stations the result was often dismaying. The Navy thus received poor service as well as unwelcome publicity for maintaining a segregated servants' branch. In an effort to standardize the training of messmen, the Bureau of Naval Personnel established a stewards school in the spring of 1943 at Norfolk and later one at Bainbridge, Maryland. The change in training did little to improve the standards of the service and much to intensify the feeling of isolation among many stewards.

LABORERS AT NAVAL AMMUNITION DEPOT.
Sailors passing 5-inch canisters, St. Julien's Creek, Virginia.

Another 12,000 Negroes served as artisans and laborers at overseas bases. Over 7,000 of these were Seabees, who, with the exception of two regular construction battalions that served with distinction in the Pacific, were relegated to "special" battalions stevedoring cargo and supplies. The rest were laborers in base companies assigned to the South Pacific area. These units were commanded by white officers, and almost all the petty officers were white.

Approximately half the Negroes in the Navy were detailed to shore billets within the continental United States. Most worked as laborers at ammunition or supply depots, at air stations, and at section bases,[3-53] concentrated in large all-black groups and sometimes commanded by incompetent white officers.[3-54]

SEABEES IN THE SOUTH PACIFIC
righting an undermined water tank.

While some billets existed in practically every important rating for graduates of the segregated specialty schools, these jobs were so few that black specialists were often assigned instead to unskilled laboring jobs.[3-55] Some of these men were among the best educated Negroes in the Navy, natural leaders capable of articulating their dissatisfaction. They resented being barred from the fighting, and their resentment, spreading through the thousands of Negroes in the shore establishment, was a prime cause of racial tension.

No black women had been admitted to the Navy. Race was not mentioned in the legislation establishing the WAVES in 1942, but neither was exclusion on account of color expressly forbidden. The WAVES and the Women's Reserve of both the Coast Guard (SPARS) and the Marine Corps therefore celebrated their second birthday exclusively white. The Navy Nurse Corps was also totally white. In answer to protests passed to the service through Eleanor Roosevelt, the Navy admitted in November 1943 that it had a shortage of 500 nurses, but since another 500 white nurses were under indoctrination and training, the Bureau of Medicine and Surgery explained, "the question relative to the necessity for accepting colored personnel in this category is not apparent."[3-56]

Another major cause of unrest among black seamen was the matter of rank and promotion. With the exception of the Coast Guard, the naval establishment had no black officers in 1943, and none were contemplated. Nor was there much opportunity for advancement in the ranks. Barred from service in the fleet, the nonrated seamen faced strong competition for the limited number of petty officer positions in the shore establishment. In consequence, morale throughout the ranks deteriorated.

The constant black complaint, and the root of the Navy's racial problem, was segregation. It was especially hard on young black recruits who had never experienced legal segregation in civilian life and on the "talented tenth," the educated Negroes, who were quickly frustrated by a policy that decided opportunity and assignment on the basis of color. They particularly resented segregation in housing, messing, and recreation. Here segregation off the job, officially sanctioned, made manifest by signs distinguishing facilities for white and black, and enforced by military as well as civilian police, was a daily reminder for the Negro of the Navy's discrimination.

34

Such discrimination created tension in the ranks that periodically released itself in racial disorder. The first sign of serious unrest occurred in June 1943 when over half the 640 Negroes of the Naval Ammunition Depot at St. Julien's Creek, Virginia, rioted against alleged discrimination in segregated seating for a radio show. In July, 744 Negroes of the 80th Construction Battalion staged a protest over segregation on a transport in the Caribbean. Yet, naval investigators cited leadership problems as a major factor in these and subsequent incidents, and at least one commanding officer was relieved as a consequence.[3-57]

Progressive Experiments

COMMANDER SARGENT

Since the inception of black enlistment there had been those in the Bureau of Naval Personnel who argued for the establishment of a group to coordinate plans and policies on the training and use of black sailors. Various proposals were considered, but only in the wake of the racial disturbances of 1943 did the bureau set up a Special Programs Unit in its Planning and Control Activity to oversee the whole black enlistment program. In the end the size of the unit governed the scope of its program. Originally the unit was to monitor all transactions involving Negroes in the bureau's operating divisions, thus relieving the Enlisted Division of the critical task of distributing billets for Negroes. It was also supposed to advise local commanders on race problems and interpret departmental policies for them. When finally established in August 1943, the unit consisted of only three officers, a size which considerably limited its activities. Still, the unit worked diligently to improve the lot of the black sailor, and eventually from this office would emerge the plans that brought about the integration of the Navy.

The Special Programs Unit's patron saint and the guiding spirit of the Navy's liberalizing race program was Lt. Comdr. Christopher S. Sargent. He never served in the unit himself, but helped find the two lieutenant commanders, Donald O. VanNess and Charles E. Dillon, who worked under Capt. Thomas F. Darden in the Plans and Operations Section of the Bureau of Naval Personnel and acted as liaison between the Special Programs Unit and its civilian superiors. A legendary figure in the bureau, the 31-year-old Sargent arrived as a lieutenant, junior grade, from Dean Acheson's law firm, but his rank and official position were no measure of his influence in the Navy Department. By birth and training he was used to moving in the highest circles of American society and government, and he had wide-ranging interests and duties in the Navy. Described by a superior as "a philosopher who could not tolerate segregation,"[3-58] Sargent waged something of a moral crusade to integrate the Navy. He was convinced that a social change impossible in peacetime was practical in war. Not only would integration build a more efficient Navy, it might also lead the way to changes in American society that would bridge the gap between the races.[3-59] In effect, Sargent sought to force the generally conservative Bureau of Naval Personnel into making rapid and sweeping changes in the Navy's racial policy.

During its first months of existence the Special Programs Unit tried to quiet racial unrest by a rigorous application of the separate but equal principle. It began attacking the concentration of Negroes in large segregated groups in the naval districts by creating more overseas billets. Toward the end of 1943, Negroes were being assigned in greater numbers to duty in the Pacific at shore establishments and aboard small defense, district, and yard craft. The Bureau of Naval Personnel also created new specialties for Negroes in the general service. One important addition was the creation of black shore patrol units for which a school was started at Great Lakes. The Special Programs Unit established a remedial training center for illiterate draftees at Camp Robert Smalls, drawing the faculty from black servicemen who had been educators in civilian life. The twelve-week course gave the students the equivalent of a fifth grade education in addition to regular recruit training. Approximately 15,000 Negroes took this training before the school was consolidated with a similar organization for whites at Bainbridge, Maryland, in the last months of the war.[3-60]

At the other end of the spectrum, the Special Programs Unit worked for the efficient use of black Class A school graduates by renewing the attack on improper assignments. The bureau had long held that the proper assignment of black specialists was of fundamental importance to morale and efficiency, and in July 1943 it had ordered that all men must be used in the ratings and for the types of work for which they had been trained.[3-61] But the unit discovered considerable deviation from this policy in some districts, especially in the south, where there was a tendency to regard Negroes as an extra labor source above the regular military complement. In December 1943 the Special Programs Unit got the bureau to rule in the name of manpower efficiency that, with the exception of special units in the supply departments at South Boston and Norfolk, no black sailor could be assigned to such civilian jobs as maintenance work and stevedoring in the continental United States.[3-62]

35

These reforms were welcome, but they ignored the basic dilemma: the only way to abolish concentrations of shore-based Negroes was to open up positions for them in the fleet. Though many black sailors were best suited for unskilled or semiskilled billets, a significant number had technical skills that could be properly used only if these men were assigned to the fleet. To relieve the racial tension and to end the waste of skilled manpower engendered by the misuse of these men, the Special Programs Unit pressed for a chance to test black seamanship. Admiral King agreed, and in early 1944 the Bureau of Naval Personnel assigned 196 black enlisted men and 44 white officers and petty officers to the USS *Mason*, a newly commissioned destroyer escort, with the understanding that all enlisted billets would be filled by Negroes as soon as those qualified to fill them had been trained. It also assigned 53 black rated seamen and 14 white officers and noncommissioned officers to a patrol craft, the PC 1264.[3-63] Both ships eventually replaced their white petty officers and some of their officers with Negroes. Among the latter was Ens. Samuel Gravely, who was to become the Navy's first black admiral.

USS MASON.
Sailors look over their new ship.

Although both ships continued to operate with black crews well into 1945, the *Mason* on escort duty in the Atlantic, only four other segregated patrol craft were added to the fleet during the war.[3-64] The *Mason* passed its shakedown cruise test, but the Bureau of Naval Personnel was not satisfied with the crew. The black petty officers had proved competent in their ratings and interested in their work, but bureau observers agreed that the rated men in general were unable to maintain discipline. The nonrated men tended to lack respect for the petty officers, who showed some disinclination to put their men on report. The Special Programs Unit admitted the truth of these charges but argued that the experiment only proved what the Navy already knew: black sailors did not respond well when assigned to all-black organizations under white officers.[3-65] On the other hand, the experiment demonstrated that the Navy possessed a reservoir of able seamen who were not being efficiently employed, and—an unexpected dividend from the presence of white noncommissioned officers—that integration worked on board ship. The white petty officers messed, worked, and slept with their men in the close contact inevitable aboard small ships, with no sign of racial friction.

Opportunity for advancement was as important to morale as assignment according to training and skill, and the Special Programs Unit encouraged the promotion of Negroes according to their ability and in proportion to their number. Although in July 1943 the Bureau of Naval Personnel had warned commanders that it would continue to order white enlisted men to sea with the expectation that they would be replaced in shore jobs by Negroes,[3-66] the Special Programs Unit discovered that rating and promotion of Negroes was still slow. At the unit's urging, the bureau advised all naval districts that it expected Negroes to be rated upward "as rapidly as practicable" and asked them to report on their rating of Negroes.[3-67] It also authorized stations to retain white petty officers for up to two weeks to break in their black replacements, but warned that this privilege must not be abused. The bureau further directed that all qualified general service candidates be advanced to ratings for which they were eligible regardless of whether their units were authorized enough spaces to take care of them. This last directive did little for black promotions at first because many local commanders ruled that no Negroes could be "qualified" since none were allowed to perform sea duties. In January 1944 the bureau had to clarify the order to make sure that Negroes were given the opportunity to advance.[3-68]

Despite these evidences of command concern, black promotions continued to lag in the Navy. Again at the Special Programs Unit's urging, the Bureau of Naval Personnel began to limit the number of rated men turned out by the black training schools so that more nonrated men already on the job might have a better chance to win ratings. The bureau instituted a specialist leadership course for rated Negroes at Great Lakes and recommended in January 1944 that two Negroes so trained be included in each base company sent out of the country. It also selected twelve Negroes with backgrounds in education and public relations and assigned them to recruiting duty around the country. The bureau expanded the black petty officer program because it was convinced by the end of 1943 that the presence of more black leaders, particularly in the large base companies, would improve discipline and raise morale. It was but a short step from this conviction to a realization that black commissioned officers were needed.

Despite its 100,000 enlisted Negroes, the absence of black commissioned officers in the fall of 1943 forced the Navy to answer an increasing number of queries from civil rights organizations and Congress.[3-69] Several times during 1942 suggestions were made within the Bureau of Naval Personnel that the instructors at the Hampton specialist school and seventy-five other Negroes be commissioned for service with the large black units, but nothing happened.

36

Secretary Knox himself thought that the Navy would have to develop a considerable body of black sailors before it could even think about commissioning black officers.[3-70] But the secretary failed to appreciate the effect of the sheer number of black draftees that overwhelmed the service in the spring of 1943, and he reckoned without the persuasive arguments of his special assistant, Adlai Stevenson.[3-71]

Secretary Knox often referred to Adlai Stevenson as "my New Dealer," and, as the expression suggested, the Illinois lawyer was in an excellent position to influence the secretary's thinking.[3-72] Although not so forceful an advocate as Christopher Sargent, Stevenson lent his considerable intelligence and charm to the support of those in the department who sought equal opportunity for the Negro. He was an invaluable and influential ally for the Special Programs Unit. Stevenson knew Knox well and understood how to approach him. He was particularly effective in getting Negroes commissioned. In September 1943 he pointed out that, with the induction of 12,000 Negroes a month, the demand for black officers would be mounting in the black community and in the government as well. The Navy could not and should not, he warned, postpone much longer the creation of some black officers. Suspicion of discrimination was one reason the Navy was failing to get the best qualified Negroes, and Stevenson believed it wise to act quickly. He recommended that the Navy commission ten or twelve Negroes from among "top notch civilians just as we procure white officers" and a few from the ranks. The commissioning should be treated as a matter of course without any special publicity. The news, he added wryly, would get out soon enough.[3-73]

There were in fact three avenues to a Navy commission: the Naval Academy, the V-12 program, and direct commission from civilian life or the enlisted ranks. But Annapolis had no Negroes enrolled at the time Stevenson spoke, and only a dozen Negroes were enrolled in V-12 programs at integrated civilian colleges throughout the country.[3-74] The lack of black students in the V-12 program could be attributed in part to the belief of many black trainees that the program barred Negroes. Actually, it never had, and in December 1943 the bureau publicized this fact. It issued a circular letter emphasizing to all commanders that enlisted men were entitled to consideration for transfer to the V-12 program regardless of race.[3-75] Despite this effort it was soon apparent that the program would produce only a few black officers, and the Bureau of Naval Personnel, at the urging of its Special Programs Unit, agreed to follow Stevenson's suggestion and concentrate on the direct commissioning of Negroes. Unlike Stevenson the bureau preferred to obtain most of the men from the enlisted ranks, and only in the case of certain specially trained men did the Navy commission civilians.

FIRST BLACK OFFICERS IN THE NAVY.
From left to right: (top row) John W. Reagan, Jesse W. Arbor, Dalton L. Baugh;
(second row) Graham E. Martin, W. O. Charles B. Lear, Frank C. Sublett;
(third row) Phillip S. Barnes, George Cooper, Reginald Goodwin;
(bottom row) James E. Hare, Samuel E. Barnes, W. Sylvester White, Dennis D. Nelson II.

The Bureau of Naval Personnel concluded that, since many units were substantially or wholly manned by Negroes, black officers could be used without undue difficulty, and when Secretary Knox, prodded by Stevenson, turned to the bureau, it recommended that the Navy commission twelve line and ten staff officers from a selected list of enlisted men.[3-76] Admiral King endorsed the bureau's recommendation and on 15 December 1943 Knox approved it, although he conditioned his approval by saying: "After you have commissioned the twenty-two officers you suggest, I think this matter should again be reviewed before any additional colored officers are commissioned."[3-77]

On 1 January 1944 the first sixteen black officer candidates, selected from among qualified enlisted applicants, entered Great Lakes for segregated training. All sixteen survived the course, but only twelve were commissioned. In the last week of the course, three candidates were returned to the ranks, not because they had failed but because the Bureau of Naval Personnel had suddenly decided to limit the number of black officers in this first group to twelve. The twelve entered the U.S. Naval Reserve as line officers on 17 March. A thirteenth man, the only candidate who lacked a college degree, was made a warrant officer because of his outstanding work in the course.

Two of the twelve new ensigns were assigned to the faculty at Hampton training school, four others to yard and harbor craft duty, and the rest to training duty at Great Lakes. All carried the label "Deck Officers Limited—only," a designation usually reserved for officers whose physical or educational deficiencies kept them from performing all the duties of a line officer. The Bureau of Naval Personnel never explained why the men were placed in this category, but it was clear that none of them lacked the physical requirements of a line officer and all had had business or professional careers in civil life.

37

Operating duplicate training facilities for officer candidates was costly, and the bureau decided shortly after the first group of black candidates was trained that future candidates of both races would be trained together. By early summer ten more Negroes, this time civilians with special professional qualifications, had been trained with whites and were commissioned as staff officers in the Medical, Dental, Chaplain, Civil Engineer, and Supply Corps. These twenty-two men were the first of some sixty Negroes to be commissioned during the war.

Since only a handful of the Negroes in the Navy were officers, the preponderance of the race problems concerned relations between black enlisted men and their white officers. The problem of selecting the proper officers to command black sailors was a formidable one never satisfactorily solved during the war. As in the Army, most of the white officers routinely selected for such assignments were southerners, chosen by the Bureau of Naval Personnel for their assumed "understanding" of Negroes rather than for their general competency. The Special Programs Unit tried to work with these officers, assembling them for conferences to discuss the best techniques and procedures for dealing with groups of black subordinates. Members of the unit sought to disabuse the officers of preconceived biases, constantly reminding them that "our prejudices must be subordinated to our traditional unfailing obedience to orders."[3-78] Although there was ample proof that many Negroes actively resented the paternalism exhibited by many of even the best of these officers, this fact was slow to filter through the naval establishment. It was not until January 1944 that an officer who had compiled an enviable record in training Seabee units described how his organization had come to see the light:

We in the Seabees no longer follow the precept that southern officers exclusively should be selected for colored battalions. A man may be from the north, south, east or west. If his attitude is to do the best possible job he knows how, regardless of what the color of his personnel is, that is the man we want as an officer for our colored Seabees. We have learned to steer clear of the "I'm from the South—I know how to handle 'em variety." It follows with reference to white personnel, that deeply accented southern whites are not generally suited for Negro battalions.[3-79]

Further complicating the task of selecting suitable officers for black units was the fact that when the Bureau of Naval Personnel asked unit commanders to recommend men for such duty many commanders used the occasion to rid themselves of their least desirable officers. The Special Programs Unit then tried to develop its own source of officers for black units. It discovered a fine reservoir of talent among the white noncommissioned officers who ran the physical training and drill courses at Great Lakes. These were excellent instructors, mature and experienced in dealing with people. In January 1944 arrangements were made to commission them and to assign them to black units.

Improvement in the quality of officers in black units was especially important because the attitude of local commanders was directly related to the degree of segregation in living quarters and recreational facilities, and such segregation was the most common source of racial tension. Although the Navy's practice of segregating units clearly invited separate living and recreational facilities, the rules were unwritten, and local commanders had been left to decide the extent to which segregation was necessary. Thus practices varied greatly and policy depended ultimately on the local commanders. Rather than attack racial practices at particular bases, the unit decided to concentrate on the officers. It explained to these leaders the Navy's policy of equal treatment and opportunity, a concept basically incompatible with many of their practices.

This conclusion was embodied in a pamphlet entitled *Guide to the Command of Negro Naval Personnel* and published by the Bureau of Naval Personnel in February 1944.[3-80] The Special Programs Unit had to overcome much opposition within the bureau to get the pamphlet published. Some thought the subject of racial tension was best ignored; others objected to the "sociological" content of the work, considering this approach outside the Navy's province. The unit argued that racial tension in the Navy was a serious problem that could not be ignored, and since human relations affected the Navy's mission the Navy should deal with social matters objectively and frankly.[3-81]

Scholarly and objective, the pamphlet was an important document in the history of race relations in the Navy. In language similar to that used in the War Department's pamphlet on race, the Bureau of Naval Personnel stated officially for the first time that discrimination flowed of necessity out of the doctrine of segregation:

The idea of compulsory racial segregation is disliked by almost all Negroes, and literally hated by many. This antagonism is in part a result of the fact that as a principle it embodies a doctrine of racial inferiority. It is also a result of the lesson taught the Negro by experience that in spite of the legal formula of "separate but equal" facilities, the facilities open to him under segregation are in fact usually inferior as to location or quality to those available to others.[3-82]

38

The guide also foreshadowed the end of the old order of things: "The Navy accepts no theories of racial differences in inborn ability, but expects that every man wearing its uniform be trained and used in accordance with his maximum individual capacity determined on the basis of individual performance."[3-83]

Forrestal Takes the Helm

The Navy got a leader sympathetic to the proposition of equal treatment and opportunity for Negroes, and possessed of the bureaucratic skills to achieve reforms, when President Roosevelt appointed Under Secretary James Forrestal to replace Frank Knox, who died suddenly on 28 April 1944. During the next five years Forrestal, a brilliant, complex product of Wall Street, would assume more and more responsibility for directing the integration effort in the defense establishment. Although no racial crusader, Forrestal had been for many years a member of the National Urban League, itself a pillar of the civil rights establishment. He saw the problem of employing Negroes as one of efficiency and simple fair play, and as the months went by he assumed an active role in experimenting with changes in the Navy's policy.[3-84]

His first experiment was with sea duty for Negroes. After the experience of the *Mason* and the other segregated ships which actually proved very little, sentiment for a partial integration of the fleet continued to grow in the Bureau of Naval Personnel. As early as April 1943, officers in the Planning and Control Activity recommended that Negroes be included in small numbers in the crews of the larger combat ships. Admiral Jacobs, however, was convinced that "you couldn't dump 200 colored boys on a crew in battle,"[3-85] so this and similar proposals later in the year never survived passage through the bureau.

Forrestal accepted Jacob's argument that as long as the war continued any move toward integrating the fighting ships was impractical. At the same time, he agreed with the Special Programs Unit that large concentrations of Negroes in shore duties lowered efficiency and morale. Forrestal compromised by ordering the bureau to prepare as an experiment a plan for the integration of some fleet auxiliary ships. On 20 May 1944 he outlined the problem for the President:

"From a morale standpoint, the Negroes resent the fact that they are not assigned to general service billets at sea, and white personnel resent the fact that Negroes have been given less hazardous assignments." He explained that at first Negroes would be used only on the large auxiliaries, and their number would be limited to not more than 10 percent of the ship's complement. If this step proved workable, he planned to use Negroes in small numbers on other types of ships "as necessity indicates." The White House answered: "OK, FDR."[3-86]

Secretary Forrestal also won the support of the Chief of Naval Operations for the move, but Admiral King still considered integration in the fleet experimental and was determined to keep strict control until the results were known. On 9 August 1944 King informed the commanding officers of twenty-five large fleet auxiliaries that Negroes would be assigned to them in the near future. As Forrestal had suggested, King set the maximum number of Negroes at 10 percent of the ship's general service. Of this number, 15 percent would be third-class petty officers from shore activities, selected as far as possible from volunteers and, in any case, from those who had served the longest periods of shore duty. Of the remainder, 43 percent would be from Class A schools and 42 percent from recruit training. The basic 10 percent figure proved to be a theoretical maximum; no ship received that many Negroes.

Admiral King insisted that equal treatment in matters of training, promotion, and duty assignments must be accorded all hands, but he left the matter of berthing to the commanding officers, noting that experience had proved that in the shore establishment, when the percentage of blacks to whites was small, the two groups could be successfully mingled in the same compartments. He also pointed out that a thorough indoctrination of white sailors before the arrival of the Negroes had been useful in preventing racial friction ashore.[3-87]

King asked all commanders concerned in the experiment to report their experiences.[3-88] Their judgment: integration in the auxiliary fleet worked. As one typical report related after several months of integrated duty:

The crew was carefully indoctrinated in the fact that Negro personnel should not be subjected to discrimination of any sort and should be treated in the same manner as other members of the crew.

The Negro personnel when they came aboard were berthed indiscriminately throughout the crew's compartments in the same manner as if they had been white. It is felt that the assimilation of the general service Negro personnel aboard this ship has been remarkably successful. To the present date there has been no report of any difficulty which could be laid to their color. It is felt that this is due in part, at least, to the high calibre of Negroes assigned to this ship.[3-89]

The comments of his commanders convinced King that the auxiliary vessels in the fleet could be integrated without incident. He approved a plan submitted by the Chief of Naval Personnel on 6 March 1945 for the gradual assignment of Negroes to all auxiliary vessels, again in numbers not to exceed 10 percent of the general service billets in any ship's complement.[3-90] A month later Negroes were being so assigned in an administratively routine manner.[3-91] The Bureau of Naval Personnel then began assigning black officers to sea duty on the integrated vessels. The first one went to the *Mason* in March, and in succeeding months others were sent in a routine manner to auxiliary vessels throughout the fleet.[3-92] These assignments were not always carried out according to the bureau's formula. The commander of the USS *Chemung*, for example, told a young black ensign:

I'm a Navy Man, and we're in a war. To me, it's that stripe that counts—and the training and leadership that it is supposed to symbolize. That's why I never called a meeting of the crew to prepare them, to explain their obligation to respect you, or anything like that. I didn't want anyone to think you were different from any other officer coming aboard.[3-93]

Admitting Negroes to the WAVES was another matter considered by the new secretary in his first days in office. In fact, the subject had been under discussion in the Navy Department for some two years. Soon after the organization of the women's auxiliary, its director, Capt. Mildred H. McAfee, had recommended that Negroes be accepted, arguing that their recruitment would help to temper the widespread criticism of the Navy's restrictive racial policy. But the traditionalists in the Bureau of Naval Personnel had opposed the move on the grounds that WAVES were organized to replace men, and since there were more than enough black sailors to fill all billets open to Negroes there was no need to recruit black women.

Actually, both arguments served to mask other motives, as did Knox's rejection of recruitment on the grounds that integrating women into the Navy was difficult enough without taking on the race problem.[3-94] In April 1943 Knox "tentatively" approved the "tentative" outline of a bureau plan for the induction of up to 5,000 black WAVES, but nothing came of it.[3-95] Given the secretary's frequent protestation that the subject was under constant review,[3-96] and his statement to Captain McAfee that black WAVES would be enlisted "over his dead body,"[3-97] the tentative outline and approval seems to have been an attempt to defer the decision indefinitely.

Secretary Knox's delay merely attracted more attention to the problem and enabled the protestors to enlist powerful allies. At the time of his death, Knox was under siege by a delegation from the Congress of Industrial Organizations (CIO) demanding a reassessment of the Navy's policy on the women's reserve.[3-98] His successor turned for advice to Captain McAfee and to the Bureau of Naval Personnel where, despite Knox's "positive and direct orders" against recruiting black WAVES, the Special Programs Unit had continued to study the problem.[3-99] Convinced that the step was just and inevitable, the unit also agreed that the WAVES should be integrated. Forrestal approved, and on 28 July 1944 he recommended to the President that Negroes be trained in the WAVES on an integrated basis and assigned "wherever needed within the continental limits of the United States, preferably to stations where there are already Negro men." He concluded by reiterating a Special Programs Unit warning: "I consider it advisable to start obtaining Negro WAVES before we are forced to take them."[3-100]

To avoid the shoals of racial controversy in the midst of an election year, Secretary Forrestal did trim his recommendations to the extent that he retained the doctrine of separate but equal living quarters and mess facilities for the black WAVES. Despite this offer of compromise, President Roosevelt directed Forrestal to withhold action on the proposal.[3-101]Here the matter would probably have stood until after the election but for Thomas E. Dewey's charge in a Chicago speech during the presidential campaign that the White House was discriminating against black women. The President quickly instructed the Navy to admit Negroes into the WAVES.[3-102]

LIEUTENANT PICKENS AND ENSIGN WILLS.
First black WAVE officers,
members of the final graduating class at Naval Reserve Midshipmen's School (WR), Northhampton,
Massachusetts.

The first two black WAVE officers graduated from training at Smith College on 21 December, and the enlistment of black women began a week later. The program turned out to be more racially progressive than initially outlined by Forrestal. He had explained to the President that the women would be quartered separately, a provision interpreted in the Bureau of Naval Personnel to mean that black recruits would be organized into separate companies. Since a recruit company numbered 250 women, and since it quickly became apparent that such a large group of black volunteers would not soon be forthcoming, some of the bureau staff decided that the Navy

40

would continue to bar black women. In this they reckoned without Captain McAfee who insisted on a personal ruling by Forrestal. She warned the secretary that his order was necessary because the concept "was so strange to Navy practice."[3-103] He agreed with her that the Negroes would be integrated along with the rest of the incoming recruits, and the Bureau of Naval Personnel subsequently ordered that the WAVES be assimilated without making either special or separate arrangements.[3-104]

By July 1945 the Navy had trained seventy-two black WAVES at Hunter College Naval Training School in a fully integrated and routine manner. Although black WAVES were restricted somewhat in specialty assignments and a certain amount of separate quartering within integrated barracks prevailed at some duty stations, the Special Programs Unit came to consider the WAVE program, which established a forceful precedent for the integration of male recruit training, its most important wartime breakthrough, crediting Captain McAfee and her unbending insistence on equal treatment for the achievement.

Forrestal won the day in these early experiments, but he was a skillful administrator and knew that there was little hope for any fundamental social change in the naval service without the active cooperation of the Navy's high-ranking officers. His meeting with Admiral King on the subject of integration in the summer of 1944 has been reported by several people. Lester Granger, who later became Forrestal's special representative on racial matters, recalled:

He [Forrestal] said he spoke to Admiral King, who was then chief of staff, and said, "Admiral King, I'm not satisfied with the situation here—I don't think that our Navy Negro personnel are getting a square break. I want to do something about it, but I can't do anything about it unless the officers are behind me. I want your help. What do you say?" He said that Admiral King sat for a moment, and looked out the window and then said reflectively, "You know, we say that we are a democracy and a democracy ought to have a democratic Navy. I don't think you can do it, but if you want to try, I'm behind you all the way." And he told me, "And Admiral King was behind me, all the way, not only he but all of the Bureau of Personnel, BuPers. They've been bricks."[3-105] Admiral Jacobs, the Chief of Naval Personnel, also pledged his support.[3-106]

SAILORS IN THE GENERAL SERVICE MOVE AMMUNITION

As news of the King-Forrestal conversation filtered through the department, many of the programs long suggested by the Special Programs Unit and heretofore treated with indifference or disapproval suddenly received respectful attention.[3-107] With the high-ranking officers cooperating, the Navy under Forrestal began to attack some of the more obvious forms of discrimination and causes of racial tension. Admiral King led the attack, personally directing in August 1944 that all elements give close attention to the proper selection of officers to command black sailors. As he put it: "Certain officers will be temperamentally better suited for such commands than others."[3-108] The qualifications of these officers were to be kept under constant review. In December he singled out the commands in the Pacific area, which had a heavy concentration of all-black base companies, calling for a reform in their employment and advancement of Negroes.[3-109]

SECURITY WATCH IN THE MARIANAS.
Ratings of these men guarding an ammunition depot include boatswain, second class, seaman, first class, and fireman, first class.

The Bureau of Naval Personnel also stepped up the tempo of its reforms. In March 1944 it had already made black cooks and bakers eligible for duty in all commissary branches of the Navy.[3-110] In June it got Forrestal's approval for putting all rated cooks and stewards in chief petty officer uniforms.[3-111] (While providing finally for the proper uniforming of the chief cooks and stewards, this reform set their subordinates, the rated cooks and stewards, even further apart from their counterparts in the general service who of course continued to wear the familiar bell bottoms.) The bureau also began to attack the concentration of Negroes in ammunition depots and base companies. On 21 February 1945 it ordered that all naval magazines and ammunition depots in the United States and, wherever practical, overseas limit their black seamen to 30 percent of the total employed.[3-112] It also organized twenty logistic support companies to replace the formless base companies sent to the Pacific in the early months of the recruitment program. Organized to perform supply functions, each company consisted of 250 enlisted men and a few officers, with a flexible range of petty officer billets.

In the reform atmosphere slowly permeating the Bureau of Naval Personnel, the Special Programs Unit found it relatively easy to end segregation in the specialist training program.[3-113] From the first, the number of Negroes eligible for specialist training had been too small to make costly duplication of equipment and services practical. In 1943, for example, the black

41

aviation metalsmith school at Great Lakes had an average enrollment of eight students. The school was quietly closed and its students integrated with white students. Thus, when the *Mason's* complement was assembled in early 1944, Negroes were put into the destroyer school at Norfolk side by side with whites, and the black and white petty officers were quartered together. As a natural consequence of the decision to place Negroes in the auxiliary fleet, the Bureau of Naval Personnel opened training in seagoing rates to Negroes on an integrated basis. Citing the practicality of the move, the bureau closed the last of the black schools in June 1945.[3-114]

Despite these reforms, the months following Forrestal's talk with King saw many important recommendations of the Special Programs Unit wandering uncertainly through the bureaucratic desert. For example, a proposal to make the logistic support companies interracial, or at least to create comparable white companies to remove the stigma of segregated manual labor, failed to survive the objections of the enlisted personnel section. The Bureau of Naval Personnel rejected a suggestion that Negroes be assigned to repair units on board ships and to LST's, LCI's, and LCT's during the expansion of the amphibious program. On 30 August 1944 Admiral King rejected a bureau recommendation that the crews of net tenders and mine ships be integrated. He reasoned that these vessels were being kept in readiness for overseas assignment and required "the highest degree of experienced seamanship and precision work" by the crews. He also cited the crowded living quarters and less experienced officers as further reasons for banning Negroes.[3-115]

There were other examples of backsliding in the Navy's racial practices. Use of Negroes in general service had created a shortage of messmen, and in August 1944 the Bureau of Naval Personnel authorized commanders to recruit among black seamen for men to transfer to the Steward's Branch. The bureau suggested as a talking point the fact that stewards enjoyed more rapid advancement, shorter hours, and easier work than men in the general service.[3-116] And, illustrating that a move toward integration was sometimes followed by a step backward, a bureau representative reported in July 1945 that whereas a few black trainees at the Bainbridge Naval Training Center had been integrated in the past, many now arriving were segregated in all-black companies.[3-117]

There were reasons for the inconsistent stance in Washington. The Special Programs Unit had for some time been convinced that only full integration would eliminate discrimination and dissolve racial tensions in the Navy, and it had understood Forrestal's desire "to do something" for the Negro to mean just that. Some senior commanders and their colleagues in the Bureau of Naval Personnel, on the other hand, while accepting the need for reform and willing to accept some racial mixing, nevertheless rejected any substantial change in the policy of restricted employment of Negroes on the grounds that it might disrupt the wartime fleet. Both sides could argue with assurance since Forrestal and King had not made their positions completely clear. Whatever the secretary's ultimate intention, the reforms carried out in 1944 were too little and too late. Perhaps nothing would have been sufficient, for the racial incidents visited upon the Navy during the last year of the war were symptomatic of the overwhelming dissatisfaction Negroes felt with their lot in the armed forces. There had been incidents during the Knox period, but investigation had failed to isolate any "single, simple cause," and troubles continued to occur during 1944.[3-118]

Three of these incidents gained national prominence.[3-119] The first was a mutiny at Mare Island, California, after an explosion destroyed two ammunition ships loading at nearby Port Chicago on 17 July 1944. The explosion killed over 300 persons, including 250 black seamen who had toiled in large, segregated labor battalions. The survivors refused to return to work, and fifty of them were convicted of mutiny and sentenced to prison. The incident became a *cause célèbre*. Finally, through the intervention of the black press and black organizations and the efforts of Thurgood Marshall and Lester Granger, the convictions were set aside and the men restored to active duty.

A riot on Guam in December 1944 was the climax of months of friction between black seamen and white marines. A series of shootings in and around the town of Agana on Christmas Eve left a black and a white marine dead. Believing one of the killed a member of their group, black sailors from the Naval Supply Depot drove into town to confront the outnumbered military police. No violence ensued, but the next day two truckloads of armed Negroes went to the white Marine camp. A riot followed and forty-three Negroes were arrested, charged with rioting and theft of the trucks, and sentenced to up to four years in prison. The authorities also recommended that several of the white marines involved be court-martialed. These men too were convicted of various offenses and sentenced.[3-120] Walter White went to Guam to investigate the matter and appeared as a principal witness before the Marine Court of Inquiry. There he pieced together for officials the long history of discrimination suffered by men of the base company. This situation, combined with poor leadership in the unit, he believed, caused the trouble. His efforts and those of other civil rights advocates led to the release of the black sailors in early 1946.[3-121]

A hunger strike developed as a protest against discrimination in a Seabee battalion at Port Hueneme, California, in March 1945. There was no violence. The thousand strikers continued to work but refused to eat for two days. The resulting publicity forced the Navy to investigate the charges; as a result, the commanding officer, the focus of the grievance, was replaced and the outfit sent overseas.

The riots, mutinies, and other incidents increased the pressure for further modifications of policy. Some senior officers became convinced that the only way to avoid mass rebellion was to avert the possibility of collective action, and collective action was less likely if Negroes were dispersed among whites. As Admiral Chester W. Nimitz, commander of the Pacific Fleet and an eloquent proponent of the theory that integration was a practical means of avoiding trouble, explained to the captain of an attack cargo ship who had just received a group of black crewmen and was segregating their sleeping quarters: "If you put all the Negroes together they'll have a chance to share grievances and to plot among themselves, and this will damage discipline and morale. If they are distributed among other members of the crew, there will be less chance of trouble. And when we say we want integration, we mean *integration.*"[3-122] Thus integration grew out of both idealism and realism.

If racial incidents convinced the admirals that further reforms were necessary, they also seem to have strengthened Forrestal's resolve to introduce a still greater change in his department's policy. For months he had listened to the arguments of senior officials and naval experts that integration of the fleet, though desirable, was impossible during the war. Yet Forrestal had seen integration work on the small patrol craft, on fleet auxiliaries, and in the WAVES. In fact, integration was working smoothly wherever it had been tried. Although hard to substantiate, the evidence suggests that it was in the weeks after the Guam incident that the secretary and Admiral King agreed on a policy of total integration in the general service. The change would be gradual, but the progress would be evident and the end assured—Negroes were going to be assigned as individuals to all branches and billets in the general service.[3-123]

Forrestal and King received no end of advice. In December 1944 a group of black publicists called upon the secretary to appoint a civilian aide to consider the problems of the Negro in the Navy. The group also added its voice to those within the Navy who were suggesting the appointment of a black public relations officer to disseminate news of particular interest to the black press and to improve the Navy's relations with the black community.[3-124] One of Forrestal's assistants proposed that an intradepartmental committee be organized to standardize the disparate approaches to racial problems throughout the naval establishment; another recommended the appointment of a black civilian to advise the Bureau of Naval Personnel; and still another recommended a white assistant on racial affairs in the office of the under secretary.[3-125]

These ideas had merit. The Special Programs Unit had for some time been urging a public relations effort, pointing to the existence of an influential black press as well as to the desirability of fostering among whites a greater knowledge of the role of Negroes in the war. Forrestal brought two black officers to Washington for possible assignment to public relations work, and he asked the director of public relations to arrange for black newsmen to visit vessels manned by black crewmen. Finally, in June 1945, a black officer was added to the staff of the Navy's Office of Public Relations.[3-126]

Appointment of a civilian aide on racial affairs was under consideration for some time, but when no agreement could be reached on where best to assign the official, Forrestal, who wanted someone he could "casually talk to about race relations,"[3-127] invited the Executive Secretary of the National Urban League to "give us some of your time for a period."[3-128] Thus in March 1945 Lester B. Granger began his long association with the Department of Defense, an association that would span the military's integration effort.[3-129]Granger's assignment was straightforward. From time to time he would make extensive trips representing the secretary and his special interest in racial problems at various naval stations.

Forrestal was sympathetic to the Urban League's approach to racial justice, and in Granger he had a man who had developed this approach into a social philosophy. Granger believed in relating the Navy's racial problems not to questions of fairness but to questions of survival, comfort, and security for all concerned. He assumed that if leadership in any field came to understand that its privilege or its security were threatened by denial of fairness to the less

43

privileged, then a meeting of minds was possible between the two groups. They would begin to seek a way to eliminate insecurity, and from the process of eliminating insecurity would come fairness. As Granger explained it, talk to the commander about his loss of efficient production, not the shame of denying a Negro a man's right to a job. Talk about the social costs that come from denial of opportunity and talk about the penalty that the privileged pay almost in equal measure to what the Negro pays, but in different coin. Only then would one begin to get a hearing. On the other hand, talk to Negroes not about achieving their rights but about making good on an opportunity. This would lead to a discussion of training, of ways to override barriers "by maintaining themselves whole."[3-130] The Navy was going to get a lesson in race relations, Urban League style.

At Forrestal's request, Granger explained how he viewed the special adviser's role. He thought he could help the secretary by smoothing the integration process in the general service through consultations with local commanders and their men in a series of field visits. He could also act as an intermediary between the department and the civil rights organizations and black press. Granger urged the formation of an advisory council, which would consist of ranking representatives from the various branches, to interpret and administer the Navy's racial policy. The need for such intradepartmental coordination seemed fairly obvious. Although in 1945 the Bureau of Naval Personnel had increased the resources of its Special Programs Unit, still the only specialized organization dealing with race problems, that group was always too swamped with administrative detail to police race problems outside Washington. Furthermore, the Seabees and the Medical and Surgery Department were in some ways independent of the bureau, and their employment of black sailors was different from that of other branches—a situation that created further confusion and conflict in the application of race policy.[3-131]

Assuming that the advisory council would require an executive agent, Granger suggested that the secretary have a full-time assistant for race relations in addition to his own part-time services. He wanted the man to be black and he wanted him in the secretary's office, which would give him prestige in the black community and increase his power to deal with the bureaus. Forrestal rejected the idea of a council and a full-time assistant, pleading that he must avoid creating another formal organization. Instead he decided to assemble an informal committee, which he invited Granger to join, to standardize the Navy's handling of Negroes.[3-132]

It was obvious that Forrestal, convinced that the Navy's senior officials had made a fundamental shift in their thinking on equal treatment and opportunity for Negroes in the Navy, was content to let specific reforms percolate slowly throughout the department. He would later call the Navy's wartime reforms "a start down a long road."[3-133] In these last months of the war, however, more barriers to equal treatment of Negroes were quietly falling. In March 1945, after months of prodding by Forrestal, the Surgeon General announced that the Navy would accept a "reasonable" number of qualified black nurses and was now recruiting for them.[3-134] In June the Bureau of Naval Personnel ordered the integration of recruit training, assigning black general service recruits to the nearest recruit training command "to obtain the maximum utilization of naval training and housing facilities."[3-135] Noting that this integration was at variance with some individual attitudes, the bureau justified the change on the grounds of administrative efficiency. Again at the secretary's urging, plans were set in motion in July for the assignment of Negroes to submarine and aviation pilot training.[3-136] At the same time Lester Granger, acting as the secretary's personal representative, was visiting the Navy's continental installations, prodding commanders and converting them to the new policy.[3-137]

THE 22D SPECIAL CONSTRUCTION BATTALION CELEBRATES V-J DAY

The Navy's wartime progress in race relations was the product of several forces. At first Negroes were restricted to service as messmen, but political pressure forced the Navy to open general service billets to them. In this the influence of the civil rights spokesmen was paramount. They and their allies in Congress and the national political parties led President Roosevelt to demand an end to exclusion and the Navy to accept Negroes for segregated general service. The presence of large numbers of black inductees and the limited number of assignments for them in segregated units prevented the Bureau of Naval Personnel from providing even a semblance of separate but equal conditions. Deteriorating black morale and the specter of racial disturbance drove the bureau to experiment with all-black crews, but the experiment led nowhere. The Navy could never operate a separate but equal fleet. Finally in 1944 Forrestal began to experiment with integration in seagoing assignments.

The influence of the civil rights forces can be overstated. Their attention tended to focus on the Army, especially in the later years of the war; their attacks on the Navy were mostly sporadic and uncoordinated and easily deflected by naval spokesmen. Equally important to race reform was the fact that the Navy was developing its own group of civil rights advocates during

44

the war, influential men in key positions who had been dissatisfied with the prewar status of the Negro and who pressed for racial change in the name of military efficiency. Under the leadership of a sympathetic secretary, himself aided and abetted by Stevenson and other advisers in his office and in the Bureau of Naval Personnel, the Navy was laying plans for a racially integrated general service when Japan capitulated.

To achieve equality of treatment and opportunity, however, takes more than the development of an integration policy. For one thing, the liberalization of policy and practices affected only a relatively small percentage of the Negroes in the Navy. On V-J day the Navy could count 164,942 enlisted Negroes, 5.37 percent of its total enlisted strength.[3-138] More than double the prewar percentage, this figure was still less than half the national ratio of blacks to whites. In August 1945 the Navy had 60 black officers, 6 of whom were women (4 nurses and 2 WAVES), and 68 enlisted WAVES who were not segregated. The integration of the Navy officer corps, the WAVES, and the nurses had an immediate effect on only 128 people. Figures for black enlisted men show that they were employed in some sixty-seven ratings by the end of the war, but steward and steward's mate ratings accounted for some 68,000 men, about 40 percent of the total black enlistment. Approximately 59,000 others were ordinary seamen, some were recruits in training or specialists striking for ratings, but most were assigned to the large segregated labor units and base companies.[3-139] Here again integrated service affected only a small portion of the Navy's black recruits during World War II.

Furthermore, a real chance existed that even this limited progress might prove to be temporary. On V-J day the Regular Navy had 7,066 Negroes, just 2.14 percent of its total.[3-140]Many of these men could be expected to stay in the postwar Navy, but the overwhelming majority of them were in the separate Steward's Branch and would remain there after the war. Black reservists in the wartime general service would have to compete with white regulars and reservists for the severely reduced number of postwar billets and commissions in a Navy in which almost all members would have to be regulars. Although Lester Granger had stressed this point in conversations with James Forrestal, neither the secretary nor the Bureau of Naval Personnel took the matter up before the end of the war. In short, after setting in motion a number of far-reaching reforms during the war, the Navy seemed in some danger of settling back into its old prewar pattern.

Still, the fact that reforms had been attempted in a service that had so recently excluded Negroes was evidence of progress. Secretary Forrestal was convinced that the Navy's hierarchy had swung behind the principle of equal treatment and opportunity, but the real test was yet to come. Hope for a permanent change in the Navy's racial practices lay in convincing its tradition-minded officers that an integrated general service with a representative share of black officers and men was a matter of military efficiency.

CHAPTER 4
World War II: The Marine Corps and the Coast Guard

The racial policies of both the Marine Corps and the Coast Guard were substantially the same as the Navy policy from which they were derived, but all three differed markedly from each other in their practical application. The differences arose partly from the particular mission and size of these components of the wartime Navy, but they were also governed by the peculiar legal relationship that existed in time of war between the Navy and the other two services.

By law the Marine Corps was a component of the Department of the Navy, its commandant subordinate to the Secretary of the Navy in such matters as manpower and budget and to the Chief of Naval Operations in specified areas of military operations. In the conduct of ordinary business, however, the commandant was independent of the Navy's bureaus, including the Bureau of Naval Personnel. The Marine Corps had its own staff personnel officer, similar to the Army's G-1, and, more important for the development of racial policy, it had a Division of Plans and Policies that was immediately responsible to the commandant for manpower planning. In practical terms, the Marine Corps of World War II was subject to the dictates of the Secretary of the Navy for general policy, and the secretary's 1942 order to enlist Negroes applied equally to the Marine Corps, which had no Negroes in its ranks, and to the Navy, which did. At the same time, the letters and directives of the Chief of Naval Operations and the Chief of Naval Personnel implementing the secretary's order did not apply to the corps. In effect, the Navy Department imposed a racial policy on the corps, but left it to the commandant to carry out that policy as he saw fit. These legal distinctions would become more important as the Navy's racial policy evolved in the postwar period.

The Coast Guard's administrative position had early in the war become roughly analogous to that of the Marine Corps. At all times a branch of the armed forces, the Coast Guard was normally a part of the Treasury Department. A statute of 1915, however, provided that during wartime or "whenever the President may so direct" the Coast Guard would operate as part of the

Navy, subject to the orders of the Secretary of the Navy.[4-1] At the direction of the President, the Coast Guard passed to the control of the Secretary of the Navy on 1 November 1941 and so remained until 1 January 1946.[4-2]

At first a division under the Chief of Naval Operations, the headquarters of the Coast Guard was later granted considerably more administrative autonomy. In March 1942 Secretary Knox carefully delineated the Navy's control over the Coast Guard, making the Chief of Naval Operations responsible for the operation of those Coast Guard ships, planes, and stations assigned to the naval commands for the "proper conduct of the war," but specifying that assignments be made with "due regard for the needs of the Coast Guard," which must continue to carry out its regular functions. Such duties as providing port security, icebreaking services, and navigational aid remained under the direct control and supervision of the commandant, the local naval district commander exercising only "general military control" of these activities in his area.[4-3] Important to the development of racial policy was the fact that the Coast Guard also retained administrative control of the recruitment, training, and assignment of personnel. Like the Marine Corps, it also had a staff agency for manpower planning, the Commandant's Advisory Board, and one for administration, the Personnel Division, independent of the Navy's bureaus.[4-4] In theory, the Coast Guard's manpower policy, at least in regard to those segments of the service that operated directly under Navy control, had to be compatible with the racial directives of the Navy's Bureau of Naval Personnel. In practice, the Commandant of the Coast Guard, like his colleague in the Marine Corps, was left free to develop his own racial policy in accordance with the general directives of the Secretary of the Navy and the Chief of Naval Operations.

The First Black Marines

These legal distinctions had no bearing on the Marine Corps' prewar racial policy, which was designed to continue its tradition of excluding Negroes. The views of the commandant, Maj. Gen. Thomas Holcomb, on the subject of race were well known in the Navy. Negroes did not have the "right" to demand a place in the corps, General Holcomb told the Navy's General Board when that body was considering the expansion of the corps in April 1941. "If it were a question of having a Marine Corps of 5,000 whites or 250,000 Negroes, I would rather have the whites."[4-5] He was more circumspect but no more reasonable when he explained the racial exclusion publicly. Black enlistment was impractical, he told one civil rights group, because the Marine Corps was too small to form racially separate units.[4-6] And, if some Negroes persisted in trying to volunteer after Pearl Harbor, there was another deterrent, described by at least one senior recruiter: the medical examiner was cautioned to disqualify the black applicant during the enlistment physical.[4-7]

Such evasions could no longer be practiced after President Roosevelt decided to admit Negroes to the general service of the naval establishment. According to Secretary Knox the President wanted the Navy to handle the matter "in a way that would not inject into the whole personnel of the Navy the race question."[4-8] Under pressure to make some move, General Holcomb proposed the enlistment of 1,000 Negroes in the volunteer Marine Corps Reserve for duty in the general service in a segregated composite defense battalion. The battalion would consist primarily of seacoast and antiaircraft artillery, a rifle company with a light tank platoon, and other weapons units and components necessary to make it a self-sustaining unit.[4-9] To inject the subject of race "to a less degree than any other known scheme," the commandant planned to train the unit in an isolated camp and assign it to a remote station.[4-10] The General Board accepted this proposal, explaining to Secretary Knox that Negroes could not be used in the Marine Corps' amphibious units because the inevitable replacement and redistribution of men in combat would "prevent the maintenance of necessary segregation." The board also mentioned that experienced noncommissioned officers were at a premium and that diverting them to train a black unit would be militarily inefficient.[4-11]

Although the enlistment of black marines began on 1 June 1942, the corps placed the reservists on inactive status until a training-size unit could be enlisted and segregated facilities built at Montford Point on the vast training reservation at Marine Barracks, New River (later renamed Camp Lejeune), North Carolina.[4-12] On 26 August the first contingent of Negroes began recruit training as the 51st Composite Defense Battalion at Montford Point under the command of Col. Samuel A. Woods, Jr. The corps had wanted to train men as typists, truck drivers, and the like—specialist skills needed in the black composite unit. Instead, the commandant established black quotas for three of the four recruiting divisions, specifying that more than half the recruits qualify in the needed skills.[4-13]

MARINES OF THE 51ST DEFENSE BATTALION
await turn on rifle range, Montford Point, 1942.

46

The enlistment process proved difficult. The commandant reported that despite predictions of black educators to the contrary the corps had netted only sixty-three black recruits capable of passing the entrance examinations during the first three weeks of recruitment.[4-14] As late as 29 October the Director of Plans and Policies was reporting that only 647 of the scheduled 1,200 men (the final strength figure decided upon for the all-black unit) had been enlisted. He blamed the occupational qualifications for the delay, adding that it was doubtful "if even white recruits" could be procured under such strictures. The commandant approved his plan for enlisting Negroes without specific qualifications and instituting a modified form of specialist training. Black marines would not be sent to specialist schools "unless there is a colored school available," but instead Marine instructors would be sent to teach in the black camp.[4-15] In the end many of these first black specialists received their training in nearby Army installations.

Segregation was the common practice in all the services in 1942, as indeed it was throughout much of American society. If this practice appeared somehow more restrictive in the Marine Corps than it did in the other services, it was because of the corps' size and traditions. The illusion of equal treatment and opportunity could be kept alive in the massive Army and Navy with their myriad units and military occupations; it was much more difficult to preserve in the small and specialized Marine Corps. Given segregation, the Marine Corps was obliged to put its few black marines in its few black units, whose small size limited the variety of occupations and training opportunities.

Yet the size of the corps would undergo considerable change, and on balance it was the Marine Corps' tradition of an all-white service, not its restrictive size, that proved to be the most significant factor influencing racial policy. Again unlike the Army and Navy, the Marine Corps lacked the practical experience with black recruits that might have countered many of the alarums and prejudices concerning Negroes that circulated within the corps during the war. The importance of this experience factor comes out in the reminiscences of a senior official in the Division of Plans and Policies who looked back on his 1942 experiences:

It just scared us to death when the colored were put on it. I went over to Selective Service and saw Gen. Hershey, and he turned me over to a lieutenant colonel [Campbell C. Johnson]— that was in April—and he was one grand person. I told him, "Eleanor [Mrs. Roosevelt] says we gotta take in Negroes, and we are just scared to death, we've never had any in, we don't know how to handle them, we are afraid of them." He said, "I'll do my best to help you get good ones. I'll get the word around that if you want to die young, join the Marines. So anybody that joins is got to be pretty good!" And it was the truth. We got some awfully good Negroes.[4-16]

Unfortunately for the peace of mind of the Marine Corps' personnel planner, the conception of a carefully limited and isolated black contingent was quickly overtaken by events. The President's decision to abolish volunteer enlistments for the armed forces in December 1942 and the subsequent establishment of a black quota for each component of the naval establishment meant that in the next year some 15,400 more Negroes, 10 percent of all Marine Corps inductees, would be added to the corps.[4-17] As it turned out the monthly draft calls were never completely filled, and by December 1943 only 9,916 of the scheduled black inductions had been completed, but by the time the corps stopped drafting men in 1946 it had received over 16,000 Negroes through the Selective Service. Including the 3,129 black volunteers, the number of Negroes in the Marine Corps during World War II totaled 19,168, approximately 4 percent of the corps' enlisted men.

The immediate problem of what to do with this sudden influx of Negroes was complicated by the fact that many of the draftees, the product of vastly inferior schooling, were incompetent. Where black volunteers had to pass the corps' rigid entrance requirements, draftees had only to meet the lowest selective service standards. An exact breakdown of black Marine Corps draftees by General Classification Test category is unavailable for the war period. A breakdown of some 15,000 black enlisted men, however, was compiled ten weeks after V-J day and included many of those drafted during the war. Category I represents the most gifted men:[4-18]

Category:	I
Percentage:	0.11

If these figures are used as a base, slightly more than 70 percent of all black enlisted men, more than 11,000, scored in the two lowest categories, a meaningless racial statistic in terms of actual numbers because the smaller percentage of the much larger group of white draftees in these categories gave the corps more whites than blacks in groups IV and V. Yet the statistic was important because low-scoring Negroes, unlike the low-scoring whites who could be scattered throughout the corps' units, had to be concentrated in a small number of segregated units to the detriment of those units. Conversely, the corps had thousands of Negroes with the mental aptitude to serve in regular combat units and a small but significant number capable of becoming officers. Yet these men were denied the opportunity to serve in combat or as officers because the segregation policy dictated that Negroes could not be assigned to a regular combat unit unless all the billets in that unit as well as all replacements were black—a practical impossibility during World War II.

Segregation, not the draft, forced the Marine Corps to devise new jobs and units to absorb the black inductees. A plan circulated in the Division of Plans and Policies called for more defense battalions, a branch for messmen, and the assignment of large black units to local bases to serve as chauffeurs, messengers, clerks, and janitors. Referring to the janitor assignment, one division official admitted that "I don't think we can get away with this type duty."[4-19] In the end the Negroes were not used as chauffeurs, messengers, clerks, and janitors. Instead the corps placed a "maximum practical number" in defense battalions. The number of these units, however, was limited, as Maj. Gen. Harry Schmidt, the acting commandant, explained in March 1943, by the number of black noncommissioned officers available. Black noncommissioned officers were necessary, he continued, because in the Army's experience "in nearly all cases to intermingle colored and white enlisted personnel in the same organization" led to "trouble and disorder."[4-20] Demonstrating his own and the Marine Corps' lack of experience with black troops, the acting commandant went on to provide his commanders with some rather dubious advice based on what he perceived as the Army's experience: black units should be commanded by men "who thoroughly knew their [Negroes'] individual and racial characteristics and temperaments," and Negroes should be assigned to work they preferred.

SHORE PARTY IN TRAINING, CAMP LEJEUNE, 1942

The points emphasized in General Schmidt's letter to Marine commanders—a rigid insistence on racial separation and a willingness to work for equal treatment of black troops— along with an acknowledgement of the Marine Corps' lack of experience with racial problems were reflected in Commandant Holcomb's basic instruction on the subject of Negroes two months later: "All Marines are entitled to the same rights and privileges under Navy Regulations," and black marines could be expected "to conduct themselves with propriety and become a credit to the Marine Corps." General Holcomb was aware of the adverse effect of white noncommissioned officers on black morale, and he wanted them removed from black units as soon as possible. Since the employment of black marines was in itself a "new departure," he wanted to be informed periodically on how Negroes adapted to Marine Corps life, what their off-duty experience was with recreational facilities, and what their attitude was toward other marines.[4-21]

D-DAY ON PELELIU.
Support troops participate in the landing of 1st Marine Division.

These were generally progressive sentiments, evidence of the commandant's desire to provide for the peaceful assimilation and advancement of Negroes in the corps. Unfortunately for his reputation among the civil rights advocates, General Holcomb seemed overly concerned with certain social implications of rank and color. Undeterred by a lack of personal experience with interracial command, he was led in the name of racial harmony to an unpopular conclusion. "It is essential," he told his commanders, "that in no case shall there be colored noncommissioned officers senior to white men in the same unit, and desirable that few, if any be of the same rank."[4-22] He was particularly concerned with the period when white instructors and noncommissioned officers were being phased out of black units. He wanted Negroes up for promotion to corporal transferred, before promotion, out of any unit that contained white corporals.

MEDICAL ATTENDANTS AT REST, PELELIU, OCTOBER, 1944

The Division of Plans and Policies tried to follow these strictures as it set about organizing the new black units. Job preference had already figured in the organization of the new Messman's Branch established in January 1943. At that time Secretary Knox had approved the reconstitution of the corps' all-white Mess Branch as the Commissary Branch and the organization of an all-black Messman's Branch along the lines of the Navy's Steward's Branch.[4-23] In authorizing the new branch, which was quickly redesignated the Steward's Branch to conform to the Navy model, Secretary Knox specified that the members must volunteer for such duty. Yet the corps, under pressure to produce large numbers of stewards in the early months of the war, showed so little faith in the volunteer system that Marine recruiters were urged to induce half of all black recruits to sign on as stewards.[4-24] Original plans called for the assignment of one steward for every six officers, but the lack of volunteers and the needs of the corps quickly caused this estimate to be scaled down.[4-25] By 5 July 1944 the Steward's Branch numbered 1,442 men, roughly 14 percent of the total black strength of the Marine Corps.[4-26] It remained approximately this size for the rest of the war.

The admonition to employ black marines to the maximum extent practical in defense battalions was based on the mobilization planners' belief that each of these battalions, with its varied artillery, infantry, and armor units, would provide close to a thousand black marines with varied assignments in a self-contained, segregated unit. But the realities of the Pacific war and the draft quickly rendered these plans obsolete. As the United States gained the ascendancy, the need for defense battalions rapidly declined, just as the need for special logistical units to move supplies in the forward areas increased. The corps had originally depended on its replacement battalions to move the mountains of supply involved in amphibious assaults, but the constant flow of replacements to battlefield units and the need for men with special logistical skill had led in the middle of the war to the organization of pioneer battalions. To supplement the work of these shore party units and to absorb the rapidly growing number of black draftees, the Division of Plans and Policies eventually created fifty-one separate depot companies and twelve separate ammunition companies manned by Negroes. The majority of these new units served in base and service depots, handling ammunition and hauling supplies, but a significant number of them also served as part of the shore parties attached to the divisional assault units. These units often worked under enemy fire and on occasion joined in the battle as they moved supplies, evacuated the wounded, and secured the operation's supply dumps.[4-27] Nearly 8,000 men, about 40 percent of the corps' black enlistment, served in this sometimes hazardous combat support duty. The experience of these depot and ammunition companies provided the Marine Corps with an interesting irony. In contrast to Negroes in the other services, black marines trained for combat were never so used. Those trained for the humdrum labor tasks, however, found themselves in the thick of the fighting on Saipan, Peleliu, Iwo Jima, and elsewhere, suffering combat casualties and winning combat citations for their units.

The increased allotment of black troops entering the corps and the commandant's call for replacing all white noncommissioned officers with blacks as quickly as they could be sufficiently trained caused problems for the black combat units. The 51st Defense Battalion in particular suffered many vicissitudes in its training and deployment. The 51st was the first black unit in the Marine Corps, a doubtful advantage considering the frequent reorganization and rapid troop turnover that proved its lot. At first the reception and training of all black inductees fell to the battalion, but in March 1943 a separate Headquarters Company, Recruit Depot Battalion, was organized at Montford Point.[4-28] Its cadre was drawn from the 51st, as were the noncommissioned officers and key personnel of the newly organized ammunition and depot companies and the black security detachments organized at Montford Point and assigned to the Naval Ammunition Depot, McAlester, Oklahoma, and the Philadelphia Depot of Supplies.

In effect, the 51st served as a specialist training school for the black combat units. When the second black defense battalion, the 52d, was organized in December 1943 its cadre, too, was drawn from the 51st. By the time the 51st was actually deployed, it had been reorganized several times and many of its best men had been siphoned off as leaders for new units. To compound these losses of experienced men, the battalion was constantly receiving large influxes of inexperienced and educationally deficient draftees and sometimes there was infighting among its officers.[4-29]

Training for black units only emphasized the rigid segregation enforced in the Marine Corps. After their segregated eight-week recruit training, the men were formed into companies at Montford Point; those assigned to the defense battalions were sent for specialist training in the weapons and equipment employed in such units, including radar, motor transport, communications, and artillery fire direction. Each of the ammunition companies sent sixty of its men to special ammunition and camouflage schools where they would be promoted to corporal when they completed the course. In contrast to the depot companies and elements of the defense battalions, the ammunition units would have white staff sergeants as ordnance specialists throughout the war. This exception to the rule of black noncommissioned officers for black units was later justified on the grounds that such units required experienced supervisors to emphasize and enforce safety regulations.[4-30] On the whole specialist training was segregated; whenever possible even the white instructors were rapidly replaced by blacks.

Before being sent overseas, black units underwent segregated field training, although the length of this training varied considerably according to the type of unit. Depot companies, for example, were labor units pure and simple, organized to perform simple tasks, and many of them were sent to the Pacific less than two weeks after activation. In contrast, the 51st Defense Battalion spent two months in hard field training, scarcely enough considering the number of raw recruits, totally unfamiliar with gunnery, that were being fed regularly into what was essentially an artillery battalion.

The experience of the two defense battalions demonstrates that racial consideration governed their eventual deployment just as it had decided their organization. With no further strategic need for defense battalions, the Marine Corps began to dismantle them in 1944, just as the two black units became operational and were about to be sent to the Central and South Pacific. The eighteen white defense battalions were subsequently reorganized as antiaircraft artillery battalions for use with amphibious groups in the forward areas. While the two black units were similarly reorganized, only they and one of the white units retained the title of defense battalion. Their deployment was also different. The policy of self-contained, segregated service was, in the case of a large combat unit, best followed in the rear areas, and the two black battalions were assigned to routine garrison duties in the backwaters of the theater, the 51st at Eniwetok in the Marshalls, the 52d at Guam. The latter unit saw nearly half its combat-trained men detailed to work as stevedores. It was not surprising that the morale in both units suffered.[4-31]

Even more explicitly racial was the warning of a senior combat commander to the effect that the deployment of black depot units to the Polynesian areas of the Pacific should be avoided. The Polynesians, he explained, were delightful people, and their "primitively romantic" women shared their intimate favors with one and all. Mixture with the white race had produced "a very high-class half-caste," mixture with the Chinese a "very desirable type," but the union of black and "Melanesian types ... produces a very undesirable citizen." The Marine Corps, Maj. Gen. Charles F. B. Price continued, had a special moral obligation and a selfish interest in protecting the population of American Samoa, especially, from intimacy with Negroes; he strongly urged therefore that any black units deployed to the Pacific should be sent to Micronesia where they "can do no racial harm."[4-32]

General Price must have been entertaining second thoughts, since two depot companies were already en route to Samoa at his request. Nevertheless, because of the "importance" of his reservations the matter was brought to the attention of the Director of Plans and Policies.[4-33] As a result, the assignment of the 7th and 8th Depot Companies to Samoa proved short-lived. Arriving on 13 October 1943, they were redeployed to the Ellice Islands in the Micronesia group the next day.

Thanks to the operations of the ammunition and depot companies, a large number of black marines, serving in small, efficient labor units, often exposed to enemy fire, made a valuable contribution. That so many black marines participated, at least from time to time, in the fighting may explain in part the fact that relatively few racial incidents took place in the corps during the war. But if many Negroes served in forward areas, they were all nevertheless severely restricted in opportunity. Black marines were excluded from the corps' celebrated combat divisions and its air arm. They were also excluded from the Women's Reserve, and not until the last months of the war did the corps accept its first black officer candidates. Marine spokesmen justified the latter exclusion on the grounds that the corps lacked facilities—that is, segregated facilities—for training black officers.[4-34]

These exclusions did not escape the attention of the civil rights spokesmen who took their demands to Secretary Knox and the White House.[4-35] It was to little avail. With the exception of the officer candidates in 1945, the separation of the races remained absolute, and Negroes continued to be excluded from the main combat units of the Marine Corps.

Personal prejudices aside, the desire for social harmony and the fear of the unknown go far toward explaining the Marine Corps' wartime racial policy. A small, specialized, and racially exclusive organization, the Marine Corps reacted to the directives of the Secretary of the Navy and the necessities of wartime operation with a rigid segregation policy, its black troops restricted to about 4 percent of its enlisted strength. A large part of this black strength was assigned to labor units where Negroes performed valuable and sometimes dangerous service in the Pacific war. Complaints from civil rights advocates abounded, but neither protests nor the cost to military efficiency of duplicating training facilities were of sufficient moment to overcome the sentiment against significant racial change, which was kept to a minimum. Judged strictly in terms of keeping racial harmony, the corps policy must be considered a success. Ironically this very success prevented any modification of that policy during the war.

The Coast Guard's pre-World War II experience with Negroes differed from that of the other branches of the naval establishment. Unlike the Marine Corps, the Coast Guard could boast a tradition of black enlistment stretching far back into the previous century. Although it shared this tradition with the Navy, the Coast Guard, unlike the Navy, had always severely restricted Negroes both in terms of numbers enlisted and jobs assigned. A small group of Negroes manned a lifesaving station at Pea Island on North Carolina's outer banks. Negroes also served as crewmen at several lighthouses and on tenders in the Mississippi River basin; all were survivors of the transfer of the Lighthouse Service to the Coast Guard in 1939. These guardsmen were almost always segregated, although a few served in integrated crews or even commanded large Coast Guard vessels and small harbor craft.[4-36] They also served in the separate Steward's Branch, although it might be argued that the small size of most Coast Guard vessels integrated in fact men who were segregated in theory.

COAST GUARD RECRUITS
at Manhattan Beach Training Station, New York.

The lot of the black Coast Guardsman on a small cutter was not necessarily a happy one. To a surprising extent the enlisted men of the prewar Coast Guard were drawn from the eastern shore and outer banks region of the Atlantic coast where service in the Coast Guard had become a strong family tradition among a people whose attitude toward race was rarely progressive. Although these men tolerated an occasional small black Coast Guard crew or station, they might well resist close service with individual Negroes. One commander reported that racial harassment drove the solitary black in the prewar crew of the cutter *Calypso* out of the service.[4-37]

Coast Guard officials were obviously mindful of such potential troubles when, at Secretary Knox's bidding, they joined in the General Board's discussion of the expanded use of Negroes in the general service in January 1942. In the name of the Coast Guard, Commander Lyndon Spencer agreed with the objections voiced by the Navy and the Marine Corps, adding that the Coast Guard problem was "enhanced somewhat by the fact that our units are small and contacts between the men are bound to be closer." He added that while the Coast Guard was not "anxious to take on any additional problems at this time, if we have to we will take some of them [Negroes]."[4-38]

When President Roosevelt made it clear that Negroes were to be enlisted, Coast Guard Commandant Rear Adm. Russell R. Waesche had a plan ready. The Coast Guard would enlist approximately five hundred Negroes in the general service, he explained to the chairman of the General Board, Vice Adm. Walton R. Sexton. Some three hundred of these men would be trained for duty on small vessels, the rest for shore duty under the captain of the port of six cities throughout the United States. Although his plan made no provision for the training of black petty officers, the commandant warned Admiral Sexton that 50 to 65 percent of the crew in these small cutters and miscellaneous craft held such ratings, and it followed that Negroes would eventually be allowed to try for such ratings.[4-39]

Further refining the plan for the General Board on 24 February, Admiral Waesche listed eighteen vessels, mostly buoy tenders and patrol boats, that would be assigned black crews. All black enlistees would be sent to the Manhattan Beach Training Station, New York, for a basic training "longer and more extensive" than the usual recruit training. After recruit training the men would be divided into groups according to aptitude and experience and would undergo advanced instruction before assignment. Those trained for ship duty would be grouped into units of a size to enable them to go aboard and assume all but the petty officer ratings of the designated ships. The commandant wanted to initiate this program with a group of 150 men. No other Negroes would be enlisted until the first group had been trained and assigned to duty for a period long enough to permit a survey of its performance. Admiral Waesche warned that the whole program was frankly new and untried and was therefore subject to modification as it evolved.[4-40]

The plan was a major innovation in the Coast Guard's manpower policy. For the first time a number of Negroes, approximately 1.6 percent of the guard's total enlisted complement, would undergo regular recruit and specialized training.[4-41] More than half would serve aboard ship at close quarters with their white petty officers. The rest would be assigned to port duty with no special provision for segregated service. If the provision for segregating nonrated Coast Guardsmen when they were at sea was intended to prevent the development of racial antagonism, the lack of a similar provision for Negroes ashore was puzzling; but whatever the Coast Guard's reasoning in the matter, the General Board was obviously concerned with the provisions for segregation in the plan. Its chairman told Secretary Knox that the assignment of Negroes to the captains of the ports was a practical use of Negroes in wartime, since these men

51

could be segregated in service units. But their assignment to small vessels, Admiral Sexton added, meant that "the necessary segregation and limitation of authority would be increasingly difficult to maintain" and "opportunities for advancement would be few." For that reason, he concluded, the employment of such black crews was practical but not desirable.[4-42]

The General Board was overruled, and the Coast Guard proceeded to recruit its first group of 150 black volunteers, sending them to Manhattan Beach for basic training in the spring of 1942. The small size of the black general service program precluded the establishment of a separate training station, but the Negroes were formed into a separate training company at Manhattan Beach. While training classes and other duty activities were integrated, sleeping and messing facilities were segregated. Although not geographically separated as were the black sailors at Camp Smalls or the marines at Montford Point, the black recruits of the separate training company at Manhattan Beach were effectively impressed with the reality of segregation in the armed forces.[4-43]

After taking a four-week basic course, those who qualified were trained as radiomen, pharmacists, yeomen, coxswains, fire controlmen, or in other skills in the seaman branch.[4-44]Those who did not so qualify were transferred for further training in preparation for their assignment to the captains of the ports. Groups of black Coast Guardsmen, for example, were sent to the Pea Island Station after their recruit training for several weeks' training in beach duties. Similar groups of white recruits were also sent to the Pea Island Station for training under the black chief boatswain's mate in charge.[4-45] By August 1942 some three hundred Negroes had been recruited, trained, and assigned to general service duties under the new program. At the same time the Coast Guard continued to recruit hundreds of Negroes for its separate Steward's Branch.

The commandant's program for the orderly induction and assignment of a limited number of black volunteers was, as in the case of the Navy and Marine Corps, abruptly terminated in December 1942 when the President ended volunteer enlistment for most military personnel. For the rest of the war the Coast Guard, along with the Navy and Marine Corps, came under the strictures of the Selective Service Act, including its racial quota system. The Coast Guard, however, drafted relatively few men, issuing calls for a mere 22,500 and eventually inducting only 15,296. But more than 12 percent of its calls (2,500 men between February and November 1943) and 13 percent of all those drafted (1,667) were Negro. On the average, 137 Negroes and 1,000 whites were inducted each month during 1943.[4-46] Just over 5,000 Negroes served as Coast Guardsmen in World War II.[4-47]

As it did for the Navy and Marine Corps, the sudden influx of Negroes from Selective Service necessitated a revision of the Coast Guard's personnel planning. Many of the new men could be assigned to steward duties, but by January 1943 the Coast Guard already had some 1,500 stewards and the branch could absorb only half of the expected black draftees. The rest would have to be assigned to the general service.[4-48] And here the organization and mission of the Coast Guard, far more so than those of the Navy and Marine Corps, militated against the formation of large segregated units. The Coast Guard had no use for the amorphous ammunition and depot companies and the large Seabee battalions of the rest of the naval establishment. For that reason the large percentage of its black seamen in the general service (approximately 37 percent of all black Coast Guardsmen) made a considerable amount of integration inevitable; the small number of Negroes in the general service (1,300 men, less than 1 percent of the total enlisted strength of the Coast Guard) made integration socially acceptable.

The majority of black Coast Guardsmen were only peripherally concerned with this wartime evolution of racial policy. Some 2,300 Negroes served in the racially separate Steward's Branch, performing the same duties in officer messes and quarters as stewards in the Navy and Marine Corps. But not quite, for the size of Coast Guard vessels and their crews necessitated the use of stewards at more important battle stations. For example, a group of stewards under the leadership of a black gun captain manned the three-inch gun on the afterdeck of the cutter *Campbell* and won a citation for helping to destroy an enemy submarine in February 1943.[4-49] The Personnel Division worked to make the separate Steward's Branch equal to the rest of the service in terms of promotion and emoluments, and there were instances when individual stewards successfully applied for ratings in general service.[4-50] Again, the close quarters aboard Coast Guard vessels made the talents of stewards for general service duties more noticeable to officers.[4-51] The evidence suggests, however, that the majority of the black stewards, about 63 percent of all the Negroes in the Coast Guard, continued to function as servants throughout the war. As in the rest of the naval establishment, the stewards in the Coast Guard were set apart not only by their limited service but also by different uniforms and the fact that chief stewards were not regarded as chief petty officers. In fact, the rank of chief steward was not introduced until the war led to an enlargement of the Coast Guard.[4-52]

52

STEWARDS AT BATTLE STATION
on the afterdeck of the cutter Campbell.

The majority of black guardsmen in general service served ashore under the captains of the ports, local district commanders, or at headquarters establishments. Men in these assignments included hundreds in security and labor details, but more and more served as yeomen, radio operators, storekeepers, and the like. Other Negroes were assigned to local Coast Guard stations, and a second all-black station was organized during the war at Tiana Beach, New York. Still others participated in the Coast Guard's widespread beach patrol operations. Organized in 1942 as outposts and lookouts against possible enemy infiltration of the nation's extensive coastlines, the patrols employed more than 11 percent of all the Coast Guard's enlisted men. This large group included a number of horse and dog patrols employing only black guardsmen.[4-53] In all, some 2,400 black Coast Guardsmen served in the shore establishment.

SHORE LEAVE IN SCOTLAND.
(The distinctive uniform of the Coast Guard steward is shown.)

The assignment of so many Negroes to shore duties created potential problems for the manpower planners, who were under orders to rotate sea and shore assignments periodically.[4-54] Given the many black general duty seamen denied sea duty because of the Coast Guard's segregation policy but promoted into the more desirable shore-based jobs to the detriment of whites waiting for rotation to such assignments, the possibility of serious racial trouble was obvious.

At least one officer in Coast Guard headquarters was concerned enough to recommend that the policy be revised. With two years' service in Greenland waters, the last year as executive officer of the USCGC *Northland*, Lt. Carlton Skinner had firsthand experience with the limitations of the Coast Guard's racial policy. While on the *Northland* Skinner had recommended that a skilled black mechanic, then serving as a steward's mate, be awarded a motor mechanic petty officer rating only to find his recommendation rejected on racial grounds. The rating was later awarded after an appeal by Skinner, but the incident set the stage for the young officer's later involvement with the Coast Guard's racial traditions. On shore duty at Coast Guard headquarters in June 1943, Skinner recommended to the commandant that a group of black seamen be provided with some practical seagoing experience under a sympathetic commander in a completely integrated operation. He emphasized practical experience in an integrated setting, he later revealed, because he was convinced that men with high test scores and specialized training did not necessarily make the best sailors, especially when their training was segregated. Skinner envisioned a widespread distribution of Negroes throughout the Coast Guard's seagoing vessels. His recommendation was no "experiment in social democracy," he later stressed, but was a design for "an efficient use of manpower to help win a war."[4-55]

Although Skinner's immediate superior forwarded the recommendation as "disapproved," Admiral Waesche accepted the idea. In November 1943 Skinner found himself transferred to the USS *Sea Cloud* (IX 99), a patrol ship operating in the North Atlantic as part of Task Force 24 reporting on weather conditions from four remote locations in northern waters.[4-56] The commandant also arranged for the transfer of black apprentice seamen, mostly from Manhattan Beach, to the *Sea Cloud* in groups of about twenty men, gradually increasing the number of black seamen in the ship's complement every time it returned to home station. Skinner, promoted to lieutenant commander and made captain of the *Sea Cloud* on his second patrol, later decided that the commandant had "figured he could take a chance on me and the *Sea Cloud*."[4-57]

It was a chance well taken. Before decommissioning in November 1944, the *Sea Cloud* served on ocean weather stations off the coasts of Greenland, Newfoundland, and France. It received no special treatment and was subject to the same tactical, operating, and engineering requirements as any other unit in the Navy's Atlantic Fleet. It passed two Atlantic Fleet inspections with no deficiencies and was officially credited with helping to sink a German submarine in June 1944. The *Sea Cloud* boasted a completely integrated operation, its 4 black officers and some 50 black petty officers and seamen serving throughout the ship's 173-man complement.[4-58] No problems of a racial nature arose on the ship, although its captain reported that his crew experienced some hostility in the various departments of the Boston Navy Yard from time to time. Skinner was determined to provide truly integrated conditions. He personally introduced his black officers into the local white officers' club, and he saw to it that when his men were temporarily detached for shore patrol duty they would go in integrated teams. Again, all these arrangements were without sign of racial incident.[4-59]

53

It is difficult to assess the reasons for the commandant's decision to organize an integrated crew. One senior personnel officer later suggested that the *Sea Cloud* was merely a public relations device designed to still the mounting criticism by civil rights spokesmen of the lack of sea duty for black Coast Guardsmen.[4-60] The public relations advantage of an integrated ship operating in the war zone must have been obvious to Admiral Waesche, although the Coast Guard made no effort to publicize the *Sea Cloud*. In fact, this absence of special attention had been recommended by Skinner in his original proposal to the commandant. Such publicity, he felt, would disrupt the military experiment and make it more difficult to apply generally the experience gained.

The success of the *Sea Cloud* experiment did not lead to the widespread integration implied in Commander Skinner's recommendation. The only other extensively integrated Coast Guard vessel assigned to a war zone was the destroyer escort *Hoquim*, operating in 1945 out of Adak in the Aleutian Islands, convoying shipping along the Aleutian chain. Again, the commander of the ship was Skinner. Nevertheless the practical reasons for Skinner's first recommendation must also have been obvious to the commandant, and the evidence suggests that the *Sea Cloud* project was but one of a series of liberalizing moves the Coast Guard made during the war, not only to still the criticism in the black community but also to solve the problems created by the presence of a growing number of black seamen in the general service. There is also reason to believe that the Coast Guard's limited use of racially mixed crews influenced the Navy's decision to integrate the auxiliary fleet in 1945. Senior naval officials studied a report on the *Sea Cloud*, and one of Secretary Forrestal's assistants consulted Skinner on his experiences and their relation to greater manpower efficiency.[4-61]

Throughout the war the Coast Guard never exhibited the concern shown by the other services for the possible disruptive effects if blacks outranked whites. As the war progressed, more and more blacks advanced into petty officer ranks; by August 1945 some 965 Negroes, almost a third of their total number, were petty or warrant officers, many of them in the general service. Places for these trained specialists in any kind of segregated general service were extremely limited, and by the last year of the war many black petty officers could be found serving in mostly white crews and station complements. For example, a black pharmacist, second class, and a signalman, third class, served on the cutter *Spencer*, a black coxswain served on a cutter in the Greenland patrol, and other black petty officers were assigned to recruiting stations, to the loran program, and as instructors at the Manhattan Beach Training Station.[4-62]

The position of instructor at Manhattan Beach became the usual avenue to a commission for a Negro. Joseph C. Jenkins went from Manhattan Beach to the officer candidate school at the Coast Guard Academy, graduating as an ensign in the Coast Guard Reserve in April 1943, almost a full year before Negroes were commissioned in the Navy. Clarence Samuels, a warrant officer and instructor at Manhattan Beach, was commissioned as a lieutenant (junior grade) and assigned to the *Sea Cloud* in 1943. Harvey C. Russell was a signal instructor at Manhattan Beach in 1944 when all instructors were declared eligible to apply for commissions. At first rejected by the officer training school, Russell was finally admitted at the insistence of his commanding officer, graduated as an ensign, and was assigned to the *Sea Cloud*.[4-63]

These men commanded integrated enlisted seamen throughout the rest of the war. Samuels became the first Negro in this century to command a Coast Guard vessel in wartime, first as captain of Lightship No. 115 and later of the USCGC *Sweetgum* in the Panama Sea Frontier. Russell was transferred from the integrated *Hoquim* to serve as executive officer on a cutter operating out of the Philippines in the western Pacific, assuming command of the racially mixed crew shortly after the war.

At the behest of the White House, the Coast Guard also joined with the Navy in integrating its Women's Reserve. In the fall of 1944 it recruited five black women for the SPARS. Only token representation, but understandable since the SPARS ceased all recruitment except for replacements on 23 November 1944, just weeks after the decision to recruit Negroes was announced. Nevertheless the five women trained at Manhattan Beach and were assigned to various Coast Guard district offices without regard to race.[4-64]

This very real progress toward equal treatment and opportunity for Negroes in the Coast Guard must be assessed with the knowledge that the progress was experienced by only a minuscule group. Negroes never rose above 2.1 percent of the Coast Guard's wartime population, well below the figures for the other services. This was because the other services

54

were forced to obtain draft-age men, including a significant number of black inductees from Selective Service, whereas the Coast Guard ceased all inductions in early 1944.

Despite their small numbers, however, the black Coast Guardsmen enjoyed a variety of assignments. The different reception accorded this small group of Negroes might, at least to some extent, be explained by the Coast Guard's tradition of some black participation for well over a century. To a certain extent this progress could also be attributed to the ease with which the directors of a small organization can reorder its policies.[4-65] But above all, the different reception accorded Negroes in the Coast Guard was a small organization's practical reaction to a pressing assimilation problem dictated by the manpower policies common throughout the naval establishment.

CHAPTER 5

A Postwar Search

The nation's military leaders and the leaders of the civil rights movement were in rare accord at the end of World War II. They agreed that despite considerable wartime improvement the racial policies of the services had proved inadequate for the development of the full military potential of the country's largest minority as well as the efficient operation and management of the nation's armed forces. Dissatisfaction with the current policy of the armed forces was a spearpoint of the increasingly militant and powerful civil rights movement, and this dissatisfaction was echoed to a great extent by the services themselves. Intimate association with minority problems had convinced the Army's Advisory Committee on Negro Troop Policies and the Navy's Special Programs Unit that new policies had to be devised and new directions sought. Confronted with the incessant demands of the civil rights advocates and presented by their own staffs with evidence of trouble, civilian leaders of the services agreed to review the status of the Negro. As the postwar era opened, both the Army and the Navy were beginning the interminable investigations that augured a change in policy.

Unfortunately, the services and the civil rights leaders had somewhat different ends in mind. Concerned chiefly with military efficiency but also accustomed to racial segregation or exclusion, most military leaders insisted on a rigid appraisal of the performance of segregated units in the war and ignored the effects of segregation on that performance. Civil rights advocates, on the other hand, seeing an opportunity to use the military as a vehicle for the extension of social justice, stressed the baneful effects of segregation on the black serviceman's morale. They were inclined to ignore the performance of the large segregated units and took issue with the premise that desegregation of the armed forces in advance of the rest of American society would threaten the efficient execution of the services' military mission. Neither group seemed able to appreciate the other's real concerns, and their contradictory conclusions promised a renewal of the discord in their wartime relationship.

Black Demands

World War II marked the beginning of an important step in the evolution of the civil rights movement. Until then the struggle for racial equality had been sustained chiefly by the "talented tenth," the educated, middle-class black citizens who formed an economic and political alliance with white supporters. Together they fought to improve the racial situation with some success in the courts, but with little progress in the executive branch and still less in the legislative. The efforts of men like W. E. B. DuBois, Walter White, and Thurgood Marshall of the NAACP and Lester Granger of the National Urban League were in the mainstream of the American reform movement, which stressed an orderly petitioning of government for a redress of grievances.

But there was another facet to the American reform tradition, one that stressed mass action and civil disobedience, and the period between the March on Washington Movement in 1940 and the threat of a black boycott of the draft in 1948 witnessed the beginnings of a shift in the civil rights movement to this kind of reform tactic. The articulate leaders of the prewar struggle were still active, and in fact would make their greatest contribution in the fight that led to the Supreme Court's pronouncement on school segregation in 1954. But their quiet methods were already being challenged by A. Philip Randolph and others who launched a sustained demand for equal treatment and opportunity in the armed forces during the early postwar period. Randolph and leaders of his persuasion relied not so much on legal eloquence in their representations to the federal government as on an understanding of bloc voting in key districts and the implicit threat of civil disobedience. The civil rights campaign, at least in the effort to end segregation in the armed forces, had the appearance of a mass movement a full decade before a weary Rosa Parks boarded a Montgomery bus and set off the all-embracing crusade of Martin Luther King, Jr.

The growing political power of the Negro and the threat of mass action in the 1940's were important reasons for the breakthrough on the color front that began in the armed forces in the

55

postwar period. For despite the measure of good will and political acumen that characterized his social programs, Harry S. Truman might never have made the effort to achieve racial equality in the services without the constant pressure of civil rights activists.

The reasons for the transformation that was beginning in the civil rights struggle were varied and complex.[5-1] Fundamental was the growing urbanization of the Negro. By 1940 almost half the black population lived in cities. As the labor shortage became more acute during the next five years, movement toward the cities continued, not only in the south but in the north and west. Attracted by economic opportunities in Los Angeles war industries, for example, over 1,000 Negroes moved to that city each month during the war. Detroit, Seattle, and San Francisco, among others, reported similar migrations. The balance finally shifted during the war, and the 1950 census showed that 56 percent of the black population resided in metropolitan areas, 32 percent in cities of the north and west.[5-2]

This mass migration, especially to cities outside the south, was of profound importance to the future of American race relations. It meant first that the black masses were separating themselves from the archaic social patterns that had ruled their lives for generations. Despite virulent discrimination and prejudice in northern and western cities, Negroes could vote freely and enjoy some protection of the law and law-enforcement machinery. They were free of the burden of Jim Crow. Along with white citizens they were given better schooling, a major factor in improving status. The mass migration also meant that this part of America's peasantry was rapidly joining America's proletariat. The wartime shortage of workers, coupled with the efforts of the Fair Employment Practices Committee and other government agencies, opened up thousands of jobs previously denied black Americans. The number of skilled craftsmen, foremen, and semiskilled workers among black Americans rose from 500,000 to over 1,000,000 during the war, while the number of Negroes working for the federal government increased from 60,000 to 200,000.[5-3]

Though much of the increase in black employment was the result of temporarily expanded wartime industries, black workers gained valuable training and experience that enabled them to compete more effectively for postwar jobs. Employment in unionized industries strengthened their position in the postwar labor movement. The severity of inevitable postwar cuts in black employment was mitigated by continued prosperity and the sustained growth of American industry. Postwar industrial development created thousands of new upper-level jobs, allowing many black workers to continue their economic advance without replacing white workers and without the attendant development of racial tensions.

The armed forces played their part in this change. Along with better food, pay, and living conditions provided by the services, many Negroes were given new work experiences. Along with many of their white fellows, they acquired new skills and a new sophistication that prepared them for the different life of the postwar industrial world. Most important, military service in World War II divorced many Negroes from a society whose traditions had carefully defined their place, and exposed them for the first time to a community where racial equality, although imperfectly realized, was an ideal. Out of this experience many Negroes came to understand that their economic and political position could be changed. Ironically, the services themselves became an early target of this rising self-awareness. The integration of the armed forces, immediate and total, was a popular goal of the newly franchised voting group, which was turning away from leaders of both races who preached a philosophy of gradual change.

The black press was spokesman for the widespread demand for equality in the armed forces; just as the growth of the black press was dramatically stimulated by urbanization of the Negro, so was the civil rights movement stimulated by the press. The Pittsburgh *Courier* was but one of many black papers and journals that developed a national circulation and featured countless articles on the subject of discrimination in the services. One black sociologist observed that it was "no exaggeration to say that the Negro press was the major influence in mobilizing Negroes in the struggle for their rights during World War II."[5-4] Sometimes inaccurate, often inflammatory, and always to the consternation of the military, the black press rallied the opposition to segregation during and after the war.

Much of the black unrest and dissatisfaction dramatized by the press continued to be mobilized through the efforts of such organizations as the National Association for the Advancement of Colored People, the National Urban League, and the Congress of Racial Equality. The NAACP, for example, revitalized by a new and broadened appeal to the black masses, had some 1,200 branches in forty-three states by 1946 and boasted a membership of more than half a million. While the association continued to fight for minority rights in the courts, to stimulate black political participation, and to improve the conditions of Negroes generally, its most popular activity during the 1940's was its effort to eliminate discrimination in the armed forces. The files of the services and the White House are replete with NAACP

56

complaints, requests, demands, and charges that involved the military departments in innumerable investigations and justifications. If the complaints effected little immediate change in policy, they at least dramatized the plight of black servicemen and mobilized demands for reform.[5-5]

Not all racial unrest was so constructively channeled during the war. Riots and mutinies in the armed services were echoed around the country. In Detroit competition between blacks and whites, many recently arrived from the south seeking jobs, culminated in June 1943 in the most serious riot of the decade. The President was forced to declare a state of emergency and dispatch 6,000 troops to patrol the city. The Detroit riot was only the most noticeable of a number of racial incidents that inevitably provoked an ugly reaction, and the postwar period witnessed an increase in antiblack sentiment and violence in the United States.[5-6] Testifying to the black community's economic and political progress during the war as well as a corresponding increase in white awareness of and protest against the mistreatment of black citizens, this antiblack sentiment was only the pale ghost of a similar phenomenon after World War I.

PRESIDENT TRUMAN ADDRESSING THE NAACP CONVENTION,
Lincoln Memorial, Washington, D.C., June 1947.
Seated at the President's left are Walter White, Eleanor Roosevelt, and Senator Wayne Morse;
visible in the rear row are Admiral of the Fleet Chester W. Nimitz, Attorney General Tom C. Clark, and Chief
Justice Fred M. Vinson.

Nevertheless, the sentiment was widespread. Traveling cross-country in a train during Christmastime, 1945, the celebrated American essayist Bernard De Voto was astonished to hear expressions of antiblack sentiment. In Wisconsin, "a state where I think I had never before heard the word 'nigger,' that [dining] car was full of talk about niggers and what had to be done about them."[5-7] A white veteran bore out the observation. "Anti-Negro talk ... is cropping up in many places ... the assumption [being] that there is more prejudice, never less.... Throughout the war the whites were segregated from the Negroes (why not say it this way for a change?) so that there were almost no occasions for white soldiers to get any kind of an impression of Negroes, favorable or otherwise." There had been some race prejudice among servicemen, but, the veteran asked, "What has caused this anti-Negro talk among those who stayed at home?"[5-8] About the same time, a U.S. senator was complaining to the Secretary of War that white and black civilians at Kelly Field, Texas, shared the same cafeterias and other facilities. He hoped the secretary would look into the matter to prevent disturbances that might grow out of a policy of this sort.[5-9]

Nor did the armed forces escape the rise in racial tension. For example, the War Department received many letters from the public and members of Congress when black officers, nearly the base's entire contingent of four hundred, demonstrated against the segregation of the officers' club at Freeman Field, Indiana, in April 1945. The question at issue was whether a post commander had the authority to exclude individuals on grounds of race from recreational facilities on an Army post. The Army Air Forces supported the post commander and suggested a return to a policy of separate and equal facilities for whites and blacks, primarily because a club for officers was a social center for the entire family. Since it was hardly an accepted custom in the country for the races to intermingle, officials argued, the Army had to follow rather than depart from custom, and, further, the wishes of white officers as well as those of Negroes deserved consideration.[5-10]

The controversy reached the desk of John McCloy, the Assistant Secretary of War, who considered the position taken by the Army Air Forces a backward step, a reversal of the War Department position in an earlier and similar case at Selfridge Field, Michigan. McCloy's contention prevailed—that the commander's administrative discretion in these matters fell short of authority to exclude individuals from the right to enjoy recreational facilities provided by the federal government or maintained with its funds. Secretary of War Stimson agreed to amend the basic policy to reflect this clarification.[5-11]

In December 1945 the press reported and the War and Navy Departments investigated an incident at Le Havre, France, where soldiers were embarking for the United States for demobilization. Officers of a Navy escort carrier objected to the inclusion of 123 black enlisted men on the grounds that the ship was unable to provide separate accommodations for Negroes. Army port authorities then substituted another group that included only one black officer and five black enlisted men who were placed aboard over the protests of the ship's officers.[5-12] The Secretary of the Navy had already declared that the Navy did not differentiate between men on account of race, and on 12 December 1945 he reiterated his statement, adding that it applied to members of all the armed forces.[5-13] Demonstrating the frequent gap between policy and practice, Forrestal's order was ignored six months later by port officials when a group of black

57

officers and men was withdrawn from a shipping list at Bremerhaven, Germany, on the grounds that "segregation is a War Department policy."[5-14]

Overt antiblack behavior and social turbulence in the civilian community also reached into the services. In February 1946 Issac Woodard, Jr., who had served in the Army for fifteen months in the Pacific, was ejected from a commercial bus and beaten by civilian police. Sergeant Woodard had recently been discharged from the Army at Camp Gordon, Georgia, and was still in uniform at the time of the brutal attack that blinded him. His case was quickly taken up by the NAACP and became the centerpiece of a national protest.[5-15] Not only did the civil rights spokesmen protest the sadistic blinding, they also charged that the Army was incapable of protecting its own members in the community.

While service responsibility for countering off-base discrimination against servicemen was still highly debatable in 1946, the right of men on a military base to protection was uncontestable. Yet even service practices on military bases were under attack as racial conflicts and threats of violence multiplied. "Dear Mother," one soldier stationed at Sheppard Field, Texas, felt compelled to write in early 1946, "I don't know how long I'll stay whole because when those Whites come over to start [trouble] again I'll be right with the rest of the fellows. Nothing to worry about. Love,..."[5-16] If the soldier's letter revealed continuing racial conflict in the service, it also testified to a growing racial unity among black servicemen that paralleled the trend in the black community. When Negroes could resolve with a new self-consciousness to "be right with the rest of the fellows," their cause was immeasurably strengthened and their goals brought appreciably nearer.

ASSISTANT SECRETARY MCCLOY

Civil rights spokesmen had several points to make regarding the use of Negroes in the postwar armed forces. Referring to the fact that World War II began with Negroes fighting for the right to fight, they demanded that the services guarantee a fair representation of Negroes in the postwar forces. Furthermore, to avoid the frustration suffered by Negroes trained for combat and then converted into service troops, they demanded that Negroes be trained and employed in all military specialties. They particularly stressed the correlation between poor leaders and poor units. The services' command practices, they charged, had frequently led to the appointment of the wrong men, either black or white, to command black units. Their principal solution was to provide for the promotion and proper employment of a proportionate share of competent black officers and noncommissioned officers. Above all, they pointed to the humiliations black soldiers suffered in the community outside the limits of the base.[5-17] One particularly telling example of such discrimination that circulated in the black press in 1945 described German prisoners of war being fed in a railroad restaurant while their black Army guards were forced to eat outside. But such discrimination toward black servicemen was hardly unique, and the civil rights advocates were quick to point to the connection between such practices and low morale and performance. For them there was but one answer to such discrimination: all men must be treated as individuals and guaranteed equal treatment and opportunity in the services. In a word, the armed forces must integrate. They pointed with pride to the success of those black soldiers who served in integrated units in the last months of the European war, and they repeatedly urged the complete abolition of segregation in the peacetime Army and Navy.[5-18]

When an executive of the National Urban League summed up these demands for President Truman at the end of the war, he clearly indicated that the changes in military policy that had brought about the gradual improvement in the lot of black servicemen during the war were now beside the point.[5-19] The military might try to ignore this fact for a little while longer, a politically sensitive President was not about to make such an error.

The Army's Grand Review

In the midst of this intensifying sentiment for integration, in fact a full year before the war ended, the Army began to search for a new racial policy. The invasion of Normandy and the extraordinary advance to Paris during the summer of 1944 had led many to believe that the war in Europe would soon be over, perhaps by fall. As the Allied leaders at the Quebec Conference in September discussed arrangements to be imposed on a defeated Germany, American officials in Washington began to consider plans for the postwar period. Among them was Assistant Secretary of War McCloy. Dissatisfied with the manner in which the Army was using black troops, McCloy believed it was time to start planning how best to employ them in the postwar Army, which, according to current assumptions, would be small and professional and would depend upon a citizen reserve to augment it in an emergency.

TRUMAN GIBSON

58

McCloy concluded that despite a host of prewar studies by the General Staff, the Army War College, and other military agencies, the Army was unprepared during World War II to deal with and make the most efficient use of the large numbers of Negroes furnished by Selective Service. Policies for training and employing black troops had developed in response to specific problems rather than in accordance with a well thought out and comprehensive plan. Because of "inadequate preparation prior to the period of sudden expansion," McCloy believed a great many sources of racial irritation persisted. To develop a "definite, workable policy, for the inclusion and utilization in the Army of minority racial groups" before postwar planning crystallized and solidified, McCloy suggested to his assistants that the War Department General Staff review existing practices and experiences at home and abroad and recommend changes.[5-20]

The Chief of Staff, General Marshall, continued to insist that the Army's racial problem was but part of a larger national problem and, as McCloy later recalled, had no strong views on a solution.[5-21] Whatever his personal feelings, Marshall, like most Army staff officers, always emphasized efficiency and performance to the exclusion of social concerns. While he believed that the limited scope of the experiment with integrated platoons toward the end of the war in Europe made the results inconclusive, Marshall still wanted the platoons' performance considered in the general staff study.[5-22]

The idea of a staff study on the postwar use of black troops also found favor with Secretary Stimson, and a series of conferences and informal discussions on the best way to go about it took place in the highest echelons of the Army during the early months of 1945. The upshot was a decision to ask the senior commanders at home and overseas for their comments. How did they train and use their black troops? What irritations, frictions, and disorders arising from racial conflicts had hampered their operations? What were their recommendations on how best to use black troops after the war? Two weeks after the war ended in Europe, a letter with an attached questionnaire was sent to senior commanders.[5-23] The questionnaire asked for such information as: "To what extent have you maintained segregation beyond the actual unit level, and what is your recommendation on this subject? If you have employed Negro platoons in the same company with white platoons, what is your opinion of the practicability of this arrangement?"

Not everyone agreed that the questionnaire was the best way to review the performance of Negroes in World War II. Truman Gibson, for one, doubted the value of soliciting information from senior commanders, feeling that these officers would offer much subjective material of little real assistance. Referring to the letter to the major senior commanders, he said:

Mere injunctions of objectivity do not work in the racial field where more often than not decisions are made on a basis of emotion, prejudice or pre-existing opinion.... Much of the difficulty in the Army has arisen from improper racial attitudes on both sides. Indeed, the Army's basic policy of segregation is said to be based principally on the individual attitudes and desires of the soldiers.

But who knew what soldiers' attitudes were? Why not, he suggested, make some scientific inquiries? Why not try to determine, for example, how far public opinion and pressure would permit the Army to go in developing policies for black troops?[5-24]

Gibson had become, perforce, an expert on public opinion. During the last several months he had suffered the slings and arrows of an outraged black press for his widely publicized analysis of the performance of black troops. Visiting black units and commanders in the Mediterranean and European theaters to observe, in McCloy's words, "the performance of Negro troops, their attitudes, and the attitudes of their officers toward them,"[5-25] Gibson had arrived in Italy at the end of February 1945 to find theater officials concerned over the poor combat record of the 92d Infantry Division, the only black division in the theater and one of three activated by the War Department. After a series of discussions with senior commanders and a visit to the division, Gibson participated in a press conference in Rome during which he spoke candidly of the problems of the division's infantry units.[5-26] Subsequent news reports of the conference stressed Gibson's confirmation of the division's disappointing performance, but neglected the reasons he advanced to explain its failure. The reports earned a swift and angry retort from the black community. Many organizations and journals condemned Gibson's evaluation of the 92d outright. Some seemed less concerned with the possible accuracy of his statement than with the effects it might have on the development of future military policy. The NAACP's *Crisis*, for example, charged that Gibson had "carried the ball for the War Department," and that "probably no more unfortunate words, affecting the representatives of the entire race, were ever spoken by a Negro in a key position in such a critical hour. We seem destined to bear the burden of Mr. Gibson's Rome adventure for many years to come."[5-27]

Other black journals took a more detached view of the situation, asserting that Gibson's remarks revealed nothing new and that the problem was segregation, of which the 92d was a notable victim. Gibson took this tack in his own defense, pointing to the irony of a situation in which "some people can, on the one hand, argue that segregation is wrong, and on the other ... blindly defend the product of that segregation."[5-28]

Gibson had defenders in the Army whose comments might well apply to all the large black units in the war. At one extreme stood the Allied commander in Italy, General Mark W. Clark, who attributed the 92d's shortcomings to "our handling of minority problems at home." Most of all, General Clark thought, black soldiers needed the incentive of feeling that they were fighting for home and country as equals. But his conclusion—"only the proper environment in his own country can provide such an incentive"—neatly played down Army responsibility for the division's problems.[5-29]

Another officer, who as commander of a divisional artillery unit was intimately acquainted with the division's shortcomings, delineated an entirely different set of causes. The division was doomed to mediocrity and worse, Lt. Col. Marcus H. Ray concluded, from the moment of its activation. Undercurrents of racial antipathy as well as distrust and prejudice, he believed, infected the organization from the outset and created an unhealthy beginning. The practice of withholding promotion from deserving black officers along with preferential assignments for white officers prolonged the malady. The basic misconception was that southern white officers understood Negroes; under such officers Negroes who conformed with the southern stereotype were promoted regardless of their abilities, while those who exhibited self-reliance and self-respect—necessary attributes of leadership—were humiliated and discouraged for their uppityness. "I was astounded," he said, "by the willingness of the white officers who preceded us to place their own lives in a hazardous position in order to have tractable Negroes around them."[5-30] In short, the men of the 92d who fought and died bravely should be honored, but their unit, which on balance did not perform well, should be considered a failure of white leadership.

COMPANY I, 370TH INFANTRY,
92D DIVISION, *advances through Cascina, Italy.*

Lt. Gen. Lucian K. Truscott, Jr., then Fifth Army commander in Italy, disagreed. Submitting the proceedings of a board of review that had investigated the effectiveness of black officers and enlisted men in the 92d Division, he was sympathetic to the frustrations encountered by the division commander, Maj. Gen. Edward M. Almond. "In justice to those splendid officers"—a reference to the white senior commanders and staff members of the division—"who have devoted themselves without stint in an endeavor to produce a combat division with Negro personnel and who have approached this problem without prejudice," Truscott endorsed the board's hard view that many infantrymen in the division "would not fight."[5-31] This conclusion was in direct conflict with the widely held and respected truism that competent leadership solved all problems, from which it followed that the answer to the problem of Negroes in combat was command. Good commanders prevented friction, performed their mission effectively, and achieved success no matter what the obstacles—a view put forth in a typical report from World War II that "the efficiency of Negro units depends entirely on the leadership of officers and NCO's."[5-32]

In fact, General Truscott's analysis of the 92d Division's problems seemed at variance with his analysis of command problems in other units, as illustrated by his later attention to problems in the all-white 34th Infantry Division.[5-33] The habit of viewing unit problems as command problems was also demonstrated by General Jacob L. Devers, who was deputy Allied commander in the Mediterranean when the 92d arrived in Italy. Reflecting later upon the 92d Division, General Devers agreed that its engineer and armor unit performed well, but the infantry did not "because their commanders weren't good enough."[5-34]

Years later General Almond, the division's commander, was to claim that the 92d Division had done "many things well and some things poorly." It fought in extremely rugged terrain against a determined enemy over an exceptionally broad front. The division's artillery as well as its technical and administrative units performed well. Negroes also excelled in intelligence work and in dealing with the Italian partisans. On the other hand, General Almond reported, infantry elements were unable to close with the enemy and destroy him. Rifle squads, platoons, and companies tended "to melt away" when confronted by determined opposition. Almond blamed this on "a lack of dedication to purpose, pride of accomplishment and devotion to duty and teammates by the majority of black riflemen assigned to Infantry Units."[5-35]

Similar judgments were expressed concerning the combat capability of the other major black unit, the 93d Infantry Division.[5-36] When elements of the 93d, the 25th Regimental Combat Team in particular, participated in the Bougainville campaign in the Solomon Islands, their performance was the subject of constant scrutiny by order of the Chief of Staff.[5-37] The combat record of the 25th included enough examples of command and individual failure to reinforce the War Department's decision in mid-1944 to use the individual units of the division in security, laboring, and training duties in quiet areas of the theater, leaving combat to more seasoned units.[5-38] During the last year of the war the 93d performed missions that were essential but not typical for combat divisions.

Analyses of the division's performance ran along familiar lines. The XIV Corps commander, under whom the division served, rated the performance of the 25th Regimental Combat Team infantry as fair and artillery as good, but found the unit, at least those parts commanded by black officers, lacking in initiative, inadequately trained, and poorly disciplined. Other reports tended to agree. All of them, along with reports on the 24th Infantry, another black unit serving in the area, were assembled in Washington for Assistant Secretary McCloy. While he admitted important limitations in the performance of the units, McCloy nevertheless remained encouraged. Not so the Secretary of War. "I do not believe," he told McCloy, "they can be turned into really effective combat troops without all officers being white."[5-39]

Black officers of the 93d, however, entertained a different view. They generally cited command and staff inefficiencies as the major cause of the division's discipline and morale problems. One respondent, a company commander in the 25th Infantry, singled out the "continuous dissension and suspicion characterizing the relations between white and colored officers of the division." All tended to stress what they considered inadequate jungle training, and, like many white observers, they all agreed the combat period was too brief to demonstrate the division's developing ability.[5-40]

92D DIVISION ENGINEERS PREPARE A FORD FOR ARNO RIVER TRAFFIC

Despite the performance of some individuals and units praised by all, the combat performance of the 92d and 93d Infantry Divisions was generally considered less than satisfactory by most observers. A much smaller group of commentators, mostly black journalists, never accepted the prevailing view. Pointing to the decorations and honors received by individuals in the two divisions, they charged that the adverse reports were untrue, reflections of the prejudices of white officers. Such an assertion presupposed that hundreds of officers and War Department officials were so consumed with prejudice that they falsified the record. And the argument from decorations, as one expert later pointed out, faltered once it was understood that the 92d and 93d Infantry Divisions combined a relatively high number of decorations with relatively few casualties.[5-41]

Actually, there was little doubt that the performance of the black divisions in World War II was generally unacceptable. Beyond that common conclusion, opinions diverged widely. Commanders tended to blame undisciplined troops and lack of initiative and control by black officers and noncommissioned officers as the primary cause of the difficulty. Others, particularly black observers, cited the white officers and their lack of racial sensitivity. In fact, as Ulysses Lee points out with careful documentation, all these factors were involved, but the underlying problem usually overlooked by observers was segregation. Large, all-black combat units submerged able soldiers in a sea of men with low aptitude and inadequate training. Segregation also created special psychological problems for junior black officers. Carefully assigned so that they never commanded white officers or men, they were often derided by white officers whose attitudes were quickly sensed by the men to the detriment of good discipline. Segregation was also a factor in the rapid transfer of men in and out of the divisions, thus negating the possible benefits of lengthy training. Furthermore, the divisions were natural repositories for many dissatisfied or inadequate white officers, who introduced a host of other problems.

Truman Gibson was quick to point out how segregation had intensified the problem of turning civilians into soldiers and groups into units. The "dissimilarity in the learning profiles" between black and white soldiers as reflected in their AGCT scores was, he explained to McCloy, primarily a result of inferior black schooling, yet its practical effect on the Army was to burden it with several large units of inferior combat ability (Table 2). In addition to the fact that large black units had a preponderance of slow learners, Gibson emphasized that nearly all black soldiers were trained near "exceedingly hostile" communities. This hostile atmosphere, he believed, had played a decisive role in their adjustment to Army life and adversely affected individual motivation. Gibson also charged the Army with promoting some black officers who lacked leadership qualifications and whose performance, consequently, was under par. He recommended a single measure of performance for officers and a single system for promotion, even if this system reduced promotions for black officers. Promotions on any basis other than merit, he concluded, deprived the Army of the best leadership and inflicted weak commanders on black units.

TABLE 2—AGCT PERCENTAGES IN SELECTED WORLD WAR II DIVISIONS

Unit	I

	(130 +)	(110
11th Armored Division	3.0	2ª
35th Infantry Division	3.3	27
92d Infantry Division (Negro)	0.4	5
93d Infantry Division (Negro)	0.1	3
100th Infantry Division	3.6	27

Source: Tables submitted by The Adjutant General to the Gillem Board, 1945.

Gibson was not trying to magnify the efficiency of segregated units. He made a special effort to compare the performance of the 92d Division with that of the integrated black platoons in Germany because such a comparison would demonstrate, he believed, that the Army's segregation policy was in need of critical reexamination. He cited "many officers" who believed that the problems connected with large segregated combat units justified their abolition in favor of the integration of black platoons into larger white units. Although such unit integration would not abolish segregation completely, Gibson concluded, it would permit the Army to use men and small units on the basis of ability alone.[5-42]

The flexibility Gibson detected among many Army officers was not apparent in the answers to the McCloy questionnaire that flowed into the War Department during the summer and fall of 1945. With few exceptions, the senior officers queried expressed uniform reactions. They reiterated a story of frustration and difficulty in training and employing black units, characterized black soldiers as unreliable and inefficient, and criticized the performance of black officers and noncommissioned officers. They were particularly concerned with racial disturbances, which, they believed, were not only the work of racial agitators but also the result of poor morale and a sense of discrimination among black troops. Yet they wanted to retain segregation, albeit in units of smaller size, and they wanted to depend, for the most part, on white officers to command these black units. Concerned with performance, pragmatic rather than reflective in their habits, the commanders showed little interest in or understanding of the factors responsible for the conditions of which they complained. Many believed that segregation actually enhanced black pride.[5-43]

These responses were summarized by the commanding generals of the major force commands at the request of the War Department's Special Planning Division.[5-44] For example, the study prepared by the Army Service Forces, which had employed a high proportion of black troops in its technical services during the war, passed on the recommendations made by these far-flung commands and touched incidentally on several of the points raised by Gibson.[5-45] Like Gibson, the Army Service Forces recommended that Negroes of little or no education be denied induction or enlistment and that no deviation from normal standards for the sake of maintaining racial quotas in the officer corps be tolerated. The Army Service Forces also wanted Negroes employed in all major forces, participating proportionately in all phases of the Army's mission, including overseas and combat assignments, but not in every occupation. For the Army Service Forces had decided that Negroes performed best as truck drivers, ammunition handlers, stevedores, cooks, bakers, and the like and should be trained in these specialties rather than more highly skilled jobs such as armorer or machinist. Even in the occupations they were best suited to, Negroes should be given from a third more to twice as much training as whites, and black units should have 25 to 50 percent more officers than white units. At the same time, the Army Service Forces wanted to retain segregated units, although it recommended limiting black service units to company size. Stating in conclusion that it sought only "to insure the most efficient training and utilization of Negro manpower" and would ignore the question of racial equality or the "wisdom of segregation in the social sense," the Army Service Forces overlooked the possibility that the former could not be attained without consideration of the latter.

The Army Ground Forces, which trained black units for all major branches of the field forces, also wanted to retain black units, but its report concluded that these units could be of battalion size. The organization of black soldiers in division-size units, it claimed, only complicated the problem of training because of the difficulty in developing the qualified black technicians, noncommissioned officers, and field grade officers necessary for such large units and finding training locations as well as assignment areas with sufficient off-base recreational facilities for large groups of black soldiers. The Army Ground Forces considered the problem of finding and training field grade officers particularly acute since black units employing black officers, at least in the case of infantry, had proved ineffective. Yet white officers put in command of black troops felt they were being punished, and their presence added to the frustration of the blacks.

The Army Ground Forces was also particularly concerned with racial disturbances, which, it believed, stemmed from conflicting white and black concepts of the Negro's place in the social

62

pattern. The Army Ground Forces saw no military solution for a problem that transcended the contemporary national emergency, and its conclusion—that the solution lay in society at large and not primarily in the armed forces—had the effect, whether or not so intended, of neatly exonerating the Army. In fact, the detailed conclusions and recommendations of the Army Ground Forces were remarkably similar to those of the Army Service Forces, but the Ground Forces study, more than any other, was shot full with blatant racism. The study quoted a 1925 War College study to the effect that the black officer was "still a Negro with all the faults and weaknesses of character inherent in the Negro race." It also discussed the "average Negro" and his "inherent characteristics" at great length, dwelling on his supposed inferior mentality and weakness of character, and raising other racial shibboleths. Burdened with these prejudices, the Army Ground Forces study concluded

that the conception that negroes should serve in the military forces, or in particular parts of the military forces, or sustain battle losses in proportion to their population in the United States, may be desirable but is impracticable and should be abandoned in the interest of a logical solution to the problem of the utilization of negroes in the armed forces.[5-46]

The Army Air Forces, another large employer of black servicemen, reported a slightly different World War II experience. Conforming with departmental policies on utilizing black soldiers, it had selected Negroes for special training on the same basis as whites with the exception of aviation cadets. Negroes with a lower stanine (aptitude) had been accepted in order to secure enough candidates to meet the quota for pilots, navigators, and bombardiers in the black units. In its preliminary report to the War Department on the employment of Negroes, the Army Air Forces admitted that individuals of both races with similar aptitudes and test scores had the same success in technical schools, could be trained as pilots and technicians in the same period of time, and showed the same degree of mechanical proficiency. Black units, on the other hand, required considerably more time in training than white units, sometimes simply because they were understrength and their performance was less effective. At the same time the Air Forces admitted that even after discounting the usual factors, such as time in service and job assignment, whites advanced further than blacks. No explanation was offered. Nevertheless, the commanding general of the Air Forces reported very little racial disorder or conflict overseas. There had been a considerable amount in the United States, however; many Air Forces commanders ascribed this to the unwillingness of northern Negroes to accept southern laws or social customs, the insistence of black officers on integrated officers' clubs, and the feeling among black fliers that command had been made an exclusive prerogative of white officers rather than a matter depending on demonstrated qualification.

In contrast to the others, the Army Air Forces revealed a marked change in sentiment over the post-World War I studies of black troops. No more were there references to congenital inferiority or inherent weaknesses, but everywhere a willingness to admit that Negroes had been held back by the white majority.

The commanding general of the Army Air Forces recommended Negroes be apportioned among the three major forces—the Army Ground Forces, the Army Service Forces, and the Army Air Forces—but that their numbers in no case exceed 10 percent of any command; that black servicemen be trained exactly as whites; and that Negroes be segregated in units not to exceed air group size. Unlike the others, the Army Air Forces wanted black units to have black commanders as far as possible and recommended that the degree of segregation in messing, recreation, and social activities conform to the custom of the surrounding community. It wanted Negroes assigned overseas in the same proportion as whites, and in the United States, to the extent practicable, only to those areas considered favorable to their welfare. Finally, the Air Forces wanted Negroes to be neither favored nor discriminated against in disciplinary matters.[5-47]

Among the responses of the subordinate commands were some exceptions to the generalizations found in those of the major forces. One commander, for example, while concluding that segregation was desirable, admitted that it was one of the basic causes of the Army's racial troubles and would have to be dealt with "one way or the other."[5-48] Another recommended dispersing black troops, one or two in a squad, throughout all-white combat units.[5-49] Still another pointed out that the performance of black officers and noncommissioned officers in terms of resourcefulness, aggressiveness, sense of responsibility, and ability to make decisions was comparable to the performance of white soldiers when conditions of service were nearly equal. But the Army failed to understand this truth, the commander of the 1st Service Command charged, and its separate and unequal treatment discriminated in a way that would affect the efficiency of any man. The performance of black troops, he concluded, depended on how severely the community near a post differentiated between the black and white soldier and how well the Negro's commander demonstrated the fairness essential to authority. The Army admitted that black units needed superior leadership, but, he added, it misunderstood what this leadership entailed. All too often commanders of black units acted under the belief that their men were different and needed special treatment, thus clearly suggesting racial inferiority. The Army, he concluded, should learn from its wartime experience the deleterious effect of segregation on motivation and ultimately on performance.[5-50]

Truman Gibson took much the same approach when he summed up for McCloy his estimate of the situation facing the Army. After rehearsing the recent history of segregation in the armed forces, he suggested that it was not enough to compare the performance of black and white troops; the reports of black performance should be examined to determine whether the performance would be improved or impaired by changing the policy of segregation. Any major Army review, he urged, should avoid the failure of the old studies on race that based differences in performance on racial characteristics and should question instead the efficiency of segregation. For him, segregation was the heart of the matter, and he counseled that "future policy should be predicated on an assumption that civilian attitudes will not remain static. The basic policy of the Army should, therefore, not itself be static and restrictive, but should be so framed as to make further progress possible on a flexible basis."[5-51]

Before passing Gibson's suggestions to the Assistant Secretary of War, McCloy's executive assistant, Lt. Col. Davidson Sommers, added some ideas of his own. Since it was "pretty well recognized," he wrote, that the Army had not found the answer to the efficient use of black manpower, a first-class officer or group of officers of high rank, supplemented perhaps with a racially mixed group of civilians, should be designated to prepare a new racial policy. But, he warned, their work would be ineffectual without specific directions from Army leaders. He wanted the Army to make "eventual nonsegregation" its goal. Complete integration, Sommers felt, was impossible to achieve at once. Classification test scores alone refuted the claim that "Negroes in general make as good soldiers as whites." But he thought there was no need "to resort to racial theories to explain the difference," for the lack of educational, occupational, and social opportunities was sufficient.[5-52]

Sommers had, in effect, adopted Gibson's gradualist approach to the problem, suggesting an inquiry to determine "the areas in which nonsegregation can be attempted first and the methods by which it can be introduced ... instead of merely generalizing, as in the past, on the disappointing and not very relevant experiences with large segregated units." He foresaw difficulties: a certain amount of social friction and perhaps a considerable amount of what he called "professional Negro agitation" because Negroes competing with whites would probably not achieve comparable ranks or positions immediately. But Sommers saw no cause for alarm. "We shall be on firm ground," he concluded, "and will be able to defend our actions by relying on the unassailable position that we are using men in accordance with their ability."

Competing with these calls for gradual desegregation was the Army's growing concern with securing some form of universal military training. Congress would discuss the issue during the summer and fall of 1945, and one of the questions almost certain to arise in the congressional hearings was the place contemplated for Negroes. Would the Army use Negroes in combat units? Would the Army train and use Negroes in units together with whites? Upon the answers to these questions hinged the votes of most, if not all, southern congressmen. Prudence dictated that the Army avoid any innovations that might jeopardize the chance for universal military training. In other words, went the prevalent view, what was good for the Army—and universal military training was in that category—had to come before all else.[5-53]

Even among officers troubled by the contradictory aspects of an issue clouded by morality, many felt impelled to give their prime allegiance to the Army as it was then constituted. The Army's impressive achievement during the war, they reasoned, argued for its continuation in conformance with current precepts, particularly in a world still full of hostilities. The stability of the Army came first; changes would have to be made slowly, without risking the menace of disruption. An attempt to mix the races in the Army seemed to most officers a dangerous move bordering on irresponsibility. Furthermore, the majority of Army officers, dedicated to the traditions of the service, saw the Army as a social as well as a military institution. It was a way of life that embraced families, wives and children. The old manners and practices were comfortable because they were well known and understood, had produced victory, and had represented a life that was somewhat isolated and insulated—particularly in the field—from the currents and pressures of national life. Why then should the old patterns be modified; why exchange comfort for possible chaos? Why should the Army admit large numbers of Negroes; what had Negroes contributed to winning World War II; what could they possibly contribute to the postwar Army?

Although opinion among Army officials on the future role of Negroes in the Army was diverse and frankly questioning in tone, opinion on the past performance of black units was not.

Commanders tended to agree that with certain exceptions, particularly small service and combat support units, black units performed below the Army average during the war and considerably below the best white units. The commanders also generally agreed that black units should be made more efficient and usually recommended they be reduced in size and filled with better qualified men. Most civil rights spokesmen and their allies in the Army, on the other hand, viewed segregation as the underlying cause of poor performance. How, then, could the conflicting advice be channeled into construction of an acceptable postwar racial policy? The task was clearly beyond the powers of the War Department's Special Planning Division, and in September 1945 McCloy adopted the recommendation of Sommers and Gibson and urged the Secretary of War to turn over this crucial matter to a board of general officers. Out of this board's deliberations, influenced in great measure by opinions previously expressed, would emerge the long-awaited revision of the Army's policy for its black minority.

The Navy's Informal Inspection

In contrast to the elaborate investigation conducted by the Army, the Navy's search for a policy consisted mainly of an informal intradepartmental review and an inspection of its black units by a civilian representative of the Secretary of the Navy. In general this contrast may be explained by the difference in the services' postwar problems. The Army was planning for the enlistment of a large cross section of the population through some form of universal military training; the Navy was planning for a much smaller peacetime organization of technically trained volunteers. Moreover, the Army wanted to review the performance of its many black combat units, whereas the naval establishment, which had excluded most of its Negroes from combat, had little to gain from measuring their wartime performance.

The character and methods of the Secretary of the Navy had an important bearing on policy. Forrestal believed he had won the senior officers to his view of equal treatment and opportunity, and to be assured of success he wanted to convince lower commanders and the ranks as well. He wrote in July 1945: "We are making every effort to give more than lip service to the principles of democracy in the treatment of the Negro and we are trying to do it with the minimum of commotion.... We would rather await the practical demonstration of the success of our efforts.... There is still a long road to travel but I am confident we have made a start." [5-54]

Forrestal's wish for a racially democratic Navy did not noticeably conflict with the traditionalists' plan for a small, technically elite force, so while the Army launched a worldwide quest in anticipation of an orthodox policy review, the Navy started an informal investigation designed primarily to win support for the racial program conceived by the Secretary of the Navy.

The Navy's search began in the last months of the war when Secretary Forrestal approved the formation of an informal Committee on Negro Personnel. Although Lester Granger, the secretary's adviser on racial matters, had originally proposed the establishment of such a committee to "help frame sound and effective racial policies,"[5-55] the Chief of Naval Personnel, a preeminent representative of the Navy's professionals, saw an altogether different reason for the group. He endorsed the idea of a committee, he told a member of the secretary's staff, "not because there is anything wrong or backward about our policies," but because "we need greater cooperation from the technical Bureaus in order that those policies may succeed."[5-56] Forrestal did little to define the group's purpose when on 16 April 1945 he ordered Under Secretary Bard to organize a committee "to assure uniform policies" and see that all subdivisions of the Navy were familiar with each other's successful and unsuccessful racial practices.[5-57]

By pressing for the uniform treatment of Negroes, Forrestal doubtless hoped to pull backward branches into line with more liberal ones so that the progressive reforms of the past year would be accepted throughout the Navy. But if Forrestal's ultimate goal was plain, his failure to give clear-cut directions to his informal committee was characteristic of his handling of racial policy. He carefully followed the recommendations of the Chief of Naval Personnel, who wanted the committee to be a military group, despite having earlier expressed his intention of inviting Granger to chair the committee. As announced on 25 April, the committee was headed by a senior official of the Bureau of Naval Personnel, Capt. Roscoe H. Hillenkoetter, with another of the bureau's officers serving as committee recorder.[5-58] Restricting the scope of the inquiry, Forrestal ordered that "whenever practical" the committee should assign each of its members to investigate the racial practices in his own organization.

Nevertheless when the committee got down to work it quickly went beyond the limited concept of its mission as advanced by the Chief of Naval Personnel. Not only did it study statistics gathered from all sections of the department and review the experiences of various commanders of black units, it also studied Granger's immediate and long-range recommendations for the department, an extension of his earlier wartime work for Forrestal. Specifically, Granger had called for the formulation of a definite integration policy and for a strenuous public relations campaign directed toward the black community. He had also called for

65

the enlistment and commissioning of a significant number of Negroes in the Regular Navy, and he wanted commanders indoctrinated in their racial responsibilities. Casting further afield, Granger had warned that discriminatory policies and practices in shipyards and other establishments must be eliminated, and employment opportunities for black civilians in the department broadened.[5-59]

The committee deliberated on all these points, and, after meeting several times, announced in May 1945 its findings and recommendations. It found that the Navy's current policies were sound and when properly executed produced good results. At the same time it saw a need for periodic reviews to insure uniform application of policy and better public relations. Such findings could be expected from a body headed by a senior official of the personnel bureau, but the committee then came up with the unexpected—a series of recommendations for sweeping change. Revealing the influence of the Special Programs Unit, the committee asked that Negroes be declared available for assignment to all types of ships and shore stations in all classifications, with selections made solely on merit. Since wholesale reassignments were impractical, the committee recommended well-planned, gradual assimilation—it avoided the word integration—as the best policy for ending the concentration of Negroes at shore activities. It also attacked the Steward's Branch as the conspicuous symbol of the Negroes' second-class status and called for the assignment of white stewards and allowing qualified stewards to transfer to general service.

The committee wanted the Judge Advocate General to assign legal advisers to all major trials, especially those involving minorities, to prevent errors in courts-martial that might be construed as discrimination. It further recommended that Negroes be represented in the secretary's public relations office; that news items concerning Negroes be more widely disseminated through bureau bulletins; and, finally, that all bureaus as well as the Coast Guard and Marine Corps be encouraged to enroll commanders in special indoctrination programs before they were assigned to units with substantial numbers of Negroes.[5-60]

GRANGER INTERVIEWING SAILORS
on inspection tour in the Pacific.

The committee's recommendations, submitted to Under Secretary Bard on 22 May 1945, were far more than an attempt to unify the racial practices of the various subdivisions of the Navy Department. For the first time, senior representatives of the department's often independent branches accepted the contention of the Special Programs Unit that segregation was militarily inefficient and a gradual but complete integration of the Navy's general service was the solution to racial problems.

Yet as a formula for equal treatment and opportunity in the Navy, the committee's recommendations had serious omissions. Besides overlooking the dearth of black officers and the Marine Corps' continued strict segregation, the committee had ignored Granger's key proposal that Negroes be guaranteed a place in the Regular Navy. Almost without exception, Negroes in the Navy's general service were reservists, products of wartime volunteer enlistment or the draft. All but a few of the black regulars were stewards. Without assurance that many of these general service reservists would be converted to regulars or that provision would be made for enlistment of black regulars, the committee's integration recommendations lacked substance. Secretary Forrestal must have been aware of these omissions, but he ignored them. Perhaps the problem of the Negro in the postwar Navy seemed remote during this last, climactic summer of the war.

GRANGER WITH CREWMEN OF A NAVAL YARD CRAFT

To document the status of the Negro in the Navy, Forrestal turned again to Lester Granger. Granger had acted more than once as the secretary's eyes and ears on racial matters, and the association between the two men had ripened from mutual respect to close rapport.[5-61] During August 1945 Granger visited some twenty continental installations for Forrestal, including large depots and naval stations on the west coast, the Great Lakes Training Center, and bases and air stations in the south. Shortly after V-J day Granger launched a more ambitious tour of inspection that found him traveling among the 45,000 Negroes assigned to the Pacific area.

Unlike the Army staff, whose worldwide quest for information stressed black performance in the familiar lessons-learned formula and only incidentally treated those factors that affected performance, Granger, a civilian, never really tried to assess performance. He was, however, a race relations expert, and he tried constantly to discover how the treatment accorded Negroes in the Navy affected their performance and to pass on his findings to local commanders. He later explained his technique. First, he called on the commanding officer for facts and opinions on the performance and morale of the black servicemen. Then he proceeded through the command, unaccompanied, interviewing Negroes individually as well as in small and large groups. Finally, he

66

returned to the commanding officer to pass along grievances reported by the men and his own observations on the conditions under which they served.[5-62]

Granger always related the performance of enlisted men to their morale. He pointed out to the commanders that poor morale was at the bottom of the Port Chicago mass mutiny and the Guam riot, and his report to the secretary confirmed the experiences of the Special Programs Unit: black performance was deeply affected by the extent to which Negroes felt victimized by racial discrimination or handicapped by segregation, especially in housing, messing, and military and civilian recreational facilities. Although no official policy on segregated living quarters existed, Granger found such segregation widely practiced at naval bases in the United States. Separate housing meant in most cases separate work crews, thereby encouraging voluntary segregation in mess halls. In some cases the Navy's separate housing was carried over into nearby civilian communities where no segregation existed before. In others shore patrols forced segregation on civilian places of entertainment, even when state laws forbade it. On southern bases, especially, many commanders willingly abandoned the Navy's ban against discrimination in favor of the racial practices of local communities. There enforced segregation was widespread, often made explicit with "colored" and "white" signs.

Yet Granger found encouraging exceptions which he passed along to local commanders elsewhere. At Camp Perry, Virginia, for example, there was a minimum of segregation, and the commanding officer had intervened to see that Virginia's segregated bus laws did not apply to Navy buses operating between the camp and Norfolk. This situation was unusual for the Navy although integrated busing had been standard practice in the Army since mid-1944. He found Camp Perry "a pleasant contrast" to other southern installations, and from his experiences there he concluded that the attitude of the commanding officer set the pace. "There is practically no limit," Granger said, "to the progressive changes in racial attitudes and relationships which can be made when sufficiently enlightened and intelligent officer leadership is in command." The development of hard and fast rules, he concluded, was unnecessary, but the Bureau of Naval Personnel must constantly see to it that commanders resisted the "influence of local conventions."

At Pearl Harbor Granger visited three of the more than two hundred auxiliary ships manned by mixed crews. On two the conditions were excellent. The commanding officer in each case had taken special pains to avoid racial differentiation in ratings, assignments, quarters, and messes; efficiency was superior, morale was high, and racial conflict was absent. On the third ship Negroes were separated; they were specifically assigned to a special bunk section in the general crew compartment and to one end of the chow table. Here there was dissatisfaction among Negroes and friction with whites.

At the naval air bases in Hawaii performance and morale were good because Negroes served in a variety of ratings that corresponded to their training and ability. The air station in Oahu, for example, had black radar operators, signalmen, yeomen, machinist mates, and others working amiably with whites; the only sign of racial separation visible was the existence of certain barracks, no different from the others, set aside for Negroes.

Morale was lowest in black base companies and construction battalions. In several instances able commanding officers had availed themselves of competent black leaders to improve race relations, but in most units the racial situation was generally poor. Granger regarded the organization of the units as "badly conceived from the racial standpoint." Since base companies were composed almost entirely of nonrated men, spaces for black petty officers were lacking. In such units the scaffold of subordinate leadership necessary to support and uphold the authority of the officers was absent, as were opportunities for individual advancement. Some units had been provisionally re-formed into logistic support companies, and newly authorized ratings were quickly filled. This partial remedy had corrected some deficiencies, but left unchanged a number of the black base companies in the Pacific area. Although construction battalions had workers of both races, Granger reported them to be essentially segregated because whites were assigned to headquarters or to supervisory posts. Some officers had carried this arbitrary segregation into off-duty areas, one commander contending that strict segregation was the civilian pattern and that everyone was accustomed to it.

The Marine Corps lagged far behind the rest of the naval establishment, and there was little pretense of conforming with the Navy's racial policy. Black marines remained rigidly segregated and none of the few black officer candidates, all apparently well qualified, had been commissioned. Furthermore, some black marines who wanted to enlist as regulars were waiting word whether they could be included in the postwar Marine Corps. Approximately 85 percent of the black marines in the Pacific area were in depot and ammunition companies and steward groups. In many cases their assignments failed to match their qualifications and previous training. Quite a few specialists complained of having been denied privileges ordinarily accorded white men of similar status—for example, opportunities to attend schools for first sergeants, musicians, and radar operators. Black technicians were frequently sent to segregated and hastily constructed schools or detached to Army installations for schooling rather than sent to Marine Corps schools. Conversely, some white enlisted men, assigned to black units for protracted periods as instructors, were often accorded the unusual privilege of living in officers' quarters and eating in the officers' mess in order to preserve racial segregation.

Most black servicemen, Granger found, resented the white fleet shore patrols in the Pacific area which they considered biased in handling disciplinary cases and reporting offenders. The commanding officer of the shore patrol in Honolulu defended the practice because he believed the use of Negroes in this duty would be highly dangerous. Granger disagreed, pointing to the successful employment of black shore patrols in such fleet liberty cities as San Diego and Miami. He singled out the situation in Guam, which was patrolled by an all-white Marine Corps guard regarded by black servicemen as racist in attitude. Frequently, racial clashes occurred, principally over the attentions of native women, but it was the concentration of Negroes in the naval barracks at Guam, Granger concluded, along with the lack of black shore patrols, that intensified racial isolation, induced a suspicion of racial policies, and aggravated resentment.

At every naval installation Granger heard vigorous complaints over the contrast between black and white ratings and promotions. Discrepancies could be explained partly by the fact that, since the general service had been opened to Negroes fairly late in the war, many white men had more than two years seniority over any black. But Granger found evidence that whites were transferred into units to receive promotions and ratings due eligible black members. In many cases, he found "indisputable racial discrimination" by commanding officers, with the result that training was wasted, trained men were prevented from acquiring essential experience and its rewards, and resentment smoldered.

Evidence of overt prejudice aside, Granger stressed again and again that the primary cause of the Navy's racial problems was segregation. Segregation was "impractical and inefficient," he pointed out, because racial isolation bred suspicion, which in turn inflamed resentment, and finally provoked insubordination. The best way to integrate Negroes, Granger felt, was to take the most natural course, that is, eliminate all special provisions, conditions, or cautions regarding their employment. "There should be no exceptional approach to problems involving Negroes," he counseled, "for the racial factor in naval service will disappear only when problems involving Negroes are accepted as part of the Navy's general program for insuring efficient performance and first-class discipline."

Despite his earlier insistence on a fair percentage of Negroes in the postwar Regular Navy, Granger conceded that the number and proportion would probably decrease during peacetime. It was hardly likely, he added, that black enlistment would exceed 5 percent of the total strength, a manageable proportion. He even saw some advantages in smaller numbers, since, as the educational standards for all enlistees rose, the integration of relatively few but better qualified Negroes would "undoubtedly make for greater racial harmony and improved naval performance."

Despite the breadth and acuity of his observations, Granger suggested remarkably few changes. Impressed by the progress made in the treatment of Negroes during the war, he apparently expected it to continue uninterrupted. Although his investigations uncovered basic problems that would continue to trouble the Navy, he did not recognize them as such. For his part, Forrestal sent Granger's voluminous reports with their few recommendations to his military staff and thanked the Urban League official for his contribution.[5-63]

Although different in approach and point of view, Granger's observations neatly complemented the findings and recommendations of the Committee on Negro Personnel. Both reinforced the secretary's postwar policy aims and both supported his gradualist approach to racial reform. Granger cited segregation, in particular the concentration of masses of black sailors, as the principal cause of racial unrest and poor morale among Negroes. The committee urged the gradual integration of the general service in the name of military efficiency. Granger and the committee also shared certain blind spots. Both were encouraged by the progress toward full-scale integration that occurred during the war, but this improvement was nominal at best, a token bow to changing conditions. Their assumption that integration would spread to all branches of the Navy neglected the widespread and deeply entrenched opposition to integration that would yield only to a strategy imposed by the Navy's civilian and military leaders. Finally, the hope that integration would spread ignored the fact that after the war few Negroes except stewards would be able to meet the enlistment requirements for the Regular Navy. In short, the postwar Navy, so far as Negroes were concerned, was likely to resemble the prewar Navy.

The search for a postwar racial policy led the Army and Navy down some of the same paths. The Army manpower planners decided that the best way to avoid the inefficient black divisions was to organize Negroes into smaller, and therefore, in their view, more efficient

68

segregated units in all the arms and services. At the same time Secretary Forrestal's advisers decided that the best way to avoid the concentration of Negroes who could not be readily assimilated in the general service was to integrate the small remnant of black specialists and leave the majority of black sailors in the separate Steward's Branch. In both instances the experiences of World War II had successfully demonstrated to the traditionalists that large-scale segregated units were unacceptable, but neither service was yet ready to accept large-scale integration as an alternative.

CHAPTER 6

New Directions

All the services developed new racial policies in the immediate postwar period. Because these policies were responses to racial stresses peculiar to each service and were influenced by the varied experiences of each, they were, predictably, disparate in both substance and approach; because they were also reactions to a common set of pressures on the services they proved to be, perhaps not so predictably, quite similar in practical consequences. One pressure felt by all the services was the recently acquired knowledge that the nation's military manpower was not only variable but also limited in quantity. Military efficiency demanded, therefore, that the services not only make the most effective use of available manpower, but also improve its quality. Since Negroes, who made up approximately 10 percent of the population, formed a substantial part of the nation's manpower, they could no longer be considered primarily a source of unskilled labor. They too must be employed appropriately, and to this end a higher proportion of Negroes in the services must be qualified for specialized jobs.

Continuing demands by civil rights groups added to the pressure on the services to employ Negroes according to their abilities. Arguing that Negroes had the right to enjoy the privileges and share the responsibilities of citizenship, civil rights spokesmen appeared determined to test the constitutionality of the services' wartime policies in the courts. Their demands placed the Truman administration on the defensive and served warning on the armed forces that never again could they look to the exclusion of black Americans as a long-term solution to their racial problems.

In addition to such pressures, the services had to reckon with a more immediate problem. Postwar black reenlistment, particularly among service men stationed overseas, was climbing far beyond expectation. As the armed forces demobilized in late 1945 and early 1946, the percentage of Negroes in the Army rose above its wartime high of 9.68 percent of the enlisted strength and was expected to reach 15 percent and more by 1947. Aside from the Marine Corps, which experienced a rapid drop in black enlistment, the Navy also expected a rise in the percentage of Negroes, at least in the near future. The increase occurred in part because Negroes, who had less combat time than whites and therefore fewer eligibility points for discharge, were being separated from service later and more slowly. The rise reflected as well the Negro's expectation that the national labor market would deteriorate in the wake of the war. Although greater opportunities for employment had developed for black Americans, civilians already filled the posts and many young Negroes preferred the job security of a military career. But there was another, more poignant reason why many Negroes elected to remain in uniform: they were afraid to reenter what seemed a hostile society and preferred life in the armed forces, imperfect as that might be. The effect of this increase on the services, particularly the largest service, the Army, was sharp and direct. Since many Negroes were poorly educated, they were slow to learn the use of sophisticated military equipment, and since the best educated and qualified men, black and white, tended to leave, the services faced the prospect of having a large proportion of their enlisted strength black and unskilled.

The Gillem Board Report

Clearly, a new policy was necessary, and soon after the Japanese surrender Assistant Secretary McCloy sent to the recently appointed Secretary of War the accumulated pile of papers on the subject of how best to employ Negroes in the postwar Army. Along with the answers to the questionnaires sent to major commanders and a collection of interoffice memos went McCloy's reminder that the matter ought to be dealt with soon. McCloy wanted to form a committee of senior officers to secure "an objective professional view" to be used as a base for attacking the whole race problem. But while he considered it important to put this professional view on record, he still expected it to be subject to civilian review.[6-1]

Robert P. Patterson became Secretary of War on 27 September 1945, after serving with Henry Stimson for five years, first as assistant and later as under secretary. Intimately concerned with racial matters in the early years of the war, Patterson later became involved in war procurement, a specialty far removed from the complex and controversial racial situation that faced the Army. Now as secretary he once again assumed an active role in the Army's black manpower problems and quickly responded to McCloy's request for a policy review.[6-2] In accordance with Patterson's oral instructions, General Marshall appointed a board, under the chairmanship of Lt. Gen. Alvan C. Gillem, Jr., which met on 1 October 1945. Three days later a formal directive signed by the Deputy Chief of Staff and approved by the Secretary of War ordered the board to "prepare a policy for the use of the authorized Negro manpower potential during the postwar period including the complete development of the means required to derive the maximum efficiency from the full authorized manpower of the nation in the event of a national emergency."[6-3] On this group, to be known as the Gillem Board, would fall the responsibility for formulating a policy, preparing a directive, and planning the use of Negroes in the postwar Army.

GENERAL GILLEM

None of the board members was particularly prepared for the new assignment. General Gillem, a Tennessean, had come up through the ranks to command the XIII Corps in Europe during World War II. Although he had written one of the 1925 War College studies on the use of black troops and had many black units in his corps, Gillem probably owed his appointment to the fact that he was a three-star general, available at the moment, and had recently been selected by the Chief of Staff to direct a Special Planning Division study on the use of black troops that had been superseded by the new board.[6-4] Burdened with the voluminous papers collected by McCloy, Gillem headed a board composed of Maj. Gen. Lewis A. Pick, a Virginian who had built the Ledo Road in the China-Burma-India theater; Brig. Gen. Winslow C. Morse of Michigan, who had served in a variety of assignments in the Army Air Forces culminating in wartime duties in China; and Brig. Gen. Aln D. Warnock, the recorder without vote, a Texan who began his career in the Arizona National Guard and had served in Iceland during World War II.[6-5] These men had broad and diverse experience and gave the board a certain geographical balance. Curiously enough, none was a graduate of West Point.[6-6]

Although new to the subject, the board members worked quickly. Less than a month after their first session, Gillem informed the Chief of Staff that they had already reached certain conclusions. They recognized the need to build on the close relationships developed between the races during the war by introducing progressive measures that could be put into operation promptly and would provide for the assignment of black troops on the basis of individual merit and ability alone. After studying and comparing the racial practices of the other services, the board decided that the Navy's partial integration had stimulated competition which improved black performance without causing racial friction. By contrast, strict segregation in the Marine Corps required longer training periods and closer supervision for black marines. In his memorandum Gillem refrained from drawing the logical conclusion and simply went on to note that the Army had, for example, integrated its black and white patients in hospitals because of the greater expense, inefficiency, and general impracticality of duplicating complex medical equipment and installations.[6-7] By inference the same disadvantages applied to maintaining separate training facilities, operational units, and the rest of the apparatus of the shrinking Army establishment. At one point in his progress report, Gillem seemed close to recommending integration, at least to the extent already achieved in the Navy. But stated explicitly such a recommendation would have been a radical step, out of keeping with the climate of opinion in the country and in the Army itself.

On 17 November 1945 the Gillem Board finished the study and sent its report to the Chief of Staff.[6-8] In six weeks the board had questioned more than sixty witnesses, consulted a mass of documentary material, and drawn up conclusions and recommendations on the use of black troops. The board declared that its recommendations were based on two complementary principles: black Americans had a constitutional right to fight, and the Army had an obligation to make the most effective use of every soldier. But the board also took into account reports of the Army's wartime experience with black units. It referred constantly to this experience, citing the satisfactory performance of the black service units and some of the smaller black combat units, in particular the artillery and tank battalions. It also described the black infantry platoons integrated into white companies in Europe as "eminently successful." At the same time large black combat units had not been satisfactory, most often because their junior officers and noncommissioned officers lacked the ability to lead. The difficulties the Army encountered in properly placing its black troops during the war, the board decided, stemmed to some extent from inadequate staff work and improper planning. Poor staff work allowed a disproportionate number of Negroes with low test scores to be allocated to combat elements. Lack of early planning, constant reorganization and regrouping of black units, and continuous shifting of individuals from one type of training to another had confused and bewildered black troops, who sometimes doubted that the Army intended to commit them to combat at all.

70

It was necessary, the board declared, to avoid repetition of this experience. Advance planning was needed to develop a broader base of trained men among black troops to provide cadres and leaders to meet national emergencies more efficiently. The Army had to realize and take advantage of the advances made by Negroes in education, industry, and government service. The wide range of skills attained by Negroes had enhanced their military value and made possible a broader selectivity with consequent benefit to military efficiency. Thus, the Army had to adopt a racial policy that provided for the progressive and flexible use of black manpower "within proportions corresponding to those in the civilian population." This policy, it added, must "be implemented *promptly* ... *must* be objective by nature ... must eliminate, at the earliest practicable moment, any special consideration based on race ... and should point towards the immediate objective of an evaluation of the Negro on the basis of individual merit and ability."

The board made eighteen specific recommendations, of which the following were the most important.

"That combat and service units be organized and activated from the Negro manpower available in the postwar Army to meet the requirements of training and expansion and in addition qualified individuals be utilized in appropriate special and overhead units." The use of qualified Negroes in overhead units was the first break with the traditional policy of segregation, for though black enlisted men would continue to eat and sleep in segregated messes and barracks, they would work alongside white soldiers and perform the same kind of duty in the same unit.

"The proportion of Negro to white manpower as exists in the civil population be the accepted ratio for creating a troop basis in the postwar Army."[6-9]

"That Negro units organized or activated for the postwar Army conform in general to other units of the postwar Army but the maximum strength of type [sic] units should not exceed that of an infantry regiment or comparable organization." Here the board wanted the Army to avoid the division-size units of World War II but retain separate black units which would be diversified enough to broaden the professional base of Negroes in the Regular Army by offering them a larger selection of military occupations.

"That in the event of universal training in peacetime additional officer supervision is supplied to units which have a greater than normal percentage of personnel falling into A.G.C.T. classifications IV and V." Such a policy had existed in World War II, but was never carried out.

"That a staff group of selected officers whose background has included commanding troops be formed within the G-1 Division of the staffs of the War Department and each major command of the Army to assist in the planning, promulgation, implementation and revision of policies affecting all racial minorities." This was the administrative machinery the board wanted to facilitate the prompt and efficient execution of the Army's postwar racial policies.

"That reenlistment be denied to regular Army soldiers who meet only the minimum standards." This provision was in line with the concept that the peacetime Army was a cadre to be expanded in time of emergency. As long as the Army accepted all reenlistments regardless of aptitude and halted black enlistments when black strength exceeded 10 percent, it would deny enlistment to many qualified Negroes. It would also burden the Army with low-scoring men who would never rise above the rank of private and whose usefulness in a peacetimecadre, which had the function of training for wartime expansion, would be extremely limited.

"That surveys of manpower requirements conducted by the War Department include recommendations covering the positions in each installation of the Army which could be filled by Negro military personnel." This suggestion complemented the proposal to use Negroes in overhead positions on an individual basis. By opening more positions to Negroes, the Army would foster leadership, maintain morale, and encourage a competitive spirit among the better qualified. By forcing competition with whites "on an individual basis of merit," the Army would become more attractive as a career to superior Negroes, who would provide many needed specialists as a "nucleus for rapid expansion of Army units in time of emergency."

"That groupings of Negro units with white units in composite organizations be continued in the postwar Army as a policy." Since World War II demonstrated that black units performed satisfactorily when grouped or operated with white combat units, the inclusion of a black service company in a white regiment or a heavy weapons company in an infantry battalion could perhaps be accomplished "without encountering insurmountable difficulties." Such groupings would build up a professional relationship between blacks and whites, but, the board warned, experimentation must not risk "the disruption of civilian racial relationships."

"That there be accepted into the Regular Army an unspecified number of qualified Negro officers ... that all officers, regardless of race, be required to meet the same standard for appointment ... be accorded equal rights and opportunities for advancement and professional improvement; and be required to meet the same standard for appointment, promotion and

71

retention in all components of the Army." The board set no limit on the number of black officers in the Army, nor did it suggest that black officers be restricted to service in black units.

Its report rendered, the board remained in existence ready to make revisions "as may be warranted" by the comments of the many individuals and agencies that were to review the policy in conformance with a directive of the Secretary of War.[6-10]

No two individuals were more intimately concerned with the course of events that led to the Gillem Board Report than John J. McCloy and Truman Gibson, and although both were about to leave government service, each gave the new Secretary of War his opinion of the report.[6-11] McCloy called the report a "fine achievement" and a "great advance over previous studies." It was most important, he said, that the board had stated the problem in terms of manpower efficiency. At the same time both men recognized ambiguities in the board's recommendations, and their criticisms were strong, precise, and, considering the conflicts that developed in the Army over these issues, remarkably acute. Both agreed the report needed a clear statement on the basic issue of segregation, and they wanted the board to eliminate the quota. Gibson pointed out that the board proposed as a long-range objective the utilization of all persons on the basis of individual ability alone. "This means, of course," he announced with more confidence than was warranted, "a completely integrated Army." In the interest of eventually achieving an integrated Army he was willing to settle for less than immediate and total integration, but nevertheless he attacked the board for what he called the vagueness of its recommendations. Progressive and planned integration, he told Secretary Patterson, demanded a clear and explicit policy stating that segregation was outmoded and integration inevitable, and the Army should move firmly and steadily from one to the other.

On some fundamental issues McCloy thought the board did "not speak with the complete clarity necessary," but he considered the ambiguity unintentional. Experience showed, he reminded the secretary, "that we cannot get enforcement of policies that permit of any possibility of misconstruction." Directness, he said, was required in place of equivocation based on delicacy. If the Gillem Board intended black officers to command white officers and men, it should have said so flatly. If it meant the Army should try unsegregated and mixed units, it should have said so. Its report, McCloy concluded, should have put these matters beyond doubt. He was equally forthright in his rejection of the quota, which he found impractical because it deprived the Army of many qualified Negroes who would be unable to enlist when the quota was full. Even if the quota was meant as a floor rather than a ceiling, McCloy thought it objectionable. "I do not see any place," he wrote, "for a quota in a policy that looks to utilize Negroes on the basis of ability."

If the Gillem Board revealed the Army's willingness to compromise in treating a pressing efficiency problem, detailed comments by interested staff agencies revealed how military traditionalists hoped to avoid a pressing social problem. For just as McCloy and Gibson criticized the board for failing to spell out concrete procedures toward integration, other staff experts generally approved the board's report precisely because its ambiguities committed them to very little. Their specific criticisms, some betraying the biases of the times, formed the basis of the standard traditionalist defense of the racial *status quo* for the next five years.

Comments from the staff's personnel organization set the tone of this criticism.[6-12] The Assistant Chief of Staff for Personnel, G-1, Maj. Gen. Willard S. Paul, approved the board's recommendations, calling them a "logical solution to the problem of effective utilization of Negro manpower." Although he thought the report "sufficiently detailed to permit intelligent, effective planning," he passed along without comment the criticisms of his subordinates. He was opposed to the formation of a special staff group. "We must soon reach the point," he wrote, "where our general staff must be able to cope with such problems without the formation of ad hoc committees or groups."[6-13]

The Assistant Chief of Staff for Organization and Training, G-3, Maj. Gen. Idwal H. Edwards, was chiefly concerned with the timing of the new policy. In trying to employ black manpower on a broader professional scale, he warned, the Army must recognize the "ineptitude and limited capacity of the Negro soldier." He wanted various phases of the new policy timed "with due consideration for all factors such as public opinion, military requirements and the military situation." If the priority given public opinion in the sequence of these factors reflected Edwards's view of their importance, the list is somewhat curious. Edwards concurred in the recommendations, although he wanted the special staff group established in the personnel office rather than in his organization, and he rejected any arbitrary percentage of black officers. More black officers could be obtained through expansion of the Reserve Officers' Training Corps, he suggested, but he rejected the board's call for special classification of all enlistees in reception and training centers, on grounds that the centers were not adequate for the task.[6-14]

The chief of the General Staff's Operations Division, Lt. Gen. John E. Hull, dismissed the Gillem report with several blunt statements: black enlisted men should be assigned to black units capable of operational use within white units at the rate of one black battalion per division; a single standard of professional proficiency should be followed for white and black officers; and "no Negro officer be given command of white troops."[6-15]

The deputy commander of the Army Air Forces, Lt. Gen. Ira C. Eaker, agreed with the board that the Army should not be "a testing ground for problems in race relationships." Neither did he think the Air Forces should organize units for the sole purpose of "advancing the prestige of one race, especially when it is necessary to utilize personnel that do not have the proper qualifications in order to keep these units up to strength." Black combat units should be limited by the 10 percent quota and by the small number of Negroes qualified for tactical training. Most Negroes should be placed in Air Forces service units, where "their wartime record was the best," even though such placement would leave the Air Forces open to charges of discrimination. The idea of experimental groupings of black and white units in composite organizations might prove "impractical," Eaker wrote to the Chief of Staff, because an Air Forces group operated as an integral unit rather than as three or four separate squadrons; units often exchanged men and equipment, and common messes were used. Composite organizations were practical "only when it is not necessary for the units to intermingle continually in order to carry on efficiently." Why intermingling could not be synonymous with efficiency, he failed to explain. The inference was clear that segregation was not only normal but best.

Yet he advocated continuing integrated flying schools and agreed that Negroes should be stationed where community attitudes were favorable. He cited the difficulties involved in stationing. For more than two years the Army Air Forces had tried to find a suitable base for its only black tactical group. Even in northern cities with large black communities—Syracuse, New York, Columbus, Ohio, and Windsor Locks, Connecticut, among others—officials had vehemently protested against having the black group.

The War Department, Eaker concluded, "should never be ahead of popular opinion on this subject; otherwise it will put itself in a position of stimulating racial disorders rather than overcoming them." Along these lines, and harking back to the Freeman Field incident, he protested against regulations reaffirmed by the Gillem Board for the joint use of clubs, theaters, post exchanges, and the like at stations in localities where such use was contrary to civilian practices.[6-16]

The Army Ground Forces headquarters concurred generally with the Gillem Board's conclusions and recommendations but suggested the Army not act alone. The headquarters recommended a policy be formulated for the entire military establishment; only then should individual elements of the armed forces come forward with their own policies. The idea that Negroes should serve in numbers proportionate to their percentage of the population and bear their share of battle losses "may be desirable but is impracticable and should be abandoned in the interest of a logical solution."[6-17] Since the abilities of Negroes were limited, the report concluded, their duties should be restricted.

The commanding general of the Army Service Forces claimed the Gillem Board Report was advocating substantially the same policy his organization had followed during the war. The Army Service Forces had successfully used an even larger percentage of Negroes than the Gillem Board contemplated. Concurring generally with the board's recommendations, he cautioned that the War Department should not dictate the use of Negroes in the field; to do so would be a serious infringement of command prerogatives that left each commander free to select and assign his men. As for the experimental groupings of black and white units, the general believed that such mixtures were appropriate for combat units but not for the separate small units common to the Army Service Forces. Separate, homogeneous companies or battalions formed during the war worked well, and experience proved mixed units impractical below group and regimental echelons.

The Service Forces commander called integration infeasible "for the present and foreseeable future." It was unlawful in many areas, he pointed out, and not common practice elsewhere, and requiring soldiers to follow a different social pattern would damage morale and defeat the Army's effort to increase the opportunities and effectiveness of black soldiers. He did not try to justify his contention, but his meaning was clear. It would be a mistake for the Army to attempt to lead the nation in such reforms, especially while reorganization, unification, and universal military training were being considered.[6-18]

Reconvened in January 1946 to consider the comments on its original report, the Gillem Board deliberated for two more weeks, heard additional witnesses, and stood firm in its conclusions and recommendations.[6-19] The policy it proposed, the board emphasized, had one purpose, the attainment of maximum manpower efficiency in time of national emergency. To achieve this end the armed forces must make full use of Negroes now in service, but future use of black manpower had to be based on the experience gained in two major wars. The board considered the policy it was proposing flexible, offering opportunity for advancement to qualified individuals and at the same time making possible for the Army an economic use of national manpower as a whole.

To its original report the board added a statement at once the hope and despair of its critics and supporters.

The Initial Objectives: The utilization of the proportionate ratio of the manpower made available to the military establishment during the postwar period. The manpower potential to be organized and trained as indicated by pertinent recommendations.

The Ultimate Objective: The effective use of *all* manpower made available to the military establishment in the event of a major mobilization at some unknown date against an undetermined aggressor. The manpower to be utilized, in the event of another major war, in the Army without regard to antecedents or race.

When, and if such a contingency arises, the manpower of the nation should be utilized in the best interests of the national security.

The Board cannot, and does not, attempt to visualize at this time, intermediate objectives. Between the first and ultimate objective, timely phasing may be interjected and adjustments made in accordance with conditions which may obtain at this undetermined date.

The board based its ultimate objective on the fact that the black community had made important advances in education and job skills in the past generation, and it expected economic and educational conditions for Negroes to continue to improve. Since such improvement would make it possible to employ black manpower in a variety of ways, the board's recommendations could be only a guide for the future, a policy that must remain flexible.

SECRETARY PATTERSON

To the specific objections raised by the reviewing agencies, the board replied that although black units eventually should be commanded by black officers "no need exists for the assignment of Negro commanders to units composed of white troops." It also agreed with those who felt it would be beneficial to correlate Army racial policies with those of the Navy. On other issues the board stood firm. It rejected the proposal that individual commanders be permitted to choose positions where Negroes could be employed in overhead installations on the grounds that this delegation of responsibility "hazards lack of uniformity and makes results doubtful." It refused to drop the quota, arguing it was needed for planning purposes. At the same time the board did admit that the 10 percent ratio, suitable for the moment, might be changed in the future in the interest of efficiency—though changed in which way it did not say.

The board rejected the proposition that the Army Service Forces and the Army Air Forces were unable to use small black units in white organizations and took a strong stand for elimination of the professional private, the career enlistee lacking the background or ability to advance beyond the lowest rank. Finally, the board rejected demands that the color line be reestablished in officers' messes and enlisted recreational facilities. "This large segment of the population contributed materially to the success attained by our military forces.... The Negro enjoyed the privileges of citizenship and, in turn, willingly paid the premium by accepting service. In many instances, this payment was settled through the medium of the supreme sacrifice."

The board's recommendations were well received, at least in the highest echelons of the War Department. General Dwight D. Eisenhower, now Chief of Staff,[6-20] quickly sent the proposed policy to the Secretary of War with a recommendation for approval "subject to such adjustment as experience shows is necessary."[6-21] On 28 February 1946 Secretary Patterson approved the new policy in a succinct restatement of the board's recommendations. The policy and the full Gillem Board Report were published as War Department Circular 124 on 27 April 1946. At the secretary's direction the circular was dispatched to the field "without delay."[6-22] On 4 March the report was released to the press.[6-23] The most exhaustive and intensive inquiry ever made by the Army into the employment of black manpower had survived the review and analysis process with its conclusions and recommendations intact.

Attitudes toward the new policy varied with interpretations of the board's statement of objectives. Secretary Patterson saw in the report "a significant development in the status of the Negro soldiers in the Army." The immediate effect of using Negroes in composite units and overhead assignments, he predicted, would be to change War Department policy on segregation.[6-24] But the success of the policy could not be guaranteed by a secretary of war, and some of his advisers were more guarded in their estimates. To Truman Gibson, once again in government service, but briefly this time, the report seemed a good beginning because it offered a new approach, one that had originated within the Army itself. Yet Gibson was wary of its chances for success: The board's recommendations, he told the Assistant Secretary of War, would make for a better Army "only if they are effectively carried out."[6-25] The newly appointed

74

assistant secretary, Howard C. Petersen, was equally cautious. Explaining the meaning of the report to the Negro Newspaper Publishers Association, he warned that "a strong policy weakly enforced will be of little value to the Army."[6-26]

Marcus H. Ray, Gibson's successor as the secretary's adviser on racial affairs,[6-27] stressed the board's ultimate objective to employ manpower without regard to race and called its recommendations "a step in the direction of efficient manpower utilization." It was a necessary step, he added, because "any racial group which lives under the stigma of implied inferiority inherent in a system of enforced separation cannot give over-all top performance in peace or in war."[6-28]

On the whole, the black community was considerably less sanguine about the new policy. The *Norfolk Journal and Guide* called the report a step in the right direction, but reserved judgment until the Army carried out the recommendations.[6-29] To a distinguished black historian who was writing an account of the Negro in World War II, the Gillem Board Report reflected the Army's ambiguity on racial matters. "It is possible," L. D. Reddick of the New York Public Library wrote, "to interpret the published recommendations as pointing in opposite directions."[6-30] One NAACP official charged that it "tries to dilute Jim-Crow by presenting it on a smaller scale." After citing the tremendous advances made by Negroes and all the reasons for ending segregation, he accused the Gillem Board of refusing to take the last step.[6-31] Most black papers adopted the same attitude, characterizing the new policy as "the same old Army." The Pittsburgh *Courier*, for one, observed that the new policy meant that the Army command had undergone no real change of heart.[6-32]Other segments of the public were more forebearing. One veterans' organization commended the War Department for the work of the Gillem Board but called its analysis and recommendations incomplete. Citing evidence that Jim Crow, not the enemy, "defeated" black combat units, the chairman of the American Veterans Committee called for an immediate end to segregation.[6-33]

Clearly, opposition to segregation was not going to be overcome with palliatives and promises, yet Petersen could only affirm that the Gillem Board Report would mean significant change. He admitted segregation's tenacious hold on Army thinking and that black units would continue to exist for some time, but he promised movement toward desegregation. He also made the Army's usual distinction between segregation and discrimination. Though there were many instances of unfair treatment during the war, he noted, these were individual matters, inconsistent with Army policy, which "has consistently condemned discrimination." Discrimination, he concluded, must be blamed on "defects" of enforcement, which would always exist to some degree in any organization as large as the Army.[6-34]

Actually, Petersen's promised "movement" toward integration was likely to be a very slow process. So substantive a change in social practice, the Army had always argued, required the sustained support of the American public, and judging from War Department correspondence and press notices large segments of the public remained unaware of what the Army was trying to do about its "Negro problem." Most military journalists continued to ignore the issue; perhaps they considered the subject of the employment of black troops unimportant compared with the problems of demobilization, atomic weaponry, and service unification. For example, in listing the principal military issues before the United States in the postwar period, military analyst Hanson Baldwin did not mention the employment of Negroes in the service.[6-35]

Given the composition of the Gillem Board and the climate of opinion in the nation, the report was exemplary and fair, its conclusions progressive. If in the light of later developments the recommendations seem timid, even superficial, it should be remembered to its credit that the board at least made integration a long-range goal of the Army and made permanent the wartime guarantee of a substantial black representation.

Nevertheless the ambiguities in the Gillem Board's recommendations would be useful to those commanders at all levels of the Army who were devoted to the racial *status quo*. Gillem and his colleagues discussed black soldiers in terms of social problems rather than military efficiency. As a result, their recommendations treated the problem from the standpoint of how best Negroes could be employed within the traditional segregated framework even while they spoke of integration as an ultimate goal. They gave their blessing to the continued existence of segregated units and failed to inquire whether segregation might not be a factor in the inefficiency and ineffectiveness of black units and black soldiers. True, they sought to use qualified Negroes in specialist jobs as a solution to better employment of black manpower, but this effort could have little practical effect. Few were qualified—and determination of qualifications was often done by those with little sympathy for the Negro and even less for the educated Negro. Black serviceman holding critical specialties and those assigned to overhead installations would never amount to more than a handful of men whose integration during duty hours only would fall far short even of tokenism.

75

To point out as the board did that the policy it was recommending no longer required segregation was meaningless. Until the Army ordered integration, segregation, simply by virtue of inertia, would remain. As McCloy, along with Gibson and others, warned, without a strong, explicit statement of intent by the Army the changes in Army practice suggested by the Gillem Board would be insignificant. The very acceptance of the board's report by officials traditionally opposed to integration should have been fair warning that the report would be difficult to use as a base for a progressive racial policy; in fact it could be used to justify almost any course of action. From the start, the War Department encountered overwhelming difficulties in carrying out the board's recommendations, and five years later the ultimate objective was still out of reach.

Clearly, the majority of Army officers viewed segregated service as the acceptable norm. General Jacob L. Devers, then commanding general of Army Ground Forces, gave a clue to their view when he told his fellow officers in 1946 that "we are going to put colored battalions in white divisions. This is purely business—the social side will not be brought into it."[6-36] Here then was the dilemma: Was not the Army a social institution as well as a fighting organization? The solution to the Army's racial problems could not be achieved by ignoring the social implications. On both counts there was a reluctance among many professional soldiers to take in Negroes. They registered acute social discomfort at the large influx of black soldiers, and many who had devoted their lives to military service had very real misgivings over using Negroes in white combat units or forming new black combat units because they felt that black fighters in the air and on the ground had performed badly in the past. To entrust the fighting to Negroes who had failed to prove their competence in this highest mission of the Army seemed to them to threaten the institution itself.

Despite these shortcomings, the work of the Gillem Board was a progressive step in the history of Army race relations. It broke with the assumption implicit in earlier Army policy that the black soldier was inherently inferior by recommending that Negroes be assigned tasks as varied and skilled as those handled by white soldiers. It also made integration the Army's goal by declaring as official policy the ultimate employment of all manpower without regard to race.

Even the board's insistence on a racial quota, it could be argued, had its positive aspects, for in the end it was the presence of so many black soldiers in the Korean War that finally ended segregation. In the meantime, controversy over the quota, whether it represented a floor supporting minimum black participation or a ceiling limiting black enlistment, continued unabated, providing the civil rights groups with a focal point for their complaints. No matter how hard the Army tried to justify the quota, the quota increased the Army's vulnerability to charges of discrimination.

Integration of the General Service

The Navy's postwar revision of racial policy, like the Army's, was the inevitable result of its World War II experience. Inundated with unskilled and undereducated Negroes in the middle of the war, the Navy had assigned most of these men to segregated labor battalions and was surprised by the racial clashes that followed. As it began to understand the connection between large segregated units and racial tensions, the Navy also came to question the waste of the talented Negro in a system that denied him the job for which he was qualified. Perhaps more to the point, the Navy's size and mission made immediately necessary what the Army could postpone indefinitely. Unlike the Army, the Navy seriously modified its racial policy in the last year of the war, breaking up some of the large segregated units and integrating Negroes in the specialist and officer training schools, in the WAVES, and finally in the auxiliary fleet and the recruit training centers.

Yet partial integration was not enough. Lester Granger's surveys and the studies of the secretary's special committee had demonstrated that the Navy could resolve its racial problems only by providing equal treatment and opportunity. But the absurdity of trying to operate two equal navies, one black and one white, had been obvious during the war. Only total integration of the general service could serve justice and efficiency, a conclusion the civil rights advocates had long since reached. After years of leaving the Navy comparatively at peace, they now began to demand total integration.

ADMIRAL DENFELD

There was no assurance, however, that a move to integration was imminent when Granger returned from his final inspection trip for Secretary Forrestal in October 1945. Both Granger and the secretary's Committee on Negro Personnel had endorsed the department's current practices, and Granger had been generally optimistic over the reforms instituted toward the end of the war. Admirals Nimitz and King both endorsed Granger's recommendations, although neither saw the need for further change.[6-37] For his part Secretary Forrestal seemed determined to maintain the momentum of reform. "What steps do we take," he asked the Chief of Naval Personnel, "to correct the various practices ... which are not in accordance with Navy standards?"[6-38]

In response the Bureau of Naval Personnel circulated the Granger reports throughout the Navy and ordered steps to correct practices identified by Granger as "not in accordance with Navy standards."[6-39] But it was soon apparent that the bureau would be selective in adopting Granger's suggestions. In November, for example, the Chief of Naval Personnel, Admiral Louis E. Denfeld, arguing that officers "could handle black personnel without any special indoctrination," urged the secretary to reject Granger's recommendation that an office be established in headquarters to deal exclusively with racial problems. At the same time some of the bureau's recruiting officials were informing Negroes that their reenlistment in the Regular Navy was to be limited to the Steward's Branch.[6-40] With the help of Admiral Nimitz, Chief of Naval Operations, Forrestal quickly put an end to this recruiting practice, but he paid no further attention to racial matters except to demand in mid-December a progress report on racial reforms in the Pacific area.[6-41] Nor did he seem disturbed when the Pacific commander reported a large number of all-black units, some with segregated recreational facilities, operating in the Pacific area as part of the permanent postwar naval organization.[6-42]

In the end the decision to integrate the general service came not from the secretary but from that bastion of military tradition, the Bureau of Naval Personnel. Despite the general reluctance of the bureau to liberalize the Navy's racial policy, there had been all along some manpower experts who wanted to increase the number of specialties open to black sailors. Capt. Hunter Wood, Jr., for example, suggested in January 1946 that the bureau make plans for an expansion in assignments for Negroes. Wood's proposal fell on the sympathetic ears of Admiral Denfeld, who considered the Granger recommendations practical for the postwar Navy. Denfeld, of course, was well aware that these recommendations had been endorsed by Admirals King and Nimitz as well as Forrestal, and he himself had gone on record as believing that Negroes in the peacetime Navy should lose none of the opportunities opened to them during the war.[6-43]

Denfeld had had considerable experience with the Navy's evolving racial policy in his wartime assignment as assistant chief of personnel where his principal concern had been the efficient distribution and assignment of men. He particularly objected to the fact that current regulations complicated what should have been the routine transfer of sailors. Simple control procedures for the segregation of Negroes in general service had been effective when Negroes were restricted to particular shore stations and duties, he told Admiral Nimitz on 4 January 1946, but now that Negroes were frequently being transferred from shore to sea and from ship to ship the restriction of Negroes to auxiliary ships was becoming extremely difficult to manage and was also "noticeably contrary to the non-differentiation policy enunciated by the Secretary of the Navy." The only way to execute that policy effectively and maintain efficiency, he concluded, was to integrate the general service completely. Denfeld pointed out that the admission of Negroes to the auxiliary fleet had caused little friction in the Navy and passed almost unnoticed by the press. Secretary Forrestal had promised to extend the use of Negroes throughout the entire fleet if the preliminary program proved practical, and the time had come to fulfill that promise. He would start with "the removal of restrictions governing the type of duty to which general service Negroes can be assigned," but would limit the number of Negroes on any ship or at any shore station to a percentage no greater than that of general service Negroes throughout the Navy.[6-44]

With the enlistment of the Chief of Naval Personnel in the cause, the move to an integrated general service was assured. On 27 February 1946 the Navy published Circular Letter 48-46: "Effective immediately all restrictions governing types of assignments for which Negro naval personnel are eligible are hereby lifted. Henceforth, they shall be eligible for all types of assignments in all ratings in all activities and all ships of naval service." The letter went on to specify that "in housing, messing, and other facilities, there would be no special accommodations for Negroes." It also directed a redistribution of personnel by administrative commands so that by 1 October 1946 no ship or naval activity would be more than 10 percent Negro. The single exception would be the Naval Academy, where a large contingent of black stewards would be left intact to serve the midshipmen's meals.

The publication of Circular Letter 48-46 was an important step in the Navy's racial history. In less than one generation, in fewer years actually than the average sailor's service life, the Navy had made a complete about-face. In a sense the new policy was a service reform rather than a social revolution; after a 23-year hiatus integration had once again become the Navy's standard racial policy. Since headlines are more often reserved for revolutions than reformations, the new policy attracted little attention. The metropolitan press gave minimum coverage to the event and never bothered to follow later developments. For the most part the black press treated the Navy's announcement with skepticism. On behalf of Secretary Forrestal, Lester Granger invited twenty-three leading black editors and publishers to inspect ships in the fleet as well as shore activities to see for themselves the changes being made. Not one accepted. As one veteran put it, the editors shrank from praising the Navy's policy change for fear of being proved hasty. They preferred to remain on safe ground, "givin' 'em hell."[6-45]

The editors had every reason to be wary: integration was seriously circumscribed in the new directive, which actually offered few guarantees of immediate change. Applying only to enlisted men in the shore establishment and on ships, the directive ignored the Navy's all-white officer corps and its nonwhite servants branch of stewards. Aimed at abolishing discrimination in the service, it failed to guarantee either through enlistment, assignment guidelines, or specific racial quotas a fair proportion of black sailors in the postwar Navy. Finally, the order failed to create administrative machinery to carry out the new policy. In a very real sense the new policy mirrored tradition. It was naval tradition to have black sailors in the integrated ranks and a separate Messman's Branch. The return to this tradition embodied in the order complemented Forrestal's philosophy of change as an outgrowth of self-realized reform. At the same time naval tradition did not include the concept of high-ranking black officers, white servants, and Negroes in specialized assignments. Here Forrestal's hope of self-reform did not materialize, and equal treatment and opportunity for Negroes in the Navy remained an elusive goal.

But Forrestal and his military subordinates made enough of a start to draw the fire of white segregationists. The secretary answered charges and demands in a straightforward manner. When, for example, a congressman complained that "white boys are being forced to sleep with these negroes," Forrestal explained that men were quartered and messed aboard ship according to their place in the ship's organization without regard to race. The Navy made no attempt to prescribe the nature or extent of their social relationships, which were beyond the scope of its authority. Although Forrestal expressed himself as understanding the strong feelings of some Americans on this matter, he made it clear that the Navy had finally decided segregation was the surest way to emphasize and perpetuate the gap between the races and had therefore adopted a policy of integration.[6-46]

What Forrestal said was true, but the translation of the Navy's postwar racial policy into the widespread practice of equal treatment and opportunity for Negroes was still before him and his officers. To achieve it they would have to fight the racism common in many segments of American society as well as bureaucratic inertia. If put into practice the new policy might promote the efficient use of naval manpower and give the Navy at least a brief respite from the criticism of civil rights advocates, but because of Forrestal's failure to give clear-cut direction—a characteristic of his approach to racial reform—the Navy might well find itself proudly trumpeting a new policy while continuing its old racial practices.

The Marine Corps

As part of the naval establishment, the Marine Corps fell under the strictures of Secretary Forrestal's announced policy of racial nondiscrimination.[6-47] At the same time the Marine Corps was administratively independent of the Chief of Naval Operations and the Chief of Naval Personnel, and Circular Letter 48-46, which desegregated the Navy's general service, did not apply to the corps. In the development of manpower policy the corps was responsible to the Navy, in organization it closely resembled the Army, but in size and tradition it was unique. Each of these factors contributed to the development of the corps' racial policy and helped explain its postwar racial practices.

Because of the similarities in organization and mission between the Army and the Marine Corps, the commandant leaned toward the Army's solution for racial problems. The Army staff had contended that racially separate service was not discriminatory so long as it was equal, and through its Gillem Board policy it accepted the responsibility of guaranteeing that Negroes would be represented in equitable numbers and their treatment and opportunity would be similar to that given whites. Since the majority of marines served in the ground units of the Fleet Marine Force, organized like the Army in regiments, battalions, and squadrons with tables of organization and equipment, the formation of racially separate units presented no great problem.

Although the Marine Corps was similar to the Army in organization, it was very different in size and tradition. With a postwar force of little more than 100,000 men, the corps was hardly able to guarantee its segregated Negroes equal treatment and opportunity in terms of specialized training and variety of assignment. Again in contrast to the Army and Navy with their long tradition of Negroes in service, the Marine Corps, with a few unauthorized exceptions, had been an exclusively white organization since 1798. This habit of racial exclusion was strengthened by those feelings of intimacy and fraternity natural to any small bureaucracy. In effect the marines formed a small club in which practically everybody knew everybody else and was reluctant to admit strangers.[6-48] Racial exclusion often warred with the corps' clear duty to provide the fair and equal service for all Americans authorized by the Secretary of the Navy. At one point the commandant, General Alexander Vandegrift, even had to remind his local commanders that black marines would in fact be included in the postwar corps.[6-49]

One other factor influenced the policy deliberations of the Marine Corps: its experiences with black marines during World War II. Overshadowing the praise commanders gave the black depot companies were reports of the trials and frustrations suffered by those who trained the large black combat units. Many Negroes trained long and hard for antiaircraft duty, yet a senior group commander found them ill-suited to the work because of "emotional instability and lack of appreciation of materiel." One battery commander cited the "mechanical ineptitude" of his men; another fell back on "racial characteristics of the Negro as a whole" to explain his unit's difficulty.[6-50] Embodying rash generalization and outright prejudice, the reports of these commanders circulated in Marine Corps headquarters, also revealed that a large group of black marines experienced enough problems in combat training to cast serious doubt on the reliability of the defense battalions. This doubt alone could explain the corps' decision to relegate the units to the backwaters of the war zone. Seeing only the immediate shortcomings of the large black combat units, most commanders ignored the underlying reasons for the failure. The controversial commander of the 51st Defense Battalion, Col. Curtis W. LeGette,[6-51] however, gave his explanation to the commandant in some detail. He reported that more than half the men in the 51st as it prepared for overseas deployment—most of them recent draftees—were in the two lowest categories, IV and V, for either general classification or mechanical aptitude. That some 212 of the noncommissioned officers of the units were also in categories IV and V was the result of the unit's effort to carry out the commandant's order to replace white noncommissioned officers as quickly as possible. The need to develop black noncommissioned officers was underscored by LeGette, who testified to a growing resentment among his black personnel at the assignment of new white noncoms. Symptomatic of the unit's basic problems in 1944 was what LeGette called an evolving "occupational neurosis" among white officers forced to serve for lengthy periods with black marines.[6-52]

GENERAL THOMAS

The marines experienced far fewer racial problems than either the Army or Navy during the war, but the difficulties that occurred were nonetheless important in the development of postwar racial policy. The basic cause of race problems was the rigid concentration of often undertrained and undereducated men, who were subjected to racial slurs and insensitive treatment by some white officials and given little chance to serve in preferred military specialties or to advance in the labor or defense units or steward details to which they were invariably consigned. But this basic cause was ignored by Marine Corps planners when they discussed the postwar use of Negroes. They preferred to draw other lessons from the corps' wartime experience. The employment of black marines in small, self-contained units performing traditional laboring tasks was justified precisely because the average black draftee was less well-educated and experienced in the use of the modern equipment. Furthermore, the correctness of this procedure seemed to be demonstrated by the fact that the corps had been relatively free of the flare-ups that plagued the other services. Many officials would no doubt have preferred to eliminate race problems by eliminating Negroes from the corps altogether. Failing this, they were determined that regular black marines continue to serve in those assignments performed by black marines during the war: in service units, stewards billets, and a few antiaircraft artillery units, the postwar successors to defense battalions.[6-53]

The development of a postwar racial policy to carry out the Navy Department's nondiscrimination order in the Marine Corps fell to the Division of Plans and Policies and its director, Brig. Gen. Gerald C. Thomas. It was a complicated task, and General Thomas and his staff after some delay established a series of guidelines intended to steer a middle path between exclusion and integration that would be nondiscriminatory. In addition to serving in the Steward's Branch, which contained 10 percent of all blacks in the corps, Negroes would serve in segregated units in every branch of the corps, and their strength would total some 2,800 men. This quota would not be like that established in the Army, which was pegged to the number of black soldiers during the war and which ultimately was based on national population ratios. The Marine Corps ratio of blacks to whites would be closer to 1 in 30 and would merely represent the estimated number of billets that might be filled by Negroes in self-sustaining segregated units.

The directorate also established a table of distribution plan that for the first time provided for black regular marines in aviation units and several other Marine Corps activities. Aviation units alone accounted for 25 percent of the marines in the postwar corps, General Thomas contended, and must absorb their proportionate share of black strength. Further, the Navy's policy of nondiscrimination demanded that all types of assignments be opened to black marines. Segregation "best suits the needs of the Marine Corps," General Thomas concluded. Ignoring the possibility of black officers and women marines, he thought that the opening of all specialties and types of duty to the enlisted ranks would find the Marine Corps "paralleling Navy policy."[6-54] Clearly, the Division of Plans and Policies wanted the corps to adopt a formula roughly analogous to the Gillem Board's separate but equal system without that body's provisions for a fixed quota, black officers, or some integrated service.

But even this concession to nondiscrimination was never approved, for the Plans and Policies Division ran afoul of a basic fact of segregation: the postwar strength of many elements of the Marine Corps was too small to support separate racial units. The Director of Aviation, for example, argued that because of the size and nature of his operation, segregated service was impossible. A substantial number of his enlisted men also did double duty by serving in air stations where Negroes could not be segregated, he explained. Only completely separate aviation units, police and maintenance, and construction units would be available for Negroes, a state of affairs "which would be open to adverse criticism." He recommended instead that Negroes in aviation be used only as stewards.[6-55] He failed to explain how this solution would escape adverse criticism.

General Thomas rejected these proposals, repeating that Secretary Forrestal's nondiscrimination policy demanded that a separate but equal system be extended throughout the Marine Corps. He also borrowed one of the Gillem Board's arguments: Negroes must be trained in the postwar military establishment in every occupation to serve as a cadre for future general mobilizations.[6-56] Thomas did not mention the fact that although large branches such as Fleet Marine Force aviation could maintain separate but equal living facilities for its black marines, even they would have to provide partially integrated training and working conditions. And the smaller organizations in the corps would be forced to integrate fully if forced to accept black marines. In short, if the corps wanted segregation it must pay the price of continued discrimination against black marines in terms of numbers enlisted and occupations assigned.

The choice was left to Commandant Vandegrift. One solution to the "Negro question," General Thomas told him, was complete integration and the abolition of racial quotas, but Thomas did not press this solution. Instead, he reviewed for Vandegrift the racial policies of the other services, pointing out that these policies had more often been devised to "appease the Negro press and other 'interested' agencies than to satisfy their own needs." Until the matter was settled on a "higher level," Thomas concluded, the services were not required to go further than had been their custom, and until Vandegrift decided on segregation or integration, setting quotas for the different branches in the corps was inappropriate. Thomas himself recommended that segregated units be adopted and that a quota be devised only after each branch of the corps reported how many Negroes it could use in segregated units.[6-57] Vandegrift approved Thomas's recommendation for segregated black units, and the Marine Corps lost the chance, temporarily, to adopt a policy in line with either the Navy's limited and integrated system or the Army's separate but equal system.

General Thomas spent the summer collecting and reviewing the proposals of the corps' various components for the employment of black marines. On the basis of this review General Vandegrift approved a postwar policy for the employment of Negroes in the Marine Corps on 26 September 1946. The policy called for the enlistment of 2,264 Negroes, 264 as stewards, the rest to serve in separate units, chiefly in ground security forces of the Fleet Marine Force in Guam and Saipan and in Marine Corps activities of the naval shore establishment. No Negroes except stewards would serve in Marine aviation, Marine forces afloat, or, with the exception of service depots, in the Marine logistic establishment.[6-58]

The policy was in effect by January 1947. In the end the Marine Corps' white-only tradition had proved strong enough to resist the progressive impulses that were pushing the other services toward some relaxation of their segregation policies. Committed to limiting Negroes to a token representation and employing black marines in rigidly self-contained units, the Marine Corps could not establish a quota for Negroes based on national racial proportions and could offer no promise of equal treatment and opportunity in work assignments and promotions.

Thus all the services emerged from their deliberations with postwar policies that were markedly different in several respects but had in common a degree of segregation. The Army, declaring that military efficiency demanded ultimate integration, temporized, guaranteeing as a first step an intricate system of separate but equal treatment and opportunity for Negroes. The Marine Corps began with the idea that separate but equal service was not discriminatory, but when equal service proved unattainable, black marines were left with separatism alone. The Navy announced the most progressive policy of all, providing for integration of its general service. Yet it failed to break the heavy concentration of Negroes in the Steward's Branch, where no whites served. And unlike the segregated Army, the integrated Navy, its admission standards too high to encourage black enlistments, did not guarantee to take any black officers or specialists.

80

None of these policies provided for the equal treatment and opportunity guaranteed to every black serviceman under the Constitution, although the racial practices of all the services stood far in advance of those of most institutions in the society from which they were derived. The very weaknesses and inadequacies inherent in these policies would in themselves become a major cause of the reforms that were less than a decade away.

CHAPTER 7

A Problem of Quotas

The War Department encountered overwhelming problems when it tried to put the Gillem Board's recommendations into practice, and in the end only parts of the new policy for the use of black manpower were ever carried out. The policy foundered for a variety of reasons: some implicit in the nature of the policy itself, others the result of manpower exigencies, and still others because of prejudices lingering in the staff, the Army, and the nation at large.

Even before the Army postwar racial policy was published in War Department Circular 124 on 27 April 1946 it met formidable opposition in the staff. Although Secretary Patterson had approved the new course of action, the Assistant Chief of Staff for Personnel, General Paul, sent a copy of what he called the "proposed" policy to the Army Air Forces for further comment.[7-1] The response of the air commander, General Carl Spaatz, revealed that he too considered the policy still open for discussion. He suggested that the Army abandon the quota in favor of admitting men on the basis of intelligence and professional ability and forbid enlistment to anyone scoring below eighty in the entry tests. He wanted the composite organizations of black and white units recommended by the board held to a minimum, and none smaller than an air group—a regimental-size unit. Black combat units should have only black service units in support. In fact, Spaatz believed that most black units should be service units, and he wanted to see Negroes employed in overhead assignments only where and when their specialties were needed. He did not want jobs created especially for them.[7-2]

These were not the only portents of difficulty for the new policy. Before its publication General Paul had announced that he would not establish a staff group on racial affairs as called for by the Gillem Board. Citing manpower shortages and the small volume of work he envisaged, Paul planned instead to divide such duties between his Welfare Branch and Military Personnel Services Group.[7-3] The concept of a central authority for the direction of racial policy was further weakened in April when Paul invited the Assistant Chief of Staff for Organization and Training, General Edwards, one of whose primary tasks was to decide the size and number of military units, to share responsibility for carrying out the recommendations of the Gillem Board.[7-4]

Assistant Secretary Petersen was perturbed at the mounting evidence of opposition. Specifically, he believed Spaatz's comments indicated a lack of accord with Army policy, and he wanted the Army Air Forces told that "these basic matters are no longer open for discussion." He also wanted to establish a troop basis that would lead, without the imposition of arbitrary percentages, to the assignment of a "fair proportion" of black troops to all major commands and their use in all kinds of duties in all the arms and services. Petersen considered the composite unit one of the most important features of the new policy, and he wanted "at least a few" such units organized soon. He mentioned the assignment of a black parachute battalion to the 82d Airborne Division as a good place to begin.

Petersen had other concerns. He was distressed at the dearth of black specialists in overhead detachments, and he wondered why War Department Circular 105, which provided for the assignment of men to critically needed specialties, explicitly excluded Negroes.[7-5] He wanted the circular revised. Above all, Petersen feared the new policy might falter from a lack of aggressive leadership. He estimated that at first it would require at least the full attention of several officers under the leadership of an "aggressive officer who knows the Army and has its confidence and will take an active interest in vigorous enforcement of the program."[7-6] By implication Petersen was asking General Paul to take the lead.

Within a week of Petersen's comments on leadership, Paul had revised Circular 105, making its provisions applicable to all enlisted men, regardless of race or physical profile.[7-7] A few days later, he was assuring Petersen that General Spaatz's comments were "inconsistent with the approved recommendations" and were being disregarded.[7-8] Paul also repeated the principal points of the new policy for the major commanders, especially those dealing with composite units and overhead assignments for black specialists. He stressed that, whenever possible, Negroes should be assigned to places where local community attitudes were most favorable and no undue burden would be imposed on local civilian facilities.[7-9]

GENERAL PAUL

81

General Paul believed the principal impediment to practical application of the new policy was not so much the opposition of field commanders as the fact that many black units continued to perform poorly. He agreed with Marcus Ray, Civilian Aide to the Secretary of War, who had predicted as early as January 1946 that the success of the Gillem Board's recommendations would depend on how many Negroes of higher than average ability the armed forces could attract and retain. Ray reasoned that among the Negroes enlisting in the Regular Army—14 percent of the 1945 total—were large numbers of noncommissioned officers in the three highest grades whose abilities were limited. They were able to maintain their ratings, usually in service units, because their duties required knowledge of neither administration nor weapons. Truckmasters, foremen, riggers, and the like, they rushed to reenlist in order to freeze themselves in grade. Since many of these men were in the two lowest test categories, they could not supply the leaders needed for black units. Ray wanted to replace these men with better educated enlistees who could be used on the broadened professional base recommended by the Gillem Board. To that end he wanted the Army to test all enlisted men, discharge those below minimum standards, and launch a recruiting campaign to attract better qualified men, both black and white.[7-10] For his part, Paul also deplored the enlistment of men who were, in his words, "mentally incapable of development into the specialists, technicians, and instructors that we must have in the post-war Regular Army."[7-11]

Here, even before the new racial policy was published, the Army staff ran head on into the realities of postwar manpower needs. In a rapid demobilization, the Army was critically short of troops, particularly for overseas replacements, and it could maintain troop strength only by accepting all the men it could get. Until Paul had more definite information on the future operations of Selective Service and the rate of voluntary Regular Army enlistments, he would have to postpone action to curtail the admission of low-scoring men. So pressing were the Army's needs that Paul could do nothing to guarantee that black strength would not greatly exceed the 10 percent figure suggested by the Gillem Board. He anticipated that by 1 July 1946 the regular and active reserve components of the Army would together be approximately 15 percent black, a percentage impossible to avoid if the Army was to retain 1.8 million men. Since all planning had been based on a 10 percent black strength, plans would have to be revised to make use of the excess. In February 1946 the Chief of Staff approved General Paul's program: Negroes would continue to be drafted at the 10 percent ratio; at the same time their enlistment in the Regular Army would continue without restriction on numbers. Negroes would be limited to 15 percent of the overseas commands, and the continental commands would absorb all the rest.[7-12]

Paul's program for absorbing Negroes faced rough going, for the already complex manpower situation was further complicated by limitations on the use of Negroes in certain overseas theaters and the demands of the War Department's major commands. The Army was prohibited by an agreement with the State Department from sending Negroes to the Panama Canal Zone; it also respected an unwritten agreement that barred black servicemen from Iceland, the Azores, and China.[7-13] Since the War Department was unable to use Negroes everywhere, the areas where they could be used had to take more. The increase in black troops provoked considerable discussion in the large Pacific and European commands because it entailed separate housing, transportation, and care for dependents—all the usual expensive trappings of segregation. Theater commanders also faced additional problems in public relations and management. As one War Department staff officer claimed, black units required more than normal administration, stricter policing, and closer supervision. This in turn demanded additional noncommissioned officers, and "more Negro bodies must be maintained to produce equivalent results."[7-14]

Both commands protested the War Department decision. Representatives from the European theater arrived in Washington in mid-February 1946 to propose a black strength of 8.21 rather than the prescribed 15 percent. Seeking to determine where black soldiers could be used "with the least harmful effect on theater operations," they discovered in conferences with representatives of the War Department staff only the places Negroes were not to be used: in infantry units, in the constabulary, which acted as a border patrol and occupation police, in highly technical services, or as supervisors of white civilian laborers.[7-15]

The commander of Army Forces, Pacific, was even more insistent on a revision, asking how he could absorb so many Negroes when his command was already scheduled to receive 50,000 Philippine Scouts and 29,500 Negroes in the second half of 1947. These two groups, which the command considered far less adaptable than white troops to occupational duties, would together make up about 40 percent of the command's total strength. Although Philippine Scouts in the theater never exceeded 31,000, the command's protest achieved some success. The

War Department agreed to reduce black troops in the Pacific to 14 percent by 1 January 1947 and 13 percent by 1 July 1947.[7-16]

No sooner had the demands of the overseas theaters been dealt with than the enlarged black quotas came under attack from the commanders of major forces. Instead of planning to absorb more Negroes, the Army Air Forces wanted to divest itself of some black units on the premise that unskilled troops were a liability in a highly technical service. General Spaatz reported that some 60 percent of all his black troops stationed in the United States in January 1946 were performing the duties of unskilled laborers and that very few could be trained for skilled tasks. He predicted that the Army Air Forces would soon have an even higher percentage of low-scoring Negroes because 15 percent of all men enlisting in his Regular Army units—expected to reach a total of 45,000 men by 1 July 1946—were black. To forestall this increase in "undesirable and uneconomical" troops, he wanted to stop inducting Negroes into the Army Air Forces and suspend all black enlistments in the Regular Army.[7-17]

The Army Air Forces elaborated on these arguments in the following months, refining both its estimates and demands. Specifically, its manpower officials estimated that to reach the 15 percent black strength ordered by 1 July 1946 the Air Forces would have to take 50,500 Negroes into units that could efficiently use only 22,000 men. This embarrassment of more than 28,000 unusable men, the Army Air Forces claimed, would require eliminating tactical units and creating additional quartermaster car companies, mess platoons, and other service organizations.[7-18] The Air staff wanted to eliminate the unwanted 28,000 black airmen by raising to eighty the minimum classification test score for Regular Army enlistment in the Army Air Forces. In the end it retreated from this proposal, and on 25 February requested permission to use the 28,000 Negroes in service units, but over and above its 400,000-man troop basis. It promised to absorb all these men into the troop basis by 30 June 1946.[7-19]

The Army staff rejected this plan on the grounds that any excess allowed above the current Air Forces troop basis would have to be balanced by a corresponding and unacceptable deficit in the Army Ground Forces and Army Service Forces.[7-20] The Army Air Forces countered with a proposal to discharge all black enlistees in excess of Air Forces requirements in the European theater who would accept discharge. It had in mind a group of 8,795 Negroes recently enlisted for a three-year period, who, in accordance with a lure designed to stimulate such enlistments, had chosen assignment in the Air Forces and a station in Europe. With a surplus of black troops, the Air Forces found itself increasingly unable to fulfill the "overseas theater of choice" enlistment contract. Since some men would undoubtedly refuse to serve anywhere but Europe, the Air staff reasoned, why not offer a discharge to all men who preferred separation over service elsewhere?

Again the Army staff turned down a request for a reduction in black troops. This time the Air Forces bowed to the inevitable—15 percent of its enlisted strength black—but grudgingly, for a quota of 50,419 Negroes, General Spaatz charged, "seriously jeopardizes the ability of the AAF to perform its assigned mission."[7-21]

The Army Service Forces also objected. When queried,[7-22] the chiefs of its technical and administrative services all agreed they could use only small percentages of black troops, and only those men in the higher categories of the classification test. From the replies of the chiefs it was plain that none of the technical services planned to use Negroes in as much as 10 percent of spaces, and several wanted to exclude black units altogether. Furthermore, the test qualifications they wanted set for many jobs were consistently higher than those achieved by the men then performing the tasks. The staff of the Army Service Forces went so far as to advocate that no more than 3.29 percent of the overhead and miscellaneous positions in the Army Service Forces be entrusted to black troops.[7-23]

These answers failed to impress the War Department's Director of Personnel and Administration and the Director of Organization and Training.[7-24] Both agreed that the technical and administrative services had failed to appreciate the problems and responsibilities outlined in War Department Circular 124; the assumption that black troops would not be used in certain types of duty in the future because they had not been so used in the past was unwarranted, General Paul added. Limited or token employment of Negroes, he declared, was no longer acceptable.[7-25]

Yet somehow the reality of black enlistments and inductions in 1946 never quite matched the Army's dire predictions. According to plans for 1 April 1946, Negroes in the continental United States would comprise 15.2 percent of the Army Service Forces, 15.4 percent of the Army Ground Forces, and 17 percent of the Army Air Forces. Actually, Negroes in continental commands on 30 April 1946 made up 14.86 percent of the Army Service Forces, 5.62 percent of the Army Ground Forces, and 11.86 percent of the Army Air Forces. The 116,752 black soldiers amounted to 12.35 percent of all troops based in the United States; overseas, the 67,372 Negroes constituted 7.73 percent of American force. Altogether, the 184,124 Negroes in the Army amounted to 10.14 percent of the whole.[7-26]

The Quota in Practice

While the solution to the problem of too many black enlistees and too many low-scoring men was obvious, it was also replete with difficulty. The difficulty came from the complex way the Army obtained its manpower. It accepted volunteers for enlistment in the Regular Army and qualified veterans for the Organized Reserves; until November 1946 it also drafted men through the Selective Service and accepted volunteers for the draft.[7-27] At the same time, under certain conditions it accepted enlistment in the Regular Army of drafted men who had completed their tours. To curtail enlistment of Negroes and discharge low-scoring professionals, the Army would be obliged to manipulate the complex regulations governing the various forms of enlistment and sidestep the egalitarian provisions of the Selective Service System at a time when the service was trying to attract recruits and avoid charges of racial discrimination. Altogether it was quite a large order, and during the next two years the Army fought the battle of numbers on many fronts.

It first took on the draft. Although to stop inducting Negroes when the administration was trying to persuade Congress to extend the draft act was politically unwise, the Army saw no way to restrict the number of Negroes or eliminate substandard men so long as Selective Service insisted on 10 percent black calls and a minimum classification test score of seventy. In April 1946 the Army issued a call for 126,000 men, boldly specifying that no Negroes would be accepted. Out of the battle of memos with Selective Service that followed, a compromise emerged: a black call of 4 percent of the total in April, a return to the usual 10 percent call for Negroes in May, and another 4 percent call in June.[7-28] No draft calls were issued in July and August, but in September the Army staff tried again, canceling the call for Negroes and rejecting black volunteers for induction.[7-29] Again it encountered resistance from the Selective Service and the black community, and when the Secretary of War was sued for violation of the Selective Service Act the Army issued a 3 percent call for Negroes in October, the last call made under the 1940 draft law. In all, 16,888 Negroes were drafted into the Army in 1946, some 10.5 percent of the total.[7-30]

The Army had more success restricting black enlistments. In April 1946, at the same time it adopted the Gillem Board recommendations, the Army began to deny enlistment or reenlistment in the Regular Army to anyone scoring below seventy on the Army General Classification Test. The only exceptions were men who had been decorated for valor and men with previous service who had scored sixty-five and were recommended for reenlistment by their commanders.[7-31] The Army also stopped enlisting men with active venereal disease, not because the Medical Department was unable to cure them but because by and large their educational levels were low and, according to the classification tests, they had little aptitude for learning. The Army stopped recruiting men for special stations, hoping a denial of the European theater and other attractive assignments would lower the number of unwanted recruits.

Using the new enlistment standards as a base, the Army quickly revised its estimated black strength downward. On 16 April 1946 the Secretary of War rescinded the order requiring major commands to retain a black strength of 15 percent.[7-32] The acting G-3 had already informed the commanding general of the Army Air Forces of the predicted drop in the number of black troops—from 13.3 percent in June 1946 to 10 percent a year later—and agreed the Army Air Forces could reduce its planned intake accordingly.[7-33] Estimating the European theater's capacity to absorb black troops at 21,845 men, approximately 10 percent of the command total, the Army staff agreed to readjust its planned allotment of Negroes to that command downward by some 1,500 spaces.[7-34]

These changes proved ill-advised, for the effort to curb the number of Negroes in the Regular Army was largely unsuccessful. The staff had overlooked the ineffectiveness of the Army's testing measures and the zeal of its recruiters who, pressed to fill their quotas, accepted enlistees without concern for the new standards. By mid-June the effect was readily apparent. The European theater, for example, reported some 19,000 Negroes in excess of billets in black units and some 2,000 men above the theater's current allotment of black troops. Assignment of Negroes to Europe had been stopped, but the number of black regulars waiting for overseas assignment stood at 5,000, a figure expected to double by the end of the summer. Some of this excess could be absorbed in eight newly created black units, but that still left black units worldwide 18 to 40 percent overstrength.[7-35]

MARCUS RAY

Notice that Negroes totaled 16 percent of the Regular Army on 1 July 1946 with the personnel staff's projections running to a 24 percent level for the next year precipitated action in the War Department. On 15 July Marcus Ray and Dean Rusk, Special Assistant to the Assistant

Secretary of War, met with representatives of the Army staff to discuss black strength. Basing his decision on the consensus of that meeting, the Secretary of War on 17 July suspended enlistment of Negroes in the Regular Army. He excepted two categories of men from this ruling. Men who qualified and had actually served for six months in any of forty-eight unusual military occupational specialties in which there were chronic manpower shortages would be enlisted without promise of specific assignment to branch or station. At the same time, because of manpower shortages, the Army would continue to accept Negroes, already regulars, who wanted to reenlist.[7-36]

While the new enlistment policy would help restore the Gillem Board's quantitative equilibrium to the Army, the secretary's exception allowing reenlistment of regulars would only intensify the qualitative imbalance between black and white soldiers. The nation's biracial educational system had produced an average black soldier who scored well below the average white soldier on all the Army's educational and training tests. The segregation policy had only complicated the problem by denying the talented Negro the full range of Army occupations and hence an equal chance for advancement. With the suspension of first-time enlistments, the qualitative imbalance was sure to grow, for now the highly qualified civilian would be passed over while the less qualified soldier was permitted to reenlist.

This imbalance was of particular concern to Marcus Ray who was present when the suspension of black enlistments had been decided upon. Ray had suggested that instead of barring all new enlistees the Army should discharge all Class V soldiers, whites and blacks alike, for the convenience of the government and recruit in their place an equal number of Class I and II candidates. Manpower officials had objected, arguing there was no point in enlisting more Negroes in Class I and II until the 10 percent ratio was again reached. Such a reduction, with current attrition, would take two years. At the same time, the Army manpower shortages made it impractical to discharge 92,000 soldiers, half of whom were white, in Class V. The organization and training representatives, on the other hand, agreed with Ray that it was in the best interest of the Army to discharge these men, pointing out that a recent increase in pay for enlisted men together with the continuing need for recruits with greater aptitude for learning would make the policy palatable to the Congress and the public.[7-37]

The conferees deferred decision on the matter, but during the following months the War Department set out to achieve a qualitative balance between its black and white recruits. On 10 August 1946 the Chief of Staff directed commanders, under the authority of Army Regulation 615-369 which defined ineptness for military service, to eliminate after six months men "incapable of serving in the Army in a desirable manner after reasonable attempts have been made to utilize their capabilities." He went on to explain that this category included those not mentally qualified, generally defined as men scoring below seventy, and those repeatedly guilty of minor offenses.[7-38] The Army reissued the order in 1947, further defining the criteria for discharge to include those who needed continued and special instruction or supervision or who exhibited habitual drunkenness, ineptness, or inability to conform to group living. A further modification in 1949 would deny reenlistment to married men who had failed during their first enlistment to make corporal or single men who did not make private first class.[7-39]

The measures were aimed at eliminating the least qualified men of both races, and in October 1946 General Paul decided the Army could now begin taking black recruits with the qualifications and background that allowed them "to become useful members of the Army."[7-40] To that end The Adjutant General announced on 2 October that as a further exception to the prohibition against black enlistments in the Regular Army all former officers and noncommissioned officers who volunteered would be accepted without limitation.[7-41] On 31 October he announced the establishment of a selective procurement program. With the exception of men who had been in certain specialized occupations for six months, all Negroes enlisting in the Regular Army had to score one hundred on the Army General Classification Test; the minimum score for white enlistees remained seventy.[7-42] At the same time, The Adjutant General rescinded for Negroes the choice-of-assignment provision of Regular Army enlistment contracts.

These measures helped lower the percentage of Negroes in the Army and reduced to some extent the differential in test scores between white and black soldiers. The percentage of Negroes dropped by 30 June 1947 to 7.91 percent of the Army, 8.99 percent of its enlisted strength and 9.4 percent of its Regular Army strength. Black enlisted strength of all the overseas commands stood at 8.75 percent, down from the 10.77 percent of the previous December. Percentages in the individual theaters reflected this trend; the European theater, for example, dropped from 10.33 percent black to 9.96, the Mediterranean theater from 10.05 to 8.03, and Alaska from 26.6 to 14.54.[7-43]

Precise figures on the number of poorly qualified troops eliminated are unknown, but the European command expected to discharge some 12,000 low-scoring and unsuitable men, many of them black, in 1947.[7-44] Several commands reported that the new regulations materially improved the quality of black units by opening vacancies to better qualified men. General Paul could argue with considerable justification that in regulating the quality of its recruits the Army was following the spirit if not the letter of the Gillem Board Report. If the Army could set high enough standards it would get good men, and to this end the General Staff's Personnel and Administration Division asked for the support of commanders.[7-45]

Although these measures were helpful to the Army, they were frankly discriminatory, and they immediately raised a storm of protest. During the summer of 1946, for example, many black soldiers and airmen complained about the Army's rejection of black enlistments for the European theater. The NAACP, which received some of the soldiers' complaints, suggested that the War Department honor its pledges or immediately release all Negroes who were refused their choice of location.[7-46] The Army did just that, offering to discharge honorably those soldiers who, denied their theater of choice, rejected any substitute offered.[7-47]

Later in 1946 a young Negro sued the Secretary of War and a Pittsburgh recruiting officer for refusing to enlist him. To make standards for black applicants substantially higher than those for whites, he alleged, violated the Preamble and Fifth Amendment of the Constitution, while the inducements offered for enlistment, for example the GI Bill of Rights, constituted a valuable property right denied him because of race. The suit asked that all further enlistments in the Army be stopped until Negroes were accepted on equal terms with whites and all special enlistment requirements for Negroes were abolished.[7-48] Commenting on the case, the chief of the War Department's Public Relations Division, Maj. Gen. Floyd L. Parks, defended the Gillem Board's 10 percent quota, but agreed that "we are on weak ground [in] having a different standard for admission between white and colored.... I think the thing to do is to put a ceiling over the number you take in, and then take the best ones."[7-49]

The suit brought to a climax the feeling of indignation against Army policy that had been growing among some civil rights activists. One organization called on the Secretary of War to abandon the Gillem Board policy "and unequivocably and equitably integrate Negroes ... without any discrimination, segregation or quotas in any form, concept or manner."[7-50] Senator Robert M. LaFollette, Jr., of Wisconsin called the decision to suspend black enlistments race discrimination.[7-51] Walter P. Reuther, president of the United Automobile Workers and the codirector of his union's Fair Practices Department, branded the establishment of a quota "undemocratic and in violation of principles for which they [Negroes] fought in the war" and demanded that black enlistment be reinstated and the quota abolished.[7-52] Invoking American tradition and the United Nations Charter, John Haynes Holmes, chairman of the board of directors of the American Civil Liberties Union, called for the abolition of enlistment quotas. The national commander of the United Negro and Allied Veterans of America announced that his organization unreservedly condemned the quota because it deliberately deprived citizens of their constitutional right to serve their country.[7-53]

The replies of the Secretary of War to all these protests were very much alike. The Army's enlistment practices, he wrote, were based on a belief that black strength in the Army ought to bear a direct relationship to the percentage of Negroes in the population. As for the basic premise of what seemed to him a perfectly logical course of action, Patterson concluded that "acceptance of the Negro-white ratio existing in the civilian population as a basis for the Army's distribution of units and personnel is not considered discriminatory."[7-54] The secretary's responses were interesting, for they demonstrated a significant change in the Army's attitude toward the quota. There is evidence that the quota was devised by the Gillem Board as a temporary expedient to guarantee the substantial participation of Negroes. It was certainly so viewed by civil rights advocates. As late as December 1946 Assistant Secretary Petersen was still echoing this view when he explained that the quota was a temporary ceiling and the Army had no right to use it as a permanent bar to black enlistment.[7-55]

Nevertheless it is also clear that the traditionalists considered the quota a means of permanently limiting black soldiers to a percentage equivalent to Negroes in the population. Assistant Secretary McCloy belonged to neither group. More than a year before in reviewing the Gillem Board's work he had declared: "I do not see any place for a quota in a policy that looks to utilization of Negroes on the basis of ability."

After a year of dealing with black overstrengths and juggling enlistment standards, General Paul and his staff thought otherwise. They believed that a ceiling must be imposed on the Army's black strength if a rapid and uncontrolled increase in the number of black troops was to be avoided. And it had to be avoided, they believed, lest it create a disproportionately large pool of black career soldiers with low aptitudes that would weaken the Army. Using the quota to limit the

86

number of black troops, they maintained, was not necessarily discriminatory. It could be defended as a logical reading of the Gillem Board's declaration that "the proportion of Negro to white manpower as exists in the civil population" should be accepted in the peacetime Army to insure an orderly and uniform mobilization in a national emergency. With the Gillem policy to support it, the Army staff could impose a strict quota on the number of black soldiers and justify different enlistment standards for blacks and whites, a course that was in fact the only alternative to the curtailment of white enlistment under the manpower restrictions being imposed upon the postwar Army.[7-56]

Paul's reasoning was eventually endorsed by the new Chief of Staff, General Omar N. Bradley, Secretary Patterson, and his successor, Secretary of the Army Kenneth C. Royall.[7-57] Beginning in mid-1947 the enlistment of Negroes was carefully geared to their percentage of the total strength of the Army, not to a fixed quota or percentage of those enlisting. This limitation on black enlistment was made more permanent in 1949 when it was included in the Army's mobilization plan, the basic manpower planning document.[7-58]

The adjustment of enlistment quotas to increase or curtail black strength quickly became routine in the Army. When the number of Negroes dropped below 10 percent of the Army's total strength in June 1947, The Adjutant General set a quota for the enlistment of black soldiers.[7-59] When this quota was met in late August, the enlistment of Negroes with no special training was reduced to 500 men per month.[7-60] As part of a Personnel and Administration Division program to increase the number and kinds of black units, the quota was temporarily increased to 3,000 men per month for four months beginning in December 1947.[7-61] Finding itself once again exceeding the 10 percent black strength figure, the Army suspended the enlistment of all Negroes for nine months beginning in April 1949.[7-62]

In effect, the Gillem Board's critics who predicted that the quota would become permanent were correct, but the quota was only the most publicized manifestation of the general scheme of apportioning manpower by race throughout the Army. General Paul had offered one solution to the problem in July 1946. He recommended that each major command and service be allocated its proportionate share of black troops; that such troops "have the over-all average frequency of AGCT grades occurring among Negro military personnel"; and that major commands and services submit plans for establishing enough units and overhead positions to accommodate their total allocations.[7-63] But Paul did not anticipate the low-scoring soldier's penchant for reenlistment or the ability of some commanders, often on the basis of this fact, to justify the rejection of further black allotments. Thus, in pursuit of a racial policy designed to promote the efficient use of manpower, the G-1 and G-3 sections of the General Staff wrestled for almost five years with the problem of racial balances in the various commands, continental armies, and training programs.

Broader Opportunities

The equitable distribution of Negroes throughout each major command and service was complicated by certain provisions of Circular 124. Along with the quota, the policy prescribed grouping black units, not to exceed regimental size, with white units in composite organizations and integrating black specialists in overhead organizations. The composite organizations were primarily the concern of the G-3 (later the Organization and Training Division) section of the General Staff, and in June 1946 its director, Lt. Gen. Charles P. Hall, brought the matter to the attention of major commanders. Although the War Department did not want to establish an arbitrary number of black combat units, Hall explained, the new policy stressed the development of such units to provide a broader base for future expansion, and he wanted more black combat units organized as rapidly as trained troops became available. To that end he called for a survey of all black units to find out their current organization and assignment.[7-64]

Army Ground Forces reported that it had formed some composite units, but its largest black unit, the 25th Regimental Combat Team, had been attached to the V Corps at Fort Jackson, South Carolina, instead of being made an organic element in a division. Practically all service group headquarters reported separate black and white battalions under their control, but many of the organizations in the Army Service Forces—those under the Provost Marshal General and the Surgeon General, for example—still had no black units, let alone composite organizations. The Caribbean Defense Command, the Trinidad Base Command, and the Headquarters Base Command of the Antilles Department reported similar situations. The Mediterranean theater was using some Negroes with special skills in appropriate overhead organizations, but in the vast European Command Negroes were assigned to separate regiments and smaller units. There were two exceptions: one provisional black regiment was attached to the 1st Infantry Division, and a black field artillery battalion was attached to each of the three occupation divisions. The Alaskan Department and the Okinawa Base Command had black units, both separate and grouped with white units, but the Yokohama Base Command continued to use specially skilled Negroes in black units because of the great demand for qualified persons in those units.[7-65]

To claim, as Hall did to Assistant Secretary Petersen, that black units were being used like white units was misleading. Despite the examples cited in the survey, many black units still remained independent organizations, and with one major exception black combat units grouped with white units were attached rather than assigned as organizational elements of a parent unit. This was an important distinction.[7-66] The constant imposition of attached status on a unit that under normal circumstances would be assigned as an organic element of a division introduced a sense of impermanence and alienation just as it relieved the division commander of considerable administrative control and hence proprietary interest in the unit.

Attached status, so common for black units, thus weakened morale and hampered training as Petersen well understood. Noting the favorable attitude of the division commander, he had asked in April 1946 if it was possible to assign the black 555th Parachute Battalion to the celebrated 82d Airborne Division.[7-67] The answer was no. The commanding general of the Army Ground Forces, General Devers, justified attachment rather than assignment of the black battalion to the 82d on the grounds that the Army's race policy called for the progressive adoption of the composite unit and attachment was a part of this process. Assignment of such units was, on the other hand, part of a long-range plan to put the new policy into effect and should still be subject to considerable study. Further justifying the *status quo*, he pointed to the division's low strength, which he said resulted from a lack of volunteers. Offering his own variation of the "Catch-22" theme, he suggested that before any black battalion was assigned to a large combat unit, the effect of such an assignment on the larger unit's combat efficiency would first have to be studied. Finally, he questioned the desirability of having a black unit assume the history of a white unit; evidently he did not realize that the intention was to assign a black unit with its black history to the division.[7-68]

GENERAL EICHELBERGER, EIGHTH ARMY COMMANDER,
inspects 24th Infantry troops, Camp Majestic, Japan, June 1947.

In the face of such arguments Hall accepted what he called the "nonfeasibility" of replacing one of the 82d's organic battalions with the 555th, but he asked whether an additional parachute battalion could be authorized for the division so that the 555th could be assigned without eliminating a white battalion. He reiterated the arguments for such an assignment, adding that it would invigorate the 555th's training, attract more and better black recruits, and better implement the provisions of Circular 124.[7-69] General Devers remained unconvinced. He doubted that assigning the black battalion to the division would improve the battalion's training, and he was "unalterably opposed" to adding an extra battalion. He found the idea unsound from both a tactical and organizational point of view. It was, he said, undesirable to reorganize a division solely to assign a black unit.[7-70]

General Hall gave up the argument, and the 555th remained attached to the 82d. Attached status would remain the general pattern for black combat units for several years.[7-71] The assignment of the 24th Infantry to the 25th Infantry Division in Japan was the major exception to this rule, but the 24th was the only black regiment left intact, and it was administratively difficult to leave such a large organization in attached status for long. The other black regiment on active duty, the 25th Infantry, was split; its battalions, still carrying their unit designations, were attached to various divisions to replace inactive or unfilled organic elements. The 9th and 10th Cavalry, the other major black units, were inactivated along with the 2d Cavalry Division in 1944, but reactivated in 1950 as separate tank battalions.

That this distinction between attached and assigned status was considered important became clear in the fall of 1947. At that time the personnel organization suggested that the word "separate" be deleted from a sentence of Circular 124: "Employment will be in Negro regiments or groups, separate battalions or squadrons, and separate companies, troops, or batteries." General Paul reasoned that the word was redundant since a black unit was by definition a separate unit. General Devers was strongly opposed to deletion on grounds that it would lead to the indiscriminate organization of small black units within larger units. He argued that the Gillem Board had provided for black units as part of larger units, but not as organic parts. He believed that a separate black unit should continue to be attached when it replaced a white unit; otherwise it would lose its identity by becoming an organic part of a mixed unit. Larger considerations seem also to have influenced his conclusion: "Our implementation of the Negro problem has not progressed to the degree where we can accept this step. We have already progressed beyond that which is acceptable in many states and we still have a considerable latitude in the present policy without further liberalizing it from the Negro viewpoint."[7-72] The Chief of Staff supported Paul's view, however, and the word "separate" was excised.[7-73]

But the practice of attaching rather than assigning black units continued until the end of 1949. Only then, and increasingly during 1950, did the Army begin to assign a number of black units as organic parts of combat divisions. More noteworthy, Negroes began to be assigned to fill the spaces in parts of white units. Thus the 3d Battalion of the 9th Infantry and the 3d Battalion of the 188th became black units in 1950.

Despite the emergence of racially composite units, the Army's execution of the Gillem Board recommendation on the integration of black and white units was criticized by black leaders. The board had placed no limitation on the size of the units to be integrated, and its call for progressive steps to utilize black manpower implied to many that the process of forming composite black and white units would continue till it included the smaller service units, which still contained the majority of black troops. It was one thing, the Army staff concluded, to assign a self-sustaining black battalion to a division, but quite another to assign a small black service unit in a similar fashion. As a spokesman for the Personnel and Administration Division put it in a 1946 address, the Army was "not now ready to mix Negro and white personnel in the same company or battery, for messing and housing." Ignoring the Navy's experience to the contrary, he concluded that to do so might provoke serious opposition from the men in the ranks and from the American public.[7-74]

Accordingly, G-1 and G-3 agreed to reject the Mediterranean theater's 1946 plan to organize composite service units in the 88th Infantry Division because such organization "involves the integration of Negro platoons or Negro sections into white companies, a combination which is not in accordance with the policy as expressed in Circular 124."[7-75] In the separate case of black service companies—for example, the many transportation truck companies and ordnance evacuation companies—theater commanders tended to combine them first into quartermaster trains and then attach them to their combat divisions.[7-76]

Despite the relaxation in the distinction between attached and assigned status in the case of large black units, the Army staff remained adamantly opposed to the combination of small black with small white units. The Personnel and Administration Division jealously guarded the orthodoxy of this interpretation. Commenting on one proposal to combine small units in April 1948, General Paul noted that while grouping units of company size or greater was permissible, the Army had not yet reached the stage where two white companies and two black companies could be organized into a single battalion. Until the process of forming racially composite units developed to this extent, he told the Under Secretary of the Army, William H. Draper, Jr., the experimental mixing of small black and white units had no place in the program to expand the use of Negroes in the Army.[7-77] He did not say when such a process would become appropriate or possible. Several months later Paul flatly told the Chief of Staff that integration of black and white platoons in a company was precluded by stated Army policy.[7-78]

Assignments

The organization of black units was primarily the concern of the Organization and Training Division; the Personnel and Administration Division's major emphasis was on finding more jobs for black soldiers in keeping with the Gillem Board's call for the use of Negroes on a broader professional scale. This could best be done, Paul decided, by creating new black units in a variety of specialties and by using more Negroes in overhead spaces in unit headquarters where black specialists would be completely interspersed with white. To that end his office prepared plans in November 1946 listing numerous occupational specialties that might be offered black recruits. It also outlined in considerable detail a proposal for converting several organizations to black units, including a field artillery (155-mm. howitzer) battalion, a tank company, a chemical mortar company, and an ordnance heavy automotive maintenance company. These units would be considered experimental in the sense that the men would be specially selected and distributed in terms of ability. The officers, Negroes insofar as practical, and cadre noncommissioned officers would be specially assigned. Morale and learning ability would be carefully monitored, and special training would be given men with below average AGCT scores. At the end of six months, these organizations would be measured against comparable white units. Mindful of the controversial aspects of his plan, Paul had a draft circulated among the major commands and services.[7-79]

The Army Ground Forces, first to answer, concentrated on Paul's proposal for experimental black units. Maj. Gen. Charles L. Bolte, speaking for the commanding general, reported that in July 1946 the command had begun a training experiment to determine the most effective assignments for black enlisted men in the combat arms. Because of troop reductions and the policy of discharging individuals with low test scores, he said, the experiment had lasted only five weeks. Five weeks was apparently long enough, however, for Brig. Gen. Benjamin F. Caffey, commander of the 25th Regimental Combat Team (Provisional), to reach some rather startling conclusions. He discovered that the black soldier possessed an untrained and undisciplined mind and lacked confidence and pride in himself. In the past the Negro had been unable to summon the physical courage and stamina needed to withstand the shocks of modern battle. Integrating individual Negroes or small black units into white organizations would therefore only lower the standard of efficiency of the entire command. He discounted the integration after the Battle of the Bulge, saying that it succeeded only because it came at the end of the war and during pursuit action. "It still remains a moot question," Caffey concluded, "as to whether the Negroes in integrated units would have fought in a tough attack or defensive battle." Curiously enough he went on to say that until Negroes reached the educational level of whites, they should be organized into small combat units—battalions and smaller—and attached to white organizations in order to learn the proper standards of military discipline, conduct, administration, and training. Despite its unfavorable opinion of experimental black units, the Army Ground Forces did not reject the whole proposal outright but asked for a postponement of six months until its own reorganization, required by the War Department, was completed.[7-80]

The other forces also rejected the idea of experimental black units. General Spaatz once again declared that the mission of the Army Air Forces was already seriously hampered by budgetary and manpower limitations and experimentation would only sacrifice time, money, manpower, and training urgently needed by the Army Air Forces to fulfill its primary mission. He believed, moreover, that such an experiment would be weighted in favor of Negroes since comparisons would be drawn between specially selected and trained black units and average white units.[7-81] In a similar vein the Director of Organization and Training, General Hall, found the conversion "undesirable at this time." He also concluded that the problem was not limited to training difficulties but involved a "combination of factors" and could be solved through the application of common sense by the local commander.[7-82]The Chiefs of Ordnance and the Chemical Corps, the technical services involved in the proposed experiment, concurred in the plan but added that they had no Negroes available for the designated units.[7-83]

In the face of this strong opposition, Paul set aside his plan to establish experimental black units and concentrated instead on the use of Negroes in overhead positions. On 10 January 1947 he drew up for the Chief of Staff's office a list of 112 military occupational specialties most commonly needed in overhead installations, including skilled jobs in the Signal, Ordnance, Transportation, Medical, and Finance Corps from which Negroes had been excluded. He called for an immediate survey of the Army commands to determine specialties to which Negroes might be assigned, the number of Negroes that could be used in each, and the number of Negroes already qualified and available for immediate assignment. Depending on the answers to this survey, he proposed that commanders assign immediately to overhead jobs those Negroes qualified by school training, and open the pertinent specialist courses to Negroes. Black quotas for the courses would be increased, not only for recruits completing basic training, who would be earmarked for assignment to overhead spaces, but also for men already assigned to units, who would be returned to their units for such assignments upon completion of their courses. Negroes thus assigned would perform the same duties as whites alongside them, but they would be billeted and messed in separate detachments or attached to existing black units for quarters and food.[7-84]

This proposal also met with some opposition. General Spaatz, for example, objected on the same grounds he had used against experimental black units. Forcing the military development of persons on the basis of color, General Ira C. Eaker, the deputy commander of Army Air Forces, argued, was detrimental to the organization as a whole. Spaatz added that it was desirable and necessary to select individual men on the basis of their potential contribution to the service rather than in response to such criteria as race.[7-85]

The Acting Deputy Chief of Staff, Maj. Gen. Henry I. Hodes, objected to the timing of the Paul proposal since it would require action by field commanders during a period when continuing mass demobilization and severe budget limitations were already causing rapid and frequent adjustments, especially in overhead installations. He also felt that sending men to school would disrupt unit activities; altogether too many men would be assigned to overhead jobs, particularly during the period when Negroes were receiving training. Finally, he believed that Paul's directive was too detailed. He doubted that it was workable because it centralized power in Washington.[7-86]

General Paul disagreed. The major flow of manpower, he maintained, was going to domestic rather than overseas installations. A relatively small shift of manpower was contemplated in his plan and would therefore cause little dislocation. The plan would provide commanders with the trained men they had been asking for. School training inevitably required men to be temporarily absent from their units, but, since commanders always complained about the scarcity of trained Negroes, Paul predicted that they would accept a temporary inconvenience in order to have their men school trained. The Gillem Board policy had been in effect for nine months, and "no material implementation by field commanders has as yet come to the attention of the division." If any changes were to be accomplished, Paul declared, "a specific directive must be issued." Since the Chief of Staff had charged the Personnel and Administration Division with implementing Gillem Board policy and since that policy expressly directed the use of Negroes in overhead positions, it seemed to Paul "inconceivable that any proposition ... designed to improve the caliber of any of their Negro personnel would be unworkable in the sense of creating a personnel shortage." He again recommended that the directive be approved and released to the public to "further the spirit and recommendations of the Gillem Board Report."[7-87]

His superiors did not agree. Instead of a directive, General Hodes ordered yet another survey to determine whether commanders were actually complying with Circular 124. He wanted all commands to itemize all the occupation specialties of major importance that contained black troops in overhead spaces.[7-88] Needless to say, the survey added little to the Army's knowledge of its racial problems. Most commanders reported full compliance with the circular and had no further recommendations.

With rare exceptions their statistics proved their claims specious. The Far East Command, for example, reported no Negroes in overhead spaces, although General MacArthur planned to incorporate about 400 Negroes into the bulk overhead units in Japan in July 1947. He reported that he would assign Negroes to overhead positions when qualified men could be spared. For the present they were needed in black units.[7-89] Other commands produced similar statistics. The Mediterranean theater, 8 percent black, had only four Negroes in 2,700 overhead spaces, a decrease over the previous year, because, as its commander explained, a shortage of skilled technicians and noncommissioned officers in black units meant that none could be spared. More than 20 percent black, the Alaskan Department had no Negroes in overhead spaces. In Europe, on the other hand, some 2,125 overhead spaces, 18.5 percent of the total, were filled by Negroes.[7-90]

Although Negroes held some 7 percent of all overhead positions in the field services, the picture was far from clear. More than 8 percent of the Army Air Forces' 105,000 overhead spaces, for example, were filled by Negroes, but the Army Ground Forces used only 473 Negroes, who occupied 5 percent of its overhead spaces. In the continental armies almost 14,000 Negroes were assigned to overhead, 13.35 percent of the total of such spaces—a more than equitable figure. Yet most were cooks, bakers, truck drivers, and the like; all finance clerks, motion picture projectionists, and personnel assistants were white. In the field commands the use of Negroes in Signal, Ordnance, Transportation, Medical, and Finance overhead spaces was at a minimum, although figures varied from one command to the other. The Transportation Corps, more than 23 percent black, used almost 25 percent of its Negroes in overhead; the Chemical Corps, 28 percent black, used more than 30 percent of its Negroes in overhead. At the same time virtually all skilled military occupational specialties were closed to Negroes in the Signal Corps, and the Chief of Finance stated flatly: "It is considered impractical to have negro overhead assigned to these [field] activities and none are utilized."[7-91]

The survey attested to a dismal lack of progress in the development of specialist training for Negroes. Although all the commanders of the zone of interior armies reported that Negroes had equal opportunity with whites to attend Army schools, in fact more than half of all the Army's courses were not open to black soldiers regardless of their qualifications. The Ordnance Department, for example, declared that all its technical courses were open to qualified Negroes, but as late as November 1947 the Ordnance School in Atlanta, Georgia, had openings for 440 whites but none for blacks.

Ironically, the results of the Hodes survey were announced just four days short of Circular 124's first birthday. Along with the other surveys and directives of the past year, it demonstrated that in several important particulars the Gillem Board's recommendations were being only partially and indifferently followed. Obviously, some way must be found to dispel the atmosphere of indifference, and in some quarters hostility, that now enveloped Circular 124.

A New Approach

A new approach was possible mainly because General Paul and his staff had amassed considerable experience during the past year in how to use black troops. They had come to understand that the problems inherent in broadening the employment of black soldiers—the procurement of desirable black recruits, their training, especially school training for military occupational specialties, and their eventual placement in spaces that used that training—were interrelated and that progress in one of these areas was impossible without advances in the other two. In November 1947 the Personnel and Administration Division decided to push for a modest step-by-step increase in the number of jobs open to Negroes, using this increase to justify an expansion of school quotas for Negroes and a special recruitment program.

91

It was a good time for such an initiative, for the Army was in the midst of an important reorganization of its program for specialist training. On 9 May 1947 the War Department had introduced a Career Guidance Program for managing the careers of enlisted men. To help each soldier develop his maximum potential and provide the most equitable system for promotions, it divided all Army jobs into several career fields—two, for example, were infantry and food service—and established certain job progressions, or ladders, within each field. An enlisted man could move up the ladder in his career field to increased responsibility and higher rank as he completed school courses, gained experience, and passed examinations.[7-92]

General Paul wanted to take advantage of this unusually fluid situation. He could point out that black soldiers must be included in the new program, but how was he to fit them in? Black units lacked the diverse jobs open to whites, and as a result Negroes were clustered in a relatively small number of military specialties with few career fields open to them. Moreover, some 111 of the Army's 124 listed school courses required an Army General Classification Test score of ninety for admission, and the Personnel and Administration Division discovered that 72 percent of Negroes enlisted between April 1946 and March 1947 as compared to 29 percent of whites scored below that minimum. Excluded from schools, these men would find it difficult to move up the career ladders.[7-93]

Concerned that the new career program would discriminate against black soldiers, Paul could not, however, agree with the solution suggested by Roy K. Davenport, an Army manpower expert. On the basis of a detailed study that he and a representative of the Personnel and Administration Division conducted on Negroes in the career program, Davenport concluded that despite significant improvement in the quality of black recruits in recent months more than half the black enlisted men would still fail to qualify for the schooling demanded in the new program. He wanted the Army to consider dropping the test score requirement for school admission and substituting a "composite of variables," including length of service in a military occupation and special performance ratings. Such a system, he pointed out, would insure the most capable in terms of performance would be given opportunities for schooling and would eliminate the racial differential in career opportunity. It was equally important, Davenport thought, to broaden arbitrarily the list of occupational specialties, open all school courses to Negroes, and increase the black quotas for courses already open to them.[7-94]

Mindful of the strong opposition to his recent attempts to train Negroes for new overhead assignments, General Paul did not see how occupational specialties could be increased until new units or converted white ones were formed, or, for that matter, how school quotas could be increased unless positions for Negroes existed to justify the training. He believed that the Army should first widen the employment of black units and individuals in overhead spaces, and then follow up with increased school quotas and special recruitment. Paul had already learned from recent surveys that the number of available overhead positions would allow only a modest increase in the number of specialized jobs available to Negroes; any significant increase would require the creation of new black units. Given the limitations on organized units, any increase would be at the expense of white units.

The Organization and Training Division had the right to decide which units would be white and which black, and considering the strong opposition in that division to the creation of more black units, an opposition that enjoyed support from the Chief of Staff's office, Paul's efforts seemed in vain. But again an unusual opportunity presented itself when the Chief of Staff approved a reorganization of the general reserve in late 1947. It established a continentally based, mobile striking force of four divisions with supporting units. Each unit would have a well-trained core of Regular Army or other troops who might be expected to remain in the service for a considerable period of time. Manpower and budget limitations precluded a fully manned and trained general reserve, but new units for the four continental divisions, which were in varying stages of readiness, were authorized.[7-95]

ARMY SPECIALISTS REPORT FOR AIRBORNE TRAINING,
Fort Bragg, North Carolina, 1948.

Here was a chance to create some black units, and Paul jumped at it. During the activation and reorganization of the units for the general reserve he persuaded the Organization and Training Division to convert nineteen white units to black: seven combat (including infantry and field artillery battalions), five combat support, and seven service units for a total of 8,000 spaces. Nine of the units were attached to general reserve divisions, including the 2d Armored, 2d Infantry, and 82d Airborne Division. The rest, nondivisional elements, were assigned to the various continental armies.[7-96]

With the spaces in hand, the Personnel and Administration Division launched a special drive in late December 1947 to secure 6,318 Negroes, 565 men per week, above the normal recruiting quotas. It called on the commanding generals of the continental armies to enlist men for three years' service in the Regular Army from among those who had previous military service, had completed high school, or had won the Bronze Star, Commendation Ribbon, or a decoration for valor, and who could make a "reasonable" score on the classification test. After basic training at Fort Dix and Fort Knox, the men would be eligible for specialized schooling and direct assignment to the newly converted units.[7-97]

The conversion of units did not expand to any great extent the range of military specialties open to Negroes because they were already serving in similarly organized units. But it did increase the number of skilled occupation slots available to them. To force a further increase in the number of school-trained Negroes, Paul asked The Adjutant General to determine how many spaces for school-trained specialists existed in the units converted from white to black and how many spaces for school-trained specialists were unfilled in black units worldwide. He wanted to increase the quotas for each school-trained specialty to insure filling all these positions.[7-98] He also arranged to increase black quotas in certain Military Police, Signal, and Medical Corps courses, and he insisted that a directive be sent to all major continental commands making mandatory the use of Negroes trained under the increased school quotas.[7-99] Moving further along these lines, Paul suggested The Adjutant General assign a black officer to study measures that might broaden the use of Negroes in the Army, increase school quotas for them, select black students properly, and assign trained black soldiers to suitable specialties.[7-100]

The Adjutant General assigned Maj. James D. Fowler, a black graduate of West Point, class of 1941, to perform all these tasks. Fowler surveyed the nineteen newly converted units and recommended that 1,134 men, approximately 20 percent of those enlisted for the special expansion of the general reserve, be trained in thirty-seven courses of instruction—an increase of 103 black spaces in these courses. Examining worldwide Army strength to determine deficiencies in school-trained specialties in black units, he recommended a total increase of 172 spaces in another thirty-seven courses. Studying the organizational tables of more than two hundred military bases, Fowler recommended that black school quotas for another eleven military occupational specialties, for which there were currently no black quotas, be set at thirty-nine spaces.

On the basis of these recommendations, the Army increased the number of courses with quotas for Negroes from 30 to 62; black quotas were increased in 14 courses; 16 others remained unchanged or their black quotas were slightly decreased. New courses were opened to Negroes in the Adjutant General's School, the airborne section of the Infantry School, and the Artillery, Armored, Engineer, Medical, Military Police, Ordnance, Quartermaster, Signal, and Transportation schools. Courses with increased quotas were in Transportation, Quartermaster, Ordnance, and Engineer schools.[7-101] The number of black soldiers in courses open to recruits quickly grew from 5 to 13.7 percent of total enrollment, and the number of courses open to Negroes rose from 30 to 48 percent of all the entry courses in the Army school system.

The Quota System: An Assessment

The conversion of nineteen units from white to black in December 1947, the procurement of 6,000 Negroes to man these units, and the increases in black quotas in the Army schools to train specialists for these and other black units worldwide marked the high point of the Army's attempt to broaden the employment of Negroes under the terms of the Gillem Board policy. As Paul well knew, the training of black troops was linked to their placement and until the great expansion of the Army in 1950 for the Korean War no other units were converted from white to black. The increase in black combat units and the spread in the range of military occupations for black troops, therefore, were never achieved as planned. The interval between wars ended just as it began with the majority of white soldiers serving in combat or administrative units and the majority of black soldiers continuing to work in service or combat support units.[7-102]

The Personnel and Organization Division made no further requests for increased school quotas for Negroes, and even those increases already approved were short-lived. As soon as the needs of the converted units were met, the school quotas for Negroes were reduced to a level sufficient to fill the replacement needs of the black units. By March 1949, spaces for black students in the replacement stream courses had declined from the 237 recommended by Major Fowler to eighty-two; the number of replacement stream courses open to Negroes fell from 48 percent of all courses offered to 19.8 percent. Fowler had expected to follow up his study of school quotas in the Military Police, Signal Corps, and Medical Corps with surveys of other schools figuring in the Career Guidance Program, but since no additional overhead positions were ever converted from white to black, no further need existed for school quota studies. The three-point study suggested by Paul to find ways to increase school quotas for Negroes was never made.

The War Department's problems with its segregation policy were only intensified by its insistence on maintaining a racial quota. Whatever the authors' intention, the quota was publicized as a guarantee of black participation. In practice it not only restricted the number of Negroes in the Army but also limited the number and variety of black units that could be formed and consequently the number and variety of jobs available to Negroes. Further, it restricted the openings for Negroes in the Army's training schools.

BRIDGE PLAYERS, SEAVIEW SERVICE CLUB, TOKYO, JAPAN, 1948

At the same time, enlistment policies combined with Selective Service regulations to make it difficult for the Army to produce from its black quota enough men with the potential to be trained in those skills required by a variety of units. Attracted by the superior economic status promised by the Army, the average black soldier continued to reenlist, thus blocking the enlistment of potential military leaders from the increasing number of educated black youths. This left the Army with a mass of black soldiers long in service but too old to fight, learn new techniques, or provide leadership for the future. Subject to charges of discrimination, the Army only fitfully and for limited periods tried to eliminate low scorers to make room for more qualified men. Yet to the extent to which it failed to attract educated Negroes and provide them with modern military skills, it failed to perform a principal function of the peacetime Army, that of preparing a cadre of leaders for future wars.

In discussing the problem of low-scoring Negroes it should be remembered that the Army General Classification Test, universally accepted in the armed services as an objective device to measure ability, has been seriously questioned by some manpower experts. Since World War II, for example, educational psychologists have learned that ethnic, cultural, and linguistic backgrounds have an important influence on performance in general testing. Davenport, who eventually became a senior manpower official in the Department of Defense has, for one, concluded that the test scores created a distorted picture of the mental ability of the black soldier. He has also questioned the fairness of the Army testing system, charging that uniform time periods were not always provided for black and white recruits taking the tests and that this injustice was only one of several inequalities of test administration that might have contributed to the substantial differences in the scores of applicants.[7-103]

The accuracy of test scores can be ignored when the subject is viewed from the perspective of manpower utilization. In the five years after World War II, the actual number of white soldiers who scored in the lowest test categories equaled or exceeded the number of black soldiers. The Army had no particular difficulty using these white soldiers to advantage, and in fact refused to discharge all Class V men in 1946. Segregation was the heart of the matter; the less gifted whites could be scattered throughout the Army but the less gifted blacks were concentrated in the segregated black units.

Reversing the coin, what could the Army do with the highly qualified black soldier? His technical skills were unneeded in the limited number and variety of black units; he was barred from white units. In an attempt to deal with this problem, the Gillem policy directed that Negroes with special skills or qualifications be employed in overhead detachments. Such employment, however, depended in great part on the willingness of commanders to use school-trained Negroes. Many of these officers complained that taking the best qualified Negroes out of black units for assignment to overhead detachments deprived black units of their leaders. Furthermore, overhead units represented so small a part of the whole that they had little effect on the Army's problem.

The racial quota also complicated the postwar reduction in Army strength. Since the strength and composition of the Army was fixed by the defense budget and military planning, the majority of new black soldiers produced by the quota could be organized into units only at the expense of white units already in existence. In light of past performance of black units and in the interests of efficiency and economy, particularly at a time of reduced operating funds and a growing cold war, how could the Army justify converting efficient white units into less capable black units? The same question applied to the formation of composite units. Grouping lower scoring black units with white units, many of the Army staff believed, would lower the efficiency of the whole and complicate the Army's relations with the civilian community. As a result, the black units remained largely separate, limited in number, and tremendously overstrength throughout the postwar period.

Some of these problems, at least, might have been solved had the Army created a special staff group to oversee the new policy, a key proposal of the Gillem Board. The Personnel and Administration Division was primarily interested in individuals, in trying to place qualified Negroes on an individual basis; the Organization and Training Division was primarily concerned with units, in trying to expand the black units to approximate the combat to service ratio of white

94

units. These interests conflicted at times, and with no single agency possessing overriding authority, matters came to an impasse, blocking reform of Army practices. Instead, the staff played a sterile numbers game, seeking to impose a strict ratio everywhere. But it was impossible to have a 10 percent proportion of Negroes in every post, in every area, in every overseas theater; it was equally impossible to have 10 percent in every activity, in every arm and service, in every type of task. Yet wherever the Army failed to organize its black strength by quota, it was open to charges of racial discrimination.

It would be a mistake to overlook the signs of racial progress achieved under the Gillem Board policy. Because of its provisions thousands of Negroes came to serve in the postwar Regular Army, many of them in a host of new assignments and occupations. But if the policy proved a qualified success in terms of numbers, it still failed to gain equal treatment and opportunity for black soldiers, and in the end the racial quotas and diverse racial units better served those who wanted to keep a segregated Army.

CHAPTER 8

Segregation's Consequences

The Army staff had to overcome tremendous obstacles in order to carry out even a modest number of the Gillem Board's recommendations. In addition to prejudices the Army shared with much of American society and the institutional inertia that often frustrates change in so large an organization, the staff faced the problem of making efficient soldiers out of a large group of men who were for the most part seriously deficient in education, training, and motivation. To the extent that it overcame these difficulties, the Army's postwar racial policy must be judged successful and, considered in the context of the times, progressive.

Nevertheless, the Gillem Board policy was doomed from the start. Segregation was at the heart of the race problem. Justified as a means of preventing racial trouble, segregation only intensified it by concentrating the less able and poorly motivated. Segregation increased the problems of all commanders concerned and undermined the prestige of black officers. It exacerbated the feelings of the nation's largest minority toward the Army and multiplied demands for change. In the end Circular 124 was abandoned because the Army found it impossible to fight another war under a policy of racial quotas and units. But if the quota had not defeated the policy, other problems attendant on segregation would probably have been sufficient to the task.

Discipline and Morale Among Black Troops

By any measure of discipline and morale, black soldiers as a group posed a serious problem to the Army in the postwar period. The standard military indexes—serious incidents statistics, venereal disease rates, and number of courts-martial—revealed black soldiers in trouble out of all proportion to their percentage of the Army's population. When these personal infractions and crimes were added to the riots and serious racial incidents that continued to occur in the Army all over the world after the war, the dimensions of the problem became clear.

In 1945, when Negroes accounted for 8.5 percent of the Army's average strength, black prisoners entering rehabilitation centers, disciplinary barracks, and federal institutions were 17.3 percent of the Army total. In 1946, when the average black strength had risen to 9.35 percent of the Army's total, 25.9 percent of the soldiers sent to the stockade were Negroes. The following tabulation gives their percentage of all military prisoners by offense:

Military Offenses

Absent without leave

Desertion

Misbehavior before the enemy

Violation of arrest or confinement

Discreditable conduct toward superior

Civil Offenses

Murder

Rape

Robbery

Manslaughter

Burglary and housebreaking

Larceny

Forgery

Assault

Source: Correction Branch, TAGO, copy in CMH.

The most common explanation offered for such statistics is that fundamental injustices drove these black servicemen to crime. Probably more to the point, most black soldiers, especially during the early postwar period, served in units burdened with many disadvantaged individuals, soldiers more likely to get into trouble given the characteristically weak leadership in these units. But another explanation for at least some of these crime statistics hinged on commanders' power to define serious offenses. In general, unit commanders had a great deal of discretion in framing the charges brought against an alleged offender; indeed, where some minor offenses were concerned officers could even conclude that a given infraction was not a serious matter at all and simply dismiss the soldier with a verbal reprimand and a warning not to repeat his offense. Whereas one commander might decide that a case called for a charge of aggravated assault, another, faced with the same set of facts, might settle for a charge of simple assault. If it is reasonable to assume that, as a part of the pattern of discrimination, Negroes accused of offenses like misconduct toward superiors, AWOL, and assault often received less generous treatment from their officers than white servicemen, then it is reasonable to suspect that statistics on Negroes involved in crime may reflect such discriminatory treatment.

The crime figures were particularly distressing to the individual black soldier, as indeed they were to his civilian counterpart, because as a member of a highly visible minority he became identified with the wrongdoing of some of his fellows, spectacularly reported in the press, while his own more typical attendance to orders and competent performance of duty were more often buried in the Army's administrative reports. In particular, Negroes among the large overseas commands suffered embarrassment. The Gillem Board policy was announced just as the Army began the occupation of Germany and Japan. As millions of veterans returned home, to be replaced in lesser numbers by volunteers, black troops began to figure prominently in the occupation forces. On 1 January 1947 the Army had 59,795 Negroes stationed overseas, 10.77 percent of the total number of overseas troops, divided principally between the two major overseas commands. By 1 March 1948, in keeping with the general reduction of forces, black strength overseas was reduced to 23,387 men, but black percentages in Europe and the Far East remained practically unchanged.[8-1] It was among these Negroes, scattered throughout Germany and Japan, that most of the disciplinary problems occurred.

During the first two years of peace, black soldiers consistently dominated the Army's serious-incident rate, a measure of indictments and accusations involving troops in crimes against persons and property. In June 1946, for example, black soldiers in the European theater were involved in serious incidents (actual and alleged) at the rate of 2.57 cases per 1,000 men. The rate among white soldiers for the same period was .79 cases per 1,000. The rate for both groups rose considerably in 1947. The figure for Negroes climbed to a yearly average of 3.94 incidents per 1,000; the figure for whites, reflecting an even greater gain, reached 1.88. These crime rates were not out of line with America's national crime rate statistics, which, based on a sample of 173 cities, averaged about 3.25 during the same period.[8-2] Nevertheless, the rate was of particular concern to the government because the majority of the civil offenses were perpetuated against German and Japanese nationals and therefore lowered the prestige and effectiveness of the occupation forces.

Less important but still a serious internal problem for the Army was a parallel rise in the incidence of venereal disease. Various reasons have been advanced for the great postwar rise in the Army's venereal disease rate. It is obvious, for example, that the rapid conversion from war to peacetime duties gave many American soldiers new leisure and freedom to engage in widespread fraternization with the civilian population. Serious economic dislocation in the conquered countries drove many citizens into a life of prostitution and crime. By the same token, the breakdown of public health services had removed a major obstacle to the spread of social disease. But whatever the reasons, a high rate of venereal disease—the overseas rate was three times greater than the rate reported for soldiers in the United States—reflected a serious breakdown in military discipline, posed a threat to the combat effectiveness of the commands, and produced lurid rumors and reports on Army morality.

As in the case of crime statistics, the rate of venereal disease for black soldiers in the overseas commands far exceeded the figure for whites. The Eighth Army, the major unit in the Far East, reported for the month of June 1946 1,263 cases of venereal disease for whites, or 139 cases per 1,000 men per year; 769 cases were reported for Negroes, or 1,186 cases per 1,000 men per year. The rates for the European Command for July 1946 stood at 806 cases per 1,000

96

Negroes per year as compared with 203 for white soldiers. The disease rate improved considerably during 1947 in both commands, but still the rates for black troops averaged 354 per 1,000 men per year in Eighth Army compared to 89 for whites. In Europe the rate was 663 per 1,000 men per year for Negroes compared to 172 for whites. At the same time the rate for all soldiers in the United States was 58 per 1,000 per year.[8-3] Some critics question the accuracy of these statistics, charging that more white soldiers, with informal access to medical treatment, were able to escape detection by the Medical Department's statisticians, at least in cases of more easily treated strains of venereal disease.

The court-martial rate for black soldiers serving overseas was also higher than for white soldiers. Black soldiers in Europe, for example, were court-martialed at the rate of 3.48 men per 1,000 during the third quarter of 1946 compared with a 1.14 rate for whites. A similar situation existed in the Far East where the black service units had a monthly court-martial rate nearly double the average rate of the Eighth Army as a whole.[8-4]

The disproportionate black crime and disease rates were symptomatic of a condition that also revealed itself in the racially oriented riots and disturbances that continued to plague the postwar Army. Sometimes black soldiers were merely reacting to blatant discrimination countenanced by their officers, to racial insults, and at times even to physical assaults, but nevertheless they reacted violently and in numbers. The resulting incidents prompted investigations, recriminations, and publicity.

Two such disturbances, more spectacular than the typical flare-up, and important because they influenced Army attitudes toward blacks, occurred at Army bases in the United States. The first was a mutiny at MacDill Airfield, Florida, which began on 27 October 1946 at a dance for black noncommissioned officers to which privates were denied admittance. Military police were called when a fight broke out among the black enlisted men and rapidly developed into a belligerent demonstration by a crowd that soon reached mob proportions. Police fire was answered by members of the mob and one policeman and one rioter were wounded. Urged on by its ringleaders, the mob then overwhelmed the main gate area and disarmed the sentries. The rioters retained control of the area until early the next day, when the commanding general persuaded them to disband. Eleven Negroes were charged with mutiny.[8-5] A second incident, a riot with strong racial overtones, occurred at Fort Leavenworth in May 1947 following an altercation between white and black prisoners in the Army Disciplinary Barracks. The rioting, caused by allegations of favoritism accorded to prisoners, lasted for two days; one man was killed and six were injured.[8-6]

Disturbances in overseas commands, although less serious, were of deep concern to the Army because of the international complications. In April 1946, for example, soldiers of the 449th Signal Construction Detachment threw stones at two French officers who were driving through the village of Weyersbusch in the Rhine Palatinate. The officers, one of them injured, returned to the village with French MP's and requested an explanation of the incident. They were quickly surrounded by about thirty armed Negroes of the detachment who, according to the French, acted in an aggressive and menacing manner. As a result, the Supreme French Commander in Germany requested his American counterpart to remove all black troops from the French zone. The U.S. commander in Europe, General Joseph T. McNarney, investigated the incident, court-martialed its instigators, and transferred the entire detachment out of the French zone. At the same time his staff explained to the French that to prohibit the stationing of Negroes in the area would be discriminatory and contrary to Army policy. Black specialists continued to operate in the French zone, although none were subsequently stationed there permanently.[8-7]

The Far East Command also suffered racial incidents. The Eighth Army reported in 1946 that "racial agitation" was one of the primary causes of assault, the most frequent violent crime among American troops in Japan. This racial agitation was usually limited to the American community, however, and seldom involved the civilian population.[8-8]

The task of maintaining a biracial Army overseas in peacetime was marked with embarrassing incidents and time-consuming investigations. The Army was constantly hearing about its racial problems overseas and getting no end of advice. For example, in May 1946 Louis Lautier, chief of the Negro Newspaper Publishers Association news service, informed the Assistant Secretary of War that fifty-five of the seventy American soldiers executed for crimes in the European theater were black. Most were category IV and V men. "In light of this fact," Lautier charged, "the blame for the comparatively high rate of crime among black soldiers belongs to the American educational system."[8-9]

But when a delegation of publishers from Lautier's organization toured European installations during the same period, the members took a more comprehensive look at the Seventh Army's race problems. They told Secretary Patterson that they found all American

97

soldiers reacting similarly to poor leadership, substandard living conditions, and menial occupations whenever such conditions existed. Although they professed to see no difference in the conduct of white and black troops, they went on to list factors that contributed to the bad conduct of some of the black troops including the dearth of black officers, hostility of military police, inadequate recreation, and poor camp location. They also pointed out that many soldiers in the occupation had been shipped overseas without basic training, scored low in the classification tests, and served under young and inexperienced noncoms. Many black regulars, on the other hand, once proud members of combat units, now found themselves performing menial tasks in the backwaters of the occupation. Above all, the publishers witnessed widespread racial discrimination, a condition that followed inevitably, they believed, from the Army's segregation policy. Conditions in the Army appeared to them to facilitate an immediate shift to integration; conditions in Europe and elsewhere made such a shift imperative. Yet they found most commanders in Europe still unaware of the Gillem Board Report and its liberalizing provisions, and little being done to encourage within the Army the sensitivity to racial matters that makes life in a biracial society bearable. Until the recommendations of the board were carried out and discrimination stopped, they warned the secretary, the Army must expect racial flare-ups to continue.[8-10]

Characteristically, the Secretary of War's civilian aide, Marcus Ray, never denied evidence of misconduct among black troops, but concentrated instead on finding the cause. Returning from a month's tour of Pacific installations in September 1946, he bluntly pointed out to Secretary Patterson that high venereal disease and court-martial rates among black troops were "in direct proportion to the high percentage of Class IV and Vs among the Negro personnel." Given Ray's conclusion, the solution was relatively simple: the Army should "vigorously implement" its recently promulgated policy, long supported by Ray, and discharge persons with test scores of less than seventy.[8-11]

The civilian aide was not insensitive to the effects of segregation on black soldiers, but he stressed the practical results of the Army's policy instead of making a sweeping indictment of segregation. For example, he criticized the report of the noted criminologist, Leonard Keeler, who had recently studied the criminal activities of American troops in Europe for the Army's Criminal Investigation Division. Ray was critical, not because Keeler had been particularly concerned with the relatively high black crime rate and its effect on Europeans, but because the report overlooked the concentration of segregated black units which had increased the density of Negroes in some areas of Europe to a point where records and reports of misconduct presented a false picture. In effect, black crime statistics were meaningless, Ray believed, as long as the Army's segregation policy remained intact. Where Keeler implied that the solution was to exclude Negroes from Europe, Ray believed that the answer lay in desegregating and spreading them out.[8-12]

It was probably inevitable that all the publicity given racial troubles would attract attention on Capitol Hill. When the Senate's Special Investigations Committee took up the question of military government in occupied Europe in the fall of 1946, it decided to look into the conduct of black soldiers also. Witnesses asserted that black troops in Europe were ill-behaved and poorly disciplined and their officers were afraid to punish them properly for fear of displeasing higher authorities. The committee received a report on the occupation prepared by its chief counsel, George Meader. A curious amalgam of sensational hearsay, obvious racism, and unimpeachable fact, the document was leaked to the press and subsequently denounced publicly by the committee's chairman, Senator Harley M. Kilgore of West Virginia. Kilgore charged that parts of the report dealing with Negroes were obviously based on hearsay. "Neither prejudice nor malice," the senator concluded, "has any place in factual reports."[8-13]

Although the committee's staff certainly had displayed remarkable insensitivity, Meader's recommendations appeared temperate enough. He wanted the committee to explore with the War Department possible solutions to the problem of black troops overseas, and he called on the War Department to give careful consideration to the recommendations of its field commanders. The European commander was already on record with a recommendation to recall all black troops from Europe, citing the absence of Negroes from the U.S. Occupation Army in the Rhineland after World War I. Lt. Gen. Lucius D. Clay, then U.S. Commander, Berlin, who later succeeded General McNarney as theater commander and military governor, wanted Negroes in the occupation army used primarily as parade troops. Meader contended that the War Department was reluctant to act on these theater recommendations because it feared political repercussions from the black community. He had no such fear: "certainly, the conduct of the negro troops, as provable from War Department records, is no credit to the negro race and proper action to solve the problem should not result in any unfavorable reaction from any intelligent negro leaders."[8-14]

98

The War Department was not insensitive to the opinions being aired on Capitol Hill. The under secretary, Kenneth C. Royall, had already dispatched a group from the Inspector General's office under Brig. Gen. Elliot D. Cooke to find out among other things if black troops were being properly disciplined and to investigate other charges Lt. Col. Francis P. Miller had made before the Special Investigations Committee. Examining in detail the records of one subordinate European command, which had 12,000 Negroes in its force of 44,000, the Cooke group decided that commanders were not afraid to punish black soldiers. Although Negroes were responsible for vehicle accidents and disciplinary infractions in numbers disproportionate to their strength, they also had a proportionately higher court-martial rate.[8-15]

While the Cooke group was still studying the specific charges of the Senate's Investigations Committee, Secretary Patterson decided on a general review of the situation. He ordered Ray to tour European installations and report on how the Gillem Board policy was being put into effect overseas. Ray visited numerous bases and housing and recreation areas in Germany, Italy, France, Switzerland, and Austria. He examined duties, living conditions, morale, and discipline. He also looked into race relations and community attitudes. His month's tour, ending on 17 December 1946, reinforced his conviction that substandard troops—black and white—were at the heart of the Army's crime and venereal disease problem. Ray supported the efforts of local commanders to discharge these men, although he wanted the secretary to reform and standardize the method of discharge. In his analysis of the overseas situation, the civilian aide avoided any specific allusion to the nexus between segregation and racial unrest. In a rare burst of idealism, however, he did condemn those who would exclude Negroes from combat units and certain occupations because of presumed prejudices on the part of the German population. To bow to such prejudices, he insisted, was to negate America's aspirations for the postwar world. In essence, Ray's formula for good race relations was quite simple: institute immediately the reforms outlined in the Gillem Board Report.

In addition to broader use of black troops, Ray was concerned with basic racial attitudes. The Army, he charged, generally failed to see the connection between prejudice and national security; many of its leaders even denied that prejudice existed in the Army. Yet to ignore the problem of racial prejudice, he claimed, condemned the Army to perpetual racial upsets. He wanted the secretary to restate the Army's racial objectives and launch an information and education program to inform commanders and troops on racial matters.[8-16]

In all other respects a lucid progress report on the Gillem Board policy, Ray's analysis was weakened by his failure to point out the effect of segregation on the performance and attitude of black soldiers. Ray believed that the Gillem Board policy, with its quota system and its provisions for the integration of black specialists, would eventually lead to an integrated Army. Preoccupied with practical and imminently possible racial reforms, Ray, along with Secretary Patterson and other reformers within the Army establishment, tended to overlook the tenacious hold that racial segregation had on Army thought.

This hold was clearly illustrated by the reaction of the Army staff to Ray's recommendations. Speaking with the concurrence of the other staff elements and the approval of the Deputy Chief of Staff, General Paul warned that very little could be accomplished toward the long-range objective of the Gillem Board—integration—until the Army completed the long and complex task of raising the quality and lowering the quantity of black soldiers. He also considered it impractical to use Negroes in overhead positions, combat units, and highly technical and professional positions in exact proportion to their percentage of the population. Such use, Paul claimed, would expend travel funds already drastically curtailed and further complicate a serious housing situation. He admitted that the deep-seated prejudice of some Army members in all grades would have a direct bearing on the progress of the Army's new racial policy.

24TH INFANTRY BAND, GIFU, JAPAN, 1947

The staff generally agreed with Ray's other recommendations with one exception: it opposed his suggestion that black units be used in the European theater's constabulary, the specially organized and trained force that patrolled the East-West border and helped police the German occupation. The theater commander had so few capable Negroes, Paul reasoned, that to siphon off enough to form a constabulary unit would threaten the efficiency of other black units. Besides, even if enough qualified Negroes were available, he believed their use in supervisory positions over German nationals would be unacceptable to many Germans.[8-17] The staff offered no evidence for this latter argument, and indeed there was none available. In marked contrast to their reaction to the French government's quartering of Senegalese soldiers in the Rhineland after World War I, the German attitude toward American Negroes immediately after World War II was notably tolerant, a factor in the popularity among Negroes of assignments to

Europe. It was only later that the Germans, especially tavern owners and the like, began to adopt the discriminatory practices of their conquerors.[8-18]

Ray's proposals and the reaction to them formed a kind of watershed in the War Department's postwar racial policy. Just ten months after the Gillem Board Report was published, the Army staff made a judgment on the policy's effectiveness: the presence of Negroes in numbers approximating 10 percent of the Army's strength and at the current qualitative level made it necessary to retain segregation indefinitely. Segregation kept possible troublemakers out of important combat divisions, promoted efficiency, and placated regional prejudices both in the Army and Congress. Integration must be postponed until the number of Negroes in the Army was carefully regulated and the quality of black troops improved. Both, the staff thought, were goals of a future so distant that segregated units were not threatened.

But the staff's views ran contrary to the Gillem Board policy and the public utterances of the Secretary of War. Robert Patterson had consistently supported the policy in public and before his advisers. Besides, it was unthinkable that he would so quickly abandon a policy developed at the cost of so much effort and negotiation and announced with such fanfare. He had insisted that the quota be maintained, most recently in the case of the European Command.[8-19] In sum, he believed that the policy provided guidelines, practical and expedient, albeit temporary, that would lead to the integration of the Army.

In face of this impasse between the secretary and the Army staff there slowly evolved what proved to be a new racial policy. Never clearly formulated—Circular 124 continued in effect with only minor changes until 1950—the new policy was based on the substantially different proposition that segregation would continue indefinitely while the staff concentrated on weeding out poorly qualified Negroes, upgrading the rest, and removing vestiges of discrimination, which it saw as quite distinct from segregation. At the same time the Army would continue to operate under a strict 10 percent quota of Negroes, though not necessarily within every occupation or specialty. The staff overlooked the increasingly evident connection between segregation and racial unrest, thereby assuring the continuation of both. From 1947 on, integration, the stated goal of the Gillem Board policy, was ignored, while segregation, which the board saw as an expedient to be tolerated, became for the Army staff a way of life to be treasured. It was from this period in 1947 that Circular 124 and the Gillem Board Report began to gain their reputations as regressive documents.

Improving the Status of the Segregated Soldier

GENERAL HUEBNER
inspects the 529th Military Police Company, Giessen, Germany, 1948.

In 1947 the Army accelerated its long-range program to discharge soldiers who scored less than seventy on the Army General Classification Test. Often a subject of public controversy, the program formed a major part of the Army's effort to close the educational and training gap between black and white troops.[8-20] Of course, there were other ways to close the gap, and on occasion the Army had taken the more positive and difficult approach of upgrading its substandard black troops by giving them extra training. Although rarely so recognized, the Army's long record of providing remedial academic and technical training easily qualified it as one of the nation's major social engineers.

In World War II thousands of draftees were taught to read and write in the Army's literacy program. In 1946 at Fort Benning an on-duty educational program was organized in the 25th Regimental Combat Team for soldiers, in this case all Negroes, with less than an eighth grade education. Although the project had to be curtailed because of a lack of specialized instructors, an even more ambitious program was launched the next year throughout the Army after a survey revealed an alarming illiteracy rate in replacement troops. In a move of primary importance to black recruits, the Far East Command, for example, ordered all soldiers lacking the equivalent of a fifth grade education to attend courses. The order was later changed to include all soldiers who failed to achieve Army test scores of seventy.[8-21]

In 1947 the European theater launched the most ambitious project by far for improving the status of black troops, and before it was over thousands of black soldiers had been examined, counseled, and trained. The project was conceived and executed by the deputy and later theater commander, Lt. Gen. Clarence R. Huebner, and his adviser on Negro affairs, Marcus Ray, now a lieutenant colonel.[8-22] These men were convinced that a program could be devised to raise the status of the black soldier. Huebner wanted to lay the foundation for a command-wide educational program for all black units. "If you're going to make soldiers out of people," he later explained, "they have the right to be trained." Huebner had specialized in training in his Army career, had written several of the Army's training manuals, and possessed an abiding faith in the ability of the Army to change men. "If your soldiers don't know how, teach them."[8-23]

100

General Huebner got his chance in March 1947 when the command decided to use some 3,000 unassigned black troops in guard duties formerly performed by the 1st Infantry Division. The men were organized into two infantry battalions,[8-24] but because of their low test scores Huebner decided to establish a twelve-to thirteen-week training program at the Grafenwohr Training Center and directed the commanding general of the 1st Division to train black soldiers in both basic military and academic subjects. Huebner concluded his directive by saying:

This is our first opportunity to put into effect in a large way the War Department policy on Negro soldiers as announced in War Department Circular No. 124, 1946. Owing to the necessity for rapid training, and to the press of occupational duties, little time has been available in the past for developing the leadership of the Negro soldier. We can now do that.... I wish you to study the program, its progress, its deficiencies and its advantages, in order that a full report may be compiled and lessons in operation and training drawn.[8-25]

As the improved military bearing and efficiency of black trainees and the subsequent impressive performance of the two new infantry battalions would suggest, the reports on the Grafenwohr training were optimistic and the lessons drawn ambitious. They prompted Huebner on 1 December 1947 to establish a permanent training center at Kitzingen Air Base.[8-26] Essentially, he was trying to combine both drill and constant supervision with a broad-based educational program. Trainees received basic military training for six hours daily and academic instruction up to the twelfth grade level for two hours more. The command ordered all black replacements and casuals arriving from the United States to the training center for classifying and training as required. Eventually all black units in Europe were to be rotated through Kitzingen for unit refresher and individual instruction. As each company completed the course at Kitzingen, the command assigned academic instructors to continue an on-duty educational program in the field. A soldier was required to participate in the educational program until he passed the general education development test for high school level or until he clearly demonstrated that he could not profit from further instruction.

Washington was quick to perceive the merit of the European program, and Paul reported widespread approval "from all concerned."[8-27] The program quickly produced some impressive statistics. Thousands of soldiers—at the peak in 1950 more than 62 percent of all Negroes in the command—were enrolled in the military training course at Kitzingen or in on-duty educational programs organized in over two-thirds of the black companies throughout the command. By June 1950 the program had over 2,900 students and 200 instructors. A year later, the European commander estimated that since the program began some 1,169 Negroes had completed fifth grade in his schools, 2,150 had finished grade school, and 418 had passed the high school equivalency test.[8-28] The experiment had a practical and long-lasting effect on the Army. For example, in 1950 a sampling of three black units showed that after undergoing training at Kitzingen and in their own units the men scored an average of twenty points higher in Army classification tests. According to a 1950 European Command estimate, the command's education program was producing some of the finest trained black troops in the Army.

REPORTING TO KITZINGEN.

Men of Company B, 371st Infantry Battalion, arrive for refresher course in basic military training.

The training program even provoked jealous reaction among some white troops who claimed that the educational opportunities offered Negroes discriminated against them. They were right, for in comparison to the on-duty high school courses offered Negroes, the command restricted courses for white soldiers to so-called literacy training or completion of the fifth grade. Command spokesmen quite openly justified the disparity on the grounds that Negroes on the whole had received fewer educational opportunities in the United States and that the program would promote efficiency in the command.[8-29]

Whether a connection can be made between the Kitzingen training program and improvement in the morale and discipline of black troops, the fact was that by January 1950 a dramatic change had occurred in the conduct of black soldiers in the European Command. The rate of venereal disease among black soldiers had dropped to an average approximating the rate for white troops (and not much greater than the always lower average for troops in the United States). This phenomenon was repeated in the serious incident rate. In the first half of 1950 courts-martial that resulted in bad conduct discharges totaled fifty-nine for Negroes, a figure that compared well with the 324 similar verdicts for the larger contingent of white soldiers.[8-30] For once the Army could document what it had always preached, that education and training were the keys to the better performance of black troops. The tragedy was that the education program was never applied throughout the Army, not even in the Far East and in the United States, where far more black soldiers were stationed than in Europe.[8-31] The Army lost yet another chance to fulfill the promise of its postwar policy.

101

In later years Kitzingen assumed the task of training black officers, a natural progression considering the attitude of General Huebner and Marcus Ray. The general and the command adviser were convinced that the status of black soldiers depended at least in part on the caliber of black officers commanding them. Huebner deftly made this point in October 1947 soon after Kitzingen opened when he explained to General Paul that he wanted more "stable, efficient, and interested Negro officers and senior non-commissioned officers" who, he believed, would set an example for the trainees.[8-32] Others shared Huebner's views. The black publishers touring Europe some months later observed that wherever black officers were assigned there was "a noticeable improvement in the morale, discipline and general efficiency of the units involved."[8-33]

The European Command had requisitioned only five black officers during the last eight months, General Paul noted; this might have caused its shortage of black officers. Still, Paul knew the problem went deeper, and he admitted that many black officers now on duty were relatively undesirable and many desirable ones were being declared surplus. He was searching for a solution.[8-34] The Personnel and Administration Division could do very little about the major cause of the shortage, for the lack of black officers was fundamentally connected with the postwar demobilization affecting all the services. Most black officers were unable to compete in terms of length of service, combat experience, and other factors that counted heavily toward retention. Consequently their numbers dropped sharply from an August 1945 high of 7,748 to a December 1947 low of 1,184. The drop more than offset the slight rise in the black percentage of the whole officer corps, .8 percent in 1945 to 1.0 percent in 1947.

At first General Paul was rather passive in his attitude toward the shortage of black officers. Commenting on Assistant Secretary of War Petersen's suggestion in May 1946 that the Army institute a special recruitment program to supplement the small number of black officers who survived the competition for Regular Army appointments, Paul noted that all appointments were based on merit and competition and that special consideration for Negroes was itself a form of discrimination.[8-35] Whether through fear of being accused of discrimination against whites or because of the general curtailment of officer billets, it was not until April 1948 that the Personnel and Administration Division launched a major effort to get more black officers.

In April 1948 General Paul had his Manpower Control Group review the officer strength of seventy-eight black units stationed in the United States. The group uncovered a shortage of seventy-two officers in the seventy-eight units, but it went considerably beyond identifying simple shortages. In estimating the number of black officers needed, the group demonstrated not only how far the Gillem Board policy had committed the Army, but in view of contemporary manpower shortages just how impossible this commitment was of being fulfilled. The manpower group discovered that according to Circular 124, which prescribed more officers for units containing a preponderance of men with low test scores, the seventy-eight units should have 187 additional officers beyond their regular allotment. Also taking into account Circular 124's provision that black officers should command black troops, the group discovered that these units would need another 477 black officer replacements. The group temporized. It recommended that the additional officers be assigned to units in which 70 percent or more of the men were in grades IV and V and without mentioning specific numbers noted that high priority be given to the replacement of white officers with Negroes. Assuming the shortages discovered in the seventy-eight units would be mirrored in the 315 black units overseas as well as other temporary units at home, the group also wanted General Paul to order a comprehensive survey of all black units.[8-36]

Paul complied with the group's request by ordering the major commanders in May to list the number of officers by branch, grade, and specialty needed to fill the vacant spaces in their black units.[8-37] But there was really little need for further surveys because the key to all the group's recommendations—the availability of suitable black officers—was beyond the immediate reach of the Army. General Paul was able to fill the existing vacancies in the seventy-eight continental units by recalling black officers from inactive duty, but the number eligible for recall or available from other sources was limited. As of 31 May 1948, personnel officials could count on only 2,794 black reserve and National Guard officers who could be assigned to extended active duty. This number was far short of current needs; Negroes would have to approximate 4.1 percent (3,000 officers) of the Army's officer corps if all the whites in black units were replaced. As for the other provisions of the Gillem Board, the Organization and Training Division urged restraint, arguing that Circular 124 was not an authorization for officers in excess of organization table ceilings, but rather that the presence of many low-scoring men constituted a basis for requesting more officers.[8-38]

General Paul did not argue the point. Admitting that the 4.1 percent figure was "an objective to be achieved over a period of time," he could do little but instruct the commanders concerned to indicate in future requisitions that they wanted black officers as fillers or replacements in black units. Clearly, as long as the number of black officers remained so low, the provisions of Circular 124 calling for black officers to replace whites or supplement the officer strength of units containing men with low test scores would have to be ignored.

There were other long-range possibilities for procuring more black officers, the most obvious the expansion of the Reserve Officers' Training Corps. As of January 1948 the Army had ROTC units at nine predominantly black colleges and universities with a total enrollment of 3,035 cadets. The Organization and Training Division contemplated adding one more unit during 1948, but after negotiations with officials from Secretary Royall's office, themselves under considerable congressional and public pressure, the division added three more advanced ROTC units, one service and two combat, at predominantly black institutions.[8-39] At the same time some hope existed for increasing the number of black cadets at West Point. The academy had nine black cadets in 1948, including five plebes. General Paul hoped that the graduation of these cadets would stimulate further interest and a corresponding increase in applications from Negroes.[8-40]

It was probably naive to assume that an increase of black cadets from four to nine would stir much interest when other statistics suggested that black officers had a limited future in the service. As Secretary Royall pointed out, even if the total number of black officers could not be quickly increased, the percentage of black officers in the Regular Army could.[8-41]Yet by April 1948 the Army had almost completed the conversion of reservists into regulars, and few black officers had been selected. In June 1945, for example, there were 8 black officers in the Regular Army; by April 1948 they numbered only 41, including 4 West Point graduates and 32 converted reservists.[8-42] The Army had also recently nominated 13 young Negroes, designated Distinguished Military Graduates of the advanced ROTC program, for Regular Army commissions.

During the Regular Army integration program, 927 Negroes and 122,520 whites applied for the Regular Army; the Army and the Air Force awarded commissions to 27,798 white officers (22.7 percent of those applying) and 96 black officers (10.3 percent of the applicants). Preliminary rejections based on efficiency and education ran close to 40 percent of the applicants of both races. The disparity in rejections by race appeared when applicants went before the Selection Board itself; only 18.55 percent of the remaining black applicants were accepted while 39.35 percent of the white applicants were selected for Regular Army commissions.[8-43]

Given statistics like these, it was difficult to stimulate black interest in a career as an Army officer, as General Paul was well aware. He had the distribution of black officers appointed to the Regular Army studied in 1947 to see if it was in consonance with the new racial policy. While most of the arms and services passed muster with the Personnel and Administration Division, Paul felt compelled to remind the Chief of Engineers, whose corps had so far awarded no Regular Army commission to the admittedly limited number of black applicants, that officers were to be accepted in the Regular Army without regard to race. He repeated this warning to the Quartermaster General and the Chief of Transportation; both had accepted black officers for the Regular Army but had selected only the smallest fraction of those applying. Although the black applicants did score slightly below the whites, Paul doubted that integration would lower the standards of quality in these branches, and he wanted every effort made to increase the number of black officers.[8-44]

The Chief of Engineers, quick to defend his record, explained that the race of candidates was difficult to ascertain and had not been considered in the selection process. Nevertheless, he had reexamined all rejected applications and found two from Negroes whose composite scores were acceptable. Both men, however, fell so short of meeting the minimum professional requirements that to appoint either would be to accord preferential treatment denied to hundreds of other underqualified applicants.[8-45] It would appear that bias and prejudice were not the only governing factors in the shortage of black officers, but rather that in some ways at least Circular 124 was making impossible demands on the Army's personnel system.

Discrimination and the Postwar Army

Training black soldiers and trying to provide them with black officers was a practical move demanded by the Army's new race policy. At the same time, often with reluctance and only after considerable pressure had been brought to bear, the Army also began to attack certain practices that discriminated against the black soldier. One was the arbitrary location of training camps after the war. In November 1946, for example, the Army Ground Forces reorganized its training centers for the Army, placing them at six installations: Fort Dix, New Jersey; Fort Bragg, North Carolina; Fort Knox, Kentucky; Fort Jackson, South Carolina; Fort Lewis, Washington, and Fort Ord, California. White enlisted and reenlisted men were sent to the training centers within the geographical limits of the Army area of their enlistment. Because it was impossible for the Army

Ground Forces to maintain separate black training cadres of battalion size at each of the six centers, all Negroes, except those slated for service in the Army Air Forces, were sent to Fort Jackson.[8-46]

The Gillem Board had called for the assignment of Negroes to localities where community attitudes were favorable, and Marcus Ray protested the Ground Forces action. "It is in effect a restatement of policy and ... has implications which will affect adversely the relationship of the Army and our Negro manpower potential.... I am certain that this ruling will have the immediate effect of crystallizing Negro objections to the enlistment of qualified men and also Universal Military Training."[8-47]

Ray reminded Assistant Secretary of War Petersen that the Fort Jackson area had been the scene of many racial disturbances since 1941 and that an increase in the black troop population would only intensify the hostile community attitude. He wanted to substitute Fort Dix and Fort Ord for Fort Jackson. He also had another suggestion: Why not assign black training companies to white battalions, especially in those training centers that drew their populations from northern, eastern, and western communities?

Petersen ignored for the time being Ray's suggestion for composite training groups, but he readily agreed on training black soldiers at more congenial posts, particularly after Ray's views were aired in the black press. Petersen also urged the Deputy Chief of Staff to coordinate staff actions with Ray whenever instructions dealing with race relations in the Army were being prepared.[8-48] At the same time, Secretary of War Patterson assured Walter White of the NAACP, who had also protested sending Negroes to Fort Jackson, that the matter was under study.[8-49] Within a matter of months Negroes entering the Army from civilian life were receiving their training at Fort Dix and Fort Ord.

Turning its back on the overt racism of some southern communities, the Army unwittingly exposed an example of racism in the west. The plan to train Negroes at Fort Ord aroused the combined opposition of the citizens around Monterey Bay, who complained to Senator William F. Knowland that theirs was a tourist area unable to absorb thousands of black trainees "without serious threat of racial conflict." The Army reacted with forthright resistance. Negroes would be trained at Fort Ord, and the Secretary of the Army would be glad to explain the situation and cooperate with the local citizenry.[8-50]

On the recommendation of the civilian aide, the Assistant Secretary of War introduced another racial reform in January 1947 that removed racial designations from overseas travel orders and authorizations issued to dependents and War Department civilian employees.[8-51] The order was strongly opposed by some members of the Army staff and had to be repeated by the Secretary of the Army in 1951.[8-52] Branding racial designations on travel orders a "continuous source of embarrassment" to the Army, Secretary Frank Pace, Jr., sought to include all travel orders in the prohibition, but the Army staff persuaded him it was unwise. While the staff agreed that orders involving travel between reception centers and training organizations need not designate race, it convinced the secretary that to abolish such designations on other orders, including overseas assignment documents, would adversely affect strength and accounting procedures as well as overseas replacement systems.[8-53] The modest reform continued in effect until the question of racial designation became a major issue in the 1960's.

Not all the reforms that followed the Gillem Board's deliberations were so quickly adopted. For in truth the Army was not the monolithic institution so often depicted by its critics, and its racial directives usually came out of compromises between the progressive and traditional factions of the staff. The integration of the national cemeteries, an emotion-laden issue in 1947, amply demonstrated that sharp differences of opinion existed within the department. Although long-standing regulations provided for segregation by rank only, local custom, and in one case—the Long Island National Cemetery—a 1935 order by Secretary of War George H. Dern, dictated racial segregation in most of the cemeteries. The Quartermaster General reviewed the practice in 1946 and recommended a new policy specifically opening new sections of all national cemeteries to eligible citizens of all races. He would leave undisturbed segregated grave sites in the older sections of the cemeteries because integration would "constitute a breach of faith with the next of kin of those now interred."[8-54] As might be expected, General Paul supported the quartermaster suggestion, as did the commander of the Army Ground Forces. The Army Air Forces commander, on the other hand, opposed integrating the cemeteries, as did the Chief of Staff, who on 22 February 1947 rejected the proposal. The existing policy was reconfirmed by the Under Secretary of War three days later, and there the matter rested.[8-55]

Not for long, for civil rights spokesmen and the black press soon protested. The NAACP confessed itself "astonished" at the Army's decision and demanded that Secretary Patterson change a practice that was both "un-American and un-democratic."[8-56] Marcus Ray predicted that continuing agitation would require further Army action, and he reminded Under Secretary

104

Royall that cemeteries under the jurisdiction of the Navy, Veterans Administration, and Department of the Interior had been integrated with considerable publicity. He urged adoption of the Quartermaster General's recommendation.[8-57] That was enough for Secretary Patterson. On 15 April he directed that the new sections of national cemeteries be integrated.[8-58]

It was a hollow victory for the reformers because the traditionalists were able to cling to the secretary's proviso that old sections of the cemeteries be left alone, and the Army continued to gather its dead in segregation and in bitter criticism. Five months after the secretary's directive, the American Legion protested to the Secretary of War over segregation at the Fort Snelling National Cemetery, Minnesota, and in August 1950 the Governor's Interracial Commission of the State of Minnesota carried the matter to the President, calling the policy "a flagrant disregard of human dignity."[8-59] The Army continued to justify segregation as a temporary and limited measure involving the old sections, but a decade after the directive the commander of the Atlanta Depot was still referring to segregation in some cemeteries.[8-60] The controversial practice would drag on into the next decade before the Department of Defense finally ruled that there would be no lines drawn by rank or race in national cemeteries.

An attempt to educate the rank and file in the Army's racial policy met some opposition in the Army staff. At General Paul's request, the Information and Education Division prepared a pamphlet intended to improve race relations through troop indoctrination.[8-61] *Army Talk 170*, published on 1 April 1947, was, like its World War II predecessors, *Command of Negro Troops* and *The Negro Soldier*, progressive for the times. While it stressed the reforms projected in the Army's policy, including eventual integration, it also clearly defended the Army's continued insistence on segregation on the grounds that segregation promoted interracial harmony. The official position of the service was baldly stated. "The Army is not an instrument of social reform. Its interest in matters of race is confined to considerations of its own effectiveness."

Even before publication the pamphlet provoked considerable discussion and soul-searching in the Army staff. The Deputy Chief of Staff, Lt. Gen. Thomas T. Handy, questioned some of the Information and Education Division's claims for black combatants. In the end the matter had to be taken to General Eisenhower for resolution. He ordered publication, reminding local commanders that if necessary they should add further instructions of their own, "in keeping with the local situation" to insure acceptance of the Army's policy. The pamphlet was not to be considered an end in itself, he added, but only one element in a "progressive process toward maximum utilization of manpower in the Army."[8-62]

Segregation in Theory and Practice

Efforts to carry out the policy set forth in Circular 124 reached a high-water mark in mid-1948. By then black troops, for so long limited to a few job categories, could be found in a majority of military occupational fields. The officer corps was open to all without the restrictions of a racial quota, and while a quota for enlisted men still existed all racial distinctions in standards of enlistment were gone. The Army was replacing white officers in black units with Negroes as fast as qualified black replacements became available. And more were qualifying every day. By 30 June 1948 the Army had almost 1,000 black commissioned officers, 5 warrant officers, and 67 nurses serving with over 65,000 enlisted men and women.[8-63]

But here, in the eyes of the Army's critics, was the rub: after three years of racial reform segregation not only remained but had been perfected. No longer would the Army be plagued with the vast all-black divisions that had segregated thousands of Negroes in an admittedly inefficient and often embarrassing manner. Instead, Negroes would be segregated in more easily managed hundreds. By limiting integration to the battalion level (the lowest self-sustaining unit in the Army system), the Army could guarantee the separation of the races in eating, sleeping, and general social matters and still hope to escape some of the obvious discrimination of separate units by making the black battalions organic elements of larger white units. The Army's scheme did not work. Schooling and specialty occupations aside, segregation quite obviously remained the essential fact of military life and social intercourse for the majority of black soldiers, and all the evidence of reasonable and genuine reform that came about under the Gillem Board policy went aglimmering. The Army was in for some rough years with its critics.

But why were the Army's senior officers, experienced leaders at the pinnacle of their careers and dedicated to the well-being of the institution they served, so reluctant to part with segregation? Why did they cling to an institution abandoned by the Navy and the Air Force,[8-64] the target of the civil rights movement and its allies in Congress, and by any reasonable judgment so costly in terms of efficient organization? The answers lie in the reasoned defense of their position developed by these men during the long controversy over the use of black troops and so often presented in public statements and documents.[8-65] Arguments for continued segregation fell into four general categories.

First, segregation was necessary to preserve the internal stability of the Army. Prejudice was a condition of American society, General of the Army Dwight D. Eisenhower told a Senate committee in 1948, and the Army "is merely one of the mirrors that holds up to our faces the United States of America." Since society separated the races, it followed that if the Army allowed black and white soldiers to live and socialize together it ran the very real risk of riots and racial disturbances which could disrupt its vital functions. Remembering the contribution of black platoons to the war in Europe, General Eisenhower, for his part, was willing to accept the risk and integrate the races by platoons, believing that the social problems "can be handled," particularly on the large posts. Nevertheless he made no move toward integrating by platoons while he was Chief of Staff. Later he explained that

the possibility of applying this lesson [World War II integration of Negro platoons] to the peacetime Army came up again and again. Objection involved primarily the social side of the soldier's life. It was argued that through integration we would get into all kinds of difficulty in staging soldiers' dances and other social events. At that time we were primarily occupied in responding to America's determination "to get the soldiers home"—so, as I recall, little progress toward integration was made during that period.[8-66]

INSPECTION BY THE CHIEF OF STAFF.
General Dwight D. Eisenhower talks with a soldier of the 25th Combat Team Motor Pool during a tour of Fort Benning, Georgia, 1947.

"Liquor and women," Lt. Gen. John C. H. Lee pronounced, were the major ingredients of racial turmoil in the Army. Although General Lee had been a prime mover in the wartime integration of combat platoons, he wanted the Army to avoid social integration because of the disturbances he believed would attend it. As General Omar N. Bradley saw it, the Army could integrate its training programs but not the soldier's social life. Hope of progress would be destroyed if integration was pushed too fast. Bradley summed up his postwar attitude very simply: "I said let's go easy—as fast as we can."

Second, segregation was an efficient way to isolate the poorly educated and undertrained black soldier, especially one with a combat occupational specialty. To integrate Negroes into white combat units, already dangerously understrength, would threaten the Army's fighting ability. When he was Chief of Staff, Eisenhower thought many of the problems associated with black soldiers, problems of morale, health, and discipline, were problems of education, and that the Negro was capable of change. "I believe," he said, "that a Negro can improve his standing and his social standing and his respect for certain of the standards that we observe, just as well as we can." Lt. Gen. Wade H. Haislip, the Deputy Chief of Staff for Administration, concluded that the Army's racial mission was education. All that Circular 124 meant, he explained, "was that we had to begin educating the Negro soldiers so they could be mixed sometime in the future." Bradley observed in agreement that "as you begin to get better educated Negroes in the service," there is "more reason to integrate." The Army was pledged to accept Negroes and to give them a wide choice of assignment, but until their education and training improved they had to be isolated.

Third, segregation was the only way to provide equal treatment and opportunity for black troops. Defending this paternalistic argument, Eisenhower told the Senate:

In general, the Negro is less well educated ... and if you make a complete amalgamation, what you are going to have is in every company the Negro is going to be relegated to the minor jobs, and he is never going to get his promotion to such grades as technical sergeant, master sergeant, and so on, because the competition is too tough. If, on the other hand, he is in smaller units of his own, he can go up to that rate, and I believe he is entitled to the chance to show his own wares.

Fourth, segregation was necessary because segments of American society with powerful representatives in Congress were violently opposed to mixing the races. Bradley explained that integration was part of social evolution, and he was afraid that the Army might move too fast for certain sections of the country. "I thought in 1948 that they were ready in the North," he added, "but not in the South." The south "learned over the years that mixing the races was a vast problem." Bradley continued, "so any change in the Army would be a big step in the South." General Haislip reasoned, you "just can't do it all of a sudden." As for the influence of those opposed to maintaining the Army's social *status quo*, Haislip, who was the Vice Chief of Staff during part of the Gillem Board period, recalled that "everybody was floundering around, trying to find the right thing to do. I didn't lose any sleep over it [charges of discrimination]." General Eisenhower, as he did so often during his career, accurately distilled the thinking of his associates:

I believe that the human race may finally grow up to the point where it [race relations] will not be a problem. It [the race problem] will disappear through education, through mutual respect,

106

and so on. But I do believe that if we attempt merely by passing a lot of laws to force someone to like someone else, we are just going to get into trouble. On the other hand, I do not by any means hold out for this extreme segregation as I said when I first joined the Army 38 years ago.

These arguments might be specious, as a White House committee would later demonstrate, but they were not necessarily guileful, for they were the heartfelt opinions of many of the Army's leaders, opinions shared by officials of the other services. These men were probably blind to the racism implicit in their policies, a racism nurtured by military tradition. Education and environment had fostered in these career officers a reverence for tradition. Why should the Army, these traditionalists might ask, abandon its black units, some with histories stretching back almost a century? Why should the ordered social life of the Army post, for so long a mirror of the segregated society of most civilian communities, be so uncomfortably changed? The fact that integration had never really been tried before made it fraught with peril, and all the forces of military tradition conspired to support the old ways.

What had gone unnoticed by Army planners was the subtle change in the attitude of the white enlisted man toward integration. Opinion surveys were rare in an institution dedicated to the concept of military discipline, but nevertheless in the five years following the war several surveys were made of the racial views of white troops (the views of black soldiers were ignored, probably on the assumption that all Negroes favored integration). In 1946, just as the Gillem Board policy was being enunciated, the Army staff found enlisted men in substantial agreement on segregation. Although most of those surveyed supported the expanded use of Negroes in the Army, an overwhelming majority voted for the principle of having racially separate working and living arrangements. Yet the pollsters found much less opposition to integration when they put their questions on a personal basis—"How do *you* feel about...?" Only southerners as a group registered a clear majority for segregated working conditions. The survey also revealed another encouraging portent: most of the opposition to integration existed among older and less educated men.[8-67]

GENERAL DAVIS

Three years later the Secretary of Defense sponsored another survey of enlisted opinion on segregation. This time less than a third of those questioned were opposed to integrated working conditions and some 40 percent were not "definitely opposed" to complete integration of both working and living arrangements. Again men from all areas tended to endorse integration as their educational level rose; opposition, on the other hand, centered in 1949 among the chronic complainers and those who had never worked with Negroes.[8-68]

In discussing prejudice and discrimination it is necessary to compare the Army with the rest of American society. Examining the question of race relations in the Army runs the risk of distorting the importance given the subject by the nation as a whole in the postwar period. While resistance to segregation was undoubtedly growing in the black community and among an increasing number of progressives in the white community, there was as yet no widespread awareness of the problem and certainly no concerted public effort to end it. This lack of perception might be particularly justified in the case of Army officers, for few of them had any experience with black soldiers and most undoubtedly were not given to wide reading and reflecting on the subject of race relations. Moreover, the realities of military life tended to insulate Army officers from the main currents of American society. Frequently transferred and therefore without roots in the civilian community, isolated for years at a time in overseas assignments, their social life often centered in the military garrison, officers might well have been less aware of racial discrimination.

Perhaps because of the insulation imposed on officers by their duties, the Army's leaders were achieving reforms far beyond those accepted elsewhere in American society. Few national organizations and industries could match the Army in 1948 for the number of Negroes employed, the breadth of responsibility given them, and the variety of their training and occupations. Looked at in this light, the Army of 1948 and the men who led it could with considerable justification be classed as a progressive force in the fight for racial justice.

Segregation: An Assessment

The gap between the Army's stated goal of integration and its continuing practices had grown so noticeable in 1948, a presidential election year, that most civil rights spokesmen and their allies in the press had become disillusioned with Army reforms. Benjamin O. Davis, still the Army's senior black officer and still after eight years a brigadier general, called the Army staff's attention to the shift in attitude. Most had greeted publication of Circular 124 as "the dawn of a new day for the colored soldier"—General Davis's words—and looked forward to the gradual eradication of segregation. But Army practices in subsequent months had brought disappointment, he warned the under secretary, and the black press had become "restless and

107

impatient." He wanted the Army staff to give "definite expression of the desire of the Department of National Defense for the elimination of all forms of discrimination-segregation from the Armed Services."[8-69] The suggestion was disapproved. General Paul explained that the Army could not make such a policy statement since Circular 124 permitted segregated units and a quota that by its nature discriminated at least in terms of numbers of Negroes assigned.[8-70]

In February 1948 the Chief of Information tried to counter criticism by asking personnel and administrative officials to collect favorable opinions from prominent civilians, "particularly Negroes and sociologists." But this antidote to public criticism failed because, as the deputy personnel director had to admit, "the Division does not have knowledge of any expressed favorable opinion either of individuals or organizations, reference our Negro policy."[8-71]

A constant concern because it marred the Army's public image, segregation also had a profound effect on the performance and well-being of the black soldier. This effect was difficult to measure but nevertheless real and has been the subject of considerable study by social scientists.[8-72] Their opinions are obviously open to debate, and in fact most of them were not fully formulated during the period under discussion. Yet their conclusions, based on modern sociological techniques, clearly reveal the pain and turmoil suffered by black soldiers because of racial separation. Rarely did the Army staff bother to delve into these matters in the years before Korea, although the facts on which the scientists based their conclusions were collected by the War Department itself. This indifference is the more curious because the Army had always been aware of what the War Department Policies and Programs Review Board called in 1947 "that intangible aspect of military life called prestige and spirit."[8-73]

Burdened with the task of shoring up its racial policy, the Army staff failed to concern itself with the effect of segregation. Yet by ignoring segregation the staff overlooked the primary cause of its racial problems and condemned the Army to their continuation. It need not have been, because as originally conceived, the Gillem Board policy provided, in the words of the Assistant Secretary of War, for "progressive experimentation" leading to "effective manpower utilization without regard to race or color."[8-74] This reasonable approach to a complex social issue was recognized as such by the War Department and by many black spokesmen. But the Gillem Board's original goal was soon abandoned, and in the "interest of National Defense," according to Secretary Royall, integration was postponed for the indefinite future.[8-75] Extension of individual integration below the company level was forbidden, and the lessons learned at the Kitzingen Training Center were never applied elsewhere; in short, progressive experimentation was abandoned.

The Gillem Board era began with Secretary Patterson accepting the theory of racially separate but equal service as an anodyne for temporary segregation; it ended with Secretary Royall embracing a permanent separate but equal system as a shield to protect the racial *status quo*. While Patterson and his assistants accepted restriction on the number of Negroes and their assignment to segregated jobs and facilities as a temporary expedient, military subordinates used the Gillem Board's reforms as a way to make more efficient a segregation policy that neither they nor, they believed, society in general was willing to change. Thus, despite some real progress on the periphery of its racial problem, the Army would have to face the enemy in Korea with an inefficient organization of its men.

The Army's postwar policy was based on a false premise. The Gillem Board decided that since Negroes had fought poorly in segregated divisions in two world wars, they might fight better in smaller segregated organizations within larger white units. Few officers really believed this, for it was commonly accepted throughout the Army that Negroes generally made poor combat soldiers. It followed then that the size of a unit was immaterial, and indeed, given the manpower that the Army received from reenlistments and Selective Service, any black unit, no matter its size, would almost assuredly be an inefficient, spiritless group of predominately Class IV and V men. For in addition to its educational limitations, the typical black unit suffered a further handicap in the vital matter of motivation. The Gillem Board disregarded this fact, but it was rarely overlooked by the black soldier: he was called upon to serve as a second-class soldier to defend what he often regarded as his second-class citizenship. In place of unsatisfactory black divisions, Circular 124 made the Army substitute three unsatisfactorily mixed divisions whose black elements were of questionable efficiency and a focus of complaint among civil rights advocates. Commanders at all levels faced a dilemma implicit in the existence of white and black armies side by side. Overwhelmed by regulations and policies that tried to preserve the fiction of separate but equal opportunity, these officers wasted their time and energy and, most often in the case of black officers, lost their self-confidence.

In calling for the integration of small black units rather than individuals, the Gillem Board obviously had in mind the remarkably effective black platoons in Europe in the last months of

108

World War II. But even this type of organization was impossible in the postwar Army because it demanded a degree of integration that key commanders, especially the major Army component commanders, were unwilling to accept.

These real problems were intensified by the normal human failings of prejudice, vested interest, well-meaning ignorance, conditioned upbringing, shortsightedness, preoccupation with other matters, and simple reluctance to change. The old ways were comfortable, and the new untried, frightening in their implications and demanding special effort. Nowhere was there enthusiasm for the positive measures needed to implement the Gillem Board's recommendations leading to integration. This unwillingness to act positively was particularly noticeable in the Organization and Training Division, in the Army Ground Forces, and even to some extent in the Personnel and Administration Division itself.

The situation might have improved had the Gillem Board been able or willing to spell out intermediate goals. For the ultimate objective of using black soldiers like white soldiers as individuals was inconceivable and meaningless or radical and frightening to many in the Army. Interim goals might have provided impetus for gradual change and precluded the virtual inertia that gripped the Army staff. But at best Circular 124 served as a stopgap measure, allowing the Army to postpone for a few more years any substantial change in race policy. This postponement cost the service untold time and effort devising and defending a system increasingly under attack from the black community and, significantly, from that community's growing allies in the administration.

CHAPTER 9
The Postwar Navy

That Army concerns and problems dominated the discussions of race relations in the armed forces in the postwar years is understandable since the Army had the largest number of Negroes and the most widely publicized segregation policy of all the services. At the same time the Army bore, unfairly, the brunt of public criticism for all the services' race problems. The Navy, committed to a policy of integration, but with relatively few Negroes in its integrated general service or in the ranks of the segregated Marine Corps and the new Air Force, its racial policy still fluid, merely attracted less attention and so escaped many of the charges hurled at the Army by civil rights advocates both in and out of the federal government. But however different or unformed their racial policies, all the services for the most part segregated Negroes in practice and all were open to charges of discrimination.

Although the services developed different racial policies out of their separate circumstances, all three were reacting to the same set of social forces and all three suffered from race prejudice. They also faced in common a growing indifference to military careers on the part of talented young Negroes who in any case would have to compete with an aging but persistent group of less talented black professionals for a limited number of jobs. Of great importance was the fact that the racial practices of the armed forces were a product of the individual service's military traditions. Countless incidents support the contention that service traditions were a transcendent factor in military decisions. Marx Leva, Forrestal's assistant, told the story of a Forrestal subordinate who complained that some admirals were still opposed to naval aviation, to which Forrestal replied that he knew some admirals who still opposed steam engines.[9-1] Forrestal's humorous exaggeration underscored the tenacity of traditional attitudes in the Navy. Although self-interest could never be discounted as a motive, tradition also figured prominently, for example, in the controversy between proponents of the battleship and proponents of the aircraft carrier. Certainly the influence of tradition could be discerned in the antipathy of Navy officials toward racial change.[9-2]

The Army also had its problems with tradition. It endured tremendous inner conflict before it decided to drop the cavalry in favor of mechanized and armored units. Nor did the resistance to armor die quickly. Former Chief of Staff Peyton C. March reported that a previous Chief of Cavalry told him in 1950 that the Army had betrayed the horse.[9-3] President Roosevelt was also a witness to how military tradition frustrated attempts to change policy. He picked his beloved Navy to make the point: "To change anything in the Na-a-vy is like punching a feather bed. You punch it with your right and you punch it with your left until you are finally exhausted, and then you find the damn bed just as it was before you started punching."[9-4] Many senior officers resisted equal treatment and opportunity simply because of their traditional belief that Negroes needed special treatment and any basic change in their status was fraught with danger.[9-5]

Still, tradition could work two ways, and in the case of the Navy, at least, the postwar decision to liberalize racial practices can be traced in part to its sense of tradition. When James Forrestal started to integrate the general service in 1944, his appeals to his senior military colleagues, the President, and the public were always couched in terms of military efficiency. But if military efficiency made the new policy announced in February 1946 inevitable, military tradition made partial integration acceptable. Black sailors had served in significant numbers in an integrated general service during the nation's first century and a half, and those in the World War II period who spoke of a traditional Navy ban against Negroes were just as wrong as those who spoke of a traditional ban on liquor. The same abstemious secretary who completely outlawed alcohol on warships in 1914 initiated the short-lived restrictions on the service of Negroes in the Navy.[9-6] Both limited integration and liquor were old traditions in the American Navy, and the influence of military tradition made integration of the general service relatively simple.

Forrestal was convinced that in order to succeed racial reform must first be accepted by the men already in uniform; integration, if quietly and gradually put into effect, would soon demonstrate its efficiency and make the change acceptable to all members of the service. Quiet gradualism became the hallmark of his effort. In August 1945 the Navy had some 165,000 Negroes, almost 5.5 percent of its total strength. Sixty-four of them, including six women, were commissioned officers.[9-7] Presumably, these men and women would be the first to enjoy the fruits of the new integration order. Their number could also be expected to increase because, as Secretary Forrestal reported in August 1946, the only quotas on enlistment were those determined by the needs of the Navy and the limitation of funds.[9-8] Even as he spoke, at least some black sailors were being trained in almost all naval ratings and were serving throughout the fleet, on planes and in submarines, working and living with whites. The signs pointed to a new day for Negroes in the Navy.

SHORE LEAVE IN KOREA.
Men of the USS Topeka land in Inch'on, 1948.

But during the chaotic months of demobilization a different picture began to emerge. Although Negroes continued to number about 5 percent of the Navy's enlisted strength, their position altered radically. The average strength figures for 1946 showed 3,300 Negroes, 16 percent of the total black strength, serving in the integrated general service while 17,300, or 84 percent, were classified as stewards. By mid-1948 the outlook was somewhat brighter, but still on the average only 38 percent of the Negroes in the Navy held jobs in the general service while 62 percent remained in the nonwhite Steward's Branch. At this time only three black officers remained on active duty. Again, what Navy officials saw as military efficiency helps explain this postwar retreat. Because of its rapidly sinking manpower needs, the Navy could afford to set higher enlistment standards than the Army, and the fewer available spaces in the general service went overwhelmingly to the many more eligible whites who applied. Only in the Steward's Branch, with its separate quotas and lower enlistment standards, did the Navy find a place for the many black enlistees as well as the thousands of stewards ready and willing to reenlist for peacetime service.

If efficiency explains why the Navy's general service remained disproportionately white, tradition explains how segregation and racial exclusion could coexist with integration in an organization that had so recently announced a progressive racial policy. Along with its tradition of an integrated general service, the Navy had a tradition of a white officer corps. It was natural for the Navy to exclude black officers from the Regular Navy, Secretary John L. Sullivan said later, just as it was common to place Negroes in mess jobs.[9-9] A *modus vivendi* could be seen emerging from the twin dictates of efficiency and tradition: integrate a few thousand black sailors throughout the general service in fulfillment of the letter of the Bureau of Naval Personnel circular; as for the nonwhite Steward's Branch and the lack of black officers, these conditions were ordinary and socially comfortable. Since most Navy leaders agreed that the new policy was fair and practical, no further changes seemed necessary in the absence of a pressing military need or a demand from the White House or Congress.

To black publicists and other advocates of civil rights, the Navy's postwar manpower statistics were self-explanatory: the Navy was discriminating against the Negro. Time and again the Navy responded to this charge, echoing Secretary Forrestal's contention that the Navy had no racial quotas and that all restrictions on the employment of black sailors had been lifted. As if suggesting that all racial distinctions had been abandoned, personnel officials discontinued publishing racial statistics and abolished the Special Programs Unit.[9-10] Cynics might have ascribed other motives for these decisions, but the civil rights forces apparently never bothered. For the most part they left the Navy's apologists to struggle with the increasingly difficult task of explaining why the placement of Negroes deviated so markedly from assignment for whites.

The Navy's difficulty in this regard stemmed from the fact that the demobilization program under which it geared down from a 3.4 million-man service to a peacetime force of less than half a million was quite straightforward and simple. Consequently, the latest state of the Negro in the Navy was readily apparent to the black serviceman and to the public. The key to service in the postwar Navy was acceptance into the Regular Navy. The wartime Navy had been composed overwhelmingly of reservists and inductees, and shortly after V-J day the Navy announced plans for the orderly separation of all reservists by September 1946. In April 1946 it discontinued volunteer enlistment in the Naval Reserve for immediate active duty, and in May it issued its last call for draftees through Selective Service.[9-11]

At the same time the Bureau of Naval Personnel launched a vigorous program to induce reservists to switch to the Regular Navy. In October 1945 it opened all petty officer ratings in the Regular Navy to such transfers and offered reservists special inducements for changeover in the form of ratings, allowance extras, and, temporarily, short-term enlistments. So successful was the program that by July 1947 the strength of the Regular Navy had climbed to 488,712, only a few thousand short of the postwar authorization. The Navy ended its changeover program in early 1947.[9-12] While it lasted, black reservists and inductees shared in the program, although the chief of the personnel recruiting division found it necessary to amplify the recruiting instructions to make this point clear.[9-13] The Regular Navy included 7,066 enlisted Negroes on V-J day, 2.1 percent of the total enlisted strength. This figure nearly tripled in the next year to 20,610, although the percentage of Negroes only doubled.[9-14]

The Steward's Branch

The major concern of the civil rights groups was not so much the number of Negroes in the Regular Navy, although this remained far below the proportion of Negroes in the civilian population, but that the majority of Negroes were being accepted for duty in the nonwhite Steward's Branch. More than 97 percent of all black sailors in the Regular Navy in December 1945 were in this branch. The ratio improved somewhat in the next six months when 3,000 black general service personnel (out of a wartime high of 90,000) transferred into the Regular Navy while more than 10,000 black reservists and draftees joined the 7,000 regulars already in the Steward's Branch.[9-15] The statistical low point in terms of the ratio of Negroes in the postwar regular general service and the Steward's Branch occurred in fiscal year 1947 when only 19.21 percent of the Navy's regular black personnel were assigned outside the Steward's Branch.[9-16] In short, more than eight out of every ten Negroes in the Navy trained and worked separately from white sailors, performing menial tasks and led by noncommissioned officers denied the perquisites of rank.

The Navy itself had reason to be concerned. The Steward's Branch created efficiency problems and was a constant source of embarrassment to the service's public image. Because of its low standards, the branch attracted thousands of poorly educated and underprivileged individuals who had a high rate of venereal disease but were engaged in preparing and serving food. Leaders within the branch itself, although selected on the basis of recommendations from superiors, examinations, and seniority, were often poor performers. Relations between the individual steward and the outfit to which he was assigned were often marked by personal conflicts and other difficulties. Consequently, while stewards eagerly joined the branch in the Regular Navy, the incidence of disciplinary problems among them was high. The branch naturally earned the opprobrium of civil rights groups, who were sensitive not only to the discrimination of a separate branch for minorities but also to the unfavorable image these men created of Negroes in the service.[9-17]

MESS ATTENDANTS, USS BUSHNELL, 1918

The Navy had a ready defense for its management of the branch. Its spokesmen frequently explained that it performed an essential function, especially at sea. Since this function was limited in scope, they added, the Navy was able to reduce the standards for the branch, thus opening opportunities for many men otherwise ineligible to join the service. In order to offer a chance for advancement the Navy had to create a separate recruiting and training system for stewards. This separation in turn explained the steward's usual failure to transfer to branches in the regular command channels. Since there were no minimum standards for the branch, it followed that most of its noncommissioned officers remained unqualified to exercise military command over personnel other than their branch subordinates. Lack of command responsibility was also present in a number of other branches not directly concerned with the operation of ships. It was not the result of race prejudice, therefore, but of standards for enlistment and types of duties performed. Nor was the steward's frequent physical separation based on race; berthing was arranged by department and function aboard large vessels. Separation did not exist on smaller ships. Messmen were usually berthed with other men of the supply department, including bakers and storekeepers. Chief stewards, however, as Under Secretary Kimball later explained, had not been required to meet the military qualifications for chief petty officer, and therefore it was "considered improper that they should be accorded the same messing, berthing, club facilities, and other privileges reserved for the highest enlisted grade of the Navy."[9-18] Stewards of the lower ranks received the same chance for advancement as members of other enlisted branches, but to grant them command responsibility would necessitate raising qualifications for the whole branch, thus eliminating many career stewards and extending steward training to include purely military subjects.[9-19]

MESS ATTENDANTS, USS WISCONSIN, 1953

There was truth in these assertions. Stewards had taken advantage of relaxed regulations, flocking into the Regular Navy during the first months of the changeover program. Many did so because they had many years invested in a naval career. Some may have wanted the training and experience to be gained from messman's service. In fact, some stewards enjoyed rewarding careers in restaurant, club, and hotel work after retirement. More surprising, considering the numerous complaints about the branch from civil rights groups, the Steward's Branch consistently reported the highest reenlistment rate in the Navy. Understandably, the Navy constantly reiterated these statistics. Actually, the stewards themselves were a major stumbling block to reform of the branch. Few of the senior men aspired to other ratings; many were reluctant to relinquish what they saw as the advantages of the messman's life. Whatever its drawbacks, messman's duty proved to be a popular assignment.[9-20]

The Navy's defense was logical, but not too convincing. Technically the Steward's Branch was open to all, but in practice it remained strictly nonwhite. Civil rights activists could point to the fact that there were six times as many illiterate whites as Negroes in the wartime Navy, yet none of these whites were ever assigned to the Steward's Branch and none transferred to that branch of the Regular Navy after the war.[9-21] Moreover, shortly after the war the Bureau of Naval Personnel predicted a 7,577-man shortage in the Steward's Branch, but the Navy made no attempt to fill the places with white sailors. Instead, it opened the branch to Filipinos and Guamanians, recruiting 3,500 of the islanders before the program was stopped on 4 July 1946, the date of Philippine independence. Some Navy recruiters found other ways to fill steward quotas. The Urban League and others reported cases in which black volunteers were rejected by recruiters for any assignment but steward duty.[9-22] Nor did civil rights spokesmen appreciate the distinction in petty officer rank the Navy made between the steward and other sailors; they continued to interpret it as part and parcel of the "injustices, lack of respect and the disregard for the privileges accorded rated men in other branches of the service."[9-23] They also resented the paternalism implicit in the secretary's assurances that messman's duty was a haven for men unable to compete.

Some individuals in the department were aware of this resentment in the black community and pushed for reform in the Steward's Branch. The Assistant Secretary of the Navy for Air, John Nicholas Brown, wanted more publicity given both in and outside the service to the fact that the branch was not restricted to any one race and, conversely, that Negroes were welcome in the general service.[9-24] In view of the strong tradition of racial separateness in the stewards rating, such publicity might be considered sheer sophistry, but no more so than the suggestion made by a senior personnel official that the Commissary Branch and Steward's Branch be combined to achieve a racially balanced specialty.[9-25] Lester Granger, now outside the official Navy family but still intimately concerned with the department's racial affairs, also pleaded for a merger of the commissary and steward functions. He reasoned that, since members of the Commissary Branch could advance to true petty officer rating, such a merger would provide a new avenue of advancement for stewards.

But more to the point Granger also pushed for reform in the standards of the Steward's Branch. He recognized that educational and other requirements had been lowered for stewards, but, he told Forrestal's successor, Secretary John L. Sullivan, there was little wisdom in "compounding past error." He also pointed out that not all messmen were in the lower intelligence classifications and recommended that the higher scoring men be replaced with low-scoring whites.[9-26]

From within the Navy itself Lt. Dennis D. Nelson, one of the first twelve Negroes commissioned and still on active duty, added his voice to the demand for reform of the Steward's Branch. An analogy may be drawn between the Navy career of Nelson and that of the legendary Christopher Sargent. Lacking Sargent's advantages of wealth and family connection, Nelson nevertheless became a familiar of Secretary Sullivan's and, though not primarily assigned to the task, made equal opportunity his preeminent concern. A highly visible member of the Navy's racial minority in Washington, he made himself its spokesman, pressing senior officials to bring the department's manpower practices closer to its stated policy. Once again the Navy experienced the curious phenomenon of a lieutenant firing off memos and letters to senior admirals and buttonholing the Secretary of the Navy.[9-27]

112

Nelson had a host of suggestions for the Steward's Branch: eliminate the branch as a racially separate division of labor in the Navy, provide permanent officer supervision for all steward units, develop capable noncommissioned officers in the branch with privileges and responsibilities similar to those of other petty officers, indoctrinate all personnel in the ramifications of the Navy's stated integration policy, and create a committee to work out the details of these changes. On several occasions Nelson tried to show his superiors how nuances in their own behavior toward the stewards reinforced, perhaps as much as separate service itself, the image of discrimination. He recommended that the steward's uniform be changed, eliminating the white jacket and giving the steward a regular seaman's look. He also suggested that petty officer uniforms for stewards be regularized. At one poignant moment this lonely officer took on the whole service, trying to change singlehandedly a thoughtless habit that demeaned both blacks and whites. He admonished the service: "refrain from the use of 'Boy' in addressing Stewards. This has been a constant practice in the Service and is most objectionable, is in bad taste, shows undue familiarity and pins a badge of inferiority, adding little to the dignity and pride of adults."[9-28]

In summing up these recommendations for the Secretary of the Navy in January 1949, Nelson reminded Sullivan that only 37 percent of the Navy's Negroes were in the general service, in contrast to 72 percent of the Negroes in the Marine Corps. He warned that this imbalance perturbed the members of the recently convened National Defense Conference on Negro Affairs and predicted it would interest those involved in the forthcoming presidential inquiry on equality in the armed forces.[9-29]

Despite its continued defense of the *status quo* in the Steward's Branch, the Bureau of Naval Personnel was not insensitive to criticism. To protect Negroes from overzealous recruiters for the branch, the bureau had announced in October 1945 that any Negro in the general service desiring transfer to the Steward's Branch had to make his request in writing.[9-30] In mid-1946 it closed the branch to first enlistment, thereby abolishing possible abuses in the recruiting system.[9-31] Later in the year the bureau tried to upgrade the quality of the branch by instituting a new and more rigorous training course for second-and third-class stewards and cooks at Bainbridge, Maryland. Finally, in June 1947 it removed from its personnel manual all remaining mention of restrictions on the transfer of messmen to the general service.[9-32] These changes were important, but they failed to attack racial separation, the major problem of the branch. Thus the controversy over messmen, in which tradition, prejudice, and necessity contended, went on, and the Steward's Branch, a symbol of discrimination in the Navy, remained to trouble both the service and the civil rights groups for some time.

Black Officers

COMMANDER NELSON

The Navy had a racial problem of more immediate concern to men like Lieutenant Nelson, one of three black officers remaining on active duty. These were the survivers of a most exclusive group that had begun its existence with much hope. In the months following graduation of the first twelve black officers and one warrant officer in March 1944, scores of Negroes had passed through the Navy's training school. By the end of the war the V-12 program had thirty-six black candidates, with three others attending the Supply Corps School at Harvard. The number of black officers had grown at an agonizingly slow rate, although in June 1944 the Secretary of the Navy approved a personnel bureau request that in effect removed any numerical quotas for black officers. Unfortunately, black officers were still limited to filling "needs as they appeared," and the need for black officers was curtailed by the restricted range of activities open to them in the segregated wartime service. Further, most nominees for commissions were selected from the ranks and depended on the sponsorship of their commanding officer who might not be able to spare a competent enlisted man who deserved promotion. Putting the matter in the best possible light, one Navy historian blamed the dearth of black officers on bureaucratic inertia.[9-33]

Despite procurement failures and within the limitations of general segregation policy, the Navy treated black officers with scrupulous fairness during the war. The Bureau of Naval Personnel insisted they be given the privileges of rank in wardroom and ashore, thus crushing an attempt by authorities at Great Lakes to underwrite a tacit ban on the use of the officers' club by Negroes. In fact, integration proved to be more the rule than the exception in training black officers. The small number of black candidates made segregated classes impractical, and after graduation of the first group of black officers at Great Lakes, Negroes were accepted in all officer candidate classes. As part of this change, the Special Programs Unit successfully integrated the Navy's officer candidate school in the posh hotels of still-segregated Miami Beach.

The officers graduated into a number of assignments. Some saw duty aboard district and yard craft, others at departmental headquarters in Washington. A few served in recruit training assignments at Great Lakes and Hampton Institute, but the majority went overseas to work in logistical and advanced base companies, the stevedore-type outfits composed exclusively of Negroes. Nelson, for example, was sent to the Marshall Islands where he was assigned to a logistic support company composed of some three hundred black sailors and noncommissioned officers with a racially mixed group of officers. Black staff officers, engineers, doctors, dentists, and chaplains were also attached to these units, where they had limited responsibilities and little chance for advancement.[9-34]

Exceptions to the assignment rule increased during the last months of the war. The Special Programs Unit had concluded that restricting black officers to district craft and shore billets might further encourage the tendency to build an inshore black Navy, and the Bureau of Naval Personnel began assigning black officers to seagoing vessels when they completed their sea duty training. By July 1945 several were serving in the fleet. To avoid embarrassment, the Chief of Naval Personnel made it a practice to alert the commanding officers of a ship about to receive a black officer so that he might indoctrinate his officers. As his assistant, Rear Adm. William M. Fechteler, explained to one such commander, "if such officers are accorded the proper respect and are required to discharge the duties commensurate with their rank they should be equally competent to white officers of similar experience."[9-35]

Fechteler's prediction proved accurate. By V-J day, the Navy's black officers, both line and staff, were serving competently in many occupations. The bureau reported that the "personnel relationship aspect" of their introduction into the service had worked well. Black officers with white petty officers and enlisted men under them handled their command responsibilities without difficulty, and in general bureau reports and field inspections noted considerable satisfaction with their performance.[9-36] But despite this satisfactory record, only three black officers remained on active duty in 1946. The promise engendered by the Navy's treatment of its black officers in the closing months of the war had not been fulfilled during the demobilization period that followed, and what had been to the civil rights movement a brightening situation rapidly became an intolerable one.

There were several reasons for the rapid demobilization of black officers. Some shared the popular desire of reserve officers to return to civilian life. Among them were mature men with substantial academic achievements and valuable technical experience. Many resented in particular their assignment to all-black labor units, and wanted to resume their civilian careers.[9-37] But a number of black officers, along with over 29,000 white reservists, did seek commissions in the Regular Navy.[9-38] Yet not one Negro was granted a regular commission in the first eighteen months after the war. Lester Granger was especially upset by these statistics, and in July 1946 he personally took up the case of two black candidates with Secretary Forrestal.[9-39]

The Bureau of Naval Personnel offered what it considered a reasonable explanation. As a group, black reserve officers were considerably overage for their rank and were thus at a severe disadvantage in the fierce competition for regular commissions. The average age of the first class of black officers was over thirty-one years. All had been commissioned ensigns on 17 March 1944, and all had received one promotion to lieutenant, junior grade, by the end of the war. When age and rank did coincide, black reservists were considered for transfer. For example, on 15 March 1947 Ens. John Lee, a former V-12 graduate assigned as gunnery officer aboard a fleet auxiliary craft, received a regular commission, and on 6 January 1948 Lt. (jg.) Edith DeVoe, one of the four black nurses commissioned in March 1945, was transferred into the Regular Navy. The following October Ens. Jessie Brown was commissioned and assigned to duty as the first black Navy pilot.

In a sense, the black officers had the cards stacked against them. As Nelson later explained, the bureau did not extend to its black line officers the same consideration given other reservists. While the first twelve black officers were given unrestricted line officer training, the bureau assigned them to restricted line positions, an added handicap when it came to promotions and retention in the postwar Navy. All were commissioned ensigns, although the bureau usually granted rank according to the candidate's age, a practice followed when it commissioned its first black staff officers, one of whom became a full lieutenant and the rest lieutenants, junior grade. As an overage reservist himself, Nelson remained on active duty after the war through the personal intervention of Secretary Forrestal. His tour in the Navy's public relations office was repeatedly extended until finally on 1 January 1950, thanks to Secretary Sullivan, he received a regular commission.[9-40]

Prospects for an increase in black officers were dim. With rare exception the Navy's officers came from the academy at Annapolis, the officer candidate program, or the Naval Reserve Officers' Training Corps (NROTC) program. Ens. Wesley A. Brown would graduate in the academy's class of 1949, the sixth Negro to attend and the first to graduate in the academy's 104-year history. Only five other Negroes were enrolled in the academy's student body in 1949, and there was little indication that this number would rapidly increase. For the most part the situation was beyond the control of the Bureau of Naval Personnel. Competition was keen for acceptance at Annapolis. The American Civil Liberties Union later asserted that the exclusion of Negroes from many of the private prep schools, which so often produced successful academy applicants, helped explain why there were so few Negroes at the academy.[9-41]

Nor were many black officers forthcoming from the Navy's two other sources. Officer candidate schools, severely reduced in size after the war and a negligible source of career officers, had no Negroes in attendance from 1946 through 1948. Perhaps most disturbing was the fact that in 1947 just fourteen Negroes were enrolled among more than 5,600 students in the NROTC program, the usual avenue to a Regular Navy commission.[9-42] The Holloway program, the basis for the Navy's reserve officer training system, offered scholarships at fifty-two colleges across the nation, but the number of these scholarships was small, the competition intense, and black applicants, often burdened by inferior schooling, did not fare well.

Statistics pointed at least to the possibility that racial discrimination existed in the NROTC system. Unlike the Army and Air Force programs, reserve officer training in the Navy depended to a great extent on state selection committees dominated by civilians. These committees exercised considerable leeway in selecting candidates to fill their state's annual NROTC quota, and their decisions were final. Not one Negro served on any of the state committees. In fact, fourteen of the fifty-two colleges selected for reserve officer training barred Negroes from admission by law and others—the exact number is difficult to ascertain—by policy. One black newspaper charged that only thirteen of the participating institutions admitted Negroes.[9-43] In all, only six black candidates survived this process to win commissions in 1948.

Lester Granger blamed the lack of black candidates on the fact that so few Negroes attended the schools; undoubtedly, more Negroes would have been enrolled in reserve officer training had the program been established at one of the predominantly black colleges. But black institutions were excluded from the wartime V-12 program, and when the program was extended to include fifty-two colleges in November 1945 the Navy again rejected the applications of black schools, justifying the exclusion, as it did for many white schools, on grounds of inadequacies in enrollment, academic credentials, and physical facilities.[9-44] Some black spokesmen called the decision discriminatory. President Mordecai Johnson of Howard University ruefully wondered how the Navy's unprejudiced and nondiscriminatory selection of fifty-two colleges managed to exclude so neatly all black institutions.[9-45]

Others disagreed. From the first the Special Programs Unit had rejected the clamor for forming V-12 units in predominantly black colleges, arguing that in the long run this could be considered enforced segregation and hardly contribute to racial harmony. Although candidates were supposed to attend the NROTC school of their choice, black candidates were restricted to institutions that would accept them. If a black school was added to the program, all black candidates would very likely gravitate toward it. Several black spokesmen, including Nelson, took this attitude and urged instead a campaign to increase the number of Negroes at the various integrated schools in the NROTC system.[9-46] Whatever the best solution, a significant and speedy increase in the number of black officers was unlikely.

Of lesser moment because of the small size of the WAVES and the Nurse Corps, the role of black women in the postwar Navy nevertheless concerned several civil rights leaders. Roy Wilkins, for one, concluded that the Navy's new policy which "hasn't worked out on the officer level ... hadn't worked on the women's level" either.[9-47] The Navy's statistics seemed to proved his contention. The service had 68 black enlisted women and 6 officers (including 4 nurses) on V-J day; a year later the number had been reduced to 5 black WAVES and 1 nurse. The Navy sought to defend these statistics against charges of discrimination. A spokesman explained that the paucity of black WAVES resulted from the fact that Negroes were barred from the WAVES until December 1944, just months before the Navy stopped recruiting all WAVES. Black WAVES who had remained in the postwar Navy had been integrated and were being employed without discrimination.[9-48]

But criticism persisted. In February 1948 the Navy could count six black WAVES out of a total enlisted force of 1,700, and during hearings on a bill to regularize the women's services several congressmen joined with a representative of the NAACP to press for a specific anti-discrimination amendment. The amendment was defeated, but not before Congressman Adam Clayton Powell charged that the status of black women in the Navy proved discrimination and demonstrated that the administration was practicing "not merely discrimination, segregation, and Jim Crowism, but total exclusion."[9-49] The same critics also demanded a similar amendment to the companion legislation on the WAC's, but it, too, was defeated.

Black nurses presented a different problem. Two of the wartime nurses had resigned to marry and the third was on inactive status attending college. The Navy, Secretary Forrestal claimed in July 1947, was finding it difficult to replace them or add to their number. Observing that black leaders had shown considerable interest in the Navy's nursing program, Forrestal noted that a similar interest had not been forthcoming from black women themselves. During the Navy's 1946 recruitment drive to attract 1,000 new nurses, only one Negro applied, and she was disqualified on physical grounds.[9-50]

Public Image and the Problem of Numbers

Individual black nurses no doubt had cogent reasons for failing to apply for Navy commissions, but the fact that only one applied called attention to a phenomenon that first appeared about 1946. Black Americans were beginning to ignore the Navy. Attempts by black reserve officers to procure NROTC applicants in black high schools and colleges proved largely unproductive. Nelson spoke before 8,500 potential candidates in 1948, and a special recruiting team reached an equal number the following year, but the combined effort brought fewer than ninety black applicants to take the competitive examination.[9-51] Recruiters had similar problems in the enlistment of Negroes for general service. Viewed from a different perspective, even the complaints and demands of black citizens, at flood tide during the war, now merely trickled into the secretary's office, reflecting, it could be argued, a growing indifference. That such unwillingness to enlist, as Lester Granger put it, should occur on the heels of a widely publicized promise of racial equality in the service was ironic. The Navy was beginning to welcome the Negro, but the Negro no longer seemed interested in joining.[9-52]

NAVAL UNIT PASSES IN REVIEW,
Naval Advanced Base, Bremerhaven, Germany, 1949.

Several reasons were suggested for this attitude. Assistant Secretary Brown placed the blame, at least in part, on the gap between policy and practice. Because of delay in abolishing old discriminatory practices, he pointed out to the Deputy Chief of Naval Operations, "the Navy's good public relations are endangered."[9-53] The personnel bureau promptly investigated, found justification for complaints of discrimination, and took corrective action.[9-54] Yet, as Nelson pointed out, such corrections, often in the form of "clarifying directives," were usually directed to specific commanders and tied to specific incidents and were ignored by other commanders as inapplicable to their own racial experiences.[9-55]Despite the existence of the racially separate Steward's Branch, the Navy's policy seemed so unassailable to the Chief of Naval Personnel that when his views on a congressional measure to abolish segregation in the services were solicited he reported without reservation that his bureau interposed no objection.[9-56]

The Navy's major racial problem by 1948 was the shockingly small number of Negroes in the service. In November 1948, a presidential election month, Negroes accounted for 4.3 percent of the navy's strength. Not only were there few Negroes in the Navy, but there were especially too few in the general service and practically no black officers, a series of statistics that made the predominately black and separate stewards more conspicuous. The Navy rejected an obvious solution, lowering recruitment standards, contending that it could not run its ships and aircraft with men who scored below ninety in the general classification test.[9-57] The alternative was to recruit among the increasing numbers of educated Negroes, as the personnel bureau had been trying to do. But here, as Nelson and others could report, the Navy faced severe competition from other employers, and here the Navy's public image had its strongest effect.

Lt. Comdr. Edward Hope, a black reserve officer assigned to officer procurement, concluded that the black community, especially veterans, distrusted all the services. Consequently, Negroes tended to disregard announced plans and policies applicable to all citizens unless they were specially labeled "for colored." Negroes tried to avoid the humiliation of applying for certain rights or benefits only to be arbitrarily rejected.[9-58] Compounding the suspicion and fear of humiliation, Hope reported, was a genuine lack of information on Navy policy that seriously limited the number of black applicants.

The cause of confusion among black students over Navy policy was easy to pinpoint, for memories of the frustrations and insults suffered by black seamen during the war were still fresh. Negroes remembered the labor battalions bossed by whites—much like the old plantation system, Lester Granger observed. Unlike the Army, the Navy had offered few black enlisted men the chance of serving in vital jobs under black commanders. This slight, according to Granger, robbed the black sailor of pride in service, a pride that could hardly be restored by the postwar image of the black sailor not as a fighting man but as a servant or laborer. Always a loyal member of the Navy team, Granger was anxious to improve the Navy's public image in the black community, and he and others often advanced plans for doing so.[9-59] But any discussion of image quickly foundered on one point: the Navy would remain suspect in the eyes of black youth and be condemned by civil rights leaders as long as it retained that symbol of racism, the racially separate Steward's Branch.

Here the practical need for change ran headlong into strong military tradition. An integrated general service was traditional and therefore acceptable; an integrated servants' branch was not. Faced with the choice of a small number of Negroes in the Navy and the attendant charges of racism or a change in its traditions, the Navy accepted the former. Lack of interest on the part of the black community was not a particularly pressing problem for the Navy in the immediate postwar years. Indeed, it might well have been a source of comfort for the military traditionalists who, armed with an unassailable integration policy, could still enjoy a Navy little changed from its prewar condition. Nevertheless, the lack of black volunteers for general service was soon to be discussed by a presidential commission, and in the next fifteen years would become a pressing problem when the Navy, the first service with a policy of integration, would find itself running behind in the race to attract minority members.

CHAPTER 10

The Postwar Marine Corps

Unlike the Army and Navy, the all-white Marine Corps seemed to consider the wartime enlistment of over 19,000 Negroes a temporary aberration. Forced by the Navy's nondiscrimination policy to retain Negroes after the war, Marine Corps officials at first decided on a black representation of some 2,200 men, roughly the same proportion as during the war. But the old tradition of racial exclusion remained strong, and this figure was soon reduced. The corps also ignored the Navy's integration measures, adopting instead a pattern of segregation that Marine officials claimed was a variation on the Army's historic "separate but equal" black units. In fact, separation was real enough in the postwar corps; equality remained elusive.

Racial Quotas and Assignments

The problem was that any "separate but equal" race policy, no matter how loosely enforced, was incompatible with the corps' postwar manpower resources and mission and would conflict with its determination to restrict black units to a token number. The dramatic manpower reductions of 1946 were felt immediately in the two major elements of the Marine Corps. The Fleet Marine Force, the main operating unit of the corps and usually under control of the Chief of Naval Operations, retained three divisions, but lost a number of its combat battalions. The divisions kept a few organic and attached service and miscellaneous units. Under such severe manpower restrictions, planners could not reserve one of the large organic elements of these divisions for black marines, thus leaving the smaller attached and miscellaneous units as the only place to accommodate self-contained black organizations. At first the Plans and Policies Division decided to assign roughly half the black marines to the Fleet Marine Force. Of these some were slated for an antiaircraft artillery battalion at Montford Point which would provide training as well as an opportunity for Negroes' overseas to be rotated home. Others were placed in three combat service groups and one service depot where they would act as divisional service troops, and the rest went into 182 slots, later increased to 216, for stewards, the majority in aviation units.

MARINE ARTILLERY TEAM.
Men of the 51st Defense Battalion in training at Montford Point with 90-mm. antiaircraft gun.

The other half of the black marines was to be absorbed by the so called non-Fleet Marine Force, a term used to cover training, security, and miscellaneous Marine units, all noncombat, which normally remained under the control of the commandant. This part of the corps was composed of many small and usually self-contained units, but in a number of activities, particularly in the logistical establishment and the units afloat, reductions in manpower would necessitate considerable sharing of living and working facilities, thus making racial separation impossible. The planners decided, therefore, to limit black assignments outside the Fleet Marine Force to naval ammunition depots at McAlester, Oklahoma, and Earle, New Jersey, where Negroes would occupy separate barracks; to Guam and Saipan, principally as antiaircraft artillery; and to a small training cadre at Montford Point. Eighty stewards would also serve with units outside the Fleet Marine Force. With the exception of the depot at Earle, all these installations had been assigned Negroes during the war. Speaking in particular about the assignment of Negroes to McAlester, the Director of the Plans and Policies Division, Brig. Gen. Gerald C. Thomas, commented that "this has proven to be a satisfactory location and type of duty for these personnel."[10-1] Thomas's conception of "satisfactory" duty for Negroes became the corps' rationale for its postwar assignment policy.

To assign Negroes to unskilled jobs because they were accustomed to such duties and because the jobs were located in communities that would accept black marines might be satisfactory to Marine officials, but it was considered racist by many civil rights spokesmen and left the Marine Corps open to charges of discrimination. The policy of tying the number of Negroes to the number of available, appropriate slots also meant that the number of black marines, and consequently the acceptability of black volunteers, was subject to chronic fluctuation. More important, it permitted if not encouraged further restrictions on the use of the remaining black marines who had combat training, thereby allowing the traditionalists to press for a segregated service in which the few black marines would be mostly servants and laborers.

The process of reordering the assignment of black marines began just eleven weeks after the commandant approved the staff's postwar policy recommendations. Informing the commandant on 6 January 1947 that "several changes have been made in concepts upon which such planning was based," General Thomas explained that the requirement for antiaircraft artillery units at Guam and Saipan had been canceled, along with the plan for maintaining an artillery unit at Montford Point. Because of the cancellation his division wanted to reduce the number of black marines to 1,500. These men could be assigned to depot companies, service units, and Marine barracks—all outside the Fleet Marine Force—or they could serve as stewards. The commandant's approval of this plan reduced the number of Negroes in the corps by 35 percent, or 700 men. Coincidental with this reduction was a 17 percent rise in spaces for black stewards to 350.[10-2]

Approval of this plan eliminated the last Negroes from combat assignments, a fact that General Thomas suggested could be justified as "consistent with similar reductions being effected elsewhere in the Corps." But the facts did not support such a palliative. In June 1946 the corps had some 1,200 men serving in three antiaircraft artillery battalions and an antiaircraft artillery group headquarters. In June 1948 the corps still had white antiaircraft artillery units on Guam and at Camp Lejeune totaling 1,020 men. The drop in numbers was explained almost entirely by the elimination of the black units.[10-3]

A further realignment of black assignments occurred in June 1947 when General Vandegrift approved a Plans and Policies Division decision to remove more black units from security forces at naval shore establishments. The men were reassigned to Montford Point with the result that the number of black training and overhead billets at that post jumped 200 percent—a dubious decision at best considering that black specialist and recruit training was virtually at a standstill. General Thomas took the occasion to advise the commandant that maintaining an arbitrary quota of black marines was no longer a consideration since a reduction in their strength could be "adequately justified" by the general manpower reductions throughout the corps.[10-4]

Actually the Marine Corps was not as free to reduce the quota of 1,500 Negroes as General Thomas suggested. To make further cuts in what was at most a token representation, approximately 1 percent of the corps in August 1947, would further inflame civil rights critics and might well provoke a reaction from Secretary Forrestal. Even Thomas's accompanying recommendation carefully retained the black strength figure previously agreed upon and actually raised the number of Negroes in the ground forces by seventy-six men. The 1,500-man minimum quota for black enlistment survived the reorganization of the Fleet Marine Force later in 1947, and the Plans and Policies Division even found it necessary to locate some 375 more billets for Negroes to maintain the figure. In August the commandant approved plans to add 100 slots for stewards and 275 general duty billets overseas, the latter to facilitate rotation and provide a broader range of assignments for Negroes.[10-5] Only once before the Korean War, and then only briefly, did the authorized strength of Negroes drop below the 1,500 mark, although because of recruitment lags actual numbers never equaled authorized strength.[10-6]

By mid-1947, therefore, the Marine Corps had abandoned its complex system of gearing the number of black marines to available assignments and, like the Army and the Air Force, had adopted a racial quota—but with an important distinction. Although they rarely achieved it, the Army and the Air Force were committed to accepting a fixed percentage of Negroes; in an effort to avoid the problems with manpower efficiency plaguing the other services, the Marine Corps established a straight *numerical* quota. Authorized black strength would remain at about 1,500 men until the Korean War. During that same period the actual percentage of Negroes in the Marine Corps almost doubled, rising from 1.3 percent of the 155,679-man corps in June 1946 to slightly more than 2 percent of the 74,279-man total in June 1950.[10-7]

Yet neither the relatively small size of the Marine Corps nor the fact that few black marines were enrolled could conceal the inefficiency of segregation. Over the next three years the personnel planning staff tried to find a solution to the problem of what it considered to be too many Negroes in the general service. First it began to reduce gradually the number of black units

118

accommodated in the Operating Force Plan, absorbing the excess black marines by increasing the number of stewards. This course was not without obvious public relations disadvantages, but they were offset somewhat by the fact that the Marine Corps, unlike the Navy, never employed a majority of its black recruits as stewards. In May 1948 the commandant approved new plans for a 10 percent decrease in the number of general duty assignments and a corresponding increase in spaces for stewards.[10-8] The trend away from assigning Negroes to general service duty continued until the Korean War, and in October 1949 a statistical high point was reached when some 33 percent of all black marines were serving as stewards. The doctrine that all marines were potential infantrymen stood, but it was small comfort to civil rights activists who feared that what at best was a nominal black representation in the corps was being pushed into the kitchen.

But they had little to fear since the number of Negroes that could be absorbed in the Steward's Branch was limited. In the end the Marine Corps still had to accommodate two-thirds of its black strength in general duty billets, a course with several unpalatable consequences. For one, Negroes would be assigned to new bases reluctant to accept them and near some communities where they would be unwelcome. For another, given the limitations in self-contained units, there was the possibility of introducing some integration in the men's living or working arrangements. Certainly black billets would have to be created at the expense of white billets. The Director of Plans and Policies warned in August 1947 that the reorganization of the Fleet Marine Force, then under way, failed to allocate spaces for some 350 Negroes with general duty contracts. While he anticipated some reduction in this number as a result of the campaign to attract volunteers for the Steward's Branch, he admitted that many would remain unassigned and beyond anticipating a reduction in the black "overage" through attrition, his office had no long-range plans for creating the needed spaces.[10-9] When the attrition failed to materialize, the commandant was forced in December 1949 to redesignate 202 white billets for black marines with general duty contracts.[10-10] The problem of finding restricted assignments for black marines in the general service lasted until it was overtaken by the manpower demands of the Korean War. Meanwhile to the consternation of the civil rights advocates, as the corps' definition of "suitable" assignment became more exact, the variety of duties to which Negroes could be assigned seemed to decrease.[10-11]

Recruitment

Postwar quotas and assignments for Negroes did nothing to curb the black community's growing impatience with separate and limited opportunities, a fact brought home to Marine Corps recruiters when they tried to enlist the Negroes needed to fill their quota. At first it seemed the traditionalists would regain their all-white corps by default. The Marine Corps had ceased drafting men in November 1945 and launched instead an intensive recruiting campaign for regular marines from among the thousands of reservists about to be discharged and regulars whose enlistments would soon expire. Included in this group were some 17,000 Negroes from among whom the corps planned to recruit its black contingent. To charges that it was discriminating in the enlistment of black civilians, the corps readily admitted that no new recruits were being accepted because preference was being given to men already in the corps.[10-12] In truth, the black reservists were rejecting the blandishments of recruiters in overwhelming numbers. By May 1946 only 522 Negroes, less than a quarter of the small postwar black complement, had enlisted in the regular service.

The failure to attract recruits was particularly noticeable in the antiaircraft battalions. To obtain black replacements for these critically depleted units, the commandant authorized the recruitment of reservists who had served less than six months, but the measure failed to produce the necessary manpower. On 28 February 1946 the commanding general of Camp Lejeune reported that all but seven Negroes on his antiaircraft artillery roster were being processed for discharge.[10-13] Since this list included the black noncommissioned instructors, the commander warned that future training of black marines would entail the use of officers as instructors. The precipitous loss of black artillerymen forced Marine headquarters to assign white specialists as temporary replacements in the heavy antiaircraft artillery groups at Guam and Saipan, both designated as black units in the postwar organization.[10-14]

It was not the fault of the black press if this expression of black indifference went unnoticed. The failure of black marines to reenlist was the subject of many newspaper and journal articles. The reason for the phenomenon advanced by the Norfolk *Journal and Guide* would be repeated by civil rights spokesmen on numerous occasions in the era before integration. The paper declared that veterans remembered their wartime experiences and were convinced that the same distasteful practices would be continued after the war.[10-15]Marine Corps officials advanced different reasons. The Montford Point commander attributed slow enlistment rates to a general postwar letdown and lack of publicity, explaining that Montford Point "had an excellent athletic program, good chow and comfortable barracks." A staff member of the Division of Plans and Policies later prepared a lengthy analysis of the treatment the Marine Corps had received in the black press. He charged that the press had presented a distorted picture of conditions faced by blacks that had "agitated" the men and turned them against reenlistment. He recommended a public relations campaign at Montford Point to improve the corps' image.[10-16] But this analysis missed the point, for while the black press might influence civilians, it could hardly instruct Marine veterans. Probably more than any other factor, the wartime treatment of black marines explained the failure of the corps to attract qualified, let alone gifted, Negroes to its postwar junior enlisted ranks.

Considering the critical shortages, temporarily and "undesirably" made up for by white marines, and the "leisurely" rate at which black reservists were reenlisting, General Thomas recommended in May 1946 that the corps recruit some 1,120 Negroes from civilian sources. This, he explained to the commandant, would accelerate black enlistment but still save some spaces for black reservists.[10-17] The commandant agreed,[10-18] and contrary to the staff's expectations, most Negroes in the postwar service were new recruits. The mass departure of World War II veterans eloquently expressed the attitude of experienced black servicemen toward the Marines' racial policy.

The word spread quickly among the new black marines. When in mid-1947 the Division of Plans and Policies was looking for ways to reduce the number of black marines in keeping with the modified manpower ceiling, it discovered that if offered the opportunity about one-third of all Negroes would apply for discharge. An even higher percentage of discharge requests was expected from among black marines overseas. The commandant agreed to make the offer, except to the stewards, and in the next six months black strength dropped by 700 men.[10-19]

Even the recruitment of stewards did not go according to predictions. Thomas had assured the commandant in the spring of 1946 that a concrete offer of steward duty to black reservists would produce the 300-man quota for the regular corps. He wanted the offer published at all separation centers and a training program for stewards instituted at Camp Lejeune.[10-20] General Vandegrift approved the proposal, but a month later the commander of Camp Lejeune reported that only three reservists and one regular had volunteered.[10-21] He advised the commandant to authorize recruitment among qualified civilians. Faced with wholesale rejection of such duty by black marines, General Thomas in March 1947 opened the Steward's Branch to Negroes with previous military service in any of the armed forces and qualifications for such work.[10-22] This ploy also proved a failure. Looking for 250 stewards, the recruiters could find but one acceptable applicant in the first weeks of the program. Retreating still further, the commandant canceled the requirement for previous military service in April, and in October dropped the requirement for "clearly established qualifications."[10-23] Apparently the staff would take a chance on any warm body.

In dropping the requirement for prior military service, the corps introduced a complication. Recruits for steward duty would be obliged to undergo basic training and their enlistment contracts would read "general duty"; Navy regulations required that subsequent reclassification to "stewards duty only" status had to be made at the request of the recruit. In August 1947 three men enlisted under the first enlistment program for stewards refused to execute a change of enlistment contract after basic training.[10-24] Although these men could have been discharged "for the good of the service," the commandant decided not to contest their right to remain in the general service. This action did not go unnoticed, and in subsequent months a number of men who signed up with the intention of becoming stewards refused to modify their enlistment contract while others, who already had changed their contract, suddenly began to fail the qualifying tests for stewards school.

The possibility of filling the quota became even more distant when in September 1947 the number of steward billets was increased to 380. Since only 57 stewards had signed up in the past twelve months, recruiters now had to find some 200 men, at least 44 per month for the immediate future. The commandant, furthermore, approved plans to increase the number of stewards to 420. In December the Plans and Policies Division, conceding defeat, recommended that the commandant arrange for the transfer of 175 men from the Navy's oversubscribed Steward's Branch. At the same time, to overcome what the division's new director, Brig. Gen. Ray A. Robinson, called "the onus attached to servant type duties," the commandant was induced to approve a plan making the rank and pay of stewards comparable to those of general duty personnel.[10-25]

These measures seemed to work. The success of the transfer program and the fact that first enlistments had finally begun to balance discharges led the recruiters to predict in March 1948 that their steward quota would soon be filled. Unfortunately, success tempted the planners to overreach themselves. Assured of a full steward quota, General Robinson recommended that approval be sought from the Secretary of the Navy to establish closed messes, along with the

120

requisite steward billets, at the shore quarters for bachelor officers overseas.[10-26] Approval brought another rise in the number of steward billets, this time to 580, and required a first-enlistment goal of twenty men per month.[10-27] The new stewards, however, were not forthcoming. After three months of recruiting the corps had netted ten men, more than offset by trainees who failed to qualify for steward school. Concluding that the failures represented to a great extent a scheme to remain in general service and evade the ceiling on general enlistment, the planners wanted the men failing to qualify discharged "for the good of the service."[10-28]

The lack of recruits for steward duty and constant pressure by stewards for transfer to general duty troubled the Marine Corps throughout the postwar period. Reviewing the problem in December 1948, the commanding general of Camp Lejeune saw three causes: "agitation from civilian sources," which labeled steward duty degrading servant's work; lack of rapid promotion; and badgering from black marines on regular duty.[10-29] But the commander's solution—a public relations campaign using black recruits to promote the attractions of steward duty along with a belated promise of more rapid promotion—failed. It ignored the central issue, the existence of a segregated branch in which black marines performed menial, nonmilitary duties.

Headquarters later resorted to other expedients. It obtained seventy-five more men from the Navy and lowered the qualification test standards for steward duty. But like earlier efforts, these steps also failed to produce enough men.[10-30] Ironically, while the corps aroused the ire of the civil rights groups by maintaining a segregated servants' branch, it was never able to attract a sufficient number of stewards to fill its needs in the postwar period.

Many of the corps' critics saw in the buildup of the Steward's Branch the first step in an attempt to eliminate Negroes from the general service. If such a scheme had ever been contemplated, it was remarkably unsuccessful, for the corps would enter the Korean War with most of its Negroes still in the general service. Nevertheless, the apprehension of the civil rights advocates was understandable because during most of the postwar period enlistment in the general service was barred to Negroes or limited to a very small number of men. Closed to Negroes in early 1947, enlistment was briefly reopened at the rate of forty men per month later that year to provide the few hundred extra men called for in the reorganization of the Operating Force Plan.[10-31] Enlistment was again opened in May 1948 when the recruiting office established a monthly quota for black recruits at ten men for general duty and eight for the Steward's Branch. The figure for stewards quickly rose to thirty per month, but effective 1 May 1949 the recruitment of Negroes for general service was closed.[10-32]

These rapid changes, indeed the whole pattern of black enlistment in the postwar Marine Corps, demonstrated that the staff's manpower practices were out of joint with the times. Not only did they invite attack from the increasingly vocal civil rights forces, but they also fostered a general distrust among black marines themselves and among those young Negroes the corps hoped to attract.

Segregation and Efficiency

The assignment policies and recruitment practices of the corps were the inevitable result of its segregation policy. Prejudice and discrimination no doubt aggravated the situation, but the policy of separation limited the ways Negroes could be employed and places to which they might be assigned. Segregation explained, for example, why Negroes were traditionally employed in certain types of combat units, and why, when changing missions and manpower restrictions caused a reduction in the number of such units, Negroes were not given other combat assignments. Most Negroes with combat military occupational specialties served in defense battalions during World War II. These units, chiefly antiaircraft artillery, were self-contained and could therefore be segregated; at the same time they cloaked a large group of men with the dignity of a combat assignment. But what was possible during the war was no longer practical and efficient in the postwar period. Some antiaircraft artillery units survived the war, but they no longer operated as battalions and were divided instead into battery-size organizations that simply could not be segregated in terms of support and recreational facilities. In fact, the corps found it impossible after the war to maintain segregation in any kind of combat unit.

Even if segregated service had been possible, the formation of all-black antiaircraft artillery battalions would have been precluded by the need of this highly technical branch for so many kinds of trained specialists. Not only would separate training facilities for the few Negroes in the peacetime corps be impossibly expensive and inefficient, but not enough black recruits were eligible for such training. A wartime comparison of the General Classification Test and Mechanical Aptitude Test scores of the men in the 52d Defense Battalion with those of men in two comparable white units showed the Negroes averaging considerably lower than the whites.[10-33] It was reasonable to expect this difference to continue since, on the whole, black recruits were scoring lower than their World War II counterparts.[10-34] Under current policies, therefore, the Marine Corps saw little choice but to exclude Negroes from antiaircraft artillery and other combat units.

Obviously the corps had in its ranks some Negroes capable of performing any task required in an artillery battalion. Yet because the segregation policy demanded that there be enough qualified men to form and sustain a whole black battalion, the abilities of these high-scoring individuals were wasted. On the other hand, many billets in antiaircraft artillery or other types of combat battalions could be filled by men with low test scores, but less gifted black marines were excluded because they had to be assigned to one of the few black units. Segregation, in short, was doubly inefficient, it kept both able and inferior Negroes out of combat units that were perpetually short of men.

Segregation also promoted inefficiency in the placement of black Marine units. While the assignment of an integrated unit with a few black marines would probably go unnoticed in most naval districts—witness the experience of the Navy itself—the task of finding a naval district and an American community where a large segregated group of black marines could be peacefully assimilated was infinitely more difficult.

The original postwar racial program called for the assignment of black security units to the Marine Barracks at McAlester, Oklahoma, and Earle, New Jersey. Noting that the station was in a strict Jim Crow area where recreational facilities for Negroes were limited and distant, the commanding officer of the Marine Barracks at McAlester recommended that no Negroes be assigned. He reminded the commandant that guard duty required marines to question and apprehend white civilian employees, a fact that would add to the racial tension in the area. His conclusions, no doubt shared by commanders in many parts of the country, summed up the problem of finding assignments for black marines: any racial incident which might arise out of disregard for local racial custom, he wrote,

would cause the Marine Corps to become involved by protecting such personnel as required by Federal law and Navy Regulations. It is believed that if one such potential incident occurred, it would seriously jeopardize the standing of the Marine Corps throughout the Southwest. To my way of thinking, the Marine Corps is not now maintaining the high esteem of public opinion, or gaining in prestige, by the manner in which its uniform and insignia are subjected to such laws. The uniform does not count, it is relegated to the background and made to participate in and suffer the restrictions and limitations placed upon it by virtue of the wearer being subject to the Jim Crow laws.[10-35]

The commander of the McAlester ammunition depot endorsed this recommendation, adding that Oklahoma was a "border" state where the Negro was not accepted as in the north nor understood and tolerated as in the south. This argument moved the Director of Plans and Policies to recommend that McAlester be dropped and the black unit sent instead to Port Chicago, California.[10-36] With the approval of the commandant and the Chief of Naval Operations, plans for the assignment were well under way in June 1947 when the commandant of the Twelfth Naval District intervened.[10-37] The presence of a black unit, he declared, was undesirable in a predominantly white area that was experiencing almost constant labor turmoil. The possibility of clashes between white pickets and black guards would invite racial conflict. His warnings carried the day, and Port Chicago was dropped in favor of the Marine Barracks, Naval Shipyard, Brooklyn, New York, with station at Bayonne, New Jersey. At the same time, because of opposition from naval officials, the plan for assigning Negroes to Earle, New Jersey, was also dropped, and the commandant launched inquiries about the depots at Hingham, Massachusetts, and Fort Mifflin, Pennsylvania.[10-38]

Fort Mifflin agreed to take fifty black marines, but several officials objected to the proposed assignment to Hingham. The Marine commander, offering what he called his unbiased opinion in the best interests of the service, explained in considerable detail why he thought the assignment of Negroes would jeopardize the fire-fighting ability of the ammunition depot. The commanding officer of the naval depot endorsed these reasons and added that assigning black marines to guard duty that included vehicle search would create a problem in industrial relations.[10-39] The commandant of the First Naval District apparently discounted these arguments, but he too voted against the assignment of Negroes on the grounds that the Hingham area lacked a substantial black population, was largely composed of restricted residential neighborhoods, and was a major summer resort on which the presence of black units would have an adverse effect.[10-40]

The commander of the Naval Base, New York, meanwhile had refused to approve a plan to assign a black unit to Bayonne, New Jersey, and suggested that it be sent to Earle, New Jersey, instead because there the unit "presented fewer problems and difficulties than at any other Naval activity." The commander noted that stationing Negroes at Bayonne would necessitate a certain amount of integration in mess and ship service facilities. Bayonne was also reputed to have the toughest gate duty in the New York area, and noncommissioned officers had to supervise a white civilian police force. At Earle, on the other hand, the facilities were completely separate, and although some complaints from well-to-do summer colonists in the vicinity could be expected, men could be bused to Newark or Jersey City for recreation. Moreover, Earle could absorb a 175-man unit.[10-41] But chief of the Navy's Bureau of Ordnance wanted to retain white marines at Earle because a recent decision to handle ammonium nitrate fertilizer there made it unwise to relieve the existing trained detachment. Earle was also using contract stevedores and expected to be using Army troops whose use of local facilities would preclude plans for a segregated barracks and mess.[10-42]

The commandant accepted these arguments and on 20 August 1947 revoked the assignment of a black unit to Earle. Still, with its ability to absorb 175 men and its relative suitability in terms of separate living facilities, the depot remained a prime candidate for black units, and in November General Vandegrift reversed himself. The Chief of Naval Operations supported the commandant's decision over the renewed objections of the Chief of the Bureau of Ordnance.[10-43] With Hingham, Massachusetts, ruled out, the commandant now considered the substitution of Marine barracks at Trinidad, British West Indies; Scotia, New York; and Oahu, Hawaii. He rejected Trinidad in favor of Oahu, and officials in Hawaii proved amenable.[10-44]

The chief of the Navy's Bureau of Supplies and Accounts objected to the use of black marines at the supply depot in Scotia, claiming that such an assignment to the Navy's sole installation in upper New York State would bring about a "weakening of the local public relations advantage now held by the Navy" and would be contrary to the Navy's best interests. He pointed out that the assignment would necessitate billeting white marine graves registration escorts and black marines in the same squad rooms. The use of black marines for firing squads at funerals, he thought, would be "undesirable." He also pointed out that the local black population was small, making for extremely limited recreational and social opportunities.[10-45] The idea of using Scotia with all these attendant inconveniences was quietly dropped, and the black marines were finally assigned to Earle, New Jersey; Fort Mifflin, Pennsylvania; and Oahu, Hawaii.

Approved on 8 November 1946, the postwar plan to assign black units to security guard assignments in the United States was not fully put into practice until 15 August 1948, almost two years later. This episode in the history of discrimination against Americans in uniform brought little glory to anyone involved and revealed much about the extent of race prejudice in American society. It was an indictment of people in areas as geographically diverse as Oklahoma, New York, Massachusetts, and New Jersey who objected to the assignment of black servicemen to their communities. It was also an indictment of a great many individual commanders, both in the Navy and Marine Corps, some perhaps for personal prejudices, others for so readily bowing to community prejudices. But most of all the blame must fall on the Marine Corps' policy of segregation. Segregation made it necessary to find assignments for a whole enlisted complement and placed an intolerable administrative burden on the corps. The dictum that black marines could not deal with white civilians, especially in situations in which they would give orders, further limited assignments since such duties were routine in any security unit. Thus, bound to a policy that was neither just nor practical, the commandant spent almost two years trying to place four hundred men.

Despite the obvious inefficiency and discrimination involved, the commandant, General Vandegrift, adamantly defended the Marine segregation policy before Secretary of the Navy Forrestal. Wartime experience showed, he maintained, oblivious to overwhelming evidence to the contrary since 1943, "that the assignment of negro Marines to separate units promotes harmony and morale and fosters the competitive spirit essential to the development of a high esprit."[10-46] His stand was bound to antagonize the civil rights camp; the black press in particular trumpeted the theme that the corps was as full of race discrimination as it had been during the war.[10-47]

Toward Integration

But even as the commandant defended the segregation policy, the corps was beginning to yield to pressure from outside forces and the demands of military efficiency. The first policy breach concerned black officers. Although a proposal for commissions had been rejected when the subject was first raised in 1944, three black candidates were accepted by the officer training school at Quantico in April 1945. One failed to qualify on physical and two on scholastic grounds, but they were followed by five other Negroes who were still in training on V-J day. One of this group, Frederick Branch of Charlotte, North Carolina, elected to stay in training through the demobilization period. He was commissioned with his classmates on 10 November 1945 and placed in the inactive reserves. Meanwhile, three Negroes in the V-12 program graduated and received commissions as second lieutenants in the inactive Marine Corps Reserve. Officer training for all these men was integrated.[10-48]

123

The first Negro to obtain a regular commission in the Marine Corps was John E. Rudder of Paducah, Kentucky, a Marine veteran and graduate of the Naval Reserve Officers' Training Corps. Analyzing the case for the commandant in May 1948, the Director of Plans and Policies noted that the law did not require the Marine Corps to commission Rudder, but that he was only the first of several Negroes who would be applying for commissions in the next few years through the Naval Reserve Officers' Training Corps. Since the reserve corps program was a vital part of the plan to expand Marine Corps officer strength, rejecting a graduate on account of race, General Robinson warned, might jeopardize the entire plan. He thought that Rudder should be accepted for duty. Rudder was appointed a second lieutenant in the Regular Marine Corps on 28 May 1948 and ordered to Quantico for basic schooling.[10-49] In 1949 Lieutenant Rudder resigned. Indicative of the changing civil rights scene was the apprehension shown by some Marine Corps officials about public reaction to the resignation. But although Rudder reported instances of discrimination at Quantico—stemming for the most part from a lack of military courtesy that amounted to outright ostracism—he insisted his decision to resign was based on personal reasons and was irreversible. The Director of Public Information was anxious to release an official version of the resignation,[10-50] but other voices prevailed, and Rudder's exit from the corps was handled quietly both at headquarters and in the press.[10-51]

The brief active career of one black officer was hardly evidence of a great racial reform, but it represented a significant breakthrough because it affirmed the practice of integrated officer training and established the right of Negroes to command. And Rudder was quickly followed by other black officer candidates, some of whom made careers in the corps. Rudder's appointment marked a permanent change in Marine Corps policy.

Enlistment of black women marked another change. Negroes had been excluded from the Women's Reserve during World War II, but in March 1949 A. Philip Randolph asked the commandant, in the name of the Committee Against Jim Crow in Military Service and Training, if black women could join the corps. The commandant's reply was short and direct: "If qualified for enlistment, negro women will be accepted on the same basis as other applicants."[10-52] In September 1949 Annie N. Graham and Ann E. Lamb reported to Parris Island for integrated training and subsequent assignment.

Yet another racial change, in the active Marine Corps Reserve, could be traced to outside pressure. Until 1947 all black reservists were assigned to inactive and unpaid volunteer reserve status, and applications for transfer to active units were usually disapproved by commanding officers on grounds that such transfers would cost the unit a loss in whites. Rejections did not halt applications, however, and in May 1947 the Director of Marine Corps Reserve decided to seek a policy decision. While he wanted each commander of an active unit left free to decide whether he would take Negroes, the director also wanted units with black enlisted men formed in the organized reserve, all-black voluntary training units recognized, and integrated active duty training provided for reservists.[10-53] A group of Negroes in Chicago had already applied for the formation of a black voluntary training unit.

General Thomas, Director of Plans and Policies, was not prepared to go the whole way. He agreed that within certain limitations the local commander should decide on the integration of black reservists into an active unit, and he accepted integrated active duty training. But he rejected the formation of black units in the organized reserve and the voluntary training program; the latter because it would "inevitably lead to the necessity for Negro officers and for authorizing drill pay" in order to avoid charges of discrimination. Although Thomas failed to explain why black officers and drill pay were unacceptable or how rejecting the program would save the corps from charges of discrimination, his recommendations were approved by the commandant over the objection of the Reserve Division.[10-54] But the Director of Reserves rejoined that volunteer training units were organized under corps regulations, the Chicago group had met all the specifications, and the corps would be subject to just criticism if it refused to form the unit. On the other hand, by permitting the formation of some all-black volunteer units, the corps might satisfy the wish of Negroes to be a part of the reserve and thus avoid any concerted attempt to get the corps to form all-black units in the organized reserve.[10-55]

At this point the Division of Plans and Policies offered to compromise. General Robinson recommended that when the number of volunteers so warranted, the corps should form black units of company size or greater, either separate or organic to larger reserve units around the country. He remained opposed to integrated units, explaining that experience proved—he neglected to mention what experience, certainly none in the Marine Corps—that integrated units served neither the best interests of the individual nor the corps.[10-56] While the commandant's subsequent approval set the stage for the formation of racially composite units in the reserve, the stipulation that the black element be of company size or larger effectively limited the degree of reform.

Black Marine unit boards ship at Morehead City, North Carolina, 1949.

The development of composite units in the reserve paralleled a far more significant development in the active forces. In 1947 the Marine Corps began organizing such units along the lines established in the postwar Army. Like the Army, the corps discovered that maintaining a quota—even when the quota for the corps meant maintaining a minimum number of Negroes in the service—in a period of shrinking manpower resources necessitated the creation of new billets for Negroes. At the same time it was obviously inefficient to assign combat-trained Negroes, now surplus with the inactivation of the black defense battalions, to black service and supply units when the Fleet Marine Force battalions were so seriously understrength. Thus the strictures against integration notwithstanding, the corps was forced to begin attaching black units to the depleted Fleet Marine Force units. In January 1947, for example, members of Headquarters Unit, Montford Point Camp, and men of the inactivated 3d Antiaircraft Artillery Battalion were transferred to Camp Geiger, North Carolina, and assigned to the all-black 2d Medium Depot Company, which, along with eight white units, was organized into the racially composite 2d Combat Service Group in the 2d Marine Division.[10-57] Although the units of the group ate in separate mess halls and slept in separate barracks, inevitably the men of all units used some facilities in common. After Negroes were assigned to Camp Geiger, for instance, recreational facilities were open to all. In some isolated cases, black noncommissioned officers were assigned to lead racially mixed details in the composite group.[10-58]

But these reforms, which did very little for a very few men, scarcely dented the Marine Corps' racial policy. Corps officials were still firmly committed to strict segregation in 1948, and change seemed very distant. Any substantial modification in racial policy would require a revolution against Marine tradition, a movement dictated by higher civilian authority or touched off by an overwhelming military need.

CHAPTER 11

The Postwar Air Force

The Air Force was a new service in 1947, but it was also heir to a long tradition of segregation. Most of its senior officers, trained in the Army, firmly supported the Army's policy of racially separate units and racial quotas. And despite continuing objections to what many saw as the Gillem Board's far too progressive proposals, the Air Force adopted the Army's postwar racial policy as its own. Yet after less than two years as an independent service the Air Force in late 1948 stood on the threshold of integration.

This sudden change in attitude was not so much the result of humanitarian promptings by service officials, although some of them forcibly demanded equal treatment and opportunity. Nor was it a response to civil rights activists, although Negroes in and outside the Air Force continued to exert pressure for change. Rather, integration was forced upon the service when the inefficiency of its racial practices could no longer be ignored. The inefficiency of segregated troops was less noticeable in the Army, where a vast number of Negroes could serve in a variety of expandable black units, and in the smaller Navy, where only a few Negroes had specialist ratings and most black sailors were in the separate Steward's Branch. But the inefficiency of separatism was plainly evident in the Air Force.

Like the Army, the Air Force had its share of service units to absorb the marginal black airman, but postwar budget restrictions had made the enlargement of service units difficult to justify. At the same time, the Gillem Board policy as well as outside pressures had made it necessary to include a black air unit in the service's limited number of postwar air wings. However socially desirable two air forces might seem to most officials, and however easy it had been to defend them as a wartime necessity, it quickly became apparent that segregation was, organizationally at least, a waste of the Air Force's few black pilots and specialists and its relatively large supply of unskilled black recruits. Thus, the inclination to integrate was mostly pragmatic; notably absent were the idealistic overtones sounded by the Navy's Special Programs Unit during the war. Considering the magnitude of the Air Force problem, it was probably just as well that efficiency rather than idealism became the keynote of change. On a percentage basis the Air Force had almost as many Negroes as the Army and, no doubt, a comparable level of prejudice among its commanders and men. At the same time, the Air Force was a new service, its organization still fluid and its policies subject to rapid modification. In such circumstances a straightforward appeal to efficiency had a chance to succeed where an idealistic call for justice and fair play might well have floundered.

Segregation and Efficiency

Many officials in the Army Air Forces had defended segregated units during the war as an efficient method of avoiding dangerous social conflicts and utilizing low-scoring recruits.[11-1] General Arnold himself repeatedly warned against bringing black officers and white enlisted men together. Unless strict unit segregation was imposed, such contacts would be inevitable, given the Air Forces' highly mobile training and operations structure.[11-2] But if segregation restricted contacts between the races it also imposed a severe administrative burden on the wartime Air Forces. It especially affected the black flying units because it ordained that not only pilots but the ground support specialists—mechanics, supply clerks, armorers—had to be black. Throughout most of the war the Air Forces, competing with the rest of the Army for skilled and high-scoring Negroes, was unable to fill the needs of its black air units. At a time when the Air Forces enjoyed a surplus of white air and ground crews, the black fighter units suffered from a shortage of replacements for their combat veterans, a situation as inefficient as it was damaging to morale.[11-3]

The shortage was compounded in the penultimate year of the war when the all-black 477th Bombardment Group was organized. (Black airmen and civil rights spokesmen complained that restricting Negroes to fighter units excluded them from many important and prestigious types of air service.) In the end the new bombardment group only served to limit black participation in the air war. Already short of black pilots, the Army Air Forces now had to find black navigators and bombardiers as well, thereby intensifying the competition for qualified black cadets. The stipulation that pilots and bombardiers for the new unit be trained at segregated Tuskegee was another obvious cause for the repeated delays in the operational date of the 477th, and its crews were finally assembled only weeks before the end of the war. Competition for black bomber crews also led to a ludicrous situation in which men highly qualified for pilot training according to their stanine scores (achievements on the battery of qualifying tests taken by all applicants for flight service) were sent instead to navigator-bomber training, for which they were only barely qualified.[11-4]

Unable to obtain enough Negroes qualified for flight training, the Army Air Forces asked the Ground and Service Forces to screen their personnel for suitable candidates, but a screening early in 1945 produced only about one-sixth of the men needed. Finally, the Air Forces recommended that the Army staff lower the General Classification Test score for pilot training from 110 to 100, a recommendation the Service and Ground Forces opposed because such a move would eventually mean the mass transfer of high-scoring Negroes to the Air Forces, thus depriving the Service and Ground Forces of their proportionate share. Although the Secretary of War approved the Air Forces proposal, the change came too late to affect the shortage of black pilots and specialists before the end of the war.

DAMAGE INSPECTION.
A squadron operations officer of the 332d Fighter Group points out a cannon hole to ground crew, Italy, 1945.

While short of skilled Negroes, the Army Air Forces was being inundated with thousands of undereducated and unskilled Negroes from Selective Service. It tried to absorb these recruits, as it absorbed some of its white draftees, by creating a great number of service and base security battalions. A handy solution to the wartime quota problem, the large segregated units eventually caused considerable racial tension. Some of the tension might have been avoided had black officers commanded black squadrons, a logical course since the Air Force had a large surplus of nonrated black officers stationed at Tuskegee.[11-5] Most were without permanent assignment or were assigned such duties as custodial responsibility for bachelor officer quarters, occupations unrelated to their specialties.[11-6]

Few of these idle black officers commanded black service units because the units were scattered worldwide while the nonrated officers were almost always assigned to the airfield at Tuskegee. Approximately one-third of the Air Forces' 1,559 black officers were stationed at Tuskegee in June 1945. Most others were assigned to the fighter group in the Mediterranean theater or the new bombardment group in flight training at Godman Field, Kentucky. Only twenty-five black officers were serving at other stations in the United States. The Second, Third, and Fourth Air Forces and I Troop Carrier Command, for example, had a combined total of seventeen black officers as against 22,938 black enlisted men.[11-7]Col. Noel F. Parrish, the wartime commander at Tuskegee, explained that the principal reason for this restriction was the prevailing fear of social conflict. If assigned to other bases, black officers might try to use the officers' clubs and other base facilities. Thus, despite the surplus of black officers only too evident at Tuskegee, their requests for transfer to other bases for assignment in their rating were usually denied on the grounds that the overall shortage of black officers made their replacement impossible.[11-8]

126

Fearing trouble between black and white officers and assuming that black airmen preferred white officers, the Air Forces assigned white officers to command black squadrons. Actually, such assignments courted morale problems and worse because they were extremely unpopular with both officers and men. Moreover, the Air Forces eventually had to admit that there was a tendency to assign white officers "of mediocre caliber" to black squadrons.[11-9] Yet few assignments demanded greater leadership ability, for these officers were burdened not only with the usual problems of a unit commander but also with the complexities of race relations. If they disparaged their troops, they failed as commanders; if they fought for their men, they were dismissed by their superiors as "pro-Negro." Consequently, they were generally a harassed and bewildered lot, bitter over their assignments and bad for troop morale.[11-10]

The social problems predicted for integration proved inevitable under segregation. Commanders found it prohibitively expensive to provide separate but equal facilities, and without them discrimination became more obvious. The walk-in protest at the Freeman Field Officers Club was but one of the natural consequences of segregation rules. And such demonstrations were only the more spectacular problems. Just as time-consuming and perhaps more of a burden were the many administrative difficulties. The Air Transport Command admitted in 1946 that it was too expensive to maintain, as the command was obligated to do, separate and equal housing and messing, including separate orderly and day rooms for black airmen. At the same time it complained of the disproportionately high percentage of black troops violating military and civil law. Although Negroes accounted for 20 percent of the command's troops, they committed more than 50 percent of its law infractions. The only connection the command was able to make between the separate, unequal facilities and the high misconduct rate was to point out that, while it had done its best to provide for Negroes, they "had not earned a very enviable record by themselves."[11-11]

COLONEL PARRISH
(*1946 photograph*).

In one crucial five-month period of the war, Army Air Forces headquarters processed twenty-two separate staff actions involving black troops.[11-12] To avoid the supposed danger of large-scale social integration, the Air Forces, like the rest of the Army during World War II, had been profligate in its use of material resources, inefficient in its use of men, and destructive of the morale of black troops.

The Air staff was not oblivious to these facts and made some adjustments in policy as the war progressed. Notably, it rejected separate training of nonrated black officers and provided for integrated training of black navigators and bombardiers. In the last days of the war General Arnold ordered his commanders to "take affirmative action to insure that equity in training and assignment opportunity is provided all personnel."[11-13] And when it came to postwar planning, the Air staff demonstrated it had learned much from wartime experience:

The degree to which negroes can be successfully employed in the Post-War Military Establishment largely depends on the success of the Army in maintaining at a minimum the feeling of discrimination and unfair treatment which basically are the causes for irritation and disorders ... in the event of a future emergency the arms will employ a large number of negroes and their contribution in such an emergency will largely depend on the training, treatment and intelligent use of negroes during the intervening years.[11-14]

But while admitting that discrimination was at the heart of its racial problem, the Air staff failed to see the connection between discrimination and segregation. Instead it adopted the recommendations of its senior commanders. The consensus was that black combat (flying) units had performed "more or less creditably," but required more training than white units, and that the ground echelon and combat support units had performed below average. Rather than abolish these below average units, however, commanders wanted them preserved and wanted postwar policy to strengthen segregation. The final recommendation of the Army Air Forces to the Gillem Board was that blacks be trained according to the same standards as whites but that they be employed in separate units and segregated for recreation, messing, and social activities "on the post as well as off," in keeping with prevailing customs in the surrounding civilian community.[11-15]

The Army Air Forces' postwar use of black troops was fairly consonant with the major provisions of the Gillem Board Report. To reduce black combat units in proportion to the reduction of its white units, it converted the 477th Bombardment Group (M) into the 477th Composite Group. This group, under the command of the Army's senior black pilot, Col. Benjamin O. Davis, Jr., included a fighter, a bombardment, and a service squadron. To provide segregated duty for its black specialists, the Army Air Forces organized regular black squadrons, mostly ammunition, motor transport, and engineer throughout its commands. To absorb the large number of unskilled Negroes, it organized one black squadron (Squadron F) in each of the ninety-seven base units in its worldwide base system to perform laboring and housekeeping chores. Finally, it promised "to the fullest possible extent" to assign Negroes with specialized skills and qualifications to overhead and special units.[11-16]

In the summer of 1947, the Army Air Forces integrated aviation training at Randolph Field, Texas, and quietly closed Tuskegee airfield, thus ending the last segregated officer training in the armed forces. The move was unrelated to the Gillem Board Report or to the demands of civil rights advocates. The Tuskegee operation had simply become impractical. In the severe postwar retrenchment of the armed forces, Tuskegee's cadet enrollment had dropped sharply, only nine men graduated in the October 1945 class.[11-17] To the general satisfaction of the black community, the few black cadets shared both quarters and classes with white students.[11-18] Nine black cadets were in training at the end of 1947.[11-19]

Another postwar reduction was not so advantageous for Negroes. By February 1946 the 477th Composite Group had been reduced to sixteen B-25 bombers, twelve P-47 fighter-bombers, and only 746 men—a 40 percent drop in four months.[11-20] Although the Tactical Air Command rated the unit's postwar training and performance satisfactory, and its transfer to the more hospitable surroundings and finer facilities of Lockbourne Field, Ohio, raised morale, the 477th, like other understaffed and underequipped organizations, faced inevitable conversion to specialized service. In July 1947 the 477th was inactivated and replaced by the 332d Fighter Group composed of the 99th, 100th, and 301st Fighter Squadrons. Black bomber pilots were converted to fighter pilots, and the bomber crews were removed from flying status.

OFFICERS' SOFTBALL TEAM
representing the 477th Composite Group, Godwin Field, Kentucky.

These changes flew in the face of the Gillem Board Report, for however slightly that document may have changed the Army's segregation policy, it did demand at least a modest response to the call for equal opportunity in training, assignment, and advancement. The board clearly looked to the command of black units by qualified black officers and the training of black airmen to serve as a cadre for any necessary expansion of black units in wartime. Certainly the conversion of black bomber pilots to fighters did not meet these modest demands. In its defense the Army Air Forces in effect pleaded that there were too many Negroes for its present force, now severely reduced in size and lacking planes and other equipment, and too many of the black troops lacked education for the variety of assignments recommended by the board.

The Army Air Forces seemed to have a point, for in the immediate postwar period its percentage of black airmen had risen dramatically. It was drafting men to replace departing veterans, and in 1946 it was taking anyone who qualified, including many Negroes. In seven months the air arm lost over half its black strength, going from a wartime high of 80,606 on 31 August 1945 to 38,911 on 31 March 1946, but in the same period the black percentage almost doubled, climbing from 4.2 to 7.92.[11-21] The War Department predicted that all combat arms would have a black strength of 15 percent by 1 July 1946.[11-22]

This prophecy never materialized in the Air Forces. Changes in enlistment standards, curtailment of overseas assignments for Negroes, and, finally, suspension of all black enlistments in the Regular Army except in certain military specialist occupations turned the percentage of Negroes downward. By the fall of 1947, when the Air Force became a separate service,[11-23] the proportion of black airmen had leveled off at nearly 7 percent. Nor did the proportion of Negroes ever exceed the Gillem Board's 10 percent quota during the next decade.

The Air Force seemed on safer ground when it pleaded that it lacked the black airmen with skills to carry out the variety of assignments called for by the Gillem Board. The Air Force was finding it impossible to organize effective black units in appreciable numbers; even some units already in existence were as much as two-thirds below authorized strength in certain ground specialist slots.[11-24] Yet here too the statistics do not reveal the whole truth. Despite a general shortage of Negroes in the high test score categories, the Air Force did have black enlisted men qualified for general assignment as specialists or at least eligible for specialist training, who were instead assigned to labor squadrons.[11-25] In its effort to reduce the number of Negroes, the service had also relieved from active duty other black specialists trained in much needed skills. Finally, the Air Force still had a surplus of black specialists in some categories at Lockbourne Field who were not assigned to the below-strength units.

Again it was not too many black enlisted men or too few black officers or specialists but the policy of strict segregation that kept the Air Force from using black troops efficiently. Insistence on segregation, not the number of Negroes, caused maldistribution among the commands. In 1947, for example, the Tactical Air Command contained some 5,000 black airmen, close to 28 percent of the command's strength. This situation came about because the command

128

counted among its units the one black air group and many of the black service units whose members in an integrated service would have been distributed throughout all the commands according to needs and abilities. The Air Force segregation policy restricted all but forty-five of the black officers in the continental United States to one base,[11-26] just as it was the Air Force's attempt to avoid integration that kept black officers from command. In November 1947, 1,581 black enlisted men and only two black officers were stationed at MacDill Field; at San Antonio there were 3,450 black airmen and again two black officers. These figures provide some clue to the cause of the riot involving black airmen at MacDill Field on 27 October 1946.[11-27]

Segregation also prevented the use of Negroes on a broader professional scale. In April 1948, 84.2 percent of Negroes in the Air Force were working in an occupational specialty as against 92.7 percent of whites, but the number of Negroes in radar, aviation specialist, wire communications, and other highly specialized skills required to support a tactical air unit was small and far below the percentage of whites. The Air Force argued that since Negroes were assigned to black units and since there was only one black tactical unit, there was little need for Negroes with these special skills.

CHECKING AMMUNITION.
An armorer in the 332d Fighter Group inspects the P-51 Mustang, Italy, 1945.

The fact that rated black officers and specialists were restricted to one black fighter group particularly concerned civil rights advocates. Without bomber, transport, ferrying, or weather observation assignments, black officers qualified for larger aircraft had no chance to diversify their careers. It was essentially the same story for black airmen. Without more varied and large black combat units the Air Force had no need to assign many black airmen to specialist training. In December 1947, for example, only 80 of approximately 26,000 black airmen were attending specialist schools.[11-28] When asked about the absence of Negroes in large aircraft, especially bombers, Air Force spokesmen cited the conversion of the 477th Composite Group, which contained the only black bomber unit, to a specialized fighter group as merely part of a general reorganization to meet the needs of a 55-wing organization.[11-29] That the one black bomber unit happened to be organized out of existence was pure accident.

The Gillem Board had sought to expand the training and placement of skilled Negroes by going outside the regular black units and giving them overhead assignments. After the war some base commanders made such assignments unofficially, taking advantage of the abilities of airmen in the overmanned, all-black Squadron F's and assigning them to skilled duties. In one instance the base commander's secretary was a member of his black unit; in another, black mechanics from Squadron F worked on the flight line with white mechanics. But whatever their work, these men remained members of Squadron F, and often the whole black squadron, rather than individual airmen, found itself functioning as an overhead unit, contrary to the intent of the Gillem Board. Even the few Negroes formally trained in a specialty and placed in an integrated overhead unit did not approximate the Gillem Board's intention of training a cadre that would be readily expandable in an emergency.

The alternative to expanded overhead assignments was continuation of segregated service units and Squadron F's, but, as some manpower experts pointed out, many special purpose units suitable for unskilled airmen were disappearing from the postwar Air Force. Experience gained through the assignment of large numbers of marginal men to such units in peacetime would be of questionable value during large-scale mobilization.[11-30] As Colonel Parrish, the wartime commander of training at Tuskegee, warned, a peacetime policy incapable of wartime application was not only unrealistic, but dangerous.[11-31]

The Air staff tried to carry out the Gillem Board's suggestion that Negroes be stationed "where attitudes are most favorable for them insofar as military factors permit," but even here the service lagged behind civilian practice. When Marcus H. Ray arrived at Wright Field, Ohio, for a two-day inspection tour in July 1946, he found almost 3,000 black civilians working peacefully and effectively alongside 18,000 white civilians, all assigned to their jobs without regard to race. "I would rate this installation," Ray reported, "as the best example of efficient utilization of manpower I have seen." He went on to explain: "The integration has been accomplished without publicity and simply by assigning workers according to their capabilities and without regard to race, creed, or color." But Ray also noted that there were no black military men on the base.[11-32] Assistant Secretary of War Petersen was impressed. "In view of the fact that the racial climate seems exceptionally favorable at Wright Field," he wrote General Carl Spaatz, "consideration should be given to the employment of carefully selected Negro military personnel with specialist ratings for work in that installation."[11-33]

The Air Force complied. In the fall of 1946 it was forming black units for assignment to Air Materiel Command Stations, and it planned to move a black unit to Wright Field in the near

129

future.[11-34] In assigning an all-black unit to Wright, however, the Air Force was introducing segregation where none had existed before, and here as in other areas its actions belied the expressed intent of the Gillem Board policy.

Impulse for Change

The problems associated with efficient use of black airmen intensified when the Air Force became an independent service in 1947. The number of Negroes fluctuated during the transition from Army Air Forces to Air Force, and as late as April 1948 the Army still retained a number of specialized black units whose members had the right to transfer to the Air Force. Estimates were that some 5,400 black airmen would eventually enter the Air Force from this source. Air Force officials believed that when these men were added to the 26,507 Negroes already in the new service, including 118 rated and 127 nonrated male officers and 4 female officers, the total would exceed the 10 percent quota suggested by the Gillem Board. Accordingly, soon after it became an independent service, the Air Force set the number of black enlistments at 300 per month until the necessary adjustments to the transfer program could be made.[11-35]

In addition to the chronic problems associated with black enlistments and quotas, four very specific problems demonstrated clearly to Air Force officials the urgent need for a change in race policy. The first of these was the distribution of black airmen which threatened the operational efficiency of the Tactical Air Command. A second, related to the first, revolved around the personnel shortages in black tactical units that necessitated an immediate reorganization of those units, a reorganization both controversial and managerially inefficient. The third and fourth problems were related; the demands of black leaders for a broader use of black servicemen suddenly intensified, dovetailing with the personal inclinations of the Secretary of the Air Force, who was making the strict segregation of black officers and specialists increasingly untenable. These four factors coalesced during 1948 and led to a reassessment of policy and, finally, to a *volte-face*.

SQUADRON F, 318TH AAF BATTALION,
in review, Lockbourne Air Force Base, Ohio, 1947.

Limiting black enlistment to 300 per month did little to ease the situation in the Tactical Air Command. There, the percentage of black personnel, although down from its postwar high of 28 percent to 15.4 percent by the end of 1947, remained several points above the Gillem Board's 10 percent quota throughout 1948. In March 1948 the command's Deputy Chief of Staff for Personnel, Col. John E. Barr, found that the large number of Negroes gave the command a surplus of "marginal individuals," men who could not be trained economically for the various skills needed. He argued that this theoretical surplus of Negroes was "potentially parasitic" and threatened the command's mission.[11-36]

At the same time, the command's personnel director found that Negroes were being inefficiently used. With one squadron designated for their black airmen, most commanders deemed surplus any Negroes in excess of the needs of that squadron and made little attempt to use them effectively. Even when some of these men were given a chance at skilled jobs in the Tactical Air Command their assignments proved short-lived. Because of a shortage of white airmen at Shaw Air Force Base, South Carolina, in early 1948, for example, Negroes from the base's Squadron F were assigned to fill all the slots in Squadron C, the base fire department. The Negroes performed so creditably that when enough white airmen to man Squadron C became available the commander suggested that the black fire fighters be transferred to Lockbourne rather than returned to their menial assignments.[11-37] The advantage of leaving the all-black Squadron C at Shaw was apparently overlooked by everyone.

Even this limited chance at occupational preferment was exceptional for black airmen in the Tactical Air Command. The command's personnel staff admitted that many highly skilled black technicians were performing menial tasks and that measures taken to raise the performance levels of other black airmen through training were inadequate. The staff also concluded that actions designed by the command to raise morale among black airmen left much to be desired. It mentioned specifically the excessively high turnover of officers assigned to black units, officers who for the most part proved mediocre as leaders. Most devastating of all, the study admitted that promotions and other rewards for duties performed by black airmen were not commensurate with those received by whites.[11-38]

Colonel Barr offered a solution that echoed the plea of Air Force commanders everywhere: revise Circular 124 to allow his organization to reduce the percentage of Negroes. Among a number of "compromise solutions" he recommended raising enlistment standards to reduce the number of submarginal airmen; designating Squadron E, the transportation squadron of the combat wings, a black unit; assigning all skilled black technicians to Lockbourne or declaring them surplus to the command; and selecting only outstanding officers to command black units.

One of these recommendations was under fire in Colonel Barr's own command. All-black transportation squadrons had already been discussed in the Ninth Air Force and had brought an immediate objection from Maj. Gen. William D. Old, its commander. Old explained that few black airmen in his command were qualified for "higher echelon maintenance activities," that is, major motor and transmission overhaul, and he had no black officers qualified to command such troops. On-the-job training would be impossible during total conversion of the squadrons from white to black; formal schooling for whole squadrons would have to be organized. Besides, Old continued, making transportation squadrons all black would only aggravate the command's race problems, for it would result in a further deviation from the "desired ratio of one to ten." Old wanted to reduce the number of black airmen in the Ninth Air Force by 1,633 men. The loss would not materially affect the efficiency of his command, he concluded. It would leave the Ninth Air Force with a ratio of one black officer to ten white and one black airman to eight white, and still permit the manning of black tactical units at full strength.[11-39] In the end none of these recommendations was followed. They needed the approval of Air Force headquarters, and as Lt. Gen. Elwood R. Quesada, commander of the Tactical Air Command, explained to General Old, the headquarters was in the midst of a lengthy review of Circular 124. In the meantime the command would have to carry on without guidance from higher headquarters.[11-40] Carry on it did, but the problems associated with the distribution of black airmen, problems the command constantly shared with Air Force headquarters, lingered throughout 1948.[11-41]

The Air Force's segregation policy had meanwhile created a critical situation in the black tactical units. The old 332d, now the 332d Fighter Wing, shared with the rest of the command the burden of too many low-scoring men—35 percent of Lockbourne's airmen were in the two lowest groups, IV and V—but here the problem was acute since the presence of so many persons with little ability limited the number of skilled black airmen that the Tactical Air Command could transfer to the wing from other parts of the command. Under direction of the command, the Ninth Air Force was taking advantage of a regulation that restricted the reenlistment of low-scoring airmen, but the high percentage of unskilled Negroes persisted at Lockbourne. Negroes in the upper test brackets were not reenlisting while the low scorers unquestionably were.[11-42]

At the same time there was a shortage of rated black officers. The 332d Fighter Wing was authorized 244 officers, but only 200 were assigned in February 1948. There was no easy solution to the shortage, a product of many years of neglect. Segregation imposed the necessity of devising a broad and long-range recruitment and training program for black officers, but not until April 1948 did the Tactical Air Command call for a steady flow of Negroes through officer candidate and flight training schools.[11-43] It hoped to have another thirty-one black pilot graduates by March 1949 and planned to recall thirty-two others from inactive status.[11-44] Even these steps could not possibly alleviate the serious shortage caused by the perennial failure to replace the wing's annual pilot attrition.

The chronic shortage of black field grade officers in the 332d was the immediate cause of the change in Air Force policy. By February 1948 the 332d had only thirteen of its forty-eight authorized field grade officers on duty. The three tactical units of the wing were commanded by captains instead of the authorized lieutenant colonels. If Colonel Davis were reassigned, and his attendance at the Air War College was expected momentarily, his successor as wing commander would be a major with five years' service.[11-45] The Tactical Air Commander was trying to have all field grade Negroes assigned to the 332d, but even that expedient would not provide enough officers.[11-46] Finally, General Quesada decided to recommend that "practically all" the key field grade positions in the 332d Wing be filled by whites.[11-47]

Subsequent discussions at Air Force headquarters gave the Air Force Chief of Staff, General Hoyt S. Vandenberg, three choices: leave Lockbourne manned exclusively by black officers; assign a white wing commander with a racially mixed staff; or permit Colonel Davis to remain in command with a racially mixed staff. Believing that General Vandenberg would approve the last course, the Tactical Air Command proceeded to search for appropriate white officers to fill the key positions under Davis.[11-48]

The deputy commander of the Ninth Air Force, Brig. Gen. Jarred V. Crabb, predicted that placing whites in key positions in the 332d would cause trouble, but leaving Davis in command of a mixed staff "would be loaded with dynamite."[11-49] The commander of the Ninth Air Force called the proposal to integrate the 332d's staff contrary to Air Force policy, which prescribed segregated units of not less than company strength. General Old was forthright:

[Integration] would be playing in the direction in which the negro press would like to force us. They are definitely attempting to force the Army and Air Force to solve the racial problem. As you know, they have been strongly advocating mixed companies of white and colored. For obvious reasons this is most undesirable and to do so would definitely limit the geographical locations in which such units could be employed. If the Air Forces go ahead and set a precedent, most undesirable repercussions may occur. Regardless of how the problem is solved, we would certainly come under strong criticism of the negro press. That must be expected.

In view of the combat efficiency demonstrated by colored organizations during the last war, my first recommendation in the interest of national defense and saving the taxpayer's money is to let the organization die on the vine. We make a big subject of giving the taxpayers the maximum amount of protection for each dollar spent, then turn around and support an organization that would contribute little or nothing in an emergency. It is my own opinion that it is an unnecessary drain on our national resources, but for political reasons I presume the organization must be retained. Therefore, my next recommended solution is to transfer all of the colored personnel from the Wing Headquarters staff to the Tactical and Service Organizations within the Wing structure and replace it with a completely white staff.[11-50]

It is difficult to estimate the extent to which these views were shared by other senior commanders, but they were widespread and revealed the tenacious hold of segregation.[11-51]

The Ninth Air Force's deputy commander offered another solution: use "whatever colored officers we have" to run Lockbourne. He urged that Colonel Davis's absence at the Air War College be considered a temporary arrangement. Meanwhile, the general added, "we can carry Lockbourne along for that period of time by close supervision from this headquarters."[11-52] As Davis later put it, cost effectiveness, not prejudice, was the key factor in the Air Force's wish to get rid of the 332d. The Air Force, he concluded, "wasn't getting its money's worth from negro pilots in a black air force."[11-53]

The Tactical Air Command's use of black troops is always singled out because of the numbers involved, but the problem was common to nearly all commands. Most Negroes in the Strategic Air Command, for example, were assigned to aviation engineer units where, as construction workers, they built roads, runways, and housing for the command's far-flung bases. These duties were transient, however, and like migrant workers at home, black construction crews were shifted from base to base as the need arose; they had little chance for promotion, let alone the opportunity to develop other skills.[11-54]

COLONEL DAVIS

The distribution of Negroes in all commands, and particularly the shortage of black specialists and officers in the 332d Fighter Wing, strongly influenced the Air Force to reexamine its racial policy, but pressures came from outside the department as well as from the black community which began to press its demands on the new service.[11-55] The prestigious Pittsburgh *Courier* opened the campaign in March 1948 by directing a series of questions on Air Force policy to the Chief of Staff. General Carl Spaatz responded with a smooth summary of the Gillem Board Report, leaning heavily on that document's progressive aims. "It is the feeling of this Headquarters," the Chief of Staff wrote, "that the ultimate Air Force objective must be to eliminate segregation among its personnel by the unrestricted use of Negro personnel in free competition for any duty within the Air Force for which they may qualify."[11-56] Unimpressed with this familiar rhetoric, the*Courier* headlined its account of the exchange, "Air Force to Keep Segregated Policy."

Assistant Secretary Eugene M. Zuckert followed General Spaatz's line when he met with black leaders at the National Defense Conference on Negro Affairs in April 1948, but his audience also showed little interest in future intentions. Putting it bluntly, they wanted to know why segregation was necessary in the Air Force. Zuckert could only assure them that segregation was a "practical military expediency," not an "endorsement of belief in racial distribution."[11-57] But the black leaders pressed the matter further. Why was it expedient in a system dedicated to consideration of the individual, asked the president of Howard University, to segregate a Negro of superior mentality? At Yale or Harvard, Dr. Mordecai Johnson continued, he would be kept on the team, but if he entered the Air Force he would be "brigaded with all the people from Mississippi and Alabama who had had education that costs $100 a year."[11-58]

Answering for the Air Force, Lt. Gen. Idwal H. Edwards, the Deputy Chief of Staff for Personnel, admitted segregation was unnecessary, promised eventual integration, but stated firmly that for the present segregation remained Air Force policy. As evidence of progress, Edwards pointed to the peaceful integration of black officers in training at Randolph Field. For one conferee this "progress" led to another conclusion: resistance to integration had to emanate from the policymakers, not from the fighting men. All Edwards could manage in the way of a reply was that Air Force policy was considered "the best way to make this thing work under present conditions."[11-59] Later Edwards, who was not insensitive to the arguments of the black leaders, told Secretary of the Air Force W. Stuart Symington that perhaps some recommendation

132

"looking toward the integration of whites and negroes in the same units may be forthcoming" from the Air Board's study of racial policy which was to commence the first week in May.[11-60]

If the logic of the black leaders impressed General Edwards, the demands themselves had little effect on policy. It remained for James C. Evans, now the adviser to Secretary of Defense Forrestal, to translate these questions and demands into recommendations for specific action. Taking advantage of a long acquaintance with the Secretary of the Air Force, Evans discussed the department's race problem with him in May 1948. Symington was sympathetic. "Put it on paper," he told Evans.[11-61]

Couching his recommendations in terms of the Gillem Board policy, Evans faithfully summarized for the secretary the demands of black leaders. Specifically, he asked that Colonel Davis, the commander of Lockbourne Air Force Base, be sent for advanced military schooling without delay. Diversification of career was long overdue for Davis, the ranking black officer in the Air Force, as it was for others who were considered indispensable because of the small number of qualified black leaders. For Davis, most of all, the situation was unfair since he had always been in command of practically all rated black officers. Nor was it good for his subordinates. The Air Force should not hesitate to assign a white replacement for Davis. In effect, Evans was telling Symington that the black community would understand the necessity for such a move.

Besides, under the program Evans was recommending, the all-black wing would soon cease to exist. He wanted the Air Force to "deemphasize" Lockbourne as the black air base and scatter the black units concentrated there. He wanted to see Negroes dispersed throughout the Air Force, either individually or in small units contemplated by the Gillem Board, but he wanted men assigned on the basis of technical specialty and proficiency rather than race. It was unrealistic, he declared, to assume all black officers could be most effectively utilized as pilots and all enlisted men as Squadron F laborers. Limiting training and job opportunity because of race reduced fighting potential in a way that never could be justified. The Air Force should open to its Negroes a wide variety of training, experience, and opportunity to acquire versatility and proficiency.[11-62]

GENERAL EDWARDS

If followed, this program would fundamentally alter Air Force racial practices. General Edwards recommended that the reply to Evans should state that certain policy changes would be forthcoming, although they would have to await the outcome of a departmental reevaluation currently under way. The suggestions had been solicited by Symington, and Edwards was anxious for Evans to understand the delay was not a device to defer action.[11-63]

Edwards was in a position to make such assurances. He was an influential member of the Air staff with considerable experience in the field of race relations. As a member of the Army staff during World War II he had worked closely with the old McCloy committee on black troops and had strongly advocated wartime experiments with the integration of small-scale units.[11-64] His background, along with his observations as chief personnel officer in the new Air Force, had taught him to avoid abstract appeals to justice and to make suggestions in terms of military efficiency. Concern with efficiency led him, soon after the Air Force became a separate service, to order Lt. Col. Jack F. Marr, a member of his staff, to study the Air Force's racial policy and practices. Testifying to Edwards's pragmatic approach, Marr later said of his own introduction to the subject: "There was no sociology involved. It was merely a routine staff action along with a bunch of other staff actions that were taking place."[11-65]

COLONEL MARR

A similar concern for efficiency, this time triggered by criticism at the National Defense Conference on Negro Affairs in April 1948 and Evans's discussions with Secretary Symington the following month, led Edwards, after talking it over with Assistant Secretary Zuckert, to raise the subject of the employment of Negroes in the Air Board in May.[11-66] In the wake of the Air Board discussion the Chief of Staff appointed a group under Maj. Gen. Richard E. Nugent, then Director of Civilian Personnel, to reexamine the service's race policy.[11-67] Nugent was another Air Force official who viewed the employment of Negroes as a problem in military efficiency.[11-68] These three, Edwards, Nugent, and Marr, were the chief figures in the development of the Air Force integration plan, which grew out of the Nugent group's study. Edwards and Nugent supervised its many refinements in the staff while Marr, whom Zuckert later described as the indispensable man, wrote the plan and remained intimately connected with it until the Air Force carried it out.[11-69] Antedating the Truman order to integrate the services, the provisions of this plan eventually became the program under which the Air Force was integrated.[11-70]

133

As it evolved during the months of deliberation,[11-71] the Air Force study of black manpower weighed Air Force practices against the Gillem Board Report and found them "considerably divergent" from the policy as outlined. It isolated several reasons for this divergence. Black airmen on the whole, as measured by classification tests, were unsuitable and inadequate for operating all-black air units organized and trained for modern combat. To achieve a balance of skills and training in black units was a "never ending problem for which there appears to be no solution under either the current Air Force policies or the policies recommended by the Gillem Board." In short, practices with respect to Negroes were "wasteful, deleterious to military effectiveness and lacking in wartime application."

Edwards and his staff saw several advantages in complete integration. Wherever qualified black airmen had been permitted to compete with whites on their individual qualifications and abilities, the Negroes "achieved a certain amount of acceptance and recognition." Students in some schools lived and learned side by side as a matter of practical necessity. "This degree of integration and acceptance on a competitive basis has been eminently successful and has to a remarkable degree solved the 'Negro problem' for the training schools involved." At some bases qualified black airmen were administratively assigned to black units but actually performed duties in white units. Some commanders had requested that these men be permanently transferred and assigned to the white units because the men deserved higher grades but could not receive them in black units and because it was poor management to have individuals performing duties for one military organization and living under the administrative jurisdiction of another.

In the end consideration of full integration was dropped in favor of a program based on the Navy's postwar integration of its general service. Edwards and his personnel staff dismissed the Navy's problems with stewards and its difficulty in enlisting skilled Negroes as temporary embarrassments with little practical consequence. This problem apparently allowed an economic and efficient use of Negroes and also "relieved the Navy of the necessity for repeated efforts to justify an untenable position." They saw several practical advantages in a similar policy for the Air Force. It would allow the elimination of the 10 percent quota. The inactivation of some black units—"and the pronounced relief of the problems involved in maintaining those units under present conditions"—could be accomplished without injustice to Negroes and with benefit to the Air Force. Nor would the integration of qualified Negroes in technical and combat units appreciably alter current practices; according to contemporary estimates such skilled men would never total more that 1 percent of the service's manpower.

The logic of social justice might have led to total integration, but it would not have solved the Air Force's pressing problem of too many unskilled blacks. It was consideration of military efficiency, therefore, that led these personnel experts to propose a system of limited integration along the lines of the Navy's postwar policy. Such a system, they concluded, would release the Air Force from its quota obligation—and hence its continuing surplus of unskilled men—and free it to assign its relatively small group of skilled black recruits where they were needed and might advance.

Although limited, the proposed reform was substantial enough to arouse opposition. General Edwards reported overwhelming opposition to any form of integration among Air Force officers, and never during the spring of 1948 did the Chief of Staff seriously consider even partial integration.[11-72] But if integration, even in a small dose, was unpalatable, widespread inefficiency was intolerable. And a new service, still in the process of developing policy, might embrace the new and the practical, especially if pressure were exerted from above. Assistant Secretary Zuckert intimated as much when he finally replied to James Evans, "You have my personal assurance that our present position is not in the interest of maintaining the status quo, but it is in anticipation of a more progressive and more satisfactory action in the relatively near future."[11-73]

CHAPTER 12
The President Intervenes

On 26 July 1948 President Harry S. Truman signed Executive Order 9981, calling on the armed forces to provide equal treatment and opportunity for black servicemen. This act has variously been described as an example of presidential initiative, the capstone of the Truman civil rights program, and the climax of the struggle for racial equality in the armed forces. But in some ways the order was simply a practical response to a presidential dilemma.

The President's order was related to the advent of the cold war. Developments in the Middle East and Europe testified to the ambitions of the Soviet Union, and many Americans feared the spread of communism throughout the world, a threat more ominous with the erosion of American military strength since World War II. In March 1947 Truman enunciated a new foreign policy calling for the containment of Soviet expansion and pledging economic and military aid to Greece and Turkey. A year later he asked Congress to adopt the Marshall Plan for

134

economic aid to Europe, authorize military training, and enact a new selective service law to maintain the armed forces at expanded levels. That same month his principal military advisers met at Key West, Florida, to discuss new military roles and missions for the armed forces, grapple with paralyzing divisions among the services, and re-form the military establishment into a genuinely unified whole.[12-1] As if to underscore the urgency of these measures, the Soviet Union began in April 1948 to harass Allied troops in Berlin, an action that would develop into a full-scale blockade by June.

Integration of the armed forces hardly loomed large on the international scene, but if the problem of race appeared insignificant to military planners, the sheer number of Negroes in the armed forces gave them new prominence in national defense. Because of postwar racial quotas, particularly in the Army and Air Force, black servicemen now constituted a significant segment of the service population, and consequently their abilities and well-being had a direct bearing on the nation's cold war defenses. The black community represented 10 percent of the country's manpower, and this also influenced defense planning. Black threats to boycott the segregated armed forces could not be ignored, and civil rights demands had to be considered in developing laws relating to selective service and universal training. Nor could the administration overlook the fact that the United States had become a leading protagonist in a cold war in which the sympathies of the undeveloped and mostly colored world would soon assume a special importance. Inasmuch as integration of the services had become an almost universal demand of the black community, integration became, willy-nilly, an important defense issue.

A second stimulus to improvement of the black serviceman's position was the Truman administration's strong civil rights program, which gave executive sanction to a national movement started some years before. The civil rights movement was the product of many factors, including the federal government's increased sense of responsibility for the welfare of all its citizens, a sense that had grown out of the New Deal and a world war which expanded horizons and increased economic power for much of the black population. The Supreme Court had recently accelerated this movement by broadening its interpretation of the Fourteenth Amendment. In the black community itself greater participation in elections and new techniques in community action were eroding discriminatory traditions and practices in many communities.

The civil rights movement had in fact progressed by 1948 to a stage at which it was politically attractive for a Democratic president to assume a vigorous civil rights stance. The urban black vote had become a major goal of Truman's election campaign, and he was being pressed repeatedly by his advisers to demonstrate his support for black interests. A presidential order on armed forces integration logically followed because the services, conspicuous practitioners of segregation and patently susceptible to unilateral action on the part of the Chief Executive, were obvious and necessary targets in the black voters' campaign for civil rights.

Finally, the integration order resulted in part from the move toward service unification and the emergence of James V. Forrestal as Secretary of Defense. Despite misgivings over centralized control of the nation's defense establishment and overconcentration of power in the hands of a Secretary of Defense, Forrestal soon discovered that certain problems rising out of common service experiences naturally converged on the office of the secretary. Both by philosophy and temperament he was disposed to avoid a clash with the services over integration. He remained sensitive to their interests and rights, and he frankly doubted the efficacy of social change through executive fiat. Yet Forrestal was not impervious to the aspirations of the civil rights activists; guided by a humane interest in racial equality, he made integration a departmental goal. His technique for achieving integration, however, proved inadequate in the face of strong service opposition, and finally the President, acting on the basis of these seemingly unrelated motives, had to issue the executive order to strengthen the defense secretary's hand.

The Truman Administration and Civil Rights

Executive and legislative interest in the civil rights of black Americans reached a level in 1948 unmatched since Reconstruction. The President himself was the catalyst. By creating a presidential committee on civil rights and developing a legislative program based on its findings, Truman brought the black minority into the political arena and committed the federal government to a program of social legislation that it has continued to support ever since. Little in the President's background suggested he would sponsor basic social changes. He was a son of the middle border, from a family firmly dedicated to the Confederate cause. His appreciation of black aspirations was hardly sophisticated, as he revealed to a black audience in 1940: "I wish to make it clear that I am not appealing for social equality of the Negro. The Negro himself knows better than that, and the highest types of Negro leaders say quite frankly they prefer the society of their own people. Negroes want justice, not social relations."[12-2]

Nor did his attitude change drastically in later years. In 1961, seven years after the Supreme Court's vital school integration decision, Truman was calling the Freedom Riders

135

"meddlesome intruders who should stay at home and attend to their own business." His suggestion to proprietors of lunch counters undergoing sit-ins was to kick out unwelcome customers.[12-3] But if he failed to appreciate the scope of black demands, Truman nevertheless demonstrated as early as 1940 an acute awareness of the connection between civil rights for blacks and civil liberties for all Americans:

In giving Negroes the rights which are theirs we are only acting in accord with our own ideals of a true democracy. If any class or race can be permanently set apart from, or pushed down below the rest in political and civil rights, so may any other class or race when it shall incur the displeasure of its more powerful associates, and we may say farewell to the principles on which we count our safety.[12-4]

He would repeat these sentiments to other gatherings, including the assembled delegates of the NAACP's 1946 convention.[12-5] The President's civil rights program would be based, then, on a practical concern for the rights of the majority. Neither his social philosophy nor his political use of black demands should detract from his achievements in the field of civil rights.

It was probably just as well that Truman adopted a pragmatic approach to civil rights, for there was little social legislation a reform president could hope to get through the postwar Congresses. Dominated by a conservative coalition that included the Dixiecrats, a group of sometimes racially reactionary southerners, Congress showed little interest in civil rights. The creation of a permanent Fair Employment Practices Commission, the one piece of legislation directly affecting Negroes and the only current test of congressional intent in civil rights, was floundering on Capitol Hill. Truman conspicuously supported the fair employment measure, but did little else specifically in the first year after the war to advance civil rights. Instead he seemed content to carry on with the New Deal approach to the problem: improve the social condition of all Americans and the condition of the minorities will also improve. In this vein his first domestic program concentrated on national projects for housing, health, and veterans' benefits.

The conversion of Harry Truman into a forceful civil rights advocate seems to have come about, at least partially, from his exposure to what he later called the "anti-minority" incidents visited on black servicemen and civilians in 1946.[12-6] Although the lynchings, property destruction, and assaults never matched the racial violence that followed World War I, they were enough to convince many civil rights leaders that the pattern of racial strife was being repeated. Some of these men, along with a group of labor executives and clergymen, formed a National Emergency Committee Against Mob Violence to warn the American public against the dangers of racial intolerance. A delegation from this committee, with Walter White as spokesman, met with the President on 19 September 1946 to demand government action. White described the scene:

The President sat quietly, elbows resting on the arms of his chair and his fingers interlocked against his stomach as he listened with a grim face to the story of the lynchings.... When I finished, the President exclaimed in his flat, midwestern accent, "My God! I had no idea it was as terrible as that! We've got to do something!"[12-7]

But the Truman administration had nearly exhausted the usual remedies open to it. The Attorney General had investigated the lynchings and Klan activities and the President had spoken out strongly and repeatedly against mob violence but without clear and pertinent civil rights legislation presidential exhortations and investigations counted for very little. Civil rights leaders like White understood this, and, given the mood of Congress, they were resigned to the lack of legislative support. Nevertheless, it was in this context that the President decided to create a committee to investigate and report on the status of civil rights in America.

The concept of a federal civil rights group had been circulating in the executive branch for some time. After the Detroit race riot in 1943, presidential assistant Jonathan Daniels had organized a committee to deal with racial troubles. Proposals to create a national organization to reduce racial tensions were advanced later in the war, principally by Saul K. Padover, a minority specialist in the Interior Department, and David K. Niles of the White House staff. Little came of the committee idea, however, because Roosevelt was convinced that any steps associated with integration would prove divisive and were unwise during wartime.[12-8] With the war over and a different political climate prevailing, Niles, now senior White House adviser on minority affairs, proposed the formation of a committee not only to investigate racial violence but also to explore the entire subject of civil rights.

WALTER WHITE

Walter White and his friends greeted the idea with some skepticism. They had come demanding action, but were met instead with another promise of a committee and the probability of interminable congressional debate and unproductive hearings.[12-9] But this time, for several reasons, it would be different. In the first place the civil rights leaders underestimated the sincerity of Truman's reaction to the racial violence. He had quickly agreed to create Niles's committee by executive order to save it from possible pigeonholing at the hands of a hostile Congress. He had also given the group, called the President's Committee on Civil Rights, a broad directive "to determine whether and in what respect current law enforcement measures and the authority and means possessed by Federal, State, and local governments may be strengthened and improved to safeguard the civil rights of the people."[12-10] The civil rights leaders also failed to gauge the effect Republican victories in the 1946 congressional elections would have on the administration. Finding it necessary to court the Negro and other minorities and hoping to confound congressional opposition, the administration sought a strong civil rights program to put before the Eightieth Congress. Thus, the committee's recommendations would get respectful attention in the White House. Finally, neither the civil rights leaders nor the President could have foreseen the effectiveness of the committee members. Serving under Charles E. Wilson, president of the General Electric Company, the group included among its fifteen members distinguished church leaders, public service lawyers, the presidents of Dartmouth College and the University of North Carolina, and prominent labor executives. The committee had two black members, Sadie T. M. Alexander, a lawyer from Philadelphia, and Channing H. Tobias, director of the Phelps-Stokes Fund. Its members not only prepared a comprehensive survey of the condition of civil rights in America but also presented to the President on 29 October 1947 a far-reaching series of recommendations, in effect a program for corrective action that would serve as a bench mark for civil rights progress for many years.[12-11]

The group recommended the concentration of civil rights work in the Department of Justice, the establishment of a permanent civil rights commission, a federal antilynching act, a permanent Fair Employment Practices Commission, and legislation to correct discrimination in voting and naturalization laws. It also examined the state of civil rights in the armed forces and incidentally publicized the long-ignored survey of black infantry platoons that had fought in Europe in 1945.[12-12] It concluded:

The injustice of calling men to fight for freedom while subjecting them to humiliating discrimination within the fighting forces is at once apparent. Furthermore, by preventing entire groups from making their maximum contribution to the national defense, we weaken our defense to that extent and impose heavier burdens on the remainder of the population.[12-13]

The committee called for sweeping change in the armed forces, recommending that Congress enact legislation, followed by appropriate administrative action, to end all discrimination and segregation in the services. Concluding that the recent service unification provided a timely opportunity for revision of existing policies and practices, the committee proposed a specific ban on discrimination and segregation in all phases of recruitment, assignment, and training, including selection for service schools and academies, as well as in mess halls, quarters, recreational facilities, and post exchanges. It also wanted commissions and promotions awarded on merit alone and asked for new laws to protect servicemen from discrimination in communities adjacent to military bases.[12-14] The committee wanted the President to look beyond the integration of people working and living on military bases, and it introduced a concept that would gain considerable support in a future administration. The armed forces, it declared, *should* be used as an instrument of social change. World War II had demonstrated that the services were a laboratory in which citizens could be educated on a broad range of social and political issues, and the administration was neglecting an effective technique for teaching the public the advantages of providing equal treatment and opportunity for all citizens.[12-15]

President Truman deleted the recommendations on civil rights in the services when he transmitted the committee's recommendations to Congress in the form of a special message on 2 February 1948. Arguing that the services' race practices were matters of executive interest and pointing to recent progress toward better race relations in the armed forces, the President told Congress that he had already instructed the Secretary of Defense to take steps to eliminate remaining instances of discrimination in the services as rapidly as possible. He also promised that the personnel policies and practices of all the services would be made uniform.[12-16]

To press for civil rights legislation for the armed forces or even to mention segregation was politically imprudent. Truman had two pieces of military legislation to get through Congress: a new draft law and a provision for universal military training. These he considered too vital to the nation's defense to risk grounding on the shoals of racial controversy. For the time being at least, integration of the armed forces would have to be played down, and any civil rights progress in the Department of Defense would have to depend on the persuasiveness of James Forrestal.

TRUMAN'S CIVIL RIGHTS CAMPAIGN
as seen by Washington Star cartoonist Clifford K. Berryman, March 14, 1948.

The basic postwar reorganization of the National Military Establishment, the National Security Act of 1947, created the Office of the Secretary of Defense, a separate Department of the Air Force, the Central Intelligence Agency, and the National Security Council. It also reconstituted the War Department as the Department of the Army and gave legal recognition as a permanent agency to the Joint Chiefs of Staff. The principle of military unification that underlay the reorganization plan was muted in the legislation that finally emerged from Congress. Although the Secretary of Defense was given authority to establish general policies and to exercise general direction and control of the services, the services themselves retained a large measure of autonomy in their internal administration and individual service secretaries retained cabinet rank. In effect, the act created a secretary without a department, a reorganization that largely reflected the viewpoint of the Navy. The Army had fought for a much greater degree of unification, which would not be achieved until the passage of the National Security Act amendments of 1949. This legislation redesignated the unified department the Department of Defense, strengthened the powers of the Secretary of Defense, and provided for uniform budgetary procedures. Although the services were to be "separately administered," their respective secretaries henceforward headed "military departments" without cabinet status.

The first Secretary of Defense, James Forrestal, was a man of exceptional administrative talents, yet even before taking office he expressed strong reservations on the wisdom of a unified military department. As early as 30 July 1945, at breakfast with President Truman during the Potsdam Conference, Forrestal questioned whether any one man "was good enough to run the combined Army, Navy, and Air Departments." What kind of men could the president get in peacetime, he asked, to be under secretaries of War, Navy, and Air if they were subordinate to a single defense secretary?[12-17] Speaking to Lester Granger that same year on the power of the Secretary of the Navy to order the Marine Corps to accept Negroes, Forrestal expressed uncertainty about a cabinet officer's place in the scheme of things. "Some people think the Secretary is god-almighty, but he's just a god-damn civilian."[12-18] Even after his appointment as defense secretary doubts lingered: "My chief misgivings about unification derived from my fear that there would be a tendency toward overconcentration and reliance on one man or one-group direction. In other words, too much central control."[12-19]

Forrestal's philosophy of management reinforced the limitations placed on the Secretary of Defense by the National Security Act. He sought a middle way in which the efficiency of a unified system could be obtained without sacrificing what he considered to be the real advantages of service autonomy. Thus, he supported a 1945 report of the defense study group under Ferdinand Eberstadt that argued for a "coordinated" rather than a "unitary" defense establishment.[12-20] Practical experience modified his fears somewhat, and by October 1948, convinced he needed greater power to control the defense establishment, Forrestal urged that the language of the National Security Act, which limited the Secretary of Defense to "general" authority only over the military departments, be amended to eliminate the word *general*. Yet he always retained his basic distrust of dictation, preferring to understand and adjust rather than to conclude and order.[12-21]

Nowhere was Forrestal's philosophy of government more evident than in his approach to the problem of integration. His office would be concerned with equal opportunity, he promised Walter White soon after his elevation to the new post, but "the job of Secretary of Defense," he warned, "is one which will have to develop in an evolutionary rather than a revolutionary manner." Further dashing hopes of sudden reform, Forrestal added that specific racial problems, as distinct from general policy matters, would remain the province of the individual services.[12-22] He retained this attitude throughout his tenure. He considered the President's instructions to end remaining instances of discrimination in the services "in accord with my own conception of my responsibilities under unification," and he was in wholehearted agreement with a presidential wish that the National Military Establishment work out the answer to its racial problems through administrative action. He wanted to see a "more nearly uniform approach to interracial problems by the three Services," but experience had demonstrated, he believed, that racial problems could not be solved simply by publishing an executive order or passing a law. Racial progress would come from education. Such had been his observation in the wartime Navy, and he was ready to promise that "even greater progress will be made in the future." But, he added, "progress must be made administratively and should not be put into effect by fiat."[12-23]

Executive fiat was just what some of Forrestal's advisers wanted. For example, his executive assistant, John H. Ohly, his civilian aide, James C. Evans,[12-24] and Truman Gibson urged the secretary to consider establishing an interservice committee along the lines of the old McCloy committee to prepare a uniform racial policy that he could apply to all the services. They wanted the committee to examine past and current practices as well as the recent reports of the

President's Advisory Commission on Universal Training and the Committee on Civil Rights and to make specific recommendations for carrying out and policing department policy. Truman Gibson went to the heart of the matter: the formulation of such an interservice committee would signal to the black community better than anything else the defense establishment's determination to change the racial situation. More and more, he warned, the discrepancies among the services' racial practices were attracting public attention. Most important to the administration was the fact that these discrepancies were strengthening opposition to universal military training and the draft.[12-25]

A. PHILIP RANDOLPH.

(Detail from painting by Betsy G. Reyneau.)

Gibson was no doubt referring to A. Philip Randolph, president of the Brotherhood of Sleeping Car Porters and organizer of the 1940 March on Washington Movement, who had spoken out against the pending legislation. Randolph was particularly concerned that the bill did not prohibit segregation, and he quoted a member of the Advisory Commission on Universal Training who admitted that the bill ignored the racial issue because "the South might oppose UMT if Negroes were included." Drafting eighteen-year olds into a segregated Army was a threat to black progress, Randolph charged, because enforced segregation made it difficult to break down other forms of discrimination. Convinced that the Pentagon was trying to bypass the segregation issue, Randolph and Grant Reynolds, a black clergyman and New York politician, formed a Committee Against Jim Crow in Military Service and Training. They planned to submit a proposal to the President and Congress for drafting a nondiscrimination measure for the armed forces, and they were prepared to back up this demand with a march on Washington—no empty gesture in an election year. Randolph had impressive backing from black leaders, among them Dr. Channing H. Tobias of the Civil Rights Committee, George S. Schuyler, columnist of the Pittsburgh *Courier*, L. D. Reddick, curator of the Schomburg Collection of the New York Public Library, and Joe Louis.[12-26]

Black spokesmen were particularly incensed by the attitude of the Secretary of the Army and his staff. Walter White pointed out that these officials continued to justify segregated units on the grounds that segregation was—he quoted them—"in the interest of national defense." White went to special pains to refute the Army's contention that segregation was necessary because the Army had to conform to local laws and customs. "How," he asked Secretary Forrestal,

can the imposition of segregation upon northern states having clear-cut laws and policies in opposition to such practices be justified by the Army?... In view of President Truman's recent report to the Congress and in view of the report of his Committee on Civil Rights condemning segregation in the Armed Forces, I am at a loss to understand the reluctance on the part of the Department of Defense to immediately eliminate all vestiges of discrimination and segregation in the Armed Forces of this country. As the foremost defender of democratic principles in international councils, the United States can ill afford to any longer discriminate against its Negro citizens in its Armed Forces solely because they were fortunate or unfortunate enough to be born Negroes.[12-27]

Forrestal stubbornly resisted the pleas of his advisers and black leaders that he assume a more active role. In the first place he had real doubts concerning his authority to do so. Forrestal was also aware of the consequences an integration campaign would have on Capitol Hill, where he was in the midst of delicate negotiations on defense measures. But most of all the role of crusader did not fit him. "I have gone somewhat slowly," Forrestal had written in late October 1947, "because I believe in the theory of having things to talk about as having been done rather than having to predict them, and ... morale and confidence are easy to destroy but not easy to rebuild. In other words, I want to be sure that any changes we make are changes that accomplish something and not merely for the sake of change."[12-28]

To Forrestal equal opportunity was not a pious platitude, but a practical means of solving the military's racial problems. Equal opportunity was the tactic he had used in the Navy where he had encouraged specialized training for all qualified Negroes. He understood that on shipboard machinists ate and bunked with machinists, firemen with firemen. Inaugurated in the fleet, the practice naturally spread to the shore establishment, and equal opportunity led inevitably to the integration of the general service. Given the opportunity to qualify for all specialties, Negroes—albeit their number was limited to the small group in the general service—quickly gained equal treatment in off-the-job activities. Forrestal intended to apply the same tactic to achieve the same results in the other services.[12-29]

As in the past, he turned first to Lester Granger, his old friend from the National Urban League. Acting on the recommendation of his special assistant, Marx Leva, Forrestal invited

139

Granger to the Pentagon to discuss the department's racial problems with a view to holding a general conference and symposium on the subject. As usual, Granger was full of ideas, and he and the secretary agreed that Forrestal should create a "critics group," which would discuss "Army and general defense policies in the use of Negro personnel."[12-30] Granger suggested a roster of black and white experts, influential in the black community and representing most shades of opinion, but he would exclude those apt to make political capital out of the issues.

The Leva-Granger conference idea fitted neatly into Forrestal's thinking. It offered the possibility of introducing to the services in a systematic and documented way the complaints of responsible black leaders while instructing those leaders in the manpower problems confronting the postwar armed forces. He hoped the conference would modify traditionalist attitudes toward integration while curbing mounting unrest in the black community. Granger and Forrestal agreed that the conference should be held soon. Although Granger wanted some "good solid white representation" in the group, Forrestal decided instead to invite fifteen black leaders to meet on 26 April in the Pentagon; he alerted the service secretaries, asking them to attend or to designate an assistant to represent them in each case.[12-31]

Announcement of the conference was upstaged in the press by the activities of some civil rights militants, including those whom Granger sought to exclude from the Forrestal conference because he thought they would make a political issue of the war against segregation. Forrestal first learned of the militants' plans from members of the National Negro Publishers Association, a group of publishers and editors of important black journals who were about to tour European installations as guests of the Army.[12-32] At Granger's suggestion Forrestal had met with the publishers and editors to explain the causes for the delay in desegregating the services. Instead, he found himself listening to an impassioned demand for immediate change. Ira F. Lewis, president of the Pittsburgh *Courier* and spokesman for the group, told the secretary that the black community did not expect the services to be a laboratory or clearinghouse for processing the social ills of the nation, but it wanted to warn the man responsible for military preparedness that the United States could not afford another war with one-tenth of its population lacking the spirit to fight. The problem of segregation could best be solved by the policymakers. "The colored people of the country have a high regard for you, Mr. Secretary, as a square shooter," Lewis concluded. And from Forrestal they expected action.[12-33]

While black newspapermen were pressing the executive branch, Randolph and his Committee Against Jim Crow were demanding congressional action. Randolph concentrated on one explosive issue, the Army's procurement of troops. The first War Department plans for postwar manpower procurement were predicated on some form of universal military training, a new concept for the United States. The plans immediately came under fire from Negroes because the Army, citing the Gillem Board Report as its authority, had specified that black recruits be trained in segregated units. The Army had also specified that the black units form parts of larger, racially mixed units and would be trained in racially mixed camps.[12-34] The President's Advisory Commission on Universal Training (the Compton Commission), appointed to study the Army's program, strongly objected to the segregation provisions, but to no avail.[12-35] As if to signal its intentions the Army trained an experimental universal military training unit in 1947 at Fort Knox that carefully excluded black volunteers.

The showdown between civil rights organizations and the administration over universal military training never materialized. Faced with chronic opposition to the program and the exigencies of the cold war, the administration quietly shelved universal training and concentrated instead on the reestablishment of the selective service system. When black attention naturally shifted to the new draft legislation, Randolph was able to capitalize on the determination of many leaders in the civil rights movement to defeat any draft law that countenanced the Army's racial policy. Appearing at the Senate Armed Services Committee hearings on the draft bill, Randolph raised the specter of civil disobedience, pledging

to openly counsel, aid, and abet youth, both white and Negro, to quarantine any Jim Crow conscription system, whether it bear the label of universal military training or selective service....

From coast to coast in my travels I shall call upon all Negro veterans to join this civil disobedience movement and to recruit their younger brothers in an organized refusal to register and be drafted....

I shall appeal to the thousands of white youths ... to demonstrate their solidarity with Negro youth by ignoring the entire registration and induction machinery....

I shall appeal to the Negro parents to lend their moral support to their sons, to stand behind them as they march with heads held high to Federal prisons as a telling demonstration to the world that Negroes have reached the limit of human endurance, that, in the words of the spiritual, we will be buried in our graves before we will be slaves.[12-36]

140

Randolph argued that hard-won gains in education, job opportunity, and housing would be nullified by federal legislation supporting segregation. How could a Fair Employment Practices Commission, he asked, dare criticize discrimination in industry if the government itself was discriminating against Negroes in the services? "Negroes are just sick and tired of being pushed around," he concluded, "and we just do not propose to take it, and we do not care what happens."[12-37]

When Senator Wayne Morse warned Randolph that such statements in times of national emergency would leave him open to charges of treason, Randolph replied that by fighting for their rights Negroes were serving the cause of American democracy. Borrowing from the rhetoric of the cold war, he predicted that such was the effect of segregation on the international fight for men's minds that America could never stop communism as long as it was burdened with Jim Crowism. Randolph threw down the gauntlet. "We have to face this thing sooner or later, and we might just as well face it now."[12-38] It was up to the administration and Congress to decide whether his challenge was the beginning of a mass movement or a weightless threat by an extremist group.

The immediate reaction of various spokesmen for the black community supported both possibilities. Also testifying before the Senate Armed Services Committee, Truman Gibson, who was a member of the Compton Commission that had objected to segregation, expressed "shock and dismay" at Randolph's pledge and predicted that Negroes would continue to participate in the country's defense effort.[12-39] For his pains Gibson was branded a "rubber stamp Uncle Tom" by Congressman Adam Clayton Powell. The black press, for the most part, applauded Randolph's analysis of the mood of Negroes, but shied away from the threat of civil disobedience. The NAACP and most other civil rights organizations took the same stand, condemning segregation but disavowing civil disobedience.[12-40]

Although the administration could take comfort in the relatively mild reaction from conservative blacks, an important element of the black community supported Randolph's stand. A poll of young educated Negroes conducted by the NAACP revealed that 71 percent of those of draft age would support the civil disobedience campaign. So impressive was Randolph's support—the New York *Times* called it a blunt warning from the black public—that one news journal saw in the campaign the specter of a major national crisis.[12-41] On the other hand, the Washington *Post* cautioned its readers not to exaggerate the significance of the protest. Randolph's words, the *Post* declared, were intended "more as moral pressure" for nondiscrimination clauses in pending draft and universal military training legislation than as a serious threat.[12-42]

Whatever its ultimate influence on national policy, the Randolph civil disobedience pledge had no visible effect on the position of the President or Congress. With a draft bill and a national political convention pending, the President was not about to change his hands-off policy toward the segregation issue in the services. In fact he showed some heat at what he saw as a threat by extremists to exploit an issue he claimed he was doing his best to resolve.[12-43] As for members of Congress, most of those who joined in the debate on the draft bill simply ignored the threatened boycott.

In contrast to the militant Randolph, the Negroes who gathered at Secretary Forrestal's invitation for the National Defense Conference on 26 April appeared to be a rather sedate group. But academic honors, business success, and gray hairs were misleading. These eminent educators, clergymen, and civil rights leaders proved just as determined as Randolph and his associates to be rid of segregation and, considering their position in the community, were more likely to influence the administration. That they were their own men quickly became apparent in the stormy course of the Pentagon meeting. They subjected a score of defense officials[12-44] to searching questions, submitted themselves to cross-examination by the press, and agreed to prepare a report for the Secretary of Defense.

While the group refrained from endorsing Randolph's position, it also refrained from criticizing him and strongly supported his thesis that segregation in itself was discrimination. Nor were its views soft-pedaled in the press release issued after the conference. The Secretary of Defense was forced to announce that the black leaders declined to serve as advisers to the National Military Establishment as long as the services continued to practice segregation. The group unanimously recommended that the armed services eliminate segregation and challenged the Army's interpretation of its own policy, insisting that the Army could abolish segregation even within the framework of the Gillem Board recommendations. The members planned no future meetings but adjourned to prepare their report.[12-45]

This adamant stand should not have surprised the Secretary of Defense. Forrestal could appreciate more than most the pressures operating on the group. In the aftermath of the report of the President's Committee on Civil Rights and in the heightened atmosphere caused by the rhetoric of the Randolph campaign, these men were also caught up in the militants' cause. If they were reluctant to attack the services too severely lest they lose their chance to influence the course of racial events in the department, they were equally reluctant to accept the pace of reform dictated by the traditionalists. In the end they chose to side with their more radical colleagues. Thus despite Lester Granger's attempt to soften the blow, the conference designed to bring the opponents together ended with yet another condemnation of Forrestal's gradualism.

Forrestal himself agreed with the goals of the conferees, he told Granger, but at the same time he refused to abandon his approach, insisting that he could not force people into cooperation and mutual respect by issuing a directive. Instead he arranged for Granger to meet with Army leaders to spread the gospel of equal opportunity and ordered a report prepared showing precisely what the Navy did during the late months of the war and "how much of it has stuck—on the question of non-segregation both in messing and barracks." The report, written by Lt. Dennis D. Nelson, was sent to Secretary of the Army Royall along with sixteen photographs picturing blacks and whites being trained together and working side by side.[12-46]

NATIONAL DEFENSE CONFERENCE ON NEGRO AFFAIRS.
Conferees prepare to meet with the press, 26 April 1948.

Given the vast size of the Army, it was perfectly feasible to open all training to qualified Negroes and yet continue for years racial practices that had so quickly proved impossible in the Navy's smaller general service. Of course, even in the Army the number of segregated jobs that could be created was limited, and in time Forrestal's tactics might, it could be argued, have succeeded despite the Army's size and the intractability of its leaders. Time, however, was precisely what Forrestal lacked, given the increasing political strength of the civil rights movement.

Sparked by Randolph's stand before the congressional committee, some members of the black community geared up for greater protests. Worse still for an administration facing a critical election, the protest was finding some support in the camps of the President's rivals. Early in May, for example, a group of prominent civil rights activists formed the Commission of Inquiry with the expressed purpose of examining the treatment of black servicemen during World War II. Organized by Randolph and Reynolds, the commission boasted Arthur Garfield Hayes, noted civil libertarian and lawyer, as its counsel. The commission planned to interrogate witnesses and, on the basis of the testimony gathered, issue a report to Congress and the public that would include recommendations on conscription legislation. Various Defense Department officials were invited to testify but only James C. Evans, who acted as department spokesman, accepted. During the inquiry, which Evans estimated was attended by 180 persons, little attention was given to Randolph's civil disobedience pledge, but Evans himself came in for considerable ridicule, and there were headlines aplenty in the black press.[12-47]

These attacks were being carried out in an atmosphere of heightened political interest in the civil rights of black servicemen. Henry A. Wallace, the Progressive Party's presidential candidate, had for some time been telling his black audiences that the administration was insincere because if it wanted to end segregation it could simply force the resignation of the Secretary of the Army.[12-48] Henry Cabot Lodge, the Republican senator from Massachusetts, called on Forrestal to make "a real attempt, well thought out and well organized," to integrate a sizable part of the armed forces with soldiers volunteering for such arrangements. Quoting from General Eisenhower's testimony before the Armed Services Committee, he reminded Forrestal that segregation was not only an undeserved and unjustified humiliation to the Negro, but a potential danger to the national defense effort. In the face of a manpower shortage, it was inexcusable to view segregation simply as a political question, "of concern to a few individuals and to a few men in public life and to be dealt with as adroitly as possible, always with an eye to the largest number of votes."[12-49]

Yet as the timing of Senator Lodge's letter suggests, the political implications of the segregation fight were a prime concern of every politician involved, and Forrestal had to act with this fact in mind. The administration considered the Wallace campaign a real but minor threat because of his appeal to black voters in the early months of the campaign.[12-50] The Republican incursion into the civil rights field was more ominous, and Forrestal, having acknowledged Lodge's letter, turned to Lester Granger for help in drafting a detailed reply. It took Granger some time to suggest an approach because he agreed with Lodge on many points but found some of his inferences as unsound as the Army's policy. For instance Lodge approved Eisenhower's comments on segregation, and the only real difference between Eisenhower and the Army staff was that Eisenhower wanted segregation made more efficient by putting smaller all-black units into racially composite organizations. Negroes opposed segregation as an insult to their race and to their manhood. Granger wanted Forrestal to tell Lodge that no group of Negroes mindful of

142

its public standing could take a position other than total opposition to segregation. Having to choose between Randolph's stand and Eisenhower's, Negroes could not endorse Eisenhower. Granger also thought Forrestal would do well to explain to Lodge that he himself favored for the other services the policy followed by the Navy in the name of improving efficiency and morale.[12-51]

A reply along these line was prepared, but Marx Leva persuaded Forrestal not to send it until the selective service bill had safely passed Congress.[12-52] Forrestal was "seriously concerned," he wrote the President on 28 May 1948, about the fate of that legislation. He wanted to express his opposition to an amendment proposed by Senator Richard B. Russell of Georgia that would guarantee segregated units for those draftees who wished to serve only with members of their own race. He also wanted to announce his intention of making "further progress" in interracial relations. To that end he had discussed with Special Counsel to the President Clark M. Clifford the creation of an advisory board to recommend specific steps his department could take in the race relations field. Reiterating a long-cherished belief, Forrestal declared that this "difficult problem" could not be solved by issuing an executive order or passing a law, "for progress in this field must be achieved by education, and not by mandate."[12-53] The President agreed to these maneuvers,[12-54] but just three days later Forrestal returned to the subject, passing along to Truman a warning from Senator Robert A. Taft of Ohio that both the Russell amendment and one proposed by Senator William Langer of North Dakota to prohibit all segregation were potential roadblocks to passage of the bill.[12-55] In the end Congress rejected both amendments, passing a draft bill without any special racial provisions on 19 June 1948.

The proposal for an advisory board proved to be Forrestal's last attempt to change the racial practices of the armed forces through gradualism. In the next few weeks the whole problem would be taken out of his hands by a White House grown impatient with his methods. There, in contrast to the comparatively weak position of the Secretary of Defense, who had not yet consolidated his authority, the full force and power of the Commander in Chief would be used to give a dramatic new meaning to equal treatment and opportunity in the armed forces. Given the temper of the times, Forrestal's surrender was inevitable, for a successful reform program had to show measurable improvements, and despite his maneuvers with the civil rights activists, the Congress, and the services, Forrestal had no success worth proclaiming in his first eight months of office.

This lack of progress disappointed civil rights leaders, who had perhaps overestimated the racial reforms made when Forrestal was Secretary of the Navy. It can be argued that as Secretary of Defense Forrestal himself was inclined to overestimate them. Nevertheless, he could demonstrate some systematic improvement in the lot of the black sailor, enough improvement, according to his gradualist philosophy, to assure continued progress. Ironically, considering Forrestal's faith in the efficacy of education and persuasion, whatever can be counted as his success in the Navy was accomplished by the firm authority he and his immediate subordinates exercised during the last months of the war. Yet this authority was precisely what he lacked in his new office, where his power was limited to only a general control over intransigent services that still insisted on their traditional autonomy.

In any case, by 1948 there was no hope for widespread reform through a step-by-step demonstration of the practicality and reasonableness of integration. Too much of the remaining opposition was emotional, rooted in prejudice and tradition, to yield to any but forceful methods. If the services were to be integrated in the short run, integration would have to be forced upon them.

Executive Order 9981

Although politics was only one of several factors that led to Executive Order 9981, the order was born during a presidential election campaign, and its content and timing reflect that fact. Having made what could be justified as a military decision in the interest of a more effective use of manpower in the armed forces, the President and his advisers sought to capitalize on the political benefits that might accrue from it.[12-56] The work of the President's Committee on Civil Rights and Truman's subsequent message to Congress had already elevated civil rights to the level of a major campaign issue. As early as November 1947 Clark Clifford, predicting the nomination of Thomas Dewey and Henry Wallace, had advised the President to concentrate on winning the allegiance of the nation's minority voters, especially the black, labor, and Jewish blocs.[12-57] Clifford had discounted the threat of a southern defection, but in the spring of 1948 southern Democrats began to turn from the party, and the black vote, an important element in the big city Democratic vote since the formation of the Roosevelt coalition, now became in the minds of the campaign planners an essential ingredient in a Truman victory. Through the efforts of Oscar Ewing, head of the Federal Security Administration and White House adviser on civil

143

rights matters, and several other politicians, Harry Truman was cast in the role of minority rights champion.[12-58]

Theirs was not a difficult task, for the President's identification with the civil rights movement had become part of the cause of his unpopularity in some Democratic circles and a threat to his renomination. He overcame the attempt to deny him the presidential nomination in June, and he accepted the strong civil rights platform that emerged from the convention. The resolution committee of that convention had proposed a mild civil rights plank in the hope of preventing the defection of southern delegates, but in a dramatic floor fight Hubert H. Humphrey, the mayor of Minneapolis and a candidate for the U.S. Senate, forced through one of the strongest civil rights statements in the history of the party. This plank endorsed Truman's congressional message on civil rights and called for "Congress to support our President in guaranteeing these basic and fundamental rights ... the right of equal treatment in the service and defense of our nation."[12-59]

Truman admitted to Forrestal that "he had not himself wanted to go as far as the Democratic platform went on the civil rights issue." The President had no animus toward those who voted against the platform; he would have done the same if he had come from their states. But he was determined to run on the platform, and for him, he later said, a platform was not a window dressing. His southern colleagues understood him. When a reporter pointed out to Governor Strom Thurmond of South Carolina that the President had only accepted a platform similar to those supported by Roosevelt, the governor answered, "I agree, but Truman really means it."[12-60] After the platform fight the Alabama and Mississippi delegates walked out of the convention. The Dixiecrat revolt was on in earnest.

Both the Democratic platform and the report of the President's Civil Rights Committee referred to discrimination in the federal government, a matter obviously susceptible to presidential action. For once the "do-nothing" Congress could not be blamed, and if Truman failed to act promptly he would only invite the wrath of the civil rights forces he was trying to court. Aware of this political necessity, the President's advisers had been studying the areas in which the President alone might act in forbidding discrimination as well as the mechanics by which he might make his actions effective. According to Oscar Ewing, the advisers had decided as early as October 1947 that the best way to handle discrimination in the federal government was to issue a presidential order securing the civil rights of both civilian government employees and members of the armed forces. In the end the President decided to issue two executive orders.[12-61]

Clifford, Ewing, and Philleo Nash, who was a presidential specialist on minority matters, worked on drafting both orders. After consulting with Truman Gibson, Nash proposed that the order directed to the services should create a committee within the military establishment to push for integration, one similar to the McCloy committee in World War II. Like Gibson, Nash was convinced that change in the armed forces racial policy would come only through a series of steps initiated in each service. By such steps progress had been made in the Navy through its Special Programs Unit and in the Army through the efforts of the McCloy committee. Nash argued against the publication of an executive order that spelled out integration or condemned segregation. Rather, let the order to the services call for equal treatment and opportunity—the language of the Democratic platform. Tie it to military efficiency, letting the services discover, under guidance from a White House committee, the inefficiency of segregation. The services would quickly conclude, the advisers assumed, that equal treatment and opportunity were impossible in a segregated system.[12-62] After a series of discussions with the President, Nash, Clifford, and Ewing drew up a version of the order to the services along the lines suggested by Nash.[12-63]

The draft underwent one significant revision at the request of the Secretary of Defense. In keeping with his theory that the services should be given the chance to work out their own methods of compliance with the order to integrate, Forrestal wanted no deadlines set. To keep antagonisms to a minimum he wanted the order to call simply for progress "as rapidly as feasible." The President agreed.[12-64]

The timing of the order was politically important to Truman, and by late July the White House was extremely anxious to publish the document. The President now had his all-important selective service legislation; he was beginning to campaign on a platform calling for a special session of Congress—a Congress dominated by Republicans, who had also just approved a party platform calling for an end to segregation in the armed forces. Haste was evident in the fact that the order, along with copies for the service secretaries, was sent to the Secretary of Defense on the morning of 26 July—the day it was issued—for comment and review by that afternoon.[12-65] The order was also submitted to Walter White and A. Philip Randolph before it was issued.[12-66]

144

Actually, the order had been read to Forrestal on the evening of the previous day, and his office had suggested one more change. Marx Leva believed that the order would be improved if it mentioned the fact that substantial progress in civil rights had been made during the war and in the years thereafter. Since a sentence to this effect had been included in Truman's civil rights message of February, Leva thought it would be well to include it in the executive order. Believing also that policy changes ought to be the work of the government or of the executive branch of the government rather than of the President alone, he offered a sentence for inclusion: "To the extent that this policy has not yet been completely implemented, such alterations or improvements in existing rules, procedures and practices as may be necessary shall be put into effect as rapidly as possible." Although Forrestal approved the sentence, it was not accepted by the President.[12-67]

Approvals were quickly gathered from interested cabinet officials. The Attorney General passed on the form and legality of the order. Forrestal was certain that Stuart Symington of the Air Force and John L. Sullivan, Secretary of the Navy, would approve the order, but he suggested that Oscar Ewing discuss the draft with Kenneth Royall. According to Ewing, the Secretary of the Army read the order twice and said, "tell the President that I not only have no objections but wholeheartedly approve, and we'll go along with it."[12-68]

The historic document, signed by Truman on 26 July 1948, read as follows:

EXECUTIVE ORDER 9981

Whereas it is essential that there be maintained in the armed services of the United States the highest standards of democracy, with equality of treatment and opportunity for all those who serve in our country's defense:

Now, therefore, by virtue of the authority vested in me as President of the United States, and as Commander in Chief of the armed services, it is hereby ordered as follows:

1. It is hereby declared to be the policy of the President that there shall be equality of treatment and opportunity for all persons in the armed services without regard to race, color, religion or national origin. This policy shall be put into effect as rapidly as possible, having due regard to the time required to effectuate any necessary changes without impairing efficiency or morale.

2. There shall be created in the National Military Establishment an advisory committee to be known as the President's Committee on Equality of Treatment and Opportunity in the Armed Services, which shall be composed of seven members to be designated by the President.

3. The Committee is authorized on behalf of the President to examine into the rules, procedures and practices of the armed services in order to determine in what respect such rules, procedures and practices may be altered or improved with a view to carrying out the policy of this order. The Committee shall confer and advise with the Secretary of Defense, the Secretary of the Army, the Secretary of the Navy, and the Secretary of the Air Force, and shall make such recommendations to the President and to said Secretaries as in the judgment of the Committee will effectuate the policy hereof.

4. All executive departments and agencies of the Federal Government are authorized and directed to cooperate with the Committee in its work, and to furnish the Committee such information or the services of such persons as the Committee may require in the performance of its duties.

5. When requested by the Committee to do so, persons in the armed services or in any of the executive departments and agencies of the Federal Government shall testify before the Committee and shall make available for the use of the Committee such documents and other information as the Committee may require.

6. The Committee shall continue to exist until such time as the President shall terminate its existence by Executive Order.

HARRY S. TRUMAN
The   White   House
July 26, 1948

As indicated by the endorsement of such diverse protagonists as Royall and Randolph, the wording of the executive order was in part both vague and misleading. The vagueness was there by design. The failure to mention either segregation or integration puzzled many people and angered others, but it was certainly to the advantage of a president who wanted to give the least offense possible to voters who supported segregation. In fact integration was not the precise word to describe the complex social change in the armed forces demanded by civil rights leaders, and the emphasis on equality of treatment and opportunity with its portent for the next generation was particularly appropriate. Truman, however, was not allowed to remain vague for long. Questioned at his first press conference after the order was issued, the President refused to set a time limit, but he admitted that he expected the order to abolish racial segregation in the armed forces.[12-69] The order was also misleading when it created the advisory committee "in" the National Military Establishment. Truman apparently intended to create a presidential committee to oversee the manpower policies of all the services, and despite the wording of the order the committee would operate as a creature of the White House, reporting to the President rather than to the Secretary of Defense.

The success of the new policy would depend to a great extent, as friends and foes of integration alike recognized, on the ability and inclination of this committee. The final choice of members was the President's, but he conspicuously involved the Democratic National Committee, the Secretary of Defense, and the Secretary of the Army. He repeatedly solicited Forrestal's suggestions, and it was apparent that the views of the Pentagon would carry much weight in the final selection. Just four days after the publication of Executive Order 9981, the President's administrative assistant, Donald S. Dawson, wrote Forrestal that he would be glad to talk to him about the seven members.[12-70] Before Forrestal replied he had Leva discuss possible nominees with the three military departments and obtain their recommendations. The Pentagon's list went to the White House on 3 August. A list compiled subsequently by Truman's advisers, chiefly Philleo Nash and Oscar Ewing, and approved by the Democratic National Committee, duplicated a number of Forrestal's suggestions; its additions and deletions revealed the practical political considerations under which the White House had to operate.[12-71]

By mid-September the committee was still unformed. The White House had been unable to get either Frank Graham, president of the University of North Carolina, a member of the President's Committee on Civil Rights, and the first choice of both the White House and the Pentagon for chairman, or Charles E. Wilson, second choice, to accept the chairmanship. Secretary of the Army Royall was particularly incensed that some of the men being considered for the committee "have publicly expressed their opinion in favor of abolishing segregation in the Armed Services. At least one of them, Lester Grainger [sic], has been critical both of the Army and of me personally on this particular matter."[12-72] Royall wanted no one asked to serve on the President's committee who had fixed opinions on segregation, and certainly no one who had made a public pronouncement on the subject. He wanted the nominees questioned to make sure they could give "fair consideration" to the subject.[12-73] Royall favored Jonathan Daniels, Ralph McGill of the Atlanta *Constitution*, Colgate Darden, president of the University of Virginia, and Douglas Southall Freeman, distinguished Richmond historian.[12-74] Names continued to be bruited about. Dawson asked Forrestal if he had any preferences for Reginald E. Gillmor, president of Sperry Gyroscope, or Julius Ochs Adler, noted publisher and former military aide to Secretary Stimson, as possibilities for chairman. Forrestal inclined toward Adler; "I believe he would be excellent although as a Southerner he might have limiting views."[12-75]

With the election imminent, the need for an announcement on the membership of the committee became pressing. On 16 September Dawson told Leva that a chairman and five of the six members had been selected and had agreed to serve: Charles Fahy, chairman, Charles Luckman, Lester Granger, John H. Sengstacke, Jacob Billikopf, and Alphonsus J. Donahue. The sixth member, still uninvited, was to be Dwight Palmer. Dawson said he would wait on this appointment until Forrestal had time to consider it, but two days later he was back, telling the secretary that the President had instructed him to release the names. There was final change: William E. Stevenson's name was substituted for Billikopf's.[12-76]

Although only two of Forrestal's nominees, Lester Granger and John Sengstacke, survived the selection process, the final membership was certainly acceptable to the Secretary of Defense. Charles Fahy was suggested by presidential assistant David K. Niles, who described the soft-voiced Georgian as a "reconstructed southerner liberal on race." A lawyer and former Solicitor General, Fahy had a reputation for sensitive handling of delicate problems, "with quiet authority and the punch of a mule." Granger's appointment was a White House bow to Forrestal and a disregard for Royall's objections. Sengstacke, a noted black publisher suggested by Forrestal and Ewing and supported by William L. Dawson, the black congressman from Chicago, was appointed in deference to the black press. Moreover, he had supported Truman's reelection "in unqualified terms." William Stevenson was the president of Oberlin College and was strongly recommended by Lloyd K. Garrison, president of the National Urban League. Finally, there was a trio of businessmen on the committee: Donahue was a Connecticut industrialist, highly recommended by Senator Howard J. McGrath of Rhode Island and Brian McMahon of Connecticut; Luckman was president of Lever Brothers and a native of Kansas City, Missouri; and Dwight Palmer was president of the General Cable Corporation.[12-77]

These were the men with whom, for a time at least, the Secretary of Defense would share his direction over the racial policies of the armed forces.

CHAPTER 13

146

Several months elapsed between the appointment of the President's Committee on Equality of Treatment and Opportunity in the Armed Services and its first meeting, a formal session with the President at the White House on 12 January 1949. Actually, certain advantages accrued from the delay, for postponing the meetings until after the President's reelection enabled the committee to face the services with assurance of continued support from the administration. Renewed presidential backing was probably necessary, considering the services' deliberations on race policy during this half-year hiatus. Their reactions to the order, logical outgrowths of postwar policies and practices, demonstrated how their perceived self-interests might subvert the President's intentions. The events of this six-month period also began to show the relative importance of the order and the parochial interests of the services as factors in the integration of the armed forces.

Public Reaction to Executive Order 9981

Considering the substantial changes it promised, the President's order provoked surprisingly little public opposition. Its publication coincided with the convening of the special session of a Congress smarting under Truman's "do-nothing" label. In this charged political atmosphere, the anti-administration majority in Congress quietly sidestepped the President's 27 July call for civil rights legislation. To do otherwise would only have added to the political profits already garnered by Truman in some important voting areas. For the same reason congressional opponents avoided all mention of Executive Order 9981, although the widely expected defeat of Truman and the consequent end to this executive sally into civil rights might have contributed to the silence. Besides, segregationists could do little in an immediate legislative way to counteract the presidential command. Congress had already passed the Selective Service Act and Defense Appropriations Act, the most suitable vehicles for amendments aimed at modifying the impact of the integration order. National elections and the advent of a new Congress precluded any other significant moves in this direction until later in the next year.

Yet if it was ignored in Congress, the order was nevertheless a clear signal to the friends of integration and brought with it a tremendous surge of hope to the black community. Publishing the order made Harry Truman the "darling of the Negroes," Roy Wilkins said later. Nor did the coincidence of its publication to the election, he added, bother a group that was becoming increasingly pragmatic about the reasons for social reform.[13-1] Both the declaredly Democratic Chicago *Defender* and Republican-oriented Pittsburgh *Courier* were aware of the implications of the order. The *Defender* ran an editorial on 7 August under the heading "Mr. Truman Makes History." The "National Grapevine" column of Charlie Cherokee in the same issue promised its readers a blow-by-blow description of the events surrounding the President's action. An interview in the same issue with Col. Richard L. Jones, black commander of the 178th Regimental Combat Team (Illinois), emphasized the beneficial effects of the proposed integration, and in the next issue, 14 August, the editor broadened the discussion with an editorial entitled "What About Prejudice?"[13-2] The *Courier*, for its part, questioned the President's sincerity because he had not explicitly called for an end to segregation. At the same time it contrasted the futility of civil disobedience with the efficiency of such an order on the services, and while maintaining its support for the candidacy of Governor Dewey the paper revealed a strong enthusiasm for President Truman's civil rights program.[13-3]

These affirmations of support for Executive Order 9981 in the major black newspapers fitted in neatly with the administration's political strategy. Nor was the Democratic National Committee averse to using the order to win black votes. For example it ran a half-page advertisement in the *Defender* under the heading "By His Deeds Shall Ye Know Him."[13-4] At the same time, not wishing to antagonize the opponents of integration further, the administration made no special effort to publicize the order in the metropolitan press. Consequently, when the order was mentioned at all, it was usually carried without comment, and the few columnists who treated the subject did so with some caution. Arthur Krock's "Reform Attempts Aid Southern Extremists" in the New York *Times*, for example, lauded the President's civil rights initiatives but warned that any attempt to force social integration would only strengthen demagogues at the expense of moderate politicians.[13-5]

If the President's wooing of the black voter was good election politics, his executive order was also a successful practical response to the threat of civil disobedience and the failure of the Secretary of Defense to strive actively for racial equality throughout the services. Declaring the President's action a substantial gain, A. Philip Randolph canceled the call for a boycott of the draft, leaving only a small number of diehards to continue the now insignificant effort. The black leaders who had participated in Secretary Forrestal's National Defense Conference gave the President their full support, and Donald S. Dawson, administrative assistant to the President, was able to assure Truman that the black press, now completely behind the committee on equal

147

treatment and opportunity, had abandoned its vigorous campaign against the Army's racial policy.[13-6]

Ironically, the most celebrated pronouncement on segregation at the moment of the Truman order came not from publicists or politicians but from the Army's new Chief of Staff, General Omar N. Bradley.[13-7] Speaking to a group of instructors at Fort Knox, Kentucky, and unaware of the President's order and the presence of the press, Bradley declared that the Army would have to retain segregation as long as it was the national pattern.[13-8] This statement prompted questions at the President's next news conference, letters to the editor, and debate in the press.[13-9] Bradley later explained that he had supported the Army's segregation policy because he was against making the Army an instrument of social change in areas of the country which still rejected integration.[13-10] His comment, as amplified and broadcast by military analyst Hanson W. Baldwin, summarized the Army's position at the time of the Truman order. "It is extremely dangerous nonsense," Baldwin declared, "to try to make the Army other than one thing—a fighting machine." By emphasizing that the Army could not afford to differ greatly in customs, traditions, and prejudices from the general population, Baldwin explained, Bradley was only underscoring a major characteristic of any large organization of conscripts. Most import, Baldwin pointed out, the Chief of Staff considered an inflexible order for the immediate integration of all troops one of the surest ways to break down the morale of the Army and destroy its efficiency.[13-11]

But such arguments were under attack by the very civil rights groups the President was trying to court. "Are we to understand that the President's promise to end discrimination," one critic asked,

was made for some other purpose than to end discrimination in its worst form—segregation? General Bradley's statement, subsequent to the President's orders, would seem to indicate that the President either did not mean what he said or his orders were not being obeyed. We should like to point out that General Bradley's reported observation ... was decidedly wide of the mark. Segregation is the legal pattern of only a few of our most backward states.... In view of the trends in law and social practice, it is high time that the Defense forces were not used as brakes on progress toward genuine democracy.[13-12]

General Bradley apologized to the President for any confusion caused by his statement, and Truman publicly sloughed off the affair, but not before he stated to the press that his order specifically directed the integration of the armed forces.[13-13] It was obvious that the situation had developed into a standoff. Some of the President's most outspoken supporters would not let him forget his integration order, and the Army, as represented by its Chief of Staff, failed to realize that events were rapidly moving beyond the point where segregation could be considered a workable policy for an agency of the United States government.

The Army: Segregation on the Defensive

The President's order heralded a series of attacks on the Army's race policy. As further evidence of the powerful pressures for change, several state governors now challenged segregation in the National Guard. Generally the race policy of the reserve components echoed that of the Regular Army, in part because it seemed logical that state units, subject to federal service, conform to federal standards of performance and organization. Accordingly, in the wake of the publication of the Gillem Board Report, the Army's Director of Personnel and Administration recommended to the Committee on National Guard Policy[13-14] that it amend its regulation on the employment of black troops to conform more closely with the new policy. Specifically, General Paul asked the committee to spell out the prohibition against integration of white and black troops below battalion level, warning that federal recognition would be denied any state unit organized in violation of this order.[13-15]

Agreeing to comply with General Paul's request, the National Guard Committee went a step further and recommended that individual states be permitted to make their own decisions on the wisdom and utility of organizing separate black units.[13-16] The Army staff rejected this proposal, however, on the grounds that it gave too much discretionary power to the state guard authorities.[13-17] Interestingly enough in view of later developments, neither the committee nor the staff disputed the War Department's right to withhold federal recognition in racial matters, and both displayed little concern for the principle of states' rights. Their attitude was important, for while the prohibition against integration sat well in some circles, it drew severe criticism in others. Unlike the Regular Army, the National Guard and the Army Reserve were composed of units deeply rooted in the local community, each reflecting the parochial attitudes of its members and its section. This truth was forcefully pointed out to the Army staff in 1946 when it tried to reactivate the 313th Infantry and designate it as a black unit in the 79th Division (Pennsylvania). Former members of the old white 313th, now prominent citizens, expressed their "very strong sentiments" on the matter, and the Army had to beat a hasty retreat. In the future, the staff decided, either black reserve units would be given the name and history of inactive black units or new units would be constituted.[13-18]

On the other hand, in 1947 citizen groups sprang up in Connecticut, New York, New Jersey, Ohio, and California to agitate among their state adjutants general for liberalization of the National Guard's racial policy. As early as February 1947 Governor James L. McConnaughy had publicly deplored segregation of Negroes in his own Connecticut National Guard. Adopting the states' rights stance more commonly associated with defenders of racial discrimination, Governor McConnaughy argued that by requiring segregation the War Department ran contrary to the wishes of individual states. Marcus Ray, the secretary's adviser on race, predicted that integration in the reserve components would continue to be a "point of increasing pressure." As he pointed out to Assistant Secretary Petersen, the Army had always supported segregation in its southern installations on the grounds that it had to conform with local mores. How then could it refuse to conform with the local statutes and customs of some northern states without appearing inconsistent? He recommended the Army amend its race policy to permit reserve components in states which wished it to integrate at a level consistent with "local community attitudes."[13-19]

The Army staff would have nothing to do with Ray's suggestion. Instead, both the Director of Personnel and Administration and the Director of Organization and Training supported a new resolution by the National Guard Policy Committee that left the number of black units and the question of their integration with white units above the company level up to the states involved. Integration at the company level was prohibited, and such integrated companies would be denied federal recognition. The committee's resolution was adopted by the Secretary of War in May 1947.[13-20]

But the fight was not over yet. In 1947 New Jersey adopted a new constitution that specifically prohibited segregation in the state militia. By extension no New Jersey National Guard unit could receive federal recognition. In February 1948 Governor McConnaughy brought Connecticut back into the fray, this time taking the matter up with the White House. A month later Governor Luther W. Youngdahl appealed to the Secretary of Defense on behalf of Negroes in the Minnesota National Guard. Secretary of the Army Royall quickly reappraised the situation and excepted New Jersey from the Army's segregation rule. Secretary Symington followed suit by excepting the New Jersey Air National Guard.[13-21]Royall also let the governors of Connecticut and Minnesota know that he would be inclined to make similar concessions to any state which, by legislative action, prohibited its governor from conforming to the federal requirements. At that time Connecticut and Minnesota had no such legislation, but Royall nevertheless agreed to refer their requests to his Committee on National Guard Policy.[13-22]

MP's HITCH A RIDE ON ARMY TANKS, AUGSBURG, GERMANY, 1949

Here the secretary did no more than comply with the National Defense Act, which required that all National Guard policy matters be formulated in the committee. Privately, Royall admitted that he did not feel bound to accept a committee recommendation and would be inclined to recognize any state prohibition against segregation. But he made a careful distinction between constitutional or legislative action and executive action in the states. A governor's decision to integrate, he pointed out, would not be recognized by the Army because such an action was subject to speedy reversal by the governor's successor and could cause serious confusion in the guard.[13-23] The majority of the National Guard Committee, supported by the Director of Organization and Training, recommended that the secretary make no exceptions to the segregation policy. The Director of Personnel and Administration, on the other hand, joined with the committee's minority in recommending that Royall's action in the New Jersey case be used as a precedent.[13-24] Commenting independently, General Bradley warned Royall that integrating individual Negroes in the National Guard would, from a military point of view, "create problems which may have serious consequences in case of national mobilization of those units."[13-25]

Here the matter would stand for some time, the Army's segregation policy intact, but an informal allowance made for excepting individual states from prohibitions against integration below the company level. Yet the publicity and criticism attendant upon these decisions might well have given the traditionalists pause. While Secretary Royall, and on occasion his superior, Secretary of Defense Forrestal, reiterated the Army's willingness to accommodate certain states,[13-26] civil rights groups were gaining allies for another proposition. The American Veterans Committee had advanced the idea that to forbid integration at the platoon level was a retreat from World War II practice, and to accept the excuse that segregation was in the interest of national defense was to tolerate a "travesty on words."[13-27] Hearings were conducted in Congress in 1949 and 1951 on bills H.R. 1403 and H.R. 1389 to prohibit segregation in the National Guard. Royall's interpretation of the National Defense Act did not satisfy advocates of a thoroughly integrated guard, for it was clear that not many states were likely to petition for permission to integrate. At the same time the exceptions to the segregation rule promised an incompatible situation between the segregated active forces and the incompletely integrated reserve organization.

Royall's ruling, while perhaps a short-term gain for traditionalists, was significant because it established a precedent that would be used by integrationists in later years. The price for defending the Army's segregation policy, guard officials discovered, was the surrender of their long-cherished claim of state autonomy. The committee's recommendation on the matter of applying the Gillem Board policy to the guard was inflexible, leaving no room for separate decisions by officials of the several states. Maj. Gen. Jim Dan Hill of the Wisconsin National Guard recognized this danger. Along with a minority of his colleagues he maintained that the decision on segregation "will have to be solved at the state level."[13-28] The committee majority argued the contrary, agreeing with Brig. Gen. Alexander G. Paxton of Mississippi that the National Defense Act of 1945 prohibited the sort of exception made in the New Jersey case. General Paxton called for a uniform policy for all guard units:

National Security is an obligation of all the states, and its necessity in time of emergency transcends all local issues. Federal recognition of the National Guard units of the several States is extended for the purpose of affording these units a Federal status under the National Defense Act. The issue in question is purely one of compliance with Federal Law.[13-29]

Here was tacit recognition of federal supremacy over the National Guard. In supporting the right of the Secretary of the Army to dictate racial policy to state guards in 1948, the National Guard Committee adopted a position that would haunt it when the question of integrating the guard came up again in the early 1960's.

Despite the publicity given to General Bradley's comments at Fort Knox, it was the Secretary of the Army, not the Chief of Staff, who led the fight against change in the Army's racial practices. As the debate over these practices warmed in the administration and the national press, Kenneth C. Royall emerged as the principal spokesman against further integration and the principal target of the civil rights forces. Royall's sincere interest in the welfare of black soldiers, albeit highly paternalistic, was not in question. His trouble with civil rights officials stemmed from the fact that he alone in the Truman administration still clung publicly to the belief that segregation was not in itself discrimination, a belief shared by many of his fellow citizens. Royall was convinced that the separate but equal provisions of the Army's Gillem Board policy were right in as much as they did provide equal treatment and opportunity for the black minority. His opinion was reinforced by the continual assurances of his military subordinates that in open competition with white soldiers few Negroes would ever achieve a proportionate share of promotions and better occupations. And when his subordinates added to this sentiment the notion that integration would disrupt the Army and endanger its efficiency, they quickly persuaded the already sympathetic Royall that segregation was not only correct but imperative.[13-30] The secretary might easily have agreed with General Paul, who told an assembly of Army commanders that aside from some needed improvement in the employment of black specialists "there isn't a single complaint anyone can make in our use of the Negro."[13-31]

Secure in his belief that segregation was right and necessary, Royall confidently awaited the judgment of the recently appointed President's committee. He was convinced that any fair judge could draw but one conclusion: under the provisions of Circular 124, Negroes had already achieved equal treatment and opportunity in the Army. His job, therefore, was relatively simple. He had to defend Army policy against outside attack and make sure it was applied uniformly throughout the service. His stand marked one of the last attempts by a major federal official to support a racially separate but equal system before the principle was finally struck down by the Supreme Court in *Brown* v. *Board of Education*.

SECRETARY ROYALL REVIEWS MILITARY POLICE,
Yokohama, Japan, 1949.]

Royall readily conceded that it was proper and necessary for Negroes to insist on integration, but, echoing a long-cherished Army belief, he adamantly opposed using the Army to support or oppose any social cause. The Army, he contended, must follow the nation, not lead it, in social matters. The Army must not experiment. When, "without prejudice to the National Defense," the Army could reduce segregation to the platoon level it would do so, but all such steps should be taken one at a time. And 1948, he told the conference of black leaders in April of that year, was not the time.[13-32]

Convinced of the rightness of the Army's policy, Secretary Royall was understandably agitated by the unfavorable publicity directed at him and his department. The publicity, he was convinced, resulted from discrimination on the part of "the Negro and liberal press" against the

150

Army's policy in favor of the Navy and Air Force. He was particularly incensed at the way the junior services had escaped the "rap"—his word—on racial matters. He ascribed it in large part, he told the Secretary of Defense in September 1948, to the "unfortunate" National Defense Conference, the gathering of black spokesmen held under Forrestal's auspices the previous spring.[13-33] The specific object of Royall's indignation was Lester Granger's final report on the work of the National Defense Conference. That report emphasized the conferees' rebuttal to Royall's defense of segregation on the grounds of military expediency and past experience with black soldiers. The Army has assumed a position, Granger claimed, that was unjustified by its own experience. Overlooking evidence to the contrary, Granger added that the Army position was at variance with the experience of the other services. His parting shot was aimed at the heart of the Army's argument: "It is as unwise as it is unsound to cite the resistance of military leadership against basic changes in policy as sufficient cause for delaying immediate and effective action."[13-34]

Adding to Royall's discomfort, Forrestal released the report on 8 September, and his letter of appreciation to Granger and the conferees assured them he would send their report to the President's committee. The New York Times promptly picked up Granger's reference to opposition among military leaders.[13-35] Royall tried to counter this attack. Since neither the President nor the Secretary of Defense had disapproved the Army's racial policy nor suggested any modifications, Royall told Forrestal he wanted him to go on record as approving the Army position. This course would doubtless be more palatable to Forrestal, Royall suggested, than having Royall announce that Forrestal had given tacit approval to the Army's policy.[13-36]

Forrestal quickly scotched this maneuver. It was true, he told Royall, that the Army's policy had not been disapproved. But neither had the Army's policy or that of the Navy or Air Force yet been reviewed by the Secretary of Defense. The President's committee would probably make such a review an early order of business. Meanwhile, the Army's race policy would continue in effect until it was altered either by Forrestal's office or by action from some other source.[13-37]

Even as Secretary Royall tried to defend the Army from the attacks of the press, the service's policy was challenged from another quarter. The blunt fact was that with the reinstitution of selective service in 1948 the Army was receiving more black recruits—especially those in the lower mental categories—than a segregated system could easily absorb. The high percentage of black soldiers so proudly publicized by Royall at the National Defense Conference was in fact a source of anxiety for Army planners. The staff particularly resented the different standards adopted by the other services to determine the acceptability of selectees. The Navy and Air Force, pleading their need for skilled workers and dependence on volunteer enlistments, imposed a higher minimum achievement score for admission than the Army, which, largely dependent upon the draft for its manpower, was required to accept men with lower scores. Thousands of Negroes, less skilled and with little education, were therefore eligible for service in the Army although they were excluded from the Navy and Air Force. Given such circumstances, it was probably inevitable that differences in racial policies would precipitate an interservice conflict. The Army claimed the difference in enlistment standards was discriminatory and contrary to the provisions of the draft law which required the Secretary of Defense to set enlistment standards. In April 1948 Secretary Royall demanded that Forrestal impose the same mental standards on all the services. He wanted inductees allocated to the services according to their physical and mental abilities and Negroes apportioned among them.

The other services countered that there were not enough well-educated people of draft age to justify raising the Army's mental standards to the Navy and Air Force levels, but neither service wanted to lower its own entrance standards to match the level necessity had imposed on the Army. The Air Force eventually agreed to enlist Negroes at a 10 percent ratio to whites, but the Navy held out for higher standards and no allocation by race. It contended that setting the same standards for all services would improve the quality of the Army's black enlistees only imperceptibly while it would do great damage to the Navy. The Navy admitted that the other services should help the Army, but not "up to the point of *unnecessarily* reducing their own effectiveness.... The modern Navy cannot operate its ships and aircraft with personnel of G.C.T. 70."[13-38] General Bradley cut to the point: if the Navy carried the day it would receive substantially fewer Negroes than the other two services and a larger portion of the best qualified.[13-39] Secretary Forrestal first referred the interservice controversy to the Munitions Board in May 1948 and later that summer to a special interservice committee. After both groups failed to reach an agreement,[13-40] Forrestal decided not to force a parity in mental standards upon the services. On 12 October he explained to the secretaries that parity could be imposed only during time of full mobilization, and since conditions in the period between October 1948 and June 1949 could not be considered comparable to those of full mobilization, parity was impossible. He promised, however, to study the qualitative needs of each service. Meanwhile, he had found no evidence that any service was discriminating in the selection of enlistees and settled for a warning that any serious discrimination by any two of the services would place "an intolerable burden" on the third.[13-41]

Convinced that Forrestal had made the wrong decision, the Army staff was nevertheless obliged to concern itself with the percentage of Negroes it would have to accept under the new selective service law. Although by November 1948 the Army's black strength had dropped to 9.83 percent of the total, its proportion of Negroes was still large when compared with the Navy's 4.3 percent, the Marine Corps' 1.79 percent, and the Air Force's 6 percent. Projecting these figures against the possible mobilization of five million men (assuming each service increased in proportion to its current strength and absorbed the same percentage of a black population remaining at 12 percent of the whole), the Army calculated that its low entrance requirements would give it a black strength of 21 percent. In the event of a mobilization equaling or surpassing that of World War II, the minimum test score of seventy would probably be lowered, and thus the Army would shoulder an even greater burden of poorly educated men, a burden that in the Army's view should be shared by all the services.[13-42]

A Different Approach

No matter how the Army tried to justify segregation or argue against the position of the Navy and Air Force, the integrationists continued to gain ground. Royall, in opposition, adopted a new tactic in the wake of the Truman order. He would have the Army experiment with integration, perhaps proving that it would not work on a large scale, certainly buying time for Circular 124 and frustrating the rising demand for change. He had expressed willingness to experiment with an integrated Army unit when Lester Granger made the suggestion through Forrestal in February 1948, but nothing came of it.[13-43] In September he returned to the idea, asking the Army staff to plan for the formation of an integrated unit about the size of a regimental combat team, along with an engineer battalion and the station complement of a post large enough to accommodate these troops. Black enlisted men were to form 10 percent of the troop basis and be used in all types of positions. Black officers, used in the same ratio as black officers in the whole Army, were to command mixed troops. General Bradley reported the staff had studied the idea and concluded that such units "did not prove anything on the subject." Royall, however, dismissed the staff's objection and reiterated his order to plan an experiment at a large installation and in a permanent unit.[13-44]

Despite the staff's obvious reluctance, Maj. Gen. Harold R. Bull, the new Director of Organization and Training, made an intensive study of the alternatives. He produced a plan that was in turn further refined by a group of senior officers including the Deputy Chief of Staff for Administration and the Chief of Information.[13-45] These officers decided that "if the Secretary of the Army so orders," the Army could activate an experimental unit in the 3d Infantry Division at Camp Campbell, Kentucky. The troops, 10 percent of them black, would be drawn from all parts of the country and include ten black officers, none above the rank of major. The unit would be carefully monitored by the Army staff, and its commander would report on problems encountered after a year's trial.

SPRING FORMAL DANCE, FORT GEORGE G. MEADE, MARYLAND, 1952

It was obvious that Forrestal wanted to avoid publicizing the project. He had his assistants, Marx Leva and John Ohly, discuss the proposal with the Secretary of the Array to impress on him the need for secrecy until all arrangements were completed. More important, he hoped to turn Royall's experiment back on the Army itself, using it to gain a foothold for integration in the largest service. Leva and Ohly suggested to Royall that instead of activating a special unit he select a Regular Army regiment—Leva recommended one from the 82d Airborne Division to which a number of black combat units were already attached—as the nucleus of the experiment. With an eye to the forthcoming White House investigation, Leva added that, while the details would be left to the Army, integration of the unit, to be put into effect "as soon as possible," should be total.[13-46]

The plan for a large-scale integrated unit progressed little beyond this point, but it was significant if only because it marked the first time since the Revolution that the Army had seriously considered using a large number of black soldiers in a totally integrated unit. The situation was not without its note of irony, for the purpose of the plan was not to abolish the racial discrimination that critics were constantly laying at the Army's doorstep. In fact, Army leaders, seriously dedicated to the separate but equal principle, were convinced the Gillem Board policy had already eliminated discrimination. Nor was the plan designed to carry out the President's order or prompted by the Secretary of Defense. Rather, it was pushed by Secretary

Royall as a means of defending the Army against the anticipated demands of the President's committee.

The plan died because, while the Army staff studied organizations and counted bodies, Royall expanded his proposal for an integrated unit to include elements of the whole national defense establishment. Several motives have been suggested for his move. By ensnaring the Navy and Air Force in the experiment, he might impress on all concerned the problems he considered certain to arise if any service attempted the integration of a large number of Negroes. An experiment involving the whole department might also divert the White House from trying to integrate the Army immediately. Besides, the scheme had an escape clause. If the Navy and Air Force refused to cooperate, and Royall thought it likely they would, given the shortage of skilled black recruits, the Army could then legitimately cancel its offer to experiment with integration and let the whole problem dissipate in a lengthy interservice argument.[13-47]

Royall formally proposed a defense-wide experiment in integration to Forrestal on 2 December. He was not oblivious to the impression his vacillation on the subject had produced and went to some lengths to explain why he had opposed such experiments in the past. Although he had been thinking about such an experiment for some time, he told Forrestal, he had publicly rejected the idea at the National Defense Conference and during the Senate hearings on the draft law because of the tense international situation and the small size of the Army at that time. His interest in the experiment revived as the size of the Army increased and similar suggestions were made by both black leaders and southern politicians, but again he had hesitated, this time because of the national elections. He was now prepared to go ahead, but only if similar action were taken by the other services.

The experimental units, he advised Forrestal, should contain both combat and service elements of considerable size, and he went on to specify their composition in some detail. The Navy and Marine Corps should include at least one shore station "where the social problems for individuals and their families will approximate those confronting the Army." To insure the experiment's usefulness, he wanted Negroes employed in all positions, including supervisory ones, for which they qualified, and he urged that attention be paid to "the problem of social relations in off-duty hours." He was candid about the plan's weaknesses. The right to transfer out of the experimental unit might confine the experiment to white and black troops who wanted it to succeed; hence any conclusions drawn might be challenged as invalid since men could not be given the right to exercise similar options in time of war. Therefore, if the experiment succeeded, it would have to be followed by another in which no voluntary options were granted. The experiment might also bring pressure from groups outside the Army, and if it failed "for any reason" the armed services would be accused of sabotage, no matter how sincere their effort. Curiously, he admitted that the plan was not favored by his military advisers. The Army staff, he noted in what must have surprised anyone familiar with the staff's consistent defense of segregation, thought the best way to eliminate segregation was to reduce gradually the size of segregated units and extend integration in schools, hospitals, and special units. Nevertheless, Royall recommended that the National Military Establishment as a whole, not the Army separately, go forward with the experiment and that it start early in 1949.[13-48]

The other services had no intention of going forward with such an experiment. The Air Force objected, as Secretary Symington explained, because the experiment would be inconclusive; too many artificial features were involved, especially having units composed of volunteers. Arbitrary quotas violated the principle of equal opportunity, he charged, and the experiment would be unfair to Negroes because the proportion of Negroes able to compete with whites was less than 1 to 10. Symington also warned against the public relations aspect of the scheme, which was of "minimal military significance but of major significance in the current public controversy on purely racial issues." The Air Force could conduct the experiment without difficulty, he conceded, for there were enough trained black technicians to man 10 percent of the positions and give a creditable performance, but these men were representative neither of the general black population of the Air Force nor of Negroes coming into the service during wartime.

Symington predicted that Negroes would suffer no matter how the experiment came out—success would be attributed to the special conditions involved; failure would reflect unjustly on the Negro's capabilities. The Air Force, therefore, preferred to refrain from participation in the experiment. Symington added that he was considering a study prepared by the Air staff over the past six months that would insure equality of treatment and increased opportunities for Negroes in the Air Force, and he expected to offer proposals to Forrestal in the immediate future.[13-49]

153

The Navy also wanted no part of the Royall experiment. Its acting secretary, John Nicholas Brown, believed that the gradual indoctrination of the naval establishment was producing the desired nondiscriminatory practices "on a sound and permanent basis without concomitant problems of morale and discipline." To adopt Royall's proposal, on the other hand, would "unnecessarily risk losing all that has been accomplished in the solution of the efficient utilization of Negro personnel to the limit of their ability."[13-50] Brown did not spell out the risk, but a Navy spokesman on Forrestal's staff was not so reticent. "Mutiny cannot be dismissed from consideration," Capt. Herbert D. Riley warned, if the Navy were forced to integrate its officers' wardrooms, staterooms, and clubs. Such integration ran considerably in advance of the Navy's current and carefully controlled integration of the enlisted general service and would, like the proposal to place Negroes in command of white officers and men, Captain Riley predicted, have such dire results as wholesale resignations and retirements.[13-51]

The decisive opposition of the Navy and Air Force convinced Forrestal that interservice integration was unworkable. In short, the Navy and Air Force had progressed in their own estimation to the point where, despite shortcomings in their racial policies rivaling the Army's, they had little to fear from the coming White House investigation. The Army could show no similar forward motion. Despite Royall's claim that he and the Army staff favored eventual integration of black soldiers through progressive reduction in the size of the Army's segregated black units, the facts indicated otherwise. For example, while Secretary of Defense Forrestal was touring Germany in late 1948 he noted in his diary of Lt. Gen. Clarence R. Huebner, now the commander of Europe: "Huebner's experience with colored troops is excellent.... He is ready to proceed with the implementation of the President's directive about nonsegregation down to the platoon level, and proposes to initiate this in the three cavalry regiments and the AA battalion up north, but does not want to do it if it is premature."[13-52]

Huebner's concern with prematurity was understandable, for the possibility of using black soldiers in the constabulary had been a lively topic in the Army for some time. Marcus Ray had proposed it in his December 1946 report to the Secretary of War, but it was quickly rejected by the Army staff. The staff had approved Huebner's decision in July 1948 to attach a black engineer construction battalion and a transportation truck company, a total of 925 men, to the constabulary. The Director of Organization and Training, however, continued to make a careful distinction between attached units and "organic assignment," adding that "the Department of the Army does not favor the organic assignment of Negro units to the Constabulary at this time."[13-53]

But by November 1948 Huebner wished to go considerably further. As he later put it, he had no need for a black infantry regiment, but since the constabulary, composed for the most part of cavalry units, lacked foot soldiers, he wanted to integrate a black infantry battalion, in platoon-size units, in each cavalry regiment.[13-54] The staff turned down his request. Arguing that the inclusion of organic black units in the constabulary "might be detrimental to the proper execution of its mission," and quoting the provision of Circular 124 limiting integration to the company level, the staff's organization experts concluded that the use of black units in the European theater below company size "would undoubtedly prove embarrassing to the Department of the Army ... in the Zone of the Interior in view of the announced Department of the Army policy." General Bull, Director of Organization and Training, informed Huebner he might use black units in composite groupings only at the company level, including his constabulary forces, "if such is desired by you," but it was "not presently contemplated that integration of Negro units on the platoon level will be approved as Department of the Army policy."[13-55] Huebner later recalled that the constabulary was his outfit, to be run his way, and "Bradley and Collins always let me do what I had to."[13-56] Still, when black infantrymen joined the constabulary in late 1948, they came in three battalion-size units "attached" for training and tactical control.[13-57]

The Truman order had no immediate effect on the Army's racial policy. The concession to state governors regarding integration of their National Guard units was beside the point, and Royall's limited offer to set up an experimental integrated unit in the Regular Army was more image than substance. Accurately summarizing the situation in March 1949, The Adjutant General informed Army commanders that although it was "strategically unwise" to republish War Department Circular 124 while the President's committee was meeting, the policies contained in that document, which was about to expire, would continue in effect until further notice.[13-58]

The Navy: Business as Usual

The Navy Department also saw no reason to alter its postwar racial policy because of the Truman order. As Acting Secretary of Navy Brown explained to the Secretary of Defense in December 1948, whites in his service had come to accept the fact that blacks must take their rightful place in the Navy and Marine Corps. This acceptance, in turn, had led to "very satisfactory progress" in the integration of the department's black personnel without producing problems of morale and discipline or a lowering of *esprit de corps*.[13-59]

Brown had ample statistics at hand to demonstrate that at least in the Navy this nondiscrimination policy was progressive. Whereas at the end of the World War II demobilization only 6 percent of the Navy's Negroes served in the general service, some two years later 38 percent were so assigned. These men and women generally worked and lived under total integration, and the men served on many of the Navy's combat ships. The Bureau of Naval Personnel predicted in early 1949 that before the end of the year at least half of all black sailors would be assigned to the general service.[13-60] In contrast to the Army's policy of separate but equal service for its black troops, the Navy's postwar racial policy was technically correct and essentially in compliance with the President's order. Yet progress was very limited and in fact in the two years under its postwar nondiscrimination policy, the Navy's performance was only marginally different from that of the other services. The number of Negroes in the Navy in December 1948, the same month Brown was extolling its nondiscrimination policy, totaled some 17,000 men, 4.5 percent of its strength and about half the Army's proportion. This percentage had remained fairly constant since World War II and masked a dramatic drop in the number of black men in uniform as the Navy demobilized. Thus while the *percentage* of the Navy's black sailors assigned to the integrated general service rose from 6 to 38, the *number* of Negroes in the general service dropped from 9,900 in 1946 to some 6,000 in 1948. Looked at another way, the 38 percent figure of blacks in the general service meant that 62 percent of all Negroes in the Navy, 10,871 men in December 1948, still served in the separate Steward's Branch.[13-61] In contrast to the Army and Air Force, the Navy's Negroes were, with only the rarest exception, enlisted men. The number of black officers in December 1948 was four; the WAVES could count only six black women in its 2,130 total. Clearly, the oft repeated rationale for these statistics—Negroes favored the Army because they were not a seafaring people—could not explain them away.[13-62]

A substantial increase in the number of Negroes would have absolved the Navy from some of the stigma of racial discrimination it endured in the late 1940's. Since the size of the Steward's Branch was limited by regulation and budget, any increase in black enlistment would immediately raise the number of Negroes serving in the integrated general service. Increased enlistments would also widen the choice of assignments, creating new opportunities for promotion to higher grades. But even this obvious and basic response to the Truman order was not forthcoming. The Navy continued to exclude many potential black volunteers on the grounds that it needed to maintain stricter mental and physical standards to secure men capable of running a modern, technically complex Navy. True, regular and reserve officers were periodically sent to black colleges to discuss naval careers with the students, but as one official, speaking of the reserves, confessed to the Fahy Committee in April 1949, "We aren't doing anything special to procure Negro officers or Negro enlisted men."[13-63]

At best, recruiting more Negroes for the general service would only partly fulfill the Navy's obligation to conform to the Truman order. It would still leave untouched the Steward's Branch, which for years had kept alive the impression that the Navy valued minority groups only as servants. The Bureau of Naval Personnel had closed the branch to first enlistments and provided for the transfer of eligible stewards to the general service, but black stewards were only transferring at the rate of seven men per month, hardly enough to alter the racial composition of the branch. In the six months following September 1948 the branch's black strength dropped by 910 men, but because the total strength of the branch also dropped, the percentage of black stewards remained constant.[13-64] What was needed was an infusion of whites, but this remedy, like an increase of black officers, would require a fundamental change in the racial attitudes of Navy leaders. No such change was evident in the Navy's postwar racial policy. While solemnly proclaiming its belief in the principle of nondiscrimination, the service had continued to sanction practices that limited integration and equal opportunity to a degree consistent with its racial tradition and manpower needs. Curiously, the Navy managed to avoid strong criticism from the civil rights groups throughout the postwar period, and the Truman order notwithstanding, it was therefore in a strong position to resist precipitous change in its racial practices.

Adjustments in the Marine Corps

Unlike the Navy, the Marine Corps did not enjoy so secure a position. Its policy of keeping black marines strictly segregated was becoming untenable in the face of its shrinking size, and by the time President Truman issued his order the corps was finding it necessary to make

155

some adjustments. Basic training, for example, was integrated in the cause of military efficiency. With fewer than twenty new black recruits a month, the corps was finding it too expensive and inefficient to maintain a separate recruit training program, and on 1 July 1949 the commandant, General Clifton B. Cates, ordered that Negroes be trained with the rest of the recruits at Parris Island, but in separate platoons.[13-65] Even this system proved too costly, however, because black recruits were forced to wait for training until their numbers built up to platoon size. Given the length of the training cycle, the camp commander had to reserve three training platoons for the few black recruits. Maj. Gen. Alfred H. Noble, the commander, repeatedly complained of the waste of instructors, time, and facilities and the "otherwise generally undesirable" features of separate black training platoons. He pointed out to the commandant that black students had been successfully assimilated into personnel administration and drill instructor schools without friction or incident, and reservist training and local intramural sports had already peacefully introduced integration to the base. Noble wanted to integrate black recruits as they arrived, absorbing them in the white training platoons then being processed. He also wanted to use selected black noncommissioned officers as instructors.[13-66]

The commandant approved the integration of recruit training on 22 September, and Noble quietly began assigning recruits without regard to color.[13-67] Integration of black noncommissioned officer platoon leaders followed, along with integration of the noncommissioned officers' club and other facilities. Noble later recalled the circumstance of the first significant instance of integration in the history of the Marine Corps:

This innovation not only produced no unfavorable reaction among the Marines, but also it had no unfavorable reaction among the civilian citizens of South Carolina in the vicinity. Of course I consulted the civilian leaders first and told them what I was going to do and got their advice and promises of help to try to stop any adverse criticisms of it. It seemed like integration was due to take place sooner or later anyway in this country, certainly in the Armed Forces, and I thought that it should take place in the Armed Forces first.[13-68]

GENERAL CATES

Since manpower restrictions also made the organization of administratively separate black units hard to justify, the postwar reduction in the number of black marines eventually led to the formation of a number of racially composite units. Where once separate black companies were the norm, by 1949 the corps had organized most of its black marines into separate platoons and assigned them as parts of larger white units. In March 1949 Secretary of the Navy Sullivan reported that with the minor exception of several black depot companies, the largest black units in the Marine Corps were platoons of forty-three men, "and they are integrated with other platoons of whites."[13-69]

The cutback in the size and kinds of black units and the integration of recruit training removed the need for the separate camp at Montford Point, home base for black marines since the beginning of World War II. The camp's last two organizations, a provisional company and a headquarters company, were inactivated on 31 July and 9 September, respectively, thus ending an era in the history of Negroes in the Marine Corps.[13-70]

Composite grouping of small black units usually provided for separate assignment and segregated facilities. As late as February 1949, the commandant made clear he had no intention of allowing the corps to drift into a *de facto* integration policy. When, for example, it came to his attention that some commanders were restricting appointment of qualified black marines to specialist schools on the grounds that their commands lacked billets for black specialists, the commandant reiterated the principle that assignment to specialty training was to be made without regard to race. At the same time he emphasized that this policy was not to be construed as an endorsement of the use of black specialists in white units. General Cates specifically stipulated that where no billets in their specialty or a related one were available for black specialists in black units, his headquarters was to be informed. The implication of this order was obvious to the Division of Plans and Policies. "This is an important one," a division official commented, "it involves finding billets for Negro specialists even if we have to create a unit to do it."[13-71] It was also obvious that when the Under Secretary of the Navy, Dan A. Kimball, reported to the Personnel Policy Board in May that "Negro Marines, including Stewards, are assigned to other [white] Marine Corps units in accord with their specialty," he was speaking of rare exceptions to the general rule.[13-72]

Cates seemed determined to ignore the military inefficiency attendant on such elaborate attempts to insure the continued isolation of black marines. The defense establishment, he was convinced, "could not be an agency for experimentation in civil liberty without detriment to its ability to maintain the efficiency and the high state of readiness so essential to national defense." Having thus tied military efficiency to segregation, Cates explained to the Assistant Secretary of

156

the Navy for Air that the efficiency of a unit was a command responsibility, and so long as that responsibility rested with the commander, he must be authorized to make such assignments as he deemed necessary. It followed, then, that segregation was a national, not a military, problem, and any attempt to change national policy through the armed forces was, in the commandant's words, "a dangerous path to pursue inasmuch as it affects the ability of the National Military Establishment to fulfill its mission." Integration must first be accepted as a national custom, he concluded, "before it could be adopted in the armed forces."[13-73] Nor was General Cates ambiguous on Marine Corps policy when it was questioned by civil rights leaders. Individual marines, he told the commander of a black depot company in a case involving opportunities available to reenlisting black marines, would be employed in the future as in the past "to serve the best interests of the Corps under existing circumstances."[13-74]

Actually, Cates was only forcibly expressing a cardinal tenet common to all the military services: the civil rights of the individual must be subordinated to the mission of the service. What might appear to a civil rights activist to be a callous and prejudiced response to a legitimate social complaint was more likely an expression of the commandant's overriding concern for his military mission. Still it was difficult to explain such elaborate precautions in a corps where Negroes numbered less than 2 percent of the total strength.[13-75] How could the integration of 1,500 men throughout the worldwide units of the corps disrupt its mission, civil rights spokesmen might well ask, especially given the evidence to the contrary in the Navy? In view of the President's order, how could the corps justify the proliferation of very small black units that severely restricted the spread of occupational opportunities for Negroes?

1ST MARINE DIVISION DRILL TEAM ON EXHIBITION
at San Diego's Balboa Stadium, 1949.

The corps ignored these questions during the summer of 1949, concentrating instead on the problem of finding racially separate assignments for its 1,000 Negroes in the general service. As the number of marines continued to drop, the Division of Plans and Policies was forced to justify the existence of black units by a series of reorganizations and redistributions. When, for example, the reorganization of the Fleet Marine Force caused the inactivation of two black depot units, the division designated a 108-man truck company as a black unit to take up the slack. At the same time the division found yet another "suitable" occupation for black marines by laying down a policy that all security detachments at inactive naval facilities were to be manned by Negroes. It also decided to assign small black units to the service battalions of the Marine divisions, maintaining that such assignments would not run counter to the commandant's policy of restricting Negroes to noncombat organizations.[13-76]

The Marine Corps, in short, had no intention of relaxing its policy of separating the races. The timing of the integration of recruit training and the breakup of some large black units perhaps suggested a general concession to the Truman order, but these administrative changes were actually made in response to the manpower restrictions of the Truman defense budget. In fact, the position of black marines in small black units became even more isolated in the months following the Truman order as the Division of Plans and Policies began devising racially separate assignments. Like the stewards before them, the security guards at closed naval installations and ammunition depots found themselves in assignments increasingly viewed as "colored" jobs. That the number of Negroes in the Marine Corps was so small aided and abetted these arrangements, which promised to continue despite the presidential order until some dramatic need for change arose.

The Air Force Plans for Limited Integration

Of all the services, the Air Force was in the best position to respond promptly to President Truman's call for equal treatment and opportunity. For some time a group of Air staff officers had been engaged in devising a new approach to the use of black manpower. Indeed their study, much of which antedated the Truman order, represented the solution of the Air Force's manpower experts to a pressing problem in military efficiency. More important than the executive order or demands of civil rights advocates, the criticism of segregation by these experts in uniform led the Air Force to accept the need for limited integration.

But there was to be no easy road to integration for the service. Considerable resistance was yet to be overcome, both in the Air staff and among senior commanders. As Secretary Zuckert later put it, while there was sentiment for integration among a few of the highest officers, "you didn't have to scratch far to run into opposition."[13-77] The Deputy Chief of Staff for Personnel, General Edwards, reported to Secretary Symington that he had found solid opposition to any proposed policy of integration in the service.[13-78] Normally such resistance would have killed the study group's proposals. In the Army, for example, opposition supported by Secretary Royall had blocked change. In the Air Force, the opposition received no such support. Indeed,

Secretary Symington proved to be the catalyst that the Army had lacked. He was the Air Force's margin of difference, transforming the study group's proposal from a staffing paper into a program for substantial change in racial policy.

In Symington the Air Force had a secretary who was not only a tough-minded businessman demanding efficiency but a progressive politician with a humanitarian interest in providing equal opportunity for Negroes. "With Symington," Eugene Zuckert has pointed out, "it was principle first, efficiency second."[13-79] Symington himself later explained the source of his humanitarian interest. "What determined me many years ago was a quotation from Bernard Shaw in Myrdal's book, *American Dilemma*, which went something like this—'First the American white man makes the negro clean his shoes, then criticizes him for being a bootblack.' All Americans should have their chance. And both my grandfathers were in the Confederate Army."[13-80] Symington had successfully combined efficiency and humanitarianism before. As president of the Emerson Electric Manufacturing Company of St. Louis, he had racially integrated a major industry carrying out vital war work in a border state, thereby increasing productivity. When he became secretary, Symington was immediately involved in the Air Force's race problems; he wanted to know, for instance, why only nine black applicants had passed the qualifying examination for the current cadet program.[13-81] When President Truman issued his executive order, Symington was ready to move. In his own words, "when Mr. Truman as Commander-in-Chief issued an order to integrate the Air Force, I asked him if he was serious. He said he was. Accordingly we did just that. I turned the actual operations of the job over to my Assistant Secretary Eugene Zuckert.... It all worked out routinely."[13-82]

To call "routine" the fundamental change that took place in Air Force manpower practices stretches the definition of the word. The integration program required many months of intensive study and planning, and many more months to carry out. Yet if integration under Symington was slow, it was also inevitable. Zuckert reported that Symington gave him about eight reasons for integration, the last "because I said do it."[13-83] Symington's tough attitude, along with the presidential order, considerably eased the burden of those in the Air Force who were expected to abandon a tradition inherited from their Army days. The secretary's diplomatic skill also softened opposition in other quarters. Symington, a master at congressional relations, smoothed the way on Capitol Hill by successfully reassuring some southern leaders, in particular Congressman Carl Vinson of Georgia, that integration had to come, but that it would come quietly and in a way least calculated to provoke its congressional opponents.[13-84]

Symington assigned general responsibility for equal opportunity matters to his assistant secretary for management, Eugene Zuckert, but the task of formulating the specific plan fell to General Edwards. To avoid conflict with some of his colleagues, Edwards resorted to the unorthodox means of ignoring the usual staff coordination. He sent his proposals directly to the Chief of Staff and then on to the secretary for approval without reference to other staff agencies, one of which, the Office of the Vice Chief of Staff, General Muir S. Fairchild, was the focal point of staff opposition.[13-85]

SECRETARY SYMINGTON

On the basis of evidence submitted by his long-standing study group, General Edwards concluded that current Air Force policy for the use of black manpower was "wasteful, deleterious to military effectiveness and lacking in wartime application." The policy of the Navy was superior, he told the Chief of Staff and the secretary, with respect to military effectiveness, economy, and morale, especially when the needs of full mobilization were considered. The Air Force would profit by adopting a policy similar to that of the Navy, and he proposed a program, to be "vigorously implemented and monitored," that would inactivate the all-black fighter wing and transfer qualified black servicemen from that wing as well as from all the major commands to white units. One exception would be that those black specialists, whose work was essential to the continued operation of their units, would stay in their black units. Some black units would be retained to provide for individuals ineligible for transfer to white units or for discharge.

The new program would abolish the 10 percent quota and develop recruiting methods to enable the Air Force to secure only the "best qualified" enlistees of both races. Men chronically ineligible for advancement, both black and white, would be eliminated. If too many Negroes enlisted despite these measures, Edwards explained that an "administratively determined ceiling of Negro intake" could be established, but the Air Force had no intention of establishing a minimum for black enlistees. As the Director of Personnel Planning put it, a racial floor was just as much a quota as a racial ceiling and had the same effect of denying opportunity to some while providing special consideration for others.[13-86]

The manpower experts had decided that the social complications of such a policy would be negligible—"more imaginary than real." Edwards referred to the Navy's experience with

158

limited integration, which, he judged, had relieved rather than multiplied social tensions between the races. Nevertheless he and his staff proposed "as a conservative but progressive step" toward the integration of living quarters that the Air Force arrange for separate sleeping quarters for blacks and whites. The so-called "barracks problem" was the principal point of discussion within the Air Force, Edwards admitted, and "perhaps the most critical point of the entire policy." He predicted that the trend toward more privacy in barracks, especially the separate cubicles provided in construction plans for new barracks, would help solve whatever problems might arise.[13-87]

While the Chief of Staff, General Vandenberg, initialed the program without comment, Assistant Secretary Zuckert was enthusiastic. As Zuckert explained to Symington, the program was predicated on free competition for all Air Force jobs, and he believed that it would also eliminate social discrimination by giving black officers and men all the privileges of Air Force social facilities. Although he admitted that in the matter of living arrangements the plan "only goes part way," he too was confident that time and changes in barracks construction would eliminate any problems.[13-88]

Symington was already familiar with most of Edwards's conclusions, for a summary had been sent him by the Assistant Vice Chief of Staff on 22 December "for background."[13-89]When he received Zuckert's comments he acted quickly. The next day he let the Secretary of Defense know what the Air Force was doing. "We propose," he told Forrestal, "to adopt a policy of integration." But he qualified that statement along the lines suggested by the Air staff: "Although there will still be units manned entirely by Negroes, all Negroes will not necessarily be assigned to these units. Qualified Negro personnel will be assigned to any duties in any Air Force activity strictly on the basis of the qualifications of the individual and the needs of the Air Force."[13-90] Symington tied the new program to military efficiency, explaining to Forrestal that efficient use of black servicemen was one of the essentials of economic and effective air power. In this vein he summarized the program and listed what he considered its advantages for the Air Force.

The proposal forwarded to the Secretary of Defense in January 1949 committed the Air Force to a limited integration policy frankly imitative of the Navy's. A major improvement over the Air Force's current practices, the plan still fell considerably short of the long-range goals enunciated in the Gillem Board Report, to say nothing of the implications of the President's equal opportunity order. Although it is impossible to say exactly why Symington decided to settle for less than full integration, there are several explanations worth considering.

In the first place the program sent to Forrestal may well not have reflected the exact views of the Air Force secretary, nor conveyed all that his principal manpower assistant intended. Actually, the concern expressed by Air Force officials for military efficiency and by civil rights leaders for equal opportunity always centered specifically on the problems of the black tactical air unit and related specialist billets at Lockbourne Air Force Base. In fact, the need to solve the pressing administrative problems of Colonel Davis's command provoked the Air staff study that eventually evolved into the integration program. The program itself focused on this command and provided for the integrated assignment of its members throughout the Air Force. Other black enlisted men, certainly those serving as laborers in the F Squadrons, scattered worldwide, did not pose a comparable manpower problem. They were ignored on the theory that abolition of the quota, along with the application of more stringent recruitment procedures, would in time rid the services of its unskilled and unneeded men.

It can be argued that the purpose of the limited integration proposal was not so much to devise a new policy as to minimize the impact of change on congressional opponents. Edwards certainly hoped that his plan would placate senior commanders and staff officers who opposed integration or feared the social upheaval they assumed would follow the abolition of all black units. This explanation would account for the cautious approach to racial mixing in the proposal, the elaborate administrative safeguards against social confrontation, and the promised reduction in the number of black airmen. Some of those pressing for the new program certainly considered the retention of segregated units a stopgap measure designed to prevent a too precipitous reorganization of the service. As Lt. Col. Jack Marr, a member of Edwards's staff and author of the staff's integration study, explained to the Fahy Committee, "we are trying to do our best not to tear the Air Force all apart and try to reorganize it overnight."[13-91] Marr predicted that as those eligible for reassignment were transferred out of black units, the units themselves, bereft of essential personnel, would become inoperative and disappear one by one.

In the end it must be admitted that race relations possess an inner dynamic, and it is impossible to relate the integration of the Air Force to any isolated decision by a secretary or proposal by a group from his military staff. The decision to integrate was the result of several disparate forces—the political interests of the administration, the manpower needs of the Air

Force, the aspirations of its black minority, and perhaps more than all the rest, the acceptance by its airmen of a different social system. Together, these factors would make successive steps to full integration impossible to resist. Integration, then, was an evolutionary process, and Symington's acceptance of a limited integration plan was only one step in a continuing process that stretched from the Air staff's study of black manpower in 1948 to the disappearance of the last black unit two years later.

CHAPTER 14
The Fahy Committee Versus the Department of Defense

Given James Forrestal's sympathy for integration, considerable cooperation could be expected between members of his department and the Committee on Equality of Treatment and Opportunity in the Armed Services, better known as the Fahy Committee. In the wake of the committee's establishment, Forrestal proposed that the service secretaries assign an assistant secretary to coordinate his department's dealings with the group and a ranking black officer from each service be assigned to advise the assistant secretaries.[14-1] His own office promised to supply the committee with vital documentation, and his manpower experts offered to testify. The service secretaries agreed to follow suit.

Willing to cooperate, Forrestal still wanted to chart his own course. Both he and his successor, Louis A. Johnson, made it quite clear that as a senior cabinet officer the Secretary of Defense was accountable in all matters to the President alone. The Fahy Committee might report on the department's racial practices and suggest changes, but the development of policy was his prerogative. Both men dealt directly with the committee from time to time, but their directives to the services on the formulation of race policy were developed independently of the White House group.[14-2] Underscoring this independent attitude, Marx Leva reminded the service secretaries that the members of the Personnel Policy Board were to work with the representatives of their respective staffs on racial matters. They were not expected "to assist Fahy."[14-3]

At the same time Secretary of Defense Forrestal was aware that the interests of a committee enjoying White House support could not be ignored. His attempt to develop a new racial policy was probably in part an effort to forestall committee criticism and in part a wish to draw up a policy that would satisfy the committee without really doing much to change things. After all, such a departmental attitude toward committees, both congressional and presidential, was fairly normal. Faced with the conflicting racial policies of the Air Force and Army, Forrestal agreed to let the services present their separate programs to the Fahy Committee, but he wanted to develop a race policy applicable to all the services.[14-4] Some of his subordinates debated the wisdom of this decision, arguing that the President had assigned that task to the Fahy Committee, but they were overruled. Forrestal ordered the newly created Personnel Policy Board to undertake, simultaneously with the committee, a study of the department's racial policy. The board was to concentrate on "breaking down the problem," as Forrestal put it, into its component parts and trying to arrive quietly at areas of agreement on a uniform policy that could be held in readiness until the Fahy Committee made its report.[14-5]

The Personnel Policy Board, established by Forrestal to help regulate the military and civilian policies of his large department, was the logical place to prepare a departmental racial policy.[14-6] But could a group basically interservice in nature be expected to develop a forceful, independent racial policy for all the services along the lines Forrestal appeared to be following? It seemed unlikely, for at their first meeting the board members agreed that any policy developed must be "satisfactory to the three services."[14-7]

Undeterred by members' calling for more investigation and debate before the board prepared a common policy, Chairman Thomas R. Reid and his chief of staff, Army Brig. Gen. Charles T. Lanham, acted.[14-8] On 28 February they drafted a directive for the Secretary of Defense that would abolish all racial quotas and establish uniform standards of induction for service which in times of emergency would include provisions for the apportionment of enlistees both qualitatively and quantitatively. Moreover, all black enlistees would be given the opportunity to serve as individuals in integrated units. The services would be completely integrated by 1 July 1950. To ease the change, Reid and Lanham would in the interim regulate the number of Negroes in integrated units, allowing not less than four men and not more than 10 percent in a company-size unit. Enlisted men could choose to serve under officers of their own race.[14-9]

Favorably received in the secretary's office, the proposed directive came too late for speedy enactment. On 3 March Forrestal resigned, and although Leva hoped the directive could be issued before Forrestal's actual departure, "in view of his long-standing interest in this field," Forrestal was obviously reluctant to commit his successor to so drastic a course.[14-10] With a final bow to his belief in service autonomy, Forrestal asked Reid and Lanham to submit their proposal to the service secretaries for review.[14-11] The secretaries approved the idea of a unified policy in principle, but each had very definite and individual views on what that policy

160

should contain and how it should be carried out. Denied firm direction from the ailing Forrestal, Reid and Lanham could do little against service opposition. Their proposal was quietly tabled while the board continued its search for an acceptable unified policy.

Perhaps it was just as well, for the Reid-Lanham draft had serious defects. It failed to address the problems of qualitative imbalance in the peacetime services, probably in deference to Forrestal's recent rejection of the Army's call for a fair distribution of high-scoring enlistees. While the proposal encouraged special training for Negroes, it also limited their assignment to a strict 10 percent quota in any unit. The result would have been an administrative nightmare, with trained men in excess of the 10 percent quota assigned to other, nonspecialty duties. As one manpower expert later admitted, "you ran the real chance of having black engineers and the like pushing wheelbarrows."[14-12]

The service objections to a carefully spelled out policy were in themselves quite convincing to Lanham and Reid. Reid agreed with Eugene Zuckert, Assistant Secretary of the Air Force, that "probably the most logical and soundest approach" was for each service to prepare a policy statement and explain how it was being carried out. The board could then prepare a general policy based on these statements, and, with the approval of the Secretary of Defense, send it to the Fahy Committee in time for its report to the President.[14-13] But if Zuckert's scheme was logical and sound, it also managed to reduce the secretary's status to final endorsement officer. Such a role never appealed to James Forrestal, and would be even less acceptable to the politically energetic Louis Johnson, who succeeded Forrestal as Secretary of Defense on 28 March 1949.

Reid appreciated this distinction, and while he was willing to abandon the idea of a policy directive spelling out matters of personnel administration, he was determined that there be a general policy statement on the subject and that it originate not with the services but with the Secretary of Defense, who would then review individual service plans for implementing his directive.[14-14] Reid set the board's staff to this task, but it took several draftings, each stronger and more specific than the last, before a directive acceptable to Reid and Lanham was devised.[14-15] Approved by the full board on 5 April 1949 and signed by Secretary Johnson the next day, the directive reiterated the President's executive order, adding that all persons would be considered on the basis of individual merit and ability and must qualify according to the prescribed standards for enlistment, promotion, assignment, and school attendance. All persons would be accorded equal opportunity for appointment, advancement, professional improvement, and retention, and although some segregated units would be retained, "qualified" Negroes would be assigned without regard to race. The secretary ordered the services to reexamine their policies and submit detailed plans for carrying out this directive.[14-16]

Although responsible for preparing the secretary's directive, Reid and Lanham had second thoughts about it. They were concerned lest the services treat it as an endorsement of their current policies. Reid pointedly explained to their representatives on the Personnel Policy Board that the service statements due by 1 May should not merely reiterate present practices, but should represent a "sincere effort" by the departments to move toward greater racial equality.[14-17] Service responses, he warned, would be scrutinized to determine "their adequacy in the light of the intent of the Secretary's policy." Reid later admitted to Secretary Johnson that the directive was so broadly formed that it "permits almost any practice under it."[14-18] He, Lanham, and others agreed that since its contents were bound to reach the press anyway, the policy should be publicized in a way that played down generalizations and emphasized the responsibilities it imposed for new directions. Johnson agreed, and the announcement of his directive, emphasizing the importance of new service programs and setting a deadline for their submission, was widely circulated.[14-19]

The directive reflected Louis Johnson's personality, ambition, and administrative strategy. If many of his associates questioned his personal commitment to the principle of integration, or indeed even his private feeling about President Truman's order, all recognized his political ambition and penchant for vigorous and direct action.[14-20] The secretary would recognize the political implications of the executive order just as he would want to exercise personal control over integration, an issue fraught with political uncertainties that an independent presidential committee would only multiply. A dramatic public statement might well serve Johnson's needs. By creating at least the illusion of forward motion in the field of race relations, a directive issued by the Secretary of Defense might neutralize the Fahy Committee as an independent force, protecting the services from outside interference while enhancing Johnson's position in the White House and with the press. A "blustering bully," one of Fahy's assistants later called Johnson, whose directive was designed, he charged, to put the Fahy Committee out of business.[14-21]

If such was his motive, the secretary was taking a chance. Announcing his directive to the press transformed what could have been an innocuous, private reaffirmation of the department's pledge of equal treatment and opportunity into a public exercise in military policymaking. The Secretary of Defense in effect committed himself to a public review of the services' racial practices. In this sense the responses he elicited from the Army and Navy were a disappointment. Both services contented themselves with an outline of their current policies and ignored the secretary's request for future plans. The Army offered statistics to prove that its present program guaranteed equal opportunity, while the Navy concluded that its practices and procedures revealed "no inconsistencies" with the policy prescribed by the Secretary of Defense.[14-22] Summing up his reaction to these responses for the Personnel Policy Board, Reid said that the Army had a poor policy satisfactorily administered, while the Navy had an acceptable policy poorly administered. Neither service complied "with the spirit or letter of the request."[14-23]

Not all the board members agreed. In the wake of the Army and Navy replies, some saw the possible need for separate service policies rather than a common policy; considering the many advances enumerated in the replies, one member even suggested that Johnson might achieve more by getting the services to prosecute their current policies vigorously. Although Chairman Reid promised that these suggestions would all be taken into consideration, he still hoped to use the Air Force response to pry further concessions out of the Army and Navy.[14-24]

The Air Force plan had been in existence for some time, its implementation delayed because Symington had agreed with Royall in January that a joint Army-Air Force plan might be developed and because he and Zuckert needed the time to sell the new plan to some of their senior military assistants.[14-25] But greater familiarity with the plan quickly convinced Royall that the Army and Air Force positions could never be reconciled, and the Air Force plan was independently presented to the Fahy Committee and later, with some revision that further liberalized its provisions, to Johnson as the Air Force reply to his directive.[14-26] The Personnel Policy Board approved the Air Force's proposal for the integration of a large group of its black personnel, and after discussing it with Fahy and the other services, Reid recommended to the Secretary of Defense that he approve it also.[14-27]

To achieve maximum benefit from the Air Force plan, Reid and his associates had to link it publicly with the inadequate replies from the other services. Disregarding the views of some board members, he suggested that Johnson reject the Army and Navy answers and, without indicating the form he thought their answers should take, order them to prepare new proposals.[14-28] Johnson would also have to ignore a warning from Secretary of the Army Royall, who had recently reminded him that Forrestal had assured Congress during the selective service hearings that the administration would not issue a preemptory order completely abolishing segregation. "I have no reason to believe that the President had changed his mind," Royall continued, "but I think you should be advised of these circumstances because if any action were later taken by you or other authority to abolish segregation in the Army I am confident that these Southern senators would remember this incident."[14-29]

Despite Royall's not so subtle warning, Reid's scheme worked. The Secretary of Defense explicitly and publicly approved the Air Force program and rejected those of the Army and Navy. Johnson told the Army, for example, that he was pleased with the progress made in the past few years, but he saw "that much remains to be done and that the rate of progress toward the objectives of the Executive Order must be accelerated."[14-30] He gave the recalcitrants until 25 May to submit "specific additional actions which you propose to take."

The Committee's Recommendations

If there was ever any question of what their programs should contain, the services had only to turn to the Fahy Committee for plenty of advice. The considerable attention paid by senior officials of the Department of Defense to racial matters in the spring of 1949 could be attributed in part to the commonly held belief that the Fahy Committee planned an integration crusade, using the power of the White House to transform the services' racial policies in a profound and dramatic way. Indeed, some members of the committee itself demanded that the chairman "lay down the law to the services."[14-31] But this approach, Charles Fahy decided, ignored both the personalities of the participants and the realities of the situation.

FAHY COMMITTEE WITH PRESIDENT TRUMAN AND ARMED SERVICES SECRETARIES.
Seated with the President are Secretary Forrestal and Committeeman A. J. Donahue.
Standing from the left: Chairman of the Personnel Policy Board Thomas R. Reid; Chief of Staff of the Personnel
Policy Board Brig. Gen. Charles T. Lanham; Committeemen John H. Sengstacke and William M. Stevenson;
Secretary Royall; Secretary Symington; Committeemen Lester Granger and Dwight R. Palmer; Secretary Sullivan;
and Charles Fahy.]

The armed forces had just won a great world war, and the opinions of the military commanders, Fahy reasoned, would carry much weight with the American public. In any conflict between the committee and the services, Fahy believed that public opinion would be likely to side with the military. He wanted the committee to issue no directive. Instead, as he reported to the President, the committee would seek the confidence and help of the armed services in working out changes in manpower practices to achieve Truman's objectives.[14-32] It was important to Fahy that the committee not make the mistake of telling the services what should be done and then have to drop the matter with no assurances that anything would be done. He was determined, rather, to obtain not only a change in policy, but also a "program in being" during the life of the committee. To achieve this change the group would have to convince the Army and the other services of the need for and justice of integration. To do less, to settle for the issuance of an integration directive alone, would leave the services the option of later disregarding the reforms on the grounds of national security or for other reasons. Fahy explained to the President that all this would take time.[14-33] "Take all the time you need," Truman told his committee.[14-34] This committee proceeded to do, gathering thousands of pages of testimony, while its staff under the direction of Executive Secretary Edwin W. Kenworthy toured military installations, analyzed the existing programs and operations of the three services, and perused the reams of pertinent historical documents.

That the committee expected the Secretary of Defense to take the lead in racial affairs, refraining from dictating policy itself, did not mean that Fahy and his associates lacked a definite point of view. From the first, Fahy understood Truman's executive order to mean unequivocally that the services would have to abandon segregation, an interpretation reinforced in a later discussion he had with the President.[14-35] The purpose of the committee, in Fahy's view, was not to impose integration on the services, but to convince them of the merits of the President's order and to agree with them on a plan to make it effective.

The trouble, the committee quickly learned, lay in trying to convince the Army of the practical necessity for integration. On one hand the Army readily admitted that there were some advantages in spreading black soldiers through the white ranks. "It might remove any false charges that equal opportunities are not provided," General Bradley testified. "It would simplify administration and the use of manpower, and it would distribute our losses in battle more nearly in proportion to the percentage of the two races."[14-36] But then the Army had so carefully and often repeated the disadvantages of integration that Bradley and others could very easily offer a logical and well-rehearsed apology for continuing the Army's current policy. Army officials repeatedly testified, for example, that their situation fundamentally differed from those of the other two services. The Army had a much higher proportion of Negroes in its ranks, 10 to 11 percent during the period of the committee's life, and in addition was required by law to accept by the thousands recruits, many of them black, whose aptitude or education would automatically disqualify them for the Air Force or Navy. Armed with these inequities, the Army remained impervious to the claims of the Navy and Air Force, defending its time-honored charge that segregation was necessary to preserve the efficiency of its combat forces. In Zuckert's opinion, the Army was trying to maintain the *status quo* at any cost.[14-37]

The Army offered other reasons. Its leaders testified that the unlimited induction of Negroes into an integrated Army would seriously affect enlistments and the morale of troops. Morale in particular affected battle efficiency. Again General Bradley testified.

I consider that a unit has high morale when the men have confidence in themselves, confidence in their fellow members of their unit, and confidence in their leaders. If we try to force integration on the Army before the country is ready to accept these customs, we may have difficulty attaining high morale along the lines I have mentioned.[14-38]

Underlying all these discussions of morale and efficiency lurked a deep-seated suspicion of the combat reliability and effectiveness of black troops and the fear that many white soldiers would refuse to serve with blacks. Many Army leaders were convinced that the performance of black troops in the past two wars did not qualify Negroes for a role in the Army's current mission, the execution of field operations in relatively small groups. These reservations were expressed frequently in Army testimony. Bradley, in defense of segregation, for example, cited the performance of the 92d Division. When asked whether a 15 percent black Army would reduce efficiency, he said, "from our experience in the past I think the time might come when it wouldn't, but the average educational standards of these men would not be up to the average of the white soldier. In modern combat a man is thrown very much on his own initiative."[14-39] This attitude was closely related to the Army's estimates of white morale: white soldiers, the argument ran, especially many among those southerners who comprised an unusually high proportion of the Army's strength, would not accept integration. Many white men would refuse

163

to take orders from black superiors, and the mutual dependence of individual soldiers and small units in combat would break down when the races were mingled.

Although these beliefs were highly debatable, they were tenaciously held by many senior officials and were often couched in terms that were extremely difficult to refute. For instance, Royall summed up the argument on morale: "I am reluctant—and I am sure all sincere citizens will be reluctant—to force a pace faster than is consistent with the efficiency and morale of the Army—or to follow a course inconsistent with the ability of the Army, in the event of war, to take the battlefield with reasonable assurance of success."[14-40]

But in time the Fahy Committee found a way, first suggested by its executive secretary, to turn the efficiency argument around. Certainly a most resourceful and imaginative man, Kenworthy had no doubt about the immorality of segregation, but he also understood, as he later told the Secretary of the Army, that whatever might be morally undeniable in the abstract, military efficiency had to govern in matters of military policy. His study of the record and his investigation of existing service conditions convinced him that segregation actually impeded military efficiency. Convinced from the start that appeals to morality would be a waste of time, Kenworthy pressed the committee members to tackle the services on their own ground—efficiency.[14-41] After seeing the Army so effectively dismiss in the name of military efficiency and national security the moral arguments against segregation as being valid but irrelevant, Kenworthy asked Chairman Fahy:

I wonder if the one chance of getting something done isn't to meet the military on their own ground—the question of military efficiency. They have defended their Negro manpower policies on the grounds of efficiency. Have they used Negro manpower efficiently?... Can it be that the whole policy of segregation, especially in large units like the 92nd and 93rd Division, ADVERSELY AFFECTS MORALE AND EFFICIENCY?[14-42]

The committee did not have to convince the Navy or the Air Force of the practical necessity for integration. With four years of experience in integrating its ships and stations, the Navy did not bother arguing the merits of integration with the committee, but instead focused its attention on black percentages and the perennial problem of the largely black Steward's Branch. Specifically, naval officials testified that integration increased the Navy's combat efficiency. Speaking for the Air Force, Symington told the committee that "in our position we believe that non-segregation will improve our efficiency in at least some instances" and consequently "it's simply been a case [of] how we are going to do it, not whether we are going to do it." Convinced of the simple justice of integration, Symington also told the committee: "You've got to clear up that basic problem in your heart before you can really get to this subject. Both Zuckert and Edwards feel right on the basic problem."[14-43]

Even while the Air Force and the Navy were assuring Fahy of their belief in the efficiency of integration, they hastened to protect themselves against a change of heart. General Edwards gave the committee a caveat on integration: "if it comes to a matter of lessening the efficiency of the Air Force so it can't go to war and do a good job, there isn't any question that the policy of non-segregation will have to go by the boards. In a case like that, I'd be one of the first to recommend it."[14-44] Secretary of the Navy Sullivan also supported this view and cautioned the committee against making too much of the differences in the services' approach to racial reforms. Each service, he suggested, should be allowed to work out a program that would stand the test of war. "If war comes and we go back [to segregation], then we have taken a very long step in the wrong direction." He wanted the committee to look to the "substance of the advance rather than to the apparent progress."[14-45]

E. W. KENWORTHY

Kenworthy predicted that attacking the Army's theory of military efficiency would require considerable research by the committee into Army policy as well as the past performance of black units. Ironically enough, he got the necessary evidence from the Army itself, in the person of Roy K. Davenport.[14-46] Davenport's education at Fisk and Columbia universities had prepared him for the scholar's life, but Pearl Harbor changed all that, and Davenport eventually landed behind a desk in the office that managed the Army's manpower affairs. One of the first black professionals to break through the armed forces racial barrier, Davenport was not a "Negro specialist" and did not wish to be one. Nor could he, an experienced government bureaucrat, be blamed if he saw in the Fahy Committee yet one more well-meaning attempt by an outside group to reform the Army. Only when Kenworthy convinced him that this committee was serious about achieving change did Davenport proceed to explain in great detail how segregation limited the availability of military occupational specialties, schooling, and assignments for Negroes.

Kenworthy decided that the time had come for Fahy to meet Davenport, particularly since the chairman was inclined to be impressed with, and optimistic over, the Army's response to

164

Johnson's directive of 6 April 1949. Fahy, Kenworthy knew, was unfamiliar with military language and the fine art practiced by military staffs of stating a purpose in technical jargon that would permit various interpretations. There was no fanfare, no dramatic scene. Kenworthy simply invited Fahy and Davenport, along with the black officers assigned by the services to assist the committee, to meet informally at his home one evening in April.[14-47]

Never one to waste time, Fahy summarized the committee's activities thus far, outlined its dealings with Army witnesses, and then handed out copies of the Army's response to Secretary Johnson's directive. Fahy was inclined to recommend approval, a course agreed to by the black officers present, but he nevertheless turned courteously to the personnel expert from the Department of the Army and asked him for his opinion of the official Army position. Davenport did not hesitate. "The directive [the Army's response to Secretary Johnson's 6 April directive] isn't worth the paper it's written on," he answered. It called for sweeping changes in the administration of the Army's training programs, he explained, but would produce no change because personnel specialists at the training centers would quickly discover that their existing procedures, which excluded so many qualified black soldiers, would fit quite comfortably under the document's idealistic but vague language. The Army's response, Davenport declared, had been very carefully drawn up to retain segregation rather than to end it.

CHARLES FAHY
(a later portrait).

Chairman Fahy seemed annoyed by this declaration. After all, he had listened intently to the Army's claims and promises and was inclined to accept the Army's proposal as a slow, perhaps, but certain way to bring about racial integration. He was, however, a tough-minded man and was greatly impressed by the analysis of the situation presented by the Army employee. When Davenport asked him to reexamine the directive with eyes open to the possibility of deceit, Fahy walked to a corner of the room and reread the Army's statement in the light of Davenport's charges. Witnesses would later remember the flush of anger that came to his face as he read. His committee was going to have to hear more from Davenport.

If efficiency was to be the keynote of the committee's investigation, Davenport explained, it would be a simple thing to prove that the Army was acting inefficiently. In a morning of complex testimony replete with statistical analysis of the Army's manpower management, he and Maj. James D. Fowler, a black West Point graduate and personnel officer, provided the committee with the needed breakthrough. Step by step they led Fahy and his associates through the complex workings of the Army's career guidance program, showing them how segregation caused the inefficient use of manpower on several counts.[14-48] The Army, for example, as part of a continuing effort to find men who *could* be trained for specialties in which it had a shortage of men, published a monthly list, the so-called "40 Report," of its authorized and actual strength in each of its 490 military occupational specialties. Each of these specialties was further broken down by race. The committee learned that no authorization existed at all for Negroes in 198 of these specialties, despite the fact that in many of them the Army was under its authorized strength. Furthermore, for many of the specialties in which there were no authorizations for Negroes no great skill was needed. In short, it was the policy of segregated service that allowed the Army, which had thousands of jobs unfilled for lack of trained specialists, to continue to deny training and assignment to thousands of Negroes whose aptitude test scores showed them at least minimally suited for those jobs. How could the Army claim that it was operating efficiently when a shortage existed and potentially capable persons were being ignored?

ROY DAVENPORT

One question led to another. If there were no authorizations for black soldiers in 198 specialties, what were the chances for qualified Negroes to attend schools that trained men for these specialties? It turned out that of the 106 school courses available after a man finished basic training, only twenty-one were open to Negroes. That is, 81 percent of the courses offered by the Army were closed to Negroes. The Army denied that discrimination was involved. Since existing black units could not use the full range of the Army's military occupational specialties, went the official line of reasoning, it would be wasteful and inefficient to train men for nonexistent jobs in those units. It followed that the Organization and Training Division must exclude many Negroes from being classified in specialties for which they were qualified and from Army schools that would train others for such unneeded specialties.

This reasoning was in the interest of segregation, not efficiency, and Davenport and others were able to prove to the committee's satisfaction that the Army's segregation policy could be defended neither in terms of manpower efficiency nor common fairness. With Davenport and Fowler's testimony, Charles Fahy later explained, he began to "see light for a solution."[14-49] He began to see how he would probably be able to gain the committee's double objective: the announcement of an integration policy for the Army and the establishment of a practical program that would immediately begin moving the Army from segregation to integration.

In fact, military efficiency was a potent weapon which, if skillfully handled, might well force the Army into important concessions leading to integration. Taking its cue from Davenport and Fowler, the committee would contend that, as the increasing complexity of war had created a demand for skilled manpower, the country could ill-afford to use any of its soldiers below their full capacity or fail to train them adequately. With a logic understandable to President and public alike, the committee could later state that since maximum military efficiency demanded that all servicemen be given an equal opportunity to discover and exploit their talents, an indivisible link existed between military efficiency and equal opportunity.[14-50] Thus equal opportunity in the name of military efficiency became one of the committee's basic premises; until the end of its existence the committee hammered away at this premise.

While the committee's logic was unassailable when applied to the plight of a relatively small number of talented and qualified black soldiers, a different solution would have to prevail when the far larger number of Negroes ineligible for Army schooling either by talent, inclination, or previous education was considered. Here the Army's plea for continued segregation in the name of military efficiency carried some weight. How could it, the Army asked, endanger the morale and efficiency of its fighting forces by integrating these men? How could it, with its low enlistment standards, abandon its racial quota and risk enlarging the already burdensome concentration of "professional black privates?" The committee admitted the justice of the Army's claim that the higher enlistment score required by the Navy and Air Force resulted in the Army's getting more than its share of men in the low-test categories IV and V. And while Kenworthy believed that immediate integration was less likely to cause serious trouble than the Army's announced plan of mixing the races in progressively smaller units, he too accepted the argument that it would be dangerous to reassign the Army's group of professional black privates to white units. Fahy saw the virtue of the Army's position here; his committee never demanded the immediate, total integration of the Army.

One solution to the problem, reducing the number of soldiers with low aptitude by forcing the other services to share equally in the burden of training and assimilating the less gifted and often black enlistee and draftee, had recently been rejected by the Navy and Air Force, a rejection endorsed by Secretary of Defense Forrestal. Even in the event that the Army could raise its enlistment standards and the other services be induced to lower theirs, much time would elapse before the concentration of undereducated Negroes could be broken up. Davenport was aware of all this when he limited his own recommendations to the committee to matters concerning the integration of black specialists, the opening of all Army schools to Negroes, and the establishment of some system to monitor the Army's implementation of these reforms.[14-51]

Having gained some experience, the committee was now able to turn the Army's efficiency argument against the racial quota. It decided that the quota had helped defeat the Gillem Board's aim of using Negroes on a broad professional scale. It pointed out that, when forced by manpower needs and the selective service law to set a lower enlistment standard, the Army had allowed its black quota to be filled to a great extent by professional privates and denied to qualified black men, who could be used on a broad professional scale, the chance to enlist.[14-52] It was in the name of military efficiency, therefore, that the committee adopted a corollary to its demand for equal opportunity in specialist training and assignment: the racial quota must be abandoned in favor of a quota based on aptitude.

Fahy was not sure, he later admitted, how best to proceed at this point with the efficiency issue, but his committee obviously had to come up with some kind of program if only to preserve its administrative independence in the wake of Secretary Johnson's directive. As Kenworthy pointed out, short of demanding the elimination of all segregated units, there was little the committee could do that went beyond Johnson's statement.[14-53] Fahy, at least, was not prepared to settle for that. His solution, harmonizing with his belief in the efficacy of long-range practical change and his estimate of the committee's strength vis-à-vis the services' strength, was to prepare a "list of suggestions to guide the Army and Navy in its [sic] determinations."[14-54] The suggestions, often referred to by the committee as its "Initial Recommendations," would in the fullness of time, Fahy thought, effect substantial reforms in the way the Negro was employed by the services.

The committee's recommendations, sent to the Personnel Policy Board in late May 1949, are easily summarized.[14-55] Questioning why the Navy's policy, "so progressive on its face," had attracted so few Negroes into the general service, the committee suggested that Negroes remembered the Navy's old habit of restricting them to servant duties. It wanted the Navy to aim

166

a vigorous recruitment program at the black community in order to counteract this lingering suspicion. At the same time the committee wanted the Navy to make a greater effort among black high school students to attract qualified Negroes into the Naval Reserve Officers' Training Corps program. To reinforce these campaigns and to remove one more vestige of racial inequality in naval service, the committee also suggested that the Navy give to chief stewards all the perquisites of chief petty officers. The lack of this rating, in particular, had continued to cast doubt on the Navy's professed policy, the committee charged. "There is no reason, except custom, why the chief steward should not be a chief petty officer, and that custom seems hardly worth the suspicion it evokes." Finally, the committee wanted the Navy to adopt the same entry standards as the Army. It rejected the Navy's claim that men who scored below ninety were unusable in the general service and called for an analysis by outside experts to determine what jobs in the Navy could be performed by men who scored between seventy and ninety. At the same time the committee reiterated that it did not intend the Navy or any of the services to lower the qualifications for their highly skilled positions.

The committee also suggested to the Air Force that it establish a common enlistment standard along with the other services. Commenting that the Air Force had apparently been able to use efficiently thousands of men with test scores below ninety in the past, the committee doubted that the contemporary differential in Air Force and Army standards was justified. With a bow to Secretary Symington's new and limited integration policy, the committee deferred further recommendations.

It showed no such reluctance when it came to the Army. It wanted the Army to abolish racial considerations in the designation of military occupational specialties, attendance at its schools, and use of its school graduates in their military specialties. In line with the establishment of a parity of enlistment standards among the services, the committee wanted the Army to abandon its racial quotas. The committee did not insist on an immediate end to segregation in the Army, believing that no matter how desirable, such a drastic change could not be accomplished, as Davenport had warned, without very serious administrative confusion. Besides, there were other pragmatic reasons for adopting the gradualist approach. For the committee to demand immediate and complete integration would risk an outcry from Capitol Hill that might endanger the whole reform program. Gradual change, on the other hand, would allow time for qualified Negroes to attend school courses, and the concept that Negroes had a right to equal educational opportunities was one that was very hard for the segregationists to attack, given the American belief in education and the right of every child to its benefits.[14-56] If the Army could be persuaded to adopt these recommendations, the committee reasoned, the Army itself would gradually abolish segregation. The committee's formula for equality of treatment and opportunity in the Army, therefore, was simple and straightforward, but each of its parts had to be accepted to achieve the whole.

As it was, the committee's program for gradual change proved to be a rather large dose for senior service officials. An Army representative on the Personnel Policy Board staff characterized the committee's work as "presumptuous," "subjective," and "argumentative." He also charged the committee with failing to interpret the executive order and thus leaving unclear whether the President wanted across-the-board integration, and if so how soon.[14-57] The Personnel Policy Board ignored these larger questions when it considered the subject on 26 May, focusing its opposition instead on two of the committee's recommendations. It wanted Secretary Johnson to make "a strong representation" to Fahy against the suggestion that there be a parity of scores for enlistment in the services. The board also unanimously opposed the committee's suggestion that the Army send all qualified Negroes to specialty schools within eighteen months of enlistment, arguing that such a policy would be administratively impossible to enforce and would discriminate against white servicemen.[14-58]

Chairman Reid temporized somewhat in his recommendations to Secretary Johnson. He admitted that the whole question of parity of entrance standards was highly controversial. He recognized the justice in establishing universal standards for enlistment through selective service, but at the same time he believed it unfair to ask any service to accept volunteers of lesser quality than it could obtain through good enlistment and recruitment methods. He wanted Johnson to concentrate his attack on the parity question.[14-59]

Before Johnson could act on his personnel group's recommendations, the Army and Navy formally submitted their second replies to his directive on the executive order. Surprisingly, the services provided a measure of support for the Fahy Committee. For its part, the Navy was under particular pressure to develop an acceptable program. It, after all, had been the first to announce a general integration policy for which it had, over the years, garnered considerable praise. But now it was losing this psychological advantage under steady and persistent criticism from civil rights leaders, the President's committee, and, finally, the Secretary of Defense himself.

Proud of its racial policy and accustomed to the rapport it had always enjoyed with Forrestal, the Navy was suddenly confronted with a new Secretary of Defense who bluntly noted its "lack of any response" to his 6 April directive, thus putting the Navy in the same league as the Army.

Secretary Johnson's rejection of the Navy's response made a reexamination of its race program imperative, but it was still reluctant to follow the Fahy Committee's proposals completely. Although the personnel bureau had already planned special recruitment programs, as well as a survey of all jobs in the Navy and the mental requirements for each, the idea of making chief petty officers out of chief stewards caused "great anger and resentment in the upper reaches of BuPers," Capt. Fred Stickney of the bureau admitted to a representative of the committee. Stickney was confident that the bureau's opposition to this change could be surmounted, but he was not so sure that the Navy would surrender on the issue of equality of enlistment standards. The committee's arguments to the contrary, the Navy remained convinced that standardizing entrance requirements for all the services would mean "lowering the calibre of men taken into the Navy."[14-60]

But even here the Navy proved unexpectedly conciliatory. Replying to the Secretary of Defense a second time on 23 May, Acting Secretary Dan Kimball committed the Navy to a program that incorporated to a great extent the recommendations of the Fahy Committee, including raising the status of chief stewards and integrating recruit training in the Marine Corps. While he did not agree with the committee's proposal for equality of enlistment standards, Kimball broke the solid opposition to the committee's recommendation on this subject by promising to study the issue to determine where men who scored less than forty-five (the equivalent of General Classification Test score ninety) could be used without detriment to the Navy.[14-61]

The question of parity of enlistment standards aside, the Navy's program generally followed the suggestions of the Fahy Committee, and Chairman Reid urged Johnson to accept it.[14-62] The secretary's acceptance was announced on 7 June and was widely reported in the press.[14-63]

To some extent the Army had an advantage over the Navy in its dealings with Johnson and Fahy. It never had an integration policy to defend, had in fact consistently opposed the imposition of one, and was not, therefore, under the same psychological pressures to react positively to the secretary's latest rebuff. Determined to defend its current interpretation of the Gillem Board policy, the Army resisted the Personnel Policy Board's use of the Air Force plan, Secretary Johnson's directive, and the initial recommendations of the Fahy Committee to pry out of it a new commitment to integrate. In lieu of such a commitment, Acting Secretary of the Army Gordon Gray[14-64] offered Secretary Johnson another spirited defense of Circular 124 on 26 May, promising that the Army's next step would be to integrate black companies in the white battalions of the combat arms. This step could not be taken, he added, until the reactions to placing black battalions in white regiments and black companies in composite battalions had been observed in detail over a period of time. Gray remained unmoved by the committee's appeal for the wider use and broader training of the talented black soldiers in the name of combat efficiency and continued to defend the *status quo*. He cited with feeling the case of the average black soldier who because of his "social environment" had most often missed the opportunity to develop leadership abilities and who against the direct competition with the better educated white soldier would find it difficult to "rise above the level of service tasks." Segregation, Gray claimed, was giving black soldiers the chance to develop leadership "unhindered and unfettered by overshadowing competition they are not yet equipped to meet." He would be remiss in his duties, he warned Johnson, if he failed to report the concern of many senior officers who believed that the Army had already gone too far in inserting black units into white units and that "we are weakening to a dangerous degree the combat efficiency of our Army."[14-65]

The Army's response found the Fahy Committee and the office of the Secretary of Defense once again in agreement. The committee rejected Gray's statement, and Kenworthy drew up a point-by-point rebuttal. He contended that unless the Army took intermediate steps, its first objective, a specific quota of black units segregated at the battalion level, would always block the realization of integration, its ultimate objective.[14-66] The secretary's Personnel Policy Board struck an even harder blow. Chairman Reid called Gray's statement a rehash of Army accomplishments "with no indication of significant change or step forward." It ignored the committee's recommendations. In particular, and in contrast to the Navy, which had agreed to restudy the enlistment parity question, the Army had rejected the committee's request that it reconsider its quota system. Reid's blunt advice to Johnson: reject the Army's reply and demand a new one by a definite and early date.[14-67]

Members of the Fahy Committee met with Johnson and Reid on 1 June. Despite the antagonism that was growing between the Secretary of Defense and the White House group, the meeting produced several notable agreements. For his part, Johnson, accepting the recommendations of Fahy and Reid, agreed to reject the Army's latest response and order the Secretary of the Army and the Chief of Staff to confer informally with the committee in an attempt to produce an acceptable program. At the same time, Johnson made no move to order a common enlistment standard; he told Fahy that the matter was extremely controversial and setting such standards would involve rescinding previous interdepartmental agreements. On the committee's behalf, Fahy agreed to reword the recommendation on schooling for all qualified Negroes within eighteen months of enlistment and to discuss further the parity issue.[14-68]

General Lanham endorsed the committee's belief that there was a need for practical, intermediate steps when he drafted a response to the Army for Secretary Johnson to sign. "It is my conviction," he wanted Johnson to say, "that the Department of the Army must meet this issue [the equal opportunity imposed by Executive Order 9981] squarely and that its action, no matter how modest or small at its inception, must be progressive in spirit and carry with it the unmistakable promise of an ultimate solution in consonance with the Chief Executive's position and our national policy."[14-69]

But the Army received no such specific instruction. Although Johnson rejected the Army's second reply and demanded another based on a careful consideration of the Fahy Committee's recommendations,[14-70] he deleted Lanham's demand for immediate steps toward providing equal opportunity. Johnson's rejection of Lanham's proposal—a tacit rejection of the committee's basic premise as well—did not necessarily indicate a shift in Johnson's position, but it did establish a basis for future rivalry between the secretary and the committee. Until now Johnson and the committee, through the medium of the Personnel Policy Board, had worked in an informal partnership whose fruitfulness was readily apparent in the development of acceptable Navy and Air Force programs and in Johnson's rejection of the Army's inadequate responses. But this cooperation was to be short-lived; it would disappear altogether as the Fahy Committee began to press the Army, while the Secretary of Defense, in reaction, began to draw closer to the Army's position.[14-71]

A Summer of Discontent

The committee approached its negotiations with the Army with considerable optimism. Kenworthy was convinced that the committee's moderate and concrete recommendations had reassured Reid and the Personnel Policy Board and would strengthen its hand in dealing with the recalcitrant Army,[14-72] and Fahy, outlining for the President the progress the committee had made with the services, said that he looked forward to his coming meetings with Gray and Bradley.[14-73]

To remove any unnecessary obstacle to what Fahy hoped would be fruitful sessions, the committee revised its initial recommendations to the Army. First, as Fahy had promised Johnson, it modified its position on guaranteeing qualified black soldiers already assigned to units the opportunity to attend Army schools within eighteen months. Calling the imbroglio over this issue a mere misunderstanding—the committee did not intend that preferential treatment be given Negroes nor that the Army train more people than it needed—Fahy explained to Johnson that the committee only wanted to make sure that qualified Negroes would have the same chance as qualified white men. It would be happy, Fahy said, to work with the Army on rewording the recommendation.[14-74] The committee also added the suggestion that so long as racial units existed, the Army might permit enlisted men in the four lowest grades, at their request, to remain in a unit predominantly composed of men of their own race. This provision, however, was not to extend to officers and noncommissioned officers in the top three grades, who received their promotions on a worldwide competitive basis. Finally, the committee offered a substitute for the numerical quota it wanted abolished. So that the Army would not get too many low-scoring recruits, either black or white, the committee proposed a separate quota for each category in the classification test scores. Only so many voluntary enlistments would be accepted in categories I through III, their numbers based on the normal spread of scores that existed in both the wartime and peacetime Army. If the Army netted more high scorers than average in any period, it would induct fewer men from the next category. It would also deny reenlistment to any man scoring less than eighty (category IV).[14-75]

After meeting first with Gray and then the Chief of Staff, Fahy called the sessions "frank and cordial" and saw some prospect of accord, although their positions were still far apart.[14-76] Just how far apart had already become apparent on 5 July when Gray presented Fahy with an outline for yet another program for using black soldiers. This new program was based in part on the comments of the field commanders, and the Director of Personnel and Administration warned that "beyond the steps listed in this plan, there is very little major compromise area left short of complete integration."[14-77] While the Army plan differed from the committee's recommendations in many ways, in essence the disagreement was limited to two fundamental points. Determined to retain segregated units, the Army opposed the reassignment of school-trained Negroes to vacancies in white units; and in order to prevent an influx of Negroes in the low achievement categories, the Army was determined to retain the numerical quota.[14-78]

The committee argued that if the Army was to train men according to their ability, hence efficiently, and in accord with the principle of equality, it must consider assigning them without regard to race. It could not see how removal of the numerical quota would result in a flood of Negroes joining the Army, but it could see how retaining the quota would prevent the enlistment of blacks for long periods of time. These two provisions—that school-trained Negroes be freely assigned and that the quota be abolished—were really the heart of the committee's plan and hope for the gradual integration of the Army. The provisions would not require the abolition of racial units "at this time," Fahy explained to President Truman, but they would gradually extend the integration already practiced in overhead installations and Army schools. The committee could not demand any less, he confessed, in light of the President's order.[14-79]

The committee and the Army had reached a stalemate. As a staff member of the Personnel Policy Board put it, their latest proposal and counterproposals were simply extensions of what had long been put forth by both parties. He advised Chairman Reid to remain neutral until both sides presented their "total proposal."[14-80] But the press was not remaining neutral. The New York *Times*, for example, accused the Army of stalling and equivocating, engaging in a "private insurrection," and trying "to preserve a pattern of bigotry which caricatures the democratic cause in every corner of the world." There was no room for compromise, the *Times* added, and President Truman could not retreat without abdicating as Commander in Chief.[14-81] Secretary Gray countered with a statement that the Army was still under injunction from the Secretary of Defense to submit a new race program, and he was contemplating certain new proposals on the military occupational specialty issue.[14-82]

The Army staff did prepare another reply for the Secretary of Defense, and on 16 September Gray met with Fahy and others to discuss it. General Wade H. Haislip, the Vice Chief of Staff, claimed privately to Gray that the new reply was almost identical with the plan presented to the committee on 5 July and that the new concessions on occupational specialties would only require the conversion of some units from white to black.[14-83] Haislip, however, had not reckoned with the concession that Gray was prepared to make to Fahy. Gray accepted in principle the committee's argument that the assignment of black graduates of specialist schools should not be limited to black units or overhead positions but could be used to fill vacancies in any unit. At the same time, he remained adamant on the quota. When the committee spoke hopefully of the advantages of an Army open to all, the Army contemplated fearfully the racial imbalance that might result. The future was to prove the committee right about the advantages, but as of September 1949 Gray and his subordinates had no intention of giving up the quota.[14-84] Gray did agree, however, to continue studying the quota issue with the committee, and Fahy optimistically reported to President Truman: "It is the Committee's expectation that it will be able within a few weeks to make a formal report to you on a complete list of changes in Army policy and practices."[14-85]

Fahy made his prediction before Secretary of Defense Johnson took a course of action that, in effect, rendered the committee's position untenable. On 30 September Johnson received from Gray a new program for the employment of black troops. Without reference to the Fahy Committee, Johnson approved the proposal and announced it to the press. Gray's program opened all military occupational specialties to all qualified men, abolished racial quotas for the Army's schools, and abolished racially separate promotion systems and standards. But it also specifically called for retention of the racial quota on enlistments and conspicuously failed to provide for the assignment of black specialists beyond those jobs already provided by the old Gillem Board policy.[14-86] Secretary Gray had asked for Fahy's personal approval before forwarding the plan discussed by the two men at such length, but Fahy refused; he wanted the plan submitted to his full committee. When Johnson received the plan he did not consult the committee at all, although he briefly referred it to the acting chairman of the Personnel Policy Board, who interposed no objection.[14-87]

It is not difficult to understand Johnson's reasons for ignoring the President's committee. He had been forced to endure public criticism over the protracted negotiations between the Army and the committee. Among liberal elements on Capitol Hill, his position—that his directive and the service replies made legislation to prohibit segregation in the services unnecessary—was

170

obviously being compromised by the lack of an acceptable Army response.[14-88] In a word, the argument over civil rights in the armed forces had become a political liability for Louis Johnson, and he wanted it out of the way. Glossing over the Army's truculence, Johnson blamed the committee and its recommendations for his problem, and when his frontal assault on the committee failed—Kenworthy reported that the secretary tried to have the committee disbanded—he had to devise another approach.[14-89] The Army's new proposal, a more reasonable-sounding document than its predecessor, provided him with a convenient opportunity. Why not quickly approve the program, thereby presenting the committee with a *fait accompli* and leaving the President with little excuse for prolonging the civil rights negotiations?

Unfortunately for Johnson the gambit failed. While Fahy admitted that the Army's newest proposal was an improvement, for several reasons he could not accept it. The assignment of black specialists to white units was a key part of the committee's program, and despite Gray's private assurances that specialists would be integrated, Fahy was not prepared to accept the Army's "equivocal" language on this subject. There was also the issue of the quota, still very much alive between the committee and the Army. The committee was bound, furthermore, to resent being ignored in the approval process. Fahy and his associates had been charged by the President with advising the services on equality of treatment and opportunity, and they were determined to be heard.[14-90] Fahy informed the White House that the committee would review the Army's proposal in an extraordinary meeting. He asked that the President meanwhile refrain from comment.[14-91]

The committee's stand received support from the black press and numerous national civil rights organizations, all of which excoriated the Army's position.[14-92] David K. Niles, the White House adviser on racial matters, warned President Truman about the rising controversy and predicted that the committee would again reject the Army's proposal. He advised the President to tell the press that Johnson's news release was merely a "progress report," that it was not final, and that the committee was continuing its investigation.[14-93] The President did just that, adding: "Eventually we will reach, I hope, what we contemplated in the beginning. You can't do it all at once. The progress report was a good report, and it isn't finished yet."[14-94] And lest his purpose remain unclear, the President declared that his aim was the racial integration of the Army.

The President's statement signaled a victory for the committee; its extent became apparent only when the Army tried to issue a new circular, revising its Gillem Board policy along the lines of the outline plan approved by Johnson on 30 September. During the weeks of protracted negotiations that followed, the committee clearly remained in control, its power derived basically from its willingness to have the differences between the committee and the Army publicized and the reluctance of the White House to have it so. The attitudes toward publicity were already noticeable when, on 11 October, Fahy suggested to Truman some possible solutions to the impasse between the committee and the Army. The Secretary of Defense could issue a supplementary statement on the Army's assignment policy, the committee could release its recommendations to the press, or the Army and the committee could resume discussions.[14-95]

President Truman ordered his military aide to read the committee's 11 October suggestion and "then take [it] up with Johnson."[14-96] As a result the Secretary of Defense retired from the controversy. Reminding Gray through intermediaries that he had approved the Army's plan in outline form, Johnson declared that it was "inappropriate" for him to approve the plan's publication as an Army circular as the Army had requested.[14-97] About the same time, Niles informed the Army that any revision of Circular 124 would have to be submitted to the White House before publication, and he candidly admitted that presidential approval would depend on the views of the Fahy Committee.[14-98] Meanwhile, his assistant, Philleo Nash, predicting that the committee would win both the assignment and quota arguments, persuaded Fahy to postpone any public statement until after the Army's revised circular had been reviewed by the committee.[14-99]

Chairman Fahy was fully aware of the leverage these actions gave his committee, although he and his associates now had few illusions about the speedy end to the contest. "I know from the best authority within P&A," Kenworthy warned the committee, that the obstructionists in Army Personnel hoped to see the committee submit final recommendations—"what its recommendations are they don't much care"—and then disband. Until the committee disbanded, its opponents would try to block any real change in Army policy.[14-100] Kenworthy offered in evidence the current controversy over the Army's instructions to its field commanders. These instructions, a copy of the outline plan approved by Secretary Johnson, had been sent to the commanders by The Adjutant General on 1 October as "additional policies" pending a revision of Circular 124.[14-101] Included in the message, of course, was Gray's order to open all military occupational specialties to Negroes; but when some commanders, on the basis of their

171

interpretation of the message, began integrating black specialists in white units, officials in the Personnel and Administration and the Organization and Training Divisions dispatched a second message on 27 October specifically forbidding such action "except on Department of Army orders."[14-102] Negroes would continue to be authorized for assignment to black units, the message explained, and to "Negro spaces in T/D [overhead] units." In effect, the Army staff was ordering commanders to interpret the secretary's plan in its narrowest sense, blocking any possibility of broadening the range of black assignments.

Kenworthy was able to turn this incident to the committee's advantage. He made a practice of never locking his Pentagon office door nor his desk drawer. He knew that Negroes, both civilian and military, worked in the message centers, and he suspected that if any hanky-panky was afoot they would discover it and he would be anonymously apprised of it. A few days after the dispatch of the second message, Kenworthy opened his desk drawer to find a copy. For the first and only time, he later explained, he broke his self-imposed rule of relying on negotiations between the military and the committee and its staff *in camera*. He laid both messages before a long-time friend of his, the editor of the Washington *Post's* editorial page.[14-103] Thus delivered to the press, the second message brought on another round of accusations, corrections, and headlines to the effect that "The Brass Gives Gray the Run-Around." Kenworthy was able to denounce the incident as a "step backward" that even violated the Gillem Board policy by allocating "Negro spaces" in overhead units. The Army staff's second message nullified the committee's recommendations since they depended ultimately on the unlimited assignment of black specialists. The message demonstrated very well, Kenworthy told the committee, that careful supervision of the Army's racial policy would be necessary.[14-104] Some newspapers were less charitable. The Pittsburgh*Courier* charged that the colonel blamed for the release of the second message had been made the "goat" in a case that involved far more senior officials, and the Washington *Post*claimed that the message "vitiates" even the limited improvements outlined in the Army's plan as approved by Secretary Johnson. The paper called on Secretary Gray to assert himself in the case.[14-105]

A furious secretary, learning of the second message from the press stories, did enter the case. Branding the document a violation of his announced policy, he had it rescinded and, publicizing a promise made earlier to the committee, announced that qualified black specialists would be assigned to some white units.[14-106] At the same time Gray was not prepared to admit that the incident demonstrated how open his plan was to evasion, just as he refused to admit that his rescinding of the errant message represented a change in policy. He would continue, in effect, the plan approved by the Secretary of Defense on 30 September, he told Fahy.[14-107]

The Army staff's draft revision of the Gillem Board circular, sent to the committee on 25 November, reflected Gray's 30 September plan.[14-108] In short, when it emerged from its journey through the various Army staff agencies, the proposed revision still contained none of the committee's key recommendations. It continued the severe restrictions on the assignment of Negroes who had specialty training; it specifically retained the numerical quota; and, with several specific exceptions, it carefully preserved the segregation of Army life.[14-109] Actually, the proposed revision amounted to little more than a repetition of the Gillem Board policy with minor modifications designed to make it easier to carry out. Fahy quickly warned the Deputy Director of Personnel and Administration that there was no chance of its winning the committee's approval.[14-110]

Assignments

The quota and assignments issues remained the center of controversy between the Army and the committee. Although Fahy was prepared to postpone a decision on the quota while negotiations continued, he was unwilling to budge on the assignments issue. As the committee had repeatedly emphasized, the question of open, integrated assignment of trained Negroes was at the heart of its program. Without it the opening of Army schools and military occupational specialties would be meaningless and the intent of Executive Order 9981 frustrated.

At first glance it would seem that the revision of Circular 124 supported the assignment of Negroes to white units, as indeed Secretary Gray had recently promised. But this was not really the case, as Kenworthy explained to the committee. The Army had always made a distinction between *specialists*, men especially recruited for critically needed jobs, and*specialties*, those military occupations for which soldiers were routinely trained in Army schools. The draft revision did not refer to this second and far larger category and was intended to provide only for the placement of the rare black specialist in white units. The document as worded even limited the use of Negroes in overhead units. Only those with skills considered appropriate by the personnel office—that is, those who possessed a specialty either inappropriate in a black unit or in excess of its needs—would be considered for racially mixed overhead units.[14-111]

172

Fahy was determined to have the Army's plan modified, and furthermore he had learned during the past few weeks how to get it done. On 9 December Kenworthy telephoned Philleo Nash at the White House to inform him of the considerable sentiment in the committee for publicizing the whole affair and read to him the draft of a press statement prepared by Fahy. As Fahy expected, the White House wanted to avoid publicity; the President, through Nash, assured the committee that the issues of assignment and quota were still under discussion. Nash suggested that instead of a public statement the committee prepare a document for the Army and the White House explaining what principles and procedures were demanded by the presidential order. In his opinion, Nash assured Kenworthy, the White House would order the Army to meet the committee's recommendations.[14-112]

White House pressure undoubtedly played a major role in the resolution of the assignment issue. When on 14 December 1949 the committee presented the Army and the President with its comments on the Army's proposed revision of Circular 124, it took the first step toward what was to be a rapid agreement on black assignments. At the same time it would be a mistake to discount the effectiveness of reasonable men of good will discussing their very real differences in an effort to reach a consensus. There is considerable evidence that when Fahy met on 27 December with Secretary Gray and General J. Lawton Collins, the Chief of Staff, he was able to convince them that the committee's position on the assignment of black graduates of specialist schools was right and inevitable.[14-113]

While neither Gray nor Collins could even remotely be described as social reformers, both were pragmatic leaders, prepared to accept changes in Army tradition.[14-114] Collins, unlike his immediate predecessors, was not so much concerned with finding the Army in the vanguard of American social practices as he was in determining that its racial practices guaranteed a more efficient organization. While he wanted to retain the numerical quota, lest the advantages of an Army career attract so large a number of Negroes that a serious racial imbalance would result, he was willing to accept a substantive revision of the Gillem Board policy.

SECRETARY OF THE ARMY GRAY

Gray was perhaps more cautious than Collins. Confessing later that he had never considered the question of equal opportunity until Fahy brought it to his attention, Gray began with a limited view of the executive order—the Army must eliminate racial discrimination, not promote racial integration. In their meeting on 27 December Fahy was able to convince Gray that the former was impossible without the latter. According to Kenworthy, Gray demonstrated an "open and unbiased" view of the problem throughout all discussions.[14-115]

The trouble was, as Roy Davenport later noted, Gordon Gray was a lawyer, not a personnel expert, and he failed to grasp the full implications of the Army staff's recommendations.[14-116] Davenport was speaking from firsthand knowledge because Gray, after belatedly learning of his experience and influence with the committee, sent for him. Politely but explicitly Davenport told Gray that the staff officers who were advising him and writing the memos and directives to which he was signing his name had deceived him. Gray was at first annoyed and incredulous; after Davenport finally convinced him, he was angry. Kenworthy, years later, wrote that the Gray-Davenport discussion was decisive in changing Gray's mind on the assignment issue and was of great help to the Fahy Committee.[14-117]

Fahy reduced the whole problem to the case of one qualified black soldier denied a job because of color and pictured the loss to the Army and the country, eloquently pleading with Gray and Collins at the 27 December meeting to try the committee's way. "I can't say you won't have problems," Fahy concluded, "but try it." Gray resisted at first because "this would mean the complete end of segregation," but unable to deny the logic of Fahy's arguments he agreed to try.[14-118] There were compromises on both sides. When Collins pointed out some of the administrative difficulties that could come from the "mandatory" language recommended by the committee, Fahy said that the policy should be administered "with latitude." To that end he promised to suggest some changes in wording that would produce "a policy with some play in the joints." The conferees also agreed that the quota issue should be downplayed while the parties continued their discussions on that subject.[14-119]

GENERAL COLLINS

Agreement followed rapidly on the heels of the meeting of the principals. Roy Davenport presented the committee members with the final draft of the Army proposal and urged that it be accepted as "the furthest and most hopeful they could get."[14-120] Lester Granger, Davenport later reported, was the first to say he would accept, with Fahy and the rest following suit,[14-121] and on 16 January 1950 the Army issued Special Regulation 600-629-1, *Utilization of Negro Manpower in the Army*, with the committee's blessing.

173

Fahy reported to Truman that the new Army policy was consistent with the executive order. Its paragraphs on assignments spelled out the principle long advocated by the committee: "Negro manpower possessing appropriate skills and qualifications will be utilized in accordance with such skills and qualifications, and will be assigned to any ... unit without regard to race or color." Adding substance to this declaration, the Army also announced that a list of critical specialties in which vacancies existed would be published periodically and ordered major commanders to assign Negroes who possessed those specialties to fill the vacancies without regard to race. The first such list was published at the same time as the new regulation. The Army had taken a significant step, Fahy told the President, toward the realization of equal treatment and opportunity for all soldiers.[14-122]

Secretary of Defense Johnson was also optimistic, but he warned Gordon Gray that many complex problems remained and asked the Army for periodic reports. His request only emphasized the fact that the Army's new regulation lacked the machinery for monitoring compliance with its provisions for integration. As the history of the Gillem Board era demonstrated, any attempt to change the Army's traditions demanded not only exact definition of the intermediate steps but also establishment of a responsible authority to enforce compliance.

Quotas

In the wake of the Army's new assignment regulation, the committee turned its full attention to the last of its major recommendations, the abolition of the numerical quota. Despite months of discussion, the disagreement between the Army and the committee over the quota showed no signs of resolution. Simply put, the Fahy Committee wanted the Army to abolish the Gillem Board's racial quota and to substitute a quota based on General Classification Test scores of enlistees. The committee found the racial quota unacceptable in terms of the executive order and wasteful of manpower since it tended to encourage the reenlistment of low-scoring Negroes and thereby prevented the enlistment of superior men. None of the Negroes graduating from high school in June 1949, for example, no matter how high their academic rating, could enlist because the black quota had been filled for months. Quotas based on test scores, on the other hand, would limit enlistment to only the higher scoring blacks and whites.

Specifically, the committee wanted no enlistment to be decided by race. The Army would open all enlistments to anyone who scored ninety or above, limiting the number of blacks and whites scoring between eighty and eighty-nine to 13.4 percent of the total Army strength, a percentage based on World War II strengths. With rare exception it would close enlistment to anyone who scored less than eighty. Applying this formula to the current Army, 611,400 men on 31 March 1949, and assessing the number of men from seventeen to thirty-four years old in the national population, the committee projected a total of 65,565 Negroes in the Army, almost exactly 10 percent of the Army's strength. In a related statistical report prepared by Davenport, the committee offered figures demonstrating that the higher black reenlistment rates would not increase the number of black soldiers.[14-123]

The Army's reply was based on the premise that "the Negro strength of the Army must be restricted and that the population ratio is the most equitable method [of] limitation." In fact, the *only* method of controlling black strength was a numerical quota of original enlistments. The personnel staff argued that enlistment specifically unrestricted by race, as the high rate of unrestricted black reenlistment had demonstrated, would inevitably produce a "very high percentage of Negroes in the Army." A quota based on the classification test scores could not limit sufficiently the number of black enlistments if, as the committee insisted, it required that identical enlistment standards be maintained for both blacks and whites. Looking at the census figure another way, the Army had its own statistics to prove its point. Basing its figures on the number of Negroes who became eighteen each month (11,000), the personnel staff estimated that black enlistments would total from 15 to 20 percent of the Army's monthly strength if an entrance quota was imposed with the cut-off score set at ninety or from 19 to 31 percent if the enlistment standards were lowered to eighty. It also pointed to the experience of the Air Force where with no quotas in the third quarter of 1949 black enlistments accounted for 16.4 percent of the total; even when a GCT quota of 100 was imposed in October and November, 10 percent of all Air Force enlistees were black.[14-124]

The committee quickly pointed out that the Army had neglected to subtract from the monthly figure of 11,000 blacks those physically and mentally disqualified (those who scored below eighty) and those in school. Using the Army's own figures and taking into account these deductions, the committee predicted that Negroes would account for 10.6 percent of the men accepted in the 8,000 monthly intake, probably at the GCT eighty level, or 5 percent of the 6,000 men estimated acceptable at the GCT ninety level.[14-125]

On 14 December 1949 the Army, offering to compromise on the quota, retired from its statistical battle with the committee. It would accept the unlimited enlistment of Negroes scoring

174

100 or better, limiting the number of those accepted below 100 so that the total black strength would remain at 10 percent of the Army's population.[14-126] Attractive to the committee because it would provide for the enlistment of qualified men at the expense of the less able, the proposal was nevertheless rejected because it still insisted upon a racial quota. Again there was a difference between the committee and the Army, but again the advantage lay with the committee, for the White House was anxious for the quota problem to be solved.[14-127]

Niles warned the President that the racial imbalance which had for so long frustrated equal treatment and opportunity for Negroes in the Army would continue despite the Army's new assignment policy unless the Army was able to raise the quality of its black enlistees. Niles considered the committee's proposal doubly attractive because, while it abolished the quota, it would also raise the level of black recruits. The proposal was sensible and fair, Niles added, and he believed it would reduce the number of black soldiers as it raised their quality. It had been used successfully by the Navy and Air Force, and, as it had in those services, would provide for the gradual dissolution of the all-black units rather than a precipitous change.[14-128] The Army staff did not agree, and as late as 28 February 1950 the Director of Personnel and Administration was recommending that the Army retain the racial quota at least for all Negroes scoring below 110 on the classification test.[14-129]

Secretary Gray, aware that the Army's arguments would not move the committee, was sure that the President did not want to see a spectacular and precipitous rise in the Army's black strength. He decided on a personal appeal to the Commander in Chief.[14-130] The Army would drop the racial quota, he told Truman on 1 March, with one proviso: "If, as a result of a fair trial of this new system, there ensues a disproportionate balance of racial strengths in the Army, it is my understanding that I have your authority to return to a system which will, in effect, control enlistments by race."[14-131] The President agreed.

At the President's request, Gray outlined a program for open recruitment, fixing April as the date when all vacancies would be open to all qualified individuals. Gray wanted to handle the changes in routine fashion. With the committee's concurrence, he planned no public announcement. From his vacation quarters in Key West, Truman added a final encouraging word: "I am sure that everything will work out as it should."[14-132] The order opening recruiting to all races went out on 27 March 1950.[14-133]

Despite the President's optimism, the Fahy Committee was beginning to have doubts about just how everything would work out. Specifically, some members were wondering how they could be sure the Army would comply with the newly approved policies. Such concern was reasonable, despite the Army's solemn commitments, when one considers the committee's lengthening experience with the Defense Department's bureaucracy and its familiarity with the liabilities of the Gillem Board policy. The committee decided, therefore, to include in its final report to the President a request for the retention of a watchdog group to review service practices. In this its views clashed directly with those of Secretary Johnson, who wanted the President to abolish the committee and make him solely responsible for the equal treatment and opportunity program.[14-134]

Niles, anxious to settle the issue, tried to reconcile the differences[14-135] and successfully persuaded the committee to omit a reference in its final report to a successor group to review the services' progress. Such a move, he told Kenworthy, would imply that, unless policed, the services would not carry out their programs. Public discussion about how long the committee was to remain in effect would also tend to tie the President's hands. Niles suggested instead that the committee members discuss the matter with the President when they met with him to submit their final report and perhaps suggest that a watchdog group be appointed or their committee be retained on a standby basis for a later review of service actions.[14-136] Before the committee met with the President on 22 May, Niles recommended to Truman that he make no commitment on a watchdog group.[14-137] Privately, Niles agreed with Clark Clifford that the committee should be retained for an indefinite period, but on an advisory rather than an operating basis so that, in Clifford's words, "it will be in a position to see that there is not a gap between policy and an administration of policy in the Defense Establishment."[14-138]

The President proceeded along these lines. Several months after the committee presented its final report, *Freedom to Serve*,[14-139] in a public ceremony, Truman relieved the group of its assignment. Commenting that the services should have the opportunity to work out in detail the new policies and procedures initiated by the committee, he told Fahy on 6 July 1950 that he would leave his order in effect, noting that "at some later date, it may prove desirable to examine the effectuation of your Committee's recommendations, which can be done under Executive Order 9981."[14-140]

An Assessment

Thus ended a most active period in the history of armed forces integration, a period of executive orders, presidential conferences, and national hearings, of administrative infighting broadcast to the public in national headlines. The Fahy Committee was the focus of this bureaucratic and journalistic excitement. Charged with examining the policies of the services in light of the President's order, the committee could have glanced briefly at current racial practices and automatically ratified Secretary Johnson's general policy statement. Indeed, this was precisely what Walter White and other civil rights leaders expected. But the committee was made of sterner stuff. With dedication and with considerable political acumen, it correctly assessed the position of black servicemen and subjected the racial policies of the services to a rigorous and detailed examination, the first to be made by an agency outside the Department of Defense. As a result of this scrutiny, the committee clearly and finally demonstrated that segregation was an inefficient way to use military manpower; once and for all it demolished the arguments that the services habitually used against any demand for serious change. Most important is the fact that the committee kept alive the spirit of reform the Truman order had created. The committee's definition of equal treatment and opportunity became the standard by which future action on racial issues in the armed forces would be measured.

Throughout its long existence, the Fahy Committee was chiefly concerned with the position of the Negro in the Army. After protracted argument it won from the Army an agreement to abolish the racial quota and to open all specialties in all Army units and all Army schools and courses to qualified Negroes. Finally, it won the Army's promise to cease restricting black servicemen to black units and overhead installations alone and to assign them instead on the basis of individual ability and the Army's need.

As for the other services, the committee secured from the Navy a pledge to give petty officer status to chief stewards and stewards of the first, second, and third class, and its influence was discernible in the Navy's decision to allow stewards to transfer to the general service. The committee also made, and the Navy accepted, several practical suggestions that might lead to an increase in the number of black officers and enlisted men. The committee approved the Air Force integration program and publicized the success of this major reform as it was carried out during 1949; for the benefit of the reluctant Army, the committee could point to the demonstrated ability of black servicemen and the widespread acceptance of integration among the rank and file of the Air Force. In regard to the Marine Corps, however, the committee was forced to acknowledge that the corps had not yet "fully carried out Navy policy."[14-141]

The Fahy Committee won from the services a commitment to equal treatment and opportunity and a practical program to achieve that end. Yet even with this victory and the strong support of many senior military officials, the possibility that determined foes of integration might erect roadblocks or that simple bureaucratic inertia would delay progress could not be discounted. There was, for example, nothing in the postwar practices of the Marine Corps, even the temporary integration of its few black recruits during basic training, that hinted at any long-range intention of adopting the Navy's integration program. And the fate of one of the committee's major recommendations, that all the services adopt equal enlistment standards, had yet to be decided. The acceptance of this recommendation hinged on the results of a Defense Department study to determine the jobs in each service that could be filled by men in the lowest mental classification category acceptable to all three services. Although the Navy and the Air Force had agreed to reexamine the matter, they had consistently opposed the application of enlistment parity in the past, and the Secretary of Defense's Personnel Policy Board had indorsed their position. Secretary Forrestal, himself, had rejected the concept, and there was nothing in the record to suggest that his successor would do otherwise. Yet the parity of enlistment standards was a vital part of the committee's argument for the abolition of the Army's racial quota. If enlistment standards were not equalized, especially in a period when the Army was turning to Selective Service for much of its manpower, the number of men in the Army's categories IV and V was bound to increase, and that increase would provide strong justification for reviving the racial quota. The Army staff was aware, as the public was not, that a resurrected quota was possible, for the President had given the Secretary of the Army authority to take such action if there was "a disproportionate balance of racial strengths."[14-142]

The Army's concern with disproportionate balance was always linked to a concern with the influx of men, mostly black, who scored poorly on the classification tests. The problem, the Army repeatedly claimed, was not the quantity of black troops but their quality. Yet at the time the Army agreed to the committee's demand to drop the quota, some 40 percent of all black soldiers scored below eighty. These men could rarely profit from the Army's agreement to integrate all specialist training and assignments. The committee, aware of the problem, had strongly urged the Army to refuse reenlistment, with few exceptions, to anyone scoring below eighty. On 11 May 1950 Fahy reminded Secretary of the Army Frank Pace, Jr., that despite the

176

Army's promise to eliminate its low scorers it continued to reenlist men scoring less than seventy.[14-143] But by July even the test score for first-time enlistment into the Army had declined to seventy because men were needed for the Korean War. The law required that whenever Selective Service began drafting men the Army would automatically lower its enlistment standards to seventy. Thus, despite the committee's recommendations, the concentration of low-scoring Negroes in the lower grades continued to increase, creating an even greater pool of men incapable of assignment to the schools and specialties open without regard to race.

The Pittsburgh Courier's reaction to the services' agreements with the Fahy Committee, May 20, 1950.

Even the Army's promise to enlarge gradually the number of specialties open to Negroes was not carried out expeditiously. By July 1950, the last month of the Fahy Committee's life, the Army had added only seven more specialties with openings for Negroes to the list of forty published seven months before at the time of its agreement with the committee. In a pessimistic mood, Kenworthy confessed to Judge Fahy[14-144] that "so long as additions are not progressively made to the critical list of MOS in which Negroes can serve, and so long as segregated units continue to be the rule, all MOS and schools can not be said to be open to Negroes because Negro units do not have calls for many of the advanced MOS." Kenworthy was also disturbed because the Army had disbanded the staff agency created to monitor the new policies and make future recommendations and had transferred both its two members to other duties. In the light of progress registered in the half year since the Army had adopted the committee's proposal, Kenworthy concluded that "the Army intends to do as little as possible towards implementing the policy which it adopted and published."[14-145]

Roy Davenport later suggested that such pessimism was ill-founded. Other factors were at work within the Army in 1950, particularly after the outbreak of war in Korea.[14-146]Davenport alluded principally to the integration of basic training centers and the assignment of greater numbers of black inductees to combat specialties—developments that were pushing the Army ahead of the integration timetable envisioned by committee members and making concern over black eligibility for an increased number of occupation categories less important.

The Fahy Committee has been given full credit for proving that segregation could not be defended on grounds of military efficiency, thereby laying the foundation for the integration of the Army. But perhaps in the long run the group's idealism proved to be equally important. The committee never lost sight of the moral implications of the services' racial policies. Concern for the rightness and wrongness of things is readily apparent in all its deliberations, and in the end the committee would invoke the words of Saint Paul to the Philippians to remind men who perhaps should have needed no such reminder that they should heed "whatsoever things are true ... whatsoever things are just." What was right and just, the committee concluded, would "strengthen the nation."[14-147]

The same ethics stood forth in the conclusion of the committee's final report, raising that practical summary of events to the status of an eloquent state paper. The committee reminded the President and its fellow citizens that the status of the individual, "his equal worth in the sight of God, his equal protection under the law, his equal rights and obligations of citizenship and his equal opportunity to make just and constructive use of his endowment—these are the very foundation of the American system of values."[14-148]

To its lasting honor the Fahy Committee succeeded in spelling out for the nation's military leaders how these principles, these "high standards of democracy" as President Truman called them in his order, must be applied in the services.

CHAPTER 15
The Role of the Secretary of Defense
1949-1951

Having ordered the integration of the services and supported the Fahy Committee in the development of acceptable racial programs, President Truman quickly turned the matter over to his subordinates in the Department of Defense, severing White House ties with the problem. Against the recommendations of some of his White House advisers, Truman adjourned the committee, leaving his executive order in effect. "The necessary programs having been adopted," he told Fahy, it was time for the services "to work out in detail the procedures which will complete the steps so carefully initiated by the committee."[15-1] In effect, the President was guaranteeing the services the freedom to put their own houses in order.

The issue of civil rights, however, was still of vital interest to one of the President's major constituencies. Black voters, recognized as a decisive factor in the November 1948 election, pressed their demands on the victorious President; in particular some of their spokesmen called on the administration to implement fully the program put forth by the Fahy Committee. These demands were being echoed in Congress by a civil rights bloc—for bloc it had now become in the wake of the election that sent Harry Truman back to the White House. No longer the concern of a congressman or two, the cause of the black serviceman was now supported by a group of politicians who, joining with civil rights leaders, pressed the Department of Defense for rapid changes in its racial practices.

The traditionalists in the armed forces also had congressional allies. In all probability these legislators would accept an integrated Navy because it involved relatively few Negroes; they might even tolerate an integrated Air Force because they lacked a proprietary attitude toward this new service; but they would fight to keep the Army segregated because they considered the Army their own.[15-2] Congressional segregationists openly opposed changes in the Army's racial policy only when they thought the time was right. They carefully avoided the subject in the months following publication of the executive order, waiting to bargain until their support became crucial to the success of such vital military legislation as the renewal of the Selective Service Act and the establishment of universal military training.

At most, Congress played only a minor role in the dramatic changes beginning in the armed forces. Champions of civil rights had little effect on service practices, although these congressmen channeled the complaints of black voters and kept the military traditionalists on the defensive. As for the congressional traditionalists, their support may have helped sustain those on the staff who resisted racial change within the Army, thus slowing down that service's integration. But the demands of congressional progressives and obstructionists tended to cancel each other out, and in the wake of the Fahy Committee's disbandment the services themselves reemerged as the preeminent factor in the armed forces racial program.

The services regained control by default. Logically, direction of racial reforms in the services should have fallen to the Secretary of Defense. In the first place, the secretary, other administration officials, and the public alike had begun to use the secretary's office as a clearinghouse for reconciling conflicting demands of the services, as an appellate court reviewing decisions of the service secretaries, and as the natural channel of communication between the services and the White House, Congress, and the public. Many racial problems had become interservice in nature, and only the Office of the Secretary of Defense possessed the administrative machinery to deal with such matters. The Personnel Policy Board or, later, the new Office of the Assistant Secretary of Defense for Manpower and Personnel might well have become the watchdog recommended by the Fahy Committee to oversee the services' progress toward integration, but neither did.

Certainly the Secretary of Defense had other matters pressing for his attention. Secretary Johnson had become the central character in the budgetary conflicts of Truman's second term, and both he and General George C. Marshall, who succeeded him as secretary on 20 September 1950, were suddenly thrust into leadership of the Korean War. In administrative matters, at least, Marshall had to concentrate on boosting the morale of a department torn by internecine budgetary arguments. Integration did not appear to have the same importance to national security as these weighty matters. More to the point, Johnson and Marshall were not social reformers. Whatever their personal attitudes, they were content to let the services set the pace of racial reform. With one notable exception neither man initiated any of the historic racial changes that took place in the armed forces during the early 1950's.

For the most part those racial issues that did involve the Secretary of Defense centered on the status of the Negro in the armed forces in general and were extraneous to the issue of integration. One of the most persistent status problems was classification by race. First posed during the great World War II draft calls, the question of how to determine a serviceman's race, and indeed the related one of who had the right to make such a determination, remained unanswered five years later. In August 1944 the Selective Service System decided that the definition of a man's race should be left to the man himself. While this solution no doubt pleased racial progressives and certainly simplified the induction process, not to speak of protecting the War Department from a ticklish court review, it still left the services the difficult and important task of designating racial categories into which men could be assigned. As late as April 1949 the Army and the Air Force listed a number of specific racial categories, one of which had to be chosen by the applicant or recruiter—the regulation left the point unclear—to identify the applicant's race. The regulation listed "white, Negro, Indian (referring to American Indian only), Puerto Rican, Cuban, Mexican, Hawaiian, Filipino, Chinese, East Indian, etc.," and specifically included mulattoes and "others of negroid race or extraction" in the Negro category, leaving other men of mixed race to be entered under their predominant race.[15-3]

The regulation was obviously subject to controversy, and in the wake of the President's equality order it is not surprising that some group—a group of Spanish-speaking Americans from

178

southern California, as it turned out—would raise the issue. Specifically, they objected to a practice of Army and Air Force recruiters, who often scratched out "white" and inserted "Mexican" in the applications of Spanish-speaking volunteers. These young men wanted to be integrated into every phase of community life, Congressman Chet Holifield told the Secretary of Defense, and he passed on a warning from his California constituents that "any attempt to forestall this ambition by treating them as a group apart is extremely repellent to them and gives rise to demoralization and hostility."[15-4] If the Department of Defense considered racial information essential, Holifield continued, why not make the determination in a less objectionable manner? He suggested a series of questions concerning the birthplace of the applicant's parents and the language spoken in his home as innocuous possibilities.

Secretary Johnson sent the congressman's complaint to the Personnel Policy Board, which, ignoring the larger considerations posed by Holifield, concentrated on simplifying the department's racial categories to five—Caucasian, Negroid, Mongolian, Indian (American), and Malayan—and making their use uniform throughout the services. The board also adopted the use of inoffensive questions to help determine the applicant's proper race category. Obviously, the board could not abandon racial designations because the Army's quota system, still in effect, depended on this information. Less clear, however, was why the board failed to consider the problem of who should make the racial determination. At any rate, its new list of racial categories, approved by the secretary and published on 11 October, immediately drew complaints from members of the department.[15-5]

NAVY CORPSMAN IN KOREA
attends wounded from the 1st Marine Division, 1950.

The secretary's racial adviser, James C. Evans, saw no need for racial designations on departmental forms, but knowing their removal was unlikely in the near future, he concentrated on trying to change the newly revised categories. He explained to the board, obviously unschooled in the nuance of racial slurs, that the word "Negroid" was offensive to many Negroes. Besides, the board's categories made no sense since Indian (American) and Malayan were not comparable to the other three entries listed. Why not, he suggested, settle for the old black, white, yellow, red, and brown designations?[15-6]

The Navy, too, objected to the board's categories. After consulting a Smithsonian ethnologist, the Under Secretary of the Navy suggested that the board create a sixth category, Polynesian, for use in shipping articles and in forms for reporting casualties. The Army, also troubled by the categories, requested they be defined. The categories were meant to provide a uniform basis for classifying military personnel, The Adjutant General pointed out, but given the variety and complexity of Army forms—he had discovered that the Army was using seven separate forms with racial entries, each with a different procedure for deciding race—uniformity was practically impossible without a careful delineation of each category.[15-7]

Its ruling under attack from the services, the board made a hasty appeal to authority. Its chief of staff, Vice Adm. John L. McCrea,[15-8] recommended that the Army and Navy consult Funk and Wagnalls *Standard Dictionary* for specific definitions of the five racial categories. That source, the admiral explained to the Under Secretary of the Navy, listed Polynesian in the Malayan category, and if the Navy decided to add race to its shipping articles, the five categories should be sufficient. The board, he added, had not meant to encourage additional use of racial information. The Navy had always used the old color categories on its shipping articles forms, the ones, incidentally, favored by Evans, and McCrea thought they generally corresponded to the categories developed by the board.[15-9] The admiral also suggested that the Army use the color system to help clarify the board's categories. He offered some generalizations on specific Army questions: "a) Puerto Ricans are officially Caucasian, unless of Indian or Negro birth; b) Filipinos are Malayan; c) Hawaiians are Malayan; d) Latin Americans are Caucasian or Indian; and e) Indian-Negro and White-Negro mixtures should be classified in accordance with the laws of the states of their birth."[15-10] The lessons on definition of race so painfully learned during World War II were ignored. Henceforth race was to be determined by a dictionary, a color scheme, and the legal vagaries found in the race laws of the several states.

The board's rulings, unscientific and open to all sorts of legal complications, could only be stopgap measures, and when on 4 January 1950 the Army again requested clarification of the racial categories, the board quickly responded. Although it continued to defend the use of racial categories, it tried to soften the ruling by stating that an applicant's declaration of race should be accepted, subject to "sufficient justification" from the applicant when his declaration created "reason to doubt." It was 5 April before the board's new chairman, J. Thomas Schneider,[15-11] issued a revised directive to this effect.[15-12]

The board's decision to accept an applicant's declaration was simply a return to the reasonable and practical method the Selective Service had been using for some time. But adopting the vague qualification "sufficient justification" invited further complaints. When the services finally translated the board's directive into a new regulation, the role of the applicant in deciding his racial identity was practically abolished. In the Army and the Air Force, for example, recruiters had to submit all unresolved identity cases to the highest local commander, whose decision, supposedly based on available documentary evidence and answers to the questions first suggested by Congressman Holifield, was final. Further, the Army and the Air Force decided that "no enlistment would be accomplished" until racial identity was decided to the satisfaction of both the applicant and the service.[15-13] The Navy adopted a similar procedure when it placed the board's directive in effect.[15-14] The new regulation promised little comfort for young Americans of racially mixed parentage and even less for the services. Contrary to the intent of the Personnel Policy Board, its directive once again placed the burden of deciding an applicant's race, with the concomitant complaints and potential civil suits, back on the services.

At the time the Army did not see this responsibility as a burden and in its quest for uniformity was willing to assume an even greater share of the decision-making in a potentially explosive issue. On 7 August the Deputy Assistant Chief of Staff, G-1, asked the Personnel Policy Board to include Army induction centers in the directive meant originally for recruiting centers only.[15-15] In effect the Army was offering to assume from Selective Service the task of deciding the race of all draftees. The board obtained the necessary agreement from Maj. Gen. Lewis B. Hershey, and Selective Service was thus relieved of an onerous task reluctantly acquired in 1944. On 29 August 1950 The Adjutant General ordered induction stations to begin entering the draftee's race in the records.[15-16]

The considerable staff activity devoted to definitions of race between 1949 and 1951 added very little to racial harmony or the cause of integration. The simplified racial categories and the regulations determining their application continued to irritate members of America's several minority groups. The ink was hardly dry on the new regulation, for example, before the director of the NAACP's Washington bureau was complaining to Secretary of the Air Force Thomas K. Finletter that the department's five categories were comparatively meaningless and caused unnecessary humiliation for inductees. He wanted racial entries eliminated.[15-17] Finletter explained that racial designations were not used for assignment or administrative purposes but solely for evaluating the integration program and answering questions from the public. His explanation prompted much discussion within the services and correspondence between them and Clarence Mitchell and Walter White of the NAACP. It culminated in a meeting of the service secretaries with the Secretary of Defense on 16 January 1951 at which Finletter reaffirmed his position.[15-18]

There was some justification for the Defense Department's position. Many of those who found racial designations distasteful also demanded hard statistical proof that members of minority groups were given equal treatment and opportunity,[15-19] and such assurances, of course, demanded racial determinations on the records. Still, not all the reasons for retaining the racial identification entry were so defensible. The Army, for example, had to maintain accurate statistics on the number of Negroes inducted because of its concern with a possible unacceptable rise in their number and the President's promise to reimpose the quota to prevent such an increase. Whatever the reasons, it was obvious that racial statistics had to be kept. It was also obvious that as long as they were kept and continued to matter, the Secretary of Defense would be saddled with the task of deciding in the end which racial tag to attach to each man in the armed forces. It was an unenviable duty, and it could be performed with neither precision nor justice.

Overseas Restrictions

Another problem involving the Secretary of Defense concerned restrictions placed on the use of black servicemen in certain foreign areas. The problem was not new. Making a distinction in cases where American troops were stationed in a country at the request of the United States government, the services excluded black troops from assignment in some Allied countries during and immediately after World War II.[15-20] The Army, for example, barred the assignment of black units to China (the Chinese government did not object to assignment of individual black soldiers up to 15 percent of any unit's strength), and the Navy removed black messmen from stations in Iceland.[15-21] Although these restrictions did not improve the racial image of the services, they were only a minor inconvenience to military officials since Negroes were for the most part segregated and their placement could be controlled easily. The armed forces continued to exclude black servicemen from certain countries into 1949 under what the Personnel Policy Board called "operating agreements (probably not in writing)" with the State Department.[15-22] But the situation changed radically when some of the services started to integrate. Efficient

180

administration then demanded that black servicemen be interchanged freely among the various duty stations. Even in the case of the still segregated Army the exclusion of Negroes from certain commands further complicated the chronic maldistribution of black soldiers throughout the service.

The interservice and departmental aspects of the problem involved Secretary of Defense Johnson. Following promulgation of his directive on racial equality and at the instigation of his Personnel Policy Board and his assistant, Najeeb Halaby, Johnson asked the Secretary of State for a formal expression of views on the use of black troops in a lengthy list of countries.[15-23] Such an expression was clearly necessary, as Air Force spokesmen pointed out. Informed of the consultations, Assistant Secretary Zuckert asked that an interim policy be formulated, so urgent had the problem become in the Air Force where new racial policies and assignments were under way.[15-24]

For his part the Secretary of State had no objection to stationing Negroes in any of the listed countries. In fact, Under Secretary James E. Webb assured Johnson, the State Department welcomed the new Defense Department policy of equal treatment and opportunity as a step toward the achievement of the nation's foreign policy objectives. At the same time Webb admitted that there were certain countries—he listed specifically Iceland, Greenland, Canada, Newfoundland, Bermuda, and British possessions in the Caribbean—where local attitudes might affect the morale of black troops and their relations with the inhabitants. The State Department, therefore, preferred advance warning when the services planned to assign Negroes to these countries so that it might consult the host governments and reduce "possible complications" to a minimum.[15-25]

This policy definition did not end the matter. In the first place the State Department decided not to restrict its list of excepted areas to the six mentioned. While it had no objection to the assignment of individual Negroes or nonsegregated units to Panama, the department informally advised the Army in December 1949, it did interpose grave objections to the assignment of black units.[15-26] Accordingly, only individual Negroes were assigned to temporary units in the Panama Command.[15-27]

Yet for several reasons, the services were uneasy about the situation. The Director of Marine Corps Personnel, for example, feared that since in the bulk reassignment of marines enlisted men were transferred by rank and military occupational specialties only, a black marine might be assigned to an excepted area by oversight. Yet the corps was reluctant to change the system.[15-28] An Air Force objection was more pointed. General Edwards worried that the restrictions were becoming public knowledge and would probably cause adverse criticism of the Air Force. He wanted the State Department to negotiate with the countries concerned to lift the restrictions or at least to establish a clear-cut, defensible policy. Secretary Symington discussed the matter with Secretary of Defense Johnson, and Halaby, knowing Deputy Under Secretary of State Dean Rusk's particular interest in having men assigned without regard to race, agreed to take the matter up with Rusk.[15-29] Secretary of the Navy Francis P. Matthews reminded Johnson that black servicemen already numbered among the thousands of Navy men assigned to four of the six areas mentioned, and if the system continued these men would periodically and routinely be replaced with other black sailors. Should the Navy, he wanted to know, withdraw these Negroes? Given the "possible unfavorable reaction" to their withdrawal, the Navy wanted to keep Negroes in these areas in approximately their present numbers.[15-30] Both the Fahy Committee and the Personnel Policy Board made it clear that they too wanted black servicemen retained wherever they were currently assigned.[15-31]

Maj. Gen. James H. Burns, Secretary Johnson's assistant for foreign military affairs, put the matter to the State Department, and James Evans followed up by discussing it with Rusk. Reassured by these consultations, Secretary Johnson issued a more definitive policy statement for the services on 5 April explaining that "the Department of State endorses the policy of freely assigning Negro personnel or Negro or non-segregated units to any part of the world to which US forces are sent; it is prepared to support the desires of the Department of Defense in this respect."[15-32] Nevertheless, since certain governments had from time to time indicated an unwillingness to accept black servicemen, Johnson directed the services to inform him in advance when black troops were to be dispatched to countries where no blacks were then stationed so that host countries might be consulted. This new statement produced immediate reaction in the services. Citing a change in policy, the Air Force issued directives opening all overseas assignments except Iceland to Negroes. After an extended discussion on the assignment of black troops to the Trieste (TRUST) area, the Army followed suit.[15-33]

Yet the problem refused to go away, largely because the services continued to limit foreign assignment of black personnel, particularly in attache offices, military assistance advisory groups, and military missions. The Army's G-3, for example, concluded in 1949 that, while the race of an individual was not a factor in determining eligibility for a mission assignment, the attitude of certain countries (he was referring to certain Latin American countries) made it advisable to inform the host country of the race of the prospective applicant. For a host country to reject a Negro was undesirable, he concluded, but for a Negro to be assigned to a country that did not welcome him would be embarrassing to both countries.[15-34] When the chief of the military mission in Turkey asked the Army staff in 1951 to reconsider assigning black soldiers to Turkey because of the attitude of the Turks, the Army canceled the assignment.[15-35]

25TH DIVISION TROOPS UNLOAD TRUCKS AND EQUIPMENT
at Sasebo Railway Station, Japan, for transport to Korea, 1950.

Undoubtedly certain countries objected to the assignment of American servicemen on grounds of race or religion, but there were also indications that racial restrictions were not always made at the behest of the host country.[15-36] In 1957 Congressman Adam Clayton Powell protested that Negroes were not being assigned to the offices of attaches, military assistance advisory groups, and military missions.[15-37] In particular he was concerned with Ethiopia, whose emperor had personally assured him that his government had no race restrictions. The Deputy Assistant Secretary of the Army admitted that Negroes were barred from Ethiopia, and although documentary evidence could not be produced, the ban was thought to have been imposed at the request of the United Nations. The State Department claimed it was unaware of any such ban, nor could it find documentation to support the Army's contention. It objected neither to the assignment of individual Negroes to attache and advisory offices in Ethiopia nor to "most" other countries.[15-38] Having received these assurances, the Department of Defense informed the services that "it was considered appropriate" to assign black servicemen to the posts discussed by Congressman Powell.[15-39]For some time, however, the notion persisted in the Department of Defense that black troops should not be assigned to Ethiopia.[15-40] In fact, restrictions and reports of restrictions against the assignment of Americans to a number of overseas posts on grounds of race or religion persisted into the 1970's.[15-41]

Congressional Concerns

Congress was slow to see that changes were gradually transforming the armed services. In its special preelection session, the Eightieth Congress ignored the recently issued Truman order on racial equality just as it ignored the President's admonition to enact a general civil rights program. But when the new Eighty-first Congress met in January 1949 the subjects of armed forces integration, the Truman order, and the Fahy Committee all began to receive attention. Debate on race in the services occurred frequently in both houses. Each side appealed to constitutional and legal principles to support its case, but the discussions might well have remained a philosophical debate if the draft law had not come up for renewal in 1950. The debate focused mostly on an amendment proposed by Senator Richard B. Russell of Georgia that would allow inductees and enlistees, upon their written declaration of intent, to serve in a unit manned exclusively by members of their own race. Russell had made this proposal once before, but because it seemed of little consequence to the still largely segregated services of 1948 it was ignored. Now in the wake of the executive order and the Fahy Committee Report, the amendment came to sudden prominence. And when Russell succeeded in discharging the draft bill with his amendment from the Senate Armed Forces Committee with the members' unanimous approval, civil rights supporters quickly jumped to the attack. Even before the bill was formally introduced on the floor, Senator Wayne Morse of Oregon told his colleagues that the Russell amendment conflicted with the stated policy of the administration as well as with sound Republican principles. He cited the waste of manpower the amendment would bring about and reminded his colleagues of the international criticism the armed forces had endured in the past because of undemocratic social practices.[15-42]

When debate began on the amendment, Senator Leverett Saltonstall of Massachusetts was one of the first to rise in opposition. While confessing sympathy for the states' rights philosophy that recognized the different customs of various sections of the nation, he branded the Russell amendment unnecessary, provocative, and unworkable, and suggested Congress leave the services alone in this matter. To support his views he read into the record portions of the Fahy Committee Report, which represented, he emphasized, the judgment of impartial civilians appointed by the President, another civilian.[15-43]

Discussion of the Russell amendment continued with opponents and defenders raising the issues of military efficiency, legality, and principles of equality and states' rights. In the end the amendment was defeated 45 to 27 with 24 not voting, a close vote if one considers that the abstentions could have changed the outcome.[15-44] A similar amendment, this time introduced by Congressman Arthur Winstead of Mississippi, was also defeated in 1951.

182

The Russell amendment was the high point of the congressional fight against armed forces integration. During the next year the integrationists took their turn, their barrage of questions and demands aimed at obtaining from the Secretary of Defense additional reforms in the services. On balance, these congressmen were no more effective than the segregationists. Secretary Johnson had obviously adopted a hands-off policy on integration.[15-45] Certainly he openly discouraged further public and congressional investigations of the department's racial practices. When the Committee Against Jim Crow sought to investigate racial conditions in the Seventh Army in December 1949, Johnson told A. Philip Randolph and Grant Reynolds that he could not provide them with military transport, and he closed the discussion by referring the civil rights leaders to the Army's new special regulation on equal opportunity published in January 1950.[15-46]

ASSISTANT SECRETARY ROSENBERG
talks with men of the 140th Medium Tank Battalion during a Far East tour.

Johnson employed much the same technique when Congressman Jacob K. Javits of New York, who with several other legislators had become interested in the joint congressional-citizen commission proposed by the Committee Against Jim Crow, introduced a resolution in the House calling for a complete investigation into the racial practices and policies of the services by a select House committee.[15-47] Johnson tried to convince Chairman Adolph J. Sabath of the House Committee on Rules that the new service policies promised equal treatment and opportunity, again using the new Army regulation to demonstrate how these policies were being implemented.[15-48] Once more he succeeded in diverting the integrationists. The Javits resolution came to naught, and although that congressman still harbored some reservations on racial progress in the Army, he nevertheless reprinted an article from *Our World* magazine in the *Congressional Record* in April 1950 that outlined "the very good progress" being made by the Secretary of Defense in the racial field.[15-49] Javits would have no reason to suspect, but the "very good progress" he spoke of had not issued from the secretary's office. For all practical purposes, Johnson's involvement in civil rights in the armed forces ended with his battle with the Fahy Committee. Certainly in the months after the committee was disbanded he did nothing to push for integration and allowed the subject of civil rights to languish.

Departmental interest in racial affairs quickened noticeably when General Marshall, Johnson's successor, appointed the brilliant labor relations and manpower expert Anna M. Rosenberg as the first Assistant Secretary of Defense for Manpower and Personnel.[15-50] Rosenberg had served on both the Manpower Consulting Committee of the Army and Navy Munitions Board and the War Manpower Commission and toward the end of the war in the European theater as a consultant to General Eisenhower, who recommended her to Marshall for the new position.[15-51] She was encouraged by the secretary to take independent control of the department's manpower affairs, including racial matters.[15-52] That she was well acquainted with integration leaders and sympathetic to their objectives is attested by her correspondence with them. "Dear Anna," Senator Hubert H. Humphrey wrote in March 1951, voicing confidence in her attitude toward segregation, "I know I speak for many in the Senate when I say that your presence with the Department of Defense is most reassuring."[15-53]

Still, to bring about effective integration of the services would take more than a positive attitude, and Rosenberg faced a delicate situation. She had to reassure integrationists that the new racial policy would be enforced by urging the sometimes reluctant services to take further steps toward eliminating discrimination. At the same time she had to promote integration and avoid provoking the segregationists in Congress to retaliate by blocking other defense legislation. The bill for universal military training was especially important to the department and to push for its passage was her primary assignment. It is not surprising, therefore, that she accomplished little in the way of specific racial reform during the first year of the Korean War.

Secretary Rosenberg took it upon herself to meet with legislators interested in civil rights to outline the department's current progress and future plans for guaranteeing equal treatment for black servicemen. She also arranged for her assistants and Brig. Gen. B. M. McFayden, the Army's Deputy G-1, to brief officials of the various civil rights organizations on the same subject.[15-54] She had congressional complaints and proposals speedily investigated, and demanded from the services periodic progress reports which she issued to legislators who backed civil rights.[15-55]

Rosenberg and her departmental colleagues were less forthcoming in some other areas of civil rights. Reflecting a desire to placate segregationist forces in Congress, they did little, for example, to promote federal protection of servicemen in cases of racial violence outside the military reservation. The NAACP had been urging the passage of such legislation for many years, and in March 1951 Clarence Mitchell called Rosenberg's attention to the mistreatment of black servicemen and their families suffered at the hands of policemen and civilians in communities

183

surrounding some military bases.[15-56] At times, Walter White charged, these humiliations and abuses by civilians were condoned by military police. He warned that such treatment "can only succeed in adversely affecting the morale of Negro troops ... and hamper efforts to secure fullhearted support of the American Negro for the Government's military and foreign policy program."[15-57]

The civil rights leaders had at least some congressional support for their demand. Congressman Abraham J. Multer of New York called on the Armed Services Committee to include in the 1950 extension of the Selective Service Act an amendment making attacks on uniformed men and women and discrimination against them by public officials and in public places of recreation and interstate travel federal offenses.[15-58] Focusing on a different aspect of the problem, Senator Humphrey introduced an amendment to the Senate version of the bill to protect servicemen detained by public authority against civil violence or punishment by extra legal forces. Both amendments were tabled before final vote on the bill.[15-59]

The matter came up again in the next Congress when Senator Herbert H. Lehman of New York offered a similar amendment to the universal military training bill.[15-60] Commenting for his department, Secretary Marshall admitted that defense officials had been supporting such legislation since 1943 when Stimson asked for help in protecting servicemen in the civilian community. But Marshall was against linking the measure to the training bill, which, he explained to Congressman Franck R. Havenner of California, was of such fundamental importance that its passage should not be endangered by consideration of extraneous issues. He wanted the problem of federal protection considered as a separate piece of legislation.[15-61]

But evidently not just yet, for when the NAACP's Mitchell, referring to Marshall's letter to Congressman Havenner, asked Rosenberg to press for separate legislation, he was told that since final congressional action was still pending on the universal military training and reserve programs it was not an auspicious moment for action on a federal protection bill.[15-62] The department's reluctance to act in the matter obviously involved more than concern with the fate of universal military training. Summing up department policy on 1 June, the day after the training bill passed the House, Rosenberg explained that the Department of Defense would not itself propose any legislation to extend to servicemen the protection afforded "civilian employees" of the federal government but would support such a proposal if it came from "any other source."[15-63] This limitation was further defined by Rosenberg's colleagues in the Defense Department. On 19 June the Assistant Secretary of Defense for Legal and Legislative Affairs, Daniel K. Edwards, rejected Mitchell's request for help in preparing the language of a bill to protect black servicemen. Mitchell had explained that discussions with congressional leaders convinced the NAACP that chances for such legislation were favorable, but the Defense Department's Assistant General Counsel declared the department did not ordinarily act "as a drafting service for outside agencies."[15-64] In fact, effective legislation to protect servicemen off military bases was more than a decade away.

Despite her concern over possible congressional opposition, Rosenberg achieved one important reform during her first year in office. For years the Army's demand for a parity of enlistment standards had been opposed by the Navy and the Air Force and had once been rejected by Secretary Forrestal. Now Rosenberg was able to convince Marshall and the armed services committees that in times of manpower shortages the services suffered a serious imbalance when each failed to get its fair share of recruits from the various so-called mental categories.[15-65] Her assistant, Ralph P. Sollat, prepared a program for her incorporating Roy K. Davenport's specific suggestions. The program would allow volunteer enlistments to continue but would require all the services to give a uniform entrance test to both volunteers and draftees. (Actually, rather than develop a completely new entrance test, the other services eventually adopted the Army's, which was renamed the Armed Forces Qualification Test.) Sollat also devised an arrangement whereby each service had to recruit men in each of the four mental categories in accordance with an established quota. Manpower experts agreed that this program offered the best chance to distribute manpower equally among the services. Approved by Secretary Marshall on 10 April 1951 under the title Qualitative Distribution of Military Manpower Program, it quickly changed the intellectual composition of the services by obliging the Navy and Air Force to share responsibility with the Army for the training and employment of less gifted inductees. For the remainder of the Korean War, for example, each of the services, not just the Army, had to take 24 percent of its new recruits from category IV, the low-scoring group. This figure was later reduced to 18 percent and finally in 1958 to 12 percent.[15-66]

The Navy and the Air Force had always insisted their high minimum entrance requirements were designed to maintain the good quality of their recruits and had nothing to do with race. Roy Davenport believed otherwise and read into their standards an intent to exclude all but a few Negroes. Rosenberg saw in the new qualitative distribution program not only the

184

chance to upgrade the Army but also a way of "making sure that the other Services had their proper share of Negroes."[15-67] Because so many Negroes scored below average in achievement tests and therefore made up a large percentage of the men in category IV, the new program served Rosenberg's double purpose. Even after discounting the influence of other factors, statistics suggest that the imposition of the qualitative distribution program operated just as Rosenberg and the Fahy Committee before her had predicted. (*Table 3*)

TABLE 3—PERCENTAGE OF BLACK ENLISTED MEN AND WOMEN

Service	1 July 1949
Army	12.4
Navy	4.7
Air Force	5.1
Marine Corps	2.1

Source: Memo for Rcd, ASD/M, 12 Sep 56, sub: Integration Percentages, ASD(M) 291.2.

The program had yet another consequence: it destroyed the Army's best argument for the reimposition of the racial quota. Upset over the steadily rising number of black enlistments in the early months of the Korean War, the Army's G-1 had pressed Secretary Pace in October 1950, and again five months later with G-3 concurrence, to reinstate a ceiling on black enlistments. Assistant Secretary Earl D. Johnson returned the request "without action," noting that the new qualitative distribution program would produce a "more equitable" solution.[15-68] The President's agreement with Secretary Gray about reimposing a quota notwithstanding, it was highly unlikely that the Army could have done so without returning to the White House for permission, and when in May 1951 the Army staff renewed its demand, Pace considered asking the White House for a quota on Negroes in category IV. After consulting with Rosenberg on the long-term effects of qualitative distribution of manpower, however, Pace agreed to drop the matter.[15-69]

Executive Order 9981 passed its third anniversary in July 1951 with little having happened in the Office of the Secretary of Defense to lift the hearts of the champions of integration. The race issues with which the Secretary of Defense concerned himself in these years—the definition of race, the status of black servicemen overseas, even the parity of enlistment standards—while no doubt important in the long run to the status of the Negro in the armed forces, had little to do with the immediate problem of segregation. Secretary Johnson had done nothing to enforce the executive order in the Army and his successor achieved little more. Willing to let the services set the pace of reform, neither secretary substantially changed the armed forces' racial practices. The integration process that began in those years was initiated, appropriately enough perhaps, by the services themselves.

CHAPTER 16
Integration in the Air Force and the Navy

The racial reforms instituted by the four services between 1949 and 1954 demonstrated that integration was to a great extent concerned with effective utilization of military manpower. In the case of the Army and the Marine Corps the reforms would be delayed and would occur, finally, on the field of battle. The Navy and the Air Force, however, accepted the connection between military efficiency and integration even before the Fahy Committee began to preach the point. Despite their very dissimilar postwar racial practices, the Air Force and the Navy were facing the same problem. In a period of reduced manpower allocations and increased demand for technically trained men, these services came to realize that racial distinctions were imposing unacceptable administrative burdens and reducing fighting efficiency. Their response to the Fahy Committee was merely to expedite or revise integration policies already decided upon.

The Air Force, 1949-1951

The Air Force's integration plan had gone to the Secretary of Defense on 6 January 1949, committing that service to a major reorganization of its manpower. In a period of severe budget and manpower retrenchment, the Air Force was proposing to open all jobs in all fields to Negroes, subject only to the individual qualifications of the men and the needs of the service.[16-1] To ascertain these needs and qualifications the Director of Personnel Planning was prepared to screen the service's 20,146 Negroes (269 officers and 19,877 airmen), approximately 5 percent of its strength, for the purpose of reassigning those eligible to former all-white units and training schools and dropping the unfit from the service.[16-2] As Secretary of the Air Force Symington made clear, his integration plan would be limited in scope. Some black service units would be retained; the rest would be eliminated, "thereby relieving the Air Force of the critical problems involved in manning these units with qualified personnel."[16-3]

In the end the integration process was not a drawn-out one; much of Symington's effort in 1949 was devoted instead to winning approval for the plan. Submitted to Forrestal on 6 January 1949, it was slightly revised after lengthy discussions in both the Fahy Committee and the Personnel Policy Board and in keeping with the Defense Secretary's equal treatment and opportunity directive of 6 April 1949. Some further delay resulted from the Personnel Policy Board's abortive attempt to achieve an equal opportunity program common to all the services. The Air Force plan was not finally approved by the Secretary of Defense until 11 May. Some in the Air Force were worried about the long delay in approval. As early as 12 January the Chief of Staff warned Symington that budget programming for the new 48-wing force required an early decision on the plan, especially in regard to the inactivation of the all-black wing at Lockbourne. Further delay, he predicted, would cause confusion in reassignment of some 4,000 troops.[16-4] In conversation with the Secretary of Defense, Symington mentioned a deadline of 31 March, but Assistant Secretary Zuckert was later able to assure Symington that the planners could tolerate a delay in the decision over integration until May.[16-5]

By then the long official silence had produced serious consequences, for despite the lack of any public announcement, parts of the plan had leaked to the press and caused some debate in Congress and considerable dissatisfaction among black servicemen. Congressional interest in the internal affairs of the armed forces was always of more than passing concern to the services. When a discussion of the new integration plan appearing in the Washington *Post* on 29 March caused a flurry of comment on Capitol Hill, Zuckert's assistant, Clarence H. Osthagen, met with the clerk of the House Armed Services Committee to "explain and clarify" for the Air Force. The clerk, Robert Harper, warned Osthagen that the impression in the House was that a "complete intermingling of Negro and white personnel was to take place" and that Congressman Winstead of Mississippi had been tempted to make a speech on the subject. Still, Harper predicted that there would be no adverse criticism of the plan in the House "at this time," adding that since that body had already passed the Air Force appropriation Chairman Carl Vinson was generally unconcerned about the Air Force racial program. Reporting on Senate reaction, Harper noted that while many members of the upper house would have liked to see the plan deferred, they recognized that the President's order made change mandatory. At any rate, Harper reassured Osthagen, the announcement of an integration plan would not jeopardize pending Air Force legislation.[16-6]

Unfortunately, the Air Force's black personnel were not so easily reassured, and the service had a morale problem on its hands during the spring of 1949. As later reported by the Fahy Committee staff, black troops generally supported the inactivation of the all-black 332d Fighter Wing at Lockbourne as a necessary step toward integration, but news reports frequently linked the disbandment of that unit to the belt tightening imposed on the Air Force by the 1950 budget. Some Negroes in the 332d concluded that the move was not directed at integration but at saving money for the Air Force.[16-7] They were concerned lest they find themselves relegated to unskilled labor units despite their training and experience. This fear was not so farfetched, considering Zuckert's private prediction that the redistribution of Lockbourne men had to be executed exactly according to the proposed program or "we would find experienced Air Force Negro technical specialists pushing wheelbarrows or driving trucks in Negro service units."[16-8]

The truth was that, while most Negroes in the Air Force favored integration, some were disturbed by the prospect of competition with whites of equivalent rank that would naturally follow. Many of the black officers were overage in grade, their proficiency geared to the F-51, a wartime piston plane, and they were the logical victims of any reduction in force that might occur in this period of reduced military budgets.[16-9] Some men doubted that the new program, as they imperfectly understood it, would truly integrate the service. They could, for example, see no way for the Air Force to break through what the press called the "community patterns" around southern bases, and they were generally suspicious of the motives of senior department officials. The Pittsburgh *Courier* summarized this attitude by quoting one black officer who expressed doubt "that a fair program will be enforced from the top echelon."[16-10]

But such suspicions were unfounded, for the Air Force's senior officials were determined to enforce the new program both fairly and expeditiously. General Vandenberg, the Chief of Staff, reported to the War Council on 11 January that the Air Force would "effect full and complete implementation" of its integration plan not only by issuing the required directives and orders, but also by assigning responsibility for monitoring the worldwide implementation of the program to his deputy for personnel. The Chief of Staff also planned to call a meeting of his senior commanders to discuss and solve problems rising from the plan and impress on them the personal attention they must give to carrying it out in the field.[16-11]

The Air Force Commanders' Conference, assembled on 12 April 1949, heard Lt. Gen. Idwal Edwards, the Deputy Chief of Staff for Personnel, explain the genesis of the integration plan and outline its major provisions. He mentioned two major steps to be taken in the first phase of the program. First, the 332d Fighter Wing would be inactivated on or before 30 June, and all blacks would be removed from Lockbourne. The commander of the Continental Air Command would create a board of Lockbourne officers to screen those assigned to the all-black base, dividing them into three groups. The skilled and qualified officers and airmen would be reassigned worldwide to white units "just like any other officers or airmen of similar skills and qualifications." General Edwards assumed that the number of men in this category would not be large. Some 200 officers and 1,500 airmen, he estimated, would be found sufficiently qualified and proficient for such reassignment. He added parenthetically that Colonel Davis understood the "implications" of the new policy and intended to recommend only an individual "of such temperament, judgment, and common sense that he can get along smoothly as an individual in a white unit, and second, that his ability is such as to warrant respect of the personnel of the unit to which he is transferred."

The technically unqualified but still "usable" men would be reassigned to black service units. The staff recognized, General Edwards added, that some Negroes were unsuited for assignment to white units for "various reasons" and had specifically authorized the retention of "this type of Negro" in black units. Finally, those who were found neither qualified nor useful would be discharged under current regulations.

The second major action would be taken at the same time as the first. All commands would similarly screen their black troops with the object of reassigning the skilled and qualified to white units and eliminating the chronically unqualified. At the same time racial quotas for recruitment and school attendance would be abolished. Henceforth, blacks would enter the Air Force under the same standards as whites and would be classified, assigned, promoted, or eliminated in accordance with rules that would apply equally to all. "In other words," Edwards commented, "no one is either helped or hindered because of the color of his skin; how far or how fast each one goes depends upon his own ability." To assure equal treatment and opportunity, he would closely monitor the problem. Edwards admitted that the subject of integrated living quarters had caused discussion in the staff, but based on the Navy's years of good experience with integrated quarters and bolstered by the probability that the number of Negroes in any white unit would rarely exceed 1 percent, the staff saw no need for separate sleeping accommodations.

General Edwards reminded the assembled commanders that, while integration was new to the Air Force, the Navy had been following a similar policy for years, encountering no trouble, even in the Deep South where black troops as well as the nearby civilian communities understood that when men left the base they must conform to the laws and customs of the community. And as a parting shot he made the commanders aware of where the command responsibility lay:

There will be frictions and incidents. However, they will be minimized if commanders give the implementation of this policy their personal attention and exercise positive command control. Unless our young commanders are guided and counselled by the senior commanders in unbiased implementation, we may encounter serious troubles which the Navy has very ably avoided. It must have your *personal attention and personal control.*[16-12]

Compelling reasons for reform notwithstanding, the effectiveness of an integration program would in the end depend on the attitude and initiative of the local commander. In the Air Force's case the ultimate effectiveness owed much to the fact that the determination of its senior officials was fully explained and widely circulated throughout the service. As Lt. Gen. Daniel (Chappie) James, Jr., later recalled, those who thought to frustrate the process were well aware that they risked serious trouble if their opposition was discovered by the senior commanders. None of the obvious excuses for preserving the racial *status quo* remained acceptable after Vandenberg and Edwards made their positions clear.[16-13]

The fact that the control of the new plan was specifically made a personal responsibility of the senior commanders spoke well for its speedy and efficient execution. This was the kind of talk commanders understood, and as the order filtered down to the lower echelons its terms became even more explicit.[16-14] "Direct attention to this changed condition is required throughout the Command," Maj. Gen. Laurence S. Kuter notified his subordinate commanders at the Military Air Transport Service. "Judgment, leadership, and ingenuity are demanded. Commanders who cannot cope with the integration of Negroes into formerly white units or activities will have no place in the Air Force structure."[16-15]

The order itself, as approved by the Secretary of Defense on 11 May 1949 and published on the same day as Air Force Letter 35-3, was unmistakable in intent and clearly spelled out a new bill of rights for Negroes in the Air Force.[16-16] The published directive differed in some respects from the version drafted by the Chief of Staff in January. Despite General Edwards's comments at the commanders' conference in April, the provision for allowing commanders to segregate barracks "if considered necessary" was removed even before the plan was first forwarded to the Secretary of Defense. This deletion was made in the Office of the Secretary of the Air Force, probably by Zuckert.[16-17] Later Zuckert commented, "I wouldn't want to give the commanders that kind of sweeping power. I would be afraid of how it might be exercised."[16-18] From the beginning, black airmen were billeted routinely in the living quarters of the units to which they were assigned.

The final version of the directive also deleted reference to a 10 percent limitation on black strength in formerly white units. Zuckert had assured the Fahy Committee this limitation was designed to facilitate, not frustrate, the absorption of Negroes into white units, and Edwards even agreed that given the determination of Air Force officials to make a success of their program, the measure was probably unnecessary.[16-19] In the end Zuckert decided to drop any reference to such limitations "because of the confusion that seemed to arise from this statement."[16-20]

ASSISTANT SECRETARY ZUCKERT

Zuckert also deleted several clauses in the supplementary letter to Air Force commanders that was to accompany and explain the order. These clauses had listed possible exemptions from the new order: one made it possible to retain a man in a black unit if he was one of the "key personnel" considered necessary for the successful functioning of a black unit, and the other allowed the local commander to keep those Negroes he deemed "best suited" for continued assignment to black units. The free reassignment of all eligible Negroes, particularly the well-qualified, was essential to the eventual dissolution of the all-black units. The Fahy Committee had objected to these provisions and considered it important for the Air Force to delete them,[16-21] but the matter was not raised during the committee hearings. There is evidence that the deletions were actually requested by the Secretary of Defense's Personnel Policy Board, whose influence in the integration of the Air Force is often overlooked.[16-22]

The screening of officers and men at Lockbourne got under way on 17 May. A board of officers under the presidency of Col. Davis, the commander of Lockbourne, and composed of representatives of Air Force headquarters, the Continental Air Command, and the Air Training Command, and important officers of Lockbourne, interviewed every officer in the wing. After considering each man's technical training, his performance, and his career field preference, the board recommended him for reassignment in a specific duty field. Although Edwards had promised that the screening boards would also judge each man's "adaptability" to integrated service, this requirement was quickly dropped by Davis and his fellow board members.[16-23] In fact, the whole idea of having screening boards was resented by some black officers. Zuckert later admitted that the screening may have been a mistake, but at the time it had been considered the best mechanism for ascertaining the proper assignment for the men.[16-24]

At the same time, a screening team in the Air Training Command gave a written examination to Lockbourne's more than 1,100 airmen and WAF's to determine if they were in appropriate military occupational specialties. A team of personnel counselors interviewed all airmen, weighed test scores, past performances, qualifications outside of assigned specialty, and choices of a career field, and then placed them in one of three categories. First, they could be earmarked for general reassignment in a specific military occupational specialty different from the one they were now in; second, they could be scheduled for additional or more advanced technical training; or third, they could be trained in their current specialties. The screeners referred marginal or extraordinary cases to Colonel Davis's board for decision.[16-25]

Concurrently with the Lockbourne processing, individual commanders established similar screening procedures wherever black airmen were then assigned. All these teams uncovered a substantial number of men and women considered eligible for further training or reassignment. (*Table 4*)

Table 4—Disposition of Black Personnel at Eight Air Force Bases, 1949

Base		Total Tested	Asgmt to Instr Duty	Asgmt to Tech S
Lockbourne				
Male		970	.32	12.08
Female		58	0.00	25.86
Lackland		247	1.62	20.65
Barksdale		158	0.00	20.25

188

Randolph	252	2.38	
Waco	146	2.06	
Mather	126	.79	
Williams	144	8.33	
Goodfellow	122	.82	
Total	2,223	1.35	

Source: President's Cmte on Equality of Treatment and Opportunity in the Armed Forces, "A First Report on the Racial Integration Program of the Air Force," 6 Feb 50, FC file.

The process of screening Lockbourne's troops was quickly completed, but the process of reassigning them was considerably more drawn-out. The reassignments were somewhat delayed in the first place by indecision, caused by budgetary uncertainties, on the future of Lockbourne itself. By 25 July, a full two months after the screening began, the Lockbourne board had recommended only 181 officers and 700 airmen to Air Force headquarters for new assignment. A short time later, however, Lockbourne was placed on inactive status and its remaining men and women, with the exception of a small caretaker detachment, were quickly reassigned throughout the Air Force.

The staff had predicted that the speed with which the integration order was carried out would follow a geographical pattern, with southern bases the last to integrate, but in fact no special pattern prevailed. For the many Negroes assigned to all-black base squadrons for administrative purposes but serving on a day-to-day basis in integrated units, the change was relatively simple. These men had already demonstrated their ability to perform their duties competently under integration, and in conformity with the new order most commanders immediately assigned them to the units in which they were already working. Except for their own squadron overhead, some base service squadrons literally disappeared when these reassignments were effected. After the screening process, most commanders also quickly reassigned troops serving in the other all-black units, such as Squadron F's, air ammunition, motor transport, vehicle repair, signal heavy construction, and aviation engineer squadrons.[16-26]

There were of course a few exceptions. Some commanders, noticeably more cautious than the majority, began the integration process with considerably less ease and speed.[16-27] As late as January 1950, for example, the Fahy Committee's executive secretary found that, with the exception of a small number of Negroes assigned to white units, the black airmen at Maxwell Air Force Base were still assigned to the all-black 3817th Base Service Squadron, the only such unit he found, incidentally, in a tour of seven installations.[16-28] But as the months went by even the most cautious commander, learning of the success of the new policy in other commands, began to reassign his black airmen according to the recommendations of the screening board. Despite the announcement that some black units would be retained, practically all units were integrated by the end of the first year of the new program. Even using the Air staff's very restricted definition of a "Negro unit," that is, one whose strength was over 50 percent black, statistics show how radical was the change in just one year. (*Table 5*)

TABLE 5—RACIAL COMPOSITION OF AIR FORCE UNITS

Month	Black Units	Integrated Units	Negroe
1949			
June	106	167	
July	89	350	
August	86	711	
September	91	863	
October	88	1,031	
November	75	1,158	
December	67	1,253	
1950			
January	59	1,301	
February	36	1,399	
March	26	1,476	
April	24	1,515	
May	24	1,506	

Tablenote 1: Figures extracted from the Marr Report; see also monthly reports on AF integration, for example Memo, Dir, Pers Plng, for Osthagen (SecAF office), 10 Mar 50, sub: Distribution of Negro Personnel, SecAF files.

Despite the predictions of some analysts, the effect of integration on black recruitment proved to be negligible. In a service whose total strength remained about 415,000 men during the first year of integration, Negroes numbered as follows (*Table 6*):

TABLE 6—BLACK STRENGTH IN THE AIR FORCE

Date	Officer Strength[1]	Enlisted Streng
December 1948	Not available	Not availab.
June 1949	319 (47)	21,782 (2,19
August 1949	330 (32)	23,568 (2,27
December 1949	368 (18)	25,523 (3,07
May 1950	341 (8)	25,367 (2,61

Tablenote 1: Includes in parentheses the Special Category Army Personnel with Air Force (SCARWAF), those soldiers assigned for duty in the Air Force but still administratively under the segregated Army, leftovers from the Department of Defense reorganization of 1947. Figures extracted from Marr Report.

The Air staff explained that the slight surge in black recruits in the early months of integration was related less to the new policy than to the abnormal recruiting conditions of the period. In addition to the backlog of Negroes who for some time had been trying to enlist only to find the Air Force quota filled, there were many black volunteers who had turned to the quota-free Air Force when the Army, its quota of Negroes filled for some time, stopped recruiting Negroes.

With Negroes serving in over 1,500 separate units there was no need to invoke the 10 percent racial quota in individual units as Vandenberg had ordered. One notable exception during the first months of the program was the Air Training Command, where the rapid and unexpected reassignment of many black airmen caused some bases, James Connally in Texas, for example, to acquire a great many Negroes while others received few or none. To prevent a recurrence of the Connally experience and "to effect a smooth operation and proper adjustment of social importance," the commander of the Air Training Command imposed an 8 to 10 percent black quota on his units and established a procedure for staggering the assignment of black airmen in small groups over a period of thirty to sixty days instead of assigning them to any particular base in one large increment. These quotas were not applied to the basic training flights, which were completely integrated. It was not uncommon to find black enlistees in charge of racially mixed training flights.[16-29] Of all Air Force organizations, the Training Command received the greatest number of black airmen as a result of the screening and reassignment. (*Table 7*)

TABLE 7—RACIAL COMPOSITION OF THE TRAINING COMMAND, DECEMBER 1949

	White
A. Flight Training	
Officers	1,345
Enlisted	3,063
Total	3,408
B. Technical Training	
Officers	1,897
Enlisted	25,838
Total	27,735
C. Indoctrination (Basic) Training	
White	7,649
Black	1,007
Total	8,656
Percent black	11.6[a]
D. Officers Candidate Training (candidates graduating from 28 November through 26 December 1949)	
White	225
Black	7
Total	232

Percent black	
E. Course Representation	

Base	No.
Chanute	
Warren	
Keesler	
Lowry	
Scott	
Sheppard	

Tablenote a: In January 1950, probably as a result of a decline in backlog and the raising of enlistment standard to GCT 100, this percentage dropped to 8.8. Tablenote b: Negroes in 61 percent of the courses offered as of 26 Dec 1949.

Source: Kenworthy Report.

At the end of the first year under the new program, the Acting Deputy Chief of Staff for Personnel, General Nugent, informed Zuckert that integration had progressed "rapidly, smoothly and virtually without incident."[16-30] In view of this fact and at Nugent's recommendation, the Air Force canceled the monthly headquarters check on the program.

To some extent the Air Force's integration program ran away with itself. Whatever their personal convictions regarding discrimination, senior Air Force officials had agreed that integration would be limited. They were most concerned with managerial problems associated with continued segregation of the black flying unit and the black specialists scattered worldwide. Other black units were not considered an immediate problem. Assistant Secretary Zuckert admitted as much in March 1949 when he reported that black service units would be retained since they performed a "necessary Air Force function."[16-31] As originally conceived, the Air Force plan was frankly imitative of the Navy's postwar program, stressing merit and ability as the limiting factors of change. The Air Force promised to discharge all its substandard men, but those black airmen either ineligible for discharge or for reassignment to specialist duty would remain in segregated units.

Yet once begun, the integration process quickly became universal. By the end of 1950, for example, the Air Force had reduced the number of black units to nine with 95 percent of its black airmen serving in integrated units. The number of black officers rose to 411, an increase of 10 percent over the previous year, and black airmen to 25,523, an increase of 15 percent, although the proportion of blacks to whites continued to remain between 6 and 7 percent.[16-32] Some eighteen months later only one segregated unit was left, a 98-man outfit, itself more than 26 percent white. Negroes were then serving in 3,466 integrated units.[16-33]

There were several reasons for the universal application of what was conceived as a limited program. First, the Air Force was in a sense the captive of its own publicity. While Secretary Symington had carefully delineated the limits of his departmental plan for the Personnel Policy Board in January 1949, he was carried considerably beyond these limits when he addressed President Truman in the open forum of the Fahy Committee's first formal meeting:

As long as you mentioned the Air Force, sir, I just want to report to you that our plan is to completely eliminate segregation in the Air Force. For example, we have a fine group of colored boys. Our plan is to take those boys, break up that fine group, and put them with the other units themselves and go right down the line all through these subdivisions one hundred percent.[16-34]

Later, Symington told the Fahy Committee that while the new program would probably temporarily reduce Air Force efficiency "we are ready, willing, and anxious to embark on this idea. We want to eliminate the fundamental aspect of class in this picture."[16-35] Clearly, the retention of large black units was incompatible with the elimination of class distinctions.

The more favorable the publicity garnered by the plan in succeeding months, the weaker the distinction became between the limited integration of black specialists and total integration. Reinforcing the favorable publicity were the monthly field reports that registered a steady drop in the number of black units and a corresponding rise in the number of integrated black airmen. This well-publicized progress provided another, almost irresistible reason for completing the task.

MUSIC MAKERS
of the U.S. Far East Air Force prepare to celebrate Christmas, Korea, 1950.

More to the point, the success of the program provided its own impetus to total integration. The prediction that a significant number of black officers and men would be ineligible for reassignment or further training proved ill-founded. The Air Force, it turned out, had few untrainable men, and after the screening process and transfer of those eligible was completed, many black units were so severely reduced in strength that their inactivation became inevitable. The fear of white opposition that had inhibited the staff planners and local commanders also proved groundless. According to a Fahy Committee staff report in March 1950, integration had been readily accepted at all levels and the process had been devoid of friction. "The men," E. W. Kenworthy reported, "apparently were more ready for equality of treatment and opportunity than the officer corps had realized."[16-36] At the same time, Kenworthy noted the effect of successful integration on the local commanders. Freed from the charges of discrimination that had plagued them at every turn, most of the commanders he interviewed remarked on the increased military efficiency of their units and the improved utilization of their manpower that had come with integration. They liked the idea of a strictly competitive climate of equal standards rigidly applied, and some expected that the Air Force example would have an effect, eventually, on civilian attitudes.[16-37]

For the Air Force, it seemed, the problem of segregation was all over but for the celebrating. And there was plenty of that, thanks to the Fahy Committee and the press. In a well-publicized tour of a cross section of Air Force installations in early 1950, Kenworthy surveyed the integration program for the committee. His favorable report won the Air Force laudatory headlines in the national press and formed the core of the Air Force section of the Fahy Committee's final report, *Freedom to Serve*.[16-38] For its part, the black press covered the program in great detail and gave its almost unanimous approval. As early as July 1949, for example, Dowdal H. Davis, president of the Negro Newspaper Publishers Association, reported on the highly encouraging reaction to the breakup of the 332d, and the headlines reflected this attitude: "The Air Force Leads the Way," the Chicago *Defender* headlined; "Salute to the Air Force," the Minneapolis *Spokesman* editorialized; and "the swiftest and most amazing upset of racial policy in the history of the U.S. Military," *Ebony* concluded. Pointing to the Air Force program as the best, the Pittsburgh *Courier* called the progress toward total integration "better than most dared hope."[16-39]

General Vandenberg and his staff were well aware of the rapid and profound change in the Air Force wrought by the integration order. From the start his personnel chief carefully monitored the program and reviewed the reports from the commands, ready to investigate any racial incidents or differences attributable to the new policy. The staff had expected a certain amount of testing of the new policy by both white and black troops, and with few exceptions the incidents reported turned out to be little more than that. Some arose from attempts by Negroes to win social acceptance at certain Air Force installations, but the majority of cases involved attempts by white airmen to introduce their black comrades into segregated off-base restaurants and theaters. Two examples might stand for all. The first involved a transient black corporal who stopped off at the Bolling Air Force Base, Washington, D.C., to get a haircut in a post exchange barbershop. He was refused service and in the absence of the post exchange officer he returned to the shop to trade words and eventually blows with the barber. The corporal was subsequently court-martialed, but the sentence was set aside by a superior court.[16-40] Another case involved a small group of white airmen who ordered refreshments at a segregated lunch counter in San Antonio, Texas, for themselves "and a friend who would join them later." The friend, of course, was a black airman. The Inspector General reported this incident to be just one of a number of attempts by groups of white and black airmen to integrate lunch counters and restaurants. In each case the commanders concerned cautioned their men against such action, and there were few reoccurrences.[16-41]

The commanders' warnings were understandable because, as any official from Secretary Symington on down would quickly explain, the Air Force did not regard itself as being in the business of forcing changes in American society; it was simply trying to make the best use of its manpower to build military efficiency in keeping with its national defense mission.[16-42] But in the end the integration order proved effective on both counts. Racial feelings, racial incidents, charges of discrimination, and the problems of procurement, training, and assignment always associated with racially designated units had been reduced by an appreciable degree or eliminated entirely. The problems anticipated from the mingling of blacks and whites in social situations had proved to be largely imaginary. The Air Force adopted a standard formula for dealing with these problems during the next decade. Incidents involving black airmen were treated as individual incidents and dealt with on a personal basis like any ordinary disciplinary case. Only when there was no alternative was an incident labeled "racial" and then the commander was expected to deal speedily and firmly with the troublemakers.[16-43] This sensible procedure freed the Air Force for a decade from the charges of on-base discrimination that had plagued it in the past.

192

Without a doubt the new policy improved the Air Force's manpower efficiency, as the experience of the 3202d Installation Group illustrates. A segregated unit serving at Eglin Air Force Base, Florida, the 3202d was composed of an all-black heavy maintenance and construction squadron, a black maintenance repair and utilities squadron, and an all-white headquarters and headquarters squadron. This rigid segregation had caused considerable trouble for the unit's personnel section, which was forced to assign men on the basis of color rather than military occupational specialty. For example, a white airman with MOS 345, a truck driver, although assigned to the unit, could not be assigned to the heavy maintenance and construction squadron where his specialty was authorized but had to be assigned to the white headquarters squadron where his specialty was not authorized. Clearly operating in an inefficient manner, the unit was charged with misassignment of personnel by the Air Inspector; in July 1950 it was swiftly and peaceably, if somewhat belatedly, integrated, and its three squadrons were converted to racially mixed units, allowing an airman to be assigned according to his training and not his color.[16-44]

The preoccupation of high officials with the effects of integration on a soldier's social life seemed at times out of keeping with the issues of national defense and military efficiency. At one of the Fahy Committee hearings, for instance, an exasperated Charles Fahy asked Omar Bradley, "General, are you running an Army or a dance?"[16-45] Yet social life on military bases at swimming pools, dances, bridge parties, and service clubs formed so great a part of the fabric of military life that the Air Force staff could hardly ignore the possibility of racial troubles in the countless social exchanges that characterized the day-to-day life in any large American institution. The social situation had been seriously considered before the new racial policy was approved. At that time the staff had predicted that problems developing out of integration would not prove insurmountable, and indeed on the basis of a year's experience a member of the Air staff declared that

at the point where the Negro and the white person are actually in contact the problem has virtually disappeared. Since all races of Air Force personnel work together under identical environmental conditions on the base, it is not unnatural that they participate together, to the extent that they desire, in certain social activities which are considered a normal part of service life. This type of integration has been entirely voluntary, without incident, and considerably more complete and more rapid than was anticipated.[16-46]

The Air staff had imposed only two rules on interracial social activities: with due regard for sex and rank all Air Force facilities were available for the unrestricted use of all its members; troublemakers would get into trouble. Under these inflexible rules, the Fahy Committee later reported, there was a steady movement in the direction of shared facilities. "Here again, mutual respect engendered on the job or in the school seemed to translate itself into friendly association."[16-47] Whether it liked it or not, the Air Force was in the business of social change.

Typical of most unit reports was one from the commander of the 1701st Air Transport Wing, Great Falls Air Force Base, Montana, who wrote Secretary Symington that the unit's eighty-three Negroes, serving in ten different organizations, lived and worked with white airmen "on an apparently equal and friendly basis."[16-48] The commander had been unable to persuade local community leaders, however, to promote equality of treatment outside the base, and beyond its movie theaters Great Falls had very few places that allowed black airmen. The commander was touching upon a problem that would eventually trouble all the services: airmen, he reported to Secretary Symington, although they have good food and entertainment on the base, sooner or later want to go to town, sit at a table, and order what they want. The Air Force was now coming into conflict with local custom which it could see no way to control. As the *Air Force Times* put it, "The Air Force, like the other services, feels circumspect policy in this regard is the only advisable one on the grounds that off-base segregation is a matter for civilian rather than military decision."[16-49]

But this problem could not detract from what had been accomplished on the bases. Judged by the standards it set for itself before the Fahy Committee, the Air Force had achieved its goals. Further, they were achieved in the period between 1949 and 1956 when the percentage of blacks in the service doubled, an increase resulting from the Defense Department's qualitative distribution of manpower rather than the removal of the racial quota.[16-50] During these years the number of black airmen rose from 5.1 to 10.4 percent of the enlisted strength and the black officers from 0.6 to 1.1 percent. Reviewing the situation in 1960, *Ebony* noted that the program begun in 1949 was working well and that white men were accepting without question progressive racial practices forbidden in their home communities. Minor racial flare-ups still occurred, but integration was no longer a major problem in the Air Force; it was a fact of life.[16-51]

The Navy and Executive Order 9981

The changing government attitude toward integration in the late 1940's had less dramatic effect on the Navy than upon the other services because the Navy was already the conspicuous possessor of a racial policy guaranteeing equal treatment and opportunity for all its members. But as the Fahy Committee and many other critics insisted, the Navy's 1946 equality guarantee was largely theoretical; its major racial problem was not one of policy but of practice as statistics demonstrated. It was true, for example, that the Navy had abolished racial quotas in recruitment, yet the small number of black sailors—17,000 during 1949, averaging 4.5 percent of the total strength—made the absence of a quota academic.[16-52] It was true that Negroes served side by side with white sailors in almost every occupation and training program in the Navy, but it was also a fact that 62 percent of all Negroes in the Navy in 1949 were still assigned to the nonwhite Steward's Branch. This figure shows that as late as December 1949 fewer than 7,000 black sailors were serving in racially integrated assignments.[16-53] Again, with only 19 black officers, including 2 nurses, in a 1949 average officer strength of 45,464, it meant little to say that the Navy had an integrated officer corps. A shadow had fallen, then, between the promise of the Navy's policy and its fulfillment, partly because of indifferent execution.

Submitted to and approved by the Secretary of Defense, the new Navy plan announced on 7 June 1949 called for a specific series of measures to bring departmental practices into line with policy.[16-54] Once he had gained Johnson's approval, Secretary of the Navy Matthews did not tarry. On 23 June he issued an explicit statement to all ships and stations, abjuring racial distinctions in the Navy and Marine Corps and ordering that all personnel be enlisted or appointed, trained, advanced or promoted, assigned and administered without regard to race, color, religion, or national origin.[16-55] Admirable and comprehensive, Matthew's statement scarcely differed in intent from his predecessor's general declaration of equal treatment and opportunity of 12 December 1945 and the more explicit directive of the Chief of Naval Operations on the same subject on 27 February 1946. Yet despite the close similarity, a reiteration was clearly necessary. As even the most ardent apologist for the navy's postwar racial policy would admit, these groundbreaking statements had not done the job, and, to satisfy the demands of the Fahy Committee and the Secretary of Defense, Secretary Matthews had to convince his subordinates that the demand for equal treatment and opportunity was serious and had to be dealt with immediately. His specific mention of the Marine Corps and the problems of enlistment, assignment, and promotion, subjects ignored in the earlier directives, represented a start toward the reform of his department's racial practices currently out of step with its expressed policy.

Yet a restatement of policy, no matter how specific, was not enough. As Under Secretary Dan A. Kimball admitted, the Navy had the formidable task of convincing its own people of the sincerity of its policy and of erasing the distrust that had developed in the black community "resulting from past discriminating practices."[16-56] Those who were well aware of the Navy's earlier failure to achieve integration by fiat were bound to greet Secretary Matthews's directive with skepticism unless it was accompanied by specific reforms. Matthews, aware of the necessity, immediately inaugurated a campaign to recruit more black sailors, commission more black officers, and remove the stigma attached to service in the Steward's Branch.

It was logical enough to start a reform of the Navy's integration program by attacking the perennial problem of too few Negroes in the general service. In his annual report to the Secretary of Defense, Matthews outlined some of the practical steps the Navy was taking to attract more qualified young blacks. The Bureau of Naval Personnel, he explained, planned to assign black sailors and officers to its recruiting service. As a first step it assigned eight Negroes to Recruitment Procurement School and subsequently to recruit duty in eight major cities with further such assignments planned when current manpower ceilings were lifted.[16-57]

The Bureau of Naval Personnel had also polled black reservists on the possibility of returning to active duty on recruiting assignments, and from this group had chosen five officers for active duty in the New York, Philadelphia, Washington, Detroit, and Chicago recruiting offices. At the same time black officers and petty officers were sent to extol the advantages of a naval career before black student bodies and citizen groups.[16-58] Their performances were exceedingly well received. The executive secretary of the Dayton, Ohio, Urban League, for example, thanked Secretary Matthews for the appearances of Lieutenant Nelson before groups of students, reporters, and community leaders in the city. The lieutenant, he added, not only "clearly and effectively interpreted the opportunities open to Negro youth in the United States Navy" but also "greatly accelerated" the community's understanding of the Navy's integration program.[16-

194

59] Nelson, himself, had been a leading advocate of an accelerated public relations program to advertise the opportunities for Negroes in the Navy.[16-60] The personnel bureau had adopted his suggestion that all recruitment literature, including photographs testifying to the fact that Negroes were serving in the general service, be widely distributed in predominantly black institutions. Manpower ceilings, however, had forced the bureau to postpone action on Nelson's suggestion that posters, films, pamphlets, and the like be used.[16-61]

An obvious concomitant to the increase in the number of black sailors was an increase in the number of black officers. The personnel bureau was well aware of this connection; Comdr. Luther C. Heinz, officer in charge of naval reserve officer training, called the shortage of Negroes in his program a particularly important problem. He promised, "in accord with the desires of the President," as he put it, to increase black participation in the Naval Reserve Officers' Training Corps, and his superior, the Chief of Naval Personnel, started a program in the bureau for that purpose.[16-62] With the help of the National Urban League, Heinz arranged a series of lectures by black officers at forty-nine black schools and other institutions to interest Negroes in the Navy's reserve officers program. In August 1949, for example, Ens. Wesley Brown, the first Negro to be graduated from Annapolis, addressed gatherings in Chicago on the opportunities for Negroes as naval officers.[16-63]

At the same time the Bureau of Naval Personnel wrote special press releases, arranged interviews for naval officials with members of the black press, and distributed publicity materials in predominantly black schools to attract candidates and to assure interested young men that race was no bar to their selection. In this connection Commander Heinz bid for and received an invitation to address the Urban League's annual conference in August 1949 to outline the Navy's program. The Chief of Naval Personnel, Rear Adm. Thomas L. Sprague, also arranged for the training of all those engaged in promoting the program—professors of naval science, naval procurement officers, and the like. In states where such assignments were considered acceptable, Sprague planned to appoint Negroes to selection committees.[16-64] In a related move he also ordered that when local law or custom required the segregation of facilities used for the administration of qualifying tests for reserve officer training, the Navy would use its own facilities for testing. This ruling was used when the 1949 examinations were given in Atlanta and New Orleans; to the delight of the black press the Navy transferred the test site to its nearby facilities.[16-65] These efforts had some positive effect. In 1949 alone some 2,700 black youths indicated an interest in the Naval Reserve Officers' Training Corps by submitting applications.[16-66]

Despite these well-intentioned efforts, the Navy failed to increase significantly the number of black officers or sailors in the next decade (Table 8). The percentage of Negroes in the Navy increased so slowly that not until 1955, in the wake of the great manpower buildup during the Korean War, did it exceed the 1949 figure. Although the percentage of black enlistments increased significantly at times—approximately 12 percent of all enlistments in 1955 were black, for example—the proportion of Negroes in the Navy's enlisted ranks was only 0.4 percent higher in 1960 than in 1949. While the number of black officers increased more than sevenfold in the same decade, it was still considerably less than 1 percent of the total officer strength, well below Army and Air Force percentages.

TABLE 8—BLACK MANPOWER, U.S. NAVY

A. Enlisted Strength		
Year	Total Strength	
1949	363,622	
1950	329,114	
1951	656,371	
1952	728,511	
1953	698,367	
1954	635,103	
1955	574,157	
1956	586,782	
1957	593,022	
1958	558,955	
1959	547,236	
1960	544,323	

B. Percentage of Blacks Enlisted in Steward's and Other Branches	
Year	*Steward's Branch*
1949	65.12
1950	57.07
1951	51.73
1952	54.95
1953	51.73
1954	53.43
1955	51.19
1956	25.38
1957	21.66
1958	23.35
C. Officer Strength (Selected Years)	
Year	*Black Officers on Active Duty*
1949	19
1951	23
1953	53
1955	81
1960	149

Source: BuPers, Personnel Statistics Branch. See especially BuPers, "Memo on Discrimination of the Negro," 24 Jan 59, BAF2-014. BuPers Technical Library. All figures represent yearly averages.

The Navy had an explanation for the small number of Negroes. The reduced manpower ceilings imposed on the Navy, even during the Korean War, had caused a drastic curtailment in recruiting. At the same time, with the brief exception of the Korean War, the Navy had depended on volunteers for enlistment and had required volunteers to score ninety or higher on the general classification test. The percentage of those who scored above ninety was lower for blacks than for whites—16 percent against 67 percent, a ratio, naval spokesmen suggested, that explained the enlistment figures. Furthermore, the low enlistment quotas produced a long waiting list of those desiring to volunteer. All applicants for the relatively few openings were thoroughly screened, and competition was so keen that any Negroes accepted for the monthly quota had to be extraordinarily well qualified.[16-67]

What the Navy's explanation failed to mention was that the rise and decline in the Navy's black strength during the 1950's was intimately related to the number of group IV enlistees being forced on the services under the provisions of the Defense Department's program for the qualitative distribution of manpower. Each service was required to accept 24 percent of all recruits in group IV from fiscal year 1953 to 1956, 18 percent in fiscal year 1957, and 12 percent thereafter. Between 1953 and 1956 the Navy accepted well above the required 24 percent of group IV men, but in fiscal year 1957 took only 15.1 percent, and in 1958 only 6.8 percent. In 1958, with the knowledge of the Secretary of Defense, all the services took in fewer of the group IV's than the distribution program required, but justified the reduction on the grounds that declining strength made it necessary to emphasize high quality in recruits. In a move endorsed by the Navy, the Air Force finally requested in 1959 that the qualitative distribution program be held in abeyance. On the basis of this request the Navy temporarily ceased to accept all group IV and some group III men, but resumed recruiting them when it seemed likely that the Secretary of Defense would refuse the request.[16-68]

CHRISTMAS IN KOREA, 1950

The correlation between the rise and fall of the group IV enlistments and the percentage of Negroes in the Navy shows that all the increases in black strength between 1952 and 1959 came not through the Navy's publicized and organized effort to attract the qualified black volunteers it had promised the Fahy Committee, but from the men forced upon it by the Defense Department's distribution program. The correlation also lends credence to the charges of some of the civil rights critics who saw another reason for the shortage of Negroes. They claimed that there had been no drop in the number of applicants but that fewer Negroes were being accepted by Navy recruiters. One NAACP official claimed that Negroes were "getting the

196

run around." Those who had fulfilled all enlistment requirements were not being informed, and others were being given false information by recruiters. He concluded that the Navy was operating under an unwritten policy of filling recruit quotas with whites, accepting Negroes only when whites were unavailable.[16-69] If these accusations were true, the Navy was denying itself the services of highly qualified black applicants at a time when the Defense Department's qualitative distribution program was forcing it to take large numbers of the less gifted. Certainly the number of Negroes capable of moving up the career and promotion ladder was reduced and the Navy left vulnerable to further charges of discrimination.

REARMING AT SEA.
Ordnancemen at work on the deck of the USS Philippine Sea, off Korea, October 1950.

As for the shortage of officers, Nelson cited the awareness among candidates that promotions were slower for blacks in the Navy than in the other services where there was "less caste and class to buck."[16-70] Nelson was aware that out of the 2,700 blacks who had indicated an interest in the reserve officer training program in 1949 only 250 actually took the aptitude tests. Of these, only two passed the tests and one of these was later rejected for poor eyesight. An Urban League spokesman believed that some failed to take the tests out of fear of failure but that many harbored a suspicion that the program was not entirely open to all regardless of race.[16-71] Reinforcing this suspicion was the fact that, despite the intentions of the Bureau of Naval Personnel and the Navy's increasing control over the appointment process, as of 1965 not a single Negro had been appointed to any of the 150-man state selection committees on reserve officer training.[16-72] Also to be considered, as the American Civil Liberties Union later pointed out, was the promotion record of black officers. As late as 1957 no black officer had ever commanded a ship, and while both black and white officers started up the same promotion ladder, the blacks were usually transferred out of the line into staff billets.[16-73]

Given the pressure on the personnel bureau to develop some respectable black manpower statistics, it is unlikely that the lack of educated, black recruits can be blamed on widespread subterfuge at the recruiting level. Far more likely is the explanation offered by Under Secretary Kimball, that the black community distrusted the Navy.[16-74] First apparent in the 1940's, this distrust lasted throughout the next decade as young Negroes continued to show a general apathy toward the Navy, which at times turned into open hostility. In September 1961 the Chief of Naval Personnel reported that recruiters were not infrequently being treated to "booing, hissing and other disorderly conduct" when they tried to discuss the opportunities for naval careers before black audiences.[16-75]

The Navy's poor reputation in the black community centered on the continued existence of the racially separate servants' branch, in the eyes of many the symbol of the service's racial exclusiveness. The Steward's Branch remained predominantly black. In 1949 it had 10,499 Negroes, 4,707 Filipinos, 741 other nonwhites, and 1 white man. Chief stewards continued to be denied the grade of chief petty officer, on the grounds that since stewards were not authorized to exercise military command over others than stewards because of their lack of military training, chief stewards were not chiefs in the military sense of the word. This difference in authority also explained, as the Chief of Naval Personnel put it, why as a general rule chief stewards were not quartered with other petty officers.[16-76] These distinctions were true also for stewards in the first, second, and third classes, a fact in their case symbolized by differences in uniform. Most of the thousands of black stewards continued to be recruited, trained, and employed exclusively in that branch, and thus for over half the Negroes—65 percent—in the 1949 Navy the chance for advancement was severely limited and the chance to qualify for a different job almost nonexistent.

BROADENING SKILLS.
Stewards on the USS Valley Forge volunteer for classes leading to advancement in other fields, Korea, 1950.

The Navy instituted several changes in the branch in the wake of the Fahy Committee's recommendations. On 25 July 1949 the Chief of Naval Personnel ordered all chief stewards designated chief petty officers with all the prerogatives of that status; in precedence they came immediately after chief dental technicians,[16-77] who were at the bottom of the list. That the change was limited to chief stewards did not go unnoticed. Joseph Evans of the Fahy Committee staff charged that the bureau "seemed to have ordered this to accede to the committee's recommendations never intending to go beyond Chief Stewards."[16-78] Nelson, by now a sort of unofficial ombudsman and gadfly for black sailors, urged his superiors to broaden the reform, and Kimball warned Admiral Sprague that limiting the change to chief stewards might be "justified on the literal statement of intention, but is vulnerable to criticism of continued discrimination." Without compelling reasons to the contrary, he added, "I do not feel that we can

197

afford to risk any possible impression of reluctant implementation of the spirit of the directive."[16-79]

Admiral Sprague got the point, and on 30 August he announced that effective with the new year, stewards—first, second, and third class—would be designated petty officers with appropriate pay, prerogatives, and precedence, and that their uniforms would be changed to conform to those of other petty officers. He also amended the bureau's manual to allow commanding officers to change the ratings of stewards without headquarters approval, thus enlarging the opportunity for stewards, in all other respects qualified, to transfer into other ratings.[16-80] These reforms brought about a slow but steady change in the assignment of black sailors. Between January 1950 and August 1953, the percentage of Negroes in the general service rose from 42 to 47 percent of the Navy's 23,000 man black strength, with a corresponding drop in the percentage of those assigned to the Steward's Branch.[16-81]

Yet these reforms were modest in terms of the pressing need for a substantive change in the racial composition of the Steward's Branch. Despite the changes in assignment policy, the Steward's Branch was still nearly 65 percent black in 1952, and the rest were mostly Filipino citizens under contract. Secretary of the Navy Kimball's observation that 133 stewards had transferred out of the branch in a recent four-month period hardly promised any speedy change in the current percentages.[16-82] In fact there was evidence even at that late date that some staff members in the personnel bureau were working at cross-purposes to the Navy's expressed policy. Worried about the shortages of volunteers for the Steward's Branch, a group of officials had met in August 1951 to discuss ways of improving branch morale. Some suggested publicizing the branch to the black press and schools, showing that Negroes were in all branches of the Navy including the Steward's. They also studied a pamphlet called "The Advantages of Stewards Duty in the Navy" that gave nine reasons why a man should become a steward.[16-83]

Obviously the Navy had to set a steady course if it intended any lasting racial reform of the Steward's Branch, but its leaders seemed ambivalent toward the problem. Despite his earlier efforts to raise the status of stewards, Kimball, in a variation on an old postwar argument, tried to show that the exclusiveness of the Steward's Branch actually worked to the Negro's advantage. As he explained to Lester Granger in November 1952, any action to effect radical or wholesale changes in ratings "would not only tend to reduce the efficiency of the Navy, but also in many instances be to the disadvantage or detriment of the individuals concerned, particularly those in the senior Steward ratings."[16-84] Supporting this line of argument, the Chief of Naval Personnel announced the reenlistment figures for the Steward's Branch—over 80 percent during the Korean War period. These figures, Vice Admiral James L. Holloway, Jr., added, proved the branch to be the most popular in the Navy and offered "a rational measure of the state of the morale and job satisfaction."[16-85]

These explanations still figured prominently in the Navy's 1961 defense of its racial statistics. Discussing the matter at a White House meeting of civil rights leaders, the Chief of Naval Personnel pointed out that all the black stewards could be replaced with Filipinos, but the Navy had refrained from such a course for several reasons. The branch still had the highest reenlistment rate. It provided jobs for those group IV men the Navy was obliged to accept but could never use in technical billets. Without the opportunity provided by the branch, moreover, "many of the rated black stewards would probably not achieve a petty officer rating at all."[16-86]

However well founded these arguments were, they did not satisfy the Navy's critics, who continued to press for the establishment of one recruitment standard and the assignment of men on the basis of interest and training rather than race. Lester Granger, for example, warned Secretary Kimball of the skepticism that persisted among sections of the black community: "As long as that branch [the Steward's Branch] is composed entirely of nonwhite personnel, the Navy is apt to be held by some to be violating its own stated policy."[16-87] To Kimball's successor, Robert B. Anderson,[16-88] Granger was even more blunt. The Steward's Branch, he declared, was "a constant irritant to the Negro public." He saw some logical reason for the continued concentration of Negroes in the branch but added "logic does not necessarily imply wisdom and I sincerely believe that it is unwise from the standpoint of efficiency and public relations to continue the Stewards Branch on its present basis."[16-89]

Granger's suggestion for change was straightforward. He wanted the Bureau of Naval Personnel to find a way to introduce a sufficiently large number of whites into the branch to transform its racial composition. The task promised to be difficult if the charges leveled in the Detroit *Free Press* were accurate. In May 1953 the paper reported incidents of naval recruiting officers who, "by one ruse or another," were shunting young volunteers, sometimes without their knowledge, into the Steward's Branch.[16-90]

Granger's suggestions were taken up by Secretary Anderson, who announced his intention of integrating the Steward's Branch and ordered the Chief of Naval Personnel to draw up plans

198

to that end.[16-91] To devise some practical measures for handling the problem, the personnel bureau brought back to active duty three officers who had been important to the development of the Navy's 1946 integration policy. Their study produced three recommendations: abolish the segregation of the Steward's Branch from the general service and separate recruitment for its members; consider consolidating the branch with the predominantly white Commissary Branch; and change the steward's insignia.[16-92]

The group acknowledged that the Steward's Branch was a "sore spot with the Negroes, and is our weakest position from the standpoint of Public Relations," and two of their recommendations were obviously aimed at immediate improvement of public relations. Combining the messmen and commissary specialists would of course create an integrated branch, which Granger estimated would be only 20 percent black, and would probably provide additional opportunities for promotions, but in the end it could not mask the fact that a high proportion of black sailors were employed in food service and valet positions. Nor was it clear how changing the familiar crescent insignia, symbolic of the steward's duties, would change the image of a separate group that still performed the most menial duties. Long-term reform, everyone agreed, demanded the presence of a significant number of whites in the branch, and there was strong evidence that the general service contained more than a few group IV white sailors. The group's proposal to abolish separate recruiting would probably increase the number of blacks in the general service and eliminate the possibility that unsuspecting black recruits would be dragooned into a messman's career; both were substantial reforms but did not guarantee that whites would be attracted or assigned to the branch.

Admiral Holloway was concerned about this latter point, which dominated his discussions with the Secretary of the Navy on 1 September 1953. He had, he told Anderson, discussed with his recruiting specialists the possibility of recruiting white sailors for the branch, and while they all agreed that whites must not be induced to join by "improper procedures," such as preferential recruitment to escape the draft, they felt that whites could be attracted to steward duty by skillful recruiters, especially in areas of the country where industrial integration had already been accomplished. His bureau was considering the abolition of separate recruiting, but to make specific recommendations on matters involving the stewards he had created an ad hoc committee, under the Deputy Chief of Naval Personnel and composed of representatives of the other bureaus. When he received this committee's views, Holloway promised to take "definite administrative action."[16-93]

INTEGRATED STEWARDS CLASS GRADUATES, GREAT LAKES, 1953

The three recommendations of the reservist experts did not survive intact the ad hoc committee's scrutiny. At the committee's suggestion, Holloway rejected the proposed merger of the commissary and steward functions on the grounds that such a move was unnecessary in an era of high reenlistment. He also decided that stewards would retain their branch insignia. He did approve, however, in a decision announced on 28 February 1954, putting an end to the separate recruitment of stewards with the exception of the contract enlistment of Filipino citizens. As Anderson assured Congressman Adam Clayton Powell of New York, only after recruit training and "with full knowledge of the opportunities in various categories of administrative specialties" would an enlistee be allowed to volunteer for messman's duty.[16-94]

Admiral Holloway promised a further search for ways to eliminate "points of friction" regarding the stewards, and naval officials discussed the problem with civil rights leaders and Defense Department officials on several occasions in the next years.[16-95] The Special Assistant to the Secretary of Defense, Adam Yarmolinsky, reported in 1961 that the Bureau of Naval Personnel "was not sanguine" about recruiting substantial numbers of white seamen for the Steward's Branch.[16-96] In answer, the Chief of Naval Personnel could only point out that no matter what their qualifications or ambitions all men assigned to the Steward's Branch were volunteers. As one commentator observed, white sailors were very rarely attracted to the messmen's field because of its reputation as a black specialty.[16-97]

Nevertheless, by 1961 a definite pattern of change had emerged in the Steward's Branch. The end of separate recruitment drastically cut the number of Negroes entering the rating, while the renewed emphasis on transferring eligible chief stewards to other specialties somewhat reduced the number of Negroes already in the branch. Between 1956 and 1961, some 600 men out of the 1,800 tested transferred to other rating groups or fields. The substantial drop in black strength resulting from these changes combined with a corresponding rise in the number of contract messmen from the western Pacific region reduced for the first time in some thirty years Negroes in the Steward's Branch to a minority. Even for those remaining in the branch, life changed considerably. Separate berthing for stewards, always justified on the grounds of different duties and hours, was discontinued, and the amount of time spent by stewards at sea, with the varied military work that sea duty involved, was increased.[16-98]

If these changes caused by the increased enlistment of stewards from the western Pacific relieved the Steward's Branch of its reputation as the black man's navy, they also perpetuated the notion that servants' duties were for persons of dark complexion. The debate over a segregated branch that had engaged the civil rights leaders and the Navy since 1932 was over, but it had left a residue of ill will; some were bitter at what they considered the listless pace of reform, a pace which left the impression that the service had been forced to change against its will. To some extent the Navy in the 1950's failed to capitalize on its early achievements because it had for so long missed the point of the integrationists' arguments about the stewards. In the fifties the Navy expended considerable time and energy advertising for black officer candidates and recruits whom they guaranteed a genuinely equal chance to participate in all specialties, but these efforts were to some extent dismissed by critics as not germane. In 1950, for example, only 114 Negroes served in the glamorous submarine assignments and even fewer in the naval air service.[16-99] Yet this obvious underrepresentation caused no great outcry from the black community. What did cause bitterness and protest in an era of aroused racial pride was the fact that servants' duties fell almost exclusively on nonwhite Americans. That these duties were popular—the 80 percent reenlistment rate in the Steward's Branch continued throughout the decade and the transfer rate into the branch almost equaled the transfer out—was disregarded by many of the more articulate spokesmen, who considered the branch an insult to the black public. As Congressman Powell informed the Navy in 1953, "no one is interested in today's world in fighting communism with a frying pan or shoe polish."[16-100] Although statistics showed nearly half the black sailors employed in other than menial tasks, Powell voiced the mood of a large segment of the black community.

WAVE RECRUITS,
Naval Training Center, Bainbridge, Maryland, 1953.

The Fahy Committee had acknowledged that manpower statistics alone were not a reliable index of equal opportunity. Convinced that Negroes were getting a full and equal chance to enlist in the general service and compete for officer commissions, the committee had approved the Navy's policy, trusting to time and equal opportunity to produce the desired result. Unfortunately for the Navy, there would be many critics both in and out of government in the 1960's who disagreed with the committee's trust in time and good intentions, for equal opportunity would remain very much a matter of numbers and percentages. In an era when a premium would be placed on the size of minority membership, the palm would go to the other services. "The blunt fact is," Granger reminded the Secretary of the Navy in 1954, "that as a general rule the most aspiring Negro youth are apt to have the least interest in a Navy career, chiefly because the Army and Air Force have up to now captured the spotlight."[16-101] A decade later the statement still held.

ADMIRAL GRAVELY
(1973 portrait).

It was ironic that black youth remained aloof from the Navy in the 1950's when the way of life for Negroes on shipboard and at naval bases had definitely taken a turn for the better. The general service was completely integrated, although the black proportion, 4.9 percent in 1960, was still far less than might reasonably be expected, considering the black population.[16-102] Negroes were being trained in every job classification and attended all the Navy's technical schools. Although not yet represented in proportionate numbers in the top grades within every rating, Negroes served in all ratings in every branch, a fact favorably noticed in the metropolitan press.[16-103] Black officers, still shockingly out of proportion to black strength, were not much more so than in the other services and were serving more often with regular commissions in the line as well as on the staff. Their lack of representation in the upper ranks demonstrated that the climb to command was slow and arduous even when the discriminatory tactics of earlier times had been removed. In 1961 the Navy could finally announce that a black officer, Lt. Comdr. Samuel L. Gravely, Jr., had been ordered to command a destroyer escort, the USS *Falgout.*[16-104]

But how were these changes being accepted among the rank and file? Comments from official sources and civil rights groups alike showed the leaven of racial tolerance at work throughout the service.[16-105] Reporter Lee Nichols, interviewing members of all the services in 1953,[16-106] found that whites expected blacks to prove themselves in their assignments while blacks were skeptical that equal opportunities for assignment were really open to them. Yet the

Nichols interviews reveal a strain of pride and wonderment in the servicemen at the profound changes they had witnessed.

In time integrated service became routine throughout the Navy, and instances of Negroes in command of integrated units increased. Bigots of both races inevitably remained, and the black community continued to resent the separate Steward's Branch, but the sincerity of the Navy's promise to integrate the service seemed no longer in doubt.

CHAPTER 17
The Army Integrates

The integration of the United States Army was not accomplished by executive fiat or at the demand of the electorate. Nor was it the result of any particular victory of the civil rights advocates over the racists. It came about primarily because the definition of military efficiency spelled out by the Fahy Committee and demonstrated by troops in the heat of battle was finally accepted by Army leaders. The Army justified its policy changes in the name of efficiency, as indeed it had always, but this time efficiency led the service unmistakably toward integration.

Race and Efficiency: 1950

The Army's postwar planners based their low estimate of the black soldier's ability on the collective performance of the segregated black units in World War II and assumed that social unrest would result from mixing the races. The Army thus accepted an economically and administratively inefficient segregated force in peacetime to preserve what it considered to be a more dependable fighting machine for war. Insistence on the need for segregation in the name of military efficiency was also useful in rationalizing the prejudice and thoughtless adherence to traditional practice which obviously played a part in the Army's tenacious defense of its policy.

An entirely different conclusion, however, could be drawn from the same set of propositions. The Fahy Committee, for example, had clearly demonstrated the inefficiency of segregation, and more to the point, some senior Army officials, in particular Secretary Gray and Chief of Staff Collins, had come to question the conventional pattern. Explaining later why he favored integration ahead of many of his contemporaries, Collins drew on his World War II experience. The major black ground units in World War II, and to a lesser degree the 99th Pursuit Squadron, he declared, "did not work out." Nor, he concluded, did the smaller independent black units, even those commanded by black officers, who were burdened with problems of discipline and inefficiency. On the other hand, the integrated infantry platoons in Europe, with which Collins had personal experience, worked well. His observations had convinced him that it was "pointless" to support segregated black units, and while the matter had "nothing to do with sociology itself," he reasoned that if integration worked at the platoon level "why not on down the line?" The best plan, he believed, was to assign two Negroes to each squad in the Army, always assuming that the quota limiting the total number of black soldiers would be preserved.[17-1]

But the Army had promised the Fahy Committee in April 1950 it would abolish the quota. If carried out, such an agreement would complicate an orderly and controlled integration, and Collins's desire for change was clearly tempered by his concern for order and control. So long as peacetime manpower levels remained low and inductions through the draft limited, a program such as the one contemplated by the Chief of Staff was feasible, but any sudden wartime expansion would change all that. Fear of such a sudden change combined with the strong opposition to integration still shared by most Army officials to keep the staff from any initiative toward integration in the period immediately after the Fahy Committee adjourned.

Even before Gray and Collins completed their negotiations with the Fahy Committee, they were treated by the Chamberlin Board to yet another indication of the scope of Army staff opposition to integration. Gray had appointed a panel of senior officers under Lt. Gen. Stephen J. Chamberlin on 18 September 1949 in fulfillment of his promise to review the Army's racial policy periodically "in the light of changing conditions and experiences of this day and time."[17-2] After sitting four months and consulting more than sixty major Army officials and some 280 officers and men, the board produced a comprehensive summary of the Army's racial status based on test scores, enlistment rates, school figures, venereal disease rates, opinion surveys, and the like.

The conclusions and recommendations of the Chamberlin Board represent perhaps the most careful and certainly the last apologia for a segregated Army.[17-3] The Army's postwar racial policy and related directives, the board assured Secretary Gray, were sound, were proving effective, and should be continued in force. It saw only one objection to segregated units: black units had an unduly high proportion of men with low classification test scores, a situation, it believed, that could be altered by raising the entrance level and improving training and leadership. At any rate, the board declared, this disadvantage was a minor one compared to the advantages of an organization that did not force Negroes into competition they were unprepared to face, did not provoke the resentment of white soldiers with the consequent risk of lowered combat effectiveness, and avoided placing black officers and noncommissioned officers in command of white troops, "a position which only the exceptional Negro could successfully fill."

A decision on these matters, the board stated, had to be based on combat effectiveness, not the use of black manpower, and what constituted maximum effectiveness was best left to the judgment of war-tested combat leaders. These men, "almost without exception," vigorously opposed integration. Ignoring the Army's continuing negotiations with the Fahy Committee on the matter, the board called for retaining the 10 percent quota. To remove the quota without imposing a higher entrance standard, it argued, would result in an influx of Negroes "with a corresponding deterioration of combat efficiency." In short, ignoring the political and budgetary realities of the day, the board called on Secretary Gray to repudiate the findings of the Fahy Committee and the stipulations of Executive Order 9981 and to maintain a rigidly segregated service with a carefully regulated percentage of black members.

While Gray and Collins let the recommendations of the Chamberlin Board go unanswered, they did very little to change the Army's racial practices in the year following their agreements with the Fahy Committee. The periodic increase in the number of critical specialties for which Negroes were to be trained and freely assigned did not materialize. The number of trained black specialists increased, and some were assigned to white units, but this practice, while substantially different from the Gillem Board's idea of limiting such integration to overhead spaces, nevertheless produced similar results. Black specialists continued to be assigned to segregated units in the majority of cases, and in the minds of most commanders such assignment automatically limited black soldiers to certain jobs and schools no matter what their qualifications. Kenworthy's blunt conclusion in May 1951 was that the Army had not carried out the policy it had agreed to.[17-4] Certainly the Army staff had failed to develop a successful mechanism for gauging its commanders' compliance with its new policy. Despite the generally progressive sentiments of General Collins and Secretary Gray's agreement with the Fahy Committee, much of the Army clung to old sentiments and practices for the same old reasons.

The catalyst for the sudden shift away from these sentiments and practices was the Korean War. Ranking among the nation's major conflicts, the war caused the Army to double in size in five months. By June 1951 it numbered 1.6 million, with 230,000 men serving in Korea in the Eighth Army. This vast expansion of manpower and combat commitment severely tested the Army's racial policy and immediately affected the racial balance of the quota-free Army. When the quota was lifted in April 1950, Negroes accounted for 10.2 percent of the total enlisted strength; by August this figure reached 11.4 percent. On 1 January 1951, Negroes comprised 11.7 percent of the Army, and in December 1952 the ratio was 13.2 percent. The cause of this striking rise in black strength was the large number of Negroes among wartime enlistments. The percentage of Negroes among those enlisting in the Army for the first time jumped from 8.2 in March 1950 to 25.2 in August, averaging 18 percent of all first-term enlistments during the first nine months of the war. Black reenlistment increased from 8.5 to 12.9 percent of the total reenlistment during the same period, and the percentage of black draftees in the total number of draftees supplied by Selective Service averaged 13 percent.[17-5]

MOVING UP.
25th Division infantrymen head for the front, Korea, July 1950.
The effect of these increases on a segregated army was tremendous. By April 1951, black units throughout the Army were reporting large overstrengths, some as much as 60 percent over their authorized organization tables. Overstrength was particularly evident in the combat arms because of the steady increase in the number of black soldiers with combat occupational specialties. Largely assigned to service units during World War II—only 22 percent, about half the white percentage, were in combat units—Negroes after the war were assigned in ever-increasing numbers to combat occupational specialties in keeping with the Gillem Board recommendation that they be trained in all branches of the service. By 1950 some 30 percent of all black soldiers were in combat units, and by June 1951 they were being assigned to the combat branches in approximately the same percentage as white soldiers, 41 percent.[17-6]

The Chief of Staff's concern with the Army's segregation policy went beyond immediate problems connected with the sudden manpower increases. Speaking to Maj. Gen. Lewis A. Craig, the Inspector General, in August 1950, Collins declared that the Army's social policy was unrealistic and did not represent the views of younger Americans whose attitudes were much more relaxed than those of the senior officers who established policy. Reporting Collins's comment to the staff, Craig went on to say the situation in Korea confirmed his own observations that mixing whites and blacks "in reasonable proportions" did not cause friction. Continued segregation, on the other hand, would force the Army to reinstate the old division-size black unit, with its ineffectiveness and frustrations, to answer the Negro's demand for equitable promotions and job opportunities. In short, both Collins and Craig agreed that the Army must eventually integrate, and they wanted the use of black servicemen restudied.[17-7]

Their view was at considerable variance with the attitude displayed by most officers on the Army staff and in the major commands in December 1950. His rank notwithstanding, Collins still had to persuade these men of the validity of his views before they would accept the necessity for integration. Moreover, with his concept of orderly and controlled social change threatened by the rapid rise in the number of black soldiers, Collins himself would need to assess the effects of racial mixing in a fluid manpower situation. These necessities explain the plethora of staff papers, special boards, and field investigations pertaining to the employment of black troops that characterized the next six months, a period during which every effort was made to convince senior officers of the practical necessity for integration. The Chief of Staff's exchange of views with the Inspector General was not circulated within the staff until December 1950. At that time the personnel chief, Lt. Gen. Edward H. Brooks, recommended reconvening the Chamberlin Board to reexamine the Army's racial policy in light of the Korean experience. Brooks wanted to hold off the review until February 1951 by which time he thought adequate data would be available from the Far East Command. His recommendation was approved, and the matter was returned to the same group which had so firmly rejected integration less than a year before.[17-8]

Even as the Chamberlin Board was reconvening, another voice was added to those calling for integration. Viewing the critical overstrength in black units, Assistant Secretary Earl D. Johnson recommended distributing excess black soldiers among other units of the Army.[17-9] The response to his proposal was yet another attempt to avoid the dictates of the draft law and black enlistments. Maj. Gen. Anthony C. McAuliffe, the G-1, advised against integrating the organized white units on the grounds that experience gained thus far on the social impact of integration was inadequate to predict its effect on "overall Army efficiency." Since the Army could not continue assigning more men to the overstrength black units, McAuliffe wanted to organize additional black units to accommodate the excess, and he asked Maj. Gen. Maxwell D. Taylor, the G-3, to activate the necessary units.[17-10]

The chief of the Army Field Forces was even more direct. Integration was untimely, General Mark W. Clark advised, and the Army should instead reimpose the quota and push for speedy implementation of the Secretary of Defense's directive on the qualitative distribution of manpower.[17-11] Clark's plea for a new quota was one of many circulating in the staff since black enlistment percentages started to rise. But time had run out on the quota as a solution to overstrength black units. Although the Army staff continued to discuss the need for the quota, and senior officials considered asking the President for permission to reinstitute it, the Secretary of Defense's acceptance of parity of enlistment standards had robbed the Army of any excuse for special treatment on manpower allotments.[17-12]

MEN OF BATTERY A,
159th Field Artillery Battalion, fire 105-mm. howitzer, Korea, August 1950.

McAuliffe's recommendation for additional black units ran into serious opposition and was not approved. Taylor's staff, concerned with the practical problems of Army organization, objected to the proposal, citing budget limitations that precluded the creation of additional units and policy restrictions that forbade the creation of new units merely to accommodate black recruits. The operations staff recommended instead that black soldiers in excess of unit strength be shipped directly from training centers to overseas commands as replacements without regard for specific assignment. McAuliffe's personnel staff, in turn, warned that on the basis of a monthly average dispatch of 25,000 replacements to the Far East Command, the portion of Negroes in those shipments would be 15 percent for May 1951, 21 percent for June, 22 percent for July, and 16 percent for August. McAuliffe listed the familiar problems that would accrue to the Far East commanders from this decision, but he was unable to break the impasse in Washington. Thus the problem of excess black manpower was passed on to the overseas commanders for resolution.[17-13]

Commanders in Korea had already begun to apply the only practical remedy. Confronted with battle losses in white units and a growing surplus of black replacements arriving in Japan, the Eighth Army began assigning individual black soldiers just as it had been assigning individual Korean soldiers to understrength units.[17-14] In August 1950, for example, initial replacements for battle casualties in the 9th Infantry of the U.S. 2d Infantry Division included two black officers and eighty-nine black enlisted men. The commander assigned them to units in his severely undermanned all-white 1st and 2d Battalions. In September sixty more soldiers from the regiment's all-black 3d Battalion returned to the regiment for duty. They were first attached but later, with the agreement of the officers and men involved, assigned to units of the 1st and 2d

Battalions. Subsequently, 225 black replacements were routinely assigned wherever needed throughout the regiment.[17-15] By December the 9th Infantry had absorbed Negroes to about their proportion of the national population, 11 percent. Of six black officers among them, one commanded Company C and another was temporarily in command of Company B when that unit fought in November on the Ch'ongch'on River line. S. L. A. Marshall later described Company B as "possibly the bravest" unit in that action.[17-16]

The practice of assigning individual blacks throughout white units in Korea accelerated during early 1951 and figured in the manpower rotation program which began in Korea during May. By this time the practice had so spread that 9.4 percent of all Negroes in the theater were serving in some forty-one newly and unofficially integrated units.[17-17] Another 9.3 percent were in integrated but predominantly black units. The other 81 percent continued to serve in segregated units: in March 1951 these numbered 1 black regiment, 10 battalions, 66 separate companies, and 7 separate detachments. Looked at another way, by May 1951 some 61 percent of the Eighth Army's infantry companies were at least partially integrated.

Though still limited, the conversion to integrated units was permanent. The Korean expedient, adopted out of battlefield necessity, carried out haphazardly, and based on such imponderables as casualties and the draft, passed the ultimate test of traditional American pragmatism: it worked. And according to reports from Korea, it worked well. The performance of integrated troops was praiseworthy with no report of racial friction.[17-18] It was a test that could not fail to impress field commanders desperate for manpower.

Training

Training units in the United States were subject to many of the stresses suffered by the Eighth Army, and without fanfare they too began to integrate. There was little precedent for the change. True, the Army had integrated officer training in World War II and basic training at the Women's Army Corps Training Center at Fort Lee, Virginia, in April 1950. But beyond that only the rare black trainee designated for specialist service was assigned to a white training unit. Until 1950 there was no effort to mix black and white trainees because the Army's manpower experts always predicted a "social problem," a euphemism for the racial conflict they feared would follow integration at large bases in the United States.

Not that demands for integration ever really ceased. Civil rights organizations and progressive lawmakers continued to press the Army, and the Selective Service System itself complained that black draftees were being discriminated against even before induction.[17-19] Because so many protests had focused on the induction process, James Evans, the Civilian Aide to the Secretary of Defense, recommended that the traditional segregation be abandoned, at least during the period between induction and first assignment.[17-20]Congressman Jacob Javits, always a critic of the Army's segregation policy, was particularly disturbed by the segregation of black trainees at Fort Dix, New Jersey. His request that training units be integrated was politely rejected in the fall of 1950 by General Marshall, who implied that the subject was an unnecessary intrusion, an attitude characteristic of the Defense Department's war-distracted feelings toward integration.[17-21]

Again, the change in Army policy came not because the staff ordered it, but because local commanders found it necessary. The commanders of the nine training divisions in the continental United States were hard pressed because the number of black and white inductees in any monthly draft call, as well as their designated training centers, depended on Selective Service and was therefore unpredictable. It was impossible for commanders to arrange for the proper number of separate white and black training units and instructors to receive the inductees when no one knew whether a large contingent of black soldiers or a large group of whites would get off the train. A white unit could be undermanned and its instructors idle while a black unit was overcrowded and its instructors overworked. This inefficient use of their valuable training instructors led commanders, first at Fort Ord and then at the other training divisions and replacement centers throughout the United States, to adopt the expedient of mixing black and white inductees in the same units for messing, housing, and training. As the commander of Fort Jackson, South Carolina, put it, sorting out the rapidly arriving inductees was "ridiculous," and he proceeded to assign new men to units without regard to color. He did, however, divert black inductees from time to time "to hold the Negro population down to a workable basis."[17-22]

The commanding general of the 9th Infantry Division at Fort Dix raised another question about integrating trainees. He had integrated all white units other than reserve units at his station, he explained to the First Army commander in January 1951, but since he was receiving many more white trainees than black he would soon be forced to integrate his two black training regiments as well by the unprecedented assignment of white soldiers to black units with black officers and noncommissioned officers.[17-23] Actually, such reverse integration was becoming commonplace in Korea, and in the case of Fort Dix the Army G-1 solved the commander's dilemma by simply removing the asterisk, which meant black, from the names of the 364th and 365th Infantry Regiments.[17-24]

The nine training divisions were integrated by March 1951, with Fort Dix, New Jersey, and Fort Knox, Kentucky, the last to complete the process. Conversion proved trouble-free and permanent; no racial incidents were reported. In June Assistant Secretary of the Army Johnson assured the Assistant Secretary of Defense for Manpower and Personnel, Anna Rosenberg, that current expansion of training divisions would allow the Army to avoid in the future even the occasional funneling of some inductees into temporarily segregated units in times of troop overstrengths.[17-25] Logic dictated that those who trained together would serve together, but despite integrated training, the plethora of Negroes in overseas replacement pipelines, and the increasing amount of integrated fighting in Korea, 98 percent of the Army's black soldiers still served in segregated units in April 1951, almost three years after President Truman issued his order.

Performance of Segregated Units

Another factor leading to a change in racial policy was the performance of segregated units in Korea. Despite "acts of heroism and capable performance of duty" by some individuals, the famous old 24th Infantry Regiment as a whole performed poorly. Its instability was especially evident during the fighting on Battle Mountain in August 1950, and by September the regiment had clearly become a "weak link in the 25th Division line," and in the Eighth Army as well.[17-26] On 9 September the division commander recommended that the regiment be removed from combat. "It is my considered opinion," Maj. Gen. William B. Kean told the Eighth Army commander, that the 24th Infantry has demonstrated in combat that

it is untrustworthy and incapable of carrying out missions expected of an Infantry Regiment. In making this statement, I am fully cognizant of the seriousness of the charges that I am making, and the implications involved.... The continued use of this Regiment in combat will jeopardize the United Nations war effort in Korea.[17-27]

Kean went on to spell out his charges. The regiment was unreliable in combat, particularly on the defensive and at night; it abandoned positions without warning to troops on its flanks; it wasted equipment; it was prone to panic and hysteria; and some of its members were guilty of malingering. The general made clear that his charges were directed at the unit as an organization and not at individual soldiers, but he wanted the unit removed and its men reassigned as replacements on a percentage basis in the other units of the Eighth Army.

General Kean also claimed to have assigned unusually able officers to the regiment, but to no avail. In attempting to lead their men in battle, all the unit's commanders had become casualties. Concluding that segregated units would not work in a combat situation, the general believed that the combat value of black soldiers would never be realized unless they were integrated into white units at a rate of not more than 10 percent.[17-28]

The 25th Division commander's charges were supported by the Eighth Army inspector general, who investigated the 24th Infantry at length but concluded that the inactivation of the 24th was unfeasible. Instead he suggested integrating Negroes in all Eighth Army units up to 15 percent of their strength by means of the replacement process. The Far East Command's inspector general, Brig. Gen. Edwin A. Zundel, concurred, stating that the rotation process would provide a good opportunity to accomplish integration and expressing hope that the theater would observe the "spirit" of the Army's latest racial regulations.[17-29]

Lt. Gen. Walton H. Walker, the Eighth Army commander, accepted the inspector general's report, and the 24th Infantry remained on duty in Korea through the winter. Zundel meanwhile continued the investigation and in March 1951 offered a more comprehensive assessment of the 24th. It was a fact, for example, that 62 percent of the unit's troops were in categories IV and V as against 41 percent of the troops in the 35th Infantry and 46 percent in the 27th, the 25th Division's white regiments. The Gillem Board had recommended supplying all such units with 25 percent more officers in the company grades, something not done for the 24th Infantry. Some observers also reported evidence in the regiment of the lack of leadership and lack of close relationships between officers and men; absence of unit *esprit de corps*; discrimination against black officers; and poor quality of replacements.

Whatever the cause of the unit's poor performance, the unanimous recommendation in the Eighth Army, its inspector general reported, was integration. Yet he perceived serious difficulty in integration. To mix the troops of the eighty-four major segregated units in the Eighth Army under wartime conditions would create an intolerable administrative burden and would be difficult for the individuals involved. If integration was limited to the 24th Infantry alone, on the other hand, its members, indeed even its former members, would share the onus of its failure. The inspector general therefore again recommended retaining the 24th, assigning additional

205

officers and noncommissioned officers to black units with low test averages, and continuing the integration of the Eighth Army.[17-30]

The Eighth Army was not alone in investigating the 24th Infantry. The NAACP was also concerned with reports of the regiment's performance, in particular with figures on the large number of courts-martial. Thirty-six of the men convicted, many for violation of Article 75 of the Articles of War (misbehavior before the enemy), had appealed to the association for assistance, and Thurgood Marshall, then one of its celebrated attorneys, went to the Far East to investigate. Granted *carte blanche* by the Far East commander, General Douglas MacArthur, Marshall traveled extensively in Korea and Japan reviewing the record and interviewing the men. His conclusions: "the men were tried in an atmosphere making justice impossible," and the NAACP had the evidence to clear most of them.[17-31] Contrasting the Army's experiences with those of the Navy and the Air Force, Marshall attributed discrimination in the military justice system to the Army's segregation policy. He blamed MacArthur for failing to carry out Truman's order in the Far East and pointed out that no Negroes served in the command's headquarters. As long as racial segregation continued, the civil rights veteran concluded, the Army would dispense the kind of injustice typical of the courts-martial he reviewed.

It would be hard to refute Marshall's contention that discrimination was a handmaiden of segregation. Not so Walter White's contention that the reports of the 24th Infantry's poor performance constituted an attempt to discredit the combat ability of black soldiers and return them to labor duties. The association's executive secretary had fought racial injustice for many decades, and, considering his World War II experiences with the breakup of the 2d Cavalry Division into labor units, his acceptance of a conspiracy theory in Korea was understandable. But it was inaccurate. The Army operated under a different social order in 1951, and many combat leaders in the Eighth Army were advocating integration. The number of black service units in the Eighth Army, some ninety in March 1951, was comparable to the number in other similar Army commands. Nor, for that matter, was the number of black combat units in the Eighth Army unusual. In March 1951 the Eighth Army had eighty-four such units ranging in size from regiment to detachment. Far from planning the conversion of black combat troops to service troops, most commanders were recommending their assignment to integrated combat units throughout Korea.

Apprised of these various conclusions, MacArthur ordered his staff to investigate the problem of segregation in the command.[17-32] The Far East Command G-1 staff incorporated the inspector general's report in its study of the problem, adding that "Negro soldiers can and do fight well when integrated." The staff went on to dismiss the importance of leadership as a particular factor in the case of black troops by observing that "no race has a monopoly on stupidity."[17-33]

Before the staff could finish its investigation, General Matthew B. Ridgway replaced MacArthur as Far East commander. Fresh from duty as Eighth Army commander, Ridgway had had close-hand experience with the 24th Infantry's problems; from both a military and a human viewpoint he had concluded that segregation was "wholly inefficient, not to say improper." He considered integration the only way to assure *esprit de corps* in any large segment of the Army. As for segregation, Ridgway concluded, "it has always seemed to me both un-American and un-Christian for free citizens to be taught to downgrade themselves this way as if they were unfit to associate with their fellows or to accept leadership themselves."[17-34] He had planned to seek authorization to integrate the major black units of the Eighth Army in mid-March, but battlefield preoccupations and his sudden elevation to theater command interfered. Once he became commander in chief, however, he quickly concurred in his inspector general's recommendation, adding that "integration in white combat units in Korea is a practical solution to the optimum utilization of Negro manpower provided the overall theater level of Negroes does not exceed 15 percent of troop level and does not exceed over 12 percent in any combat unit."[17-35]

The 24th Infantry's experiences struck yet another blow at the Army's race policy. Reduce the size of black units, the Gillem Board had reasoned, and you will reduce inefficiency and discrimination. Such a course had not worked. The same troubles that befell the 92d Division in Italy were now being visited in Korea on the 24th Infantry, a unit rich with honors extending back to the Indian fighting after the Civil War, the War with Spain, and the Philippine Insurrection. The unit could also boast among its medal of honor winners the first man to receive the award in Korea, Pfc. William Thompson of Company M. Before its inactivation in 1951 the 24th had yet another member so honored, Sgt. Cornelius H. Carlton of Company H.

Final Arguments

206

To concentrate on the widespread sentiment for integration in the Far East would misrepresent the general attitude that still prevailed in the Army in the spring of 1951. This attitude was clearly reflected again by the Chamberlin Board, which completed its reexamination of the Army's racial policy in light of the Korean experience in April. The board recognized the success of integrated units and even cited evidence indicating that racial friction had decreased in those units since the men generally accepted any replacement willing to fight. But in the end the board retreated into the Army's conventional wisdom: separate units must be retained, and the number of Negroes in the Army must be regulated.[17-36]

The board's recommendations were not approved. Budgetary limitations precluded the creation of more segregated units and the evidence of Korea could not be denied. Yet the board still enjoyed considerable support in some quarters. The Vice Chief of Staff, General Haislip, who made no secret of his opposition to integration, considered it "premature" to rely and act solely on the experience with integration in Korea and the training divisions, and he told Secretary Pace in May 1951 that "no action should be taken which would lead to the immediate elimination of segregated units."[17-37] And then there was the assessment of Lt. Gen. Edward M. Almond, World War II commander of the 92d Division and later X Corps commander in Korea and MacArthur's chief of staff. Twenty years after the Korean War Almond's attitude toward integration had not changed.

I do not agree that integration improves military efficiency; I believe that it weakens it. I believe that integration was and is a political solution for the composition of our military forces because those responsible for the procedures either do not understand the characteristics of the two human elements concerned, the white man and the Negro as individuals. The basic characteristics of Negro and White are fundamentally different and these basic differences must be recognized by those responsible for integration. By trial and error we must test the integration in its application. These persons who promulgate and enforce such policies either have not the understanding of the problem or they do not have the intestinal fortitude to do what they think if they do understand it. There is no question in my mind of the inherent difference in races. This is not racism—it is common sense and understanding. Those who ignore these differences merely interfere with the combat effectiveness of battle units.[17-38]

The opinions of senior commanders long identified with segregated units in combat carried weight with the middle-ranking staff officers who, lacking such experience, were charged with devising policy. Behind the opinions expressed by many staff members there seemed to be a nebulous, often unspoken, conviction that Negroes did not perform well in combat. The staff officers who saw proof for their convictions in the troubles of the 24th Infantry ignored the possibility that segregated units, not individual soldiers, was the problem. Their attitude explains why the Army continued to delay changes made imperative by its experience in Korea.

It also explains why at this late date the Army turned to the scientific community for still another review of its racial policy. The move originated with the Army's G-3, Maj. Gen. Maxwell D. Taylor, who in February called for the collection of all information on the Army's experiences with black troops in Korea. If the G-1, General McAuliffe, did not consider the available data sufficient, General Taylor added, he would join in sponsoring further investigation in the Far East.[17-39] The result was two studies. The G-1 sent an Army personnel research team, which left for Korea in April 1951, to study the Army's regulations for assigning men under combat conditions and to consider the performance of integrated units.[17-40] On 29 March, Maj. Gen. Ward S. Maris, the G-4, requested the Operations Research Office, a contract agency for the Army, to make a study of how best to use black manpower in the Army.[17-41] The G-1 investigation, undertaken by manpower experts drawn from several Army offices, concentrated on the views of combat commanders; the contract agency reviewed all available data, including a detailed battlefield survey by social scientists. Both groups submitted preliminary reports in July 1951.

Their findings complemented each other. The G-1 team reported that integration of black soldiers into white combat units in Korea had been accomplished generally "without undue friction and with better utilization of manpower." Combat commanders, the team added, "almost unanimously favor integration."[17-42] The individual soldier's own motivation determined his competence, the team concluded. The contract agency, whose report was identified by the code name Project CLEAR,[17-43] observed that large black units were, on average, less reliable than large white units, but the effectiveness of small black units varied widely. The performance of individual black soldiers in integrated units, on the other hand, approximated that of whites. It found that white officers commanding black units tended to attribute their problems to race; those commanding integrated units saw their problems as military ones. The contract team also confirmed previous Army findings that efficient officers and noncommissioned officers, regardless of race, were accepted by soldiers of both races. Integration, it decided, had not lowered white morale, but it had raised black morale. Virtually all black soldiers supported integration, while white soldiers, whatever their private sentiments, were not overtly hostile. In most situations, white attitudes toward integration became more favorable with firsthand experience. Although opinions varied, most combat commanders with integration experience believed that a squad should contain not more than two Negroes. In sum, the Project CLEAR group concluded that segregation hampered the Army's effectiveness while integration increased it. Ironically, this conclusion practically duplicated the verdict of the Army's surveys of the integration of black and white units in Europe at the end of World War II.

General Collins immediately accepted the Project CLEAR conclusions when presented to him verbally on 23 July 1951.[17-44] His endorsement and the subsequent announcement that the Army would integrate its forces in the Far East implied a connection which did not exist. Actually, the decision to integrate in Korea was made before Project CLEAR or the G-1 study appeared. This is not to denigrate the importance of these documents. Their justification of integration in objective, scientific terms later helped convince Army traditionalists of the need for worldwide change and absolved the Secretary of the Army, his Chief of Staff, and his theater commander of the charge of having made a political and social rather than a military decision.[17-45]

Integration of the Eighth Army

On 14 May 1951 General Ridgway forced the issue of integration by formally requesting authority to abolish segregation in his command. He would begin with the 24th Infantry, which he wanted to replace after reassigning its men to white units in Korea. He would then integrate the other combat units and, finally, the service units. Where special skills were not a factor Ridgway wanted to assign his black troops throughout the theater to a maximum of 12 percent of any unit. To do this he needed permission to integrate the 40th and 45th Divisions, the federalized National Guard units then stationed in Japan. He based his proposals on the need to maintain the combat effectiveness of his command where segregated units had proved ineffective and integrated units acceptable.[17-46]

When it finally arrived, the proposal for wide-scale integration of combat units encountered no real opposition from the Army staff. General Ridgway had rehearsed his proposal with the G-3 when the latter visited the Far East in April. Taylor "heartily approved," calling the times auspicious for such a move.[17-47] Of course his office quickly approved the plan, and McAuliffe in G-1 and the rest of the staff followed suit. There was some sentiment on the staff, eventually suppressed, for retaining the 24th Infantry as an integrated unit since the statutory requirement for the four black regiments had been repealed in 1950.[17-48] The staff did insist, over the G-1's objections, on postponing the integration of the two National Guard divisions until their arrival in Korea, where the change could be accomplished through normal replacement-rotation procedures.[17-49] There were other minor complications and misunderstandings between the Far East Command and the Army staff over the timing of the order, but they were easily ironed out.[17-50] Collins discussed the plan with the appropriate congressional chairmen, Ridgway further briefed the Secretary of Defense during General Marshall's 1951 visit to Japan, and Secretary of the Army Pace kept the President informed.[17-51]

GENERAL RIDGWAY

Pace had succeeded Gordon Gray as secretary in April 1950 and participated in the decisions leading to integration. A Harvard-trained lawyer with impressive managerial skills, Pace did not originate any of the Army's racial programs, but he fully supported the views of his Chief of Staff, General Collins.[17-52] Meeting with his senior civilian assistants, the G-1 and G-3 of the Army, and Assistant Secretary of Defense Rosenberg on 9 June, Pace admitted that their discussions were being conducted "probably with a view to achieving complete integration in the Army." Nevertheless, he stressed a cautionary approach because "once a step was taken it was very much harder to retract." He was particularly worried about the high percentage of black soldiers, 12.5 percent of the Army's total, compared with the percentage of Negroes in the other services. He summarized the three options still under discussion in the Department of the Army: Ridgway's call for complete integration in Korea, followed by integration of Army elements in Japan, with a 10 percent limit on black replacements; Mark Clark's proposal to ship black combat battalions to Korea to be used at the division commanders' discretion, with integration limited to combat-tested individuals and then only in support units; and, finally, the Army staff's decision to continue sending replacements for use as the Far East Command saw fit.

Commenting on the Ridgway proposal, one participant pointed out that a 10 percent limit on black replacements, even if integration spread to the European Command, would mean that the majority of the Army's Negroes would remain in the United States. Rosenberg, however, preferred the Ridgway plan. Stressing that it was an Army decision and that she was "no crusader," she nevertheless reminded Secretary Pace that the Army needed to show some progress. Rosenberg mentioned the threat of a Congress which might force more drastic measures upon the Army and pointedly offered to defer answering her many congressional inquisitors until the Army reached a decision.[17-53]

The decision was finally announced on 1 July 1951. A message went out to General Ridgway approving "deactivation of the 24th Infantry and your general plan for integration of Negroes into all units (with the temporary exception of the 40th and 45th Divisions)."[17-54] The staff wanted the move to be gradual, progressive, and secret to avoid any possible friction in the Eighth Army and to win general acceptance for integration. But it did not remain secret for long. In the face of renewed public criticism for its segregated units and after lengthy staff discussion, the Army announced the integration of the Far East Command on 26 July, the third anniversary of the Truman order.[17-55] Prominent among the critics of the Army's delay was General MacArthur, who publicly blamed President Truman for the continued segregation of his former command. The charge, following as it did the general's dismissal, was much discussed in the press and the Department of Defense. Easily disputed, it was eventually overtaken by the fact of integration.

Three problems had to be solved in carrying out the integration order. The first, inactivation of the 24th Infantry and the choice of a replacement, was quickly overcome. From the replacements suggested, Ridgway decided on the 14th Infantry, which had been recently assigned, minus men and equipment, to the Far East Command. It was filled with troops and equipment from the 34th Infantry, then training replacements in Japan. On 1 October it was assigned to the 24th's zone of responsibility in the 25th Division's line. The 24th Infantry, its men and equipment transferred to other infantry units in Korea, was inactivated on 1 October and "transferred to the control of the Department of the Army."[17-56]

The second problem, integration of units throughout the command, proved more difficult and time-consuming. Ridgway considered the need most urgent in the infantry units and wanted their integration to take precedence. The 3d Battalion of the 9th Infantry was reorganized first, many of its black members scattered throughout other infantry units in the 2d Division. But then things got out of phase. To speed the process the Army staff dropped its plan for inactivating all segregated units and decided simply to remove the designation "segregated" and assign white soldiers to formerly all-black units. Before this form of integration could take place in the 3d Battalion, 15th Infantry, the last major black infantry unit, the 64th Tank Battalion and the 58th Armored Field Artillery Battalion began the process of shifting their black troops to nearby white units. The 77th Engineer Combat Company was the last combat unit to lose the asterisk, the Army's way of designating a unit black.[17-57] The command was originally committed to an Army contingency plan that would transfer black combat troops found superfluous to the newly integrated units to service units, but this proved unnecessary. All segregated combat troops were eventually assigned to integrated combat units.[17-58]

To soften the emotional aspects of the change, troop transfers were scheduled as part of the individual soldier's normal rotation. By the end of October 1951 the Eighth Army had integrated some 75 percent of its infantry units. The process was scheduled for completion by December, but integration of the rest of its combat units and the great number of service units dragged on for another half year. It was not until May 1952 that the last divisional and nondivisional organizations were integrated.[17-59]

The third and greatest problem in the integration of the Far East Command was how to achieve a proportionate distribution of black troops throughout the command. Ridgway was under orders to maintain black strength at a maximum 12 percent except in combat infantry units, where the maximum was 10 percent. The temporary restriction on integrating the 40th and 45th Divisions and the lack of specially trained Negroes eligible for assignment to the Japan Logistical Command added to the difficulty of achieving this goal, but the basic cause of delay was the continued shipment of black troops to the Far East in excess of the prescribed percentage. During the integration period the percentage of black replacements averaged between 12.6 and 15 percent and occasionally rose above 15 percent.[17-60] Ridgway finally got permission from Washington to raise the ratio of black soldiers in his combat infantry units to 12 percent, and further relief could be expected in the coming months when the two National Guard divisions began integrating.[17-61] Still, in October 1951 the proportion of Negroes in the Eighth Army had risen to 17.6 percent, and the flow of black troops to the Far East continued unabated, threatening the success of the integration program. Ridgway repeatedly appealed for relief, having been warned by his G-1 that future black replacements must not exceed 10 percent if the integration program was to continue successfully.[17-62]

209

Ridgway was particularly concerned with the strain on his program caused by the excessive number of black combat replacements swelling the percentage of Negroes in his combat units. By September black combat strength reached 14.2 percent, far above the limits set by the Army staff. Ridgway wanted combat replacements limited to 12 percent. He also proposed that his command be allowed to request replacements by race and occupational specialty in order to provide Army headquarters with a sound basis for allotting black enlisted men to the Far East. While the Army staff promised to try to limit the number of black combat troops, it rejected the requisition scheme. Selection for occupational specialist training was not made by race, the G-1 explained, and the Army could not control the racial proportions of any particular specialty. Since the Army staff had no control over the number of Negroes in the Army, their specialties or the replacement needs of the command, no purpose would be served by granting such a request.[17-63]

Yet Ridgway's advice could not be ignored, because by year's end the whole Army had developed a vested interest in the success of integration in the Far East. The service was enjoying the praise of civil rights congressmen, much of the metropolitan press, and even some veterans' groups, such as the Amvets.[17-64] Secretary Pace was moved to call the integration of the Eighth Army a notable advance in the field of human relations.[17-65] But most of all, the Army began to experience the fruits of racial harmony. Much of the conflict and confusion among troops that characterized the first year of the war disappeared as integration spread, and senior officials commented publicly on the superior military efficiency of an integrated Army in Korea.[17-66] As for the men themselves, their attitudes were in sharp contrast to those predicted by the Army traditionalists. The conclusion of some white enlisted men, wounded and returned from Korea, were typical:

Far as I'm concerned it [integration] worked pretty good.... When it comes to life or death, race does not mean any difference.... It's like one big family.... Got a colored guy on our machine gun crew—after a while I wouldn't do without him.... Concerning combat, what I've seen, an American is an American. When we have to do something we're all the same.... Each guy is like your own brother—we treated all the same.... Had a colored platoon leader. They are as good as any people.... We [an integrated squad] had something great in common, sleeping, guarding each other—sometimes body against body as we slept in bunkers.... Takes all kinds to fight a war.[17-67]

Integration was an established fact in Korea, but the question remained: could an attitude forged in the heat of battle be sustained on the more tranquil maneuver grounds of central Europe and the American south?

COLOR GUARD, 160TH INFANTRY, KOREA, 1952.
Integration of the European and Continental Commands

Since the Army was just 12 percent Negro in September 1951, it should have been possible to solve Ridgway's problem of black overstrength simply by distributing black soldiers evenly throughout the Army. But this solution was frustrated by the segregation still in force in other commands. Organized black units in the United States were small and few in number, and black recruits who could not be used in them were shipped as replacements to the overseas commands, principally in the Far East and Europe.[17-68] Consequently, Ridgway's problem was not an isolated one; his European counterpart was operating a largely segregated command almost 13 percent black. The Army could not prevent black overstrengths so long as Negroes were ordered into the quota-free service by color-blind draft boards, but it could equalize the overstrength by integrating its forces all over the world.

This course, along with the knowledge that integration was working in the Far East and the training camps, was leading senior Army officials toward full integration. But they wanted certain reassurances. Believing that integration of the continental commands would create, in the words of the G-1, "obstacles and difficulties vastly greater than those in FECOM," the Army staff wanted these problems thoroughly analyzed before taking additional moves, "experimental or otherwise," to broaden integration.[17-69] General Collins, although personally committed to integration, voiced another widespread concern over extending integration beyond the Far East units. Unlike the Navy and the Air Force, which were able to secure more highly qualified men on a volunteer basis, the Army had long been forced to accept anyone meeting the draft's minimum standards. This circumstance was very likely to result, he feared, in an army composed to an unprecedented degree of poorly educated black soldiers, possibly as much as 30 percent in the near future.[17-70]

The Army's leaders received the necessary reassurances in the coming months. The Secretary of Defense laid to rest their fear that the draft-dependent Army would become a dumping ground for the ignorant and untrainable when, in April 1951, he directed that troops must be distributed among the services on a qualitative basis. Assistant Secretary of the Army Johnson asked Professor Eli Ginzberg, a social scientist and consultant to the Army, to explain to the Army Policy Council the need for aggressive action to end segregation.[17-71]And once again, but this time with considerable scientific detail to support its recommendations, the Project CLEAR final report told Army leaders that the service should be integrated worldwide. Again the researchers found that the Army's problem was not primarily racial, but a question of how best to use underqualified men. Refining their earlier figures, they decided that black soldiers were best used in integrated units at a ratio of 15 to 85. Integration on the job was conducive to social integration, they discovered, and social integration, dependent on several variables, was particularly amenable to firm policy guidance and local control. Finally, the report found that integration on military posts was accepted by local civilians as a military policy unlikely to affect their community.[17-72]

The Chief of Staff approved the Project CLEAR final report, although his staff had tried to distinguish between the report's view of on-the-job integration and social integration, accepting the former with little reservation, but considering the latter to be "weak in supporting evidence." The personnel staff continued to stress the need to reimpose a racial quota quickly without waiting for black enrollment to reach 15 percent as the Project CLEAR report suggested. It also believed that integration should be limited to the active federal service, exempting National Guard units under state control. General McAuliffe agreed to drop racial statistics but warned that investigation of discrimination charges depended on such statistics. He also agreed that blacks could be mixed with whites at 10 to 20 percent of the strength of any white unit, but to assign whites in similar percentages to black units "would undoubtedly present difficulties and place undue burdens on the assigned white personnel." Finally, McAuliffe stressed that commanders would have flexibility in working out the nonoperational aspects of integration so long as their methods and procedures were consistent with Army policy.[17-73]

These reservations aside, McAuliffe concluded that integration was working in enough varied circumstances to justify its extension to the entire Army. General Collins agreed, and on 29 December 1951 he ordered all major commanders to prepare integration programs for their commands. Integration was the Army's immediate goal, and, he added, it was to be progressive, in orderly stages, and without publicity.[17-74]

The Chief of Staff's decision was especially timely for the European Command where General Thomas T. Handy faced manpower problems similar to if not so critical as those in the Far East. During 1951 Army strength in Europe had also risen sharply—from 86,000 to 234,000 men. Black strength had increased even more dramatically, from 8,876 (or 11 percent) to 27,267 (or 13 percent). The majority of black soldiers in Europe served in segregated units, the number of which more than doubled because of the Korean War. From sixty-six units in June 1950, the figure rose to 139 in March 1952. Most of these units were not in divisions but in service organizations; 113 were service units, of which fifty-three were transportation units.

Again as in the Far East, some integration in Europe occurred in response to the influx of new soldiers as well as to Army directives. Handy integrated his Noncommissioned Officers' Academy in 1950 in an operation involving thousands of enlisted men. After he closed the segregated Kitzingen Training Center in February 1951, black troops were absorbed into other training and replacement centers on an integrated basis. For some time Army commanders in Europe had also been assigning certain black soldiers with specialist training to white units, a practice dramatically accelerated in 1950 when the command began receiving many Negroes with occupation specialties unneeded in black units. In March 1951 Handy directed that, while the assignment of Negroes to black units remained the first priority, Negroes possessing qualifications unusable or in excess of the needs of black units would be assigned where they could be used most effectively.[17-75] Consequently, by the end of 1951 some 7 percent of all black enlisted men, 17 percent of the black officers, and all black soldiers of the Women's Army Corps in the command were serving in integrated units.

In sharp contrast to the Far East Command, there was little support among senior Army officials in Europe for full integration. Sent by Assistant Secretary Johnson to brief European commanders on the Army's decision, Eli Ginzberg met with almost universal skepticism. Most commanders were unaware of the Army's success with integration in the Far East and in the training divisions at home; when so informed they were quick to declare such a move impractical for Europe. They warned of the social problems that would arise with the all-white civilian population and predicted that the Army would be forced to abandon the program in midstream.[17-76]

There were exceptions. Lt. Gen. Manton S. Eddy, the commander of the Seventh Army, described the serious operational problems caused by segregation in his command. Most of his black units were unsatisfactory, and without minimizing the difficulties he concluded in 1951 that integration was desirable not only for the sake of his own mission but for the Army's efficiency and the nation's world leadership. Officers at Headquarters, Supreme Allied Powers, Europe, also recited personnel and training problems caused in their command by segregation, but here, Ginzberg noted, the attitude was one of cautious silence, an attitude that made little difference because General Eisenhower's command was an international organization having nothing to do with the Army's race policies. It would, however, be of some interest during the 1952 political campaign when some commentators made the false claim that Eisenhower had integrated American units in Europe.[17-77]

Obviously it was going to take more than a visit from Ginzberg to move the European Command's staff, and later in the year Collins took the matter up personally with Handy. This consultation, and a series of exchanges between McAuliffe and command officials, led Collins to ask Handy to submit an integration plan as quickly as possible.[17-78] Handy complied with a proposal that failed on the whole to conform to the Army's current plans for worldwide integration and was quickly amended in Washington. The European Command would not, Collins decreed, conduct a special screening of its black officers and noncoms for fitness for combat duty. The command would not retain segregated service units, although the Army would allow an extension of the program's timetable to accomplish the integration of these units. Finally, the command would stage no publicity campaign but would instead proceed quietly and routinely. The program was to begin in April 1952.[17-79]

Integration of the European Command proceeded without incident, but the administrative task was complicated and frequently delayed by the problem of black overstrength. Handy directed that Negroes be assigned as individuals in a 1 to 10 ratio in all units although he would tolerate a higher ratio in service and temporary duty units during the early stages of the program.[17-80] This figure was adjusted upward the following year to a maximum of 12 percent black for armor and infantry units, 15 percent for combat engineers and artillery, and 17.5 percent for all other units. During the process of integrating the units, a 25 percent black strength was authorized.[17-81]

The ratios were raised because the percentage of Negroes in the command continued to exceed the 1 to 10 ratio and was still increasing. In September 1953 the new commander, General Alfred M. Gruenther, tried to slow the rate of increase.[17-82] He got Washington to halt the shipment of black units, and he himself instituted stricter reenlistment standards in Europe. Finally, he warned that with fewer segregated units to which black troops might be assigned, the racial imbalance was becoming more critical, and he asked for a deferment of the program's completion.[17-83] The Army staff promised to try to alleviate the racial disproportions in the replacement stream, but asked Gruenther to proceed as quickly as possible with integration.[17-84]

There was little the Army staff could do. The continental commands had the same overstrength problem, and the staff considered the European Command an inappropriate place to raise black percentages. By mid-1953 Negroes accounted for some 16 percent of Army personnel in Europe and, more important to the command, the number of Negroes with combat occupation specialties continued to increase at the same rate. As an alternative to the untenable practice of reclassifying combat-trained men for noncombat assignments purely on account of race, Gruenther again raised the acceptable ratio of blacks in combat units. At the same time he directed the Seventh Army commander to treat ratios in the future merely as guidelines, to be adhered to as circumstances permitted.[17-85] The percentage of Negroes in the command leveled off at this time, but not before the black proportion of the command's transportation units reached 48.8 percent. Summing up his command's policy on integration, Gruenther concluded: "I cannot permit the assignment of large numbers of unqualified personnel, regardless of race, to prejudice the operation readiness of our units in an effort to attain 100 percent racial integration, however desirable that goal may be."[17-86] A heavy influx of white replacements with transportation specialties allowed the European Command to finish integrating the elements of the Seventh Army in July 1954.[17-87] The last black unit in the command, the 94th Engineer Battalion, was inactivated in November.

Integration of black troops in Europe proved successful on several counts, with the Army, in Assistant Secretary Fred Korth's words, "achieving benefits therefrom substantially greater than we had anticipated at its inception."[17-88] The command's combat readiness increased, he claimed, while its racial incidents and disciplinary problems declined. The reaction of the soldiers was, again in Korth's words, "generally good" with incidents stemming from integration "fewer and much farther between." Moreover, the program had been a definite advantage in

212

counteracting Communist propaganda, with no evidence of problems with civilians arising from social integration. More eloquent testimony to the program's success appeared in the enthusiasm of the European Command's senior officials.[17-89] Their fears and uncertainties eased, they abruptly reversed their attitudes and some even moved from outright opposition to praise for the program as one of their principal achievements.

The smaller overseas commands also submitted plans to Army headquarters for the breakup of their segregated units in 1951, and integration of the Alaskan Command and the rest proceeded during 1952 without incident.[17-90] At the same time the continental Army commands, faced with similar manpower problems, began making exceptions, albeit considerably more timidly than the great overseas commands, to the assignment of Negroes to black units. As early as September 1951 the Army G-1 discovered instances of unauthorized integration in every Army area,[17-91] the result of either unrectified administrative errors or the need to find suitable assignments for black replacements. "The concern shown by you over the press reaction to integrating these men into white units," the Sixth Army commander, Lt. Gen. Joseph M. Swing, reported to the Army staff, "causes me to guess that your people may not realize the extent to which integration has already progressed—at least in the Sixth Army."[17-92] Swing concluded that gradual integration had to be the solution to the Army's race problems everywhere. McAuliffe agreed with Swing that the continental commands should be gradually integrated, but, as he put it, "the difficulty is that my superiors are not prepared to admit that we are already launched on a progressive integration program" in the United States. The whole problem was a very touchy one, McAuliffe added.[17-93]

The Army staff had agreed to halt the further integration of units in the United States until the results of the overseas changes had been carefully analyzed. Nevertheless, even while the integration of the Far East forces was proceeding, General McAuliffe's office prepared a comprehensive two-phase plan for the integration of the continental armies. It would consolidate all temporary units then separated into racial elements, redistributing all Negroes among the organized white units; then, Negroes assigned to black components of larger white units would be absorbed into similar white units through normal attrition or by concentrated levies on the black units. McAuliffe estimated that the whole process would take two years.[17-94]

VISIT WITH THE COMMANDER.
Soldiers of the Ordnance Branch, Berlin Command, meet with Brig. Gen. Charles F. Craig.

McAuliffe's plan was put into effect when General Collins ordered worldwide integration in December 1952. The breakdown of the "10 percent Army" proceeded uneventfully, and the old black units disappeared. The 9th and 10th Cavalry Regiments, now converted into the 509th and 510th Tank Battalions (Negro), received white replacements and dropped the racial designation. The 25th Infantry, now broken down into smaller units, was integrated in September 1952. On 12 October 1953 Assistant Secretary of Defense John Hannah announced that 95 percent of the Army's Negroes were serving in integrated units with the rest to be so assigned not later than June 1954.[17-95] His estimate was off by several months. The European Command's 94th Engineer Battalion, the last major all-black unit, was inactivated in November 1954, several weeks after the Secretary of Defense had announced the end of all segregated units.[17-96]

BROTHERS UNDER THE SKIN,
inductees at Fort Sam Houston, Texas, 1953.

Like a man who discovers that his profitable deeds are also virtuous, the Army discussed its new racial policy with considerable pride. From company commander to general officer the report was that the Army worked better, integration was desirable, and despite all predictions to the contrary, it was a success. Military commentators in and out of uniform stoutly defended the new system against its few critics.[17-97] Most pointed to Korea as the proving ground for the new policy. Assistant Secretary of Defense Hannah generalized about the change to integration: "Official analyses and reports indicate a definite increase in combat effectiveness in the overseas areas.... From experience in Korea and elsewhere, Army commanders have determined, also, that more economical and effective results accrue from the policies which remove duplicate facilities and operations based upon race."[17-98] The Army, it would seem, had made a complete about-face in its argument from efficiency.

But integration did more than demonstrate a new form of military efficiency. It also stilled several genuine fears long entertained by military leaders. Many thoughtful officials had feared that the social mingling that would inevitably accompany integration in the continental United States might lead to racial incidents and a breakdown in discipline. The new policy seemed to prove this fear groundless.[17-99] A 1953 Army-sponsored survey reported that, with the single major exception of racially separate dances for enlisted men at post-operated service clubs on

213

southern bases, segregation involving uniformed men and women now stopped at the gates of the military reservation.[17-100] Army headquarters, carefully monitoring the progress of social integration, found it without incident.[17-101] At the same time the survey revealed that some noncommissioned officers' clubs and enlisted men's clubs tended to segregate themselves, but no official notice was taken of this tendency, and not one such instance was a source of racial complaint in 1953. The survey also discovered that racial attitudes in adjacent communities had surprisingly little influence on the relations between white and black soldiers on post. Nor was there evidence of any appreciable resentment toward integration on the part of white civilian employees, even when they worked with or under black officers and enlisted men.

The on-post dance, a valuable morale builder, was usually restricted to one race because commanders were afraid of arousing antagonism in nearby communities. But even here restrictions were not uniform. Mutual use of dance floors by white and black couples was frequent though not commonplace and was accepted in officers' clubs, many noncommissioned officers' clubs, and at special unit affairs. The rules for social integration were flexible, and many adjustments could be made to the sentiments of the community if the commander had the will and the tact. Some commanders, unaware of what was being accomplished by progressive colleagues, were afraid to establish a precedent, and often avoided practices that were common elsewhere. Social scientists reviewing the situation suggested that the Army should acquaint the commanders with the existing wide range of social possibilities.

Fear of congressional disapproval, another reason often given for deferring integration, was exaggerated, as a meeting between Senator Richard B. Russell and James Evans in early 1952 demonstrated. At the request of the manpower secretary, Evans went to Capitol Hill to inform the chairman of the Armed Services Committee that for reasons of military efficiency the Army was going to integrate. Senator Russell observed that he had been unable to do some things he wanted to do "because your people [black voters] weren't strong enough politically to support me." Tell the secretary, Russell added, "that I won't help him integrate, but I won't hinder him either—and neither will anyone else."[17-102] The senator was true to his word. News of the Army's integration program passed quietly through the halls of Congress without public or private protest.

Much opposition to integration was based on the fear that low-scoring black soldiers, handicapped by deficiencies in schooling and training, would weaken integrated units as they had the all-black units. But integration proved to be the best solution. As one combat commander put it, "Mix 'um up and you get a strong line all the way; segregate 'um and you have a point of weakness in your line. The enemy hits you there, and it's bug out."[17-103] Korea taught the Army that an integrated unit was not as weak as its weakest men, but as strong as its leadership and training. Integration not only diluted the impact of the less qualified by distributing them more widely, but also brought about measurable improvement in the performance and standards of a large number of black soldiers.

Closely related to the concern over the large number of ill-qualified soldiers was the fear of the impact of integration on a quota-free Army. The Project CLEAR team concluded that a maximum of 15 to 20 percent black strength "seems to be an effective interim working level."[17-104] General McAuliffe pointed out in November 1952 that he was trying to maintain a balanced distribution of black troops, not only geographically but also according to combat and service specialties (*see Tables 9 and 10*). Collins decided to retain the ceiling on black combat troops—no more than 12 percent in any combat unit—but he agreed that a substantially higher percentage was acceptable in all other units.[17-105]

TABLE 9—WORLDWIDE DISTRIBUTION OF ENLISTED PERSONNEL BY RACE, OCTOBER 1952

(In Thousands)

Category	European Command	Far East Command	
White	212.1	293.1	
Black	35.6	41.5	
Total	247.7	334.6	
Percent black	14.4	12.4	

Tablenote a: Restrictions remained in effect on the assignment of Negroes to certain stations in USARPAC, TRUST, and USARCARIB.

Source: Memo, Chief, Per and Dist Br, G-1, for ACofS, G-1, 8 Oct 52, sub: Distribution of Negro Enlisted Personnel, G-1, 291.2.

TABLE 10—DISTRIBUTION OF BLACK ENLISTED PERSONNEL BY BRANCH AND RANK, 31 OCTOBER 1952

214

Branch	
Armor	
Artillery	
Infantry	
Adjutant General's Corps	
Chemical Corps	
Corps of Engineers	
Military Police Corps	
Finance Corps	
Army Medical Service	
Ordnance Corps	
Quartermaster Corps	
Signal Corps	
Transportation Corps	
Women's Army Corps	
No Branch assignment[a]	
Total	1

Tablenote a: In training.

Tablenote b: Figures show black percentage of total Army enlistments.

Tablenote c: Discrepancy with Table 9, which is based on September figures.

Source: STM-30, 31 Oct 52.

These percentages were part of a larger concern over the number of Negroes in the Army as a whole. Based on the evidence of draft-swollen enlistment statistics, it seemed likely that the 15 to 20 percent figure would be reached or surpassed in 1953 or 1954, and there was some discussion in the staff about restoring the quota. But such talk quickly faded as the Korean War wound down and the percentage declined. Negroes constituted 14.4 percent of enlisted strength in December 1952 and leveled off by the summer of 1955 at 11.9 percent. Statistics for the European Command illustrated the trend. In June 1955, Negroes accounted for 3.6 percent of the command's officer strength and 11.4 percent of its enlisted strength. The enlisted figure represents a drop from a high of 16.1 percent in June 1953. The percentage of black troops was down to 11.2 percent of the command's total strength—officers, warrant officers, and enlisted men—by June 1956. The reduction is explained in part by a policy adopted by all commands in February 1955 of refusing, with certain exceptions, to reenlist three-year veterans who scored less than ninety in the classification tests. In Europe alone some 5,300 enlisted men were not permitted to reenlist in 1955. Slightly more than 25 percent were black.[17-106]

The racial quota, in the guise of an "acceptable" percentage of Negroes in individual units, continued to operate long after the Army agreed to abandon it. No one, black or white, appears to have voiced in the early 1950's the logical observation that the establishment of a racial quota in individual Army units—whatever the percentage and the grounds for that percentage—was in itself a residual form of discrimination. Nor did anyone ask how establishing a race quota, clearly distinct from restricting men according to mental, moral, or professional standards, could achieve the "effective working level" posited by the Army's scientific advisers.

These questions would still be pertinent years later because the alternative to the racial quota—the enlistment and assignment of men without regard for color—would continue to be unacceptable to many. They would argue that to abandon the quota, as the services did in the 1960's, was to violate the concept of racial balance, which is yet another hallmark of an egalitarian society. For example, during the Vietnam War some black Americans complained that too many Negroes were serving in the more dangerous combat arms. Since men were assigned without regard to race, these critics were in effect asking for the quota again, reminding the service that the population of the United States was only some 11 percent black. And during discussions of the all-volunteer Army a decade later, critics would be asking how the white majority would react to an army 30 or even 50 percent black.

These considerations were clearly beyond the ken of the men who integrated the Army in the early 1950's. They concentrated instead on the perplexities of enlisting and assigning vast numbers of segregated black soldiers during wartime and closely watched the combat performance of black units in Korea. Integration provided the Army with a way to fill its depleted combat units quickly. The shortage of white troops forced local commanders to turn to the growing surplus of black soldiers awaiting assignment to a limited number of black units. Manpower restrictions did not permit the formation of new black units merely to accommodate the excess, and in any case experience with the 24th Infantry had strengthened the Army staff's conviction that black combat units did not perform well. However commanders may have felt about the social implications of integration, and whatever they thought of the fighting ability of black units, the only choice left to them was integration. When the Chief of Staff ordered the integration of the Far East Command in 1951, what had begun as a battlefield expedient became official policy.

Segregation became unworkable when the Army lost its power to limit the number of black soldiers. Abandonment of the quota on enlistments, pressed on the Army by the Fahy Committee, proved compatible with segregated units only so long as the need for fighting men was not acute. In Korea the need became acute. Ironically, the Gillem Board, whose work became anathema to the integrationists, accurately predicted the demise of segregation in its final report, which declared that in the event of another major war the Army would use its manpower "without regard to antecedents or race."

CHAPTER 18
Integration of the Marine Corps

Even more so than in the Army, the history of racial equality in the Marine Corps demonstrates the effect of the exigencies of war on the integration of the armed forces. The Truman order, the Fahy Committee, even the demands of civil rights leaders and the mandates of the draft law, all exerted pressure for reform and assured the presence of some black marines. But the Marine Corps was for years able to stave off the logical outcome of such pressures, and in the end it was the manpower demands of the Korean War that finally brought integration.

In the first place the Korean War caused a sudden and dramatic rise in the number of black marines: from 1,525 men, almost half of them stewards, in May 1949, to some 17,000 men, only 500 of them serving in separate stewards duty, in October 1953.[18-1] Whereas the careful designation of a few segregated service units sufficed to handle the token black representation in 1949, no such organization was possible in 1952, when thousands of black marines on active duty constituted more than 5 percent of the total enlistment. The decision to integrate the new black marines throughout the corps was the natural outcome of the service's early experiences in Korea. Ordered to field a full division, the corps out of necessity turned to the existing black service units, among others, for men to augment the peacetime strength of its combat units. These men were assigned to any unit in the Far East that needed them. As the need for more units and replacements grew during the war, newly enlisted black marines were more and more often pressed into integrated service both in the Far East and at home.

Most significantly, the war provided a rising generation of Marine Corps officers with a first combat experience with black marines. The competence of these Negroes and the general absence of racial tension during their integration destroyed long accepted beliefs to the contrary and opened the way for general integration. Although the corps continued to place special restrictions on the employment of Negroes and was still wrestling with the problem of black stewards well into the next decade, its basic policy of segregating marines by race ended with the cancellation of the last all-black unit designation in 1951. Hastily embraced by the corps as a solution to a pressing manpower problem, integration was finally accepted as a permanent manpower policy.

Impetus for Change

This transformation seemed remote in 1949 in view of Commandant Clifton B. Cates's strong defense of segregation. At that time Cates made a careful distinction between allocating men to the services without regard to race, which he supported, and ordering integration of the services themselves. "Changing national policy in this respect through the Armed Forces," he declared, "is a dangerous path to pursue inasmuch as it effects [sic] the ability of the National Military Establishment to fulfill its mission."[18-2] Integration of the services had to follow, not precede, integration of American society.

The commandant's views were spelled out in a series of decisions announced by the corps in the wake of the Secretary of the Navy's call for integration of all elements of the Navy Department in 1949. On 18 November 1949 the corps' Acting Chief of Staff announced a new racial policy: individual black marines would be assigned in accordance with their specialties to vacancies "in any unit where their services can be effectively utilized," but segregated black units would be retained and new ones created when appropriate in the regular and reserve components of the corps. In the case of the reserve component, the decision on the acceptance of an applicant was vested in the unit commander.[18-3] On the same day the commandant made it

216

clear that the policy was not to be interpreted too broadly. Priority for the assignment of individual black marines, Cates informed the commander of the Pacific Department, would be given to the support establishment and black officers would be assigned to black units only.[18-4]

Further limiting the chances that black marines would be integrated, Cates approved the creation of four new black units. The Director of Personnel and the Marine Quartermaster had opposed this move on the grounds that the new units would require technical billets, particularly in the supply specialties, which would be nearly impossible to fill with available enlisted black marines. Either school standards would have to be lowered or white marines would have to be assigned to the units. Cates met this objection by agreeing with the Director of Plans and Policies that no prohibition existed against racial mixing in a unit during a period of on-the-job training. The Director of Personnel would decide when a unit was sufficiently trained and properly manned to be officially designated a black organization.[18-5] In keeping with this arrangement, for example, the commanding general of the 2d Marine Division reported in February 1950 that his black marines were sufficiently trained to assume complete operation of the depot platoon within the division's service command. Cates then designated the platoon as a unit suitable for general duty black marines, which prompted the Coordinator of Enlisted Personnel to point out that current regulations stipulated "after a unit has been so designated, all white enlisted personnel will be withdrawn and reassigned."[18-6]

Nor were there any plans for the general integration of black reservists, although some Negroes were serving in formerly all-white units. The 9th Infantry Battalion, for instance, had a black lieutenant. As the assistant commandant, Maj. Gen. Oliver P. Smith, put it on 4 January 1950, black units would be formed "in any area where there is an expressed interest" provided that the black population was large enough to support it.[18-7] When the NAACP objected to the creation of another all-black reserve unit in New York City as being contrary to Defense Department policy, the Marine Corps justified it on the grounds that the choice of integrated or segregated units must be made by the local community "in accord with its cultural values."[18-8] Notwithstanding the Secretary of the Navy's integration order and assignment policies directed toward effective utilization, it appeared that the Marine Corps in early 1950 was determined to retain its system of racially segregated units indefinitely.

But the corps failed to reckon with the consequences of the war that broke out suddenly in Korea in June. Two factors connected with that conflict caused an abrupt change in Marine race policy. The first was the great influx of Negroes into the corps. Although the commandant insisted that race was not considered in recruitment, and in fact recruitment instructions since 1948 contained no reference to the race of applicants, few Negroes had joined the Marine Corps in the two years preceding the war.[18-9] In its defense the corps pointed to its exceedingly small enlistment quotas during those years and its high enlistment standards, which together allowed recruiters to accept only a few men. The classification test average for all recruits enlisted in 1949 was 108, while the average for black enlistees during the same period was 94.7. New black recruits were almost exclusively enlisted for stewards duty.[18-10]

A revision of Defense Department manpower policy combined with the demands of the war to change all that. The imposition of a qualitative distribution of manpower by the Secretary of Defense in April 1950 meant that among the thousands of recruits enlisted during the Korean War the Marine Corps would have to accept its share of the large percentage of men in lower classification test categories. Among these men were a significant number of black enlistees who had failed to qualify under previous standards. They were joined by thousands more who were supplied through the nondiscriminatory process of the Selective Service System when, during the war, the corps began using the draft. The result was a 100 percent jump in the number of black marines in the first year of war, a figure that would be multiplied almost six times before war inductions ran down in 1953. (*Table 11*)

TABLE 11—BLACK MARINES, 1949-1955

Date	Officers	
July 1949	0	
July 1950	0	
January 1951	2	
July 1951	3	
January 1952	3	
July 1952	NA	
January 1953	10	
July 1953	13	

217

November 1953	18	
June 1954	19	
January 1955	19	

A second factor forcing a change in racial policy was the manpower demands imposed upon the corps by the war itself. When General MacArthur called for the deployment of a Marine regimental combat team and supporting air group on 2 July 1950, the Secretary of the Navy responded by sending the 1st Provisional Marine Brigade, which included the 5th Marine Regiment, the 1st Battalion of the 11th Marines (Artillery), and Marine Air Group 33. By 13 September the 1st Marine Division and the 1st Marine Air Wing at wartime strength had been added. Fielding these forces placed an enormous strain on the corps' manpower, and one result was the assignment of a number of black service units, often combined with white units in composite organizations, to the combat units.

The pressures of battle quickly altered this neat arrangement. Theoretically, every marine was trained as an infantryman, and when shortages occurred in combat units commanders began assigning black replacements where needed. For example, as the demand for more marines for the battlefield grew, the Marine staff began to pull black marines from routine duties at the Marine Barracks in New Jersey, Pennsylvania, and Hawaii and send them to Korea to bring the fighting units up to full strength. The first time black servicemen were integrated as individuals in significant numbers under combat conditions was in the 1st Provisional Marine Brigade during the fighting in the Pusan Perimeter in August 1950. The assignment of large numbers of black marines throughout the combat units of the 1st Marine Division, beginning in September, provided the clearest instance of a service abandoning a social policy in response to the demands of the battlefield. The 7th Marines, for example, an organic element of the 1st Marine Division since August 1950, received into its rapidly expanding ranks, along with many recalled white reservists and men from small, miscellaneous Marine units, a 54-man black service unit. The regimental commander immediately broke up the black unit, assigning the men individually throughout his combat battalions.

That the emergency continued to influence the placement of Negroes is apparent from the distribution of black marines in March 1951, when almost half were assigned to combat duty in integrated units.[18-11] Before the war was over, the 1st Marine Division had several thousand black marines, serving in its ranks in Korea, where they were assigned to infantry and signal units as well as to transportation and food supply organizations. One of the few black reserve officers on active duty found himself serving as an infantry platoon commander in Company B of the division's 7th Marines.

The shift to integration in Korea proved uneventful. In the words of the 7th Marines commander: "Never once did any color problem bother us.... It just wasn't any problem. We had one Negro sergeant in command of an all-white squad and there was another—with a graves registration unit—who was one of the finest Marines I've ever seen."[18-12] Serving for the first time in integrated units, Negroes proceeded to perform in a way that not only won many individuals decorations for valor but also won the respect of commanders for Negroes as fighting men. Reminiscing about the performance of black marines in his division, Lt. Gen. Oliver P. Smith remembered "they did everything, and they did a good job because they were integrated, and they were with good people."[18-13] In making his point the division commander contrasted the performance of his integrated men with the Army's segregated 24th Infantry. The observations of field commanders, particularly the growing opinion that a connection existed between good performance and integration, were bound to affect the deliberations of the Division of Plans and Policies when it began to restudy the question of black assignments in the fall of 1951.

As a result of the division's study, the Commandant of the Marine Corps announced a general policy of racial integration on 13 December 1951, thus abolishing the system first introduced in 1942 of designating certain units in the regular forces and organized reserves as black units.[18-14] He spelled out the new order in some detail on 18 December, and although his comments were addressed to the commanders in the Fleet Marine Force, they were also forwarded to various commands in the support establishment that still retained all-black units. The order indicated that the practices now so commonplace in Korea were about to become the rule in the United States.[18-15] Some six months later the commandant informed the Chief of Naval Personnel that the Marine Corps had no segregated units and while integration had been gradual "it was believed to be an accomplished fact at this time."[18-16]

MARINES ON THE KANSAS LINE, KOREA.
Men of the 1st Marines await word to move out.

The change was almost immediately apparent in other parts of the corps, for black marines were also integrated in units serving with the fleet. Reporting on a Mediterranean tour of the 3d Battalion, 6th Marines (Reinforced), from 17 April to 20 October 1952, Capt. Thomas L. Faix, a member of the unit, noted: "We have about fifteen Negro marines in our unit now, out of fifty men. We have but very little trouble and they sleep, eat and go on liberty together. It would be hard for many to believe but the thought is that here in the service all are facing a common call or summons to service regardless of color."[18-17] Finally, in August 1953, Lt. Gen. Gerald C. Thomas, who framed the postwar segregation policy, announced that "integration of Negroes in the Corps is here to stay. Colored boys are in almost every military occupation specialty and certainly in every enlisted rank. I believe integration is satisfactory to them, and it is satisfactory to us."[18-18]

MARINE REINFORCEMENTS.
A light machine gun squad of 3d Battalion, 1st Marines, arrives during the battle for "Boulder City."

Assignments

The 1951 integration order ushered in a new era in the long history of the Marine Corps, but despite the abolition of segregated units, the new policy did not bring about completely unrestricted employment of Negroes throughout the corps. The commandant had retained the option to employ black marines "where their services can be effectively utilized," and in the years after the Korean War it became apparent that the corps recognized definite limits to the kinds of duty to which black marines could be assigned. Following standard assignment procedures, the Department of Personnel's Detail Branch selected individual staff noncommissioned officers for specific duty billets. After screening the records of a marine and considering his race, the branch could reject the assignment of a Negro to a billet for any reason "of overriding interest to the Marine Corps."[18-19]

By the same token, the assignment of marines in the lower ranks was left to the individual commands, which filled quotas established by headquarters. Commanders usually filled the quotas from among eligible men longest on station, but whether or not Negroes were included in a transfer quota was left entirely to the discretion of the local commander. The Department of Personnel reserved the right, however, to make one racial distinction in regard to bulk quotas: it regulated the number of black marines it took from recruit depots as replacements, as insurance against a "disproportionate" number of Negroes in combat units. Under the screening procedures of Marine headquarters and unit commanders, black enlisted men were excluded from assignment to reserve officer training units, recruiting stations, the State Department for duty at embassies and legations, and certain special duties of the Department of Defense and the Navy Department.[18-20]

For the service to reserve the right to restrict the assignment of Negroes when it was of "overriding interest to the Marine Corps" was perhaps understandable, but it was also susceptible to considerable misinterpretation if not outright abuse. The Personnel Department was "constantly" receiving requests from commanders that no black noncoms be assigned to their units. While some of these requests seemed reasonable, the chief of the division's Detail Branch noted, others were not. Commanders of naval prison retraining centers did not want black noncommissioned officers assigned because, they claimed, Negroes caused unrest among the prisoners. The Marine Barracks in Washington, D.C., where the commandant lived, did not want black marines because of the ceremonial nature of its mission. The Marine Barracks at Dahlgren, Virginia, did not want Negroes because conflicts might arise with civilian employees in cafeterias and movies. Other commanders questioned the desirability of assigning black marines to the Naval Academy, to inspector-instructor billets in the clerical and supply fields, and to billets for staff chauffeurs. The Detail Branch wanted a specific directive that listed commands to which black marines should not be assigned.[18-21]

Restrictions on the assignment of black marines were never codified, but the justification for them changed. In place of the "overriding interest to the Marine Corps" clause, the corps began to speak of restrictions "solely for the welfare of the individual Marine." In 1955 the Director of Personnel, Maj. Gen. Robert O. Bare, pointed to the unusually severe hardships imposed on Negroes in some communities where the attitude toward black marines sometimes interfered with their performance of duty. Since civilian pressures could not be recognized officially, Bare reasoned, they had to be dealt with informally on a person-to-person basis.[18-22] By this statement he meant the Marine Corps would informally exclude Negroes from certain assignments. Of course no one explained how barring Negroes from assignment to recruitment, inspector-instructor, embassy, or even chauffeur duty worked for "the welfare of the individual Marine." Such an explanation was just what Congressman Powell was demanding in January 1958 when he asked why black marines were excluded from assignments to the American Embassy in Paris.[18-23]

Community attitudes toward Negroes in uniform had become a serious matter in all the services by the late 1950's, and concern for the welfare of black marines was repeatedly voiced by Marine commanders in areas as far-flung as Nevada, Florida, and southern California.[18-24] But even here there was reason to question the motives of some local commanders, for during a lengthy discussion in the Personnel Department some officials asserted that the available evidence indicated no justification for restricting assignments. Anxiety over assignments anywhere in the United States was unfounded, they claimed, and offered in support statistics demonstrating the existence of a substantial black community in all the duty areas from which Negroes were unofficially excluded. The Assignment and Classification Branch also pointed out that the corps had experienced no problems in the case of the thirteen black marines then assigned to inspector-instructor duty, including one in Mobile, Alabama. The branch went on to discuss the possibility of assigning black marines to recruiting duty. Since recruiters were assigned to areas where they understood local attitudes and customs, some officials reasoned, Negroes should be used to promote the corps among potential black enlistees whose feelings and attitudes were not likely to be understood by white recruiters.

These matters were never considered officially by the Marine Corps staff, and as of 1960 the Inspector General was still keeping a list of stations to which Negroes would not be assigned. But the picture quickly changed in the next year, and by June 1962 all restrictions on the assignment of black marines had been dropped with the exception of several installations in the United States where off-base housing was unavailable and some posts overseas where the use of black marines was limited because of the attitudes of foreign governments.[18-25]

TRAINING EXERCISES
on Iwo Jima, March 1954.

The perennial problem of an all-black Steward's Branch persisted into the 1960's. Stewards served a necessary though unglamorous function in the Marine Corps, and education standards for such duty were considerably lower than those for the rest of the service. Everyone understood this, and beyond the stigma many young people felt was attached to such duties, many Negroes particularly resented the fact that while the branch was officially open to all, somehow none of the less gifted whites ever joined. Stewards were acquired either by recruiting new marines with stewards-duty-only contracts or by accepting volunteers from the general service. The evidence suggests that there was truth in the commonly held assumption among stewards that when a need for more stewards arose, "volunteers" were secured by tampering with the classification test scores of men in the general service.[18-26]

The commandant seemed less concerned with methods than results when stewards were needed. In June 1950 he had reaffirmed the policy of allowing stewards to reenlist for general duty, but when he learned that some stewards had made the jump to general duty without being qualified, he announced that men who had signed contracts for stewards duty only were not acceptable for general duty unless they scored at least in the 31st percentile of the qualifying tests. To make the change to general duty even less attractive, he ruled that if a steward reenlisted for general duty he would have to revert to the rank of private, first class.[18-27] Such measures did nothing to improve the morale of black stewards, many of whom, according to civil rights critics, felt confined forever to performing menial tasks, nor did it prevent constant shortages in the Steward's Branch and problems arising from the lack of men with training in modern mess management.

The corps tried to attack these problems in the mid-1950's. At the behest of the Secretary of the Navy it eliminated the stewards-duty-only contract in 1954; henceforth all marines were enlisted for general duty, and only after recruit training could volunteers sign up for stewards duty. Acceptance of men scoring below ninety in the classification tests would be limited to 40 percent of those volunteering each month for stewards duty.[18-28] The corps also instituted special training in modern mess management for stewards. In 1953 the Quartermaster General had created an inspection and demonstration team composed of senior stewards to instruct members of the branch in the latest techniques of cooking and baking, supervision, and management.[18-29] In August 1954 the commandant established an advanced twelve-week course for stewards based on the Navy's successful system.

MARINES FROM CAMP LEJEUNE ON THE USS VALLEY FORGE
for training exercises, 1958.

These measures, however, did nothing to cure the chronic shortage of men and the attendant problems of increased work load and low morale that continued to plague the

220

Steward's Branch throughout the 1950's. Consequently, the corps still found it difficult to attract enough black volunteers to the branch. In 1959, for example, the branch was still 8 percent short of its 826-man goal.[18-30] The obvious solution, to use white volunteers for messman duty, would be a radical departure from tradition. True, before World War II white marines had been used in the Marine Corps for duties now performed by black stewards, but they had never been members of a branch organized exclusively for that purpose. In 1956 tradition was broken when white volunteers were quietly signed up for the branch. By March 1961 the branch had eighty white men, 10 percent of its total. Reviewing the situation later that year, the commandant decided to increase the number of white stewards by setting a racial quota on steward assignment. Henceforth, he ordered, half the volunteers accepted for stewards duty would be white.[18-31]

COLONEL PETERSEN
(1968 photograph).

The new policy made an immediate difference. In less than two months the Steward's Branch was 20 percent white. In marked contrast to the claims of Navy recruiters, the marines reported no difficulty in attracting white volunteers for messman duties. Curiously, the volunteers came mostly from the southeastern states. As the racial composition of the Steward's Branch changed, the morale of its black members seemed to improve. As one senior black warrant officer later explained, simply opening stewards duty to whites made such duty acceptable to many Negroes who had been prone to ask "if it [stewards duty] was so good, why don't you have some of the whites in it."[18-32] When transfer to general service assignments became easy to obtain in the 1960's, the Marine Corps found that only a small percentage of the black stewards now wished to make the change.

There were still inequities in the status of black marines, especially the near absence of black officers (two on active duty in 1950, nineteen in January 1955) and the relatively slow rate of promotion among black marines in general. The corps had always justified its figures on the grounds that competition in so small a service was extremely fierce, and, as the commandant explained to Walter White in 1951, a man had to be good to compete and outstanding to be promoted. He cited the 1951 selection figures for officer training: out of 2,025 highly qualified men applying, only half were selected and only half of those were commissioned.[18-33] Promotion to senior billets for noncommissioned officers was also highly competitive, with time in service an important factor. It was unlikely in such circumstances that many black marines would be commissioned from the ranks or a higher percentage of black noncommissioned officers would be promoted to the most senior positions during the 1950's.[18-34] The Marine Corps had begun commissioning Negroes so recently that the development of a representative group of black officers in a system of open competition was of necessity a slow and arduous task. The task was further complicated because most of the nineteen black officers on active duty in 1955 were reservists serving out tours begun in the Korean War. Only a few of them had made the successful switch from reserve to regular service. The first two were 2d Lt. Frank E. Petersen, Jr., the first black Marine pilot, and 2d Lt. Kenneth H. Berthoud, Jr., who first served as a tank officer in the 3d Marine Division. Both men would advance to high rank in the corps, Petersen becoming the first black marine general.

SERGEANT MAJOR HUFF

As for the noncommissioned officers, there were a number of senior enlisted black marines in the 1950's, many of them holdovers from the World War II era, and Negroes were being promoted to the ranks of corporal and sergeant in appreciable numbers.

But the tenfold increase in the number of black marines during the Korean War caused the ratio of senior black noncommissioned officers to black marines to drop. Here again promotion to higher rank was slow. The first black marine to make the climb to the top in the integrated corps was Edgar R. Huff. A gunnery sergeant in an integrated infantry battalion in Korea, Huff later became battalion sergeant major in the 8th Marines and eventually senior sergeant major of the Marine Corps.[18-35]

By 1962 there were 13,351 black enlisted men, 7.59 percent of the corps' strength, and 34 black officers (7 captains, 25 lieutenants, and 2 warrant officers) serving in integrated units in all military occupations. These statistics illustrate the racial progress that occurred in the Marine Corps during the 1950's, a change that was both orderly and permanent, and, despite the complicated forces at work, in essence a gift to the naval establishment from the Korean battlefield.

CHAPTER 19

221

On 30 October 1954 the Secretary of Defense announced that the last racially segregated unit in the armed forces of the United States had been abolished.[19-1] Considering the department's very conservative definition of a segregated unit—one at least 50 percent black—the announcement celebrated a momentous change in policy. In the little more than six years since President Truman's order, all black servicemen, some quarter of a million in 1954, had been intermingled with whites in the nation's military units throughout the world. For the services the turbulent era of integration had begun.

The new era's turbulence was caused in part by the decade-long debate that immediately ensued over the scope of President Truman's guarantee of equal treatment and opportunity for servicemen. On one side were ranged most service officials, who argued that integration, now a source of pride to the services and satisfaction to the civil rights movement, had ceased to be a public issue. Abolishing segregated units, they claimed, fulfilled the essential elements of the executive order, leaving the armed forces only rare vestiges of discrimination to correct. Others, at first principally the civil rights bloc in Congress and civil rights organizations, but later black servicemen themselves, contended that the Truman order committed the Department of Defense to far more than integration of military units. They believed that off-base discrimination, so much more apparent with the improvement of on-base conditions, seriously affected morale and efficiency. They wanted the department to challenge local laws and customs when they discriminated against black servicemen.

This interpretation made little headway in the Department of Defense during the first decade of integration. Both the Eisenhower and Kennedy administrations made commitments to the principle of equal treatment within the services, and both admitted the connection between military efficiency and discrimination, but both presumed, at least until 1963, severe limitations on their power to change local laws and customs. For their part, the services constantly referred to the same limitations, arguing that their writ in regard to racial reform ran only to the gates of the military reservation.

Yet while there was no substantive change in the services' view of their racial responsibilities, the Department of Defense was able to make significant racial reforms between 1954 and 1962. More than expressing the will of the Chief Executive, these changes reflected the fact that military society was influenced by some of the same forces that were operating on the larger American society. Possessed of a discipline that enabled it to reform rapidly, military society still shared the prejudices as well as the reform impulses of the body politic. Racial changes in the services during the first decade of integration were primarily parochial responses to special internal needs; nevertheless, they took place at a time when civil rights demands were stirring the whole country. Their effectiveness must be measured against the expectations such demands were kindling in the black community.

The Civil Rights Revolution

The post-World War II civil rights movement was unique in the nation's history. Contrasting this era of black awakening with the post-Civil War campaign for black civil rights, historian C. Vann Woodward found the twentieth century phenomenon "more profound and impressive ... deeper, surer, less contrived, more spontaneous."[19-2] Again in contrast to the original, the so-called second reconstruction period found black Americans uniting in a demand for social justice so long withheld. In 1953, the year before the Supreme Court decision to desegregate the schools, Clarence Mitchell of the NAACP gave voice to the revolutionary rise in black expectations:

Twenty years ago the Negro was satisfied if he could have even a half-decent school to go to (and took it for granted that it would be a segregated school) or if he could go to the hotel in town or the restaurant maybe once a year for some special interracial dinner and meeting. Twenty years ago much of the segregation pattern was taken for granted by the Negro. Now it is different.[19-3]

The difference was understandable. The rapid urbanization of many black Americans, coupled with their experience in World War II, especially in the armed forces and in defense industries, had enhanced their economic and political power and raised their educational opportunities. And what was true for the war generation was even truer for its children. Possessed of a new self-respect, young Negroes began to demonstrate confidence in the future and a determination to reject the humiliation of second-class citizenship. Out of this attitude grew a widespread demand among the young for full equality, and when this demand met with opposition, massive participation in civil rights demonstrations became both practical and inevitable. Again historian Woodward's observations are pertinent:

More than a black revolt against whites, it was in part a generational rebellion, an uprising of youth against the older generation, against the parental "uncle Toms" and their inhibitions. It

222

even took the N.A.A.C.P. and CORE (Congress of Racial Equality) by surprise. Negroes were in charge of their own movement, and youth was in the vanguard.[19-4]

CLARENCE MITCHELL

To a remarkable extent, this youthful vanguard was strongly religious and nonviolent. The influence of the church on the militant phase of the civil rights movement is one of the movement's salient characteristics.

This black awakening paralleled a growing realization among an increasing number of white Americans that the demands of the civil rights leaders were just and that the government should act. World War II had made many thoughtful Americans aware of the contradiction inherent in fighting fascism with segregated troops. In the postwar years, the cold war rivalry for the friendship and allegiance of the world's colored peoples, who were creating a multitude of new states, added a pragmatic reason for ensuring equal treatment and opportunity for black Americans. A further inducement, and a particularly forceful one, was the size of the northern black vote, which had become the key to victory in several electorally important states and had made the civil rights cause a practical political necessity for both major parties.

The U.S. Supreme Court was the real pacesetter. Significantly broadening its interpretation of the Fourteenth Amendment, the Court reversed a century-old trend and called for federal intervention to protect the civil rights of the black minority in transportation, housing, voting, and the administration of justice. In the *Morgan* v. *Virginia* decision of 1946,[19-5] for example, the Court launched an attack on segregation in interstate travel. In another series of cases it proclaimed the right of Negroes to be tried only in those courts where Negroes could serve on juries and outlawed the all-white primary system, which in some one-party states had effectively barred Negroes from the elective process. The latter decision partly explains the rise in the number of qualified black voters in twelve southern states from 645,000 in 1947 to some 1.2 million by 1952. However, many difficulties remained in the way of full enfranchisement. The poll tax, literacy tests, and outright intimidation frustrated the registration of Negroes in many areas, and in some rural counties black voter registration actually declined in the early 1960's. But the Court's intervention was crucial because its decisions established the precedent for federal action that would culminate in the Voting Rights Act of 1965.

These judicial initiatives whittled away at segregation's hold on the Constitution, but it was the Supreme Court's rulings in the field of public education that dealt segregation a mortal blow. Its unanimous decision in the case of *Oliver Brown et al.* v. *Board of Education of Topeka, Kansas*, on 17 May 1954[19-6] not only undermined segregation in the nation's schools, but by an irresistible extension of the logic employed in the case also committed the nation at its highest levels to the principle of racial equality. The Court's conclusion that "separate educational facilities are inherently unequal" exposed segregation in all public areas to renewed judicial scrutiny. It was, as Professor Woodward described it, the most far-reaching Court decision in a century, and it marked the beginning of the end of Jim Crow's reign in America.[19-7]

But it was only the beginning, for the Court's order that the transition to racially nondiscriminatory school systems be accomplished "with all deliberate speed"[19-8] encountered massive resistance in many places. Despite ceaseless litigation and further affirmations by the Court, and despite enforcement by federal troops in the celebrated cases of Little Rock, Arkansas, and Oxford, Mississippi, and by federal marshals in New Orleans, Louisiana,[19-9] elimination of segregated public schools was painfully slow. As late as 1962, for example, only 7.6 percent of the more than three million Negroes of school age in the southern and border states attended integrated schools.

The executive branch also took up the cause of civil rights, albeit in a more limited way than the courts. The Eisenhower administration, for instance, continued President Truman's efforts to achieve equal treatment and opportunity for black servicemen. Just before the *Brown* decision the administration quickly desegregated most dependent schools on military bases. It also desegregated the school system of Washington, D.C., and, with a powerful push from the Supreme Court in the case of the *District of Columbia* v. *John R. Thompson Co.* in 1953,[19-10] abolished segregation in places of public accommodation in the nation's capital. Eisenhower also continued Truman's fight against discrimination in federal employment, including jobs covered by government contracts, by establishing watchdog committees on government employment policy and government contracts.

Independent federal agencies also began to attack racial discrimination. The Interstate Commerce Commission, with strong assistance from the courts, made a series of rulings that by 1961 had outlawed segregation in much interstate travel. The Federal Housing Authority, following the Supreme Court's abrogation of the state's power to enforce restrictive covenants in the sale of housing, began in the early 1950's to push toward a federal open-occupancy policy in

223

public housing and all housing with federally guaranteed loans. The U.S. Commission on Civil Rights, an investigatory agency appointed by the President under the Civil Rights Act of 1957, examined complaints of voting discrimination and denials of equal protection under the law. Both Eisenhower and Kennedy dispatched federal officials to investigate and prosecute violations of voting rights in several states.

But civil rights progress was still painfully slow in the 1950's. The fight for civil rights in that decade graphically demonstrated a political fact of life: any profound change in the nation's social system requires the concerted efforts of all three branches of the national government. In this case the Supreme Court had done its part, repeatedly attacking segregation in many spheres of national life. The executive branch, on the other hand, did not press the Court's decisions as thoroughly as some had hoped, although Eisenhower certainly did so forcibly and spectacularly with federal troops at Little Rock in 1957. The dispatch of paratroopers to Little Rock,[19-11] a memorable example of federal intervention and one popularly associated with civil rights, had, in fact, little to do with civil rights, but was rather a vivid example of the exercise of executive powers in the face of a threat to federal judicial authority. Where the *Brown* decision was concerned, Eisenhower's view of judicial powers was narrow and his leadership antithetical to the Court's call for "all deliberate speed." He even withheld his support in school desegregation cases. Eisenhower was quite frank about the limitations he perceived in his power and, by inference, his duty to effect civil rights reforms. Such reforms, he believed, were a matter of the heart and, as he explained to Congressman Powell in 1953, could not be achieved by means of laws or directives or the action of any one person, "no matter with how much authority and forthrightness he acts."[19-12]

Despite the President's reluctance to lead in civil rights matters, major blame for the lack of substantial progress must be assigned to the third branch of government. The 1957 and 1960 civil rights laws, pallid harbingers of later powerful legislation in this field, demonstrated Congress's lukewarm commitment to civil rights reform that severely limited federal action. The reluctance of Congress to enact the reforms augured in the *Brown* decision convinced many Negroes that they would have to take further measures to gain their full constitutional rights. They had seen presidents and federal judges embrace principles long argued by civil rights organizations, but to little avail. Seven years after the *Brown* decision, Negroes were still disfranchised in large areas of the south, still endured segregated public transportation and places of public accommodation, and still encountered discrimination in employment and housing throughout the nation. Nor had favorable court decisions and federal attempts at enforcement reversed the ominous trend in black unemployment rates, which had been rising for a decade. Above all, court decisions could not spare Negroes the sense of humiliation that segregation produced. Segregation implied racial inferiority, a "constant corroding experience," as Clarence Mitchell once called it. It was segregation's seeming imperviousness to governmental action in the 1950's that caused the new generation of civil rights leaders to develop new civil rights techniques.

Their new methods forced the older leaders, temporarily at least, into eclipse. No longer could they convince their juniors of the efficacy of legal action, and the 1950's ended with the younger generation taking to the streets in the first spontaneous battles of their civil rights revolution. Under the direction of the Southern Christian Leadership Council and its charismatic founder, Martin Luther King, Jr., the strategy of massive civil disobedience, broached in 1948 by A. Philip Randolph, became a reality. Other organizations quickly joined the battle, including the Student Nonviolent Coordinating Committee (SNCC), also organized by Dr. King but soon destined to break away into more radical paths, and the Congress of Racial Equality (CORE), an older organization, now expanded and under its new director, James Farmer, rededicated to activism.

Rosa Parks's refusal to move to the rear of the Montgomery bus in 1955 and the ensuing successful black boycott that ended the city's segregated transportation pointed the way to a wave of nonviolent direct action that swept the country in the 1960's. Thousands of young Americans, most notably in the student-led sit-ins enveloping the south in 1960[19-13] and the scores of freedom riders bringing chaos to the transportation system in 1961, carried the civil rights struggle into all corners of the south. "We will wear you down by our capacity to suffer," Dr. King warned the nation's majority, and suffer Negroes did in the brutal resistance that met their demands. But it was not in vain, for police brutality, mob violence, and assassinations set off hundreds of demonstrations throughout the country and made civil rights a national political issue.

The stage was set for a climatic scene, and onto that stage walked the familiar figure of A. Philip Randolph, calling for a massive march on Washington to demand a redress of black grievances. This time, unlike the response to his 1940 appeal, the answer was a promise of

224

support from both races. The churches joined in, many labor leaders, including Walter Reuther, enlisted in the demonstration, and even the President, at first opposed, gave his blessing to the national event. A quarter of a million people, about 20 percent of them white, marched to the Lincoln Memorial on 28 August 1963 to hear King appeal to the nation's conscience by reciting his dream of a just society. In the words of the Kerner Commission:

It [the march] was more than a summation of the past years of struggle and aspiration. It symbolized certain new directions: a deeper concern for the economic problems of the masses, more involvement of white moderates and new demands from the most militant, who implied that only a revolutionary change in American institutions would permit Negroes to achieve the dignity of citizens.[19-14]

Limitations on Executive Order 9981

The decade of national civil rights activity that culminated symbolically at the Lincoln Memorial in 1963 was closely mirrored in the Department of Defense, where the services' definition of equal treatment and opportunity underwent a marked evolution. Here, a decade that had begun with the department's placing severe limitations on its defense of black servicemen's civil rights ended with the department's joining the vanguard of the civil rights movement.

In the early 1950's the services were constantly referring to the limitations of Executive Order 9981. The Air Force could not intervene in local custom, Assistant Secretary Zuckert told Clarence Mitchell in 1951. Social change in local communities must be evolutionary, he continued, either ignoring or contrasting the Air Force's own social experience.[19-15]Defending the practice of maintaining large training camps in localities discriminating against black soldiers, the Army Chief of Staff explained to Senator Homer Ferguson of Michigan that while its facilities were open to all soldiers regardless of race, the Army had no control over nearby civilian communities. There was little its commanders could do beyond urging local civic organizations to cooperate.[19-16] The Deputy Chief of Naval Personnel was even more blunt. "The housing situation at Key West is not within the control of the Navy," he told the Assistant Secretary of Defense in 1953. Housing was segregated, he admitted, but it was the Federal Housing Authority, not the Navy, that controlled the location of off-base housing for black sailors.[19-17]

These excuses for not dealing with off-base discrimination continued throughout the decade. As late as 1959, discussing a case of racial discrimination near an Army base in Germany, a Defense Department spokesman explained to Congressman James Roosevelt that "since the incident did not take place on one of our military bases, we are not in a position to offer direct relief in the situation...."[19-18] Even James Evans, the racial counselor, came to use this explanation. "Community mores with respect to race vary," Evans wrote in 1956, and "such matters are largely beyond direct purview of the Department of Defense."[19-19]

Understandably, in view of the difficulties they perceived, the services tried to avoid the whole problem. In 1954, for example, a group of forty-eight black soldiers traveling on a bus in Columbia, South Carolina, were arrested and fined when they protested the attempted arrest of one of them for failing to comply with the state's segregated seating law. In the ensuing furor, Secretary of Defense Charles E. Wilson explained to President Eisenhower that soldiers were subject to community law and his department contemplated no investigation or disciplinary action in the case. In view of the civil rights issues involved, Wilson continued,[19-20] the Judge Advocate General of the Army discussed the matter with the Justice Department and referred related correspondence to that department "for whatever disposition it considered appropriate." "This reply," an assistant noted on Wilson's file copy of the memo for the President, "gets them off our neck, but I don't know about Brownell's [the Attorney General]."[19-21]

But the services never did get "them" off their neck, and to a large extent defense officials could only blame themselves for their troubles. Their attitude toward extending their standards of equal treatment and opportunity to local communities implied a benign neutrality on their part in racial disputes involving servicemen. This attitude was belied by the fact that on numerous and sometimes celebrated occasions the services helped reinforce local segregation laws. In 1956, for example, Secretary of the Air Force Harold E. Talbott explained that military commanders were expected to foster good relations with local authorities and in many areas were obliged to "require" servicemen to conform to the dictates of local law "regardless of their own convictions or personal beliefs."[19-22]

This requirement could be rather brutal in practice and placed the services, the nation's leading equal opportunity employer, in questionable company. In 1953 a black pilot stationed at Craig Air Force Base, Alabama, refused to move to the rear of a public bus until the military police ordered him to comply with the state law. The Air Force officially reprimanded and eventually discharged the pilot. The position of the Air Force was made clear in the reprimand:

Your actions in this instance are prejudicial to good order and military discipline and do not conform to the standards of conduct expected of a commissioned officer of the United

225

States Air Force. As a member of the Armed Forces, you are obliged to abide by all municipal and state laws, regardless of your personal feelings or Armed Forces policy relative to the issue at hand. Your open violation of the segregation policy established by this Railroad Company and the State of Alabama is indicative of extremely poor judgment on your part and reflects unfavorably on your qualifications as a commissioned officer.[19-23]

As the young pilot's commanding officer put it, the lieutenant had refused to accept the fact that military personnel must use tact and diplomacy to avoid discrediting the United States Air Force.[19-24]

Tact and diplomacy were also the keynote when the services helped enforce the local segregation practices of the nation's allies. This became increasingly true even in Europe in the 1950's, although never with as much publicity as the events connected with the carrier *Midway's* visit to Capetown, South Africa, in 1955. Its captain, on the advice of the U.S. consul, agreed to conform with a local law that segregated sailors when they were ashore. This agreement became public knowledge while the ship was en route, but despite a rash of protests and congressional demands that the visit be canceled, the *Midway* arrived at Capetown. Later a White House spokesman tried to put a good face on the incident:

We believe that a far greater blow was struck for the cause of equal justice when 23,000 South Africans came aboard the Midway on a non-segregated basis—when the whole community saw American democracy in action—than could have been made if we had decided to by-pass Capetown. Certainly no friends for our cause would have been gained in that way![19-25]

The black serviceman lacked the civilian's option to escape community discrimination. For example, one black soldier requested transfer because of discrimination he was forced to endure in the vicinity of Camp Hanford, Washington. His request was denied, and in commenting on the case the Army's G-1 gave a typical service excuse when he said that the Army could not practically arrange for the mass reassignment of black soldiers or the restriction of their assignments to certain geographical areas to avoid discrimination.[19-26] The Air Force added a further twist. Replying to a similar request, a spokesman wrote that limiting the number of bases to which black airmen could be assigned would be "contrary to the policy of equality of treatment."[19-27] There was, however, one exception to the refusal to alter assignments for racial reasons. Both the Air Force and the Army had an established and frequently reiterated policy of not assigning troops involved in interracial marriages to states where such unions were illegal.[19-28]

At times the services' respect for local laws and ordinances forced them to retain some aspects of the segregation policies so recently abolished. Answering a complaint made by Congressman Powell in 1956, for example, The Adjutant General of the Army explained that off-duty entertainment did not fall within the scope of the Truman order. Since most dances were sponsored by outside groups, they had to take place "under conditions cited by them." To insist on integration in this instance, The Adjutant General argued, would mean cancellation of these dances to the detriment of the soldiers' morale. For that reason, segregated dances would continue on post.[19-29]

This response illustrates the services' approach to equal opportunity and treatment during the Eisenhower administration. The President showed a strong reluctance to interfere with local laws and customs, a reluctance that seemed to flow out of a pronounced constitutional scruple against federal intervention in defiance of local racial laws. The practical consequence of this scruple was readily apparent in the armed forces throughout his administration. In 1955, for example, a black veteran called the President's attention to the plight of black soldiers, part of an integrated group, who were denied service in an Alabama airport and left unfed throughout their long journey. Answering for the President, Maxwell M. Rabb, Secretary to the Cabinet, reaffirmed Eisenhower's dedication to equal opportunity but added that it was not in the scope of the President's authority "to intervene in matters which are of local or state-wide concern and within the jurisdiction of local legislation and determination."[19-30] Again to a black soldier complaining of being denied service near Fort Bragg, North Carolina, a White House assistant, himself a Negro, replied that "outside of an Army post, there is little that the Federal Government can do, except to appeal to the decency of the citizens to treat men in uniform with courtesy and respect." He then suggested a course of action for black soldiers:

The President's heart bleeds when any Americans are victims of injustice, and he is doing everything he possibly can to rectify this situation in our country.

You can hold up his hand by carrying on, despite the unpleasant things that are happening to you at this moment, realizing that, on this end, we will work all the harder to make your sacrifices worthwhile.[19-31]

But as the record suggests, this promise to rectify the situation was never meant to extend beyond the gates of the military reservation. Thus, the countless incidents of blatant discrimination encountered by black GI's would continue largely unchallenged into the 1960's, masking the progress made by the Eisenhower administration in ordering the sometimes reluctant services to adopt reforms. This presidential resolution was particularly obvious in the integration of civilian facilities at Navy shipyards and installations and in schools for dependent children on military posts.

Integration of Navy Shipyards

The Navy employed many thousands of civilians, including a large number of Negroes, at some forty-three installations from Virginia to Texas. At the Norfolk shipyard, for example, approximately 35 percent of the 15,000 employees were black. To the extent dictated by local laws and customs, black employees were segregated and otherwise discriminated against. The degree of segregation depended upon location, and, according to a 1953 newspaper survey, ranged "from minor in most instances to substantial in a few cases."[19-32]

In January 1952 the Chief of the Office of Industrial Relations, Rear Adm. W. McL. Hague, all but absolved Navy installations from the provisions of Executive Order 9980.[19-33]He announced that segregation would continue if "the station is subject to local laws of the community in which located, and the laws of the community require segregated facilities," or if segregation were "the norm of the community and conversion to common facilities would, in the judgment of the commanding officer, result in definite impediment to productive effort." Known officially as "OIR Notice CP75," Hague's statement left little doubt that segregation would remain the norm in most instances. It specified that a change to integrated facilities would be allowed only after the commander had decided that it could be accomplished without "inordinate interference with the Station's ability to carry out its mission." If other facilities stood nearby, the change would be allowed only after he had coordinated with the naval district commander.[19-34] Shortly thereafter the Acting Secretary of the Navy expressed his agreement with Hague's statement,[19-35] thus elevating it to an official expression of Navy policy.

CONGRESSMAN POWELL

Official protestations to the contrary, the Navy was again segregating people by race. Evans, in the Department of Defense, charged that this was in fact the "insidious intent" of Hague's notice. He pointed out to Assistant Secretary of Defense Rosenberg that signs and notices of segregation were reappearing over drinking fountains and toilets at naval installations which had abandoned such practices, that men in uniform were now subjected to segregation at such facilities, and that the local press was making the unrefuted claim that local law was being reestablished on federal properties.[19-36] Somewhat late to the battle, Dennis D. Nelson seemingly a permanent fixture in the Pentagon, spoke out against his department's policy, but from a different angle. He warned the Secretary of the Navy through his aide that Notice 75 was embarrassing not only for the Navy but for the White House as well.[19-37]

Nelson was right of course. The notice quickly won the attention of civil rights leaders. Walter White condemned the policy, but his protest, along with the sharp complaints of the NAACP's Clarence Mitchell and Jerry Gilliam and the arguments of the Urban League's Lester Granger, failed to move Secretary of the Navy Dan A. Kimball.[19-38] The secretary insisted that integrating these installations might jeopardize the fulfillment of the Navy's mission, dependent as it was on the "efficiency and whole-hearted cooperation" of the employees. "In a very realistic way," he told Walter White, the Navy must recognize and conform to local labor customs and usages.[19-39] Answering Rosenberg's inquiry on the subject, the Navy gave its formula for change:

This Department cannot take the initiative in correcting this social ill but must content itself with being alert to take advantage of the gradual dissolution of these racial prejudices which can be effectively brought about only by a process of social education and understanding. This Department is ever ready to dissolve segregation practices of long standing as soon as that can be done without decreasing the effectiveness of our activities.[19-40]

President Eisenhower's newly appointed Secretary of the Navy, Robert B. Anderson, endorsed Notice 75 along the same lines, informing Mitchell that the Navy would "measure the pace of non-segregation by the limits of what is practical and reasonable in each area."[19-41]

But what seemed practical and reasonable in the Navy was not necessarily so in the White House, where the President had publicly pledged his administration to the abolition of segregation in the federal government. Should Eisenhower falter, there was always his 1952 campaign ally, Congressman Powell, to remind him of his "forthright stand on segregation when federal funds are expended."[19-42] In colorful prose that pulled no punches, Powell reminded the President of his many black supporters and pressed him on the Navy's continuing segregation. Although he denied Powell's charge of obstructionist tactics in the executive branch, the President had in fact been told by Maxwell Rabb, now serving as his minority affairs assistant, that "some government agencies were neglecting their duty."[19-43] The President responded to this news promptly enough by ordering Rabb to supervise the executive agencies in their application of the presidential racial policy. Rabb thereafter discussed the Navy's policy with Secretary Anderson and his assistants on 11 June 1953.

With his policy openly contradicting the President's, Anderson was in an awkward position. He had been unaware of the implications of the problem, he later explained, and had accepted his predecessor's judgment. His mistake, he pled, was one of timing not intent.[19-44] Yet Anderson had conducted a wide correspondence on the subject, discussed the matter with Lester Granger, and as late as 28 May was still defending Notice 75, telling Special White House Assistant Wilton B. Persons that it represented a practical answer to a problem that could not be corrected by edict. Nor could he introduce any changes, he maintained, adopting his predecessor's argument that the Navy should "be alert to take advantage of its [segregation's] gradual dissolution through the process of social education and understanding."[19-45]

But neither the civil rights leaders nor the White House could be put off with gradualism. Anderson's stand was roundly criticized. In an address to the NAACP annual convention, Walter White plainly referred to the secretary's position as a "defiance of President Eisenhower's order."[19-46] If such barbed criticism left the secretary unmoved, Rabb carried a stronger weapon, and in their 11 June meeting the two men discussed the President's order to integrate federally owned or controlled properties, the possibility of a Supreme Court decision on the same subject, and, more to the point, Powell's public statements concerning segregation at the Norfolk and Charleston naval shipyards.[19-47]

SECRETARY ANDERSON
talks to a member of the fleet.

Anderson then proceeded to reverse his position. He began by ordering a survey of a group of southern installations to estimate the effect of integration on their civilian programs. He learned segregation could be virtually eliminated at these shipyards and stations within six months, although Under Secretary Charles S. Thomas, who prepared the report, agreed with the local commanders that an integration directive would be certain to cause trouble. But the formula chosen by the commanders for eliminating segregation, in which Thomas concurred, might well have given Anderson pause. They wanted to remove racial signs from drinking fountains and toilets, certain that the races would continue using separate facilities, and leave the problem of segregated cafeterias till later. It was the unanimous opinion of those involved, Thomas reported, that the situation should not be forced by "agitators," a category in which they all placed Powell.

On 20 August Anderson directed commanders of segregated facilities to proceed steadily toward complete elimination of racial barriers. Furthermore, each commander was to submit a progress report on 1 November and at sixty-day intervals thereafter.[19-48] Although the secretary was concerned with the possible reaction of the civil rights groups were integration not achieved in the first sixty days, he was determined to give local commanders some leeway in carrying out his order.[19-49] But he made it clear to the press that he did not intend "to put up with inaction."

He need not have worried. Evans reported on 29 October that integration of the Charleston shipyard was almost complete and had occurred so far without incident. In fact, he told Assistant Secretary of Defense John A. Hannah, the reaction of the local press and community had been "surprisingly tolerant and occasionally favorable."[19-50] Evans, however, apparently overlooked an attempt by some white employees to discourage the use of integrated facilities. Although there was no disorder, the agitators were partly successful; the Chief of Industrial Relations reported that white usage had dropped severely.[19-51] Nevertheless by 14 January 1954 this same officer could tell Secretary Anderson that all racial barriers for civilian employees had been eliminated without incident.[19-52]

Dependent Children and Integrated Schools

The Department of Defense's effort to integrate schools attended by servicemen's children proved infinitely more complex than integrating naval shipyards. In a period when national attention was focused on the constitutional implications of segregated education, the Eisenhower administration was thrust into a dispute over the intent of federal aid to education and eventually into a reappraisal of the federal role in public education. Confusing to the Department of Defense, the President's personal attitude remained somewhat ambiguous throughout the controversy. He had publicly committed himself to ending segregation in federally financed institutions, yet he had declared scruples against federal interference with state laws and customs that would prevent him from acting to keep such a pledge when all its ramifications were revealed.

In fact not one but four separate categories of educational institutions came under scrutiny. Only the first category, schools run by the U.S. Office of Education for the Department of Defense overseas and on military reservations in the United States, operated exclusively with federal funds. The next two categories, schools operated by local school districts on military reservations and schools on federal land usually adjacent to a military reservation, were supported by local and state funds with federal subsidies. The fourth and by far the largest group contained the many community schools attended by significant numbers of military dependents. These schools received considerable federal support through the impact aid program.

The federal support program for schools in "federally impacted" areas added yet another dimension to the administration's reappraisal. The impact aid legislation (Public Laws 815 and 874),[19-53] like similar programs during World War II, was based on the premise that a school district derived no tax from land occupied by a federal installation but usually incurred an increase in school enrollment. In many cases the enrollment of military dependents was far greater than that of the communities in the school district. Actually, these programs were not limited to the incursion of military families; the most extreme federal impact in terms of enrollment percentages was found in remote mountain districts where in some cases almost all students were children of U.S. Forest Service or National Park Service employees.

In recognition of these inequities in the tax system, Congress gave such school systems special "in-lieu of tax" support. Public Law 815 provided for capital projects, land, buildings, and major equipment; Public Law 874 gave operating support in the form of salaries, supplies, and the like. If, for example, a school district could prove at least 3 percent of its enrollment federally connected, it was eligible to receive from the U.S. Office of Education a grant equal to the district's cost of instruction for federally connected students. If it could show federally connected enrollment necessitated additional classrooms, the school district was eligible for federally financed buildings. Such schools were usually concentrated in military housing areas, but examples existed of federally financed schools, like federal dependents, scattered throughout the school district. Students from the community at large attended the federally constructed schools and the school district continued to receive state support for all students. Although Public Law 874 was far more important in terms of general application and fiscal impact, its companion piece, Public Law 815, was more important to integration because it involved the construction of schools. From the beginning Congress sought to prevent these laws from becoming a means by which federal authorities exercised control over the operation of school districts. It stipulated that "no department, officer or employee of the United States shall exercise any direction, supervision or control over the personnel, curriculum or program of instruction" of any local school or school system.[19-54] The firmness of this admonition, an indication of congressional opinion on this important issue, later played a decisive part in the integration story.

Attacks on segregation in schools attended by military dependents did not begin until the early fifties when the Army, in answer to complaints concerning segregated schools in Texas, Oklahoma, and Virginia, began using a stock answer to the effect that the schools were operated by state agencies as part of the state school system subject to state law.[19-55] Trying to justify the situation to Clarence Mitchell, Assistant Public Secretary of the Army Fred Korth cited Public Law 874, whose intent, he claimed, was that educating children residing on federal property was the responsibility of "the local educational agency."[19-56]

Senator Humphrey, for one, was not to be put off by such an interpretation. He reminded Assistant Secretary Rosenberg that President Truman had vetoed an education bill in 1951 because of provisions requiring segregation in schools on federal property. As a member of the subcommittee that guided Public Law 874 through Congress, Humphrey could assure Rosenberg that at no time did Congress include language requiring segregation in post schools. Thanks to the Army's interpretation, he observed, local community segregation practices were being extended for the first time to federal property under the guise of compliance with federal law. He predicted further incursions by the segregationists if this move was left unchallenged.[19-57]

After conferring with both Humphrey and Mitchell, Rosenberg took the matter of segregated schools on military posts to the U.S. Commissioner of Education, Earl J. McGrath. With Secretary of Defense Lovett's approval she put the department on record as opposed to segregated schools on posts because they were "violative not only of the policy of the Department" but also of "the policy set forth by the President."[19-58] Evidently McGrath saw Public Law 874 in the same light, for on 15 January 1953 he informed Rosenberg that if the Department of Defense outlawed segregated dependent schooling and local educational agencies were unable to comply, his office would have to make "other arrangements" for the children.[19-59]

Commissioner McGrath proposed that his office discuss the integration question further with Defense Department representatives but the change in administrations interrupted these negotiations and Rosenberg's successor, John A. Hannah, made it clear that there would be no speedy change in the racial composition of post schools. Commenting at Hannah's request on the points raised by McGrath, the Army's principal personnel officer concluded that integration should be considered a departmental goal, but one that should be approached by steps "consistent with favorable local conditions as determined by the installation commander concerned." In his opinion, committing the department to integration of all on-post schools, as the Assistant Secretary of Defense had proposed earlier, would create teacher procurement problems and additional financial burdens.[19-60] This cautious endorsement of integrated schools was further qualified by the Secretary of the Army. It was a "desirable goal," he told Hannah, but "positive steps to eliminate segregation ... should be preceded by a careful analysis of the impact on each installation concerned."[19-61] Hannah then broke off negotiations with the Office of Education.

The matter was rescued from bureaucratic limbo when in answer to a question during his 19 March 1953 press conference President Eisenhower promised to investigate the school situation, adding:

I will say this—I repeat it, I have said it again and again: whenever Federal funds are expended for anything, I do not see how any American can justify—legally, or logically, or morally—a discrimination in the expenditure of those funds as among our citizens. All are taxed to provide these funds. If there is any benefit to be derived from them, I think they must all share, regardless of such inconsequential factors as race and religion.[19-62]

The sweeping changes implied in this declaration soon became apparent. Statistics compiled as a result of the White House investigation revealed that federal dependents attended thousands of schools, a complex mix of educational institutions having little more in common than their mutual dependence in whole or part on federal funds.[19-63] Most were under local government control and the great majority, including the community public schools, were situated a long distance from any military base. The President was no doubt unaware of the ramifications of federal enrollment and impacted aid on the nation's schools when he made his declaration, and, given his philosophy of government and the status of civil rights at the time, it is not surprising that his promise to look into the subject came to nothing. From the beginning Secretary of Defense Wilson limited the department's campaign against segregated schools to those on federal *property* rather than those using federal *funds*. And even this limited effort to integrate schools on federal property encountered determined opposition from many local officials and only the halfhearted support of some of the federal officials involved.

The Department of Defense experienced few problems at first as it integrated its own schools. Its overseas schools, especially in Germany and Japan, had always been integrated, and its schools in the United States now quickly followed suit. Eleven in number, they were paid for and operated by the U.S. Commissioner of Education because the states in which they were located prohibited the use of state funds for schools on federal property. With only minimal public attention, all but one of these schools was operating on an integrated basis by 1953. The exception was the elementary school at Fort Benning, Georgia, which at the request of the local school board remained a white-only school. On 20 March 1953 the new Secretary of the Army, Robert T. Stevens, informed the White House that this school had been ordered to commence integrated operations in the fall.[19-64]

The integration of schools operated by local school authorities on military posts was not so simple, and before the controversy died down the Department of Defense found itself assuming responsibility for a number of formerly state-operated institutions. As of April 1953, twenty-one of these sixty-three schools in the United States were operating on a segregated basis. (*Table 12*)

TABLE 12—DEFENSE INSTALLATIONS WITH SEGREGATED PUBLIC SCHOOLS

State

Alabama (C)[1]	Maxwell Air Force Base
	Craig Air Force Base
Arkansas (S)[2]	Pine Bluff Arsenal (Army)
Florida (C)	MacDill Air Force Base
	Eglin Air Force Base
	Tyndall Air Force Base
	Naval Air Station, Pensacola
	Patrick Air Force Base
Maryland (S)	Andrews Air Force Base

230

	Naval Air Station, Patuxent
	Naval Powder Factory, Indianhead
Oklahoma (C)	Fort Sill (Army)
Texas (C)	Fort Bliss (Army)
	Fort Hood (Army)
	Fort Sam Houston (Army)
	Randolph Air Force Base
	Reese Air Force Base
	Shepherd Air Force Base
	Lackland Air Force Base
Virginia (C)	Fort Belvoir (Army)
	Langley Air Force Base

Tablenote 1: (C) indicates segregation required by state constitution. Tablenote 2: (S) indicates segregation required by state statute.

The Secretary of the Army promised to investigate the possibility of integrating schools on Army bases and to consider further action with the Commissioner of Education "as the situation is clarified." He warned the President that to "prod the commissioner" into setting up integrated federal schools when segregated state schools were available would invite charges in the press and Congress of squandering money. Moreover, newly assembled faculties would have state accreditation problems.[19-65] Admitting that there were complicating factors, the President ignored the secretary's warnings and noted that if integrated schools could not be provided by state authorities "other arrangements will be considered."[19-66]

Others in the administration took these complications more seriously. Oveta Culp Hobby, Secretary of Health, Education, and Welfare, was concerned with the attitude of Congress and the press. She pleaded for more time to see what the Supreme Court would rule on the subject and to study the effect of the conversion to federally operated schools "so that we can feel confident of our ground in the event further action should be called for." Going a step further than the Secretary of the Army, Hobby suggested delaying action on the twenty-one segregated schools on posts "for the immediate present."[19-67]

In marked contrast to Hobby's recommendation, and incidentally buttressing popular belief in the existence of an interdepartmental dispute on the subject, Secretary of Defense Wilson told the President that he wanted to end segregation in all schools on military installations "as swiftly as practicable." He admitted it would be difficult, as a comprehensive and partially covert survey of the school districts by the local commanders had made clear. The commanders found, for example, that the twenty-one school districts involved would not operate the schools as integrated institutions. Wilson also stressed that operating the schools under federal authority would be very expensive, but his recommendation was explicit. There should be no exact timetable, but the schools should be integrated before the 1955 fall term.[19-68]

Although both Wilson and Hobby later denied that the Department of Health, Education, and Welfare was opposed to integrating the schools, rumors and complaints persisted throughout the summer of 1953 that Hobby opposed swift action and had carried her opposition "to the cabinet level."[19-69] Lending credence to these rumors, President Eisenhower later admitted that there was some foot-dragging in his official family. He had therefore ordered minority affairs assistant Rabb, already overseeing the administration's fight against segregated shipyards, to "track down any inconsistencies of this sort in the rest of the departments and agencies of the government."[19-70]

The interdepartmental dispute was quickly buried by Wilson's dramatic order of 12 January 1954. Effective as of that date, the secretary announced, "no new school shall be opened for operation on a segregated basis, and schools presently so conducted shall cease operating on a segregated basis, as soon as practicable, and under no circumstances later than September 1, 1955."[19-71] Wilson promised to negotiate with local authorities, but if they were unable to comply the Commissioner of Education would be requested to provide integrated facilities through the provisions of Public Law 874. Interestingly, the secretary's order predated the Supreme Court decision on segregated education by some four months.

The order prompted considerable public response. The Anti-Defamation League of B'nai B'rith telegraphed "hearty approval of your directive ... action is consonant with democratic ideals and in particular with the military establishment's successful program of integration in the armed forces."[19-72] Walter White added the NAACP's approval in a similar vein, and many individual citizens offered congratulations.[19-73] But not all the response was favorable. Congressman

231

Arthur A. Winstead of Mississippi asked the secretary to outline for him "wherein you believe that procedure will add anything whatsoever to the defense of this country. Certainly it appears to me that you have every reason anyone could desire to refuse to take action which is in total violation of certain state laws."[19-74]

The three services quickly responded to the order. By 18 February all had issued specific directives for enforcing it. The Secretary of the Navy, for example, declared that the "policy of non-segregation" would apply

to the operation of existing schools and school facilities hereafter constructed on Navy and Marine Corps installations within the United States, Alaska, Hawaii, Puerto Rico and the Virgin Islands, the area in which Public Law 874 and ... 815 ... are operative.... In the case of PL 874 this area will be extended, effective 1 July 1954, to include Wake Island ... the same policy of non-segregation will apply in all Navy-operated schools for dependent children of military and civilian personnel of the Department of Defense.[19-75]

Any local school official hoping for a reprieve from the deadlines expressed in these orders was likely to be disappointed. In response to queries on the subject, the services quoted their instructions, and if they excused continued segregation during the 1954 school year they were adamant about the September 1955 integration date.[19-76] The response of Secretary of the Air Force Talbott to one request for an extension revealed the services' determination to stick to the letter of the Wilson order. Talbott agreed with the superintendent of the Montgomery County, Alabama, school board that local school boards were best qualified to run the schools for dependent children of the military, but he refused to extend the deadline. "Unilateral action in the case of individual Air Force base schools would be in violation of the directive," he explained, adding: "At such time as the Alabama legislature acts to permit your local board of education to operate the school at Maxwell AFB on an integrated basis, the Air Force will return operational responsibility for the school to the local board at the earliest practicable date."[19-77]

As a result of this unified determination on the part of departmental officials, the Office of the Assistant Secretary of Defense could announce in December 1954 that two of the schools, the one at Craig Air Force Base, Alabama, and Fort Belvoir, Virginia, were integrated; two others, the Naval Air Station school at Pensacola, Florida, and Reese Air Force Base, Texas, had been closed; the remaining seventeen would be fully integrated by the September 1955 deadline.[19-78] Lee Nichols, a prolific writer on integration, reported in November 1955 that schools segregated for generations suddenly had black and white children sitting side by side. This move by the armed forces, he pointed out, could have far-reaching effects. Educators from segregated community schools would be watching the military experiment closely for lessons in how to comply with the Supreme Court's desegregation order.[19-79]

Strictly speaking there were more than twenty-one segregated schools operating on federal installations. A small group of institutions built and operated by local authorities stood on land leased from the services. At the time of Secretary Wilson's order this category of schools included three with 75-year leases, those at Fort Meade, Maryland, and Fort Bliss and Biggs Air Force Base, Texas, and one with a 25-year lease at Pine Bluff Arsenal, Arkansas.[19-80] The Air Force's general counsel believed the lease could be broken in light of the Wilson order, but the possibility developed that some extensions might be granted to these schools because of the lease complication.[19-81] The Secretary of the Army went right to the point, asking the Assistant Secretary of Defense, Carter L. Burgess, for an extension in the case of Fort Meade pending Maryland's integration of its schools under the Supreme Court's decision.[19-82] In response Burgess ordered, as of 1 June 1955, the exemption of four schools. "No attempt shall be made," he informed the services, "to break the lease or take over operation of the schools pending further instruction from the Secretary of Defense."[19-83]

It was some time before the question of temporary extensions was resolved. Two of the leased property schools, Biggs and Fort Bliss, were integrated before the September deadline as a result of a change in state law in the wake of the Supreme Court's decision. Then, on 16 July 1956, the Assistant Secretary of the Army reported that the phased integration of Fort Meade's elementary school had started.[19-84] The Pine Bluff Arsenal case was still unresolved in 1956, but since at that time there were no black dependents at the installation it was not considered so pressing by Burgess, who allowed the extension to continue beyond 1956. Besides, it turned out there were still other schools in this category that the Navy had temporarily exempted from the September 1955 deadline. The school at the Patuxent River Naval Air Station, for example, which had no black dependents eligible for attendance, was allowed to continue to operate as usual while negotiations were under way for the transfer of the school and property to the St. Mary's County, Maryland, school board.[19-85] A lease for the temporary use of buildings by local authorities for segregated schools on the grounds of the New Orleans Naval Air Station was

232

allowed to run on until 1959 because of technicalities in the lease, but not, however, without considerable public comment.[19-86]

READING CLASS IN THE MILITARY DEPENDENTS SCHOOL,
Yokohama, Japan, 1955.

The Department of Defense could look with pride at its progress. In less than three years after President Eisenhower had promised to look into segregated schools for military dependents, the department had integrated hundreds of classrooms, inducing local authorities to integrate a series of schools in areas that had never before seen blacks and whites educated together. It had even ordered the integration of classes conducted on post by local universities and voluntarily attended by servicemen in off-duty hours.[19-87] Yet many dependent schools were untouched because Wilson's order applied only to schools on federal property. It ignored the largest category of dependent schools, those in the local community that because of heavy enrollment of federal dependents were supported in whole or part by federal funds. In these institutions some 28,000 federal dependents were being educated in segregated classes. Integration for them would have to await the long court battles that followed *Brown v. Board of Education.*

This dreary prospect had not always seemed so inevitable. Although Wilson's order ignored local public schools, civil rights advocates did not, and the problem of off-base segregation, typified by the highly publicized school at the Little Rock Air Force Base in 1958, became an issue involving not only the Department of Defense but the whole administration. The decision to withhold federal aid to school districts that remained segregated in defiance of court orders was clearly beyond the power of the Department of Defense. In a memorandum circulated among Pentagon officials in October 1958, Assistant Secretary of Health, Education, and Welfare Elliot C. Richardson discussed the legal background of federal aid to schools attended by military dependents, especially congressional intent and the definition of "suitable" facilities as expressed in Public Laws 815 and 874. He also took up the question of whether to provide off-base integrated schooling, balancing the difficult problem of protecting the civil rights of federal employees against the educational advantages of a state-sponsored education system. Richardson mentioned the great variation in school population—some bases having seven high school aged children one year, none the next—and the fact that the cost of educating the 28,087 dependents attending segregated schools in 1957 would amount to more than $49 million for facilities and $8.7 million annually for operations. He was left with one possible conclusion, that "irrespective of our feelings about the unsuitability of segregated education as a matter of principle, we are constrained by the legislative history, the settled administrative construction, and the other circumstances surrounding the statutes in question to adhere to the existing interpretation of them."[19-88]

Richardson might be "constrained" to accept the *status quo,* but some black parents were not. In the fall of 1958 matters came to a head at the school near the Little Rock air base. Here was a new facility, built by the local school board exclusively with federal funds, on state land, and intended primarily for the education of dependents living at a newly constructed military base. On the eve of the school's opening, the Pulaski County school board informed the Air Force that the school would be for white students only. The decision was brought to the President's attention by a telegram from a black sergeant's wife whose child was denied admission.[19-89] The telegram was only the first in a series of protests from congressmen, civil rights organizations, and interested citizens. For all the Defense Department had a stock answer: there was nothing the Air Force could do. The service neither owned nor operated the school, and the impact aid laws forbade construction of federal school facilities if the local school districts could provide public school education for federal dependents.[19-90]

The department would not get off the hook so easily; the President wanted something done about the Little Rock school, although he wanted his interest kept quiet.[19-91] Yet any action would have unpleasant consequences. If the department transferred the father, it was open to a court suit on his behalf; if it tried to force integration on the local authorities, they would close the school. Since neither course was acceptable, Assistant Secretary of Defense Charles C. Finucane ordered his troubleshooter, Stephen Jackson, to Little Rock to investigate.[19-92]

Before he went to Little Rock, Jackson met with officials from the Department of Health, Education, and Welfare and decided, with the concurrence of the Department of Justice, that the solution lay in government purchase of the land. The school would then be on a military base and subject to integration. Should local authorities refuse to operate the integrated on-base school, the Air Force would do so. In that event, Jackson warned local officials on his arrival in Arkansas, the school district would lose much of its federal enrollment and hence its very important federal subsidy. Nor could the board be assured that the federal acquisition would be limited to one school. Jackson later admitted the local black school had also been constructed

233

with federal funds, and he could not guarantee that it would escape federal acquisition. Board members queried Jackson on this point, introducing the possibility that the federal government might try to acquire local high schools, also attended in large numbers by military dependents and also segregated. Jackson assured the school board that the department "had no desire to change the community patterns where schools were already in existence merely because they received federal aid,"[19-93] a statement that amounted to a new federal policy.

Jackson failed to convince the board, and in late October 1958 it rejected the government's offer to run an integrated school on land purchased from them.[19-94] Jackson thereupon met with justice officials and together they decided that sometime before 1 January 1959 the Justice Department would acquire title to the school land for one year by taking a leasehold through the right of eminent domain. They did not at that time, however, formulate any definite plan of action to accomplish the school take-over.[19-95]

It was just as well, for soon after this decision was reached the NAACP brought up the subject of dependent schools near the Air Force bases at Blytheville, Arkansas, and Stewart, Tennessee.[19-96] Air Force Deputy Assistant Secretary James P. Goode was quick to point out that there were at least five other segregated schools constructed with federal funds, situated near Air Force bases, and attended almost exclusively by federal dependents. He also predicted that a careful survey would reveal perhaps another fifteen schools in segregated districts serving only Air Force dependents. In light of these facts, and with a frankly confessed aversion to the administration's acquisition of the properties by right of eminent domain, Goode preferred to have the schools integrated in an orderly manner through the supervision of the federal courts.[19-97]

This attitude was to prevail for some time in the Department of Defense. In April 1961, for example, the Assistant Secretary for Manpower informed a Senate subcommittee that, while schools under departmental jurisdiction were integrated "without reservation and with successful results," many children of black servicemen stationed in Georgia, Alabama, Mississippi, and elsewhere still attended segregated off-post schools. Adjacent to military posts and attended "in whole or in part by federal dependents," these schools "conformed to state rather than federal laws."[19-98] And as late as May 1963, a naval official admitted there was no way for the Navy to require school officials in Key West, Florida, to conform to the Department of Defense's policy of equal opportunity.[19-99]

Yet even as the principle of noninterference with racial patterns of the local community emerged intact from the lengthy controversy, exceptions to its practical application continued to multiply. In the fall of 1959, less than a year after the administration suspended its campaign to integrate off-base schools in Arkansas, black Air Force dependents quietly entered the Little Rock school. At the same time, schools catering predominantly to military dependents near bases in Florida and Tennessee integrated with little public attention.[19-100] Under pressure from the courts, and after President Eisenhower had discussed the case in a national press conference in terms of the proper use of impact aid in segregated districts, the city of Norfolk, Virginia, agreed to integrate its 15,000 students, roughly one-third of whom were military dependents.[19-101]

The controversy over schools for dependents demonstrated the limits of federal intervention in the local community on behalf of the civil rights of servicemen. Before these limits could be breached a new administration would have to redefine the scope of the Defense Department's power. Nevertheless, the armed forces had scored some dramatic successes in the field of race relations by 1960. Some five million servicemen, civilians, and their dependents were proving the practicality of integration on the job, in schools, and in everyday living. Several writers even suggested that the services' experience had itself become a dynamic force for social change in the United States.[19-102] The New York *Times's* Anthony Lewis went so far as to say that the successful integration of military society led to the black crusade against discrimination in civilian society.[19-103] Others took the services' influence for granted, as Morton Puner did when he observed in 1959 that "the armed services are more advanced in their race relations than the rest of the United States. Perhaps it is uniquely fitting that this should be so, that in one of the greatest peacetime battles of our history, the armed forces should be leading the way to victory."[19-104]

As such encomiums became more frequent, successful integration became a source of pride to the services. Military commanders with experience in Korea had, according to Assistant Secretary of Defense Hannah, universally accepted the new order as desirable, conceding that integration worked "very well" despite predictions to the contrary.[19-105] Nor was this attitude limited to military commanders, for there had been considerable change in sentiment among senior defense officials. Citing the major economies realized in the use of manpower and facilities, Secretary Wilson reported to President Eisenhower in March 1955 that the results of integration were encouraging:

Combat effectiveness is increased as individual capabilities rather than racial designations determine assignments and promotions. Economics in manpower and funds are achieved by the elimination of racially duplicated facilities and operations. Above all, our national security is improved by the more effective utilization of military personnel, regardless of race.[19-106]

In other reports he expatiated on this theme, explaining how integration cut down racial incidents in the services and improved "national solidarity and strength."[19-107] After years of claiming the contrary, defense officials were justifying integration in the name of military efficiency.

Certainly racial incidents in the armed forces practically disappeared in the immediate post-integration period, and the number of complaints about on-base discrimination that reached the Pentagon from individual black servicemen dropped dramatically. Moreover, supporting Secretary Wilson's claim of national solidarity, major civil rights organizations began to cite the racial experiences of the armed forces to strengthen their case against segregated American society. Civil rights leaders continued to press for action against discrimination outside the military reservation, but in the years after Korea their sense of satisfaction with the department's progress was quite obvious. At its national conventions in 1953 and 1954, for example, the NAACP officially praised the services for their race policy. As one writer observed, integration not only increased black support for the armed forces and black commitment to national defense during the cold war, but it also boosted the department's prestige in the black and white community alike, creating indirect political support for those politicians who sponsored the racial reforms.[19-108]

But what about the black serviceman himself? A Negro enlisting in the armed forces in 1960, unlike his counterpart in 1950, entered an integrated military community. He would quickly discover traces of discrimination, especially in the form of unequal treatment in assignments, promotions, and the application of military justice, but for a while at least these would seem minor irritants to a man who was more often than not for the first time close to being judged by ability rather than race.[19-109] It was a different story in the civilian community, where the black serviceman's uniform commanded little more respect than it did in 1950. Eventually this contrast would become so intolerable that he and his sympathizers would beleaguer the Department of Defense with demands for action against discrimination in off-base housing, schools, and places of public accommodation.

CHAPTER 20
Limited Response to Discrimination

The good feelings brought on by the integration of the armed forces lasted less than a decade. By the early 1960's the Department of Defense and the civil rights advocates had begun once more to draw apart, the source of contention centering on their differing interpretations of the scope of the Truman order. The Defense Department professed itself unable to interfere with community laws and customs even when those laws and customs discriminated against men in uniform. The civil rights leaders, however, rejected the federal government's acceptance of the *status quo.* Reacting especially to the widespread and blatant discrimination encountered by servicemen both in communities adjacent to bases at home and abroad and in the reserve components of the services in many parts of the country, they stepped up demands for remedial action against a situation that they believed continued at the sufferance of the armed forces.

Nor were their demands limited to the problem of discrimination in the local community. Civil rights spokesmen backed the complaints of those black servicemen who had begun to question their treatment in the military community itself. Lacking what many of them considered an effective procedure for dealing with racial complaints, black servicemen usually passed on their grievances to congressmen and various civil rights organizations, and these, in turn, took the problems to the Defense Department. The number of complaints over inequalities in promotion, assignment, and racial representation never matched the volume of those on discrimination in the community, nor did their appearance attest to a new set of problems or any particular increase in discrimination. It seemed rather that the black serviceman, after the first flush of victory over segregation, was beginning to perceive from the vantage of his improved position that other and perhaps more subtle barriers stood in his way. Whatever the reason, complaints of discrimination within the services themselves, rarely heard in the Pentagon in the late 1950's, suddenly reappeared.[20-1] Actually, the complaints about discrimination both in the local civilian community and on the military reservation called for a basic alteration in the way the services interpreted their policies of equal treatment and opportunity. In the end it would prove easier for the services to attack the gaudier but ultimately less complicated problems outside their gates.

It would be a mistake to equate the notice given the persistent but subtle problem of on-base discrimination with the sometimes brutal injustice visited on black servicemen off-base in the early 1960's. Black servicemen often found the short bus ride from post to town a trip into

235

the past, where once again they were forced to endure the old patterns of segregation. Defense Department officials were aware, for example, that decent housing open to black servicemen was scarce. With limited income, under military orders, and often forced by circumstances to reside in the civilian community, black servicemen were, in the words of Robert S. McNamara, President Kennedy's Secretary of Defense, "singularly defenseless against this bigotry."[20-2] While the services had always denied responsibility for combating this particular form of discrimination, many in the black community were anxious to remind them of John F. Kennedy's claim in the presidential campaign of 1960 that discrimination in housing could be alleviated with a stroke of the Chief Executive's pen.

But housing was only part of a larger pattern of segregation that included restrictions on black servicemen's use of many places of public accommodation such as restaurants, theaters, and saloons, some literally on the doorstep of military reservations. James Evans listed some twenty-seven military installations in the United States where in 1961 segregation in transportation and places of public accommodation was established in adjacent communities by law or custom.[20-3] Moreover, instances of blatant Jim Crow tactics were rapidly multiplying near bases in Japan, Germany, the Philippines, and elsewhere as host communities began to adopt the prejudices of their visitors.[20-4] The United States Commission on Civil Rights charged that black servicemen were often reluctant to complain to their superiors or the Inspector General because of the repeated failure of local commands to show concern for the problem and suspicion that complainers would be subjected to reprisals.[20-5]

Civil rights leaders were particularly distressed by this form of discrimination, which, considering the armed forces' persistent declaration of impotence in the matter, seemed destined to remain a permanent condition of service life. "These problems involve factors which are not directly under the control of the Department of Defense," Assistant Secretary for Manpower Carlisle P. Runge noted in a typical response.[20-6] Similar sentiments were often expressed by local commanders, although some tried to soften their refusal to act with the hope that the military example might change local community attitudes in the long run.[20-7] Congressman Charles C. Diggs, Jr., did not share this hope. Citing numerous examples for the President of discrimination against black servicemen, he charged that, far from influencing local communities to change, commanders actually cooperated in discrimination by punishing or otherwise identifying protesting servicemen as troublemakers.[20-8]

CIVIL RIGHTS LEADERS AT THE WHITE HOUSE.
Attorney General Robert F. Kennedy poses with
(from left) Martin Luther King, Jr., Roy Wilkins, Whitney M. Young, Jr., and A. Philip Randolph.

Especially galling to civil rights leaders was the conviction that the armed forces had set up artificial and self-imposed barriers to a needed social reform. In the end this conviction seemed to spur them on. The American Veterans Committee, for example, demanded that when a community "mistreats American troops, such as in Montgomery, Alabama, or flaunts its Ku Klux Klan membership, as does Selma, Alabama, the entire area should be placed 'off limits' to purchases by Defense installations and by Servicemen."[20-9] Others were convinced that the federal government was in effect supporting segregation through its widespread economic assistance programs to state and local governments and to private institutions in the fields of employment, housing, education, health service, military affairs, and agriculture. In August 1961 a group of fifty civil rights leaders petitioned the President to end such federal support.[20-10] On a more modest scale, the Congress of Racial Equality asked the Army in August 1962 to declare segregated restaurants in Aberdeen, Maryland, off limits to all military personnel. The activist group justified its demand by stating that "the Army declares dangerous or immoral establishments off limits to soldiers and what is more dangerous or immoral in a democracy than racial intolerance?"[20-11] In this they failed to distinguish between the commander's proper response to what was illegal, for example prostitution, and what was still legal, for example, segregated housing.

The Kennedy Administration and Civil Rights

The strong connection between black morale and military efficiency made it likely that the new Secretary of Defense would be intimately concerned with problems of discrimination. Highly trained in modern managerial techniques, Robert S. McNamara came to the Pentagon with the idea of instituting a series of fundamental changes in the management of the armed forces through manpower reorganization and what was becoming known as systems analysis. Whatever his attitude toward racial justice, his initial interest in the Defense Department's black employees, military and civilian, was closely linked to his concern for military efficiency. Less than a week on the job, he called for information on the status of Negroes in the department. He had heard that some services were better integrated than others, and he wanted his Assistant

236

Secretary for Manpower to investigate. He wanted to know if there was a "fair" proportion of Negroes in the higher civilian grades. If not, he asked, "what do you recommend be done about it?"[20-12] These questions, and indeed all action on civil rights matters originating in his office in the months to come, indicated that McNamara, like his predecessors, would limit his reforms to discrimination within the services themselves. But as time passed, McNamara, like President Kennedy, would warm to the civil rights cause and eventually both would become firmly committed.

The Kennedy administration has been closely identified with civil rights, yet the President's major biographers and several of his assistants agree that his commitment to civil rights reform did not emerge full-blown on inauguration day. It was only in the last months of his administration that Kennedy, subjected to civil rights demands and sharing the interests and experiences of his brother Robert, the Attorney General, threw himself wholeheartedly into the civil rights fray.[20-13] As senator and later as President, Kennedy was sympathetic to the aspirations of the black minority, appreciated its support in his campaign, but regarded civil rights as one, and not the most pressing, problem facing the Chief Executive. Even his administrations's use of federal marshals during the freedom rides in 1961 and its use of both marshals and troops at Oxford, Mississippi, in 1962 and troops again in Alabama in 1963 were justified in the name of enforcement of federal judicial processes. Well into 1963 he studiously downplayed the civil rights issues involved.

Kennedy was convinced that the only answer to the injustices suffered by Negroes was a series of strong laws, but he was also certain that such legislation was impossible to achieve in 1961. To urge it on an unwilling Congress would only jeopardize his legislative program, increase the black minority's feeling of frustration, and divide the nation in a period of national crisis. Discussing the Civil Rights Commission's "non-negotiable" demands concerning the organized reserves, for example, commission member Father Theodore Hesburgh remembered the President saying:

Look, I have a serious problem in West Berlin, and I do not think this is the proper time to start monkeying around with the Army.... I have no problem with the principle of this, and we'll certainly be doing it, but at this precise moment I have to keep uppermost in mind that I may need these units ... and I can't have them in the midst of a social revolution while I'm trying to do this.[20-14]

Kennedy temporized. He would promptly and positively endorse the principle of equal rights and enforce the civil rights decisions of the Supreme Court through negotiation, moral suasion, executive order, and, when necessary, through the use of federal marshals.[20-15] The Justice Department meanwhile would pursue a vigorous course of litigation to insure the franchise for Negroes from which, he believed, all civil blessings flowed.

Civil rights was not mentioned in Kennedy's first State of the Union message. With the exception of a measure to outlaw literacy and poll tax requirements for voting, no civil rights bills were sent to the Eighty-seventh Congress. Yet at one of his first press conferences, the President told newsmen that a plan to withhold federal funds in certain segregation cases would be included in a general study "of where the Federal Government might usefully place its power and influence to expand civil rights."[20-16] On 6 March 1961 he signed Executive Order 10925, which combined the committees on government contracts and employment policy into a single Committee on Equal Employment Opportunity chaired by the Vice President.[20-17] His order, he believed, specified sanctions "sweeping enough to ensure compliance."[20-18] Finally, in November 1962, after numerous and increasingly pointed reminders from civil rights advocates, the President issued Executive Order 11063, directing executive agencies to take action against discrimination in the sale or lease of federal housing or any housing bought with loans from or insured by the federal government.[20-19]

Besides executive orders, the White House had other ways, less formal but perhaps more efficient, of getting the federal bureaucracy to move on civil rights. Upon the recommendation of Special Assistant Frederick G. Dutton, the President created the Civil Rights Subcabinet Group in March 1961 to coordinate the administration's civil rights actions. Under Dutton's chairmanship, this group included the assistant secretaries responsible for racial matters in their respective agencies, with White House Special Civil Rights Assistant Harris Wofford serving as executive secretary.[20-20] The group regularly scrutinized the racial programs of the various departments, demanding reports and investigations of racial matters and insuring that the interests and criticisms of the administration were quickly disseminated at the operations level of the federal agencies affected.[20-21]

There is evidence that the subcabinet group was responsible for considerable cross-fertilization of civil rights programs among the departments. For example, it appears to have used the experience of black servicemen in interstate travel to move the Department of Justice and,

237

with the assistance of Attorney General Kennedy, the Interstate Commerce Commission toward eliminating such discrimination.[20-22] And it was through the subcabinet group that the Attorney General's interest in minority voting rights was translated into a voting registration campaign among servicemen.[20-23]

The existence of this group, with its surveys, questions, and investigations, put constant pressure on the armed services. They were not singled out for special treatment, but they obviously attracted the attention of both the White House and the civil rights organizations because their commitment to equal treatment and opportunity affected so many people and their past successes and remaining problems were having a decided impact on American society. In the words of presidential assistant Wofford, the Defense Department was "a world within itself," a world which by its magnitude could make a "significant contribution by its example" to the solution of the nation's racial problems.[20-24]

The size of the department's racial program alluded to by Wofford also invited the attention of a federal agency outside White House control. The United States Commission on Civil Rights was continually investigating the services, probing allegations of discrimination against black servicemen and evaluating the role of the department in community race relations.[20-25] Of particular interest to an understanding of racial policy in the 1960's is the commission's comprehensive survey, titled "The Services and Their Relations with the Community," which concluded that the continued existence of community discrimination against servicemen and their dependents had a detrimental effect on the morale and efficiency of significant numbers of them. The commission cataloged the traditional alibis of military commanders: "it is not the mission of the services to concern themselves with the practices of the local community"; the commander's responsibility "stops at the gate"; harmonious relations with the community must be maintained; and, finally, in order to achieve harmony, servicemen must comply with local laws and customs. Yet when it came to other areas of community relations, particularly where the general health, welfare, and morale of the servicemen were involved, the commission found that commanders did not hesitate to ally themselves with servicemen, local community controversy and opposition notwithstanding. The commission wanted the services to take a similar stand against racial discrimination in the community. Although its specific recommendations differed little from those of civil rights leaders, its position as an independent federal agency and its access to the news media added a constant and special pressure on the services.[20-26]

Another pressure on the armed forces in the early sixties was exerted by the civil rights bureaucracy in the White House itself. Various presidential assistants subjected the services' reports on progress in the equal opportunity field to unprecedented scrutiny, asking questions that forced the Defense Department to explain or justify its racial policies and practices.[20-27] In March 1961, civil rights assistants on the President's staff inquired about the number of Negroes on the Defense Department's military and civilian screening boards.[20-28]Later, Special Assistant Frank D. Reeves inquired about the employees working in the executive area of the department and suggested that the front offices do something about hiring more black office workers.[20-29] And again as a result of a number of questions raised about the Navy's race policy, presidential assistant Wofford sponsored a White House meeting on 18 September 1961 for several civil rights representatives and Adam Yarmolinsky, Special Assistant to the Secretary of Defense, with the Chief of Naval Personnel, Vice Adm. William R. Smedberg. Beginning with Yarmolinsky's probing questions concerning the perennial problem of racial composition of the Steward's Branch, the meeting evolved into a general review of the Navy's recent problems and achievements in race relations.[20-30]

At times this White House scrutiny could be aggressively critical. There was, for example, small comfort for Defense Department officials in Dutton's review of department comments on the recommendations of the Civil Rights Leadership Conference submitted to the White House in August 1961.[20-31] Dutton wanted to know more about the department's inquiry into possible racial discrimination in the sentences meted out by military courts. He was concerned with the allegation, categorically denied by the Defense Department, that black servicemen with school-aged dependents were being moved off bases to avoid integrating base schools. He wanted a prompt investigation. Dutton was impatient with the Navy's explanation for the continuing predominance of Negroes in the Steward's Branch, and he was especially critical of the racial situation in the National Guard. He wanted a progress report on these points. Finally, he was unhappy with the lack of Negroes in officer training, an executive area, he claimed, in which civilian agencies were forging ahead. He wanted something done about that also.[20-32]

The disquietude White House staff members produced among Defense Department officials was nothing compared to the trauma induced by the President's personal attention. John Kennedy rarely intervened but he did so on occasion quickly and decisively and in a way

238

illustrative of his administration's civil rights style. He acted promptly, for example, when he noticed an all-white unit from the Coast Guard Academy marching in his inaugural parade. His call to the Secretary of the Treasury Douglas Dillon on inauguration night led to the admission of the first black students to the Coast Guard Academy. He elaborated on the incident during his first cabinet meeting, asking each department head to analyze the minority employment situation in his own department. He was also upset to see "few, if any" black honor guardsmen in the units that greeted visiting Ghanian President Kwame Nkrumah on 13 March, an observation not lost on Secretary McNamara. "Would it be possible," the new defense chief asked his manpower assistant, "to introduce into these units a reasonable number of negro personnel?"[20-33] An immediate survey revealed that Negroes accounted for 14 percent of the Air Force honor unit, 8 percent of the Army's, and 2.2 percent of the Marines Corps'. The 100-man naval unit had no black members.[20-34]

PRESIDENT KENNEDY AND PRESIDENT ALLESSANDRI OF CHILE
review an all-white honor guard unit, White House, 1962.

These were minor incidents, yet Kennedy's interest was bound to make a difference. As Evans wryly put it in regard to the survey of blacks in the honor guard: "Pending any further instructions it is submitted that the alert which has been given in person and by telephone in connection with the securing of the above data may be adequate for accomplishing the objectives contemplated in the [McNamara] memorandum."[20-35] If not conducive to substantive change in the lot of the black serviceman, the President's intervention signaled in a way clearly understood by Washington bureaucrats that a new style in executive politics was at hand and a new awareness of the racial implications of their actions was expected of them.[20-36]

The Department of Defense, 1961-1963

The White House approach to civil rights matters was faithfully adopted in McNamara's department. Despite a reputation for foot-dragging in some quarters—Deputy Secretary Roswell L. Gilpatric admitted that neither he nor McNamara was especially interested in personnel matters and that some of their early appointments in the personnel field were inappropriate—[20-37]the secretary and his assistants issued a spate of directives and policy memorandums and inaugurated a whole series of surveys and investigations. Yarmolinsky was later able to recall eleven major papers produced by the secretary's office during the first thirty months of McNamara's incumbency. Evans's more comprehensive list of actions taken by the office of the secretary's manpower assistant with regard to equal opportunity contained some forty items.[20-38] These totals did not include 1,717 racial complaints the Defense Department investigated and adjudicated before September 1963 nor the scores of contract compliance reviews conducted under the equal opportunity clauses in defense contracts.[20-39]

The number of Department of Defense rulings that pertained directly to black servicemen was matched by the comprehensiveness of their subject matter. Many concerned the recruitment of Negroes and the increase in their proportion of the military establishment. Others pertained to off-base matters, ranging from prohibitions against the use of segregated facilities during field exercises to the use of military units in ceremonies and shows involving segregated audiences. Continued segregation in the reserves, the racial policies of the United Services Organization, and even the racial rule of morticians who dealt with the services came in for attention.

Yet if these investigations and directives bespoke a quickened tempo in the fight for equal treatment and opportunity in the armed forces, they did not herald a substantive reinterpretation of policy. The Defense Department continued to limit its actions to matters obviously and directly within its purview. The same self-imposed restriction that kept McNamara's immediate predecessors from dealing with the most pressing demands for reforms by black servicemen and the civil rights leaders continued to be observed. This fact was especially clear in the case of the Defense Department's four major policy pronouncements involving the complex problem of discrimination visited upon servicemen and their dependents outside the gates of the military reservation.

Discrimination Off the Military Reservation

In the first of these directives, which was derived from President Kennedy's executive order on equal employment opportunity,[20-40] Secretary McNamara laid down that no departmental facility could be used by employee recreational organizations that practiced racial or religious discrimination. Included were facilities financed from nonappropriated funds as well as all organizations to which civilian as well as military personnel belonged.[20-41] A straightforward enough commitment to a necessary racial reform, the secretary's order could by logical extension also be viewed as carrying the department's fight against racial discrimination into the civilian community. Yet precisely because of these implications, the directive was subjected to later

239

clarification. Official interpretation revealed that secretarial rhetoric aside, the Department of Defense was not yet ready to involve civilians in its equality crusade.

The problem emerged when the commander of Maxwell Air Force Base, in keeping with his reading of the McNamara order, prohibited the use of Maxwell's dining halls for a segregated luncheon of the American Legion's Boys' State and its playing fields for the segregated Maxwell Little League teams. Assistant Secretary Runge quickly reassured Senator Lister Hill of Alabama that the 28 April order was limited to employee organizations and so informed the Under Secretary of the Air Force.[20-42] But a further clarification and, in effect, a further restriction of the department's policy in discrimination cases was issued when the Civil Rights Commission became interested in the case. "If these activities are not covered by the April 28 directive," the commission's staff director-designate wanted to know, "what is the position of the Department of Defense on them?"[20-43] Runge's response, cleared through Special Assistant Yarmolinsky, was hardly reassuring to the commission. The department did not inquire into the racial rules of private organizations that used departmental facilities, Runge explained, nor did it object when its departmentally sponsored teams and groups played or performed with segregated private recreational groups.[20-44]

With the effect of a stone dropped into water, the implications of the anti-discrimination memorandum continued to ripple outward. The commander of Brookley Air Force Base, Alabama, canceled the sale of subsidized tickets to the Mobile Bears baseball games by the base's civilian welfare council on the grounds that the ball park's segregated seating of Air Force personnel violated the secretary's order. Inquiries from Capitol Hill set off another round of clarifications.[20-45] While the secretary's manpower advisers were inclined to support the base commander's action, some of the department's legal advisers had reservations. Canceling the sale of tickets, a lawyer in the general counsel's office noted, was consistent with one construction of the secretary's memorandum but was not the "inevitable interpretation" since it was the ball club and not the Air Force recreational organization that discriminated.[20-46] Another departmental lawyer warned that if the commander's interpretation was sustained the department would next have to prohibit welfare groups from selling unsubsidized tickets to events where the seating or even perhaps the performers themselves were segregated.[20-47]

Yarmolinsky ignored such speculations, and on 4 August 1961 informed special presidential assistant Dutton that the secretary's office approved the base commander's action. Although the sale of tickets did not technically violate Executive Order 10925, the department's sponsorship and subsidy of segregated events, he said, "is, in our opinion, not consonant with the clear intent of the President's memorandum."[20-48] Yarmolinsky suggested the White House might want to consider proposing to the ball club that the air base would resume the sale of tickets if it could sell a block of unsegregated seats. The White House reply was postponed until after the passage of the foreign aid bill, but the Air Force eventually received notice to proceed along these lines.[20-49]

On 19 June 1961 Deputy Secretary Gilpatric issued a second major policy statement. This one ostensibly dealt with the availability of integrated community facilities for servicemen, but was in fact far wider in scope, and brought the department nearer the uncharted shoals of community race relations. A testament to the extraordinary political sensitivity of the subject was the long time the document spent in the drafting stage. Its wording incorporated the suggestions of representatives of the three service secretaries and was carefully reviewed by the President's civil rights advisers, who wanted the draft shown to the President "because of his particular interest in Civil Rights matters."[20-50] With their request in mind, and because of what he considered "the tense situation now existent in the South," Runge urged the secretary to send the President the memorandum. Before doing so McNamara asked his general counsel, Cyrus R. Vance, to discuss the draft with the under secretaries of the services and Assistant Attorney General Nicholas B. Katzenbach and Burke Marshall. At the suggestion of the justice officials, the draft was slightly revised; then it was sent once again to the services for review. Finally on 19 June 1961, and only after Yarmolinsky had rejected certain minor alterations suggested by the services, was the memorandum issued under Gilpatric's signature and its provisions passed down to the local commanders by the service secretaries.[20-51]

The policy that emerged from all this careful labor committed the services to very little change. In the first place the title, The Availability of Facilities to Military Personnel, was vague, a legacy of the department's fear of congressional retaliation for any substantive move in the politically sensitive area of race relations. Actually the secretary's office was primarily concerned with discrimination in places of public accommodation such as swimming pools, recreational facilities, meeting halls, and the like while the explosive subject of off-base housing was ignored. Although the order's ambiguity did not preclude initiatives in the housing field by some zealous commanders, neither did it oblige any commander to take any specific action, thus providing a convenient excuse for no action at all.[20-52] Commanders, for example, were ordered to provide integrated facilities off post for servicemen "to the extent possible," a significant qualification in areas where such facilities were not available in the community. Commanders were also "expected to make every effort" to obtain integrated facilities off base through the good offices of their command-community relations committees. In effect the department was asking its commanders to achieve through tact what the courts and the Justice Department were failing to achieve through legal process.

Where the order was specific, it carefully limited the extent of reforms. It barred the use of military police in the enforcement of local segregation laws, a positive step but a limited reform since only in very rare instances had military police ever been so employed. The order also provided "as circumstances warranted" for legal assistance to servicemen to insure that they were afforded due process of law in cases growing out of the enforcement of local segregation ordinances. Again what seemed a broad commitment and extensive interference with local matters was in practice very carefully circumscribed, as demonstrated by the Air Force policy statement issued in the wake of the secretary's order.

The Air Force announced that in the case of discrimination in the community, the local Air Force commander and his staff judge advocate would interview the aggrieved serviceman to ascertain the facts and advise him of his legal recourses, "but will neither encourage nor discourage the filing of a criminal complaint." The purpose of the policy, the Air Force Chief of Staff explained, was to assist servicemen and at the same time avoid disrupting good community relations. The commander should remain interested, but he should leave the work to his judge advocate so that the commander would not personally be "caught in the middle" to the detriment of his community relations program. If local authorities refused to cooperate, the matter should be referred to higher authority who might pursue it with local government officials. Such procedures might keep the commander from becoming embroiled in locally sensitive issues.[20-53] In short, discrimination was to be fought through voluntary action at the local command level, but nothing was to be done that might compromise the commander's standing with the local authorities.

McNamara's office displayed the same good intentions and crippling inhibitions when it considered policy on the participation of servicemen in civil rights demonstrations. The secretary had inherited a policy from his predecessor who, in the wake of a series of sit-in demonstrations involving black airmen in the spring of 1960, had approved a plan devised by the judge advocate generals of the services and other Defense Department officials. Declaring such activity "inappropriate" in light of the services' mission, these officials banned the participation of servicemen in civil rights demonstrations and gave local commanders broad discretionary powers to prevent such participation, including the right to declare the place of demonstration off limits or to restrict servicemen to the base. Although all the services adopted the new policy, only the Air Force published detailed instructions.[20-54]

This prohibition did not deter all black servicemen, and some commanders, in their zeal to enforce departmental policy, went beyond the methods McNamara's predecessor had recommended. Such was the case during a series of sit-ins at Killeen, Texas, near the Army's Fort Hood, where, as reported in the national press and subsequently investigated by the United States Commission on Civil Rights, the commander used military police to break up two demonstrations.[20-55] The secretary's office reacted quickly to the incidents. A prohibition against the use of military police to quell civil rights demonstrations was quickly included in the secretary's policy statement, The Availability of Facilities to Military Personnel, then being formulated. "This memorandum," Assistant Secretary Runge assured McNamara, "should preclude any further such incidents."[20-56] In specific reference to the situation in the Fort Hood area, the Deputy Under Secretary of the Army reported that as a result of a new policy and the emphasis placed on personal contact by commanders with local community representatives, "a cordial relationship now exists between Fort Hood and the surrounding communities."[20-57]

But to ban the use of military police and to urge commanders to deal with local business leaders to end segregation actually begged the question. Significantly, the much-heralded memorandum on the availability of integrated facilities failed to review the rules governing participation in demonstrations, a subject of pressing interest to an increasing number of Negroes as the civil rights struggle moved into a more active phase. Bothered by this failure, Air Force representatives on the policy drafting team had wanted to provide local commanders with guidance before civil rights incidents occurred. The Justice officials who reviewed the memorandum at McNamara's invitation, however, were reluctant to see specific reference to such incidents incorporated, and the matter was ignored.[20-58]

In fact, Justice officials were not the only ones reluctant to see the issue raised. It was a common belief in the Defense Department that military service placed some limitations on a

241

man's basic liberties. Because servicemen were assigned to their duty station, subject to immediate transfers and on duty twenty-four hours a day, they were allowed no opportunity for participating in demonstrations.[20-59] The department's general counsel was even more specific, saying that a prohibition against picketing would not conflict with the department's anti-discrimination policies and could be lawfully imposed by the services. "Indeed," he believed, "the role of the military establishment in our society required the imposition of such a limitation on the off-duty activities of service personnel."[20-60] Blessed by such authority, the 1960 prohibition against participation in civil rights demonstrations remained in effect for more than three years.[20-61]

Such restrictions could not last much longer. Given the civil rights temper of the times—1963 witnessed the mammoth march on Washington, the introduction of President Kennedy's civil rights bill, and the landmark directive of the Secretary of Defense on equal opportunity in the armed forces—a total prohibition on servicemen's participation in demonstrations appeared more and more incongruous. Finally, on 16 July 1963, McNamara relaxed the department's policy. Still declaring such participation inappropriate and unnecessary for servicemen in view of their "special obligations of citizenship," he nevertheless lifted the ban on military participation in demonstrations, provided that the uniform was not worn; such activity took place during off-duty hours, off the military reservation, and did not constitute a breach of law and order; and no violence was reasonably likely to result.[20-62]

SECRETARY OF DEFENSE MCNAMARA

Again an apparent liberalization of departmental racial policy actually promised very little change. First, the continuing prohibitions on participation in demonstrations were so broad and so vague that they could be interpreted to cover almost any civil rights activity. Then, too, the secretary left the interpretation of his order to the judgment of local commanders, a dubious blessing in the eyes of the civil libertarians and concerned servicemen in light of the narrow constructions commanders had given recent Defense Department memorandums. Finally, the relaxation of the ban was applicable only to the continental United States. In response to a request for guidance from the European commander, the Joint Chiefs of Staff informed all overseas commanders that as guests of Allied nations, U.S. servicemen had no right to picket, demonstrate, or otherwise participate in any act designed to "alter the policies, practices, or activities of the local inhabitants who are operating within the framework of their own laws."[20-63]

The fourth major memorandum on racial matters outlined the department's application of Executive Order 11063 on housing. Racial discrimination in off-base housing had become perhaps the chief complaint of black servicemen who were further incensed by many local commanders who maintained lists of segregated houses in their base housing offices. In some cases commanders referred their black servicemen to the Urban League or similar organizations for help in finding suitable housing.[20-64] Demands that the services do something about the situation were rebuffed. As the Assistant Secretary of Defense explained to a White House official, the Department of Defense had "virtually no direct involvement" in off-base housing, the segregation of which was "not readily susceptible to change by actions that are within the control of the military departments."[20-65]

Several of McNamara's assistants disagreed. They drafted a housing order for the secretary but not without opposition at first from some of their colleagues. An Army representative, for example, suggested a counterproposal that commanders be ordered to work through the federal agencies established in various geographical areas of the country by Executive Order 11063. An Air Force spokesman recommended the creation of special regional and local community committees, chaired by representatives of the Housing and Home Finance Agency and including members from all major federal agencies. For his part, Stephen S. Jackson, a special assistant in the manpower office, thought these service proposals had merit, and he wanted to postpone action until they had been discussed with other interested federal agencies.[20-66]

McNamara, however, "readily agreed" with his housing experts that a letter on nondiscrimination in family housing was necessary. On 8 March 1963 he informed the service secretaries that effective immediately all military leases for family housing, that is, contracts for private housing rented by the services for servicemen, would contain a nondiscrimination clause in accordance with the President's executive order. He also ordered military bases to maintain listings only on nonsegregated private housing.[20-67] Again an attempt to bring about a needed change was severely limited in effectiveness by the department's concern for the scope of the commander's authority in the local community. The application of the President's order would end segregation in leased housing, but only a small percentage of black servicemen lived in such housing. The majority of service families lived off base in private housing, which the new order,

242

except for banning the listing of segregated properties by base housing offices, ignored. Barring the use of segregated private housing to all servicemen, a more direct method of changing the racial pattern surrounding military installations, would have to wait for a substantive change in departmental thinking.

Reserves and Regulars: A Comparison

While the interest of both civil rights advocates and defense officials was focused on off-base concerns during the early 1960's, discrimination continued to linger in the armed forces. A particularly sensitive issue to the services, which in the public mind had complete jurisdiction over all men in uniform, was the position of the Negro in the reserve components. To generalize on the racial policies of the fifty-four National Guard organizations is difficult, but whereas some state guards had been a progressive force in the integration of the services in the early postwar period, others had become symbols of racism by 1961. Some fourteen years after the Truman order, ten states with large black populations and understaffed guard units still had no Negroes in the guard. The Kennedy administration was not the first to wrestle with the problem of applying a single racial policy to both the regulars and the guard. It was aware that too much tampering with the politically influential and volatile guard could produce an explosion. At the same time any appearance of timidity courted antagonism from another quarter.

From the beginning the new administration found itself criticized by civil rights organizations, including the U.S. Commission on Civil Rights, for not moving quickly against segregated National Guard units.[20-68] A delegation from the NAACP's 1961 convention visited Assistant Secretary Runge in July and criticized—to the exclusion of all other subjects—discrimination in the National Guard. This group wanted the federal government to withhold funds from states that continued to bar black participation. Repeating the old claim that special federal-state relationships precluded direct action by the Secretary of Defense, Runge nevertheless promised the delegates a renewed effort to provide equal opportunity. He also made a somewhat irrelevant reference to the recent experience of a black citizen in Oklahoma who had secured admission to the state guard by a direct appeal to the governor.[20-69] How futile such appeals would be in some states was demonstrated a week later when the Adjutant General of Florida declared that since the guard was a volunteer organization and his state had always drawn its members from among white citizens, Florida was under no obligation to enlist black men.[20-70]

That the new administration had quietly adopted different policies toward the guard and the regular forces was confirmed when Runge responded to a report prepared by the American Veterans Committee on the lack of racial progress in the guard. The veterans group called on the administration to use the threat of withdrawal of federal recognition to alter guard practices.[20-71] The administration refused. A policy of force might be acceptable for the active armed forces, but voluntary persuasion seemed more appropriate for the National Guard. Enunciating what would become the Defense Department's position on the National Guard through 1963, Runge declared that the federal government had no legal authority to force integration on the guard when it was not serving in a federal status. Furthermore, withdrawal of federal recognition or withholding federal funds as a means of bringing about integration, though legally sound, would cause some states to reject federal support and inactivate their units, thereby stripping the country of a portion of its military reserve and damaging national security. Citing the progress being made by persuasion, Runge predicted that some recalcitrant states might in time voluntarily move toward integration.[20-72] Noting instances of recent progress and citing legal restrictions against forcing state compliance, McNamara endorsed the policy of encouraging voluntary compliance.[20-73]

Although unauthorized, similar patterns of discrimination persisted in parts of the organized reserves. Reserve units had links with both the regular forces and the guard. Like the regulars, the reserve was legally a creature of the federal government and subject to policies established by the Secretary of Defense. Moreover, the reserve drew much of its manpower from the pool of soldiers separating from active duty with a reserve obligation still to fulfill, and within some limits the Defense Department could assign such men to units in a manner that could influence the reserve's racial composition. But like the guard, the reserve also had a distinct local flavor, serving almost as a social club in some parts of the country. This characteristic was often an important factor in maintaining a unit at satisfactory strength. Since segregation sometimes went hand in hand with the clublike atmosphere, the services feared that a strong stand on integration might cause a severe decline in the strength of some units.[20-74] When the Army staff reviewed the situation in 1956, therefore, it had not pressed for integration of all units, settling instead for merely "encouraging" commanders to open their units to Negroes.[20-75]

The move toward complete integration of the reserves was slow. In 1956, for example, more than 75 percent of the Army's reserve units in southern states were still segregated. The other services followed a similar pattern; in 1962 more than 40 percent of all reserve units in the country were white; the Army retained six all-black reserve units as well. Racial exclusion persisted in the Reserve Officers' Training Corps also, although here the fault was probably not so much a matter of reserve policy as the lingering segregation pattern in some state school systems. At the same time, the reserves had more blacks in nondrill status than in drill status. In other words, more blacks were in reserve pools where, unassigned to specific units, they did not participate in active duty training. In 1962, some 75 percent of the black reservists in the Army and Air Force, 85 percent in the Navy, and 38 percent in the Marine Corps were assigned to such pools. For many reservists, paid drill status was desirable; apart from the money received for such active duty, they had the opportunity to gain credit toward retirement and pensions.

Deputy Secretary of Defense Gilpatric reminded the services in April 1962 that the Truman order applied to the reserves and called on the under secretaries to integrate the all-black and all-white units "as rapidly as is consistent with military effectiveness."[20-76] He also wanted a review of black assignments for the purpose of removing the disproportionate number of Negroes in pools "consistent with the military requirements and the skills of the personnel involved."

A defense manpower team surveyed the reserves in November 1962. It tried to soften the obvious implication of its racial statistics by pointing out that the all-black units were limited to two Army areas, and action had already been taken by the Third Army and Fourth Army commanders to integrate the six units as soon as possible. The team also announced initiation of a series of administrative safeguards against discrimination in the enlistment and assignment of men to drilling units. As for the all-white units, the reviewers cautioned that discrimination was not necessarily involved since Negroes constituted a relatively small proportion of the strength of the reserves—4.8 percent of the Army, 4.4 percent of the Air Force, and an estimated 3.2 percent of the Navy. Furthermore, the data neither proved nor disproved allegations of discrimination since the degree to which individuals volunteered, the skills and aptitudes they possessed, and the needs of the services were all factors in the assignment and use of the men involved.[20-77]

Pleas of an absence of legal authority in regard to the National Guard and generalized promises of racial reform in the reserves were not going to still the complaints of the civil rights organizations nor discourage the interest of their allies in the administration. Clearly, the Department of Defense would be hearing more about race in the reserve components in the months to come.

The sudden reemergence in the early 1960's of complaints of discrimination in the regular forces centered around a familiar litany: the number of Negroes in some of the services still fell significantly short of the black percentage of the national population; and separate standards, favorable to whites, prevailed in the promotion and assignment systems of all the services. There had to be some discrimination involved, Congressman Diggs pointed out to the Secretary of the Air Force in July 1960. With extensive help from the services, Diggs had been investigating servicemen's complaints for some time. While his major concern remained the discrimination suffered by black servicemen off base, he nevertheless concluded that the service regulations developed in consultation with the Fahy Committee more than a decade earlier had not been fully implemented and discriminatory practices existed "in varying degrees" at military installations around the world. Diggs admitted that a black serviceman might well charge discrimination to mask his failure to compete successfully for a job or grade, but to accept such failures as a universal explanation for the disproportionate number of Negroes in the lower ranks and undesirable occupations was to accept as true the canard that Negroes as a group were deficient. Diggs's conclusion, which he pressed upon the department with some notice in the press, was that some black servicemen were being subtly but deliberately and arbitrarily restricted to inferior positions because their military superiors exercised judgments based on racial considerations. These judgments, he charged, were inconsistent with the spirit of the Truman order.[20-78]

At first glance the 1963 study of racial discrimination by the U.S. Commission on Civil Rights seemed to contradict Diggs's charges. The commission concluded that taken as a whole the status of black servicemen had improved considerably since the Truman order. It noted that black representation had remained relatively constant since the early days of integration, 8.2 percent of the total, 9.2 percent of the enlisted strength, and approached national population averages. The percentage of black officers, 1.6 percent of all officers, while admittedly low, had been rising steadily and compared favorably with the number of black executives in the civilian economy. The occupational status of the black enlisted man had also undergone steady improvement since the early days of integration, especially when one compared the number and variety of military occupation specialties held by black servicemen with opportunities in the rest of the civil service and the business community.

Finally, and perhaps most important, the commission found that in their daily operations, military installations were "generally free from the taint of racial discrimination."[20-79] It confirmed the general assessments of the Anti-Defamation League of B'nai B'rith and the American Veterans Committee among others, pointing out that black and white servicemen not only worked side by side, but also mingled in off-duty hours.[20-80] In sum, the study demonstrated general satisfaction with the racial situation on military bases. Its major concern, and indeed the major concern of Diggs and most black servicemen, remained the widespread discrimination prevailing against black servicemen in the local community.

These important generalizations aside, the commission nevertheless offered impressive statistical support for some of Diggs's charges when it investigated the diverse and conflicting enlistment and assignment patterns of the different services. The Navy and Marine Corps came in for special criticism. Even when the complexities of mental aptitude requirements and use of draftees versus enlistees were discounted, the commission found that these two services consistently employed a significantly smaller percentage of Negroes than the Army and Air Force. A similar disparity existed in assignment procedures. The commission found that both services failed to match the record of the civilian economy in the use of Negroes in technical, mechanical, administrative, clerical, and craft fields. It suspected that the services' recruiting and testing methods intensified these differences and wondered whether they might not operate to exclude Negroes in some instances.

Despite general approval of conditions on the bases, the commission found what it called "vestiges of discrimination on some bases." It reported some segregated noncommissioned officer clubs, some segregated transportation of servicemen to the local community, and some discriminatory employment patterns in the hiring of civilians for post jobs. Partly the legacy of the old segregated services, this discrimination, the commission concluded, was to a greater extent the result of the intrusion of local civilian attitudes. The commission's attention to outside influences on attitudes at the base suggested that it found the villain of the Diggs investigation, the prejudiced military official, far too simplistic an explanation for what was in reality institutional racism, a complex mixture of sociological forces and military traditions acting on the services. The Department of Defense's manpower experts dwelt on these forces and traditions when they analyzed recruitment, promotion, and assignment trends for McNamara in 1963.[20-81]

They found a general increase in black strength ratios between 1949 and 1962 (*Table 13*). They blamed the "selective" recruiting practices in vogue before the Truman order for the low enlistment ratios in 1949, just as they attributed the modest increases since that time to the effects of the services' equal treatment and opportunity programs. In the judgment of these analysts, racial differences in representation since the Truman order, and indeed most of the other discrepancies between black and white servicemen, could usually be explained by the sometimes sharp difference in aptitude test results (*Table 14*). A heritage of the Negro's limited, often segregated and inferior education and his economic and related environmental handicaps, low aptitude scores certainly explained the contrast in disqualification rates (*Tables 15 and 16*). By 1962 fully half of all Negroes—as compared to 8 percent of all whites—failed to qualify for service under minimum mental test standards. In some southern states, the draftee rejection rate for Negroes exceeded 80 percent.

TABLE 13—BLACK STRENGTH IN THE ARMED FORCES FOR SELECTED YEARS
(In Percentage)

	Army		Navy	
Year	Enlisted Men	Officers	Enlisted Men	
1949	12.4	1.8	4.7	
1954	13.7	3.0	3.6	
1962	12.2	3.2	5.2	

TABLE 14—ESTIMATED PERCENTAGE DISTRIBUTION OF DRAFT-AGE MALES IN U.S.
POPULATION BY AFQT GROUPS
(Based on Preinduction Examination, 1959-1962)

Group	White
I	11.8
II	31.3
III	31.9
IV	19.0

245

V	6.0

TABLE 15—RATE OF MEN DISQUALIFIED FOR SERVICE IN 1962
(In Percentage)

Cause	
Medical and other	
Mental test failure	
Total	

TABLE 16—REJECTION RATES FOR FAILURE TO PASS ARMED FORCES MENTAL TEST,
1962

	Area
Grand total, Continental United States	
Total, white	
Total, black	
First Army: Connecticut, Maine, Massachusetts, New Hampshire, New Jersey, New York, Rhode Island, Vermont	
White	
Black	
Second Army: Delaware, Washington, D.C., Kentucky, Maryland, Ohio, Pennsylvania, Virginia, West Virginia	
White	
Black	
Third Army: Alabama, Florida, Georgia, Mississippi, North Carolina, South Carolina, Tennessee	
White	
Black	
Fourth Army: Arkansas, Louisiana, New Mexico, Oklahoma, Texas	
White	
Black	
Fifth Army: Colorado, Illinois, Iowa, Michigan, Minnesota, Missouri, Nebraska, North Dakota, South Dakota, Wisconsin, Wyomir	
White	
Black	
Sixth Army: Arizona, California, Idaho, Montana, Nevada, Oregon, Utah, Washington	
White	
Black	

This problem became critical for black enlistments in the mid-1950's when the services, with less need for new servicemen, raised the mental standards for enlistees, denying Group IV men the right to enlist. (An exception to this pattern was the Navy's decision to accept Group IV enlistments in 1956 and 1957 to replace post-Korean enlistment losses.) In terms of total black representation, however, the new mental standards made a lesser difference (*Table 17*). Denying Group IV men enlistment during the 1950's only increased their number in the draft pool, and when the Army stepped up draft inductions in the early 1960's the number of Group IV men in uniform, including Negroes, rapidly increased.

TABLE 17—NONWHITE INDUCTIONS AND FIRST ENLISTMENTS, FISCAL YEARS 1953-
1962[1]

Fiscal Year	Total Accessions (000) [1]	DOD
1953	886.1	12.8
1954	576.3	10.0
1955	622.6	10.6
1956	481.9	11.2
1957	456.7	9.1
1958	367.1	7.9
1959	392.0	7.1
1960	389.4	8.1
1961	394.7	8.2
1962	518.6	9.7
Total	5,085.4	9.9

Tablenote 1: Includes inductions and male "non-prior service" enlistments into the Regular components.

Tablenote 2: The Army was the only service drafting men during this decade.

While the Army's dependence on the draft, and thus Group IV men, explained part of the continuing high percentage of Negroes in that service, the Defense Department manpower group was at a loss to explain the notable variation in black enlistments among the services. All employed similar enlistment standards, yet during the period 1958—1960, for example, black enlistment in the Army and Air Force averaged 7 percent, the Marine Corps 6 percent, and the Navy 2.7 percent. Nor could the analysts isolate the factors contributing to the low officer ratios in all four services. Almost all military officers during the period under analysis were college graduates, Negroes comprised about 4 percent of all male college graduates, yet only the Army maintained a black officer ratio approaching that figure. (*See Table 17.*)

The inability of many black servicemen to score highly in the tests might also explain why training in some technical occupations continued more restricted for them (*Tables 18 and 19*). In contrast to ground combat and service occupations, which required little formal school training, some occupation groups—electronics, for example—had high selection standards. The Defense Department group admitted that occupations for blacks in the armed forces had also been influenced by historical patterns of segregated assignments to food service and other support occupations. Among men with twenty or more years in uniform, 40 percent of the blacks and 12 percent of the whites were assigned to service occupations. But this pattern was changing, the analysts pointed out. The reduction in the differential between whites and blacks in service occupations among more recent recruits clearly reflected the impact of policies designed to equalize opportunities (*Table 20*). These policies had brought about an increasing proportion of Negroes in white collar skills as well as in ground combat skills.

TABLE 18—DISTRIBUTION OF ENLISTED PERSONNEL IN EACH MAJOR OCCUPATION, 1956

Occupation	
Electronics	
Other technical	
Admin. & clerical	
Mechanics & repairmen	
Crafts	
Services	
Ground combat	

TABLE 19—OCCUPATIONAL GROUP DISTRIBUTION BY RACE. ALL DOD, 1962

	Percentage Distribution	
	Negroes	
Ground combat	23.7	

247

Electronics	7.0	14.9
Other technical	6.8	7.7
Admin. & clerical	21.5	19.2
Mechanics & repairmen	15.1	26.0
Crafts	5.6	6.6
Services	20.3	10.7
Total	100.0	100.0

TABLE 20—OCCUPATIONAL GROUP DISTRIBUTION OF ENLISTED PERSONNEL BY
LENGTH OF SERVICE AND RACE

Occupational Group	0-4 Years		4-8 Years	
	White	Black	White	Black
Ground combat	20.3	32.7	9.8	17.7
Electronics	14.1	5.6	19.7	10.3
Other technical	7.5	7.1	7.3	7.0
Admin. & clerical	18.3	22.3	17.5	22.6
Mechanics	23.9	12.8	29.6	20.5
Crafts	5.3	4.0	6.9	7.4
Services	10.6	15.5	9.2	15.1

This change was dramatically highlighted by the occupational distribution of naval personnel in 1962 (*Table 21*). Among General Qualification Test Groups I and II, the percentage of Negroes assigned to service occupations, mainly stewards, commissarymen, and the like, declined from 22 percent of those with more than twelve years' service to 2 percent of those with less than twelve years' service, with sharp increases in the "other technical" group, mainly medical and dental specialists, and smaller increases in other technical skills. A similar trend also appeared in the lower mental categories. One persisting occupational difference was the tendency to assign a relatively large percentage of Negroes with high aptitudes to "other technical" skills and those of low aptitude to service occupations. The group admitted that these differences required further analysis.

TABLE 21—PERCENTAGE DISTRIBUTION OF NAVY ENLISTED PERSONNEL BY RACE,
AFQT GROUPS AND OCCUPATIONAL AREAS, AND LENGTH OF SERVICE, 1962

AFQT Group and Occupational Area[1]
Groups I and II
Electronics
Other technical
Admin. & clerical
Mechanics & repairmen
Crafts
Services
Total
Group III
Electronics
Other technical
Admin. & clerical
Mechanics & repairmen
Crafts
Services
Total

248

Group IV	
Electronics	
Other technical	
Admin. & clerical	
Mechanics & repairmen	
Crafts	
Services	
Total	

Tablenote 1: Excludes personnel not classified by occupation, such as recruits and general duty seamen.

Reporting on promotions, the Defense Department group found that the relatively limited advancement of black officers was caused chiefly by their disadvantage in point of time in service and grade, branch of service, and educational background (*Table 22*). Although the difference in grade distribution among black and white enlisted men was much smaller, it too seemed related to disadvantages in education and service occupation. Again, for Negroes entering the services since 1950, the grade distribution had become similar to that of whites. The Navy's experience illustrated this point. In the case of those entering the Navy since the Korean War, the grade distribution of whites and nonwhites within the first three mental categories was nearly identical (*Table 23*). The divergences were much wider among the more senior men in the service groups, but this was probably due at least in part to the concentration of senior black servicemen in relatively overmanned specialties, such as food service, where promotional opportunities were limited. With this exception little evidence exists that whites enjoyed an advantage over blacks in the matter of promotions in the enlisted ranks.

TABLE 22—PERCENTAGE DISTRIBUTION OF BLACKS AND WHITES BY PAY GRADE, ALL DOD, 1962

Grade	
Officers	
O-1 to O-2	
O-3	
O-4	
O-5	
O-6 to O-10	
Total	
Enlisted Men	
E-1 to E-3	
E-4	
E-5	
E-6	
E-7 to E-9	
Total	

TABLE 23—PERCENTAGE DISTRIBUTION OF NAVY ENLISTED PERSONNEL BY RACE, AFQT GROUPS, PAY GRADE, AND LENGTH OF SERVICE, 1962

Pay grade	0-12 Y.
	White
E-1 to E-3	50.0
E-4	22.5
E-5	17.8
E-6	8.3
E-7 to E-9	1.4
Total	100.0

E-1 to E-3	60.6
E-4	20.7
E-5	13.1
E-6	5.1
E-7 to E-9	.5
Total	100.0
E-1 to E-3	77.1
E-4	13.0
E-5	7.9
E-6	1.9
E-7 to E-9	.1
Total	100.0

Tablenote a: Less than .05 percent.

All these figures could be conjured up when the services had to answer complaints of discrimination, but more often than not the services contented themselves with a vague defense of the *status quo*[20-82] Such answers were clearly unacceptable to civil rights leaders and their allies in the administration, and it is not surprising that the complaints persisted. To the argument that higher enlistment standards were a matter of military economy during a period of partial mobilizations, those concerned about civil rights responded that, since marginal manpower was a necessary ingredient of full mobilization, the services should learn to deal in peacetime with what would be a wartime problem.[20-83] To pleas of helplessness against off-base discrimination, the activists argued that these practices had demonstrably adverse effects on the morale of more than 9 percent of the armed forces and were, therefore, a clear threat to the accomplishment of the services' military mission.[20-84]

Integration of black servicemen and general political and economic gains of the black population had combined in the last decade to create a ground swell for reform that resulted in ever more frequent and pressing attacks on the community policies of the Department of Defense. Some members of the administration rode with the reform movement. Although he was speaking particularly of increased black enrollment at the military academies, Special White House Assistant Wofford betrayed the reformer's attitude toward the whole problem of equal opportunity when he told James Evans "I am sure that much work has been done, but there is, of course, still a long way to go."[20-85] But by 1962 the services had just about exhausted the traditional reform methods available to them. To go further, as Wofford and the civil rights advocates demanded, meant a fundamental change in the department's commitment to equal treatment and opportunity. The decision to make such a change was clearly up to Secretary McNamara and the Kennedy administration.

CHAPTER 21
Equal Treatment and Opportunity Redefined

By 1962 the civil rights leaders and their allies in the Kennedy administration were pressing the Secretary of Defense to end segregation in the reserve components and in housing, schools, and public accommodations in communities adjacent to military installations. Such an extension of policy, certainly the most important to be contemplated since President Truman's executive order in 1948, would involve the Department of Defense in the fight for servicemen's civil rights, thrusting it into the forefront of the civil rights movement.

Given the forces at work in the department, it was by no means certain in 1962 that the fight against discrimination would be extended beyond those vestiges that continued to exist in the military community itself. In Robert McNamara the department had an energetic secretary, committed to the principle of equal treatment and opportunity, and, since his days with the Ford Motor Company in Michigan, a member of the NAACP. But, as his directives indicated, McNamara had much to learn in the field of race relations. As he later recalled: "Adam [Yarmolinsky] was more sensitive to the subject [race relations] in those days than I was. I was concerned. I recognized what Harry Truman had done, his leadership in the field, and I wanted to continue his work. But I didn't know enough."[21-1]

The Secretary Makes a Decision

Some of McNamara's closest advisers and some civil rights advocates in the Kennedy administration, increasingly critical of current practices, were anxious to instruct the secretary in

250

the need for a new racial outlook. But their efforts were counterbalanced by the influence of defenders of the *status quo*, primarily the manpower bureaucrats in the secretary's office and their colleagues in the services. These men opposed substantive change not because they objected to the reformers' goals but because they doubted the wisdom and propriety of interfering in what they regarded as essentially a domestic political issue.

Superficially, the department's racial policy appears to have been shaped by a conflict between traditionalists and progressives, but it would be a mistake to apply these labels mechanically to the men involved. There were among them several shades of opinion, and they were affected as well by complex political and social pressures. Many of those involved in the debate shared a similar goal. A continuum existed, one defense official later suggested, that ranged from a few people who wanted for a number of reasons to do nothing—who even wanted to tolerate the continued segregation of National Guard units called to active duty in 1961—to men of considerable impatience who thought the off-limits sanction was a neglected and obvious weapon which ought to be invoked at once.[21-2] Nevertheless, these various views tended to coalesce into a series of mutually exclusive arguments that can be analyzed.[21-3]

One group, from whom Adam Yarmolinsky, McNamara's special assistant, might be singled out as the most prominent member, developed arguments for a new racial policy that would encourage the services to modify local laws and customs in ways more favorable to black servicemen. Unlike earlier reformers in the department who acted primarily out of an interest in military efficiency, these men were basically civil libertarians, or "social movers," as Secretary of the Air Force Zuckert called them. They were allied with like-minded new frontiersmen, including the President's special counsel on minority affairs and Attorney General Kennedy, who were convinced that Congress would enact no new civil rights legislation in 1962. The services, this group argued, had through their recent integration found themselves in the vanguard of the national campaign for equal treatment and opportunity for Negroes, and to some it seemed only logical that they be used to retain that lead for the administration. These men had ample proof, they believed, for the proposition that the services' policies had already influenced reforms elsewhere. They saw a strong connection, for example, between the new Interstate Commerce Commission's order outlawing segregation in interstate travel and the services' efforts to secure equal treatment for troops in transit. In effect, in the name of an administration handicapped by an unwilling legislature, they were asking the services to fly the flag of civil rights.

If their motives differed from those of their predecessors, their rhetoric did not. Yarmolinsky and his colleagues argued that racial discrimination, particularly discrimination in housing and public accommodations, created a serious morale problem among black GIs, a contention strongly supported by the recent Civil Rights Commission findings. While the services had always denied responsibility for combating discrimination outside the military reservation, these officials were confident that the connection between this discrimination and military efficiency could be demonstrated. They were also convinced that segregated housing and the related segregation of places of public accommodation were particularly susceptible to economic pressure from military authorities.

ADAM YARMOLINSKY

This last argument was certainly not new. For some time civil rights spokesmen had been urging the services to use economic pressure to ease discrimination. Specifically, Congressman Powell, and later a number of civil rights groups, had called on the armed forces to impose off-limits sanctions for all servicemen against businesses that discriminated against black servicemen. Clear historical precedent seemed to exist for the action demanded by the controversial Harlem legislator because from earliest time the services had been declaring establishments and whole geographical areas off limits to their officers and men in order to protect their health and welfare. In view of the services' contention that equal treatment and opportunity were important to the welfare of servicemen, was it not reasonable, the spokesmen could ask, for the armed forces to use this powerful economic weapon against those who discriminated?

Those defense officials calling for further changes also argued that even the limited reforms already introduced by the administration faced slow going in the Department of Defense. This point was of particular concern to Robert Kennedy and his assistants in the Justice Department who agreed that senior defense officials lacked neither the zeal nor the determination to advance the civil rights of black servicemen but that the uniformed services were not, as Deputy Secretary Gilpatric expressed it, "putting their hearts and souls into really carrying out all of these directives and policies." Reflecting on it later, Gilpatric decided that the problem in the armed forces was one of pace. The services, he believed, were willing enough to carry out the policies, but in their own way and at their own speed, to avoid the appearance of acting as the agent of another federal department.

251

All these arguments failed to convince Assistant Secretary for Manpower Runge, some officials in the general counsel's office, and principal black adviser on racial affairs James Evans, among others. This group and their allies in the services could point to a political fact of life: to interfere with local segregation laws and customs, specifically to impose off-limits sanctions against southern businessmen, would pit the administration against powerful congressmen, calling down on it the wrath of the armed services and appropriation committees. To the charge that this threat of congressional retaliation was simply an excuse for inaction, the services could explain that unlike the recent integration of military units, which was largely an executive function with which Congress, or at least some individual congressmen, reluctantly went along, sanctions against local communities would be considered a direct threat by scores of legislators. "Even one obscure congressman thus threatened could light a fire over military sanctions," Evans later remarked, "and there were plenty of folks around who were eager to fan the flames."

Even more important, the department's equal opportunity bureaucracy argued, was the need to protect the physical well-being of the individual black soldier. In a decade when civil rights beatings and murders were a common occurrence, these men knew that Evans was right when he said "by the time Washington could enter the case the young man could be injured or dead." Operating under the principle that the safety and welfare of the individual transcended the civil rights of the group, these officials wanted to forbid the men, both the black and the increasing number of white activists, to disobey local segregation laws and customs.

The opponents of intervention pointed out that the services would be ill-advised to push for changes outside the military reservation until the reforms begun under Truman were completely realized inside the reservation. Ignoring the argument that discrimination in the local community had a profound effect on morale, they wanted the services to concentrate instead on the necessary but minor reforms within their jurisdiction. To give the local commander the added responsibility for correcting discrimination in the community, they contended, might very well dilute his efforts to correct conditions within the services. And to use servicemen to spearhead civil rights reform was a misuse of executive power. With support from the department's lawyers, they questioned the legality of using off-limits sanctions in civil rights cases. They constantly repeated the same refrain: social reform was not a military function. As one manpower spokesman put it to the renowned black civil rights lawyer, Thurgood Marshall, "let the Army tend its own backyard, and let other government agencies work on civil rights."[21-4]

Runge and the rest were professional manpower managers who had a healthy respect for the chance of command error and its effect on race relations nationally. In this they found an ally in Secretary of the Air Force Eugene M. Zuckert, one of the architects of Air Force integration in 1949. American commanders lacked training in the delicate art of community relations, Zuckert later explained, and should even a few of them blunder they could bring on a race crisis of major proportions. He sympathized with the activists' goals and was convinced that the President as Commander in Chief could and should use the armed forces for social ends; but these social objectives had to be balanced against the need to preserve the military forces for their primary mission. Again on the practical level, Deputy Secretary of Defense Gilpatric was concerned with the problems of devising general instructions that could be applied in all the diverse situations that might arise at the hundreds of bases and local communities involved.[21-5]

Many of the manpower officials carefully differentiated between equal treatment, which had always been at the heart of the Defense Department's reforms, and civil rights, which they were convinced were a constitutional matter and belonged in the hands of the courts and the Justice Department. The principle of equal treatment and opportunity was beyond criticism. Its application, a lengthy and arduous task that had occupied and still concerned the services' racial advisers, had brought the Department of Defense to unparalleled heights of racial harmony. Convinced that the current civil rights campaign was not the business of the Defense Department, they questioned the motives of those who were willing to make black GI's the stalking horse for their latest and perhaps transient enthusiasm, in the process inviting congressional criticism of the department's vital racial programs. In short, Assistant Secretary Runge and his colleagues argued that the administration's civil rights campaign should be led by the Justice Department and by the Department of Health, Education, and Welfare, not the Defense Department, which had other missions to perform.

Such were the rationalizations that had kept the Department of Defense out of the field of community race relations for over a decade, and the opponents of change in a strong position. Their opposition was reasonable, their allies in the services were legion, they were backed by years of tradition, and, most important, they held the jobs where the day-to-day decisions on racial matters were made. To change the *status quo*, to move the department beyond the notion that the guarantee of equal rights stopped at the boundaries of military installations, might seem "desirable and indeed necessary" to Yarmolinsky and his confreres,[21-6] but it would take something more than their eloquent words to bring about change.

Yarmolinsky was convinced that the initiative for such a change had to come from outside the department. Certain that any outside investigation would quickly reveal the connection between racial discrimination in the community and military efficiency, he wanted the Secretary of Defense to appoint a committee of independent citizens to investigate and report on the situation.[21-7] The idea of a citizens' committee was not new. The Fahy Committee provided a recent precedent, and in August 1961 Congressman Diggs had asked the Secretary of Defense to consider the appointment of such a group, a suggestion rejected at the time by Assistant Secretary Runge.[21-8] But Yarmolinsky enjoyed opportunities unavailable to the Michigan congressman; he had the attention and the support of Robert McNamara. In the latter's words: "Adam suggested another broad review of the place of the Negro in the Department. The committee was necessary because the other sources—the DOD manpower reports and so forth—were inadequate. They didn't provide the exact information I needed. This is what Adam and I decided."[21-9] This decision launched the Department of Defense into one of the most important civil rights battles of the 1960's.

The Gesell Committee

On 24 June 1962 John F. Kennedy announced the formation of the President's Committee on Equality of Opportunity in the Armed Forces, popularly designated the Gesell Committee after its chairman, Gerhard A. Gesell.[21-10] It was inevitable that the Gesell Committee should be compared to the Fahy Committee, given the similarity of interests, but in fact the two groups had little in common and served different purposes. The Fahy Committee had been created to carry out President Truman's equal treatment and opportunity policy. The Gesell Committee, on the other hand, was less concerned with carrying out existing policy than with developing a new policy for the Department of Defense. The Fahy Committee operated under an executive order and sought an acceptable integration program from each service. The Gesell Committee enjoyed no such advantage, although the Truman order was technically still in effect and could have been used to support it. (The Kennedy administration ignored this possibility, and Yarmolinsky warned one presidential aide that the Truman order should be quietly revoked lest someone question why the Gesell Committee had not been afforded similar stature.)[21-11]

Again unlike the Fahy Committee, which forced its attention upon a generally reluctant Defense Department at the behest of the President, the Gesell Committee was created by the Secretary of Defense; the presidential appointment of its members bestowed an aura of special authority on a group that lacked the power of its predecessor to make and review policy. McNamara later put it quite bluntly: "The committee was the creature of the Secretary of Defense. Calling it a President's committee was just windowdressing. The civil rights people didn't have a damn thing to do with it. We wanted information, and that's just what the Gesell people gave us."[21-12] In fact, Yarmolinsky conceived the project, named it, nominated its members, and drew up its directives. Only when it was well along was the project passed to the White House for review of the committee's makeup and guidelines.[21-13]

This special connection between the Department of Defense and the Gesell Committee influenced the course of the investigation. True to his concept of the committee as a fact-finding team, McNamara personally remained aloof from its proceedings, never trying to influence its investigation or findings. Ironically, Gesell would later complain about this remoteness, regretting the secretary's failure to intervene in the case of the recalcitrant National Guard.[21-14] He could harbor no complaint, however, against the secretary's special assistant, Yarmolinsky, who carefully guided the committee's investigation to the explosive subject of off-base discrimination. Even while expressing the committee's independence, Gesell recognized Yarmolinsky's influence. "It was perfectly clear," Gesell later noted, "that Yarmolinsky was interested in the off-base housing and discrimination situation, but he had no solution to suggest. He wanted the committee to come up with one."[21-15] Yarmolinsky formally spelled out this interest when he devised the group's presidential directive. The committee, he informed Vice President Lyndon B. Johnson during March 1962, would devote itself to those measures that should be taken to improve the effectiveness of current policies and procedures in the services and to the methods whereby the Department of Defense could improve equality of opportunity for members of the armed forces and their dependents in the civilian community.[21-16]

The citizens chosen for this delicate task, "integrationists all,"[21-17] were men with backgrounds in the law and the civil rights movement, their nearest common denominators being Yale University and acquaintance with Yarmolinsky, a graduate of Yale Law School.[21-18] Chairman Gesell was a Washington lawyer, educated at Yale, an acquaintance of

253

Yarmolinsky's with whom he shared a close mutual friend, Burke Marshall, also from Yale and the head of the Department of Justice's Civil Rights Division. Gesell always assumed that this friendship with Marshall explained his selection by the Kennedy administration for such a sensitive task.[21-19] Black committeemen were Nathaniel S. Colley, a California lawyer, civil rights advocate associated with the NAACP, and former law school classmate of Yarmolinsky's; John H. Sengstacke, publisher of the Chicago *Defender* and a member of the Fahy Committee; and Whitney M. Young, Jr., of the National Urban League. The other members were Abe Fortas, a prominent Washington attorney and former Yale professor; Benjamin Muse, a leader of the Southern Regional Council and a noted student of the civil rights movement; and Louis Hector, also a Yale-educated lawyer, who was called in to replace ailing Dean Joseph O'Meara of the Notre Dame Law School. Gesell arranged for the appointment of Laurence I. Hewes III, of Yale College and Law School, as the committee's counsel.

Some of the members had definite ideas on how the committee should operate. Warning of a new mood in the black community where "impatience and expectations" were far different from what they were at the time of the Fahy Committee, Whitney Young wanted the committee to prepare a frank and honest report free of the "taint of whitewash." To that end he wanted the group's directive interpreted in its broadest sense as leading to a wide-ranging examination of off-base housing, recreation, and educational opportunity, among other subjects. He wanted an investigation at the grass roots level, and he offered specific suggestions about the size and duties of the staff to achieve this. Young also recommended commissioning "additional citizen teams" to assist in some of the numerous and necessary field trips and wanted the committee to use Congressman Diggs and his files.[21-20]

Benjamin Muse, on the other hand, considered direct, personal investigation of specific grievances too time-consuming. He wanted the group to concentrate instead on the command level, holding formal conferences with key staff officials. The best way to impress upon the services that the White House was serious, he told Gesell, was to learn the opinions of these officials and to elicit, "subject to our private analysis and discount," a great deal of helpful information.[21-21]

Chairman Gesell compromised. He wanted the group to develop some broad recommendations on the basis of a limited examination of specific complaints. President Kennedy agreed. He told Gesell: "don't go overboard and try to visit every base, but unless you see at least some bases you will never understand the situation."[21-22] White House assistant Lee C. White suggested that while the committee had no deadline it should be advised that a report would be needed in June if any legislative proposals were to be submitted to Congress. At the same time he wanted the White House to make clear that the members, "and particularly the Negro members," would be left free to act as they chose.[21-23]

In the end the committee's operations owed something to all these suggestions. The group worked out of a small office near the White House and pointedly distant from the Pentagon. Its formal meetings were rare—only seven in all—and were used primarily to hear the presentations of service officials and consider the committee's findings. At a meeting in November 1962, for instance, Gesell arranged for five Air Force base commanders to discuss the application of the equal opportunity policy in their commands and in neighboring communities and describe their own duties as they saw them.[21-24]

The chairman explained that the infrequent meetings were used mostly for "needling people and asking for statistics." Some black members at first opposed asking the services for statistical data on the grounds that such requests would reinforce the tendency to identify servicemen by race, thus encouraging racial assignments and, ultimately, racial quotas. The majority, however, was convinced of the need for statistical material, and in the end the requests for such information enjoyed the committee's unanimous support.[21-25]

Most of the committee's work was done in a "shirt sleeve" atmosphere, as its chairman described it, with a staff of four people.[21-26] Members, alone and in groups, studied the mountains of racial statistics, some prepared by the staff of the Civil Rights Commission, and the lengthy answers to committee questionnaires prepared by the services. The services also arranged for on-site inspections by committee members.[21-27] The field trips proved to be of paramount importance, not only in ascertaining the conditions of black servicemen and their dependents but also in fixing the extent of the local commander's responsibility for race relations. Operating usually in two-man biracial teams, the committee members would separate to interview the commander, local businessmen, and the men themselves. The firsthand information thus gathered had a profound influence on the committee's thinking, an influence readily discernible in its recommendations to the President.

The committee concluded from its investigations that serious discrimination against black servicemen and their families existed at home and abroad within the services and in the civilian

254

community, and that this discrimination affected black morale and military efficiency. Regarding evidence of discrimination within the services, the committee isolated a series of problems existing "both service-wide and at particular bases."[21-28] Specifically, the group was not convinced by official reasons for the disproportionately small number of Negroes in some services, especially among the noncommissioned officers and in the officer corps. Chairman Gesell called the dearth of black officers a "shocking condition."[21-29]His group was particularly concerned with the absence of black officers on promotion boards and the possibility of unfairness in the promotion process where photos and racial and religious information were included in the selection files made available to these boards. It also noted the failure of the services to increase the number of black ROTC graduates. The committee considered and rejected the idea of providing preferential treatment for Negroes to achieve better representation in the services and in the higher grades.[21-30]

Overrepresentation of black enlisted men in certain supply and food services was obvious.[21-31] Here the committee was particularly critical of the Navy and the Marine Corps. On another score, the Chief of Naval Personnel noted that the committee "considers the Navy and Marines far behind the Army and Air Force, particularly in the area of community relations," a criticism, he admitted, "to some extent" justified.[21-32] So apparent was the justification that, at the suggestion of the Secretary of the Navy, Gesell discussed with Under Secretary Paul B. Fay, Jr., ways to better the Navy's record in its "areas of least progress."[21-33] Gesell later concluded that the close social contact necessary aboard ship had been a factor in the Navy's slower progress.[21-34] Whatever the reason, the Navy and Marine Corps fell statistically short of the other services in every category measured by the Gesell group.

The "sex thing," as Gesell referred to the interracial problems arising from off-duty social activities, also proved to be important, especially for noncommissioned officer and service clubs and base-sponsored activities in the community. The committee itself had persuaded the National United Services Organization to integrate its facilities, and it wanted local commanders to follow up by inviting black civilians to participate in USO dances and entertainments.[21-35] The committee also discussed discrimination in military police assignments, segregation in local transport and on school buses, and the commander's attitude toward interracial associations both on and off the military reservation.

Despite its criticism of the imperfect application of service race policies—some service-wide, others confined to certain bases—the committee reported to the President that the services had made "an intelligent and far-reaching advance toward complete integration, and, with some variations from service to service, substantial progress toward equality of treatment and opportunity."[21-36] Gesell called the services the nation's "pace setter," and he was convinced that they had not received sufficient credit for their racial achievements, which were "way ahead of General Motors and the other great corporations."[21-37] That the services were more advanced than other segments of American society in terms of equal treatment and opportunity was beyond dispute; nevertheless, serious problems connected with racial prejudice and the armed forces' failure to understand the fundamental needs of black servicemen remained. The committee's investigation, with its emphasis on off-base realities and its dependence on statistics and other empirical data, did not lend itself to more than a superficial treatment of these subtle and stubborn, if unmeasurable, on-base problems.

The committee believed that some of what appeared discriminatory was in reality the working of such factors as the black serviceman's lack of seniority, deficiencies in education, and lack of interest in specific fields and assignments. Looking beyond these, the fruits of institutional racism, the committee concluded that much of the substantiated discrimination disclosed in its investigations had proved to be limited in scope. But whether limited or widespread, discrimination had to be eliminated. Prompt attention to even minor incidents of discrimination would contribute substantially to morale and serve to keep before all servicemen the standard of conduct decreed by executive policy.[21-38]

The committee was considerably less sanguine over conditions encountered by black servicemen off military bases. In eloquent paragraphs it outlined for the President the injustices suffered by these men and their families in some American communities, the effect of these practices on morale, and the consequent danger to the mission of the armed forces. It reviewed the services' efforts to eliminate segregated housing, schooling, and public accommodations around the military reservations and found them wanting. Local commanders, the committee charged, were often naive about the existence of social problems and generally did not keep abreast of departmental policy specifying their obligations; they were especially ill-informed on the McNamara-Gilpatric directives and memorandums on equal treatment. Often quizzed on the subject, the commanders told the committee that they enjoyed very fine community relationships.

To this Whitney Young would answer that fine community relationships and racial injustice were not necessarily exclusive.[21-39]

This community-based discrimination, the committee found, had become a greater trial for black servicemen and their families because of its often startling contrast to their life in the services. There was even evidence that some of the off-base segregation, especially overseas, had been introduced through the efforts of white servicemen. Particularly irritating to the committee were restrictions placed on black participation in civil rights demonstrations protesting such off-base conditions. The committee wanted the restrictions removed.[21-40]

In the end the committee's reputation would rest not so much on its carefully developed catalog of racial discrimination. After all, others, most notably the Civil Rights Commission, had recently documented the problems encountered by black servicemen, although not in the detail offered by the Gesell group, and had convincingly tied this discrimination to black morale and military efficiency. The committee's major contribution lay rather in its establishment of a new concept in command responsibility that directly attacked the traditional parochialism of the services' social concerns:

It should be the policy of the Department of Defense and part of the mission of the chain of command from the Secretaries of the Services to the local base commander not only to remove discrimination within the Armed Forces, but also to make every effort to eliminate discriminatory practices as they affect members of the Armed Forces and their dependents within the neighboring civilian communities.[21-41]

In effect the committee proposed a new racial policy for the Department of Defense, one that would translate the services' promise of equality of treatment and opportunity into a declaration of civil liberties. To that end it recommended the adoption of a set of techniques radically new to the thinking of the military commanders, one that grew out of the committee's own experiences in the field.

Chairman Gesell later recollected how this recommendation developed:

I remember in particular our experiences at the bases at Augusta and Pensacola. This made a strong impression on me. I saw discrimination on bases right under the noses of the commanders who were often not even aware of it. And I saw much discrimination in communities around the bases. Sometimes unbelievable. At Pensacola, for example, I found that the Station had never used Negroes for guard duty at the main gate where they would be seen by the public, black and white. We told this to the commander and reminded him of the effect that it had on black morale. He changed it immediately. On base the housing for blacks was segregated off to one side in poor run-down shacks below the railroad tracks. We told the commander who admitted that he had some substandard housing units but was unaware of any segregation in housing. The commander promised to report to us about this in two weeks. He did later report: "the whole housing area has been bulldozed and all housing on base integrated." It was examples like this that convinced me that there was much the commanders could do.[21-42]

This sense of racial progress made a vivid impression on committee member Muse who later recalled that "it was amazing how much activity our presence stirred up. It showed that a lot could be done by commanders."[21-43] Gesell and Muse were particularly impressed by how local commanders, acting firmly but informally, could achieve swift breakthroughs. But actually, as the Gesell-Young trip to Pensacola demonstrated, often more than the base commander was involved in these dramatic reforms. A week after their trip to Florida, Gesell and Young had a casual chat with Under Secretary Fay about conditions at Pensacola, particularly housing conditions, that, they claimed, had contributed to a "literally disgraceful" state of black morale, leading black sailors "almost to the point of rebellion." Although the base commander seemed concerned, he had deferred to his military superior who lacked the "philosophical outlook oriented toward the successful implementation of equal opportunity policies." Fay was quick to see the point. He pledged the Navy to a "constructive effort" to eliminate the problem at Pensacola "prior to the Committee's reporting date [to the President] of 1 June."[21-44] In a matter of hours Fay was arranging to send the Inspector General to Pensacola, but the matter did not end there. In late May committee counsel Hewes asked the Assistant Secretary of Defense concerned with military installations about housing at Pensacola, thus setting off yet another investigation of the base.[21-45]

Gesell saw the reforms at Pensacola as a direct result of his own suggestion to a commander. He seemed unaware that his remarks to Fay had set in motion a chain of action behind the scenes. In the weeks following, black servicemen were moved from the substandard segregated housing to integrated Navy-controlled housing both on and off base. The local commander also arranged for the desegregation of some off-base social facilities in a effort to improve black morale.[21-46] If the changes at Pensacola appear more closely related to the committee's political clout in Washington than to the commander's interest in reform, they also demonstrate the power for reform that the commander could exercise. This was the committee's main point, that equal opportunity was a command responsibility.[21-47] But it would be hard to sell in the Department of Defense where, as Gesell himself later admitted, resistance to what was perceived as a political matter was common to most American military officers.[21-48]

The most controversial recommendation, however, was that the armed forces should, when necessary, exercise economic sanctions against recalcitrant businesses. In the name of troop morale and military efficiency, the committee wanted commanders to put public accommodations off limits for all servicemen, and it wanted the Secretary of Defense, as a last resort, to close the military installations in communities that persisted in denying black servicemen their civil rights.[21-49] Again, Gesell elaborated on the power of base commanders and recommended tactics.

There was also much that they could do in the community to improve the lot of their blacks. If only they were sensitive to the situation.... For example, we visited the local community leaders. I would put it to the local banker who held the mortgage on the local bowling alley: "what would you do if you were a commander and some of your men were barred from the local bowling alley?" He got the point and the alley outside the base was desegregated overnight. To another I said, "you know, I'm just a lawyer down here on a temporary job, and I can only talk with you about these things. But you can't tell about those guys in Washington. They will have to be closing some bases soon. Now put yourself in their shoes. Which would you shut, those bases that don't have race problems or those that do?" Again, they got the point. In other words, an implied economic threat by the commander would work well. Hell, the commanders were always getting good citizenship awards and ignoring the major citizenship problem of the era. Commanders were local heroes, and they had plenty of influence. They use it. The trouble was most commanders were ignorant of the ferment among their own men on this subject. In all my trips I hinted at sanctions and base closings. The dutch uncle approach. I wanted the commanders to do the same. I talked economics to the community leaders. It opened their eyes. The commanders could do the same.[21-50]

The committee further refined its concepts of economic sanctions during the course of its hearings. Commanders were frequently quizzed on the probable effects of the imposition of off-limits sanctions or base closings.[21-51] Despite the reluctance of most commanders to invoke sanctions, committee members, assuming that no community would long persist in a social order detrimental to its economic welfare, came to the belief that ultimately only a firm and uncompromising policy of economic sanctions would eliminate off-base discrimination. The committee was obviously aware of the controversial aspects of its recommendation, and it stressed that the department's objective should always be "the preservation of morale, not the punishment of local communities which have a tradition of segregation."[21-52]

Mindful of the wish expressed by the White House staff that a report be submitted by mid-1963, the committee, acting unanimously, completed on 13 June 1963 an initial report on discrimination in the services and the local community, postponing the results of its time-consuming and less-pressing investigation of the National Guard and overseas posts until a later date.[21-53] Complete accord among the members had not been automatic. The chairman later recalled that the group's black members had remained somewhat aloof during the months of investigation, perhaps because at first they felt the report might be a whitewash of executive policy, but that they became "enthusiastic" when they read his draft and quickly joined in the preparation of the final version.[21-54]

The reason for this enthusiasm was a report that faithfully reflected the realities of discrimination suffered by black servicemen and proposed solutions based on conclusions drawn by the members from their months of discussion and investigation. The committee's conclusions and recommendations were the natural reaction of a group of humane and sensible men to the overwhelming evidence of continued discrimination against black servicemen. National policy, the committee told the President, required that this discrimination be eliminated, for

equal opportunity for the Negro will exist only when it is possible for him to enter upon a career of military service with assurance that his acceptance and his progress will be in no way impeded by reason of his color. Clearly, distinctions based on race prevent full utilization of Negro military personnel and are inconsistent with the objectives of our democratic society.[21-55]

257

The committee wanted responsibility for eliminating these color distinctions in the services shifted to the local commander. Commanders, it believed, needed to improve their communication with black servicemen and should be "held accountable to discover and remedy discrimination" in their commands. The committee, in short, wanted racial sensitivity made a function of command.

Command responsibility for equal opportunity, the committee emphasized, was particularly important "in the area of most pressing concern, off-base discrimination." It wanted local commanders to attack discrimination in the community by seeking the voluntary compliance of local businessmen and by establishing biracial community committees. The committee asserted that despite the services' claims to the contrary the Department of Defense had made no serious effort to achieve off-base compliance with its anti-discrimination measures through voluntary action. Commanders had been given little guidance thus far, and a carefully planned program of voluntary action should be given a chance. If it failed, commanders should be able to employ sanctions against the offending businesses; if sanctions failed, the services should consider closing installations in offending areas. The committee again stressed the need to fix responsibility for the program on local commanders. A commander's performance should be monitored and rated, and offices should be established in the Department of Defense and in the individual services to devise programs, monitor their progress, and bring base commanders into close working relationship with other interested and responsible federal agencies.

Although their recommendations were later excoriated by critics as a radical usurpation of state sovereignty and a threat to civil liberties, the committee had meant only to provide a graduated solution to a national defense problem. Let reform begin with the local commander's improving conditions on his base and pressing for voluntary changes in the local community. Only when this tactic failed—and the committee predicted that failure would be a rare occurrence—should the services employ economic sanctions.

A firm philosophical assumption underlay all these recommendations. The committee believed that the armed forces, a worldwide symbol of American society, had to be the leader in the quest for racial justice. Social reform, therefore, both within the services and where it affected servicemen in the community beyond, was a legitimate military function. To the extent that these reforms were successful, the armed forces would not only be protecting the civil rights of black servicemen but also providing a standard against which civilian society could measure its conduct and other nations could judge the country's adherence to its basic principles.[21-56]

Reaction to a New Commitment

The Gesell Committee's conclusion that discrimination in the community was tied to military efficiency meshed well with the civil rights philosophy of the New Frontier. Responding to the committee's report, President Kennedy cited "the interests of national defense, national policy and basic considerations of human decency" to justify his administration's interest in opening public accommodations and housing to black servicemen. He considered it proper to ask the "military community to take a leadership role" in the matter and asked Secretary McNamara to review the committee's recommendations.[21-57] The secretary, in turn, personally asked the service secretaries to comment on the recommendations and assigned the Deputy Under Secretary of the Army (Manpower), Alfred B. Fitt, to act as coordinator and draw up the Defense Department's reply.[21-58]

The comments thus solicited revealed that some of McNamara's senior subordinates had not been won over by the committee's arguments that the services should take an active role in community race relations.[21-59] The sticking point at all levels involved two important recommendations: the rating of commanders on their handling of racial matters and the use of economic sanctions. In regard to the proposal to close bases in communities that persisted in racial discrimination, the Secretary of the Navy said bluntly: "Do not concur. Base siting is based upon military requirements."[21-60] These officials promised that commanders would press for voluntary compliance, but for more aggressive measures they preferred to wait for the passage of federal legislation—they had in mind the administration's civil rights bill then being considered by Congress—which would place the primary responsibility for the protection of a serviceman's civil rights in another federal department. The Secretary of the Air Force suggested that the services continue to plan, but defer action on the committee's recommendations until Congress acted on the civil rights bill.[21-61]

ALFRED FITT

Despite the opposition to these recommendations, Fitt saw room for compromise between the committee and the services. Noting, for example, that the services wanted to do their own monitoring of their commander's performance, Fitt agreed this would be acceptable so long as the Secretary of Defense could monitor the monitors. Adding that officers, like other human beings, tended to concentrate on the tasks that would be reviewed by superiors, he wanted to see a judgment of a commander's ability to handle discrimination matters included in the narrative portion of his efficiency report. On the question of sanctions, Fitt pointed out to McNamara that the services now understood that their equal opportunity responsibilities extended beyond the limits of the military reservation but that several of their objections to the use of sanctions were sound. He suggested the secretary approve the use of sanctions in discrimination cases but place severe restraints on their imposition, restricting the decision to the secretary's office.

This suggestion no doubt pleased McNamara. Although the committee's recommendations might be the logical outcome of its investigations, in the absence of a strong federal civil rights law even a sympathetic secretary of defense could not accept such radical changes in the services' community relations programs without reservations. Nor, as Gesell later admitted, could a secretary of defense chance the serious compromise to the administration's effort to win passage of such a law that could be caused by some "too gung-ho" commander left to impose sanctions on his own.[21-62] The secretary agreed with the committee that much could be done by individual commanders in a voluntary way to change the customs of the local community, and he wanted the emphasis to be kept there.

Unlike Gesell, who doubted the effectiveness of directives and executive edicts ("trouble-making" he called them), McNamara considered equal opportunity matters "an executive job that should be handled by the Departments, using directives."[21-63] Armed with the committee's call for action and the services' agreement in principle, McNamara turned to the preparation of a directive, the main outline of which he transmitted to the President on 24 July after review by Burke Marshall in the Department of Justice. As McNamara explained to Marshall, "I would like to be able to tell him [the President] that you have read same and offer no objection."[21-64]

The Secretary of Defense promised the President to "eliminate the exceptions and guard the continuing reality" of racial equality in the services. In the light of the committee's conclusion that off-base discrimination reduced military effectiveness, he pledged that "the military departments will take a leadership role in combating discrimination wherever it affects the military effectiveness" of servicemen. McNamara admitted having reservations about some of the committee's recommendations, especially the closing of bases near communities that constantly practiced discrimination; such closings, he declared, were not feasible "at this time." Nevertheless he agreed with the committee that off-limits sanctions should be available to the services, for "certainly the damage to military effectiveness from off-base discrimination is not less than that caused by off-base vice, as to which the off-limits sanction is quite customary."[21-65] He failed to add that even though sanctions against vice were regularly applied by the local commander, sanctions against discrimination would be reserved to higher authority.

The directive, in reality an outline of the Department of Defense's civil rights responsibilities and the prototype of subsequent secretarial orders dealing with race, was published on 26 July 1963, the fifteenth anniversary of Harry Truman's executive order. It read in part:

II. Responsibilities.

A. Office of the Secretary of Defense:

1. Pursuant to the authority vested in the Secretary of Defense and the provisions of the National Security Act of 1947, as amended, the Assistant Secretary of Defense (Manpower) is hereby assigned responsibility and authority for promoting equal opportunity for members of the Armed Forces.

In the performance of this function he shall (a) be the representative of the Secretary of Defense in civil rights matters, (b) give direction to programs that promote equal opportunity for military personnel, (c) provide policy guidance and review policies, regulations and manuals of the military departments, and (d) monitor their performance through periodic reports and visits to field installations.

2. In carrying out the functions enumerated above, the Assistant Secretary of Defense (Manpower) is authorized to establish the Office of Deputy Assistant Secretary of Defense (Civil Rights).

B. The Military Departments:

1. The military departments shall, with the approval of the Assistant Secretary of Defense (Manpower), issue appropriate instructions, manuals and regulations in connection with the leadership responsibility for equal opportunity, on and off base, and containing guidance for its discharge.

2. The military departments shall institute in each service a system for regularly reporting, monitoring and measuring progress in achieving equal opportunity on and off base.

C. Military Commanders:

Every military commander has the responsibility to oppose discriminatory practices affecting his men and their dependents and to foster equal opportunity for them, not only in areas under his immediate control, but also in nearby communities where they may live or gather in off-duty hours. In discharging that responsibility a commander shall not, except with the prior approval of the Secretary of his military department, use the off-limits sanction in discrimination cases arising within the United States.[21-66]

After some thirty months in office, Robert McNamara had made a most decisive move in race relations. In the name of fulfilling Harry Truman's pledge of equal treatment and opportunity he announced an aggressive new policy. Not only would the department work to eliminate discrimination in the armed forces, but when servicemen were affected it would work in the community as well. Even more ominous to the secretary's critics was the fact that the new policy revealed McNamara's willingness, under certain circumstances, to use the department's economic powers to force these changes. This directive marked the beginning of McNamara's most active period of participation in the civil rights revolution of the 1960's.

But the secretary's move did not escape strong criticism. The directive was denounced as infamous and shocking, as biased, impractical, undemocratic, brutally authoritarian, and un-American. If followed, critics warned, it would set the military establishment at war with society, inject the military into civilian political controversies in defiance of all traditions to the contrary, and burden military commanders with sociological tasks beyond their powers and to the detriment of their military mission.[21-67]

"It is hard to realize that your office would become so rotten and degraded," one critic wrote McNamara. "In my opinion you are using the tactics of a dictator.... It is a tragic event when the Federal Government is again trying to bring Reconstruction Days into the South. Again the military is being used to bring this about." Did businesses not have the right to choose their customers? Did local authorities not have the right to enforce the law in their communities? And surely the white soldier deserved the freedom to choose his associates.[21-68] Another correspondent reproached McNamara: "you have, without conscience and with total disregard for the honorable history of the Military of our Great Nation, signed our freedom away." And still another saw her white supremacy menaced: "We have a bunch of mad dogs in Washington and if you and others like you are not stopped, our children will curse us. We don't want black grandchildren and we won't have them. If you want to dance with them—you have two legs, start dancing."

Not all the correspondents were racist or hysterical. Some thoughtful citizens were concerned with what they considered extramilitary and illegal activities on the part of the services and took little comfort from the often repeated official statement that the Secretary of Defense had no present plans for the use of sanctions and hoped that they would never have to be used.[21-69]

Some defenders of the directive saw the whole controversy over sanctions as a red herring dragged across the path of a genuine equal treatment and opportunity program.[21-70]During congressional debate on the directive, the use of off-limits sanctions quickly became the respectable issue behind which those opposed to any reform could rally. The Senate debated the subject on 31 July; the House on 7 August. During lengthy sessions on those days, opponents cast the controversy in the familiar context of states' rights, arguing that constitutional and legal points were involved. As Congressman Durward G. Hall of Missouri put it: "The recommendations made in the report and in the directive indicate a narrowness of vision which, in seeing only the civil rights issue, has blinded itself to the question of whether it is proper to use the Armed Forces to enforce a moral or social, rather than a legal, issue in the civilian sector."[21-71]

Opponents argued generally that the directive represented government by fiat, an unprecedented extension of executive power that imposed the armed forces on civilian society in a new and illegal way. If the administration was already empowered to protect the civil rights of some citizens, why, they asked, was it pushing so hard for a civil rights bill? The fact was, several legislators argued, the Department of Defense was interfering with the civil rights of businessmen and practicing a crude form of economic blackmail.[21-72]

Critics also discussed the directive in terms of military efficiency. The secretary had given the commanders a new mission, Senator John Stennis of Mississippi noted, that "can only be detrimental to military tradition, discipline, and morale." Elaborating on this idea, Congressman L. Mendel Rivers of South Carolina predicted that the new policy would destroy the merit promotion system. Henceforth, Rivers forecast, advancement would depend on acceptance of integration; henceforth, racial quotas would "take the place of competence for purposes of promotion." Others were alarmed at the prospect of civil rights advisers on duty at each base and

260

outside the regular chain of command. This outrage, Congressman H. R. Gross of Iowa charged, "would create the biggest army of snoopers and informers that the military has ever heard of."

Some legislators saw sinister things afoot in the Pentagon. Senator Herman E. Talmadge of Georgia thought he recognized a return to the military districting of Reconstruction days, and Congressman F. Edward Hebert of Louisiana warned that "everybody should be prepared for the midnight knock on the door." Congressman Otto E. Passman of Louisiana thought it most likely that Attorney General Kennedy was behind the whole thing; "a tragic state of affairs," he said, if the Justice Department was directing "the missions of the Military Establishment." Congressman Hebert found yet another villain in the piece. Adam Yarmolinsky, whom he incorrectly identified as the author of the McNamara directive, had, Hebert accused, "one objective in mind—with an almost satanielike zeal—the forced integration of every facet of the American way of life, using the full power of the Department of Defense to bring about this change."[21-73] In line with these suspicions, some legislators reported that the secretary's new civil rights deputy, Alfred B. Fitt, was circulating among southern segregationist businessmen with, in Senator Barry M. Goldwater's words, "a dossier gleaned from Internal Revenue reports." Senator Stennis suspected that the Secretary of Defense had come under the influence of "obscure men," and he warned against their revolutionary strategy: "It had been apparent for some time that the more extreme exponents of revolutionary civil rights action have wanted to use the military in a posture of leadership to bring about desegregation outside the boundaries of military bases."[21-74]

The congressional critics had a strategy of their own. They would try to persuade McNamara to rescind or modify his directive, and, failing that, they would try to change the new defense policy by law. Senators Goldwater, J. William Fulbright of Arkansas, and Robert C. Byrd of West Virginia, along with some of their constituents, debated with McNamara while no less than the chairman of the House Armed Services Committee, Carl Vinson of Georgia, introduced a bill aimed at outlawing all integration activity by military officers.[21-75] Their campaign came to naught because the new policy had its own supporters in Congress,[21-76] and the great public outcry against the directive, so ardently courted by its congressional opponents, failed to materialize. Judging by the press, the public showed little interest in the Gesell Committee's report and comment on the secretary's directive was regional, with much of it coming from the southern press. Certainly the effect of the directive could not compare with the furor set off by the Truman order in 1948.

The attitude of the press merely underscored a fact already obvious to many politicians on Capitol Hill in 1963—equal opportunity in the armed forces had dwindled to the status of a minor issue in the greater civil rights struggle engulfing the nation. The media reaction also suggested that prolonged attacks against the committee and the directive were for hometown consumption and not a serious effort to reverse policy. In effect a last hurrah for the congressional opponents of integration in the armed forces, the attacks failed to budge the Secretary of Defense and marked the end of serious congressional attempts to influence armed forces racial policy.[21-77] The threat of congressional opposition, at times real and sometimes imagined, had discouraged progressive racial policies in the Department of Defense for over a quarter of a century. Its abrupt and public demise robbed the traditionalists in the Department of Defense of a cherished excuse for inaction.

The Gesell Committee: Final Report

While the argument over the McNamara directive raged, the Gesell Committee worked quietly if intermittently on the final segment of its investigation, the status of blacks stationed overseas and in the National Guard. President Kennedy's death in November 1963 introduced an element of uncertainty in a group serving at the pleasure of the Chief Executive. Special Presidential Counsel Lee C. White arranged for Gesell to meet with President Lyndon B. Johnson, and Gesell offered to disband the committee if Johnson wished. The President left it in being. As Gesell later observed: "The committee felt that Johnson understood us and our work in a way better than Kennedy who had no clear idea on how to go with the race issue. We had no trouble with Johnson who could have stopped us if he wanted."[21-78]

The committee's operations became even more informal in this final stage. Its investigations completed, its staff dissolved, and its members (now one man short with the resignation of Nathaniel Colley) scattered, the committee operated out of Gesell's law office. He was almost exclusively responsible for its final report.[21-79] This informality masked the protracted negotiations that the committee conducted with the National Guard Bureau over the persistent exclusion of Negroes. It also masked the solid investigation by individual committee members and the voluminous evidence gathered by the staff in support of the group's final report.

These investigations and the documentary evidence again confirmed the findings of the Civil Rights Commission, although the Gesell Committee's emphasis was different. It dismissed

261

the problem of assignment of Negroes to overseas stations. The percentage of Negroes, both officers and men, sent overseas approximated their percentage in the continental United States, and with rare and "understandable" exceptions—it cited South Africa—overseas assignments in the armed forces were made routinely without regard for race.[21-80]The committee also quickly dismissed the problem of discrimination on overseas bases, which it considered "minimal," and as in the United States chiefly the result of poor communication between commanders and men. The group concentrated instead on discrimination off base, especially in Germany. Back from a firsthand look in April 1964, Benjamin Muse reported that local American commanders seemed unwilling to take the matter seriously, but he considered it delicate and complex, principally because prejudice had been most often introduced by American servicemen. He suggested that off-limits sanctions should also be imposed in Germany but "only after consultation and on a basis of mutual understanding with German municipal authorities."[21-81]

The committee wanted the recommendations on off-base discrimination contained in its initial report also applied overseas. Ignoring the oft made distinction about the guest status of overseas service, it wanted the Department of State enlisted in a campaign against discrimination in public accommodations, including the use of off-limits sanctions when necessary. The committee also called for a continuing review to insure equal opportunity in assignments to attache and mission positions.

The committee devoted the largest portion of its final report to the National Guard, "the only branch of the Armed Forces," it told President Johnson, "which has not been fully integrated."[21-82] Chairman Gesell later reported that when the segregated state guards were pressured they "resisted like hell."[21-83] This resistance had a political dimension, but when Attorney General Kennedy chided that "you are killing us with the Guard," Gesell replied that the committee took orders from the President and would ignore the political problems involved. Nevertheless, before the committee issued its report Gesell sent the portions on the National Guard to the Justice Department for comment, as one justice official noted, "apparently ... in the hope that its recommendation will not prove embarrassing to the administration."[21-84]

The committee admitted that its investigation of the National Guard was incomplete because of the variation in state systems and the absence of statistical data on recruitment, assignment, and promotion in some state guards. It had no doubt, however, of the central premise that discrimination existed. For example, until 1963 ten states with large black populations had no black guardsmen at all. Membership in the guard, the committee concluded, was a distinct advantage for some individuals, providing the chance to perform their military obligation without a lengthy time away from home or work. Because of the peculiar relationship between the reserve and regular systems, National Guard service had important advantages in retirement benefits for others. These advantages and benefits should, in simple fairness, be open to all, but beyond the basic constitutional rights involved there were practical reasons for federal insistence on integration. The committee accepted the National Guard Bureau's conclusion that, since guard units were subject to integration when federalized, their morale and combat efficiency would be improved if their members were accustomed to service with Negroes in all ranks during training.[21-85]

The committee stressed executive initiatives. It wanted the President to declare the integration of the National Guard in the national interest. It wanted the Department of Defense to demand pertinent racial statistics from the states. For psychological advantages, it wanted the recent liberalization of guard policies toward Negroes widely publicized. Again suggesting voluntary methods as a first step, the committee called for the use of economic sanctions if voluntary methods failed. The President should lose no time in applying the provisions of the new Civil Rights Act of 1964, which forbade the use of federal funds in discriminatory activities, to offending states. As it had been in the case of discrimination in local communities, the committee was optimistic about the success of voluntary compliance. Citing its own efforts and those of the National Guard Bureau,[21-86] the committee reported that the last ten states to hold out had now begun to integrate their guard units at least on a token basis. In fact, the committee's report had to be revised at the last minute because Alabama and Mississippi enrolled Negroes in their enlisted ranks.

Chairman Gesell circulated a draft report containing these findings and recommendations among committee members in September 1964.[21-87] His colleagues suggested only minor revisions, although Whitney Young thought that some of the space spent on complimenting the services could be better used to emphasize the committee's recommendations for further reform. He did not press the point but noted wryly: "if we were as sensitive about the feelings of the victims of discrimination as we are of the perpetuators, we wouldn't have most of these problems to begin with."[21-88] Maj. Gen. Winston P. Wilson, the Chief of the National Guard Bureau, also reviewed the draft and found it "entirely fair, temperate and well-founded."[21-89] The committee's final report was sent to the President on 20 November 1964. A month later Johnson sent it along to McNamara with the request that he be kept informed on progress of the negotiations between the secretary and the governors on integration of the National Guard.[21-90]

The radical change in the civil rights orientation of the Department of Defense demanded by the administration's civil rights supporters was obviously a task too controversial for the department to assume in 1963 on its own initiative. It was, as a member of the Gesell Committee later remarked, a task that only a group of independent citizens reporting to the President could effectively suggest.[21-91] In the end the committee did all that its sponsors could have wanted. It confirmed the persistence of discrimination against black servicemen both on and off the military base and effectively tied that discrimination to troop morale and military efficiency. The committee's conclusions, logically derived from the connection between morale and efficiency, introduced a radically expanded concept of racial responsibility for the armed forces.

Although many people strongly associate the Gesell Committee with the use of economic coercion against race discrimination in the community, the committee's emphasis was always on the local commander's role in achieving voluntary compliance with the department's equal opportunity policies. Economic sanction was conceived of as a last resort. The directive of the Secretary of Defense that endorsed these recommendations was also denounced for embracing sanctions, although here the charges were even less appropriate because the use of sanctions was severely circumscribed. It remained to be seen how far command initiative and voluntary compliance could be translated by the services into concrete gains.

CHAPTER 22
Equal Opportunity in the Military Community

When Secretary McNamara issued his equal opportunity directive in 1963, all segregated public accommodations, schools, and even housing near military reservations became potential targets of the Department of Defense's integration drive. This change in policy was substantive, but the traditionalists who feared the sudden intrusion of the services into local community affairs and the reformers who later charged McNamara with procrastination missed the point. More than a declaration of racial principles, the directive was a guideline for the progressive application of a series of administrative pressures. Endorsing the Gesell Committee's concept of command responsibility, McNamara enjoined the local commander to oppose discrimination and foster equal opportunity both on and off the military base. He also endorsed the committee's recommendation for the use of economic sanctions in cases where voluntary compliance could not be obtained. By demanding the approval of the service secretaries for the use of sanctions, McNamara served notice that this serious application of the commander's authority would be limited and infrequent. He avoided altogether the committee's call for closing military bases.

The secretary's critics overlooked the fact that no exact timetable was set for the reforms outlined in the directive, and actually several factors were operating against precipitate action on discrimination outside the military reservation. Strong sentiment existed among service officials for leaving off-base discrimination problems to the Department of Justice, and, as early reactions to the committee report revealed, the committee's findings did little to alter these feelings. More important, the inclination to postpone the more controversial aspects of the equal opportunity directive received support from the White House itself. Political wisdom dictated that the Department of Defense refrain from any dramatic move in the civil rights field while Congress debated the civil rights bill, a primary legislative goal of both the Kennedy and Johnson administrations. "Avoid civil rights spectaculars" was the White House's word to the executive departments while the civil rights act hung fire.[22-1]

The lack of pressure by black servicemen and civil rights advocates lent itself to official procrastination. Civil rights organizations, preoccupied with racial unrest throughout the nation and anxious for the passage of new civil rights legislation, seemed to lose some of their intense interest in service problems. They paid scant attention to the directive beyond probing for the outer limits of the new policy. In the months following the directive, officials of the NAACP and other organizations shot off a spate of requests for the imposition of off-limits sanctions against certain businesses and schools and in some cases even whole towns and cities.[22-2] When Defense Department officials made clear that sanctions were to be a last, not first, resort and offered the cooperation of local commanders for a joint effort against local discrimination through voluntary compliance, the demands of the civil rights organizations petered out.[22-3]

According to a 1964 survey of black servicemen and veterans, this group enjoyed military life more than whites and were more favorably disposed toward the equal opportunity efforts of the Department of Defense.[22-4] They continued to complain, but the volume of their complaints was considerably reduced. One unsettling note: although fewer in number, the complaints were often addressed to the White House, the Justice Department, the civil rights organizations, or the Secretary of Defense, thus confirming the Gesell Committee's finding that black servicemen continued to distrust the services' interest in or ability to administer justice.[22-5]

The Secretary of Defense's manpower staff processed all these complaints. It dismissed those considered unrelated to race but forwarded many to the individual services with requests for immediate remedial action. Significantly, those involving the violation of a serviceman's civil rights off base continued to be sent to the Justice Department for disposition. Defense Department officials themselves adjudicated the hundreds of discrimination cases involving civilian employees.[22-6]

In the weeks and months following publication of the equal opportunity directive, official replies to the demands and complaints of black servicemen and their allies in the civil rights organizations continued to be carefully circumscribed. Whatever skepticism such restricted application of the Gesell recommendations may have produced among the civil rights leaders, the department found itself surprisingly free from outside pressure. It was able to set the pace of its own reform and to avoid meanwhile a clash with either reformers or segregationists over major civil rights issues of the day.

Creating a Civil Rights Apparatus

The Defense Department could do little about discrimination either on or off the military reservation until it was better organized for the task. The secretary needed new bureaucratic tools with which to develop new civil rights procedures, unite the disparate service programs, and document whatever failures might occur. He created a civil rights secretariat, assigning to his manpower assistant, Norman S. Paul,[22-7] the responsibility for promoting equal opportunity in the armed forces. Although racial affairs had always been considered among the manpower secretary's general duties, with precedents reaching back through the Personnel Policy Board to World War II when Assistant Secretary of War John J. McCloy supervised the employment of black troops, McNamara now significantly increased these responsibilities. The assistant secretary would represent him "in civil rights matters," would direct the department's equal opportunity programs, and would provide policy guidance for the military departments, reviewing their policies, regulations, instructions, and manuals and monitoring their performance.[22-8] To carry out these functions, the Secretary of Defense authorized his assistant to create a deputy assistant secretary for civil rights.[22-9] Again a precedent existed for the secretary's move. In January 1963 Paul had assigned an assistant to coordinate the department's racial activities.[22-10] The reorganization transferred the person and duties of the secretary's civilian aide, James C. Evans, to the Office of the Deputy Assistant Secretary for Civil Rights. The new organization was thus provided with a pedigree traceable to World War I and the work of Emmett J. Scott,[22-11] although Evans' move to the deputy's staff was the only connection between Scott and that office. The civilian aides, limited by the traditionally indifferent attitudes of the services toward equal opportunity programs, had been used to advise civilian officials on complaints from the black community, especially black servicemen, and to rationalize service policies for civil rights organizations. The new civil rights office, reflecting McNamara's positive intentions, was organized to monitor and instruct military departments.

The civil rights deputy was a relatively powerless bureaucrat. He might investigate discrimination and isolate its causes, but he enjoyed no independent power to reform service practices. His substantive dealings with the services had to be staffed through his superior, the Assistant Secretary for Manpower, a man to whom equal opportunity was but one of many problems and who might well question new or aggressive civil rights tactics. Such an attitude was understandable in an official with little or no experience in civil rights matters and no day-to-day contact with civil rights operations. Norman Paul, whose experience was in legislative liaison, might also be especially sensitive to the possibility of congressional or public criticism.[22-12] Indicative of the assistant secretary's attitude toward his civil rights deputy was the fact that the position was reorganized and retitled, with some significant corresponding changes in function each time, a bewildering five times in ten years.[22-13] To add to the problems of the civil rights office, nine different men were to occupy the deputy's position, three of them in the capacity of acting deputy, in that same decade.[22-14]

The organization of the equal opportunity program of the Secretary of Defense was not without its critics. Some wanted to enhance the prestige of the equal opportunity program by creating a separate assistant secretary for civil rights.[22-15] Such an official, accountable to the Secretary of Defense alone, would be free to direct the services' racial activities and, they agreed, would also serve as a highly visible symbol to servicemen and civil rights advocates alike of the department's determination to execute its new policy. Others, however, defended the existing organization, arguing that racial discrimination was a manpower problem, and the number of assistant secretaries was fixed by law and the chance of congressional approval for yet another manpower position was remote.[22-16]

These organizational problems had yet to appear in July 1963 when at Yarmolinsky's suggestion Secretary McNamara appointed Alfred B. Fitt the first civil rights deputy. Since 1961 the Army's Deputy Under Secretary for Manpower, Fitt had recently been on loan to the Office of the Secretary of Defense to coordinate the department's responses to the Gesell Committee. He was the author of the equal opportunity directive signed by McNamara, and his personal views on the subject, while consistent with those of Yarmolinsky and McNamara, were often expressed in more advanced terms. Going beyond the usual arguments for equal treatment based on morale and military efficiency, Fitt referred to the black servicemen's struggle as a moral issue. He was glad, he later confessed, to be on the right side of such an issue, and he felt indebted to the positive racial policies of Kennedy and Johnson and their Secretary of Defense.[22-17] He quickly gathered around him a staff of like-minded experts who proceeded to their first task, a review of the services' outline plans called for in the secretary's directive.[22-18]

ARRIVING IN VIETNAM.
101st Airborne Division troops aboard the USNS General Le Roy Eltinge.

Although merely outlines of proposed service programs, the three plans submitted in July and August nevertheless reflected the emphasis on off-base discrimination preached by the Gesell Committee and endorsed by the Secretary of Defense.[22-19] The plans also revealed the services' essential satisfaction with their current on-base programs, although each outlined further reforms within the military community. The Navy, for example, announced reforms in recruitment methods, and the Army planned the development of more racially equitable training programs and job assignments. All three services discussed new provisions for monitoring their equal opportunity programs, with the Army including explicit provisions for the processing of servicemen's racial complaints. And to insure the coordination of equal opportunity matters in future staff decisions, each service also announced (the Navy in a separate staff action) the formation of an equal opportunity organization in its military staff: an Equal Rights Branch in the office of the Army's Deputy Chief of Staff for Personnel, an Equal Opportunity Group in the Air Force's Directorate of Personnel Planning to work in conjunction with its Secretary's Committee on Equal Opportunity, and an Ad Hoc Committee in the Navy's Bureau of Personnel.

The outline plans revealed that the services entertained differing interpretations of the McNamara call for command responsibility in equal opportunity matters. The Gesell Committee had considered this responsibility of fundamental importance and wanted the local commander held accountable and his activities in this area made part of his performance rating. There was some disagreement among manpower experts on this point. How, one critic asked, could the services set up standards against which a commander's performance might be fairly judged? How could they insure that an overzealous commander might not, in the interest of a higher efficiency report, upset anti-discrimination programs that called for subtle negotiation?[22-20] But to Chairman Gesell the equal opportunity situation demanded action, and how could this demand be better impressed on the commander than by the knowledge that his performance was being measured?[22-21] The point of this argument, which the committee accepted, was that unless personal responsibility was fixed, policies and directives on equal opportunity were just so much rhetoric.

Only the Army's outline plan explicitly adopted the committee's controversial recommendation that "the effective performance of commanders in this area will be considered along with other responsibilities in determining his overall manner of duty performance." The Navy equivocated. Commanders would "monitor continually racial matters with a goal toward improvement." The Inspectors General of the Navy and Marine Corps were "instructed to appraise" all command procedures. The Air Force expected base base commanders to concern themselves with the welfare nondiscriminatory treatment of its servicemen when they were away from the base, but it left them considerable freedom in the matter. "The military mission is predominant," the Air Force announced, and the local commander must be given wide latitude in dealing with discrimination cases since "each community presented a different situation for which local solutions must be developed."

The decision by the Navy and Air Force to exempt commanders from explicit responsibility in equal opportunity matters came after some six months of soul-searching. Under Secretary of the Navy Fay agreed with his superior that the Navy's equal opportunity "image" suffered in comparison to the other services and the percentage of Negroes in the Navy and Marine Corps left much to be desired. But when ordered by Secretary Fred Korth to develop a realistic approach to equal opportunity in consultation with the Gesell Committee, Fay's response tended to ignore service shortcomings and, most significantly, failed to fix responsibility for equal opportunity matters. He proposed to revise Navy instructions to provide for increased liaison between local commanders and community leaders and monitor civil rights cases involving naval personnel, but his response neither discussed new ways to increase job opportunities for Negroes nor mentioned making equal opportunity performance a part of the military efficiency rating system.[22-22] His elaborate provisions for monitoring and reporting notwithstanding, his efforts appeared primarily cosmetic.

DIGGING IN.
Men of M Company, 7th Marines, construct a defense bunker during "Operation Desoto," Vietnam.

Undoubtedly, the Navy's image in the black community needed some refurbishing. Despite substantial changes in the racial composition of the Steward's Branch in recent years, Negroes continued to avoid naval service, as a special Navy investigation later found, because "they have little desire to become stewards or cooks."[22-23] Fay believed that the shortage of Negroes was part of a general problem shared by all the services. His public relations proposals were designed to overcome the difficulty of attracting volunteers. His recommendations were approved by Secretary Korth in February 1963 and disseminated throughout the Navy and Marine Corps for execution.[22-24] With only minor modification they were also later submitted to the Secretary of Defense as the Navy's outline plan.

Even as Fay settled on these modest changes, signs pointed to the possibility that the department's military leaders would be amenable to more substantial reform. The Chief of Naval Personnel admitted that the Gesell Committee's charges against the service were "to some extent" justified and warned naval commanders that if they failed to take a more positive approach to equal opportunity they would be ordered to take actions difficult for both the Navy and the community. Better "palatable evolutionary progress," he counseled, than "bitter revolutionary change."[22-25]

Air Force officials had also considered the problem of command responsibility in the months before submitting their outline plan. As early as December 1962, Under Secretary Joseph V. Charyk admitted the possibility of confusion over what the policy of base commanders should be concerning off-base segregation. He proposed that the staff consider certain "minimum" actions, including "mandatory evaluation of all officers concerning their knowledge of this program and the extent to which they have complied with the policy of anti-discrimination."[22-26] Secretary Zuckert discussed Charyk's proposal with his assistants on 23 January 1963. It was also considered by McNamara, who then passed it to the other services, calling on them to develop similar programs.[22-27] Finally, Air Force officials discussed command responsibility in preparing their critique of Gesell Committee recommendations, and Secretary Zuckert informed Assistant Secretary of Defense Paul that "the responsibility for this [the Air Force's anti-discrimination] program will be clearly designated down to base level."[22-28] Despite this attention, the subject of specific command responsibility was not clearly delineated in the Air Force's outline plan.

Paul ignored the critical differences in the services' outline plans when he approved all three without distinction on 13 September.[29] Alfred Fitt later explained why the Department had not insisted the services adopt the committee's specific recommendations on command responsibility. Commenting on the committee's call for the appointment of a special officer at each base to transmit black servicemen's grievances to base commanders, Fitt acknowledged that most Negroes were reluctant to complain, but said the services were aware of this reluctance and had already devised means to overcome it. Problems in communication, he pointed out, were leadership problems, and commanders must be left free to find their own method of learning about conditions in their commands. As for the committee's suggestion that equal opportunity initiatives in the local community be made a consideration in the promotion of the commander, the Defense Department had temporized. Such initiatives, Fitt explained, might be considered part of the commander's total performance, but it should never be the governing factor in determining advancement.[22-30]

Yet the principle of command responsibility was not completely ignored, for Paul made his approval of the plans contingent on several additional service actions. Each service had to prepare for commanders an instruction manual dealing with the discharge of their equal opportunity responsibilities, develop an equal opportunity information program for the periodic orientation of all personnel, and institute some method of insuring that all new commanders promptly reviewed equal opportunity programs applicable to their commands. The secretary also set deadlines for putting the plans into effect. The preparation of these comprehensive regulations and manuals, however, took much longer than expected, a delay, Fitt admitted, that slowed equal opportunity progress to some extent.[22-31] In fact, it was not until January 1965 that the last of the basic service regulations on equal opportunity was published.[22-32]

There were several reasons for the delay. The first was the protracted congressional debate over the civil rights bill. Some service officials strongly supported the stand that off-base complaints of black servicemen were chiefly the concern of the Justice Department. On a more practical level, however, the Department of Defense was reluctant to issue new directives while legislation bearing directly on discrimination affecting servicemen was being formulated. Accepting these arguments, Paul postponed the services' submission of new regulations and manuals until the act assumed final form.

The delayed publication of the service regulations could also be blamed in part on the confusion that surrounded the announcement of a new Defense policy on attendance at segregated meetings. The issue arose in early 1964 when Fitt discovered some defense employees accepting invitations to participate in segregated affairs while others refused on the basis of the secretary's equal opportunity directives. Inconsistency on such a delicate subject disturbed the civil rights deputy. The services had fortuitously avoided several potentially embarrassing incidents when officials were invited to attend segregated functions, and Fitt warned Paul that "if we don't erect a better safeguard than sheer chance, we're bound somewhere, sometime soon to look foolish and insensitive."[22-33] He wanted McNamara to issue a policy statement on the subject, admittedly a difficult task because it would be hard to write and would require White House clearance that might not be forthcoming. For the short run Fitt wanted to deal with the problem at a regular staff meeting where he could discuss the matter and coordinate his strategy without the delay of publishing new regulations.

As it turned out, anxiety over White House approval proved groundless. "The President has on numerous occasions made clear his view that Federal officials should not participate in segregated meetings," White House Counsel Lee C. White informed all department and agency heads, and he suggested that steps be taken in each department to inform all employees.[22-34] The Deputy Secretary of Defense, Cyrus R. Vance, complied on 7 July by issuing a memorandum to the services prohibiting participation in segregated meetings. Adding to the text prepared in the White House, he ordered that this prohibition be incorporated in regulations then being prepared, a move that necessitated additional staffing of the developing equal opportunity regulations.[22-35]

Objections to the prohibition were forthcoming. Continuing on a tack he had pursued for several years, the Air Force Deputy Special Assistant for Manpower, Personnel, and Organization, James P. Goode, objected to the application of the Vance memorandum to base commanders. These men had to maintain good relations with community leaders, he argued, and good relations were best fostered by the commander's joining local community organizations such as the Rotary Club and the Chamber of Commerce, which were often segregated. These civic and social organizations offered an effective forum for publicizing the objectives of the Department of Defense, and to forbid the commander's participation because of segregation would seriously reduce his local influence. Goode wanted the order "clarified" to exclude local community organizations from its coverage on the grounds that including them would be "detrimental to the best interests of all military personnel and their dependents and would result in a corresponding reduction in military effectiveness."[22-36]The Defense Department would have nothing to do with the idea. Such an exception to the rule, the civil rights deputy declared, would not constitute a clarification, but rather a nullification of the order. The Air Force request was rejected.[22-37]

The confusion surrounding the publication of service regulations suggested that without firm and comprehensive direction from the Office of the Secretary of Defense the services would never develop effective or uniform programs. Service officials argued that commanders had always been allowed to execute racial policy without specific instructions. They feared popular reaction to forceful regulations, and, in truth, they were already being subjected to congressional criticism over minor provisions of the Gesell Committee's report. Even the innocuous suggestion that officers be appointed to channel black servicemen's complaints was met with charges of "snooping" and "gestapo" tactics.[22-38]

Although both the Gesell Committee and Secretary McNamara had made clear that careful direction was necessary, the manpower office of the Department of Defense temporized. Instead of issuing detailed guidelines to the services that outlined their responsibilities for enforcing the provision of the secretary's equal opportunity directive, instead of demanding a strict accounting from commanders of their execution of these responsibilities, Paul asked the services for outline plans and then indiscriminately approved these plans even when they passed over real accountability in favor of vaguely stated principles. The result was a lengthy period of bureaucratic confusion. Protected by the lack of specific instructions the services went through an Alfonse-Gaston routine, each politely refraining from commitment to substantial measures while waiting to see how far the others would go.[22-39]

The immediate test for the services' belatedly organized civil rights apparatus was the racial discrimination lingering within the armed forces themselves. The Civil Rights Commission and the Gesell Committee had been concerned with the exceptions to the services' generally satisfactory equal opportunity record. It was these exceptions, such chronic problems as underrepresentation of Negroes in some services, in the higher military grades, and in skilled military occupations, that continued to concern the Defense Department civil rights organization and the services as they tried to carry out McNamara's directive. Seemingly minor compared to the discrimination faced by black servicemen outside the military reservation, racial problems within the military family and how the services dealt with them would have direct bearing on the tranquility of the armed forces in the 1970's.

LISTENING TO THE SQUAD LEADER.
Men of Company D, 21st Infantry, prepare to move out, Quang Tin Province, Vietnam.

Two pressing needs, and obviously interrelated ones, were to attract a greater number of young blacks to a military career and improve the status of Negroes already in uniform. These were not easy, short-term tasks. In the first place the Negro, ironically in view of the services' now genuine desire to have him, was no longer so interested in joining. As explained by Defense Department civil rights officials, the past attitudes and practices of the services, especially the treatment of Negroes during World War II, had created among black opinion-makers an indifference toward the services as a vocation.[22-40] Lacking encouragement from parents, teachers, and peers, black youths were increasingly reluctant to consider a military career. For their part the services tried to counter this attitude with an energetic public relations program.[22-41] Encouraged by the department's civil rights experts they tried to establish closer relations with black students. They even reorganized their recruitment programs, and the Secretary of Defense himself initiated a program to attract more black ROTC cadets.[22-42] Service representatives also worked with teachers and school officials to inform students on military career opportunities.

Enlistment depended not only on a man's desire to join but also on his ability to qualify. Following the publication of a presidential task force report on the chronic problem of high draft rejection rates, the Army inaugurated in August 1964 a Special Training and Enlistment Program (STEP), an experiment in the "military training, education, and physical rehabilitation of men who cannot meet current mental or medical standards for regular enlistment in the Army."[22-43] Aimed at increasing enlistments by providing special training after induction for those previously rejected as unqualified, the program provided for the enlistment of 8,000 substandard men, which included many Negroes. Before the men could be enlisted, however, Congress killed the program, citing its cost and duplication of the efforts of the Job Corps. It was not until 1967 that the idea of accepting many young men ineligible for the draft because of mental or educational deficiencies was revived when McNamara launched his Project 100,000.[22-44]

The services were unable to bring off a dramatic change in black enlistment patterns in the 1960's. With the exception of the Marine Corps, in which the proportion of black enlisted men increased 4 percent, the percentage of Negroes in the services remained relatively stationary between 1962 and 1968 (*Table 24*). In 1968, when Negroes accounted for 11 percent of the American population, their share of the enlisted service population remained at 8.2, with significant differences among the services. Nor did there seem much chance of increasing the number of black servicemen since the percentage of Negroes among draftees and first-time enlistees was rising very slowly while black reenlistment rates, for some twenty years a major factor in holding black strength steady, began to decline (*Table 25*). Actually, enlistment figures for both whites and blacks declined, a circumstance usually attributed to the unpopularity of the Vietnam War, although in the midst of the war, in 1967, black first-term reenlistment rates continued to exceed white rates 2 to 1.

TABLE 24—BLACK PERCENTAGES, 1962-1968

Year	Army		Navy	
	Officers	Enlisted Men	Officers	Enlisted Men
1962	3.2	12.2	.2	5.2
1964	3.4	13.4	.3	5.8
1965	3.5	13.9	.3	5.8
1967	3.4	12.1	.3	4.7
1968	3.3	12.6	.4	5.0

Source: Records of ASD (M) 291.2.

TABLE 25—RATES FOR REENLISTMENTS, 1964-1967

Year	Army		Navy
	White	Black	White
1964	18.5	49.3	21.6
1965	13.7	49.3	24.2
1966	20.0	66.5	17.6
1967	12.9	31.7	16.7

Source: Records of ASD (M) 291.2; see especially Paul Memo.

The low percentage of black officers, a matter of special concern to the Civil Rights Commission and the Gesell Committee as well as the civil rights organizations, remained relatively unchanged in the 1960's (*see Table 24*). Nor could any dramatic rise in the number of black officers be expected. Between 1963 and 1968 the three service academies graduated just fifty-one black officers, an impressive statistic only in the light of the record of a total of sixty black graduates in the preceding eighty-six years. Furthermore, there were only 116 black cadets in 1968, a vast proportional increase over former years but also an indication of the small number of black officers that could be expected from that source during the next four years (*Table 26*). Since cadets were primarily chosen by congressional nomination and from other special categories, little could be done, many officials assumed, to increase substantially the number of black cadets and midshipmen. An imaginative effort by Fitt in early 1964, however, proved this assumption false. Fitt got the academies to agree to take all the qualified Negroes he could find and some senators and congressmen to relinquish some of their appointments to the cause. He then wrote every major school district in the country, seeking black applicants and assuring them that the academies were truly open to all those qualified. Even though halfway through the academic year, Fitt's "micro-personnel operation," as he later called it, yielded appointments for ten Negroes. Unfortunately, his successor did not continue the effort.[22-45]

TABLE 26—BLACK ATTENDANCE AT THE MILITARY ACADEMIES, JULY 1968

Academy	Class of 1969	Class of 1970	Class
Army	10	7	
Navy	2	8	
Air Force	6	10	
Totals	18	25	

Source: Office, Deputy Assistant Secretary of Defense (Civil Rights).

The ROTC program at predominantly black colleges had always been the chief source of black officers, but here, again, there was little hope for immediate improvement. With the exception of a large increase in the number of black Air Force officers graduating from five black colleges, the percentage of officers entering the service from these institutions remained essentially unchanged throughout the 1960's despite the services' new equal opportunity programs (*Table 27*). Some civil rights leaders had been arguing for years that the establishment of ROTC units at predominantly black schools merely helped perpetuate the nation's segregated college system. Fitt agreed that as integrated education became more commonplace the number of black ROTC graduates would increase in predominantly white colleges, but meanwhile he considered units at black schools essential. Among the approximately 140 black colleges without ROTC affiliation, some could possibly qualify for units, and in February 1965 Fitt's successor, Stephen N. Shulman, called for the formation of more ROTC units as an equal opportunity measure.[22-46] The Army responded by creating a unit at Arkansas A&M Normal College, and the Navy opened a unit at Prairie View A&M in the President's home state of Texas. Balancing the expectations implied by the formation of these new units were the growing antiwar sentiment among college students and the special competition for black college graduates in the private business community, both of which made ROTC commissions less attractive to many black students.

TABLE 27—ARMY AND AIR FORCE COMMISSIONS GRANTED AT PREDOMINANTLY BLACK SCHOOLS

School	
A&T College, N.C.	
Central State College, Ohio	
Florida A&M College	

269

Hampton University, Va.	29
Lincoln University, Pa.	19
Morgan State College, Md.	21
Prairie View A&M College, Tex.	20
South Carolina State College	16
Southern University, La.	23
Tuskegee Institute, Ala.	14
Virginia State College	21
West Virginia State College	22
Howard University, Washington, D.C.	19
Total	286
Percentage of total such commissions granted	2.4

	Army Commission
School	
A&T College, N.C.	
Howard University, Washington, D.C.	
Maryland State College	
Tennessee A&I University	
Tuskegee Institute, Ala.	
Total	

Source: Office, Deputy Assistant Secretary of Defense (Civil Rights).

Chance of promotion for officers and men was one factor in judging equal treatment and opportunity in the services. A statistical comparison of the ranks of enlisted black servicemen between 1964 and 1966 reveals a steady advance (*Table 28*). With the exception of the Air Force, the percentage of Negroes in the higher enlisted ranks compared favorably with the total black percentage in each service. The advance was less marked for officers, but here too the black share of the O-4 grade (major or lieutenant commander) was comparable with the black percentage of the service's total strength. The services could declare with considerable justification that reform in this area was necessarily a drawn-out affair; promotion to the senior ranks must be won against strong competition.

TABLE 28—PERCENTAGE OF NEGROES IN CERTAIN MILITARY RANKS, 1964-1966

	E-6 (Staff Sergeant or Petty Offi
Army	
Navy	
Marine Corps	
Air Force	
	O-4 (Major or Lieutenant Co
Army	
Navy	
Marine Corps	
Air Force	

Source: Office, Deputy Assistant Secretary of Defense (Civil Rights).

The department's civil rights office forwarded to the services complaints from black servicemen who, despite the highest efficiency ratings and special commendations from commanders, failed to win promotions. "Almost uniformly," the office reported in 1965, "the reply comes back from the service that there had been no bias, no partiality, no prejudice operating in detriment on the complainant's consideration for promotion. They reply the best qualified was promoted, but this was not to say that the complainant did not have a very good record."[22-47] While black officers might well have been subtly discriminated against in matters of promotion, they also, it should be pointed out, shared in the general inflation in

270

efficiency ratings, common in all the services, that resulted in average officers being given "highest efficiency ratings."

In addition to complaining of direct denial of promotion opportunity, so-called "vertical mobility," some black officers alleged that their chances of promotion had been systematically reduced by the services when they failed to provide Negroes with "horizontal mobility," that is, with a wide variety of assignments and all-important command experience which would justify their future advancement. Supporting these claims, the civil rights office reported that only 5 Negroes were enrolled at the senior service schools in 1965, 4 black naval officers with command experience were on active duty, and 26 black Air Force officers had been given tactical command experience since 1950. The severely limited assignment of black Army officers at the major command headquarters, moreover, illustrated the "narrow gauge" assignment of Negroes.[22-48] This picture seemed somewhat at variance with Deputy Assistant Secretary Shulman's assurances to the Kansas Conference on Civil Rights in May 1965 that "we have paid particular attention to the assignment of Negro officers to the senior Service schools, and to those positions of command that are so vital to officer advancement to the highest rank."[22-49]

Since promotion in the military ranks depended to a great extent on a man's skills, training in and assignment to vital job categories were important to enlisted men. Here, too, the statistics revealed that the percentage of Negroes in the technical occupations, which had begun to rise in the years after Korea, had continued to increase but that a large proportion still held unskilled or semiskilled military occupational specialties (Table 29). Eligibility for the various military occupations depended to a great extent on the servicemen's mental aptitude, with men scoring in the higher categories usually winning assignment to technical occupations. When the Army began drafting large numbers of men in the mid-1960's, the number of men in category IV, which included many Negroes, began to go up. Given the fact that many Negroes with the qualifications for technical training were ignoring the services for other vocations while the less qualified were once again swelling the ranks, the Department of Defense could do little to insure a fair representation of Negroes in technical occupations or increase the number of black soldiers in higher grades. The problem tended to feed upon itself. Not only were the statistics the bane of civil rights organizations, but they also influenced talented young blacks to decide against a service career, in effect creating a variation of Gresham's law in the Army wherein men of low mentality were keeping out men of high intelligence. There seemed little to be done, although the department's civil rights office pressed the services to establish remedial training for category IV men so that they might become eligible for more technical assignments.

TABLE 29—DISTRIBUTION OF SERVICEMEN IN OCCUPATIONAL GROUPS BY RACE, 1967

Group / Activity	White		Number	P
	Number	Percent Dist.		
Combat troops	324,560	12.1	55,518	
Electronics				
repairmen	239,595	9.0	13,843	
Communications				
specialists	191,372	7.2	12,856	
Medical personnel	101,793	3.8	11,074	
Other technicians	52,132	1.9	3,812	
Administrative				
personnel	430,186	16.1	55,543	
Mechanical				
repairmen	498,899	18.6	39,820	
Draftsmen	144,070	5.4	15,728	
Service & supply				
personnel	283,976	10.6	53,136	
Miscellaneous / unknown	245,055	9.1	14,964	
Trainees[a]	166,478	6.2	18,753	
Total	2,678,116	100.0	295,047	

Tablenote a: Represents an Army category only.

Source: Bahr, "The Expanding Role of the Department of Defense As an Instrument of Social Change." Bahr's table is based on unpublished data from the DASD (CR).

271

If a man's assignment and promotion depended ultimately on his aptitude category, that category depended upon his performance in the Armed Forces Qualifying Test and other screening tests usually administered at induction. These tests have since been widely criticized as being culturally biased, more a test of an individual's understanding of the majority race's cultural norms than his mental aptitude. Even the fact that the tests were written also left them open to charges of bias. Some educational psychologists have claimed that an individual's performance in written tests measured his cultural and educational background, not his mental aptitude. It is true that the accuracy of test measurements was never reassessed in light of the subsequent performance of those tested. The services paid little attention to these serious questions in the 1960's, yet as a Defense Department task force studying the administration of military justice was to observe later:

the most important determination about a serviceman's future career (both in and out of the service) is made almost solely on the basis of the results of these tests: where he will be placed, how and whether he will be promoted during his hitch, and whether what he will learn in the service will be saleable for his post-service career.[22-50]

The Department of Defense depended on the "limited predictive capability of these tests," the task force charged, in deciding whether a serviceman was assigned to a "soft core" field, that is, given a job in such categories as transportation or supply, or whether he could enter one of the more profitable and prestigious "hard core" fields that would bring more rapid advancement.

Accurate and comprehensive testing and the measurement of acquired skills was obviously an important and complex matter, but in 1963 it was ignored by both the Civil Rights Commission and the Gesell Committee. President Kennedy, however, seemed aware of the problem. Before leaving for Europe in the summer of 1963 he called on the Secretary of Defense to consider establishing training programs keyed primarily to the special problems of black servicemen found ineligible for technical training. According to Lee White, the President wanted to use new training techniques "and other methods of stimulating interest and industry" that might help thousands of men bridge "the gap that presently exists between their own educational and cultural backgrounds and those of the average white serviceman."[22-51]

Because of the complexity of the problem, White agreed with Fitt that the program should be postponed pending further study, but the President's request happened to coincide with a special survey of the deficiencies and changes in recruit training then being made by Under Secretary of the Army Stephen Ailes.[22-52] Ailes offered to develop a special off-duty training program in line with the President's request. The program, to begin on a trial basis in October 1963, would also include evaluation counseling to determine if and when trainees should be assigned to technical schools.[22-53] Such a program represented a departure for the services, which since World War II had consistently rejected the idea frequently advanced by sociologists that the culturally, environmentally, and educationally deprived were denied equal opportunity when they were required to compete with the middle-class average.[22-54] Although no specific, measurable results were recorded from this educational experiment, the project was eventually blended into the Army's Special Training and Enlistment Program and finally into McNamara's Project 100,000.[22-55]

Beyond considering the competence of black servicemen, the Department of Defense had to face the possibility that discrimination was operating at least in some cases of assignment and promotion. Abolishing the use of racial designations on personnel records was one obvious way of limiting such discrimination, and throughout the mid-1960's the department sought to balance the conflicting demands for and against race labeling. Along with the integration of military units in the 1950's, the services had narrowed their multiple and cumbersome definition of races to a list of five groups. Even this list, a compromise drawn up by the Defense Department's Personnel Policy Board, was criticized. Reflecting the opinion of the civil rights forces, Evans declared that the definition of five races and twelve subcategories was scientifically inaccurate, statistically complicated, and racially offensive. He wanted a simple "white, nonwhite" listing of servicemen.[22-56] The subject continued to be discussed throughout the 1960's, the case finally going to the Director of the Bureau of the Budget, the ultimate authority on government forms. In August 1969 the director announced a uniform method for defining the races in federal statistics. The collectives "Negro and Other Races," "All Other Rates," or "All Other" would be acceptable to designate minorities; the terms "White," "Negro," and "Other Races" would be acceptable in distinguishing between the majority, principal minority, and other races.[22-57]

It was the use to which these definitions were put more than their number that had concerned civil rights leaders since the 1950's. Under pressure from civil rights organizations, some congressmen, and the Office of the Secretary of Defense, the services began to abandon some of the least justifiable uses of racial designations, principally those used on certain inductees' travel orders, reassignment orders, and reserve rosters.[22-58] But change was not widespread, and as late as 1963 the services still distinguished by race in their basic personnel records, casualty reports, statistical and command strength reports, personnel control files, and over twenty-five other departmental forms.[22-59] They continued to defend the use of racial designations on the grounds that measurement of equal opportunity programs and detection of discrimination patterns depended on accurate racial data.[22-60] Few could argue with these motives, although critics continued to question the need for race designations on records that were used in assignment and promotion processes. When public opposition developed to the use of racial entries on federal forms in general, the President's Committee on Equal Opportunity appointed a subcommittee in 1963 under Civil Service Chairman John W. Macy, Jr., to investigate. After much deliberation this group conducted a statistical experiment within the Department of Agriculture to discover whether employees could be identified by racial groups in a confidential manner separate from other personnel data.[22-61]

SUPPLYING THE SEVENTH FLEET.
USS Procyon crewmen rig netload of supplies for a warship.

The civil rights staff of the Defense Department was also interested in further limiting the use of race in departmental forms. In April 1963 Assistant Secretary Paul ordered a review of military personnel records and reporting forms to determine where racial entries were included unnecessarily.[22-62] His review uncovered twenty-five forms used in common by the services and the Office of the Secretary of Defense that contained racial designations. On 3 March 1964 Paul discreetly ordered the removal of race designations on all but nine of these forms, those concerning biostatistical, criminal, and casualty figures.[22-63] His order did not, however, extend to another group of forms used by individual services for their own purposes, and later in the year Fitt drafted an order that would have eliminated all racial designations in the services except an entry for data processing systems and one for biostatistical information. The directive also would have allowed racial designations on forms that did not identify individuals, arranged for the disposition of remains and casualty reporting, described fugitives and other "wanted" types, and permitted other exceptions granted at the level of the Assistant Secretary of Defense or that of the service secretary. Finally it would have set up a system for purging existing records and removing photographs from promotion board selection folders.[22-64] The services strongly objected to a purge of existing records on the grounds of costliness, and they were particularly opposed to the removal of photographs. Photographs were traditional and remained desirable, Deputy Under Secretary of the Army Roy K. Davenport explained, because they were useful in portraying individual physical characteristics unrelated to race.[22-65] Davenport added, however, that photographs could be eliminated from promotion board materials.

These proposals marked a high point in the effort to simplify and reduce the use of racial designations by the Department of Defense. Although several versions of Fitt's 1964 draft order were discussed in later years, none was ever published.[22-66] Nor did the Bureau of the Budget, to which the matter was referred for the development of a government-wide policy, publish any instructions. In fact, by the mid-1960's an obvious trend had begun in the Department of Defense toward broader use of racial indicators but narrower definition of race.

Several changes in American society were responsible for the changes. The need for more exact racial documentation overcame the argument for removing racial designations, for the civil rights experts both within and outside the department demanded more detailed racial statistics to protect and enlarge the equal opportunity gains of the sixties. The demand was also supported by representatives of the smaller racial minorities who, joining in the civil rights revolution, developed a self-awareness that made detailed racial and ethnic statistics mandatory. The shift was made possible to a great extent by the change in public opinion toward racial minorities. As one civil rights official later noted, the change in attitude had caused black servicemen to reconsider their belief that detrimental treatment necessarily followed racial identification.[22-67] Ironically, just a decade after the McNamara directive on equal opportunity, a departmental civil rights official, himself a Negro, was defending the use of photographs in the selection process on the grounds that such procedures were necessary in any large organization where individuals were relatively unknown to their superiors.[22-68] So strong had the services' need for black officers become, it could be argued, that a promotion board's knowledge of a candidate's race redounded to the advantage of the black applicants. For whatever reason, the pressure to eliminate racial indicators from personnel forms had largely disappeared at the end of the 1960's.

The Gesell Committee's investigations also forced the Department of Defense to consider the possibility of discrimination in the rarefied area of embassy and special mission assignments and the certainty of discrimination against black servicemen in local communities near some overseas bases. Concerning the former, the staff of the civil rights deputy concluded that such assignments were voluntary and based on special selection procedures. Race was not a factor

273

except for three countries where assignments were "based on politically ethnic considerations."[22-69] Nevertheless, Fitt began to discuss with the services ways to attract more qualified black volunteers for assignments to attaché, mission, and military assistance groups.

The department was less responsive to the Gesell Committee's recommendations on racial restrictions encountered off base overseas. The services, traditionally, had shunned consideration of this matter, citing their role as guests. When the Department of Defense outlined the commander's responsibility regarding off-base discrimination overseas, it expressly authorized commanders to impose sanctions in foreign communities, yet just five weeks later the services clarified the order for the press, explaining that sanctions would be limited to the United States.[22-70] A spokesman for the U.S. Army in Germany admitted that discrimination continued in restaurants and bars, adding that such discrimination was illegal in Germany and was limited to the lowest class establishments.[22-71] Supporting these conclusions was a spate of newspaper reports of segregated establishments in certain areas of Okinawa and the neighborhood around an Army barracks near Frankfurt, Germany.[22-72]

Despite these continuing press reports, the services declared in mid-1965 that the "overwhelming majority" of overseas installations were free of segregation problems in housing or public accommodations. One important exception to this overwhelming majority was reported by General Paul Freeman, the commander of U.S. Army Forces in Europe. He not only admitted that the problem existed in his command but also concluded that it had been imported from the United States. The general had met with Gerhard Gesell and subsequently launched a special troop indoctrination program in Europe on discrimination in public accommodations. He also introduced a voluntary compliance program to procure open housing.[22-73]

The Gesell Committee had repeatedly asserted that discrimination existed only in areas near American bases, and its most serious manifestations were "largely inspired by the attitude of a minority of white servicemen" who exerted social pressure on local businessmen. It was, therefore, a problem for American forces, and not primarily one for its allies. The civil rights office, however, preferred to consider the continuing discrimination as an anti-American phenomenon rather than a racial problem.[22-74] Fitt and his successor seemed convinced that such discrimination was isolated and its solution complex because of the difficulty in drawing a line between the attitudes of host nations and American GI's. Consequently, the problem continued throughout the next decade, always low key, never widespread, a problem of black morale inadequately treated by the department.

The failure to solve the problem of racial discrimination overseas and, indeed, the inability to liquidate all remaining vestiges of discrimination within the military establishment, constituted the major shortfall of McNamara's equal opportunity policy. With no attempt to shift responsibility to his subordinates,[22-75] McNamara later reflected with some heat on the failure of his directive to improve treatment and opportunities for black servicemen substantially and expeditiously: "I was naive enough in those days to think that all I had to do was show my people that a problem existed, tell them to work on it, and that they would then attack the problem. It turned out of course that not a goddamn thing happened."[22-76]

Although critical of his department's performance, McNamara would probably admit that more than simple recalcitrance was involved. For example, the services' traditional opposition to outside interference with the development of their personnel policies led naturally to their opposition to any defense programs setting exact command responsibilities or dictating strict monitoring of their racial progress. Defense officials, respecting service attitudes, failed to demand an exact accounting. Again, the services' natural reluctance to court congressional criticism, a reluctance shared by McNamara and his defense colleagues, led them all to avoid unpopular programs such as creating ombudsmen at bases to channel black servicemen's complaints. As one manpower official pointed out, all commanders professed their intolerance of discrimination in their commands, yet the prospect of any effective communication between these commanders and their subordinates suffering such discrimination remained unlikely.[22-77] Again defense officials, restrained by the White House from antagonizing Congress, failed to insist upon change.

Finally, while it was true that the services had not responded any better to McNamara's directive than to any of several earlier and less noteworthy calls for racial equality within the military community, it was not true that the reason for the lack of progress lay exclusively with the service. Against the background of the integration achievements of the previous decade, a feeling existed among defense officials that such on-base discrimination as remained was largely a matter of detail. Even Fitt shared the prevailing view. "In three years of close attention to such matters, I have observed [no] ... great gains in on-base equality," because, he explained to his superior, *"the basic gains were made in the 1948-1953 period."*[22-78] It must be remembered that discrimination operating within the armed forces was less tractable and more difficult to solve

274

than the patterns of segregation that had confronted the services of old or the off-base problems confronting them in the early 1960's. The services had reached what must have seemed to many a point of diminishing returns in the battle against on-base discrimination, a point at which each successive increment of effort yielded a smaller result than its predecessor.

No one—not the Civil Rights Commission, the Gesell Committee, the civil rights organizations, and, judging from the volume of complaints, not even black servicemen themselves—seriously tried to disabuse these officials of their satisfaction with the pace of reform. Certainly no one equated the importance of on-base discrimination with the blatant off-base discrimination that had captured everyone's attention. In fact, problems as potentially explosive as the discrimination in the administration of military justice were all but ignored during the 1960's.[22-79]

USAF GROUND CREW, TAN SON NHUT AIR BASE, VIETNAM,
relaxes over cards in the alert tent.

The sense of satisfaction that pervaded Fitt's comment, however understandable, was lamentable because it helped insure that certain inequities in the military community would linger. The failure of Negroes to win skilled job assignments and promotions, for example, would remain to fester and contribute significantly to the bitterness visited upon a surprised Department of Defense in later years. In brief, because the services had become a model of racial equality when judged by contemporary standards, the impulse of almost all concerned was to play down the reforms still needed on base and turn instead to the pressing and spectacular challenges that lay in wait outside the gates.

CHAPTER 23

From Voluntary Compliance to Sanctions

The Defense Department's attitude toward off-base discrimination against servicemen underwent a significant change in the mid-1960's. At first Secretary McNamara relied on his commanders to win from the local communities a voluntary accommodation to his equal opportunity policy. Only after a lengthy interval, during which the accumulated evidence demonstrated that voluntary compliance would, in some cases, not be forthcoming, did he take up the cudgel of sanctions. His use of this powerful economic weapon proved to be circumscribed and of brief duration, but its application against a few carefully selected targets had a salubrious and widespread effect. At the same time developments in the civil rights movement, especially the passage of strong new legislation in 1964, permitted servicemen to depend with considerable assurance upon judicial processes for the redress of their grievances.

Sanctions were distasteful, and almost everyone concerned was anxious to avoid their use. The Gesell Committee wanted them reserved for those recalcitrants who had withstood the informal but determined efforts of local commanders to obtain voluntary compliance. McNamara agreed. "There were plenty of things that the commanders could do in a voluntary way," he said later, and he wanted to give them time "to get to work on this problem."[23-1] His principal civil rights assistants considered it inappropriate to declare businesses or local communities off limits while the services were still in the process of developing voluntary action programs and before the full impact of new federal civil rights legislation on those programs could be tested. As for the services themselves, each was on record as being opposed to any use of sanctions in equal opportunity cases. The 1963 equal opportunity directive of the Secretary of Defense reflected this general reluctance. It authorized the use of sanctions, but in such a carefully restricted manner that for three years agencies of the Department of Defense never seriously contemplated using them.

Development of Voluntary Action Programs

Despite this obvious aversion to the use of sanctions in equal opportunity cases, the public impression persisted that Secretary McNamara was trying to use military commanders as instruments for forcing the desegregation of civilian communities. Actually, the Gesell Committee and the McNamara directive had demanded no such thing, as the secretary's civil rights deputy was repeatedly forced to point out. Military commanders, Fitt explained, were obligated to protect their men from harm and to secure their just treatment. Therefore, when "harmful civilian discrimination" was directed against men in uniform, "the wise commander seeks to do something about it." Commanders, he observed, did not issue threats or demand social reforms; they merely sought better conditions for servicemen and their families through cooperation and understanding. As for the general problem of racial discrimination in the United States, that was a responsibility of the civilian community, not the services.[23-2]

Exhibiting a similar concern for the sensibilities of congressional critics, Secretary McNamara assured the Senate Armed Services Committee that he had no plans "to utilize military personnel as a method of social reform." At the same time he reiterated his belief that

275

troop efficiency was affected by segregation, and added that when such a connection was found to exist "we should work with the community involved." He would base such involvement, he emphasized, on the commander's responsibility to maintain combat readiness and effectiveness.[23-3] Similar reassurances had to be given the military commanders, some of whom saw in the Gesell recommendations a demand for preferential treatment for Negroes and a level of involvement in community affairs that would interfere with their basic military mission.[23-4] To counter this belief, Fitt and his successor hammered away at the Gesell Committee's basic theme: discrimination affects morale; morale affects military efficiency. The commander's activities in behalf of equal opportunity for his men in the community is at least as important as his interest in problems of gambling, vice, and public health, and is in furtherance of his military mission.[23-5]

McNamara's civil rights assistants tried to provide explicit guidance on the extent to which it was proper for base commanders to become involved in the community. Fitt organized conferences with base commanders to develop techniques for dealing with off-base discrimination, and his office provided commanders with legal advice to counter the arguments of authorities in segregated communities. Fitt also encouraged commanders to establish liaison with local civil rights groups whose objectives and activities coincided with departmental policy. At his request, Assistant Secretary of Defense for Manpower Paul devised numerous special instructions and asked the services to issue regulations supporting commanders in their attempts to change community attitudes toward black servicemen. These regulations, in turn, called on commanders to enlist community support for equal treatment and opportunity measures, utilizing in the cause their command-community relations committees. Consisting of base officials and local business and community leaders, these committees had originally been organized by the services to improve relations between the base and town. Henceforth, they would become the means by which the local commanders might introduce measures to secure equal treatment for servicemen.[23-6]

FIGHTER PILOTS ON THE LINE.
Col. Daniel (Chappie) James, Jr., commander of an F-4 jet, and his pilot readying for takeoff from a field in Thailand.

Perhaps the most important, certainly most controversial, of Fitt's moves[23-7] was the establishment of a system to measure the local commanders' progress against off-base discrimination. His vehicle was a series of off-base equal opportunity inventories, the first comprehensive, statistical record of discrimination affecting servicemen in the United States. Based on detailed reports from every military installation to which 500 or more servicemen were assigned, the first inventory covered some 305 bases in forty-eight states and the District of Columbia and nearly 80 percent of the total military population stationed in the United States. Along with detailed surveys of public transportation, education, public accommodations, and housing, the inventory reported on local racial laws and customs, police treatment of black servicemen, the existence of state and local agencies concerned with equal opportunity enforcement, and the base commander's use of command-community relations committees.[23-8]

The first inventory confirmed the widespread complaints of special discrimination encountered by black servicemen. It also uncovered interesting patterns in that discrimination. In matters of commercial transportation, local schools, and publicly owned facilities such as libraries and stadiums, the problem of discrimination against black servicemen was confined almost exclusively to areas around installations in the south. But segregated public accommodations such as motels, restaurants, and amusements, a particularly virulent form of discrimination for servicemen, who as transients had to rely on such businesses, existed in all parts of the country including areas as diverse as Iowa, Alaska, Arizona, and Illinois. Discrimination in these states was especially flagrant since all except Arizona had legislation prohibiting enforced segregation of public accommodations. Discrimination in the sale and rental of houses showed a similar pattern. Only thirty installations out of the 305 reporting were located in states with equal housing opportunity statutes. These were in northern states, stretching from Maine to California. At the same time, some of these installations reported discrimination in housing despite existing state legislation forbidding such practices. No differences were reported in the treatment of black and white servicemen with respect to civilian law enforcement except that in some communities black servicemen were segregated when taken into custody for criminal violations.

Generally, the practice of most forms of discrimination was more intense in the south, but the record of other sections of the country was no better than mixed, even where legislation forbade such separate and unequal treatment. Obviously there was much room for progress, and as indicated in the inventory much still could be done within the armed forces themselves. The reports revealed that almost one-third of the commands inventoried failed to form the command-community relations committees recommended by the Gesell Committee and ordered in the services' equal opportunity directives. Of the rest, only sixty-one commands had invited local black leaders to participate in what were supposed to be biracial groups.

The purpose of the follow-up inventories—three were due from each service at six-month intervals—was to determine the progress of local commanders in achieving equal opportunity for their men. The Defense Department showed considerable energy in extracting from commanders comprehensive information on the state of equal opportunity in their communities.[23-9] In fact, this rather public exposition proved to be the major reporting system on equal opportunity progress, the strongest inducement for service action, and the closest endorsement by the department of the Gesell Committee's call for an accountability system.

The first follow-up inventory revealed some progress in overcoming discrimination near military installations, but progress was slight everywhere and in some areas of concern nonexistent. Discrimination in schooling for dependents off base, closely bound to the national problem of school desegregation, remained a major difficulty. Commanders reported that discrimination in public accommodations was more susceptible to command efforts, but here, too, in some parts of the country, communities were resisting change. A Marine Corps commander, for example, reported the successful formation of a command-community relations committee at his installation near Albany, Georgia, but to inquiries concerning the achievements of this committee the commander was forced to reply "absolutely none."[23-10]

Some forms of discrimination seemed impervious to change. Open housing, for one, was the exception rather than the rule throughout the country. One survey noted the particular difficulty this created for servicemen, especially the many enlisted men who lived in trailers and could find no unsegregated place to park.[23-11] At times the commanders' efforts to improve the situation seemed to compound the problem. The stipulation that only open housing be listed with base housing officers served more to reduce the number of listings than to create opportunities for open housing. Small wonder then that segregated housing, "the most pervasive and most intractable injustice of all," in Alfred Fitt's words, was generally ignored while the commanders and civil rights officials concentrated instead on the more easily surmountable forms of discrimination.[23-12]

At least part of the reason for the continued existence of housing discrimination against servicemen lay in the fact that the Department of Defense continued to deny itself the use of its most potent equal opportunity weapon. Well into 1964, Fitt could report that no service had contemplated the use of sanctions in an equal opportunity case.[23-13] Nor had housing discrimination ever figured prominently in any decision to close a military base. At Fitt's suggestion, Assistant Secretary Paul proposed that community discrimination patterns be listed as one of the reasons for closing military bases.[23-14] Although the Assistant Secretary for Installations and Logistics, Thomas D. Morris, agreed to consult such information during deliberations on closings, he pointed out that economics and operational suitability were the major factors in determining a base's value.[23-15] As late as December 1964, an official of the Office of the Secretary of Defense was publicly explaining that "discrimination in the community is certainly a consideration, but the military effectiveness and justification of an installation must be primary."[23-16]

Clearly, voluntary compliance had its limits, and Fitt said as much on the occasion of his departure after a year's assignment as the civil rights deputy. Reviewing the year's activities for Gesell, Fitt concluded that "we have done everything we could think of" in formulating civil rights policy and in establishing a monitoring system for its enforcement. He was confident that the department's campaign against discrimination had gained enough momentum to insure continued progress. If, as he put it, the "off-base lot of the Negro serviceman will not in my time be the same as that of his white comrade-in-arms" he was nevertheless satisfied that the Department of Defense was committed to equal opportunity and that commitment was "bound to be beneficial."[23-17]

Fitt's assessment was accurate, no doubt, but not exactly in keeping with the optimistic spirit of the Gesell Committee and Secretary McNamara's subsequent equal opportunity commitment to the President. Obviously more could be achieved through voluntary compliance if the threat of legal sanctions were available. In the summer of 1964, therefore, the Defense Department's manpower officials turned to new federal civil rights legislation for help.

Civil Rights, 1964-1966

The need for strong civil rights legislation had become increasingly apparent in the wake of *Brown* v. *Board of Education*.[23-18] With that decision, the judicial branch finally lined up definitively with the executive in opposition to segregation. But the effect of this united opposition was blunted by the lack of a strong civil rights law, something that President Kennedy

277

had not been able to wrestle from a reluctant legislative branch. The demands of the civil rights movement only underscored the inability of court judgments and executive orders alone to guarantee the civil rights of all Americans. Such a profound social change in American society required the concerted action of all three branches of government, and by 1963 the drive for strong civil rights legislation had made such legislation the paramount domestic political issue. Lyndon Johnson fully understood its importance. "We have talked long enough in this country about equal rights," he told his old colleagues in Congress, "we have talked for one hundred years or more. It is time now to write the next chapter, and to write it in the books of law."[23-19]

He was peculiarly fitted for the task. A southerner in quest of national support, Johnson was determined for very practical reasons to carry out the civil rights program of his slain predecessor and to end the long rule of Jim Crow in many areas of the country. He let it be known that he would accept no watered-down law.

I made my position [on the civil rights bill] unmistakably clear: We were not prepared to compromise in any way. "So far as this administration is concerned," I told a press conference, "its position is firm." I wanted absolutely no room for bargaining.... I knew that the slightest wavering on my part would give hope to the opposition's strategy of amending the bill to death.[23-20]

Certainly this pronouncement was no empty rhetoric, coming as it did from a consummate master of the legislative process who enjoyed old and close ties with congressional leaders.

Johnson was also philosophically committed to change. "Civil rights was really something that was, by this time, burning pretty strongly in Johnson," Harris L. Wofford later noted.[23-21] The new President exhorted his countrymen: "To the extent that Negroes were imprisoned, so was I ... to the extent that Negroes were free, really free, so was I. And so was my country."[23-22] Skillfully employing the wave of sympathy for equal rights that swept the country after John Kennedy's death, President Johnson procured a powerful civil rights act, which he signed on 2 July 1964.[23-23]

The object of the Civil Rights Act of 1964 was no less than the overthrow of segregation in America. Its major provisions outlawed discrimination in places of amusement and public accommodation, in public education, labor unions, employment, and housing. It called for federal intervention in voting rights cases and established a Community Relations Service in the Department of Commerce to arbitrate racial disputes. The act also strengthened the Civil Rights Commission and broadened its powers. It authorized the United States Attorney General and private citizens to bring suit in discrimination cases, outlining the procedures for such cases. Most significant were the sweeping provisions of the law's Title VI that forbade discrimination in any activity or program that received federal financial assistance. This added the threat of economic sanctions against any of those thousands of institutions, whether public or private, which, while enjoying federal benefactions, discriminated against citizens because of race. Accurately characterized as the "most effective instrument yet found for the elimination of racial discrimination,"[23-24] Title VI gave the federal government leave to cut segregation and discrimination out of the body politic. In Professor Woodward's words, "a national consensus was in the making and a peaceful solution was in sight."[23-25]

The 1964 presidential election was at hand to test this consensus. Given the Republican candidate's vehement opposition to the Civil Rights Act, Lyndon Johnson's overwhelming victory was among other things widely interpreted as a national plebiscite for the new law. The President, however, preferred a broader interpretation. Believing that "great social change tends to come rapidly in periods of intense activity before the impulse slows,"[23-26] he considered his victory a mandate for further social reform. On the advice of the Justice Department and the Civil Rights Commission, he called on Congress to eliminate the "barriers to the right to vote."[23-27]

In common with its predecessors, the 1964 Civil Rights Act had only touched lightly on the serious obstacles in the way of black voters. Although some 450,000 Negroes were added to the voting rolls in the southern states in the year following passage of the 1964 law, the civil rights advocates were calling for stronger legislation. With bipartisan support, the President introduced a measure aimed directly at states that discriminated against black voters, providing for the abolition of literacy tests, appointment of federal examiners to register voters for all elections, and assignment of federal supervisors for those elections. The Twenty-fourth Amendment, adopted in February 1964, had eliminated the poll tax in federal elections, and the President's new measure carried a strong condemnation of the use of the poll tax in state elections as well.

In all of his efforts the President had the unwitting support of the segregationists, who treated the nation to another sordid racial spectacular. In February 1965 Alabama police jailed

Martin Luther King, Jr., and some 2,000 members of his voting rights drive, and a generally outraged nation watched King's later clash with the police over a voting rights march. This time he and his followers were stopped at a bridge in Selma, Alabama, by state troopers using tear gas and clubs. The incident climaxed months of violence that saw the murder of three civil rights workers in Philadelphia, Mississippi; the harassment of the Mississippi Summer Project, a voting registration campaign sponsored by several leading civil rights organizations; and ended in the assassination of a white Unitarian minister, James Reeb, of Washington, D.C., one of the hundreds of clergymen, students, and other Americans who had joined in the King demonstrations. Addressing a joint session of Congress on the voting rights bill, the President alluded to the Selma incident, declaring: "Their cause must be our cause too. Because it is not just Negroes, but really it is all of us who must overcome the crippling legacy of bigotry and injustice. And we shall overcome."[23-28]

MEDICAL EXAMINATION.
Navy doctor on duty, Yokosuka, Japan.

The President's bill passed easily with bipartisan support, and he signed it on 6 August 1965. Two days later federal examiners were on the job in three states. The act promised a tremendous difference in the political complexion of significant portions of the country. In less than a year federal examiners certified 124,000 new voters in four states and almost half of all eligible Negroes were registered to vote in the states and counties covered by the law. Another result of the new legislation was that the Attorney General played an active role in the 1966 defeat of the state poll tax laws in *Harper* v. *Virginia Board of Elections.*[23-29]

Useful against legalized discrimination, chiefly in the south, the civil rights laws of the mid-1960's were conspicuously less successful in those areas where discrimination operated outside the law. In the great urban centers of the north and west, home of some 45 percent of the black population, *de facto* segregation in housing, employment, and education had excluded millions of Negroes from the benefits of economic progress. This ghettoization, this failure to meet human needs, led to the alienation of many young Americans and a bitter resentment against society that was dramatized just five days after the signing of the 1965 voting rights act when the Watts section of Los Angeles exploded in flames and violence. There had been racial unrest before, especially during the two previous summers when flare-ups occurred in Cambridge (Maryland), Philadelphia, Jacksonville, Brooklyn, Cleveland, and elsewhere, but Watts was a different matter. Before the California National Guard with some logistical help from the Army quelled the riots, thirty-four people were killed, some 4,000 arrested, and $35 million worth of property damaged or destroyed. The greatest civil disturbance since the 1943 Detroit riot, Watts was but the first in a series of urban disturbances which refuted the general belief that the race problem had been largely solved in cities of the north and the west.[23-30]

Discrimination in housing was a major cause of black urban unrest, and housing was foremost among the areas of discrimination still untouched by federal legislation. The housing provision of the 1964 Civil Rights Act was severely limited, and Johnson rejected the idea of yet another executive order proposed by his Committee on Equal Opportunity in Housing. Like the order signed by Kennedy, it could cover only new housing and even that with dubious legality. Johnson, relying on the civil rights momentum developed over the previous years, decided instead to press for a comprehensive civil rights bill that would outlaw discrimination in the sale of all housing. The new measure was also designed to attack several other residual areas of discrimination, including jury selection and the physical protection of Negroes and civil rights workers. Although he enjoyed a measure of bipartisan support for these latter sections of the bill, the President failed to overcome the widespread opposition to open housing, and the 1966 civil rights bill died in the Senate, thereby postponing an effective law on open housing until after the assassination of Dr. King in 1968.

The spectacle of demonstrators and riots in northern cities and the appearance in 1966 of the "black power" slogan considered ominous by many citizens were blamed for the bill's failure. Another and more likely cause was that in violating the sanctity of the all-white neighborhood Johnson had gone beyond any national consensus on civil rights. In August 1966, for example, a survey by the Louis Harris organization revealed that some 46 percent of white America would object to having a black family as next-door neighbors and 70 percent believed that Negroes "were trying to move too fast." Of particular importance to the Department of Defense, which would be taking some equal opportunity steps in the housing field in the next months, was the fact that this opposition was not translated into a general rejection of the concept of equal opportunity. In fact, although the bill failed to win enough votes to apply the Senate's cloture rule, the President could boast that he won a clear majority in both houses. His defeat slowed the pace of the civil rights movement and postponed a solution to a major domestic problem;

postponed, because, as Roy Wilkins reminded his fellow citizens at the time, "the problem is not going away ... the Negro is not going away."[23-31]

The Civil Rights Act and Voluntary Compliance

The enactment of new civil rights legislation in 1964 had thrust the armed forces into the heart of the civil rights movement in a special way. As Secretary McNamara himself reminded his subordinates, President Johnson was determined to have each federal department develop programs and policies that would give meaning to the new legislation. That legislation, he added, created "new opportunities" to win full equality for all servicemen. The secretary made the usual connection between discrimination and military efficiency, adding that "this reason alone" compelled departmental action.[23-32] Obviously other reasons existed, and when McNamara called on all commanders to support their men in the "lawful assertion of the rights guaranteed" by the act he was making his more than 300 local commanders agents of the new federal legislation.

Defense officials quickly arranged for the publication of directives and regulations applying the provisions of the new law to the whole defense establishment. To insure, as McNamara put it, that military commanders understood their responsibility for seeing that those in uniform were accorded fair treatment as prescribed by the new law, Assistant Secretary Paul had already ordered the services to advise the rank and file of their rights and instruct commanders to seek civilian cooperation for the orderly application of the act to servicemen.[23-33] After considering the service comments solicited by his civil rights deputy,[23-34] Paul issued a departmental instruction on 24 July that prescribed specific policies and procedures for processing the requests of uniformed men and women for legal action under Titles II (Public Accommodations), III (Public Facilities), and IV (Public Education) of the act. The instruction encouraged, but did not compel, the use of command assistance by servicemen who wished to request suit by the U.S. Attorney General.[23-35]

Finally in December, McNamara issued a directive spelling out his department's obligations under the act's controversial Title VI, Nondiscrimination in Federally Assisted Programs.[23-36] This directive was one of a series requested by the White House from various governmental agencies and reviewed by the Justice Department and the Bureau of the Budget in an attempt to coordinate the federal government's activities under the far-reaching Title VI provision.[23-37] After arranging for the circulation of the directive throughout the services, Secretary McNamara explained in considerable detail how grants and loans of federal funds, transfer, sale, or lease of military property, and in fact any federal assistance would be denied in cases where discrimination could be found. Although this directive would affect the Department of Defense chiefly through the National Guard and various civil defense programs, it was nevertheless a potential source of economic leverage for use by the armed forces in the fight against discrimination.[23-38] Furthermore, this directive, unlike McNamara's equal opportunity directive of the previous year, was supported by federal legislation and thus escaped the usual criticism suffered by his earlier directives on discrimination.

The Department of Defense's voluntary compliance program in off-base discrimination cases had its greatest success in the months following the passage of the Civil Rights Act. Given the passage of the act and other federal legislation, pronouncements of the federal courts, and the broad advance of racial tolerance throughout the nation, the Defense Department's civil rights officials came to expect that most discrimination could be dealt with in a routine manner. As Robert E. Jordan III, a staff assistant to the department's civil rights deputy, put it, the use of sanctions would not "normally" be invoked when the Civil Rights Act or other laws could provide a judicial remedy.[23-39] Fitt predicted that only a "very tiny number" of requests by servicemen for suits under the act would ever be processed all the way through to the courts. He expected to see many voluntary settlements achieved by commanders spurred to action by the filing of requests for suit.[23-40]

By early 1965 local commanders had made "very good progress," according to one Defense Department survey, in securing voluntary compliance with Title II of the act for public accommodations frequented by servicemen. Each service had reported "really surprising examples of progress" in obtaining integrated off-base housing in neighborhoods adjoining military installations and heavily populated by service families. The services also reported good progress in obtaining integrated off-duty education for servicemen, as distinct from their dependents in the public schools.[23-41] At the same time lesser but noticeable progress was reported in Titles II and III cases. In the first off-base inventory some 145 installations in twenty states had reported widespread discrimination in nearby restaurants, hotels, bars, bowling alleys, and other Title II businesses; forty installations in nine states reported similar discrimination in libraries, city parks, and stadiums (Title III categories). Each succeeding inventory reported impressive reductions in these figures.

280

Defense Department officials observed that the amount of progress depended considerably on the size of the base, its proximity to the local community, and the relationship between the commander and local leaders. Progress was most notable at large bases near towns. The influence of the Civil Rights Act on cases involving servicemen was also readily apparent. But above all, these officials pointed to the personal efforts of the local commander as the vital factor. Many commanders were able to use the off-base inventory itself as a weapon to fight discrimination, especially when the philosophy of "if everybody else desegregates I will" was so prevalent. Nor could the effect of commanders' achievements be measured merely in terms of hotels and restaurants open to black servicemen. The knowledge that his commander was fighting for his rights in the community gave a tremendous boost to the black serviceman's morale. It followed that when a commander successfully forced a change in the practices of a business establishment, even one only rarely frequented by servicemen, he stirred a new pride and self-respect in his men.[23-42]

The Limits of Voluntary Compliance

If the Civil Rights Act strengthened the hands of the commander, it also quickly revealed the ultimate limits of voluntary compliance itself. The campaign against Titles II and III discrimination was only one facet of the Department of Defense's battle against off-base discrimination, which also included major attacks against discrimination in the National Guard, in the public schools, and, finally, in housing. It was in these areas that the limits of voluntary compliance were reached, and the technique was abandoned in favor of economic sanctions.

Because of its intimate connection with the Department of Defense, the National Guard appeared to be an easy target in the attack against off-base discrimination. Although Secretary McNamara had accepted his department's traditional voluntary approach toward ending discrimination in this major reserve component,[23-43] the possibility of using sanctions against the guard had been under discussion for some time. As early as 1949 the legal counsel of the National Guard Bureau had concluded that the federal government had the right to compel integration.[23-44] Essentially the same stand was taken in 1961 by the Defense Department's Assistant General Counsel for Manpower.[23-45]

These opinions, along with the 1947 staff study on the guard and the 1948 New Jersey case,[23-46] provided support extending over more than a decade for the argument that the federal government could establish racial policies for the National Guard. Indeed, there is no evidence of opposition to this position in the 1940's, and southern guard leaders openly accepted federal supremacy during the period when the Army and Air Force were segregated. But in the 1960's, long after the services had integrated their active forces and seemed to be moving toward a similar policy for the guard, doubts about federal authority over a peacetime guard appeared. The National Guard Bureau disputed the 1949 opinion of its legal counsel and the more recent one from the Defense Department and stressed the political implications of forcing integration; a bureau spokesman asserted that "an ultimatum to a governor that he must commit political suicide in order to obtain federal support for his National Guard will be rejected." Moreover, if federal officials insisted on integration, the bureau foresaw a deterioration of guard units to the detriment of national security.[23-47]

AUTO PILOT SHOP.

Airmen check out equipment, Biggs Air Force Base, Texas.

The National Guard Bureau supported voluntary integration, and its chiefs tried in 1962 and 1963 to prod state adjutants general into taking action on their own account. Citing the success some states, notably Texas, enjoyed in continuing the integration their units first experienced during federalized service in the Berlin call-up, Maj. Gen. D. W. McGowan warned other state organizations that outright defiance of federal authorities could not be maintained indefinitely and would eventually lead to integration enforced by Washington.[23-48] Replies from the state adjutants varied, but in some cases it became clear that the combination of persuasion and quiet pressure might bring change. The Louisiana adjutant general, for example, reported that considering the feelings in his state's legislature any move toward integration would require "a selling job." At the same time, he carefully admitted, "some of these days, the thing [integration] is probably inevitable."[23-49] The administration, however, continued to take the view that integration of the National Guard was a special problem because the leverage available to implement it was in no way comparable to the federal government's control over the active forces or the organized reserves.

Progress toward total integration continued through 1963 and 1964, although slowly.[23-50] Near the end of 1964, the National Guard Bureau announced that every state National Guard was integrated, though only in token numbers in some cases.[23-51] Even this slight victory could not be claimed by the Department of Defense or its National Guard Bureau, but was the result of the pressure exerted on states by the Gesell Committee.

The Civil Rights Act of 1964 altered the Defense Department's attitude toward the National Guard. Title VI of the act undercut all arguments against federal supremacy over the guard, for it no longer mattered who had technical responsibility for units in peacetime. In practical terms, the power to integrate clearly rested now with the federal government, which in a complete reversal of its earlier policy showed a disposition to use it. On 15 February 1965 Deputy Secretary of Defense Vance ordered the Army and Air Force to amend National Guard regulations to eliminate any trace of racial discrimination and "to ensure that the policy of equal opportunity and treatment is clearly stated."[23-52] Vance's order produced a speedy change in the states, so much so that later in 1965 the Department of Defense was finally able to oppose New York Congressman Abraham J. Multer's biannual bill to withhold federal aid from segregated guard units on the grounds that there were no longer any such units.[23-53]

Lack of equal opportunity in the National Guard might have been resented by civil rights groups, but black servicemen themselves suffered more generally and more deeply from discrimination visited on their children. Alfred Fitt summarized these feelings in 1964:

The imposition of unconstitutionally segregated schooling on their children is particularly galling for the Negro serviceman. As comparative transients—and as military men accustomed to avoiding controversy with civilian authorities—they cannot effectively sue for the constitutional rights of their sons and daughters. Yet they see their children, fresh from the integrated environment which is the rule on military installations, condemned to schools which are frequently two, even three grades behind the integrated schools these same children had attended on-base or at their fathers' previous duty stations.[23-54]

There was much to be said for the Defense Department's theory that an appeal for voluntary compliance would produce much integration in off-base schools attended by military dependents. That these children were the offspring of men serving in defense of their country was likely to have considerable impact in the south, especially, with its strong military traditions. That the children had in most cases already attended integrated schools, competing and learning with children of another race, was likely to make their integration more acceptable to educators.

Beyond these special reasons, the services could expect help from new legislation and new administration rulings. The Civil Rights Act of 1960, for example, had authorized the Department of Health, Education, and Welfare to provide integrated education for military dependents in areas where public schools were discontinued. In March 1962 Secretary of Health, Education, and Welfare Abraham Ribicoff announced that racially segregated schools were no longer "suitable" institutions under the terms of Public Laws 815 and 879 and that beginning in September 1963 his department would "exercise sound discretion, take appropriate steps" to provide integrated education for military dependents. If the children were withdrawn from local school systems to achieve this, he warned, so too the federal aid.[23-55] Lending credence to Ribicoff's warning, his department undertook a survey in the fall of 1962 of selected military installations to determine the educational status of military dependents.[23-56] On 17 September 1962 Attorney General Kennedy filed suit in Richmond to bar the use of federal funds in the segregated schools of Prince George County, Virginia, the location of Fort Lee.[23-57] Finally, in January 1963, the Department of Health, Education, and Welfare announced that unless state officials relented it would start a crash program of construction and operation of integrated schools for military dependents in Alabama, Georgia, Mississippi, and South Carolina.[23-58]

Some local commanders took immediate advantage of these emotional appeals and administration pressures. The commandant of the Marine Corps Schools, Quantico, for example, won an agreement from Stafford County, Virginia, authorities that the county would open its high school and two elementary schools to Marine Corps dependents without regard to race. The commandant also announced that schools in Albany, Georgia, had agreed to take military dependents on an integrated basis.[23-59] The Air Force announced that schools near Eglin, Whiting, and MacDill Air Force Bases in Florida as well as those near six bases in Texas, including Sheppard and Connally, would integrate. The Under Secretary of the Navy reported similar successes in school districts in Florida, Tennessee, and Texas. And the commander of Fort Belvoir started discussions with the Fairfax County, Virginia, school board looking toward the speedy desegregation of schools near the fort.

Lest any commander hesitate, the Department of Defense issued a new policy in regard to the education of military dependents. On 15 July 1963 Assistant Secretary Paul directed all local commanders in areas where public education was still segregated—large parts of some fifteen states—to counsel parents on the procedures available for the transfer of their children to integrated schools, on how to appeal assignment to segregated schools, and on legal action as an alternative to accepting local school board decisions to bar their children.[23-60] In December

1963 Fitt drew up contingency plans for the education of dependent children in the event of local school closings.[23-61] In April of 1964 Fitt reminded the services that Defense Department policy called for the placement of military dependents in integrated schools and that commanders were expected to make "appropriate efforts" on behalf of the children to eliminate any deviation from that policy.[23-62] In effect, base commanders were being given a specific role in the fight to secure for black and white dependents equal access to public schools.

The action taken by base commanders under this responsibility might alter patterns of segregated education in some areas, but in the long run any attempt to integrate schools through a program of voluntary compliance appeared futile. At the end of the 1964 school year more than 76,300 military dependents, including 6,177 black children, at forty-nine installations attended segregated schools. Another 14,390 children on these same bases attended integrated schools, usually grade school, on the military base itself.[23-63] Because of the restrictions against base closings and off-limits sanctions, there was little hope that base commanders could produce any substantial improvement in this record. Fitt admitted that the Department of Defense could not compel the integration of a school district. He recognized that it was impossible to establish an accredited twelve-grade system at the forty-nine installations, yet at the same time he considered it "incompatible with military requirements" to assign black servicemen with children to areas where only integrated schools were available. Even the threat to deny impacted-area aid was limited because in many communities the services' contracts with local school districts to educate dependent children was contingent on continuous federal aid. If the aid was stopped the schools would be closed, leaving service children with no schools to attend.[23-64]

The only practical recourse for parents of military dependents, Fitt believed, was to follow the slow process of judicial redress under Title IV of the civil rights bill then moving through Congress. Anticipating the new law, Fitt asked the services to provide him with pertinent data on all school districts where military dependents attended segregated schools. He planned to use this information in cooperation with the Departments of Justice and Health, Education, and Welfare for use in federal suits. He also requested reports on the efforts made by local commanders to integrate schools used by dependent children and the responses of local school officials to such efforts.[23-65] Later, after the new law had been signed by the President, Norman Paul outlined for the services the procedures to be used for lodging complaints under Titles IV and VI of the Civil Rights Act and directed that local commanders inform all parents under their command of the remedies afforded them under the new legislation.[23-66]

With no prospect in sight for speedy integration of schools attended by military dependents, the Department of Defense summarily ended the attendance of uniformed personnel at all segregated educational institutions. With the close of the 1964 spring semester, Paul announced, no Defense Department funds would be spent to pay tuition for such schooling.[23-67] The economic pressure implicit in this ruling, which for some time had been applied to the education of civilian employees of the department, allowed many base commanders to negotiate an end to segregation in off-base schools.[23-68]

The effort of the Department of Defense to secure education for its military dependents in integrated schools was, on the whole, unsuccessful. Integration, when it finally came to most of these institutions later in the 1960's, came principally through the efforts of the Department of Health, Education, and Welfare to enforce Title VI of the Civil Rights Act of 1964. Yet the role of local military commanders in the effort to secure integrated schools cannot be ignored, for with the development of a new policy toward off-base facilities in 1963 the commander became a permanent and significant partner in the administration's fight to desegregate the nation's schools. In contrast to earlier times when the Department of Defense depended on moral suasion to desegregate schools used by servicemen's children, its commanders now educated parents on their legal rights, collected data to support class action suits, and negotiated with school boards. If the primary impetus for this activity was the Civil Rights Act of 1964, the philosophy of the Gesell Committee and the Secretary of Defense's directive were also implicit.

Discrimination in the sale and lease of housing continued to be the most widespread and persistent form of racial injustice encountered by black servicemen, and a most difficult one to fight. The chronic shortage of on-base accommodations, the transient nature of a military assignment, and the general reluctance of men in uniform to protest publicly left the average serviceman at the mercy of local landlords and real estate interests. Nor did he have recourse in law. No significant federal legislation on the subject existed before 1969, and state laws (by 1967 over half the states had some form of prohibition against discrimination in public housing and twenty-one states had open housing laws) were rather limited, excluding owner-occupied dwellings, for example, from their provisions. Even President Kennedy's 1962 housing order was restricted to future building and to housing dependent on federal financing.

283

Both the Civil Rights Commission and the Gesell Committee studied the problem in some detail and concluded that the President's directive to all federal agencies to use their "good offices" to push for open housing in federally supported housing had not been followed in the Department of Defense. The Civil Rights Commission, in particular, painted a picture of a Defense Department alternating between naivete and indifference in connection with the special housing problems of black servicemen.[23-69] White House staffer Wofford later decided that the Secretary of Defense was dragging his feet on the subject of off-base housing, although Wofford admitted that each federal agency was a forceful advocate of action by other agencies.[23-70]

SUBMARINE TENDER DUTY.
A senior chief boatswain mate and master diver at his station on the USS Hunley.

The Assistant Secretary for Manpower conceded in November 1963 that little had been done, but, citing the widely misunderstood off-base inventory, he pleaded the need to avoid retaliation by segregationist forces in Congress both on future authorizations for housing and on the current civil rights legislation. He recommended that the Department of Defense complete and disseminate to local commanders information packets containing relevant directives, statistics, and legal procedures available in the local housing field.[23-71]

McNamara approved this procedure, again investing local commanders with responsibility for combating a pervasive form of discrimination with a voluntary compliance program. Specifically, local commanders were directed to promote open housing near their bases, expanding their open housing lists and pressing the problem of local housing discrimination on their biracial community committees for solution. They were helped by the secretary's assistants. His civil rights and housing deputies became active participants in the President's housing committee, transmitting to local military commanders the information and techniques developed in the executive body. McNamara's civil rights staff inaugurated cooperative programs with state and municipal equal opportunity commissions and other local open housing bodies, making these community resources available to local commanders. Finally, in February 1965, the Department of Defense entered into a formal arrangement with the Federal Housing Administration to provide commanders with lists of all housing in their area covered by the President's housing order and to arrange for the lease of foreclosed Federal Housing Authority properties to military personnel.[23-72]

These activities had little effect on the military housing situation. An occasional apartment complex or trailer court got integrated, but no substantial progress could be reported in the four years following Secretary McNamara's 1963 equal opportunity directive. On the contrary, the record suggests that many commanders, discouraged perhaps by the overwhelming difficulties encountered in the fair housing field, might agree with Fitt: "I have no doubt that I did nothing about it [housing discrimination] in 1963-4 because I was working on forms of discrimination at once more blatant and easier to overcome. I did not fully understand the impact of housing discrimination, and I did not know what to do about it."[23-73]

A special Defense Department housing survey of thirteen representative communities, including a study of service families in the Washington, D.C., area, documented this failure. The survey described a housing situation as of early 1967 in which progress toward open off-base housing for servicemen was minimal. Despite the active off-base programs sponsored by local commanders, discrimination in housing remained widespread.[23-74] and based on four years' experience the Department of Defense had to conclude that appeals to the community for voluntary compliance would not produce integrated housing for military families on a large scale. Still, defense officials were reluctant to substitute more drastic measures. Deputy Secretary Vance, for one, argued in early 1967 that nationwide application of off-limits sanctions would raise significant legal issues, create chaotic conditions in the residential status of all military personnel, downgrade rather than enhance the responsibility of local commanders to achieve their equal opportunity goals, and, above all, fail to produce more integrated housing. Writing to the chairman of the Action Coordinating Committee to End Segregation in the Suburbs (ACCESS),[23-75] he asserted that open housing for servicemen would be achieved only through the "full commitment at every level of command to the proposition of equal treatment."[23-76]

But even as Vance wrote, the department's housing policy was undergoing substantial revision. And, ironically, it was the very group to which Vance was writing that precipitated the change. It was the members of ACCESS who climaxed their campaign against segregated apartment complexes in the Washington suburbs with a sit-down demonstration in McNamara's reception room in the Pentagon on 1 February, bringing the problem to the personal attention of a Secretary of Defense burdened with Vietnam.[23-77] Although strongly committed to the principle of equal opportunity and always ready to support the initiatives of his civil rights

284

assistants,[23-78] McNamara had largely ignored the housing problem. Later he castigated himself for allowing the problem to drift for four years.

I get charged with the TFX. It's nothing compared to the Bay of Pigs or my failure for four years to integrate off-base military housing. I don't want you to misunderstand me when I say this, but the TFX was only money. We're talking about blood, the moral foundation of our future, the life of the nation when we talk about these things.[23-79]

McNamara was being unnecessarily harsh with himself. There were several reasons, quite unrelated to either the Secretary of Defense or his assistants, that explain the failure of voluntarism to integrate housing used by servicemen. A major cause—witness the failure of President Johnson's proposed civil rights bill in 1966—was that open housing lacked a national consensus or widespread public support. Voluntary compliance was successful in other areas, such as public accommodation, transportation, and to some extent even in dependent schooling, precisely because the requests of local commanders were supported by a growing national consensus and the force of national legislation. In dealing with housing discrimination, however, these same commanders faced public indifference or open hostility without the comforting support of federal law. Even with the commander's wholehearted commitment to open housing, a commitment that equal opportunity directives from the services could by no means insure, his effectiveness against such widespread discrimination was questionable. Nothing in his training prepared him for the delicate negotiations involved in obtaining integrated housing. Moreover, it was extremely difficult if not impossible to isolate the black serviceman's housing plight from that of other black citizens; thus, an open housing campaign really demanded comprehensive action by the whole federal government. The White House had never launched a national open housing campaign; it was not, indeed, until 16 February 1967 that President Johnson submitted a compulsory national open housing bill to Congress.[23-80]

Whatever the factors contributing to the lack of progress, McNamara admitted that "the voluntary program had failed and failed miserably."[23-81] Philosophically, Robert McNamara found this situation intolerable. He had become interested in the "unused potential" of his department to change American society as it affected the welfare of servicemen. As Fitt explained, the secretary believed

any department which administers 10% of the gross national product, with influence over the lives of 10 million people, is bound to have an impact. The question is whether it's going to be a dumb, blind impact, or a marshaled and ordered impact. McNamara wanted to marshal that impact by committing defense resources to social goals that were still compatible with the primary mission of security.[23-82]

Clearly, the Secretary of Defense considered open housing for service families one of these goals, and when his attention was drawn to the immediacy of the problem by the ACCESS demonstration he acted quickly. At his instigation Vance ordered the local commanders of all services to conduct a nationwide census of all apartment houses, housing developments, and mobile home courts consisting of five or more rental units within normal commuting distance of all installations having at least 500 servicemen. He also ordered the commanders to talk to the owners or operators of these properties personally and to urge them to open their properties to all servicemen. He organized an Off-base Equal Opportunity Board, consisting of the open housing coordinators of each service and his office to monitor the census. Finally, he announced the establishment of a special action program under the direction of Thomas D. Morris, now the Assistant Secretary for Manpower. Aimed at the Washington, D.C., area specifically, the program was designed to serve as a model for the rest of the country.[23-83]

Vance also notified the service secretaries that subsequent to the census all local commanders would be asked to discuss the census findings with local community leaders in an effort to mobilize support for open housing. Later Assistant Secretary Morris, with the help of the acting civil rights deputy, L. Howard Bennett, spelled out a program for "aggressive" negotiation with community leaders and cooperation with other government agencies, in effect a last-ditch attempt to achieve open housing for servicemen through voluntary compliance. Underscoring the urgency of the housing campaign, the department demanded a monthly report from all commanders on their open housing activities,[23-84] and Morris promptly launched a proselytizing effort of his own in the metropolitan Washington area. Described simply by McNamara as "a decent man," Morris spoke indefatigably before civil leaders and realtors on behalf of open housing.[23-85]

The department's national housing census confirmed the gloomy statistics projected from earlier studies indicating that housing discrimination was widespread and intractable and damaging to servicemen's morale.[23-86] McNamara decided that local commanders "were not going to involve themselves," and for the first time since sanctions were mentioned in his equal opportunity directive some four years before, he decided to use them in a discrimination case.

285

The Secretary of Defense himself, not the local commander nor the service secretaries, made the decision: housing not opened to *all* servicemen would be closed to *all* servicemen.[23-87] Aware of the controversy accompanying such action, the secretary's legal counsel prepared a justification. Predictably, the department's lawyer argued that sanctions against discrimination in off-base housing were an extension of the commander's traditional right to forbid commerce with establishments whose policies adversely affected the health or morals of his men. Acutely conscious of the lack of federal legislation barring housing discrimination, Vance and his legal associates were careful to distinguish between an owner's legal right to choose his tenants and the commander's power to impose a military order on his men.

Although committed to a nationwide imposition of sanctions on housing if necessary, the Secretary of Defense hoped that the example of a few cases would be sufficient to break the intransigence of offending landlords; certainly a successful test case would strengthen the hand of the commanders in their negotiations with community leaders. Metropolitan Washington was the obvious area for the first test case, and the Maryland General Assembly further focused attention on that region when on 28 February 1967 it called on the Secretary of Defense to end housing discrimination for all military personnel in the state.[23-88] On the night of 21 June, Gerhard Gesell received an unexpected phone call: there would be something in tomorrow's paper, Robert McNamara told him, that should be especially interesting to the judge.[23-89] And there was, indeed, on the front page. As of 1 July, all military personnel would be forbidden to lease or rent housing in any segregated apartment building or trailer court within a three-and-a-half-mile radius of Andrews Air Force Base, Maryland. Citing the special housing problems of servicemen returning from Vietnam, McNamara pointed out that in the Andrews area of Maryland less than 3 percent of some 22,000 local apartment units were open to black servicemen. The Andrews situation, he declared, was causing problems "detrimental to the morale and welfare of the majority of our Negro military families and thus to the operational effectiveness of the base."[23-90]

The secretary's rhetoric, skillfully justifying sanctions in terms of military efficiency and elementary fairness for returning combat veterans, might have explained the singular lack of adverse congressional reaction to the order. No less a personage than Chairman L. Mendel Rivers of the House Armed Services Committee admitted that he had no objection to the sanctions near Andrews. Asked about possible sanctions elsewhere, Rivers added that he would cross that bridge later.[23-91]

Rivers and his congressional allies would have little time for reflection, because McNamara quickly made it clear that the Andrews action was only a first step. Sanctions were imposed in rapid succession on areas surrounding four other military installations in Maryland, Fort George G. Meade, Aberdeen Proving Ground, Edgewood Arsenal, and Fort Holabird.[23-92] More pressure was placed on segregationists when McNamara announced on 8 September his intention to extend the sanctions nationwide. He singled out California, where the Defense Department census had shown black servicemen barred from a third of all rental units, for special attention. In fact, off-limits sanctions imposed on broad geographical areas were used only once more—in December 1967 against multiple rental properties in the northern Virginia area.[23-93] In the meantime, the Department of Defense had developed a less dramatic but equally effective method of exerting economic pressure on landlords. On 17 July 1967 McNamara ordered the establishment of housing referral offices at all installations where more than 500 men were assigned. All married servicemen seeking off-base housing were required to obtain prior clearance from these offices before entering into rental agreements with landlords.[23-94]

Finally, in the wake of the passage of the Civil Rights Act of 1968 and the Supreme Court's ruling against housing discrimination in *Jones* v. *Mayer*, McNamara's successor, Clark M. Clifford, was able to combine economic threats with new legal sanctions against landlords who continued to discriminate. On 20 June 1968 Clifford ordered the services to provide advice and legal assistance to servicemen who encountered discrimination in housing. The services were also to coordinate their housing programs with the Departments of Housing and Urban Development and Justice, provide assistance in locating nondiscriminatory rental units, and withhold authorization for servicemen to sign leases where discriminatory practices were evident. In a separate action the manpower assistant secretary also ordered that housing referral offices be established on all bases to which 100—as opposed to the earlier 500—military personnel were assigned.[23-95]

FIRST AID.
Soldier of the 23d Infantry gives water to heat stroke victim during "Operation Wahiawa," Vietnam.

The result of these directives was spectacular. By June 1968 the ratio of off-base housing units carried on military referral listings—that is, apartment and trailer court units with open

286

housing policies assured in writing by the owner or certified by the local commander—rose to some 83 percent of all available off-base housing for a gain of 247,000 units over the 1967 inventory.[23-96] In the suburban Washington area alone, the number of housing units opened to all servicemen rose more than 300 percent in 120 days—from 15,000 to more than 50,000 units.[23-97] By the end of 1968 some 1.17 million rental units, 93 percent of all those identified in the 1967 survey, were open to all servicemen.[23-98] Still, these impressive gains did not signal the end of housing discrimination for black servicemen. The various Defense Department sanctions excluded dwellings for four families or less, and the evidence suggests that the original and hastily compiled off-base census on which all the open housing gains were measured had ignored some particularly intransigent landlords in larger apartment houses and operators of trailer courts on the grounds that their continued refusal to negotiate with commanders had made the likelihood of integrating their properties extremely remote.

The campaign for open housing is the most noteworthy chapter in the fight for equality of treatment and opportunity for servicemen. The efforts of the Department of Defense against other forms of off-base discrimination were to a great extent successful because they coincided with court rulings and powerful civil rights legislation. The campaign for open housing, on the other hand, was launched in advance of court and congressional action and in the face of much popular feeling against integrated housing. McNamara's fight for open housing demonstrates, as nothing had before, his determination to use, if necessary, the department's economic powers in the civilian community to secure equal treatment and opportunity for servicemen. In the name of fair housing, McNamara invested not only his own prestige but also the Defense Department's manpower and financial resources. In effect, this willingness to use the extreme weapon of off-limits sanctions revitalized the idea of using the Department of Defense as an instrument of social change in American society.

McNamara's willingness to push the department beyond the national consensus on civil rights (as represented by the contemporary civil rights laws) also signified a change in his attitude. Unlike Yarmolinsky and Robert Kennedy, McNamara limited his attention to discrimination's effect on the individual serviceman and, ultimately, on the military efficiency of the armed forces. Despite his interest in the cause of civil rights, he had, until the open housing campaign, always circumscribed the department's equal opportunity program to fit a more traditional definition of military mission. Seen in this light, McNamara's attack against segregated housing represented not only the substitution of a new and more powerful technique—sanctions—for one that had been found wanting—voluntary compliance, but also a substantial evolution in his own social philosophy. He later implied as much.

We request cooperation and seek voluntary compliance [in obtaining open housing].... I am fully aware that the Defense Department is not a philanthropic foundation or a social-welfare institution. But the Department does not intend to let our Negro servicemen and their families continue to suffer the injustices and indignities they have in the past. I am certain my successors will pursue the same policy.[23-99]

By 1967 the major programs derived from Secretary McNamara's equal opportunity policy had been defined, and the Department of Defense could look back with pride on the substantial and permanent changes it had achieved in the treatment of black servicemen in communities near military bases.[23-100] Emphasizing voluntary compliance with its policy, the department had proved to be quite successful in its campaign against discrimination in off-base recreation, public transportation and accommodation, in the organized reserves, and even, to a limited extent, in off-base schools. It was logical that the services should seek voluntary compliance before resorting to more drastic methods. As the Gesell Committee had pointed out, base commanders had vast influence in their local communities, influence that might be used in countless ways to alter the patterns of off-base discrimination. For the first time the armed forces had fought discrimination by making the local commander responsible for a systematic program of negotiations in the community.

But voluntary compliance had its limits. Its success depended in large measure on the ability and will of local commanders, who, for the most part, were unprepared by training or temperament to deal with the complex and explosive problems of off-base discrimination. Even if the commander could qualify as a civil rights reformer, he had little time or incentive for a duty that would go unrecognized in terms of his efficiency rating yet must compete for his attention with other necessary duties that were so recognized. Finally, the successful use of voluntary compliance techniques depended on the implied threat of legal or economic pressures, yet, for a considerable period following McNamara's 1963 directive, no legal strictures against some forms of discrimination existed, and the use of economic sanctions had been so carefully circumscribed by defense officials as to render the possibility of their use extremely remote.

287

The decision to circumscribe the use of economic sanctions against off-base discrimination made sense. Closing a base because of discrimination in nearby communities was practically if not politically impossible and might conceivably become a threat to national security. As to sanctions aimed at specific businesses, the secretary's civil rights assistants feared the possibility that the abrupt or authoritarian imposition of sanctions by an insensitive or unsympathetic commander might sabotage the department's whole equal opportunity program in the community. They were determined to leave the responsibility for sanctions in the hands of senior civilian officials. In the end it was the most senior of these officials who acted. When his attention turned to the problem of discrimination in off-base housing for black servicemen in 1967, Secretary McNamara quickly decided to use sanctions against a discriminatory practice widely accepted and still legal under federal law.

The combination of voluntary compliance techniques and economic sanctions, in tandem with the historic civil rights legislation of the mid-1960's, succeeded in eliminating most of the off-base discrimination faced by black servicemen. Ironically, in view of its unquestioned control in the area, the Department of Defense failed to achieve an equal success against discrimination within the military establishment itself. Complaints concerning the number, promotion, assignment, and punishment of black servicemen, a limited problem in the mid-1960's, went mostly unrecognized. Relatively speaking, they were ignored by the Gesell Committee and the civil rights organizations in the face of the more pressing off-base problems and only summarily treated by the services, which remained largely silent about on-base and in-house discrimination. Long after off-base discrimination had disappeared as a specific military problem, this neglected on-base discrimination would rise up again to trouble the armed forces in more militant times.[23-101]

CHAPTER 24
Conclusion

The Defense Department's response to the recommendations of the Gesell Committee marked the close of a well-defined chapter in the racial history of the armed forces. Within a single generation, the services had recognized the rights of black Americans to serve freely in the defense of their country, to be racially integrated, and to have, with their dependents, equal treatment and opportunity not only on the military reservation but also in nearby communities. The gradual compliance with Secretary McNamara's directives in the mid-1960's marked the crumbling of the last legal and administrative barriers to these goals.

Why the Services Integrated

In retrospect, several causes for the elimination of these barriers can be identified. First, if only for the constancy and fervor of its demands, was the civil rights movement. An obvious correlation exists between the development of this movement and the shift in the services' racial attitudes. The civil rights advocates—that is, those spokesmen of the rapidly proliferating civil rights organizations and their allies in Congress, the White House, and the media—formed a pressure group that zealously enlisted political support for equal opportunity measures. Their metier was presidential politics. In several elections they successfully traded their political assistance, an unknown quantity, for specific reform. Their influence was crucial, for example, in Roosevelt's decision to enlist Negroes for general service in the World War II Navy and in all branches of the Army and in Truman's proclamation of equal treatment and opportunity; it was notable in the adjudication of countless discrimination cases involving individual black servicemen both on and off the military base. Running through all their demands and expressed more and more clearly during this period was the conviction that segregation itself was discrimination. The success of their campaign against segregation in the armed forces can be measured by the extent to which this proposition came to be accepted in the counsels of the White House and the Pentagon.

Because the demands of the civil rights advocates were extremely persistent and widely heard, their direct influence on the integration of the services has sometimes been overstressed. In fact, for much of the period their most important demands were neutralized by the logical-sounding arguments of those defending the racial *status quo*. More to the point, the civil rights revolution itself swept along some important defense officials. Thus the reforms begun by James Forrestal and Robert McNamara testified to the indirect but important influence of the civil rights movement.

Resisting the pressure for change was a solid bloc of officials in the services which held out for the retention of traditional policies of racial exclusion or segregation. Professed loyalty to military tradition was all too often a cloak for prejudice, and prejudice, of course, was prevalent in all the services just as it was in American society. At the same time traditionalism simply reflected the natural inclination of any large, inbred bureaucracy to preserve the privileges and order of an earlier time. Basically, the military traditionalists—that is, most senior officials and commanders

288

of the armed forces and their allies in Congress—took the position that black servicemen were difficult to train and undependable in battle. They cited the performance of large black combat units during the world wars as support for their argument. They also rationalized their opposition to integration by saying that the armed forces should not be an instrument of social change and that the services could only reflect the social mores of the society from which they sprang. Thus, in their view, integration not only hindered the services' basic mission by burdening them with undependable units and marginally capable men, but also courted social upheaval in military units.

Eventually reconciled to the integration of military units, many military officials continued to resist the idea that responsibility for equal treatment and opportunity of black servicemen extended beyond the gates of the military reservation. Deeply ingrained in the officer corps was the conviction that the role of the military was to serve, not to change, society. To effect social change, the traditionalist argued, would require an intrusion into politics that was by definition militarism. It was the duty of the Department of Justice and other civilian agencies, not the armed forces, to secure those social changes essential for the protection of the rights of servicemen in the civilian community.[24-1] If these arguments appear to have overlooked the real causes of the services' wartime racial problems and ignored some of the logical implications of Truman's equal treatment and opportunity order, they were nevertheless in the mainstream of American military thought, ardently supported, and widely proclaimed.

The story of integration in the armed forces has usually, and with some logic, been told in terms of the conflict between the "good" civil rights advocates and the "bad" traditionalists. In fact, the history of integration goes beyond the dimensions of a morality play and includes a number of other influences both institutional and individual.

VIETNAM PATROL.
Men of the 35th Infantry advance during "Operation Baker."

The most prominent of these institutional factors were federal legislation and executive orders. After World War II most Americans moved slowly toward acceptance of the proposition that equal treatment and opportunity for the nation's minorities was both just and prudent.[24-2] A drawn-out process, this acceptance was in reality a grudging concession to the promptings of the civil rights movement; translated into federal legislation, it exerted constant pressure on the racial policy of the armed forces. The Selective Service Acts of 1940 and 1948, for example, provided an important reason for integrating when, as interpreted by the executive branch, their racial provisions required each service to accept a quota of Negroes among its draftees. The services could evade the provisions of the acts for only so long before the influx of black draftees in conjunction with other pressures led to alterations in the old racial policies. Truman's order calling for equality of treatment and opportunity in the services was also a major factor in the racial changes that took place in the Army in the early 1950's. To a great extent the dictates of the civil rights laws of 1964 and 1965 exerted similar pressure on the services and account for the success of the Defense Department's comprehensive response during the mid-1960's to the discrimination faced by servicemen in the local community.

Questions concerning the effect of law on social custom, and particularly the issue of whether government should force social change or await the popular will, are of continuing interest to the sociologist and the political scientist. In the case of the armed forces, a sector of society that habitually recognizes the primacy of authority and law, the answer was clear. Ordered to integrate, the members of both races adjusted, though sometimes reluctantly, to a new social relationship. The traditionalists' genuine fear that racial unrest would follow racial mixing proved unfounded. The performance of individual Negroes in the integrated units demonstrated that changed social relationships could also produce rapid improvement in individual and group achievement and thus increase military efficiency. Furthermore, the successful integration of military units in the 1950's so raised expectations in the black community that the civil rights leaders would use that success to support their successful campaign in the 1960's to convince the government that it must impose social change on the community at large.[24-3]

Paralleling the influence of the law, the quest for military efficiency was another institutional factor that affected the services' racial policies. The need for military efficiency had always been used by the services to rationalize racial exclusion and segregation; later it became the primary consideration in the decision of each service to integrate its units. Reinforcing the efficiency argument was the realization by the military that manpower could no longer be considered an inexhaustible resource. World War II had demonstrated that the federal government dare not ignore the military and industrial potential of any segment of its population. The reality of the limited national manpower pool explained the services' guarantee that Negroes would be included in the postwar period as cadres for the full wartime mobilization of black manpower. Timing was somewhat dependent on the size and mission of the individual service; integration came to each when it became obvious that black manpower could not be used efficiently in separate organizations. In the case of the largest service, the Army, the Fahy Committee used the failure to train and use eligible Negroes in unfilled jobs to convince senior officials that military efficiency demanded the progressive integration of its black soldiers, beginning with those men eligible for specialist duties. The final demonstration of the connection between efficiency and integration came from those harried commanders who, trying against overwhelming odds to fight a war in Korea with segregated units, finally began integrating their forces. They found that their black soldiers fought better in integrated units.

MARINE ENGINEERS IN VIETNAM.
Men of the 11th Engineer Battalion move culverts into place in a mountain stream during "Operation Pegasus."

Later, military efficiency would be the rationale for the Defense Department's fight against discrimination in the local community. The Gesell Committee was used by Adam Yarmolinsky and others to demonstrate to Secretary McNamara if not to the satisfaction of skeptical military traditionalists and congressional critics that the need to solve a severe morale problem justified the department's intrusion. Appeals to military efficiency, therefore, became the ultimate justification for integrating the units of the armed forces and providing for equal treatment of its members in the community.

Beyond the demands of the law and military efficiency, the integration of the armed forces was also influenced by certain individuals within the military establishment who personified America's awakening social conscience. They led the services along the road toward integration not because the law demanded it, nor because activists clamored for it, nor even because military efficiency required it, but because they believed it was right. Complementing the work of these men and women was the opinion of the American serviceman himself. Between 1940 and 1965 his attitude toward change was constantly discussed and predicted but only rarely solicited by senior officials. Actually his opinion at that time is still largely unknown; documentary evidence is scarce, and his recollections, influenced as they are by the intervening years of the civil rights movement, are unreliable. Yet it was clearly the serviceman's generally quiet acceptance of new social practices, particularly those of the early 1950's, that ratified the services' racial reforms. As a perceptive critic of the nation's racial history described conditions in the services in 1962:

There was a rising tide of tolerance around the nation at that time. I was thrilled to see it working in the services. Whether officers were working for it or not it existed. From time to time you would find an officer imbued with the desire to improve race relations.... It was a marvel to me, in contrast to my recent investigations in the South, to see how well integration worked in the services.[24-4]

Indeed, it could be argued, American servicemen of the 1950's became a positive if indirect cause of racial change. By demonstrating that large numbers of blacks and whites could work and live together, they destroyed a fundamental argument of the opponents of integration and made further reforms possible if not imperative.

How the Services Integrated, 1946-1954

The interaction of all these factors can be seen when equal treatment and opportunity in the armed forces is considered in two distinct phases, the first culminating in the integration of all active military units in 1954, the second centering around the decision in 1963 to push for equal opportunity for black servicemen outside the gates of the military base.[24-5]

The Navy was the acknowledged pioneer in integration. Its decision during World War II to assign black and white sailors to certain ships was not entirely a response to pressures from civil rights advocates, although Secretary James Forrestal relied on his friends in the Urban League, particularly Lester Granger, to teach him the techniques of integrating a large organization. Nor was the decision solely the work of racial reformers in the Bureau of Naval Personnel, although this small group was undoubtedly responsible for drafting the regulations that governed the changes in the wartime Navy. Rather, the Navy began integrating its general service because segregation proved painfully inefficient. The decision was largely the result of the impersonal operation of the 1940 draft law. Although imperfectly applied during the war, the anti-discrimination provision of that law produced a massive infusion of black inductees. The Army, with its larger manpower base and expandable black units, could evade the implications of a nondiscrimination clause, but the sheer presence of large numbers of Negroes in the service, more than any other force, breached the walls of segregation in the Navy.

LOADING A ROCKET LAUNCHER.
Crewmen of the USS Carronade participating in a coordinated gunfire support action near Chu Lai, Vietnam.

The Navy experiment with an all-black crew had proved unsatisfactory, and only so many shore-based jobs were considered suitable for large segregated units. Bowing to the argument that two navies—one black, one white—were both inefficient and expensive, Secretary Forrestal began to experiment with integration during the last months of the war and finally announced a policy of integration in February 1946. The full application of this new policy would wait for some years while the Navy's traditional racial attitudes warred with its practical desire for efficiency.

The Air Force was the next to end segregation. Again, immediate outside influences appeared to be slight. Despite the timing of the Air Force integration directive in early 1949 and Secretary Stuart Symington's discussions of the subject with Truman and the Fahy Committee, plans to drop many racial barriers in the Air Force had already been formulated at the time of the President's equal opportunity order in 1948. Nor is there any evidence of special concern among Air Force officials about the growing criticism of their segregation policy. The record clearly reveals, however, that by late 1947 the Air staff had become anxious over the manpower requirements of the Gillem Board Report, which enunciated the postwar racial policy that the Air Force shared with the Army.

The Gillem Board Report would hardly be classified as progressive by later standards; its provisions for reducing the size of black units and integrating a small number of black specialists were, in a way, an effort to make segregation less wasteful. Nevertheless, with all its shortcomings, this postwar policy contained the germ of integration. It committed the Army and Air Force to total integration as a long-range objective, and, more important, it made permanent the wartime policy of allotting 10 percent of the Army's strength to Negroes. Later branded by the civil rights spokesmen as an instrument for limiting black enlistment, the racial quota committed the Army and its offspring, the Air Force, not only to maintaining at least 10 percent black strength but also to assigning black servicemen to all branches and all job categories, thereby significantly weakening the segregated system. Although never filled in either service, the quotas guaranteed that a large number of Negroes would remain in uniform after the war and thus gave both services an incentive to desegregate.

Once again the Army could postpone the logical consequences of its racial policy by the continued proliferation of its segregated combat and service units. But the new Air Force almost immediately felt the full force of the Gillem Board policy, quickly learning that it could not maintain 10 percent black strength separate but equal. It too might have continued indefinitely enlarging the number of service units in order to absorb black airmen. Like the Army, it might even have ignored the injunction to assign a quota of blacks to every military occupation and to every school. But it was politically impossible for the Air Force to do away with its black flying units, and it became economically impossible in a time of shrinking budgets and manpower cuts to operate separate flying units for the small group of Negroes involved. It was also unfeasible, considering the small number of black rated officers and men, to fill all the positions in the black air units and provide at the same time for the normal rotation and advanced training schedules. Facing these difficulties and mindful of the Navy's experience with integration, the Air Force began serious discussion of the integration of its black pilots and crews in 1947, some months before Truman issued his order.

Committed to integrating its air units and rated men in 1949, the Air staff quietly enlarged its objectives and broke up all its black units, thereby making the Air Force the first service to achieve total integration. There were several reasons for this rapid escalation in what was to have been a limited program. As devised by General Edwards and Colonel Marr of the Air staff the plan demanded that all black airmen in each command be conscientiously examined so that all might be properly reassigned, further trained, retained in segregated units, or dismissed. The removal of increasing numbers of eligible men from black units only hastened the end of those organizations, a tendency ratified by the trouble-free acceptance of the program by all involved.

The integration of the Army was more protracted. The Truman order in 1948 and the Fahy Committee, the White House group appointed to oversee the execution of that order, focused primarily on the segregated Army. There is little doubt that the President's action had a political dimension. Given the fact that the Army had become a major target of the President's own Civil Rights Commission and that it was a highly visible practitioner of segregation, the equal opportunity order would almost have had to be part of the President's plan to unite the nation's minorities behind his 1948 candidacy. The order was also a logical response to the threat of civil disobedience issued by A. Philip Randolph and endorsed by other civil rights advocates. In a matter of weeks after Truman issued his integration order, Randolph dropped his opposition to the 1948 draft law and his call for a boycott of the draft by Negroes.

It remained for the Fahy Committee to translate the President's order into a working program leading toward integration of the Army. Like Randolph and other activists, the

291

committee quickly concluded that segregation was a denial of equal treatment and opportunity and that the executive order, therefore, was essentially a call for the services to integrate. After lengthy negotiations, the committee won from the Army an agreement to move progressively toward full integration. Gradual integration was disregarded, however, when the Army, fighting in Korea, was forced by a direct threat to the efficiency of its operations to begin wide-scale mixing of the races. Specifically, the proximate reason for the Army's integration in the Far East was the fact that General Ridgway faced a severe shortage of replacements for his depleted white units while accumulating a surplus of black replacements. So pressing was his need that even before permission was received from Washington integration had already begun on the battlefield. The reason for the rapid integration of the rest of the Army was more complicated. The example of Korea was persuasive, as was the need for a uniform policy, but beyond that the rapid modernization of the Army was making obsolete the large-scale labor units traditionally used by the Army to absorb much of its black quota. With these units disappearing, the Army had to find new jobs for the men, a task hopelessly complicated by segregation.

The postwar racial policy of the Marine Corps struck a curious compromise between that of the Army and of the Navy. Adopting the former's system of segregated units and the latter's rejection of the 10 percent racial quota, the corps was able to assign its small contingent of black marines to a few segregated noncombatant duties. But the policy of the corps was only practicable for its peacetime size, as its mobilization for Korea demonstrated. Even before the Army was forced to change, the Marine Corps, its manpower planners pressed to find trained men and units to fill its divisional commitment to Korea, quietly abandoned the rules on segregated service.

While progressives cited the military efficiency of integration, traditionalists used the efficiency argument to defend the racial *status quo*. In general, senior military officials had concluded on the basis of their World War II experience that large black units were ineffective, undependable in close combat, and best suited for supply assignments. Whatever their motives, the traditionalists had reached the wrong conclusion from their data. They were correct when they charged that, despite competent and even heroic performance on the part of some individuals and units, the large black combat units had, on average, performed poorly during the war. But the traditionalists failed, as they had failed after World War I, to see the reasons for this poor performance. Not the least of these were the benumbing discrimination suffered by black servicemen during training, the humiliations involved in their assignments, and the ineptitude of many of their leaders, who were most often white.

AMERICAN SAILORS
help evacuate Vietnamese child.

Above all, the postwar manpower planners drew the wrong conclusion from the fact that the average General Classification Test scores of men in World War II black units fell significantly below that of their white counterparts. The scores were directly related to the two groups' relative educational advantages which depended to a large extent on their economic status and the geographic region from which they came. This mental average of servicemen was a unit problem, for at all times the total number of white individuals who scored in low-aptitude categories IV and V greatly outnumbered black individuals in those categories. This greater number of less gifted white servicemen had been spread thinly throughout the services' thousands of white units where they caused no particular problem. The lesser number of Negroes with low aptitude, however, were concentrated in the relatively few black units, creating a serious handicap to efficient performance. Conversely, the contribution of talented black servicemen was largely negated by their frequent assignment to units with too many low-scoring men. Small units composed in the main of black specialists, such as the black artillery and armor units that served in the European theater during World War II, served with distinction, but these units were special cases where the effect of segregation was tempered by the special qualifications of the carefully chosen men. Segregation and not mental aptitude was the key to the poor performance of the large black units in World War II.

Postwar service policies ignored these facts and defended segregation in the name of military efficiency. In short, the armed forces had to make inefficiency seem efficient as they explained in paternalistic fashion that segregation was best for all concerned. "In general, the Negro is less well educated than his brother citizen that is white," General Eisenhower told the Senate Armed Forces Committee in 1948, "and if you make a complete amalgamation, what you are going to have is in every company the Negro is going to be relegated to the minor jobs ... because the competition is too rough."[24-6]

Competence in a great many skills became increasingly important for servicemen in the postwar period as the trend toward technical complexity and specialization continued in all the

292

services. Differences in recruiting gave some services an advantage. The Navy and Air Force, setting stricter standards of enlistment, could fill their ranks with high-scoring volunteers and avoid enlisting large groups of low-scoring men, often black, who were eventually drafted for the Army. While this situation helped reduce the traditional opposition to integration in the Navy and Air Force, it made the Army more determined to retain separate black units to absorb the large number of low-scoring draftees it was obligated to take. A major factor in the eventual integration of the Army—and the single most significant contribution of the Secretary of Defense to that end—was George Marshall's decision to establish a parity of enlistment standards for the services. On the advice of his manpower assistant, Anna Rosenberg, Marshall abolished the special advantage enjoyed by the Navy and Air Force, making all the services share in the recruitment of low-scoring men. The common standard undercut the Army's most persuasive argument for restoring a racial quota and maintaining segregated units.

BOOBY TRAP VICTIM
from Company B, 47th Infantry, resting on buddy's back, awaits evacuation.

In the years from 1946 to 1954, then, several forces converged to bring about integration of the regular armed forces. Pressure from the civil rights advocates was one, idealistic leadership another. Most important, however, was the services' realization that segregation was an inefficient way to use the manpower provided by a democratic draft law or a volunteer system made democratic by the Secretary of Defense. Each service reached its conclusion separately, since each had a different problem in the efficient use of manpower and each had its own racial traditions. Accordingly, the services saw little need to exchange views, develop rivalries, or imitate one another's racial policies. There were two exceptions to this situation: both the Army and Air Force naturally considered the Navy's integration experience when they were formulating postwar policies, and the Navy and Air Force fought the Army's proposals to experiment with integrated units and institute a parity of enlistment standards.

Equal Treatment and Opportunity

Segregation officially ended in the active armed forces with the announcement of the Secretary of Defense in 1954 that the last all-black unit had been disbanded. In the little more than six years after President Truman's order, some quarter of a million blacks had been intermingled with whites in the nation's military units worldwide. These changes ushered in a brief era of good feeling during which the services and the civil rights advocates tended to overlook some forms of discrimination that persisted within the services. This tendency became even stronger in the early 1960's when the discrimination suffered by black servicemen in local communities dramatized the relative effectiveness of the equal treatment and opportunity policies on military installations. In July 1963, in the wake of another presidential investigation of racial equality in the armed forces, Secretary of Defense McNamara outlined a new racial policy. An extension of the forces that had produced the abolition of segregated military units, the new policy also vowed to carry the crusade for equal treatment and opportunity for black servicemen outside the military compound into the civilian community beyond. McNamara's 1963 directive became the model for subsequent racial orders in the Defense Department.

This enlargement of the department's concept of equal treatment and opportunity paralleled the rise of the modern civil rights movement, which was reaching its apogee in the mid-1960's. McNamara later acknowledged the influence of the civil rights activists on his department during this period. But the department's racial progress cannot be explained solely as a reaction to the pressures exerted by the civil rights movement. Several other factors lay behind the new and broader policy. The Defense Department was, for instance, under constant pressure from black officers and men who were not only reporting inequities in the newly integrated services and complaining of the remaining racial discrimination within the military community but were also demanding the department's assistance in securing their constitutional rights from the communities outside the military bases. This was particularly true in the fields of public education, housing, and places of entertainment.

The services as well as the Defense Department's manpower officials resisted these demands and continued in the early 1960's to limit their racial reforms to those necessary but exclusively internal matters most obviously connected with the efficient operation of their units. Reinforcing this resistance was the reluctance on the part of most commanders to break with tradition and interfere in what they considered community affairs. Nor had McNamara's early policy statements in response to servicemen's demands come to grips with the issue of discrimination in the civilian community. At the same time, some reformers in the Defense Department had allied themselves with like-minded progressives throughout the administration and were searching for a way to carry out President Kennedy's commitment to civil rights. These individuals were determined to use the services' early integration successes as a stepping-stone to

293

further civil rights reforms while the administration's civil rights program remained bogged down in Congress.

Although these reformers believed that the armed forces could be an effective instrument of social change for society at large, they clothed their aims in the garb of military efficiency. In fact, military efficiency was certainly McNamara's paramount concern when he supported the idea of enlarging the scope of his department's racial programs and when in 1962 he readily accepted the proposal to appoint the Gesell Committee to study the services' racial program.

The Gesell Committee easily documented the connection, long suspected by the reformers, between discrimination in the community and poor morale among black servicemen and the link between morale and combat efficiency. More important, with its ability to publicize the extent of discrimination against black servicemen in local communities and to offer practical recommendations for reform, the committee was able to stimulate the secretary into action. Yet not until his last years in office, beginning with his open housing campaign in 1967, did McNamara, who had always championed the stand of Adam Yarmolinsky and the rest, become a strong participant.

McNamara promptly endorsed the Gesell Committee's report, which called for a vigorous program to provide equal opportunity for black servicemen, ordering the services to launch such a program in communities near military bases and making the local commander primarily responsible for its success. He soft-pedaled the committee's controversial provision for the use of economic sanctions against recalcitrant businessmen, stressing instead the duty of commanders to press for changes through voluntary compliance. These efforts, according to Defense Department reports, achieved gratifying results in the next few years. In conjunction with other federal officials operating under provisions of the 1964 Civil Rights Act, local commanders helped open thousands of theaters, bowling alleys, restaurants, and bathing beaches to black servicemen. Only in the face of continued opposition to open housing by landlords who dealt with servicemen, and then not until 1967, did McNamara decide to use the powerful and controversial weapon of off-limits sanctions. In short order his programs helped destroy the patterns of segregation in multiple housing in areas surrounding most military bases.

The federal government's commitment to civil rights, manifest in Supreme Court decisions, executive orders, and congressional actions, was an important support for the Defense Department's racial program during this second part of the integration era. It is doubtful whether many of the command initiatives recommended by the Gesell Committee would have succeeded or even been tried without the court's 1954 school ruling and the Civil Rights Act of 1964. Yet in several important instances, such as the McNamara 1963 equal opportunity directive and the open housing campaign in 1967, the department's actions antedated federal action. Originally a follower of civilian society in racial matters, the armed forces moved ahead in the 1950's and by the mid-1960's had become a powerful stimulus for change in civilian practices in some areas of the country.[24-7]

Achievements of the services should not detract from the primacy of civil rights legislation in the reforms of the 1960's. The sudden fall of barriers to black Americans was primarily the result of the Civil Rights Acts. But the fact and example of integration in the armed forces was an important cause of change in the communities near military bases. Defense officials, prodding in the matter of integrated schooling for dependent children, found the mere existence of successfully integrated on-base schooling a useful tool in achieving similar schooling off-base. The experience of having served in the integrated armed forces, shared by so many young Americans, also exercised an immeasurable influence on the changes of the 1960's. Gesell Committee member Benjamin Muse recalled hearing a Mississippi hitchhiker say in 1961 at the height of the anti-integration, anti-Negro fever in that area: "I don't hold with this stuff about 'niggers'. I had a colored buddy in Korea, and I want to tell you he was all right."[24-8]

CAMARADERIE.
A soldier of Company C, 7th Infantry, lights a cigarette for a marine from D Company, 26th Marines, during "Operation Pegasus" near Khe Sanh.

In retrospect, the attention paid by defense officials and the services to off-base discrimination in the 1960's may have been misdirected; many of these injustices would eventually have succumbed to civil rights legislation. Certainly more attention could have been paid to the unfinished business of providing equal treatment and opportunity for black servicemen within the military community. Discrimination in matters of promotion, assignment, and military justice, overlooked by almost everyone in the early 1960's, was never treated with the urgency it deserved. To have done so might have averted at least some of the racial turmoil visited on the services in the Vietnam era.

But these shortcomings merely point to the fact that the services were the only segment of American society to have integrated, however imperfectly, the races on so large a scale. In doing so they demonstrated that a policy of equal treatment and opportunity is more than a legal concept; it also ordains a social condition. Between the enunciation of such a policy and the achievement of its goals can fall the shadow of bigotry and the traditional way of doing things. The record indicates that the services surmounted bigotry and rejected the old ways to a gratifying degree. To the extent that they were successful in bringing the races together, their efficiency prospered and the nation's ideal of equal opportunity for all citizens was fortified.

Unfortunately, the collapse of the legal and administrative barriers to equal treatment and opportunity in the armed forces did not lead immediately to the full realization of this ideal. Equal treatment and opportunity would remain an elusive goal for the Department of Defense for years to come. The post-1965 period comprises a new chapter in the racial history of the services. The agitation that followed the McNamara era had different roots from the events of the previous decades. The key to this difference was suggested during the Vietnam War by the Kerner Commission in its stark conclusion that "our nation is moving toward two societies, one black, one white—separate but unequal."[24-9] In contrast to the McNamara period of integration, when civil rights advocates and Defense Department officials worked toward a common goal, subsequent years would be marked by an often greater militancy on the part of black servicemen and a new kind of friction between a fragmented civil rights movement and the Department of Defense. Clearly, in coping with these problems the services will have to move beyond the elimination of legal and administrative barriers that had ordered their racial concerns between 1940 and 1965.

Note on Sources

The search for source materials used in this volume provided the writer with a special glimpse into the ways in which various government agencies have treated what was until recently considered a sensitive subject. Most important documents and working papers concerning the employment of black servicemen were, well into the 1950's and in contrast to the great bulk of personnel policy papers, routinely given a security classification. In some agencies the "secret" or "confidential" stamp was considered sufficient to protect the materials, which were filed and retired in a routine manner and, therefore, have always been readily available to the persistent and qualified researcher. But, as any experienced staff officer could demonstrate, other methods beyond mere classification can be devised to prevent easy access to sensitive material.

Thus, subterfuges were employed from time to time by officials dealing with racial subjects. In some staff agencies, for example, documents were collected in special files, separated from the normal personnel or policy files. In other instances the materials were never retired in a routine matter, but instead remained for many years scattered in offices of origin or, less often, in some central file system. If some officials appear to have been overly anxious to shield their agency's record, they also, it should be added, possessed a sense of history and the historical import of their work. Though the temptation may have been strong within some agencies to destroy papers connected with past controversies, most officials scrupulously preserved not only the basic policy documents concerning this specialized subject, but also much of the back-up material that the historian treasures.

The problem for the modern researcher is that these special collections and reserved materials, no longer classified and no longer sensitive, have fallen, largely unnoted, into a sea of governmental paper beyond the reach of the archivist's finding aids. The frequently expressed comment of the researcher, "somebody is withholding something," should, for the sake of accuracy, be changed to "somebody has lost track of something."

This material might never have been recovered without the skilled assistance of the historical offices of the various services and Office of the Secretary of Defense. At times their search for lost documents assumed the dimensions of a detective story. In partnership with Marine Corps historian Ralph Donnelly, for example, the author finally traced the bulk of the World War II racial records of the Marine Corps to an obscure and unmarked file in the classified records section of Marine Corps headquarters. A comprehensive collection of official documents on the employment of black personnel in the Navy between 1920 and 1946 was unearthed, not in the official archives, but in a dusty file cabinet in the Bureau of Naval Personnel's Management Information Division.

The search also had its frustrations, for some materials seem permanently lost. Despite persistent and imaginative work by the Coast Guard's historian, Truman Strobridge, much of the documentary record of that service's World War II racial history could not be located. The development of the Coast Guard's policy has had to be reconstructed, painstakingly and laboriously, from other sources. The records of many Army staff agencies for the period 1940-43 were destroyed on the assumption that their materials were duplicated in The Adjutant General's files, an assumption that frequently proved to be incorrect. Although generally intact, the Navy's records of the immediate post-World War II period also lack some of the background staff work on the employment of black manpower. Fortunately for this writer, the recent, inadvertent destruction of the bulk of the Bureau of Naval Personnel's classified wartime records occurred after the basic research for this volume had been completed, but this lamentable accident will no doubt cause problems for future researchers.

Thanks to the efforts of the services' historical offices and the wonder of photocopying, future historians may be spared some of the labor connected with the preparation of this volume. Most of the records surviving outside regular archives have been identified and relocated for easy access. Copies of approximately 65 percent of all documents cited in this volume have been collected and are presently on file in the Center of Military History, from which they will be retired for permanent preservation.

Official Archival Material

The bulk of the official records used in the preparation of this volume is in the permanent custody of the National Archives and Records Service, Washington, D.C. The records of most military agencies for the period 1940-54 are located in the Modern Military Records Branch or in the Navy and Old Army Branch of the National Archives proper. Most documents dated after 1954, along with military unit records (including ships' logs), are located in the General Archives Division in the Washington National Records Center, Suitland, Maryland. The Suitland center also holds the other major group of official materials, that is, all those documents still administered by the individual agencies but stored in the center prior to their screening and acquisition by the National Archives. These records are open to qualified researchers, but access to them is controlled by the records managers of the individual agencies, a not altogether felicitous arrangement for the researcher, considering the bulk of the material and its lack of organization.

The largest single group of materials consulted were those of the various offices of the Army staff. Although these agencies have abandoned the system of classifying all documents by a decimal-subject system, the system persisted in many offices well into the 1960's, thereby enabling the researcher to accomplish a speedy, if unrefined, screening of pertinent materials. Even with this crutch, the researcher must still comb through thousands of documents created by the Secretary of War (later Secretary of the Army), his assistant secretary, the Chief of Staff, and the various staff divisions, especially the Personnel (G-1), Organization and Training (G-3), and Operations Divisions, together with the offices of The Adjutant General, the Judge Advocate General, and the Inspector General. The War Department Special Planning Division's files are an extremely important source, especially for postwar racial planning, as are the records of the three World War II major commands, the Army Ground, Service, and Air Forces. Although illuminating in regard to the problem of racial discrimination, the records of the office of the secretary's civilian aide are less important in terms of policy development. Finally, the records of the black units, especially the important body of documents related to the tribulations of the 92d Infantry Division in World War II and the 24th Infantry Regiment in Korea, are also vital sources for this subject.

The records managers in the Office of the Secretary of Defense also used the familiar 291.2 classification to designate materials related to the subject of Negroes. (An exception to this generalization were the official papers of the secretary's office during the Forrestal period when a Navy file system was generally employed.) The most important materials on the subject of the Defense Department's racial interests are found in the records of the Office of the Secretary of Defense. The majority of these records, including the voluminous files of the Assistant Secretary (Manpower) so helpful for the later sections of the study, have remained in the custody of the department and are administered by the Office of the Deputy Assistant Secretary of Defense (Administration). After 1963 the Office of the Deputy Assistant Secretary (Civil Rights) and its successor organizations loom as a major source. Many of the official papers were eventually filed with those of the Assistant Secretary (Manpower) or have been retained in the historical files of the Equal Opportunity Office of the Secretary of Defense. The records of the Personnel Policy Board and the Office of the General Counsel, both part of the files of the Office of the Secretary of Defense, are two more important sources of materials on black manpower.

A subject classification system was not universally applied in the Navy Department during the 1940's and even where used proved exceedingly complicated. The records of the Office of the Secretary of the Navy are especially strong in the World War II period, but they must be supplemented with the National Archives' separate Forrestal papers file. Despite the recent loss of records, the files of the Bureau of Naval Personnel remain the primary source for documents on the employment of black personnel in the Navy. Research in all these files, even for the World War II period, is best begun in the Records Management offices of those two agencies. More readily accessible, the records of the Chief of Naval Operations and the General Board, both of considerable importance in understanding the Navy's World War II racial history, are located in the Operational Archives Branch, Naval Historical Division, Washington Navy Yard. This office has recently created a special miscellaneous file containing important documents of interest to the researcher on racial matters that have been gleaned from various sources not easily available to the researcher.

Copies of all known staff papers concerning black marines and the development of the Marine Corps' equal opportunity program during the integration period have been collected and filed in the reference section of the Director of Marine Corps History and Museums, Headquarters, U.S. Marine Corps. Likewise, most of the very small selection of extant official Coast Guard records on the employment of Negroes have been identified and collected by the Coast Guard historian. The log of the *Sea Cloud*, the first Coast Guard vessel in modern times to boast a racially mixed crew, is located in the Archives Branch at Suitland.

The Air Force has retained control of a significant portion of its postwar personnel records, and the researcher would best begin work in the Office of the Administrative Assistant, Secretary of the Air Force. This office has custody of the files of the Secretary of the Air Force, his assistant secretaries, the Office of the Chief of Staff, and the staff agencies pertinent to this story, especially the Deputy Chief of Staff, Personnel, and the Director of Military Personnel. The records of black air units, as well as the extensive and well-indexed collection of official unit and base histories and studies and reports of the Air staff that touch on the service's racial policies, are located in the Albert F. Simpson Historical Research Center, Maxwell AFB, Alabama. These records are supplemented, and sometimes duplicated, by the holdings of the Suitland Records Center and the Office of Air Force History, Bolling Air Force Base, Washington, D.C. Other Air Force files of interest, particularly in the area of policy planning, can be found in the holdings of the National Archives' Modern Military Branch.

The records of the Selective Service System also provide some interesting material, but most of this has been published by the Selective Service in its *Special Groups* (Special Monograph Number 10, 2 vols. [Washington: Government Printing Office, 1953]). Far more important are the records of the War Manpower Commission, located in the National Archives, which, when studied in conjunction with the papers of the Secretaries of War and Navy, reveal the influence of the 1940 draft law on the services' racial policies.

Personal Collections

The official records of the integration of the armed forces are not limited to those documents retired by the governmental agencies. Parts of the story must also be gleaned from documents that for various reasons have been included in the personal papers of individuals. Documents created by government officials, as well as much unofficial material of special interest, are scattered in a number of institutional or private repositories. Probably the most noteworthy of these collections is the papers of the President's Committee on Equality of Treatment and Opportunity in the Armed Forces (the Fahy Committee) in the Harry S. Truman Library. In addition to this central source, the Truman Library also contains materials contributed by Philleo Nash, Oscar Chapman, and Clark Clifford, whose work in the White House was intimately, if briefly, concerned with armed forces integration. The President's own papers, especially the recently opened White House Secretary's File, contain a number of important documents.

Documents of special interest can also be found in the Roosevelt Papers at the Franklin D. Roosevelt Library and among the various White House files preserved in the Dwight D. Eisenhower Library. The Central White House file in the John F. Kennedy Library, along with the papers of Harris Wofford and Gerhard Gesell, are essential to the history of equal opportunity in the early 1960's. Most of these collections are well indexed.

The James V. Forrestal Papers, Princeton University Library, while helpful in tracing the Urban League's contribution to the Navy's integration policy, lack the focus and comprehensiveness of the Forrestal Papers in the National Archives' Office of the Secretary of the Navy file. Another collection of particular interest for the naval aspects of the story is the Dennis D. Nelson Papers, in the custody of the Nelson family in San Diego, California, with a microfilm copy on file in the Navy's Operational Archives Branch in Washington. The heart of this collection is the materials Nelson gathered while writing "The Integration of the Negro in the United States Navy, 1776-1947," a U.S. Navy monograph prepared in 1948. The Nelson collection also contains a large group of newspaper clippings and other rare secondary materials of special interest. The Maxie M. Berry Papers, in the custody of the equal opportunity officer of the U.S. Coast Guard headquarters, offer a rare glimpse into the life of black Coast Guardsmen during World War II, especially those assigned to the all-black Pea Island Station, North Carolina.

The U.S. Army Military History Research Collection at Carlisle Barracks, Pennsylvania, has acquired the papers of James C. Evans, the long-time Civilian Aide to the Secretaries of War and Defense, and those of Lt. Gen. Alvan C. Gillem, Jr., the chairman of the Army's special personnel board that bears his name. The Evans materials contain a rare collection of clippings and memorandums on integration in the armed forces; the Gillem Papers are particularly interesting for the summaries of testimony before the Gillem Board.

The papers of the National Association for the Advancement of Colored People in the Manuscript Division, Library of Congress, are useful, especially if used in conjunction with that library's Arthur B. Spingarn Papers, in assessing the role of the civil rights leaders in bringing about black participation in World War II. The collection of secondary materials on Negroes in the armed forces in the Schomburg Collection, New York Public Library, however, is disappointing, considering the prominence of that institution.

Finally, the U.S. Army Center of Military History, Washington, D.C., has on file those materials collected by the author in the preparation of this volume, including not only those items cited in the footnotes, but also copies of hundreds of official documents and correspondence with various participants, together with the unique body of documents and notes collected by Lee Nichols in his groundbreaking research on integration. Of particular importance among the documents in the Center of Military History are copies of many Bureau of Naval Personnel documents, the originals of which have since been destroyed, as well as copies of the bulk of the papers produced by the Fahy Committee.

Interviews

The status of black servicemen in the integration era has attracted considerable attention among oral history enthusiasts. The author has taken advantage of this special source, but oral testimony concerning integration must be treated cautiously. In addition to the usual dangers of fallible memory that haunt all oral history interviews, the subjects of some of these interviews, it should be emphasized, were separated from the events they were recalling by a civil rights revolution that has changed fundamentally the attitudes of many people, both black and white. In some instances it is readily apparent that the recollections of persons being interviewed have been colored by the changes of the 1950's and 1960's, and while their recitation of specific events can be checked against the records, their estimates of attitudes and influences, not so easily verified, should be used cautiously. Much of this danger can be avoided by a skillful interviewer with special knowledge of integration. Because of the care that went into the interviews conducted in the U.S. Air Force Oral History Program, which are on file at the Albert F. Simpson Historical Research Center, they are particularly dependable. This is especially true of those used in this study, for they were conducted by Lt. Col. Alan Gropman and Maj. Alan Osur, both serious students of the subject. Particular note should be made of the especially valuable interviews with former Secretary of the Air Force Eugene M. Zuckert and several of the more prominent black generals.

The extensive Columbia University Oral History Collection has several interviews of special interest, in particular the very revealing interview with the National Urban League's Lester Granger. Read in conjunction with the National Archives' Forrestal Papers, this interview is a major source for the Navy's immediate postwar policy changes. Similarly, the Kennedy Library's oral history program contains several interviews that are helpful in assessing the role of the services in the Kennedy administration's civil rights program. Of particular interest are the interviews with Harris Wofford, Roy Wilkins, and Theodore Hesburgh.

The U.S. Marine Corps Oral History Program, whose interviews are on file in Marine Corps headquarters, and the U.S. Navy Oral History Collection, copies of which can be found in the Navy's Operational Archives Branch, contain several interviews of special interest to researchers in racial history. Mention should be made of the Marine Corps interviews with Generals Ray A. Robinson and Alfred G. Noble and the Navy's interviews with Captains Mildred McAfee Horton and Dorothy Stratton, leaders of the World War II WAVES and SPARS.

Finally, included in the files of the Center of Military History is a collection of notes taken by Lee Nichols, Martin Blumenson, and the author during their interviews with leading figures in the integration story. The Nichols notes, covering the series of interviews conducted by that veteran reporter in 1953-54, include such items as summaries of conversations with Harry S. Truman, Truman K. Gibson, Jr., and Emmett J. Scott.

Printed Materials

Many of the secondary materials found particularly helpful by the author have been cited throughout the volume, but special attention should be drawn to certain key works in several categories. In the area of official works, Ulysses Lee's *The Employment of Negro Troops* in the United States Army in World War II series (Washington: Government Printing Office, 1966) remains the definitive account of the Negro in the World War II Army. The Bureau of Naval Personnel's

"The Negro in the Navy," Bureau of Naval Personnel History of World War II (mimeographed, 1946, of which there is a copy in the bureau's Technical Library in Washington), is a rare item that has assumed even greater significance with the loss of so much of the bureau's records. Presented without attribution, the text paraphrases many important documents accurately. Margaret L. Geis's "Negro Personnel in the European Command, 1 January 1946-30 June 1950," part of the Occupation Forces in Europe series (Historical Division, European Command, 1952), Ronald Sher's "Integration of Negro and White Troops in the U.S. Army, Europe, 1952-1954" (Historical Division, Headquarters, U.S. Army, Europe, 1956), and Charles G. Cleaver, "Personnel Problems," vol. III, pt. 2, of the "History of the Korean War" (Military History Section, Headquarters, Far East Command, 1952), are important secondary sources for guiding the student through a bewildering mass of materials. Alan M. Osur's *Blacks in the Army Air Forces During World War II: The Problem of Race Relations* (Washington: Government Printing Office, 1977) and Alan Gropman's *The Air Force Integrates, 1945-1964* (Washington: Government Printing Office, 1978), both published by the Office of Air Force History, and Henry I. Shaw, Jr., and Ralph W. Donnelly's *Blacks in the Marine Corps* (Washington: Government Printing Office, 1975) provided official, comprehensive surveys of their subjects. Finally, there is in the files of the Center of Military History a copy of the transcripts of the National Defense Conference on Negro Affairs (26 April 1948). Second only to the transcripts of the Fahy Committee hearings in comprehensiveness on the subject of postwar racial policies, this document also provides a rare look at the attitudes of the traditional black leadership at a crucial period.

As the footnotes indicate, congressional documents and newspapers were also important resources mined in the preparation of this volume. Of particular interest, the Center of Military History has on file a special guide to some of these sources prepared by Lt. Col. Reinhold S. Schumann (USAR). This guide analyzes the congressional and press reaction to the 1940 and 1948 draft laws and to the Fahy and Gesell Committee reports.

In his *Blacks and the Military in American History: A New Perspective* (New York: Praeger, 1974), Jack D. Foner provides a fine general survey of the Negro in the armed forces, including an accurate summary of the integration period. Among the many specialized studies on the integration period itself, cited throughout the text, several might provide a helpful entree to a complicated subject. The standard account is Richard M. Dalfiume's *Desegregation of the United States Armed Forces: Fighting on Two Fronts, 1939-1953* (Columbia, Missouri: University of Missouri Press, 1969). Carefully documented and containing a very helpful bibliography, this work tends to emphasize the influence of the civil rights advocates and Harry Truman on the integration process. The reader will also benefit from consulting Lee Nichols's pioneer work, *Breakthrough on the Color Front* (New York: Random House, 1954). Although lacking documentation, Nichols's journalistic account was devised with the help of many of the participants and is still of considerable value to the student. The reader may also want to consult Richard J. Stillman II's short survey, *Integration of the Negro in the U.S. Armed Forces* (New York: Praeger, 1968), principally for its statistical information on the post-Korean period.

The role of President Truman and the Fahy Committee in the integration of the armed forces has been treated in detail by Dalfiume and by Donald R. McCoy and Richard T. Ruetten in *Quest and Response: Minority Rights and the Truman Administration* (Lawrence, Kansas: The University of Kansas Press, 1973). A valuable critical appraisal of the short-range response of the Army to the Fahy Committee's work appeared in Edwin W. Kenworthy's "The Case Against Army Segregation," *Annals of the American Academy of Political and Social Science* 275 (May 1951):27-33. In addition, the reader may want to consult William C. Berman's *The Politics of Civil Rights in the Truman Administration* (Columbus: Ohio State University Press, 1970) for a general survey of civil rights in the Truman years.

The expansion of the Defense Department's equal treatment and opportunity policy in the 1960's is explained by Adam Yarmolinsky in *The Military Establishment: Its Impacts on American Society* (New York: Harper & Row, 1971). This book is the work of a number of informed specialists sponsored by the 20th Century Fund. A general survey of President Kennedy's civil rights program is presented by Carl M. Brauer in his *John F. Kennedy and the Second Reconstruction* (New York: Columbia University Press, 1977). The McNamara era is treated in Fred Richard Bahr's "The Expanding Role of the Department of Defense as an Instrument of Social Change" (Ph.D. dissertation, George Washington University, 1970).

Concerning the rise of the civil rights movement itself, the reader would be advised to consult C. Vann Woodward's masterful *The Strange Career of Jim Crow*, 3d ed. rev. (New York: Oxford University Press, 1974), and the two volumes composed by Gesell Committee member Benjamin Muse, *Ten Years of Prelude: The Story of Integration Since the Supreme Court's 1954 Decision* (New York: The Viking Press, 1964), and *The American Negro Revolution: From Nonviolence to Black Power, 1963-1967* (Bloomington: University of Indiana Press, 1968). Important aspects of the civil rights movement and its influence on American servicemen are discussed by Jack Greenberg in *Race Relations and American Law* (New York: Columbia University Press, 1959) and Eli Ginzberg, *The Negro Potential* (New York: Columbia University Press, 1956).

Finally, many of the documents supporting the history of the integration of the armed forces, including complete transcripts of the Fahy Committee hearings and the Conference on Negro Affairs, have been compiled by the author and Bernard C. Nalty in the multivolumed *Blacks in the United States Armed Forces: Basic Documents* (Wilmington: Scholarly Resources, 1977).

Index

301

302

303

304

305

306

307

310

311

314

315

316

317

318

319

320

U.S. GOVERNMENT PRINTING OFFICE: 1981 0-305-168

Footnote 1: Oscar Handlin, "The Goals of Integration," *Daedalus 95* (Winter 1966): 270.(Back)

Footnote 1-1: Gunnar Myrdal, *The American Dilemma: The Negro Problem and Modern Democracy*, rev. ed. (New York: Harper Row, 1962), p. lxi.(Back)

Footnote 1-2: Benjamin Quarles, *The Negro in the American Revolution* (Chapel Hill: University of North Carolina Press, 1961), pp. 182-85. The following brief summary of the Negro in the pre-World War II Army is based in part on the Quarles book and Roland C. McConnell, *Negro Troops of Antebellum Louisiana: A History of the Battalion of Free Men of Color* (Baton Rouge: Louisiana State University Press, 1968); Dudley T. Cornish, *Sable Arm: Negro Troops in the Union Army, 1861-1865* (New York: Norton, 1966); William H. Leckie, *The Buffalo Soldiers: A Narrative of the Negro Cavalry in the West* (Norman: University of Oklahoma Press, 1969); William Bruce White, "The Military and the Melting Pot: The American Army and Minority Groups, 1865-1924" (Ph.D. dissertation, University of Wisconsin, 1968); Marvin E. Fletcher, *The Black Soldier and Officer in the United States Army, 1891-1917* (Columbia: University of Missouri Press, 1974); Arthur E. Barbeau and Florette Henri, *Unknown Soldiers: Black American Troops in World War I* (Philadelphia: Temple University Press, 1974). For a general survey of black soldiers in America's wars, see Jack Foner, *Blacks and the Military in American History: A New Perspective* (New York: Praeger, 1974).(Back)

Footnote 1-3: Estimates vary; exact racial statistics concerning the nineteenth century Navy are difficult to locate. See Enlistment of Men of Colored Race, 23 Jan 42, a note appended to Hearings Before the General Board of the Navy, 1942, Operational Archives, Department of the Navy (hereafter OpNavArchives). The following brief summary of the Negro in the pre-World War II Navy is based in part on Foner's *Blacks and the Military in American History* as well as Harold D. Langley, "The Negro in the Navy and Merchant Service, 1798-1860," *Journal of Negro History* 52 (October 1967):273-86; Langley's *Social Reform in the United States Navy 1798-1862*, (Urbana: University of Illinois Press, 1967) Peter Karsten, *The Naval Aristocracy: The Golden Age of Annapolis and the Emergence of Modern American Navalism* (New York: The Free Press, 1972); Frederick S. Harrod, *Manning the New Navy: The Development of a Modern Naval Enlisted Force, 1899-1940* (Westport: Greenwood Press, 1978).(Back)

Footnote 1-4: Ltr, Rear Adm C. W. Nimitz, Actg Chief, Bureau of Navigation, to Rep. Hamilton Fish, 17 Jun 37, A9-10, General Records of the Department of the Navy (hereafter GenRecsNav).(Back)

Footnote 1-5: Memo, H. A. Badt, Bureau of Navigation, for Officer in Charge, Public Relations, 24 Jul 40, sub: Negroes in U.S. Navy, Nav-641, Records of the Bureau of Naval Personnel (hereafter BuPersRecs).(Back)

Footnote 1-6: 163 U.S. 537 (1896). In this 1896 case concerning segregated seating on a Louisiana railroad, the Supreme Court ruled that so long as equality of accommodation existed, segregation could not in itself be considered discriminatory and therefore did not violate the equal rights provision of the Fourteenth Amendment. This "separate but equal" doctrine would prevail in American law for more than half a century.(Back)

Footnote 1-7: Foner, *Blacks and the Military in American History*, p. 66.(Back)

Footnote 1-8: Ulysses Lee, *The Employment of Negro Troops*, United States Army in World War II (Washington: Government Printing Office, 1966), p. 5. See also Army War College Historical Section, "The Colored Soldier in the U.S. Army," May 1942, p. 22, copy in CMH.(Back)

Footnote 1-9: For a modern analysis of the two incidents and the effect of Jim Crow on black units before World War I, see John D. Weaver, *The Brownsville Raid* (New York: W. W. Norton Co., 1970); Robert V. Haynes, *A Night of Violence: The Houston Riot of 1917* (Baton Rouge: Louisiana State University Press, 1976).(Back)

Footnote 1-10: On the racial attitudes of the Wilson administration, see Nancy J. Weiss, "The Negro and the New Freedom: Fighting Wilsonian Segregation," *Political Science Quarterly* 84 (March 1969):61-79.(Back)

Footnote 1-11: *Special Report of the Provost Marshal General on Operations of the Selective Service System to December 1918* (Washington: Government Printing Office, 1919), p. 193.(Back)

Footnote 1-12: The development of post-World War I policy is discussed in considerable detail in Lee, *Employment of Negro Troops*, Chapters I and II. See also U.S. Army War College Miscellaneous File 127-1 through 127-23 and 127-27, U.S. Army Military History Research Collection, Carlisle Barracks (hereafter AMHRC).(Back)

Footnote 1-13: The 1940 strength figure is extrapolated from Misc Div, AGO, Returns Sec, 9 Oct 39-30 Nov 41. The figures do not include some 3,000 Negroes in National Guard units under state control.(Back)

Footnote 1-14: This discussion of civil rights in the pre-World War II period draws not only on Lee's *Employment of Negro Troops*, but also on Lee Finkle, *Forum for Protest: The Black Press During World War II* (Cranbury: Fairleigh Dickinson University Press, 1975); Harvard Sitkoff, "Racial Militancy and Interracial Violence in the Second World War," *Journal of American History* 58 (December 1971):661-81; Reinhold Schumann, "The Role of the National Association for the Advancement of Colored People in the Integration of the Armed Forces According to the NAACP Collection in the Library of Congress" (1971), in CMH; Richard M. Dalfiume, *Desegregation of the United States Armed Forces: Fighting on Two Fronts, 1939-1953* (Columbia: University of Missouri Press, 1969).(Back)

Footnote 1-15: The Jim Crow era is especially well described in Rayford W. Logan's *The Negro in American Life and Thought: The Nadir, 1877-1901* (New York: Dial, 1954) and C. Vann Woodward's *The Strange Career of Jim Crow*, 3d ed. rev. (New York: Oxford University Press, 1974).(Back)

Footnote 1-16: Frank Freidel, *F.D.R. and the South* (Baton Rouge: Louisiana State University Press, 1965), pp. 71-102. See also Bayard Rustin, *Strategies for Freedom: The Changing Patterns of Black Protest* (New York: Columbia University Press, 1976), p. 16.(Back)

Footnote 1-17: Pittsburgh *Courier*, December 21, 1940.(Back)

Footnote 1-18: *The Crisis* 47 (July 1940):209.(Back)

Footnote 1-19: Myrdal, *American Dilemma*, p. 744.(Back)

Footnote 1-20: Lee Finkle, "The Conservative Aims of Militant Rhetoric: Black Protest During World War II," *Journal of American History* 60 (December 1973):693.(Back)

Footnote 1-21: Some impression of the extent of this campaign and its effect on the War Department can be gained from the volume of correspondence produced by the Pittsburgh*Courier* campaign and filed in AG 322.99 (2-23-38)(1).(Back)

Footnote 1-22: The Army's plans and amendments are treated in great detail in Lee, *Employment of Negro Troops*.(Back)

Footnote 1-23: Hearings Before the Committee on Military Affairs. House of Representatives, 76th Cong., 3d sess., on H.R. 10132, *Selective Compulsory Military Training and Service*, pp. 585-90.(Back)

Footnote 1-24: *Congressional Record*, 76th Cong., 3d sess., vol. 86, p. 10890.(Back)

Footnote 1-25: 54 *U.S. Stat.* 885(1940).(Back)

Footnote 1-26: Ibid. Fish commanded black troops in World War I. Captain of Company K, Fifteenth New York National Guard (Colored), which subsequently became the 369th Infantry, Fish served in the much decorated 93d Division in the French sector of the Western Front.(Back)

Footnote 1-27: See especially Ltr, Houston to CofS, 1 Aug and 29 Aug 34; Ltr, CofS to Houston, 20 Aug 34; Ltr, Maj Gen Edgar T. Conley, Actg AG, USA, to Walter White, 25 Nov 35; Ltr, Houston to Roosevelt, 8 Oct 37; Ltr, Houston to SW, 8 Oct 37. See also Elijah Reynolds, *Colored Soldiers and the Regular Army* (NAACP Pamphlet, December 10, 1934). All in C-376, NAACP Collection, Library of Congress.(Back)

Footnote 1-28: Ibid. Ltr, Houston to CofS, 1 Aug 34.(Back)

Footnote 1-29: *The Crisis* 46 (1939):49, 241, 337.(Back)

Footnote 1-30: Ltr, Presley Holliday to White, 11 Sep 39; Ltr, White to Holliday, 15 Sep 39. Both in C-376, NAACP Collection, LC.(Back)

Footnote 1-31: Ltr, White to Roosevelt, 15 Sep 39, in C-376, NAACP Collection, LC. This letter was later released to the press.(Back)

Footnote 1-32: Memo, Marshall for White, 28 Oct 39; Ltr, Secy to the President to White, 17 Oct 39. Both in C-376, NAACP Collection, LC.(Back)

Footnote 1-33: Memo, White for Roy Wilkins et al., Oct 39; Ltr, Houston to White, Oct 39; Memo, Wilkins to White, 23 Oct 39. All in C-376, NAACP Collection, LC.(Back)

Footnote 1-34: Walter White, "Conference at White House, Friday, September 27, 11:35 A.M.," Arthur B. Spingarn Papers, Library of Congress. See also White's *A Man Called White* (New York: Viking Press, 1948), pp. 186-87.(Back)

Footnote 1-35: Ltr, White to Stephen Early, 21 Oct 40. See also Memo, White for R. S. W. [Roy Wilkins], 18 Oct 40. Both in C-376, NAACP Collection, LC. See also Ltr, S. Early to White, 18 Oct 40, Incl to Ltr, White to Spingarn, 24 Oct 40, Spingarn Papers, LC.(Back)

Footnote 1-36: White, *A Man Called White*, pp. 187-88.(Back)

Footnote 1-37: Roy Wilkins Oral History Interview, Columbia University Oral History Collection. See also A. Philip Randolph, "Why Should We March," *Survey Graphic* 31 (November 1942), as reprinted in John H. Franklin and Isidore Starr, eds., *The Negro in Twentieth Century America* (New York: Random House, 1967).(Back)

Footnote 1-38: White, *A Man Called White*, pp. 190-93.(Back)

Footnote 1-39: Herbert Garfinkle, *When Negroes March: The March on Washington Movement in the Organizational Politics of FEPC* (Glencoe: The Free Press, 1959), provides a comprehensive account of the aims and achievements of the movement.(Back)

Footnote 2-1: This survey of the Army and the Negro in World War II is based principally on Lee's *Employment of Negro Troops*. A comprehensive account of the development of policy, the mobilization of black soldiers, and their use in the various theaters and units of World War II, this book is an indispensable source for any serious student of the subject.(Back)

Footnote 2-2: For examples of how World War I military experiences affected the thinking of the civil rights advocates and military traditionalists of World War II, see Lester B. Granger Oral History Interview, 1960, Columbia University Oral History Collection; Interview, Lee Nichols with Lt. Gen. John C. H. Lee (c. 1953). For the influence of World War II on a major contributor to postwar racial policy, see Interview, Lee Nichols with Harry S. Truman, 24 Jun 53. Last two in Nichols Collection, CMH. These interviews are among many compiled by Nichols as part of his program associated with the production of *Breakthrough on the Color Front* (New York: Random House, 1954). Nichols, a journalist, presented this collection of interviews, along with other documents and materials, to the Center of Military History in 1972. The interviews have proved to be a valuable supplement to the official record. They capture the thoughts of a number of important participants, some no longer alive, at a time relatively close to the events under consideration. They have been checked against the sources whenever possible and found accurate.(Back)

Footnote 2-3: Memo, ACofS, G-3, for CofS, 3 Jun 40, sub: Employment of Negro Manpower, G-3/6541-527.(Back)

Footnote 2-4: Memo, TAG for CG's et al., 16 Oct 40, sub: War Department Policy in Regard to Negroes, AG 291.21 (10-9-40) M-A-M.(Back)

Footnote 2-5: The foregoing impressions are derived largely from Interviews, Lee Nichols with James C. Evans, who worked for Judge Hastie during World War II, and Ulysses G. Lee (c. 1953). Both in Nichols Collection, CMH.(Back)

Footnote 2-6: Memo, William H. Hastie for SW, with attachment, 22 Sep 41, sub: Survey and Recommendations Concerning the Integration of the Negro Soldiers Into the Army, G-1/15640-120. See also Intervs, Nichols with Evans and Lee.(Back)

Footnote 2-7: Stimson, a Republican, had been appointed by Roosevelt in 1940, along with Secretary of the Navy Frank Knox, in an effort to enlist bipartisan support for the administration's foreign policy in an election year. Stimson brought a wealth of experience with him to the office, having served as Secretary of War under William Howard Taft and Secretary of State under Herbert Hoover. The quotations are from Stimson Diary, 25 October 1940, Henry L. Stimson Papers, Yale University Library.(Back)

Footnote 2-8: Henry L. Stimson and McGeorge Bundy, *On Active Service in Peace and War* (New York: Harper and Brothers, 1947), pp. 461-64. The quotations are from Stimson Diary, 24 Jan 42.(Back)

Footnote 2-9: Memo, USW for CofS, 6 Oct 41, G-1/15640-120.(Back)

Footnote 2-10: Memo, CofS for SW, 1 Dec 41, sub: Report of Judge William H. Hastie, Civilian Aide to the Secretary of War, dated 22 Sep 41, OCS 20602-219.(Back)

Footnote 2-11: Ibid. See also Forrest C. Pogue, *George C. Marshall: Organizer of Victory* (New York: The Viking Press, 1973), pp. 96-99.(Back)

Footnote 2-12: The Army staff's mobilization planning for black units in the 1930's generally relied upon the detailed testimony of the commanders of black units in World War I. This testimony, contained in documents submitted to the War Department and the Army War College, was often critical of the Army's employment of black troops, although rarely critical of segregation. The material is now located in the U.S. Army's Military History Research Collection, Carlisle Barracks, Pennsylvania. For discussion of the post-World War I review of the employment of black troops, see Lee's *Employment of Negro Troops*, Chapter I, and Alan M. Osur's *Blacks in the Army Air Forces During World War II: The Problem of Race Relations* (Washington: Government Printing Office, 1977), Chapter I.(Back)

Footnote 2-13: Memo, USW for Maj Gen William Bryden (principal deputy chief of staff), 10 Jan 42, OCS 20602-250.(Back)

Footnote 2-14: Col Eugene R. Householder, TAGO, Speech Before Conference of Negro Editors and Publishers, 8 Dec 41, AG 291.21 (12-1-41) (1).(Back)

Footnote 2-15: Lee, *Employment of Negro Troops*, ch. VI.(Back)

Footnote 2-16: Noteworthy is the fact that for several reasons not related to race (for instance, language and nationality) the German Army also organized separate units. Its 162d Infantry Division was composed of troops from Turkestan and the Caucasus, and its 5th SS Panzer Division had segregated Scandinavian, Dutch, and Flemish regiments. Unlike the racially segregated U.S. Army, Germany's so-called Ost units were only administratively organized into separate divisions, and an Ost infantry battalion was often integrated into a "regular" German infantry regiment as its fourth infantry battalion. Several allied armies also had segregated units, composed, for example, of Senegalese, Gurkhas, Maoris, and Algerians.(Back)

Footnote 2-17: Memo, ASW for Judge Hastie, 2 Jul 42, ASW 291.2, NT 1942.(Back)

Footnote 2-18: Strength of the Army, 1 Jan 46, STM-30, p. 61.(Back)

Footnote 2-19: Lee, *Employment of Negro Troops*, pp. 241-57. For an extended discussion of Army test scores and their relation to education, see Department of the Army, *Marginal Man and Military Service: A Review* (Washington: Government Printing Office, 1966). This report was prepared for the Deputy Under Secretary of the Army for Personnel Management by a working group under the leadership of Dr. Samuel King, Office of the Chief of Research and Development.(Back)

Footnote 2-20: For discussion of how Selective Service channeled manpower into the armed forces, see Selective Service System, Special Monograph Number 10, *Special Groups* (Washington: Government Printing Office, 1953), ch. VIII, and Special Monograph Number 12, *Quotas, Calls, and Inductions* (Washington: Government Printing Office, 1948), chs. IV-VI.(Back)

Footnote 2-21: Lee, *Employment of Negro Troops*, p. 113.(Back)

Footnote 2-22: The Army's air arm was reorganized several times. Designated as the Army Air Corps in 1926 (the successor to the historic Army Air Service), it became the Army Air Forces in the summer of 1941. This designation lasted until a separate U.S. Air Force was created in 1947. Organizationally, the Army was divided in March 1942 into three equal parts: the Army Ground Forces, the Army Service Forces (originally Services of Supply), and the Army Air Forces. This division was administrative. Each soldier continued to be assigned to a branch of the Army, for example, Infantry, Artillery, or Air Corps, a title retained as the name of an Army branch.(Back)

Footnote 2-23: Memo, CofAC for G-3, 31 May 40, sub: Employment of Negro Personnel in Air Corps Units, G-3/6541-Gen-527.(Back)

Footnote 2-24: USAF Oral History Program, Interv with Maj Gen Noel F Parrish (USAF, Ret.), 30 Mar 73.(Back)

Footnote 2-25: William H. Hastie, *On Clipped Wings: The Story of Jim Crow in the Army Air Corps* (New York: NAACP, 1943). Based on War Department documents and statistics, this famous pamphlet was essentially an attack on the Army Air Corps. For a more comprehensive account of the Negro and the Army Air Forces, see Osur, *Blacks in the Army Air Forces During World War II*.(Back)

Footnote 2-26: For a detailed discussion of the black training program, see Osur, *Blacks in the Army Air Forces During World War II*, ch. III; Lee, *Employment of Negro Troops*, pp. 461-66; Charles E. Francis, *The Tuskegee Airmen: The Story of the Negro in the U.S. Air Force* (Boston Bruce Humphries, 1955).(Back)

Footnote 2-27: Memo, CofAS for ASW, 12 Jan 43, ASW 291.2.(Back)

Footnote 2-28: Ltr, Walter White to Gen Marshall, 22 Dec 41, AG 291.21 (12-22-41).(Back)

Footnote 2-29: See C-279, 2, Volunteer Division Folder, NAACP Collection, Manuscripts Division, LC.(Back)

Footnote 2-30: Ltr, CofS to Dorothy Canfield Fisher, 16 Feb 42, OCS 20602-254.(Back)

Footnote 2-31: Draft Memo (initialed E.W.C.) for Gen Edwards, G-3 Negro File, 1942-44. See also Lee, *Employment of Negro Troops*, pp. 152-57.(Back)

Footnote 2-32: Ltr, Paul V. McNutt to SW, 17 Feb 43, AG 327.31 (9-19-40) (1) sec. 12.(Back)

Footnote 2-33: Ltr, SW to McNutt, 20 Feb 43, AG 327.31 (9-19-40) (1) sec. 12.(Back)

Footnote 2-34: Ltr, McNutt to SW, 23 Mar 43, AG 327.31 (9-19-40) (1) sec. 12.(Back)

Footnote 2-35: The danger was further reduced when, as part of a national manpower allocation reform, President Roosevelt removed the Bureau of Selective Service from the War Manpower Commission's control and restored it to its independent status as the Selective Service System on 5 December 1943. See Stimson and Bundy, *On Active Service*, pp. 483-86; Theodore Wyckoff, "The Office of the Secretary of War Under Henry L. Stimson," in CMH.(Back)

Footnote 2-36: Strength of the Army, 1 Jan 46, STM-30, p. 60.(Back)

Footnote 2-37: Memo, Dir of Mil Pers, SOS, for G-1, 12 Sep 42, SPGAM/322.5 (WAAC) (8-24-42). See also Edwin R. Embree, "Report of Informal Visit to Training Camp for WAAC's Des Moines, Iowa" (c. 1942), SPWA 291.21. For a general description of Negroes in the Women's Army Auxiliary Corps, see Mattie E. Treadwell, *The Women's Army Corps*, United States Army in World War II (Washington: Government Printing Office, 1954), especially Chapter III. See also Lee, *Employment of Negro Troops*, pp. 421-26.(Back)

Footnote 2-38: Inactivation of the 2d Cavalry Division began in February 1944, and its headquarters completed the process on 10 May. The 9th Cavalry was inactivated on 7 March, the 10th Cavalry on 20 March 1944.(Back)

Footnote 2-39: Ltr, SW to Rep. Hamilton Fish, 19 Feb 44, reprinted in U.S. Congress, House, *Congressional Record*, 78th Cong., 2d sess., pp. 2007-08.(Back)

Footnote 2-40: War Department Pamphlet 20-6, *Command of Negro Troops*, 29 February 1944.(Back)

Footnote 2-41: Army Service Forces Manual M-5, *Leadership and the Negro Soldier*, October 1944, p. iv.(Back)

Footnote 2-42: Lee, *Employment of Negro Troops*, p. 84; for a full discussion of morale, see ch. XI. See also David G. Mandelbaum, *Soldier Groups and Negro Soldiers* (Berkeley: University of California Press, 1952); Charles Dollard and Donald Young, "In the Armed Forces," *Survey Graphic* 36 (January 1947):66ff.(Back)

Footnote 2-43: Memo, G-1 for CofS, 18 Jul 42; DF, G-1 to TAG, 11 Aug 42. Both in AG 334 (Advisory Cmte on Negro Trp Policies, 11 Jul 42) (1).(Back)

Footnote 2-44: The committee included the Assistant Chiefs of Staff, G-1, of the War Department General Staff, the Air Staff, and the Army Ground Forces; the Director of

Personnel, Army Service Forces; General Davis, representing The Inspector General, and an acting secretary. The Civilian Aide to the Secretary of War was not a member, although Judge Hastie's successor was made an *ex officio* member in March 1943. See Min of Mtg of Advisory Cmte, Col J. S. Leonard, 22 Mar 43, ASW 291.2 NTC.(Back)

Footnote 2-45: See, for example, Memo, Recorder, Cmte on Negro Troop Policies (Col John H. McCormick), for CofS, sub: Negro Troops, WDCSA 291.2 (12-24-42).(Back)

Footnote 2-46: Memo, Hastie for SW, 22 Sep 41, sub: Survey and Recommendations Concerning the Integration of the Negro Soldier Into the Army, G-1/15640-120.(Back)

Footnote 2-47: On 16 January 1942 the Navy announced that "in deference to the wishes of those for whom the plasma is being provided, the blood will be processed separately so that those receiving transfusions may be given blood of their own race." Three days later the Chief of the Bureau of Medicine, who was also the President's personal physician, told the Secretary of the Navy, "It is my opinion that at this time we cannot afford to open up a subject such as mixing blood or plasma regardless of the theoretical fact that there is no chemical difference in human blood." See Memo, Rear Adm Ross T. McIntire for SecNav, 19 Jan 42, GenRecsNav. See also Florence Murray, ed., *Negro Handbook, 1946-1947*(New York: A. A. Wyn, 1948), pp. 373-74. For effect of segregated blood banks on black morale, see Mary A. Morton, "The Federal Government and Negro Morale," *Journal of Negro Education* (Summer 1943): 452, 455-56.(Back)

Footnote 2-48: Eli Ginzberg, *The Negro Potential* (New York: Columbia University Press, 1956), p. 85. Ginzberg points out that only about one out of ten black soldiers in the upper two mental categories became an officer, compared to one out of four white soldiers.(Back)

Footnote 2-49: Memo, DCofS to CG, AAF, 10 Aug 42, sub: Professional Qualities of Officers Assigned to Negro Units, WDGAP 322.99; Memo, CG, VII Corps, to CG, AGF, 28 Aug 42, same sub, GNAGS 210.31.(Back)

Footnote 2-50: Brig Gen B. O. Davis, "History of a Special Section Office of the Inspector General (29 June 1941 to 16 November 1944)," p. 8, in CMH.(Back)

Footnote 2-51: Ltr, TAG to CG, AAF, et al., 13 May 42, AG 291.21 (3-31-42).(Back)

Footnote 2-52: Stimson's comments were not limited to overseas areas. To a request by the Second Army commander that Negroes be excluded from maneuvers in certain areas of the American south he replied: "No, get the Southerners used to them!" Memo, ACofS, WPD, for CofS, 25 Mar 42, sub: The Colored Troop Problem, OPD 291.2. Stimson's comments are written marginally in ink and initialed "H.L.S."(Back)

Footnote 2-53: Memo, G-1 for TAG, 4 Apr 42, and Revised Proposals, 22 Apr and 30 Apr 42. All in G-1/15640-2.(Back)

Footnote 2-54: Memo, Civilian Aide to SW, 17 Nov 42, ASW 291.2 NT.(Back)

Footnote 2-55: See, for example, AAF Central Decimal Files for October 1942-May 1944 (RG 18). For an extended discussion of this subject, see Lee, *Employment of Negro Troops*, ch XI-XIII.(Back)

Footnote 2-56: Memo, Brig Gen B. O. Davis for the IG, 24 Dec 42, IG 333.9-Great Britain.(Back)

Footnote 2-57: Memo, ASW for CofS, 3 Jul 43, sub: Negro Troops, ASW 291.2 NT. The Judge Advocate General described disturbances of this type as military "mutiny." See The Judge Advocate General, *Military Justice, 1 July 1940 to 31 December 1945*, p. 60, in CMH.(Back)

Footnote 2-58: Lee, *Employment of Negro Troops*, p. 83.(Back)

Footnote 2-59: Ltr, TAG to Dr. Amanda V. G. Hillyer, Chmn Program Cmte, D.C. Branch, NAACP, 12 Apr 41, AG 291.21 (2-28-41) (1).(Back)

Footnote 2-60: Research Branch, Special Service Division, "What the Soldier Thinks," 8 December 1942, and "Attitudes of the Negro Soldier," 28 July 1943. Both cited in Lee,*Employment of Negro Troops*, pp. 304-06. For detailed analysis, see Samuel A. Stouffer et al., *Studies in Social Psychology in World War II*, vol. I, *The American Soldier: Adjustment During Army Life* (Princeton: Princeton University Press, 1949), pp. 556-80. For a more personal view of black experiences in World War II service clubs, see Margaret Halsey's*Color Blind: A White Woman Looks at the Negro* (New York: Simon and Schuster, 1946). For a comprehensive expression of the attitudes of black soldiers, see Mary P. Motley, ed.,*The Invisible Soldier: The Experience of the Black Soldier, World War II* (Detroit: Wayne State University Press, 1975), a compilation of oral histories by World War II veterans. Although these interviews were conducted a quarter of a century after the event and in the wake of the modern civil rights movement, they provide useful insight to the attitude of black soldiers toward discrimination in the services.(Back)

Footnote 2-61: Office of War Information, The Negroes' Role in the War: A Study of White and Colored Opinions (Memorandum 59, Surveys Division, Bureau of Special Services), 8 Jul 43, in CMH.(Back)

326

Footnote 2-62: Special Services Division, "What the Soldier Thinks," Number 2, August 1943, pp. 58-59, SSD 291.2.(Back)

Footnote 2-63: Dollard and Young, "In the Armed Forces," p. 68.(Back)

Footnote 2-64: New York *Times*, December 2, 1943.(Back)

Footnote 2-65: Gibson, a lawyer and a graduate of the University of Chicago, became Judge Hastie's assistant in 1940. After Hastie's resignation on 29 January 1943, Gibson served as acting civilian aide and assumed the position permanently on 21 September 1943. See Memo, ASW for Admin Asst (John W. Martyn), 21 Sep 43, ASW 291.2 NT-Civ Aide.(Back)

Footnote 2-66: Memo, Gibson to ASW, 3 Nov 43, ASW 291.2 NT. See also New York *Times*, December 2, 1943.(Back)

Footnote 2-67: For discussion of Gibson's attitude and judgments, see Interv, author with Evans, 3 Jun 73.(Back)

Footnote 2-68: Memo, Chmn, Advisory Cmte, for CofS, 3 Jul 43, sub: Negro Troops, ASW 291.2 NT. This was not sent until 6 July.(Back)

Footnote 2-69: Memo, CofS for CG, AAF, et al., 13 Jul 43, sub: Negro Troops, WDCSA 291.21.(Back)

Footnote 2-70: Memo, Advisory Cmte for CofS, 16 Mar 43, sub: Inflammatory Publications, ASW 291.2 NT Cmte; Memo, CG, 4th Service Cmd, ASF, to CG, ASF, 12 Jul 43, sub: Disturbances Among Negro Troops, with attached note initialed by Gen Marshall, WDCSA 291.2 (12 Jul 43).(Back)

Footnote 2-71: Memo, J. J. McC (John J. McCloy) for Gen Marshall, 21 Jul 43, with attached note signed "GCM," ASW 291.2 NT.(Back)

Footnote 2-72: Min of Mtg of Advisory Cmte on Negro Troop Policies, 29 Feb 44, ASW 291.2 Negro Troops Cmte; Lee, *Employment of Negro Troops*, pp. 449-50.(Back)

Footnote 2-73: Memo, ASW for SW, 2 Mar 44, inclosing formal recommendations, WDCSA 291.2/13 Negroes (1944).(Back)

Footnote 2-74: Pogue, *Organizer of Victory*, p. 99.(Back)

Footnote 2-75: Memo, CG, AGF, for CG's, Second Army, et al., n.d., sub: Efficiency Ratings of Commanders of Negro Units Scheduled for Overseas Shipment, GNGAP-L 201.61/9.(Back)

Footnote 2-76: WD PAM 20-6, *Command of Negro Troops*, 29 Feb 44.(Back)

Footnote 2-77: The Army Service Forces published a major supplement to War Department Pamphlet 20-6 in October 1944, see Army Service Forces Manual M-5, *Leadership and the Negro Soldier*.(Back)

Footnote 2-78: Ltr, TAG to CG, AAF, et al., 8 Jul 44, sub: Recreational Facilities, AG 353.8 (5 Jul 44) OB-S-A-M.(Back)

Footnote 2-79: Actually, the use of officers' clubs by black troops was clearly implied if not ordained in paragraph 19 of Army Regulation 210-10, 20 December 1940, which stated that any club operating on federal property must be open to all officers assigned to the post, camp, or station. For more on the Freeman Field incident, see Chapter 5, below.(Back)

Footnote 2-80: Memo, Secy, Advisory Cmte, for Advisory Cmte on Special Troop Policies, 13 Jun 45, sub: Minutes of Meeting, ASW 291.2 NT.(Back)

Footnote 2-81: Ltr, Actg SW for Gov. Chauncey Sparks of Alabama, 1 Sep 44, WDCSA 291.2 (26 Aug 44).(Back)

Footnote 2-82: Ltr, ASW to Herbert B. Elliston, Editor, Washington *Post*, 5 Aug 43, ASW 291.2 NT (Gen).(Back)

Footnote 2-83: Ltr, USW to Roane Waring, National Cmdr, American Legion, 5 May 43, SW 291.2 NT. Integrated hospitals did not appear until 1943. See Robert J. Parks, "The Development of Segregation in U.S. Army Hospitals, 1940-1942," *Military Affairs* 37 (December 1973): 145-50.(Back)

Footnote 2-84: Ltr, ASW to SecNav, 22 Aug 45, ASW 291.2 NT (Gen).(Back)

Footnote 2-85: Ltr, William Hastie to Lee Nichols, 15 Jul 53, in Nichols Collection, CMH; see also Lee, *Employment of Negro Troops* pp. 15-20; Army War College Misc File 127-1 through 127-22, AMHRC.(Back)

Footnote 2-86: As published in Mobilization Regulation 1-2 (1938 and May 1939 versions), par. 11d, and 15 Jul 39 version, par. 13b.(Back)

Footnote 2-87: Lee, *Employment of Negro Troops*, p. 50.(Back)

Footnote 2-88: TAG Ltr, 26 Apr 41, AG 352 (4-10-41) M-M-C.(Back)

Footnote 2-89: Davis, "History of a Special Section Office of the Inspector General."(Back)

Footnote 2-90: Eleven of these were candidates at the Infantry School, 2 at the Field Artillery School, 7 at the Quartermaster School, and 1 each at the Cavalry, Ordnance, and

Finance Schools. Memo, TAG for Admin Asst, OSW, 16 Sep 41, sub: Request of the Civ Aide to the SW for Data Relative to Negro Soldiers, AG 291.21 (9-12-41) M; Memo, TAG for Civ Aide to SW, 18 Nov 41, sub: Request for Data Relative to Negro Soldiers Admitted to OCS, AG 291.21 (10-30-41) RB.(Back)

Footnote 2-91: Ltr, Hastie to SW, 8 May 41, ASW 291.2 NT.(Back)

Footnote 2-92: Memo, ACofS, G-3, for CofS, 12 May 41, sub: Negro Officers; Memo, ACofS, G-3, for ACofS, G-1 (ATTN: Col Wharton), 12 Jun 41, same sub. Both in WDGOT 291.2.(Back)

Footnote 2-93: Pogue, *Organizer of Victory*, p. 96.(Back)

Footnote 2-94: Memo, Hastie for ASW, 5 Sep 41, G-1/15640-120; Ltr, Hastie to Nichols, 15 Jul 53; Tab C to AG 320.2 (11-24-42).(Back)

Footnote 2-95: Telg, Walter White, NAACP, to SW and President Roosevelt, 23 Oct 41, AG 291.21 (10-23-41) (3); Ltr, Edgar W. Brown to President Roosevelt and SW, 15 Oct 41, AG 291.2 (10-15-41) (1). See also Memo, ACofS, G-3, for CofS, 23 Oct 41, sub: Negro Officer Candidate Schools, G-3/43276.(Back)

Footnote 2-96: Ltr, Horace Wilkinson to Rep. John J. Sparkman (Alabama), 24 Aug 43; Ltr, TAG to Rep. John Starnes (Alabama), 15 Sep 43. Both in AG 095 (Wilkinson) (28 Aug 43). See also Interv, Nichols with Ulysses Lee, 1953.(Back)

Footnote 2-97: Ltr, SGS to Sen. Carl Hayden (Arizona), 12 Dec 41, AG 352 (12-12-41). See also Memo, ACofS, G-3, for CofS, 23 Oct 41, sub: Negro Officer Candidate Schools, G-3/43276.(Back)

Footnote 2-98: Dollard and Young, "In the Armed Forces."(Back)

Footnote 2-99: Memos, Hastie for ASW, 4 Nov 42 and 15 Dec 42; Ltr, Maj Gen A. D. Bruce, Cmdr, Tank Destroyer Center, to ASW, 31 Dec 42. All in ASW 291.2 NT (12-2-42).(Back)

Footnote 2-100: For a detailed discussion, see Lee, *Employment of Negro Troops*, Chapter XXII.(Back)

Footnote 2-101: Ltr, Lt Gen John C. H. Lee to Commanders of Colored Troops, ComZ, 26 Dec 44, sub: Volunteers for Training and Assignment as Reinforcements, AG 322X353XSGS.(Back)

Footnote 2-102: Revised version of above, same date. Copies of both versions in CMH. Later General Eisenhower stated that he had decided to employ the men "as individuals," but the evidence is clear that he meant platoons in 1944, see Ltr, D.D.E. to Gen Bruce C. Clarke, 29 May 63, in CMH.(Back)

Footnote 2-103: The 92d Division was assigned to the Mediterranean theater.(Back)

Footnote 2-104: Davis, "History of a Special Section Office of the Inspector General," p. 19.(Back)

Footnote 2-105: ETO I&E Div Rpt E-118 Research Br, The Utilization of Negro Infantry Platoons in White Companies, Jun 45; ASF I&E Div Rpt B-157, Opinions About Negro Infantry Platoons in White Companies of Seven Divisions, 3 Jul 45. For a general critique of black performance in World War II, see Chapter 5 below.(Back)

Footnote 2-106: Memo, CG, ASF, to ASW, 11 Jul 45, ASW 291.2 NT.(Back)

Footnote 2-107: The percentage of high school graduates and men scoring in AGCT categories I, II, and III among the black infantry volunteers was somewhat higher than that of all Negroes in the European theater. As against 22 percent high school graduates and 29 percent in the first three test score categories for the volunteers, the percentages for all Negroes in the theater were 18 and 17 percent. At the same time the averages for black volunteers were considerably below those for white riflemen, of whom 41 percent were high school graduates and 71 percent in the higher test categories—figures that tend to refute the general's argument. See ASF I&E Div Rpt B-157, 3 Jul 45.(Back)

Footnote 2-108: Msg, Hq ComZ, ETO, Paris, France (signed Bradley), to WD 3 Jul 45. For similar reports from the field see, for example, Ltr, Brig Gen R. B. Lovett, ETO AG, to TAG, 7 Sep 45, sub: The Utilization of Negro Platoons in White Companies; Ltr, Hq USFET to TAG, 24 Oct 45, same sub. Both in AG 291.2 (1945).(Back)

Footnote 2-109: Memo, CofS for ASW, 25 Aug 45, WDCSA 291.2 Negroes (25 Aug 45).(Back)

Footnote 2-110: Ltr, ASW to SecNav, 22 Aug 45, ASW 291.2 NT (Gen).(Back)

Footnote 3-1: All statistics in this chapter are taken from the files of the U.S. Navy, Bureau of Naval Personnel (hereafter cited as BuPers).(Back)

Footnote 3-2: After some delay and considerable pressure from civil rights sources, the Navy identified Miller, awarded him the Navy Cross, and promoted him to mess attendant, first class. Miller was later lost at sea. See Dennis D. Nelson, *The Integration of the Negro Into the U.S.*

Navy (New York: Farrar, Straus and Young, 1951), pp. 23-25. The Navy further honored Miller in 1973 by naming a destroyer escort (DE 1091) after him.(Back)

Footnote 3-3: There were exceptions to this generalization. The Navy had 43 black men with ratings in the general service in December 1941: the 6 regulars from the 1920's, 23 others returned from retirement, and 14 members of the Fleet Reserve. See U.S. Navy, Bureau of Naval Personnel, "The Negro in the Navy in World War II" (1947) (hereafter "BuPers Hist"), p. 1. This study is part of the bureau's unpublished multivolume administrative history of World War II. A copy is on file in the bureau's Technical Library. The work is particularly valuable for its references to documents that no longer exist.(Back)

Footnote 3-4: One of Theodore Roosevelt's Rough Riders, a World War I field artillery officer, and later publisher of the Chicago *Daily News*, Knox was an implacable foe of the New Deal but an ardent internationalist, strongly sympathetic to President Roosevelt's foreign policy.(Back)

Footnote 3-5: In 1940 the bureaus were answerable only to the Secretary of the Navy and the President, but after a reorganization of 1942 they began to lose some of their independence. In March 1942 President Roosevelt merged the offices of the Chief of Naval Operations and Commander in Chief, U.S. Fleet, giving Admiral Ernest J. King, who held both titles, at least some direction over most of the bureaus. Eventually the Chief of Naval Operations would become a figure with powers comparable to those exercised by the Army's Chief of Staff. See Julius A. Furer, *Administration of the Navy Department in World War II* (Washington: Government Printing Office, 1959), pp. 113-14. This shift in power was readily apparent in the case of the administration of the Navy's racial policy.(Back)

Footnote 3-6: Ltr, SecNav to Lt. Gov. Charles Poletti (New York), 24 Jul 40, Nav-620-AT, GenRecsNav.(Back)

Footnote 3-7: Idem to Sen. Arthur Capper (Kansas), 1 Aug 40, QN/P14-4, GenRecsNav.(Back)

Footnote 3-8: Memo, Rear Adm W. R. Sexton, Chmn of Gen Bd, for Capt Morton L. Deyo, 17 Sep 40, Recs of Gen Bd, OpNavArchives.(Back)

Footnote 3-9: Idem for SecNav, 17 Sep 40, sub: Enlistment of Colored Persons in the U.S. Navy, Recs of Gen Bd, OpNavArchives. 1st Ind to Ltr, Natl Public Relations Comm of the Universal Negro Improvement Assn to SecNav, 4 Oct 41; Memo, Chief, BuNav, for CNO, 24 Oct 41, and 2d Ind to same, CNO to SecNav (Public Relations). Both in BuPers QN/P14-4 (411004), GenRecsNav. For examples of the Navy's response on race, see Ltr, Ens Ross R. Hirshfield, Off of Pub Relations, to Roberson County Training School, 25 Oct 41; Ltr, Ens William Stucky to W. Henry White, 4 Feb 42. Both in QN/P14-4. BuPersRecs.(Back)

Footnote 3-10: Quoted in White, *A Man Called White*, p. 191.(Back)

Footnote 3-11: Ibid.(Back)

Footnote 3-12: Memo, W. A. Allen, Office of Public Relations, for Lt Cmdr Smith, BuPers, 29 Jan 42, BuPers QN/P-14, BuPersRecs.(Back)

Footnote 3-13: Ltr, Chief, BuNav, to Chmn, Gen Bd, 22 Jan 42, sub: Enlistment of Men of Colored Race in Other Than Messman Branch, Recs of Gen Bd, OpNavArchives.(Back)

Footnote 3-14: Ibid.(Back)

Footnote 3-15: The FEPC was established 25 June 1941 to carry out Roosevelt's Executive Order 8802 against discrimination in employment in defense industries and in the federal government.(Back)

Footnote 3-16: "BuPers Hist," pp. 4-5; Ltr, Mark Ethridge to Lee Nichols. 14 Jul 53, in Nichols Collection, CMH.(Back)

Footnote 3-17: Ltr, SecNav to Gifford Pinchot, 19 Jan 42, 54-1-15, GenRecsNav.(Back)

Footnote 3-18: Quoted in "BuPers Hist," p. 5.(Back)

Footnote 3-19: Memo, SecNav for Chmn, Gen Bd, 16 Jan 42, sub: Enlistment of Men of Colored Race in Other Than Messman Branch, Recs of Gen Bd, OpNavArchives.(Back)

Footnote 3-20: Enlistment of Men of Colored Race (201), 23 Jan 42, Hearings Before the General Board of the Navy, 1942; Memo, Chmn, Gen Bd, for SecNav, 3 Feb 42, sub: Enlistment of Men of Colored Race in Other Than Messman Branch. Both in Recs of Gen Bd, OpNavArchives.(Back)

Footnote 3-21: Quoted in "BuPers Hist," p. 6.(Back)

Footnote 3-22: Memo, SecNav for Chmn, Gen Bd, 14 Feb 42, Recs of Gen Bd, OpNavArchives. The quotation is from the Knox Memo and is not necessarily in the exact words of the President.(Back)

Footnote 3-23: Memos, Chmn, Gen Bd, for Chief, BuNav, Cmdt, CG, and Cmdt, MC, 18 Feb 42, sub: Enlistment of Men of Colored Race in Other Than Messman Branch. For examples of responses, see Ltr, Cmdt, to Chmn, Gen Bd, 24 Feb 42, same sub; Memo, Chief, BuNav, for

Chmn, Gen Bd, 7 Mar 42, same sub; Memo, CNO for Chief, BuNav, 25 Feb 42, same sub, with 1st Ind by CINCUSFLT, 28 Feb 42, same sub. The final enlistment plan is found in Memo, Chmn, Gen Bd, for SecNav, 20 Mar 42, same sub (G. B. No 421). All in Recs of Gen Bd, OpNavArchives. It was transmitted to the President in Ltr, SecNav to President, 27 Mar 42, P14-4/MM, GenRecsNav.(Back)

Footnote 3-24: Memo, President for Secy of Navy, 31 Mar 42, Franklin D. Roosevelt Library, Hyde Park, New York.(Back)

Footnote 3-25: New York *Times*, January 10 and March 20, 1942.(Back)

Footnote 3-26: Office of SecNav, Press Release, 7 Apr 42.(Back)

Footnote 3-27: "The Navy Makes a Gesture," *Crisis* 49 (May 1942):51. The National Negro Congress quotation reprinted in Dennis D. Nelson's summary of reactions to the Secretary of the Navy's announcement. See Nelson, "The Integration of the Negro in the United States Navy, 1776-1947" (NAVEXOS-P-526), p. 38. (This earlier and different version of Nelson's published work, derived from his master's thesis, was sponsored by the U.S. Navy.)(Back)

Footnote 3-28: Although essentially correct, the critics were technically inaccurate since some Negroes would be assigned to Coast Guard cutters which qualified as sea duty.(Back)

Footnote 3-29: Quoted in Nelson, "The Integration of the Negro," p. 37.(Back)

Footnote 3-30: *Opportunity* (May 1942), p. 82.(Back)

Footnote 3-31: Memo, Chief, BuNav, for SecNav, 17 Apr 42, sub: Training Facilities for Negro Recruits, Nav-102; Memo, SecNav for Rear Adm Randall Jacobs, 21 Apr 42, 54-1-22. Both in GenRecsNav.(Back)

Footnote 3-32: Memo, SecNav for Chmn, Gen Bd, 7 Mar 42, GenRecsNav.(Back)

Footnote 3-33: For a discussion of Armstrong's philosophy from the viewpoint of an educated black recruit, see Nelson, "Integration of the Negro," pp. 28-34. See also Ltr, Nelson to author, 10 Feb 70, CMH files.(Back)

Footnote 3-34: With the exception of machinist school, where blacks were in training twice as long as whites, specialist training for Negroes and whites was similar in length. See "BuPers Hist," pp. 28-30, 60-61.(Back)

Footnote 3-35: BuPers, "Reports, Schedules, and Charts Relating to Enlistment, Training, and Assignment of Negro Personnel," 5 Jun 42, Pers-617, BuPersRecs.(Back)

Footnote 3-36: In May 1942 the name of the Bureau of Navigation was changed to the Bureau of Naval Personnel to reflect more accurately the duties of the organization.(Back)

Footnote 3-37: Memo, Chief, NavPers, for CO, Great Lakes NTC, 23 Apr 43. P14-1, BuPersRecs.(Back)

Footnote 3-38: "BuPers Hist," p. 54.(Back)

Footnote 3-39: Ibid., p. 9.(Back)

Footnote 3-40: Memo, SW for SecNav, 16 Feb 42, sub: Continuing of Voluntary Recruiting by the Navy, QN/P14-4, GenRecsNav.(Back)

Footnote 3-41: Idem for President, 16 Mar 42, copy in QN/P14-4, GenRecsNav.(Back)

Footnote 3-42: Memo, President for SW, 20 Mar 42, copy in QN/P14-4, GenRecsNav.(Back)

Footnote 3-43: Executive Order 9279, 5 Dec 42.(Back)

Footnote 3-44: Memo, SecNav for Rear Adm Randall Jacobs, 5 Dec 43, 54-1-22, GenRecsNav.(Back)

Footnote 3-45: Ltr, Paul McNutt to SecNav, 17 Feb 43, WMC Gen files, NARS.(Back)

Footnote 3-46: Memo, President for SecNav, 22 Feb 43, FDR Library.(Back)

Footnote 3-47: Ltr, Knox to McNutt, 26 Feb 43, WMC Gen files.(Back)

Footnote 3-48: Ltr, McNutt to Knox, 23 Mar 43, WMC Gen files.(Back)

Footnote 3-49: Ltr, SecNav to Paul McNutt, 13 Apr 43; Ltr, McNutt to Knox, 23 Apr 43; both in WMC Gen files.(Back)

Footnote 3-50: Selective Service System, *Special Groups*, vol. II, pp. 198-201. See also Memos, Director of Planning and Control, BuPers, for Chief, BuPers, 25 Feb 43, sub: Increase in Colored Personnel for the Navy; and 1 Apr 43, sub; Increase in Negro Personnel in Navy. Both in P-14, BuPersRecs.(Back)

Footnote 3-51: Memos, SecNav for President, 25 Feb and 14 Apr 43, quoted in "BuPers Hist," pp. 13-14; Memo, Actg Chief, NavPers, for SecNav, 24 Feb 43, sub: Employment of Colored Personnel in the Navy, Pers 10, GenRecsNav. For Roosevelt's approval see "BuPers Hist," p. 14.(Back)

Footnote 3-52: "BuPersHist," p. 41.(Back)

Footnote 3-53: Naval districts organized section bases during the war with responsibility, among other things, for guarding beaches, harbors, and installations and maintaining equipment.(Back)

Footnote 3-54: See CNO ALNAV, 7 Aug 44, quoted in Nelson, "Integration of the Negro," p. 46.(Back)

Footnote 3-55: Memo, Actg Chief, NavPers, for Cmdts, AlNav Districts et al., 26 Sep 44, sub: Enlisted Personnel—Utilization of in Field for which Specifically Trained, Pers 16-3/MM, BuPersRecs.(Back)

Footnote 3-56: Ltr, Eleanor Roosevelt to SecNav, 20 Nov 43; Ltr, SecNav to Mrs. Roosevelt, 27 Nov 43; both in BUMED-S-EC, GenRecsNav. Well known for her interest in the cause of racial justice, the President's wife received many complaints during the war concerning discrimination in the armed forces. Mrs. Roosevelt often passed such protests along to the service secretaries for action. Although there is no doubt where Mrs. Roosevelt's sympathies lay in these matters, her influence was slight on the policies and practices of the Army or Navy. Her influence on the President's thinking is, of course, another matter. See White, *A Man Called White*, pp. 168-69, 190.(Back)

Footnote 3-57: For a discussion of these racial disturbances, see "BuPers Hist," pp. 75-80.(Back)

Footnote 3-58: Interv, Lee Nichols with Rear Adm. R. H. Hillenkoetter, 1953, in Nichols Collection, CMH.(Back)

Footnote 3-59: Nichols, *Breakthrough on the Color Front*, pp. 54-59. Nichols supports his affectionate portrait of Sargent, who died shortly after the war, with interviews of many wartime officials who worked in the Bureau of Naval Personnel with Sargent. See Nichols Collection, CMH. See also *Christopher Smith Sargent, 1911-1946*, a privately printed memorial prepared by the Sargent family in 1947, copy in CMH.(Back)

Footnote 3-60: For further discussion, see Nelson, "Integration of the Negro," pp. 124-46.(Back)

Footnote 3-61: BuPers Ltr, Pers 106-MBR, 12 Jul 43.(Back)

Footnote 3-62: "BuPers Hist," p. 53.(Back)

Footnote 3-63: Memo, Chief, BuPers, for CINCUSFLEET, 1 Dec 43, sub: Negro Personnel, P16/MM, BuPersRecs. The latter experiment has been chronicled by its commanding officer, Eric Purdon, in *Black Company: The Story of Subchaser 1264* (Washington: Luce, 1972).(Back)

Footnote 3-64: Memo, CNO for Cmdt, First and Fifth Naval Districts, 10 May 44, sub: Assignment of Negro Personnel, P-16-3/MM, BuPersRecs.(Back)

Footnote 3-65: For an assessment of the performance of the *Mason's* crew. see "BuPers Hist," pp. 42-43 and 92.(Back)

Footnote 3-66: BuPers Ltr, P16-3, 12 Jul 43, sub: The Expanded Use of Negroes, BuPersRecs.(Back)

Footnote 3-67: Ltr, Chief, NavPers, to Cmdts, All Naval Districts, 19 Aug 43, sub: Advancement in Rating re: Negro Personnel, P17-2/MM, BuPersRecs.(Back)

Footnote 3-68: BuPers Cir Ltr 6-44, 12 Jan 44.(Back)

Footnote 3-69: News that the Navy had inadvertently commissioned a black student at Harvard University in the spring of 1942 produced the following reaction in one personnel office: "LtCmdr B ... [Special Activities Branch, BuPers] says this is true due to a slip by the officer who signed up medical students at Harvard. Cmdr. B. says this boy has a year to go in medical school and hopes they can get rid of him some how by then. He earnestly asks us to be judicious in handling this matter and prefers that nothing be said about it." Quoted in a Note, H. M. Harvey to M Mc (ca. 20 Jun 42), copy on file in the Dennis D. Nelson Collection, San Diego, California.(Back)

Footnote 3-70: Ltr, SecNav to Sen. David I. Walsh (Massachusetts), 21 May 42, 51-1-26; see also idem to Sen. William H. Smathers (Florida), 7 Feb 42, Nav-32-C. Both in GenRecsNav.(Back)

Footnote 3-71: Interv, Lee Nichols with Lester Granger, 1953, in Nichols Collection, CMH.(Back)

Footnote 3-72: Kenneth S. Davis, *The Politics of Honor: A Biography of Adlai E. Stevenson* (New York: Putnam, 1957), p. 146; Ltr, A. E. Stevenson to Dennis D. Nelson, 10 Feb 48, Nelson Collection, San Diego, California.(Back)

Footnote 3-73: Memo, Stevenson for the Secretary [Knox], 29 Sep 43, 54-1-50, GenRecsNav.(Back)

Footnote 3-74: The V-12 program was designed to prepare large numbers of educated men for the Navy's Reserve Midshipmen schools and to increase the war-depleted student bodies of many colleges. The Navy signed on eligible students as apprentice seamen and paid their academic expenses. Eventually the V-12 program produced some 80,000 officers for the wartime Navy. For an account of the experiences of a black recruit in the V-12 program, see Carl T. Rowan, "Those Navy Boys Changed My Life," *Reader's Digest* 72 (January 1958):55-58. Rowan, the celebrated columnist and onetime Deputy Assistant Secretary of State for Public Affairs, was one of the first Negroes to complete the V-12 program. Another was Samuel Gravely.(Back)

Footnote 3-75: BuPers Cir Ltr 269-43, 15 Dec 43.(Back)

Footnote 3-76: Memo, SecNav for Chief, NavPers, 20 Nov 43, 54-1-50; Memo, Chief, NavPers, for SecNav, 2 Dec 43, sub: Negro Officers. Both in GenRecsNav.(Back)

Footnote 3-77: Memo, SecNav for Rear Adm Jacobs, 15 Dec 43, quoted in "BuPers Hist," p. 33.(Back)

Footnote 3-78: Quoted in Record of "Conference With Regard to Negro Personnel," held at Hq, Fifth Naval District, 26 Oct 43, Incl to Ltr, Chief, NavPers, to All Sea Frontier Cmds et al., 5 Jan 44, sub: Negro Personnel—Confidential Report of Conference With Regard to the Handling of, Pers 1013, BuPers Recs. The grotesque racial attitudes of some commanders, as well as the thoughtful questions and difficult experiences of others, were fully aired at this conference.(Back)

Footnote 3-79: Ibid.(Back)

Footnote 3-80: NavPers 15092, 12 Feb 44.(Back)

Footnote 3-81: "BuPers Hist," pt. II, pp. 2-3.(Back)

Footnote 3-82: NavPers 15092, 12 Feb 44, p. 10.(Back)

Footnote 3-83: Ibid., p. 1.(Back)

Footnote 3-84: See Columbia University Oral Hist Interv with Granger; USAF Oral History Program, Interview with James C. Evans, 24 Apr 73.(Back)

Footnote 3-85: Interv, Lee Nichols with Vice Adm Randall Jacobs, 29 Mar 53, in Nichols Collection, CMH.(Back)

Footnote 3-86: Memo, SecNav for President, 20 May 44, Forrestal file, GenRecsNav.(Back)

Footnote 3-87: Ltr, CNO to CO, USS *Antaeus* et al., 9 Aug 44, sub: Negro Enlisted Personnel—Assignment of to Ships of the Fleet, P16-3/MM, OpNavArchives.(Back)

Footnote 3-88: Idem to Cmdr, *Antaeus* et al., 9 Jan 45, P16-3, OpNavArchives.(Back)

Footnote 3-89: Ltr, CO, USS *Antaeus*, to Chief, NavPers, 16 Jan 45, sub: Negro Enlisted Personnel—Assignment of to Ships of the Fleet, Ag67/P16-3/MM; see also Memo, Cmdr D. Armstrong for ComSerForPac, 29 Dec 44, sub: Negro Enlisted Personnel (General Service Ratings) Assignment of to Ships of the Fleet; Ltr, ComSerForPac to Chief, NavPers, 2 Jan 45, with CINCPac&POA end thereto, same sub; Ltrs to Chief, NavPers, from CO, USS *Laramie*, 17 Jan 45, USS *Mattole*, 19 Jan 45, with ComSerForLant end, and USS *Ariel*, 1 Feb 45. All Incl to Memo, Chief, NavPers, for CINCUSFLEET, 6 Mar 45, sub: Negro Personnel—Expanded Use of, Pers 2119 FB. All in OpNavArchives.(Back)

Footnote 3-90: Memo, Chief, NavPers, for CINCUSFLEET, 6 Mar 45, sub: Negro Personnel—Expanded Use of, with 1st Ind, from Fleet Adm, USN, for Vice CNO, 28 Mar 45, same sub, FFI/P16-3/MM, OpNavArchives.(Back)

Footnote 3-91: BuPers Cir Ltr 105-45, 13 Apr 45, sub: Negro General-Service Personnel, Assignment of to Auxiliary Vessels of the Fleet.(Back)

Footnote 3-92: Ltr, Chief, NavPers, to CO, USS *Mason*, 16 Mar 45, sub: Negro Officer—Assignment of, Pers 2119-FB; see also idem to CO, USS *Kaweah*, 16 Jul 45, sub: Negro Officer—Assignment of to Auxiliary Vessel of the Fleet, AO 15/P16-1; idem to CO, USS *Laramie*, 21 Aug 45, same sub, AO 16/P16-1. All in OpNavArchives.(Back)

Footnote 3-93: Quoted in Rowan, "Those Navy Boys Changed My Life." pp 57-58.(Back)

Footnote 3-94: Ltr, Mildred M. Horton to author, 14 Mar 75, CMH files.(Back)

Footnote 3-95: Memo, Chief, NavPers, for SecNav, 27 Apr 43, Pers 17MD, BuPersRecs, Memo, SecNav for Adm Jacobs, 29 Apr 43, 54-1-43, GenRecsNav.(Back)

Footnote 3-96: See, for example, Ltr, SecNav to Algernon D. Black, City-Wide Citizen's Cmte on Harlem, 23 Apr 43, 54-1-43, GenRecsNav.(Back)

Footnote 3-97: Quoted in Ltr, Horton to author, 14 Mar 75.(Back)

Footnote 3-98: Memo, Ralph Bard for Forrestal, 4 May 44, sub: Navy Policy on Recruitment of Negro Females as WAVES; Ltr, Nathan Cowan, CIO, to Forrestal, 20 May 44, 54-1-1. Both in GenRecsNav.(Back)

Footnote 3-99: Memo, J. V. F. (Forrestal) for Adm Denfeld (ca. 7 Jun 44); Memo, Capt Mildred McAfee for Adm Denfeld, 7 Jun 44; both in 54-1-4, GenRecsNav. See also Memo, Chief, NavPers, for SecNav, 11 May 44, sub: Navy Policy on Recruitment of Negro Females as WAVES, Pers 17, GenRecsNav.(Back)

Footnote 3-100: Memo, Forrestal for President, 28 Jul 44, 54-1-4, GenRecsNav.(Back)

Footnote 3-101: Memo, Lt Cmdr John Tyree (White House aide) for Forrestal, 9 Aug 44, 54-1-4, GenRecsNav.(Back)

Footnote 3-102: Navy Dept Press Release, 19 Oct 44.(Back)

Footnote 3-103: Oral History Interview, Mildred McAfee Horton, 25 Aug 69, Center of Naval History.(Back)

Footnote 3-104: Ltr, Asst Chief, NavPers, to CO, NavTraScol (WR), Bronx, N.Y., 8 Dec 44, sub: Colored WAVE Recruits, Pers-107, BuPersRecs.(Back)

Footnote 3-105: Quoted in the Columbia University Oral History Interview with Granger. Granger's incorrect reference to Admiral King as "chief of staff" is interesting because it illustrates the continuing evolution of that office during World War II.(Back)

Footnote 3-106: James V. Forrestal, "Remarks for Dinner Meeting at National Urban League," 12 Feb 58, Box 31, Misc file, Forrestal Papers, Princeton Library. Forrestal's truncated version of the King meeting agreed substantially with Granger's lengthier remembrance.(Back)

Footnote 3-107: Intervs, Lee Nichols with Adm Louis E. Denfeld (Deputy Chief of Naval Personnel, later CNO) and with Cmdr Charles Dillon (formerly of BuPers Special Unit), 1953; both in Nichols Collection, CMH.(Back)

Footnote 3-108: ALNAV, 7 Aug 44, quoted in Nelson, "Integration of the Negro," p. 46.(Back)

Footnote 3-109: Dir, CNO, to Forward Areas, Dec 44, quoted in Nelson's "Integration of the Negro," p. 51.(Back)

Footnote 3-110: BuPers Cir Ltr 72-44, 13 Mar 44, sub: Negro Personnel of the Commissary Branch, Assignment to Duty of.(Back)

Footnote 3-111: Idem, 182-44, 29 Jun 44, "Uniform for Chief Cooks and Chief Stewards and Cooks and Stewards."(Back)

Footnote 3-112: Idem, 45-18, 21 Feb 45, and 45-46, 31 May 45, sub: Negro Enlisted Personnel—Limitation on Assignment of to Naval Ammunition Depots and Naval Magazines.(Back)

Footnote 3-113: There is some indication that integration was already going on unofficially in some specialist schools; see Ltr, Dr. M. A. F. Ritchie to James C. Evans, 13 Aug 65, CMH files.(Back)

Footnote 3-114: BuPers Cir Ltr 194-44, sub: Advanced Schools, Nondiscrimination in Selection of Personnel for Training in; Ltr, Chief, NavPers, to CO, AdComd, NavTraCen, 12 Jun 45, sub: Selection of Negro Personnel for Instruction in Class "A" Schools, 54-1-21, GenRecsNav.(Back)

Footnote 3-115: Memo, CNO for Chief, NavPers, 30 Aug 44, sub: Negro Personnel—Assignment to ANs and YMs, P13-/MM, BuPersRecs.(Back)

Footnote 3-116: BuPers Cir Ltr 227-44, 12 Aug 44, sub: Steward's Branch, Procurement of From General-Service Negroes.(Back)

Footnote 3-117: Memo, Lt William H. Robertson, Jr., for Rear Adm William M. Fechteler, Asst Chief, NavPers, 20 Jul 45, sub: Conditions Existing at NTC, Bainbridge, Md., Regarding Negro Personnel, Reported on by Lt Wm. H. Robertson, Jr., Pers-2119-FB, BuPersRecs.(Back)

Footnote 3-118: "BuPers Hist," p. 75.(Back)

Footnote 3-119: Nelson, "Integration of the Negro," ch. VIII.(Back)

Footnote 3-120: Henry I. Shaw, Jr., and Ralph W. Donnelly, *Blacks in the Marine Corps* (Washington: Government Printing Office, 1975), pp. 44-45.(Back)

Footnote 3-121: White's testimony before the Court of Inquiry was attached to a report by Maj Gen Henry L. Larsen to CMC (ca. 22 Jan 45), Ser. No. 04275, copy in CMH.(Back)

Footnote 3-122: As quoted in White, *A Man Called White*, p. 273. For a variation on this theme, see Interv, Nichols with Hillenkoetter.(Back)

Footnote 3-123: Ltr, Rear Adm Hillenkoetter to Nichols, 22 May 53; see also Intervs, Nichols with Granger, Hillenkoetter, Jacobs, Thomas Darden, Dillon, and other BuPers officials. In contrast to the Knox period, where the files are replete with Secretary of the Navy memos, BuPers letters, and General Board reports on the development of the Navy's racial policy, there is scant documentation on the same subject during the early months of the Forrestal administration. This is understandable because the subject of integration was extremely delicate and not readily susceptible to the usual staffing needed for most policy decisions. Furthermore, Forrestal's laconic manner of expressing himself, famous in bureaucratic Washington, inhibited the usual flow of letters and memos.(Back)

Footnote 3-124: Ltr, John H. Sengstacke to Forrestal, 19 Dec 44, 54-1-9, GenRecsNav; Interv, Nichols with Granger.(Back)

333

Footnote 3-125: Memo, Under Sec Bard for SecNav, 1 Jan 45; Memo, H Struve Hensel (Off of Gen Counsel) for Forrestal, 5 Jan 45; both in 54-1-9, Forrestal file, GenRecsNav.(Back)

Footnote 3-126: Memo, SecNav for Eugene Duffield (Asst to Under Sec), 16 Jan 45, 54-1-9; idem for Rear Adm A. Stanton Merrill (Dir of Pub Relations), 24 Mar and 4 May 45, 54-1-16. All in Forrestal file, GenRecsNav.(Back)

Footnote 3-127: Quoted in Forrestal, "Remarks for Dinner of Urban League." (Back)

Footnote 3-128: Ltr, SecNav to Lester Granger, 1 Feb 45, Forrestal file, GenRecsNav.(Back)

Footnote 3-129: Ltrs, Granger to Forrestal, 19 Mar and 3 Apr 45, 54-1-13, Forrestal file, GenRecsNav. Granger and Forrestal had attended Dartmouth College, but not together as Forrestal thought. For a detailed and affectionate account of their relationship, see Columbia University Oral History Interview with Granger.(Back)

Footnote 3-130: Columbia University Oral Hist Interv with Granger.(Back)

Footnote 3-131: Memo, Chief, NavPers, for Cmdr Richard M. Paget (Exec Office of the SecNav), 21 Apr 45, sub: Organization of Advisory Cmte, Pers 2119, GenRecsNav. See also "BuPers Hist," pt. II, p. 3.(Back)

Footnote 3-132: Ltr, Granger to SecNav, 19 Mar 45; Ltrs, SecNav to Granger, 26 Mar and 5 Apr 45. All in 54-1-13, Forrestal file, GenRecsNav. The activities of the intradepartmental committee will be discussed in Chapter 5.(Back)

Footnote 3-133: Ltr, Forrestal to Marshall Field III (publisher of *PM*), 14 Jul 45, 54-1-13, Forrestal file, GenRecsNav.(Back)

Footnote 3-134: Memo, SecNav for Rear Adm W. J. C. Agnew, Asst Surg Gen, 28 Jan 45; Memo, Surg Gen for Eugene Duffield, 19 Mar 45; both in 54-1-3, Forrestal file, GenRecsNav. By V-J day the Navy had four black nurses on active duty.(Back)

Footnote 3-135: Ltr, Chief, NavPers, to Cmdts, All Naval Districts, 11 Jun 45, sub: Negro Recruit Training—Discontinuance of Special Program and Camps for, P16-3/MM, BuPersRecs.(Back)

Footnote 3-136: Memo, SecNav for Artemus L. Gates, Asst Sec for Air, et al. 16 Jul 45; Ltr, SecNav to Granger, 14 Jul 45; both in 54-1-20, GenRecsNav.(Back)

Footnote 3-137: Ltr, Granger to Forrestal, 4 Aug 45, 54-1-13, GenRecsNav.(Back)

Footnote 3-138: Pers 215-BL, "Enlisted Strength—U.S. Navy," 26 Jul 46, BuPersRecs.(Back)

Footnote 3-139: Pers 215-12-EL, "Number of Negro Enlisted Personnel on Active Duty," 29 Nov 45 (statistics as of 31 Oct 45), BuPersRecs.(Back)

Footnote 3-140: Pers-215-BL, "Enlisted Strength—U.S. Navy," 26 Jul 46.(Back)

Footnote 4-1: 38 *U.S. Stat. at L* (1915), 800-2. Since 1967 the Coast Guard has been a part of the Department of Transportation.(Back)

Footnote 4-2: Executive Order 8928, 1 Nov 41. A similar transfer under provisions of the 1915 law was effected during World War I. The service's predecessor organizations, the Revenue Marine, Revenue Service, Revenue-Marine Service, and the Revenue Cutter Service, had also provided the Navy with certain specified ships and men during all wars since the Revolution.(Back)

Footnote 4-3: Ltr, SecNav to CominCh-CNO, 30 Mar 42, sub: Administration of Coast Guard When Operating Under Navy Department, quoted in Furer, *Administration of the Navy Department in World War II*, pp. 608-10.(Back)

Footnote 4-4: For a survey of the organization and functions of the U.S. Coast Guard Personnel Division, see USCG Historical Section, *Personnel*, The Coast Guard at War, 25:16-27.(Back)

Footnote 4-5: Quoted in Navy General Board, "Plan for the Expansion of the USMC," 18 Apr 41 (No. 139), Recs of Gen Bd, OpNavArchives.(Back)

Footnote 4-6: Ltr, CMC to Harold E. Thompson, Northern Phila. Voters League, 6 Aug 40, AQ-17, Central Files, Headquarters, USMC (hereafter MC files).(Back)

Footnote 4-7: Memo, Off in Charge, Eastern Recruiting Div, for CMC, 16 Jan 42, sub: Colored Applicants for Enlistment in the Marine Corps, WP 11991, MC files.(Back)

Footnote 4-8: Memo, SecNav for Adm W. R. Sexton, 14 Feb 42, P14-4, Recs of Gen Bd, OpNavArchives. The quotation is from the Knox Memo and is not necessarily in the President's exact words.(Back)

Footnote 4-9: In devising plans for the composite battalion the Director of Plans and Policies rejected a proposal to organize a black raider battalion. The author of the proposal had explained that Negroes would make ideal night raiders "as no camouflage of faces and hands would be necessary." Memo, Col Thomas Gale for Exec Off, Div of Plans and Policies, 19 Feb 42, AO-250, MC files.(Back)

Footnote 4-10: Memo, CMC for Chmn of Gen Bd, 27 Feb 42, sub: Enlistment of Men of the Colored Race in Other Than Messman Branch, AO-172, MC files.(Back)

Footnote 4-11: Memo, Chmn of Gen Bd for SecNav, 20 Mar 42, sub: Enlistment of Men of the Colored Race in Other Than Messman Branch (G.B. No. 421), Recs of Gen Bd, OpNavArchives.(Back)

Footnote 4-12: Memo, CMC for District Cmdrs, All Reserve Districts Except 10th, 14th, 15th, and 16th, 25 May 42, sub: Enlistment of Colored Personnel in the Marine Corps, Historical and Museum Division, Headquarters, U.S. Marine Corps (hereafter Hist Div, HQMC). For further discussion of the training of black marines and other matters pertaining to Negroes in the Marine Corps, see Shaw and Donnelly, *Blacks in the Marine Corps*. This volume by the corps' chief historian and the former chief of its history division's reference branch is the official account.(Back)

Footnote 4-13: Memo, CMC for Off in Charge, Eastern, Central, and Southern Recruiting Divs, 15 May 42, sub: Enlistment of Colored Personnel in the Marine Corps, AP-54 (1535), MC files. The country was divided into four recruiting divisions, but black enlistment was not opened in the west coast division on the theory that there would be few volunteers and sending them to North Carolina would be unjustifiably expensive. Only white marines were trained in California. This circumstance brought complaints from civil rights groups. See, for example, Telg, Walter White to SecNav, 14 Jul 42, AP-361, MC files.(Back)

Footnote 4-14: Memo, CMC for SecNav, 23 Jun 42, AP-54 (1535-110), MC files.(Back)

Footnote 4-15: Memo, Dir, Div of Plans and Policies, for CMC, 29 Oct 42, sub: Enlistment of Colored Personnel in the Marine Corps Reserve, AO-320, MC files.(Back)

Footnote 4-16: USMC Oral History Interview, General Ray A. Robinson (USMC Ret.), 18-19 Mar 68, p. 136, Hist Div, HQMC.(Back)

Footnote 4-17: Memo, CMC for Chief, NavPers, 1 Apr 43, sub: Negro Registrants To Be Inducted Into the Marine Corps, AO-320-2350-60, MC files.(Back)

Footnote 4-18: Memo, Dir, Pers, for Dir, Div of Plans and Policies, 21 Jul 48, sub: GCT Percentile Equivalents for Colored Enlisted Marines in November 1945 and in March 1948, sub file: Negro Marines—Test and Testing, Ref Br, Hist Div, HQMC.(Back)

Footnote 4-19: Unsigned Memo for Dir, Plans and Policies Div, 26 Dec 42, sub: Colored Personnel, with attached handwritten note, AO-320, MC files.(Back)

Footnote 4-20: Ltr, Actg CMC to Major Cmdrs, 20 Mar 43, sub: Colored Personnel, AP-361, MC files.(Back)

Footnote 4-21: Ltr of Instruction No. 421, CMC to All CO's, 14 May 43, sub: Colored Personnel, MC files.(Back)

Footnote 4-22: Ibid. The subject of widespread public complaint when its existence became known after the war, the instruction was rescinded. See Memo, J. A. Stuart, Div of Plans and Policies, for CMC, 14 Feb 46, sub: Ltr of Inst #421 Revocation of, AO-1, copy in Ref Br, Hist Div, HQMC.(Back)

Footnote 4-23: Memo, CMC for SecNav, 30 Dec 42, sub: Change of Present Mess Branch in the Marine Corps to Commissary Branch and Establishment of a Messman's Branch and Ranks Therein, with SecNav approval indicated, AO-363-341. See also Memo, CMC for Chief, NavPers, 30 Dec 42, sub: Request for Allotment to MC..., A-363; Memo, Dir, Div of Plans and Policies, for CMC, 23 Nov 42, sub: Organization of Mess Branch (Colored), AO-283. All in MC files.(Back)

Footnote 4-24: Memo, Dir of Recruiting for Off in Charge, Eastern Recruiting Div et al., 25 Feb 42, sub: Messman Branch, AP-361-1390; Memo, CMC for SecNav, 3 Apr 43, sub: Change in Designation..., AO-340-1930. Both in MC files.(Back)

Footnote 4-25: Memo, Dir, Plans and Policies, for CMC, 18 May 43, sub: Assignment of Steward's Branch Personnel, AO-371, MC files.(Back)

Footnote 4-26: Memo, H. E. Dunkelberger, M-1 Sec, Div of Plans and Policies, for Asst CMC, 5 Jul 44, sub: Steward's Branch Personnel, AO-660, MC files.(Back)

Footnote 4-27: Shaw and Donnelly, *Blacks in the Marine Corps*, pp. 29-46. See also, HQMC Div of Public Information, "The Negro Marine, 1942-1945," Ref Br, Hist Div, HQMC.(Back)

Footnote 4-28: Memo, CO, 51st Def Bn, for Dir, Plans and Policies, 29 Jan 43, sub: Colored Personnel, Ref Br, Hist Div, HQMC.(Back)

Footnote 4-29: For charges and countercharges on the part of the 51st's commanders, see Hq, 51st Defense Bn, "Record of Proceedings of an Investigation," 27 Jun 44; Memo, Lt Col Floyd A. Stephenson for CMC, 30 May 44, sub: Fifty-First Defense Battalion, Fleet Marine Force, with indorsements and attachments; Memo, CO, 51st Def Bn, for CMC, 20 Jul 44, sub: Combat Efficiency, Fifty-First Defense Battalion. All in Ref Br, Hist Div, HQMC.(Back)

Footnote 4-30: Shaw and Donnelly, *Blacks in the Marine Corps*, p. 31.(Back)

Footnote 4-31: For a discussion of black morale in the combat-trained units, see USMC Oral History Interview, Obie Hall, 16 Aug 72, Ref Br, and John H. Griffin, "My Life in the Marine Corps," Personal Papers Collection, Museums Br. Both in Hist Div, HQMC.(Back)

Footnote 4-32: Ltr, Maj Gen Charles F. B. Price to Brig Gen Keller E. Rockey, 24 Apr 43; 26132, Ref Br, Hist Div, HQMC.(Back)

Footnote 4-33: Brig Gen Rockey for S-C files, 4 Jun 43, Memo, G. F. Good, Div of Plans and Policies, to Dir, Div of Plans and Policies, 3 Sep 43. Both attached to Price Ltr, see n. 32 above.(Back)

Footnote 4-34: Ltr, Phillips D. Carleton, Asst to Dir, MC Reserve, to Welford Wilson, U.S. Employment Service, 27 Mar 43, AF-464, MC files. For more on black officers in the Marine Corps, see Chapter 9.(Back)

Footnote 4-35: See, for example, Ltr, Mary Findley Allen, Interracial Cmte of Federation of Churches, to Mrs. Roosevelt (ca. 9 Mar 43); Memo, SecNav for Rear Adm Jacobs, 22 Mar 43, P-25; Memo, R. C. Kilmartin, Jr., Div of Plans and Policies, for Dir, Div of Plans and Policies, 25 Sep 43, AO-434. All in Hist Div, HQMC.(Back)

Footnote 4-36: Capt. Michael Healy, who was of Irish and Afro-American heritage, served as commanding officer of the *Bear* and other major Coast Guard vessels. At his retirement in 1903 Healy was the third ranking officer in the U.S. Revenue Cutter Service. See Robert E. Greene, *Black Defenders of America, 1775-1973* (Chicago: Johnson Publishing Company, 1974), p. 139. For pre-World War II service of Negroes in the Coast Guard, see Truman R. Strobridge, *Blacks and Lights: A Brief Historical Survey of Blacks and the Old U.S. Lighthouse Service* (Office of the USCG Historian, 1975); H. Kaplan and J. Hunt, *This Is the United States Coast Guard* (Cambridge, Md.: Cornell Maritime Press, 1971); Rodney H. Benson, "Romance and Story of Pea Island Station," *U.S. Coast Guard Magazine* (November 1932):52; George Reasons and Sam Patrick, "Richard Etheridge—Saved Sailors," Washington *Star*, November 13, 1971. For the position of Negroes on the eve of World War II induction, see Enlistment of Men of Colored Race (201), 23 Jan 42, Hearings Before the General Board of the Navy, 1942.(Back)

Footnote 4-37: Interv, author with Capt W. C. Capron, USCGR, 20 Feb 75, CMH files.(Back)

Footnote 4-38: Enlistment of Men of Colored Race (201), 23 Jan 42, Hearings Before the General Board of the Navy, 1942.(Back)

Footnote 4-39: Memo, Cmdt, CG, for Adm Sexton, Chmn of Gen Bd, 2 Feb 42, sub: Enlistment of Men of the Colored Race in Other Than Messman Branch, attached to Enlistment of Men of Colored Race (201), 23 Jan 42, Hearings Before the General Board of the Navy, 1942.(Back)

Footnote 4-40: Memo, Cmdt, CG, for Chmn of Gen Bd, 24 Feb 42. sub: Enlistment of Men of the Colored Race in Other Than Messman Branch, P-701, attached to Recs of Gen Bd, No 421 (Serial 204-X), OpNavArchives.(Back)

Footnote 4-41: Unless otherwise noted, all statistics on Coast Guard personnel are derived from Memo, Chief, Statistical Services Div, for Chief, Pub Information Div, 30 Mar 54, sub: Negro Personnel, Officers and Enlisted; Number of, Office of the USCG Historian; and "Coast Guard Personnel Growth Chart," *Report of the Secretary of the Navy-Fiscal 1945*, p. A-15.(Back)

Footnote 4-42: Memo, Chmn of Gen Bd for SecNav, 20 Mar 42, sub: Enlistment of Men of the Colored Race in Other Than Messman Branch, G.B. No. 421 (Serial 204), OpNavArchives.(Back)

Footnote 4-43: Interv, author with Ira H. Coakley, 26 Feb 75, CMH files. Coakley was a recruit in one of the first black training companies at Manhattan Beach.(Back)

Footnote 4-44: For a brief account of the Coast Guard recruit training program, see Nelson, "Integration of the Negro," pp. 84-87, and "A Black History in World War II," *Octagon*(February 1972): 31-32.(Back)

Footnote 4-45: Log of Pea Island Station, 1942, Berry Collection, USCG Headquarters.(Back)

Footnote 4-46: Selective Service System, *Special Groups*, 2:196-201.(Back)

Footnote 4-47: Testimony of Coast Guard Representatives Before the President's Committee on Equality of Treatment and Opportunity in the Armed Services, 18 Mar 49, p. 8.(Back)

Footnote 4-48: USCG Public Relations Div, Negroes in the U.S. Coast Guard, July 1943, Office of the USCG Historian.(Back)

Footnote 4-49: Ltr, Cmdt, USCG, to Cmdr, Third CG District, 18 Jan 52, sub: ETHERIDGE, Louis C; ... Award of the Bronze Star Medal, P15, BuPersRecs; USCG Pub Rel Div, Negroes in the U.S. Coast Guard, Jul 43.(Back)

Footnote 4-50: USCG Pers Bull 37-42, 31 Mar 43, sub: Apprentice Seamen and Mess Attendants, Third Class, Advancement of, USCG Cen Files 61A701.(Back)

Footnote 4-51: Intervs, author with Cmdt Carlton Skinner, USCGR, 18 Feb 75, and with Capron, CMH files.(Back)

Footnote 4-52: For discussion of limited service of Coast Guard stewards, see Testimony of Coast Guard Representatives Before the President's Committee on Equality of Treatment and Opportunity in the Armed Services, 18 Mar 49, pp. 27-31.(Back)

Footnote 4-53: USCG Historical Section, The Coast Guard at War, 18:1-10, 36.(Back)

Footnote 4-54: USCG Pers Bull 44-42, 25 Jun 42, sub: Relief of Personnel Assigned to Seagoing Units, USCG Cen Files 61A701.(Back)

Footnote 4-55: Interv, author with Skinner; Ltr, Skinner to author, 29 Jun 75, in CMH files. The Skinner memorandum to Admiral Waesche, like so many of the personnel policy papers of the U.S. Coast Guard from the World War II period, cannot be located. For a detailed discussion of Skinner's motives and experiences, see his testimony before the President's Committee on Equality of Treatment and Opportunity in the Armed Services, 25 Apr 49, pp. 1-24.(Back)

Footnote 4-56: A unique vessel, the *Sea Cloud* was on loan to the government for the duration of the war by its owner, the former Ambassador to Russia, Joseph Davies. Davies charged a nominal sum and extracted the promise that the vessel would be restored to its prewar condition as one of the world's most famous private yachts.(Back)

Footnote 4-57: Interv, author with Skinner.(Back)

Footnote 4-58: Log of the *Sea Cloud* (IX 99), Aug-Nov 44, NARS, Suitland.(Back)

Footnote 4-59: Interv, author with Skinner.(Back)

Footnote 4-60: Interv, author with Rear Adm R. T. McElligott, 24 Feb 75, CMH files. For an example of the Coast Guard reaction to civil rights criticism, see Ltr, USCG Public Relations Officer to Douglas Hall, Washington *Afro-American*, July 12, 1943, CG 051, Office of the USCG Historian.(Back)

Footnote 4-61: Ltr, Skinner to author, 2 Jun 75.(Back)

Footnote 4-62: USCG Historical Section, The Coast Guard at War, 23:53; Intervs, author with Lt Harvey C. Russell, USCGR, 14 Feb 75, and with Capron, CMH files.(Back)

Footnote 4-63: "A Black History in WWII," pp. 31-34. For an account of Samuels' long career in the Coast Guard, see Joseph Greco and Truman R. Strobridge, "Black Trailblazer Has Colorful Past," *Fifth Dimension* (3d Quarter, 1973); see also Interv, author with Russell.(Back)

Footnote 4-64: USCG Historical Section, The Coast Guard at War, 25:25. See also Oral History Interview, Dorothy C. Stratton, 24 Sep 70, Center of Naval History.(Back)

Footnote 4-65: For discussion of this point, see Testimony of Coast Guard Representatives Before the President's Committee on Equality of Treatment and Opportunity in the Armed Services, 18 Mar 49, pp. 25-26.(Back)

Footnote 5-1: This discussion is based in great part on Arnold M. Rose, "The American Negro Problem in the Context of Social Change," *Annals of the Academy of Political Science* 257 (January 1965):1-17; Rustin, *Strategies for Freedom*, pp. 26-46; Leonard Broom and Norval Glenn, *Transformation of the Negro American* (New York: Harper and Row, 1965); St. Clair Drake and Horace Cayton, *Black Metropolis: A Study of Negro Life in a Northern City* (New York: Harcourt Brace, 1970); John Hope Franklin, *From Slavery to Freedom: A History of Negro America*, 3d ed. (New York: Knopf, 1967); Woodward's *The Strange Career of Jim Crow*; Seymour Wolfbein, "Postwar Trends in Negro Employment," a report by the Occupational Outlook Division, Bureau of Labor Statistics, in CMH; Oscar Handlin, "The Goals of Integration," and Kenneth B. Clark, "The Civil Rights Movement: Momentum and Organization," both in *Daedalus* 95 (Winter 1966).(Back)

Footnote 5-2: For a discussion of this trend, see Bureau of Labor Statistics, "Social and Economic Conditions of Negroes in the United States" (Current Population Reports P23, October 1967); see also Charles S. Johnson, "The Negro Minority," *Annals of the Academy of Political Science* 223 (September 1942):10-16.(Back)

Footnote 5-3: Selective Service System, *Special Groups*, vol. I, pp. 177-78; see also Robert C. Weaver, "Negro Labor Since 1929," *The Journal of Negro History* 35 (January 1950):20-38.(Back)

Footnote 5-4: E. Franklin Frazier, *The Negro in the United States* (New York: Macmillan, 1957), p. 513.(Back)

Footnote 5-5: Clark, "The Civil Rights Movement," pp. 240-47.(Back)

Footnote 5-6: *Report of the National Advisory Commission on Civil Disorders, 1 March 1968*, Kerner Report (Washington: Government Printing Office, 1968), pp. 104-05; see also Dalfiume, *Desegregation of the U.S. Armed Forces*, pp. 132-34. For a detailed account of the major riot, see R. Shogan and T. Craig, *The Detroit Race Riot: A Study in Violence* (New York: Chilton Books, 1964).(Back)

337

Footnote 5-7: Bernard De Voto, "The Easy Chair" *Harper's* 192 (January 1946):38-39.(Back)

Footnote 5-8: Ltr, John H. Caldwell (Hartsdale, New York) to the Editor, *Harper's* 192 (March 1946): unnumbered front pages.(Back)

Footnote 5-9: Ltr, Sen. W. Lee O'Daniel of Texas to SW, 27 Feb 46, ASW 291.2 (1946).(Back)

Footnote 5-10: This important incident in the Air Force's racial history has been well documented. See AAF Summary Sheet, 5 May 45, sub: Racial Incidents at Freeman Field and Ft. Huachuca, Arizona, and Memo, Maj Gen H. R. Harmon, ACofS, AAF, for DCofS, 29 May 45, both in WDGAP 291.2. See also Memo, The Inspector General for DCofS, 1 May 45, sub: Investigation at Freeman Field, WDSIG 291.2 Freeman Field, and Memo, Truman Gibson for ASW, 14 May 45, ASW 291.2 NT. For a critical contemporary analysis, see Hq Air Defense Command, "The Training of Negro Combat Units by the First Air Force" (Monograph III, May 1946), vol. 1; ch. III, AFSHRC. The incident is also discussed in Osur, *Blacks in the Army Air Forces During World War II*, ch. VI, and in Alan L. Gropman's *The Air Force Integrates, 1943-1964* (Washington: Government Printing Office, 1978). Gropman's work is the major source for the history of Negroes in the postwar Air Force.(Back)

Footnote 5-11: Memo, ASW for SW, 4 Jun 45; Memo, SGS for DCofS, 7 Jun 45, sub: Report of Advisory Committee on Special Troop Policies, both in ASW 291.2 (NT).(Back)

Footnote 5-12: OPD Summary Sheet to CofS, 2 Apr 46, CS 291.2 Negroes; Memo, WD Bureau of Public Relations for Press, 5 Jan 46; Ltr, Exec to Actg ASW to P. Bernard Young, Jr., Norfolk *Journal and Guide*, 14 Dec 45, ASW 291.2.(Back)

Footnote 5-13: ALNAV 423-45, 12 Dec 45.(Back)

Footnote 5-14: Memo, Marcus H. Ray, Civ Aide to SW, for ASW, 11 Jun 46, ASW 291.2 (NT).(Back)

Footnote 5-15: See Ltr, Walter White, Secy, NAACP, to SW, 6 May 46, and a host of letters in SW 291.2 file. See also copies of NAACP press releases on the subject in CMH files.(Back)

Footnote 5-16: Ltr, 28 Feb 46, copy in SW 291.2.(Back)

Footnote 5-17: For a summary of these views, see Warman Welliver, "Report on the Negro Soldier," *Harper's* 192 (April 1946):333-38 and back pages.(Back)

Footnote 5-18: Murray, *Negro Handbook, 1946-1947*, pp. 369-70.(Back)

Footnote 5-19: Ltr, Exec Secy, National Urban League, to President Truman, 27 Aug 45, copy in Forrestal file, GenRecsNav.(Back)

Footnote 5-20: Memos, McCloy for Advisory Committee on Special Troop Policies, 31 Jul and 1 Sep 44, sub: Participation of Negro Troops in the Post-War Military Establishment; Memo, ASW for SW, 10 Jan 46, same sub, all in ASW 291.2 (NT).(Back)

Footnote 5-21: Ltr, John J. McCloy to author, 18 Sep 69, CMH files.(Back)

Footnote 5-22: Memo, CofS for McCloy, 25 Aug 45, WDCSA 291.2 Negroes (25 Aug 45).(Back)

Footnote 5-23: Ltr, TAG to CinC, Southwest Pacific Area, et al., 23 May 45, sub: Participation of Negro Troops in Post-War Military Establishment, AG 291.2 (23 May 45). On the high-level discussions, see Memo, Maj Gen W. F. Tompkins, Dir, Special Planning Div, for ACofS, G-1, and Personnel Officers of the Air, Ground, and Service Forces, 24 Feb 45, same sub; DF, G-1, WDGS (Col O. G. Haywood, Exec), 8 Mar 45, same sub; Memo, Col G. E. Textor, Dep Dir, WDSSP, for ACofS, G-1, 10 Mar 45, same sub; Memo for the File (Col Lawrence Westbrook), 16 Mar 45; Memo, Maj Bell I. Wiley for Col Mathews, 18 Apr 45, all in AG 291.2.(Back)

Footnote 5-24: Memo, Gibson for ASW, 30 May 45, ASW 291.2 (NT).(Back)

Footnote 5-25: Ltr, Gibson to Gen John C. H. Lee, CG, ComZ, ETOUSA, 31 Mar 45, ASW 291.2 (NT).(Back)

Footnote 5-26: Memo, Truman Gibson for Maj Gen O. L. Nelson, 12 Mar 45, sub: Report on Visit to 92d Division (Negro Troops), ASW 291.2.(Back)

Footnote 5-27: "Negro Soldier Betrayed," *Crisis* 52 (April 1945):97; "Gibson Echo," ibid. (July 1945):193.(Back)

Footnote 5-28: Washington *Afro-American*, April 15, 1945, quoted in Lee, *Employment of Negro Troops*, p. 579. For details of the Gibson controversy, see Lee, pp. 575-79.(Back)

Footnote 5-29: Mark W. Clark, *A Calculated Risk* (New York: Harper & Brothers, 1950), pp. 414-15.(Back)

Footnote 5-30: Ltr, Ray to Gibson, 14 May 45, WDGAP 291.2. Ray later succeeded Gibson as Civilian Aide to the Secretary of War.(Back)

338

Footnote 5-31: 1st Ind, Hq Fifth Army (signed L. K. Truscott, Jr.), 30 Jul 45, to Proceedings and Board of Review, 92d Inf Div, Fifth Army files.(Back)

Footnote 5-32: WD file 291.2 (Negro Troop Policy), 1943-1945, is full of statements to this effect. The quote is from 2d Ind, Hq USASTAF, 26 Jul 45, attached to AAF Summary Sheets to CofS, 17 Sep 45, sub: Participation of Negro Troops in the Post-War Military Establishment, AG 291.2 (23 May 45).(Back)

Footnote 5-33: L. K. Truscott, Jr., *Command Missions: A Personal Story* (New York: Dutton, 1959), see pages 461-62 and 471-72 for comparison of Truscott's critical analysis of problems of the 34th and 92d Infantry Divisions.(Back)

Footnote 5-34: Interv, author with General Jacob Devers, 30 Mar 71, CMH files.(Back)

Footnote 5-35: Ltr, Lt Gen Edward M. Almond to Brig Gen James L. Collins, Jr., 1 Apr 72, CMH files. General Almond's views are thoroughly explored in Paul Goodman, *A Fragment of Victory* (Army War College, 1952). For an objective and detailed treatment of the 92d Division, see Lee, *Employment of Negro Troops*, Chapter XIX, and Ernest F. Fisher, Jr., *Cassino to the Alps*, United States Army in World War II (Washington: Government Printing Office, 1977), Chapter XXIII.(Back)

Footnote 5-36: A third black division, the 2d Cavalry, never saw combat because it was disbanded upon arrival in the Mediterranean theater.(Back)

Footnote 5-37: Rad, Marshall to Lt Gen Millard Harmon, CG, USAFISPA, 18 Mar 44, CM-OUT 7514 (18 Mar 44).(Back)

Footnote 5-38: Lee, *Employment of Negro Troops*, pp. 498-517. Lee discusses here the record of the 93d Infantry Division and War Department decisions concerning its use.(Back)

Footnote 5-39: The above digested reports and quotations are from Lee, *Employment of Negro Troops*, pp. 513-17.(Back)

Footnote 5-40: USAFFE Board Reports No. 185, 20 Jan 45, and 221, 25 Feb 45, sub: Information on Colored Troops. These reports were prepared at the behest of the commanding general of the Army Ground Forces during the preparation of Bell I. Wiley's *The Training of Negro Troops* (AGF Study No. 36, 1946). The quotation is from Exhibit K of USAFFE Board Report No. 221.(Back)

Footnote 5-41: E. W. Kenworthy, "The Case Against Army Segregation," *Annals of the American Academy of Political Science* 275 (May 1952):28-29. A low decoration to casualty ratio is traditionally used as one measure of good unit performance. However, so many different unit attitudes and standards for decorations existed during World War II that any argument over ratios can only be self-defeating no matter what the approach.(Back)

Footnote 5-42: Memo, Gibson for ASW, 23 Apr 45, sub: Report of Visit to MTO and ETO, ASW 291.2 (NT); see also Interv, Bell I. Wiley with Truman K. Gibson, Civilian Aide to Secretary of War, 30 May 45, CMH files.(Back)

Footnote 5-43: Eventually over thirty-five commands responded to the McCloy questionnaire. For examples of the attitudes mentioned above, see Ltr, HQ, U.S. Forces, European Theater (Main) to TAG, 1 Oct 45, sub: Study of Participation of Negro Troops in the Postwar Establishment; Ltr, HQ, U.S. Forces, India, Burma Theater, to TAG, 28 Aug 45, same sub; Ltr, GHQ USARPAC to TAG, 3 Sep 45, same sub. All in AG 291.2 (23 May 45). Some of these and many others are also located in WDSSP 291.2 (1945).(Back)

Footnote 5-44: Memo, Dir, WDSSP, for CG's, ASF et al., 23 May 45, sub: Participation of Negro Troops in the Postwar Military Establishment, AG 291.2 (23 May 45).(Back)

Footnote 5-45: Memo, CofS, ASF, for Dir, Special Planning Division, WDSS, 1 Oct 45, sub: Participation of Negro Troops in the Postwar Military Establishment, WDSSP 291.2 (2 Oct 45). On the use of Negroes in the Signal Corps, see the following volumes in the United States Army in World War II series: Dulany Terrett, *The Signal Corps: The Emergency*(Washington: Government Printing Office, 1956); George Raynor Thompson et al., *The Signal Corps: The Test* (Washington: Government Printing Office, 1957); George Raynor Thompson and Dixie R. Harris, *The Signal Corps: The Outcome* (Washington: Government Printing Office, 1966).(Back)

Footnote 5-46: Memo, Ground AG, AGF, for CofSA, 28 Nov 45, sub: Participation of Negro Troops in the Postwar Military Establishment, with Incl, WDSSP 291.2 (27 Dec 45).(Back)

Footnote 5-47: Memo, CG, AAF, for CofSA, 17 Sep 45, sub: Participation of Negro Troops in the Postwar Military Establishment, WDSSP 291.2 (1945). For the final report of 2 Oct 45, which summed up the previous recommendations, see Summary Sheet, AC/AS-1 for Maj Gen C. C. Chauncey, DCofAS, 2 Oct 45, same sub and file.(Back)

Footnote 5-48: Ltr, OCSigO (Col David E. Washburn, Exec Off) to WDSSP, 31 Jul 45, sub: Participation of Negro Troops in the Postwar Military Establishment, WDSSP 291.2 (1945).(Back)

Footnote 5-49: Ltr, Maj Gen James L. Collins, CG, Fifth Service Cmd, to CG, ASF, 24 Jul 45, sub: Participation of Negro Troops in the Postwar Military Establishment, WDSSP 291.2.(Back)

Footnote 5-50: Memo, CG, First Service Cmd, for CG, ASF, 23 Jul 45, sub: Participation of Negro Troops in the Postwar Military Establishment, WDSSP 291.2 (1945).(Back)

Footnote 5-51: Memo, Truman Gibson for ASW, 8 Aug 45, ASW 291.2.(Back)

Footnote 5-52: Memo, Exec Off, ASW, for McCloy, 28 Aug 45, ASW 291.2 (NT).(Back)

Footnote 5-53: Memos, Col Frederick S. Skinner for Dir, Special Planning Div, WDSS, 25 May and 2 Jun 45, sub: Participation of Negro Troops in the Postwar Military Establishment, WDSSP 291.2 (1945).(Back)

Footnote 5-54: Ltr, Forrestal to Field, 14 Jul 45, 54-1-13, Forrestal file, GenRecsNav.(Back)

Footnote 5-55: Ltr, Lester Granger to SecNav, 19 Mar 45, 54-1-13, Forrestal file, GenRecsNav.(Back)

Footnote 5-56: Memo, Chief, NavPers, for Cmdr Richard M. Paget (Exec Off, SecNav), 21 Apr 45, sub: Formation of Informal Cmte to Assure Uniform Policies on the Handling of Negro Personnel, P-17, BuPersRecs.(Back)

Footnote 5-57: Memo, SecNav for Cmdr Richard M. Paget, 16 Apr 45, 54-1-19, Forrestal file, GenRecsNav.(Back)

Footnote 5-58: Other members of the committee included four senior Navy captains and representatives of the Marine Corps and Coast Guard. Memo, SecNav for Under SecNav, 25 Apr 45, QB495/A3-1, GenRecsNav.(Back)

Footnote 5-59: Ltr, Granger to SecNav, 19 Mar 45, 54-1-13, Forrestal file, GenRecsNav.(Back)

Footnote 5-60: Memo, Cmte on Personnel for Under SecNav, 22 May 45, sub: Report and Recommendations of Committee on Negro Personnel, P. 16-3, GenRecsNav.(Back)

Footnote 5-61: Columbia University Oral Hist Interv with Granger.(Back)

Footnote 5-62: Granger's findings and an account of his inspection technique are located in Ltrs, Granger to SecNav, 4 Aug, 10 Aug, 27 Aug, and 31 Oct 45; and in "Minutes of Press Conference Held by Mr. Lester B. Granger," 1 Nov 45. All in 54-1-13, Forrestal file, GenRecsNav. See also Columbia University Oral Hist Interv with Granger.(Back)

Footnote 5-63: Memo, J.F. [James Forrestal] for Vice Adm Jacobs (Chief of Naval Personnel), 23 Aug 45; Ltr, SecNav to Granger, 29 Dec 45, both in 54-1-13, Forrestal file, GenRecsNav.(Back)

Footnote 6-1: Memo, McCloy for SW, 17 Sep 45, SW 291.2; Ltr, McCloy to author, 25 Sep 69, CMH files.(Back)

Footnote 6-2: See, for example, Memo, SW for CofS, 7 Nov 45, SW 291.2; see also Ltr, McCloy to author, 25 Sep 69.(Back)

Footnote 6-3: Quoted in Memo, Gen Gillem for CofS, 17 Nov 45, sub: Report of Board of General Officers on Utilization of Negro Manpower in the Post-War Army, copy in CSGOT 291.2 (1945) BP.(Back)

Footnote 6-4: Interv, Capt Alan Osur, USAF, with Lt Gen Alvan C. Gillem (USA Ret.), 3 Feb 72, copy in CMH.(Back)

Footnote 6-5: Memo, Maj Gen Ray Porter, Dir, Spec Planning Div, for Gillem, 28 Sep 45, sub: War Department Special Board on Negro Manpower, WDCSA 320.2.(Back)

Footnote 6-6: In a later comment on the selections, McCloy said that the geographical spread and lack of West Point representation was accidental and that the use of general officers reflected the importance of the subject to him and to Patterson. See Ltr, McCloy to author, 25 Sep 69, and Ltr, Gen Morse to author, 10 Sep 74, CMH files.(Back)

Footnote 6-7: Memo, Gen Gillem for CofS, 26 Oct 45, sub: Progress Rpt on Board Study of Utilization of Negro Manpower in the Post-War Army, WDCSA 291.2; see also Interv, Osur with Gillem.(Back)

Footnote 6-8: Memo, Gillem for CofS, 17 Nov 45, sub: Report of Board of General Officers on the Utilization of Negro Manpower in the Post-War Army. Unless otherwise noted this section is based on the report.(Back)

Footnote 6-9: The 10 percent quota that eventually emerged from the Gillem Board was an approximation; Gillem later recalled that the World War II enlisted ratio was nearer 9.5 percent, but that General Eisenhower, the Chief of Staff, saying he could not remember that, suggested making it "an even 10 percent." See Interv, Osur with Gillem.(Back)

Footnote 6-10: Memo, Brig Gen H. I. Hodes, ADCofS, for Gillem, 24 Nov 45, sub: War Department Special Board on Negro Management, WDCSA 320.2 (17 Nov 45).(Back)

340

Footnote 6-11: Memo, Civilian Aide for ASW, 13 Nov 45, ASW 291.2 Negro Troops (Post War); Ltr, idem to SW, 13 Nov 45; Memo, McCloy for Patterson, 24 Nov 45; Memo, Gibson for SW, 28 Nov 45. Last three in SW 291.2. The Gibson quote is from the 28 November memo.(Back)

Footnote 6-12: For examples of this extensive review of the Gillem Board Report in G-1, see the following Memos: Col J. F. Cassidy (Exec Office, G-1) for Col Parks, 10 Dec 45; Chief, Officer Branch, G-1, for Exec Off, G-1 Policy Group, 14 Dec 45; Actg Chief, Req and Res Br, for Chief, Policy Control Group, 14 Dec 45; Lt Col E. B. Jones, Special Projects Br, for G-1, 19 and 21 Dec 45, sub: Policy for Utilization of Negro Manpower in Post-War Army. All in WDGAP 291.2.(Back)

Footnote 6-13: Memo, Gen Paul, G-1, for CofS, 27 Dec 45, sub: Policy for Utilization of Negro Manpower in Post-War Army, WDGAP 291.2 (24 Nov 45).(Back)

Footnote 6-14: G-3 Summary Sheet to ADCofS, 2 Jan 46, sub: War Department Special Board on Negro Manpower, WDGCT 291.21 (24 Nov 45).(Back)

Footnote 6-15: Memo, Lt Gen John E. Hull, ACofS, OPD (signed Brig Gen E. D. Post, Dep Chief, Theater Gp, OPD), for ACofS, G-3, 4 Jan 46, sub: War Department Special Board on Negro Manpower, WDGCT 291.21.(Back)

Footnote 6-16: 1st Ind, Lt Gen Ira C. Eaker, Deputy Cmdr, AAF, to CofS, 19 Dec 45, sub: War Department Special Board on Negro Manpower, copy at Tab H, Supplemental Report of Board of Officers on Utilization of Negro Manpower in the Post-War Army, 26 Jan 46, copy in CMH.(Back)

Footnote 6-17: Memo, Lt Col S. R. Knight (for CG, AGF) for CofS, 18 Dec 45, sub: Army Ground Forces Comments and Recommendations on Report of the War Department Special Board (Gillem) on Negro Manpower, dated 17 Nov 45, GNGPS 370.01 (18 Dec 45); AGF Study, "Participation of Negro Troops in the Postwar Military Establishment," 28 Nov 45, forwarded to CofS, ATTN: Dir, WD Special Planning Div, GNDCG 370.01 (28 Nov 45).(Back)

Footnote 6-18: Memo, Maj Gen Daniel Noce, Actg CofS, ASF, for CofS, 28 Dec 45, sub: War Department Special Board on Negro Manpower, copy at Tab J, Supplemental Report of War Department Special Board on Negro Manpower, 26 Jan 46, CMH files.(Back)

Footnote 6-19: Supplemental Report of War Department Special Board on Negro Manpower, "Policy for Utilization of Negro Manpower in the Post-War Army," 26 Jan 46. The following quotations are taken from this amended version of the Gillem Board Report, a copy of which, with all tabs and annexes, is in CMH.(Back)

Footnote 6-20: Eisenhower succeeded Marshall as Chief of Staff on 19 November 1945.(Back)

Footnote 6-21: Memo, CofS for SW, 1 Feb 46, sub: Supplemental Report of Board of Officers on Utilization of Negro Manpower in the Post-War Army, WDCSA 320.2 (1 Feb 46).(Back)

Footnote 6-22: Ltr, TAG for CG's, AGF et al., 6 May 46, sub: Utilization of Negro Manpower in the Post-War Army, WDGAP 291.2.(Back)

Footnote 6-23: WD Press Release, 4 Mar 46, "Report of Board of Officers on Utilization of Negro Manpower in the Post-War Army."(Back)

Footnote 6-24: Memo, SW for CofS, 28 Feb 46, WDCSA 320.2 (28 Feb 46).(Back)

Footnote 6-25: Memo, Truman Gibson, Expert Consultant to the SW, for Howard C. Petersen, 28 Feb 46, ASW 291.2 Negro Troops (Post-War).(Back)

Footnote 6-26: Remarks of the Assistant Secretary of War at Luncheon for Negro Newspaper Publishers Association, 1 Mar 46, ASW 291.2.(Back)

Footnote 6-27: Ray, a former commander of an artillery battalion in the 92d Infantry Division, was appointed civilian aide on 2 January 1946; see WD Press Release, 7 Jan 46.(Back)

Footnote 6-28: Ltr, Marcus Ray to Capt Warman K. Welliver, 10 Apr 46, copy in CMH. Welliver, the commander of a black unit during the war, was a student of the subject of Negroes in the Army; see his "Report on the Negro Soldier."(Back)

Footnote 6-29: Norfolk *Journal and Guide*, March 9, 1946.(Back)

Footnote 6-30: Ltr, L. D. Reddick, N.Y. Pub. Lib., to SW, 12 Mar 46, SW 291.(Back)

Footnote 6-31: Ltr, Bernard Jackson, Youth Council, NAACP Boston Br, to ASW, 4 Apr 46, ASW 291.2 (NT).(Back)

Footnote 6-32: Pittsburgh *Courier*, May 11, 1946.(Back)

Footnote 6-33: Ltr, Charles G. Bolte, Chmn, Amer Vets Cmte, to SW, 8 Mar 46; see also Ltr, Ralph DeNat, Corr Secy, Amer Vets Cmte, to SW, 28 May 46, both in SW 291.2 (Cmte) (9 Aug 46).(Back)

Footnote 6-34: Ltrs, ASW to Bernard H. Solomon and to Bernard Jackson, 9 Apr 46, both in ASW 291.2.(Back)

341

Footnote 6-35: Hanson Baldwin, "Wanted: An American Military Policy," *Harper's* 192 (May 1946):403-13.(Back)

Footnote 6-36: Remarks by Gen J. L. Devers, Armored Conference Report, 16 May 46.(Back)

Footnote 6-37: Ltr, CINCPAC&POA to SecNav via Ch, NavPers, 30 Oct 45, sub: Negro Naval Personnel—Pacific Ocean Areas, and 2d Ind, CNO, 7 Dec 45, same sub, both in P16-3/MM, OpNavArchives.(Back)

Footnote 6-38: Memo, J. F. for Adm Jacobs, 23 Aug 45, 54-1-13, Forrestal file, GenRecsNav.(Back)

Footnote 6-39: Memo, Asst Ch, NavPers, for SecNav, 10 Sep 45, sub: Ur Memo of August 23, 1945, Relative to Lester B. Granger ... 54-1-13, Forrestal file, GenRecsNav.(Back)

Footnote 6-40: 1st Ind, Chief, NavPers, to Ltr, CINCPAC&POA to SecNav, 30 Oct 45, sub: Negro Personnel—Pacific Ocean Areas (ca. 15 Nov 45), P16-3MM, OpNavArchives; Memo, M. F. Correa (Admin Asst to SecNav) for Capt Robert N. McFarlane, 30 Nov 45, 54-1-13, Forrestal file, GenRecsNav.(Back)

Footnote 6-41: Forrestal's request for a progress report was circulated in CNO Dispatch 142105Z Dec 45 to CINCPAC&POA, quoted in Nelson, "Integration of the Negro," p. 58.(Back)

Footnote 6-42: Memo, CINCPAC&POA for CNO, 5 Jan 46, sub: Negro Naval Personnel—Pacific Ocean Areas, P10/P11, OpNavArchives.(Back)

Footnote 6-43: Admiral Denfeld's statement to the black press representatives in this regard is referred to in Memo, Capt H. Wood, Jr., for Chief, NavPers, 2 Jan 46, P16-3/MM, BuPersRecs.(Back)

Footnote 6-44: Ltr, Chief, NavPers, to CNO, 4 Jan 46, sub: Assignment of Negro Personnel, P16-3MM, BuPersRecs.(Back)

Footnote 6-45: As reported in Ltr, Granger to author, 25 Jun 69, CMH files.(Back)

Footnote 6-46: Ltr, Congressman Stephen Pace of Georgia to Forrestal, 22 Jun 46; Ltr, Forrestal to Pace, 14 Aug 46, both in 54-1-13, Forrestal file, GenRecsNav.(Back)

Footnote 6-47: The latest pronouncement of that policy was ALNAV 423-45.(Back)

Footnote 6-48: See USMC Oral History Interviews, Lt Gen James L. Underhill, 25 Mar 68, and Lt Gen Ray A. Robinson, 18 Mar 68, both in Hist Div, HQMC.(Back)

Footnote 6-49: Memo, CO, 26th Marine Depot Co., Fifth Service Depot, Second FMF, Pacific, for CMC, 2 Nov 45, with Inds, sub: Information Concerning Peacetime Colored Marine Corps, Request for; Memos, CMC for CG, FMF (Pacific), et al., 11 Dec 45, sub: Voluntary Enlistments, Negro Marines, in Regular Marine Corps, Assignment of Quotas; idem for Cmdr, MCAB, Cherry Point, N.C., et al., 14 Dec 45. Unless otherwise noted, all documents cited in this section are located in Hist Div, HQMC.(Back)

Footnote 6-50: AAA Gp, 51st Defense Bn, FMF, Montford Pt., Gp Cmdr's Endorsement on Annual Record Practice, Year 1943, 20 Dec 43; AAA Gp, 51st Defense Bn, FMF, Montford Pt., Battery Cmdr's Narrative Report of Record Practice, 1943, 21 Dec 43; idem, Battery Cmdr's Narrative Rpt (signed R. H. Twisdale) (ca. 20 Dec 43).(Back)

Footnote 6-51: For the extensive charges and countercharges concerning the controversy between Colonel LeGette and his predecessor in the 51st, see files of Hist Div, HQMC.(Back)

Footnote 6-52: Memo, CO, 51st Defense Bn, FMF, for CMC, 20 Jul 44, sub: Combat Efficiency, Fifty-First Defense Battalion, Serial 1085.(Back)

Footnote 6-53: Shaw and Donnelly, *Blacks in the Marine Corps*, pp 47-49; Interv, James Westfall with Col Curtis W. LeGette (USMC, Ret.), 8 Feb 72, copy in CMH.(Back)

Footnote 6-54: Memo, Dir, Div of Plans and Policies, for CMC, 8 Apr 46, sub: Negro Personnel in the Post-War Marine Corps. This memo was not submitted for signature and was superseded by a memo of 13 May 46.(Back)

Footnote 6-55: Memos, Dir, Aviation, for CMC, 26 Apr 46, sub: Negro Personnel in the Post-War Marine Corps, and 31 May 46, sub: Enlistment of Negroes "For Duty in Aviation Units Only."(Back)

Footnote 6-56: Div of Plans and Policies (signed G. C. Thomas), Consideration of Non-Concurrence, 2 May 46, attached to Memo, Dir, Aviation, for CMC, 26 Apr 46.(Back)

Footnote 6-57: Memo, Dir, Div of Plans and Policies, for CMC, 13 May 46, sub: Negro Personnel in the Post-War Marine Corps.(Back)

Footnote 6-58: Idem for CMC, 25 Sep 46, sub: Post-War Negro Personnel Requirements. For examples of the proposals submitted by the various components, see Memo, F. D. Beans, G-3, for G-1, 6 Aug 46, sub: Employment of Colored Personnel in the Fleet Marine Force (Ground) (less Service Ground) and in Training Activities; Memo, Lt Col Schmuck, G-3, for Col Stiles, 10 Jun 46, sub: Utilization of Negro Personnel in Post-War Infantry Units of the Fleet

Marine Force; Memo, QMC for CMC, 4 Sep 46, sub: Negro Personnel in the Post-War Marine Corps.(Back)

Footnote 7-1: DF, ACofS, G-1, to CG, AAF, 15 Mar 46, sub: Utilization of Negro Manpower in the Postwar Army, WDGAP 291.2.(Back)

Footnote 7-2: Memo, CG, AAF, for ACofS, G-1, 3 Apr 46, sub: Utilization of Manpower in the Postwar Army, WDGAP 291.2.(Back)

Footnote 7-3: DF, ACofS, G-1, to ASW, 26 Mar 46, sub: Implementation of WD Cir 124, WDGAP 291.2.(Back)

Footnote 7-4: Idem to ACofS, G-3, 29 Apr 46, sub: Implementation of WD Cir 124, WDGAP 291.2.(Back)

Footnote 7-5: WD Cir 105, 10 Apr 46.(Back)

Footnote 7-6: Memo, ASW for ACofS, G-1, 27 Apr 46, ASW 291.2.(Back)

Footnote 7-7: G-1 Summary Sheet for CofS, 3 May 46, sub: Changes to WD Cir 105, 1946, WDGAP 291.2. Revision appeared as WD Circular 142, 17 May 46.(Back)

Footnote 7-8: DF, ACofS, G-1, to ASW, 13 May 46, sub: Utilization of Negro Manpower in Postwar Army, WDGAP 291.2.(Back)

Footnote 7-9: Ltr, TAG to CG's, AGF, AAF, and ASF, 6 May 46, sub: Utilization of Negro Manpower in Postwar Army, AGAM-PM 291.2 (30 Apr 46); idem to CG's, 10 Jun 46, same sub, same file (4 Jun 46).(Back)

Footnote 7-10: Memo, Marcus H. Ray for ASW, 22 Jan 46, ASW 291.2.(Back)

Footnote 7-11: Memo, ACofS, G-1, for CofS, 25 Jan 46, sub: Utilization of Negro Manpower in the Postwar Army, WDGAP 291.2.(Back)

Footnote 7-12: DF, ACofS, G-1, 23 Jan 46, sub: Utilization of Negro Personnel, WDGAP 291.2 (23 Jan 46); Ltr, TAG to CG's, Major Forces, and Overseas Cmdrs, 4 Feb 46, same sub, AG 291.2 (31 Jan 46) OB-S-A-M.(Back)

Footnote 7-13: G-1 Memo for Rcd, Col Coyne, Operations Gp, 19 Feb 47, WDGAP 291.2; prohibitions for certain areas are discussed in detail in Chapter 15.(Back)

Footnote 7-14: Memo, Actg Chief, Pac Theater Sec, OPD, for Maj Gen H. A. Craig, Dep ACofS, OPD, 12 Feb 46, sub: Utilization of Negro Manpower, WDGOT 291.2.(Back)

Footnote 7-15: Memo, Chief, Eur Sec, OPD, for Maj Gen Howard A. Craig, Dep ACofS, OPD, 15 Feb 46, sub: Utilization of Negro Personnel, WDGOT 291.2.(Back)

Footnote 7-16: Memo for Rcd, Lt Col French, Theater Group, OPD, 7 May 46, sub: Negro Enlisted Strength, Pacific Theater, 1947, WDGOT 291.2. For a discussion of the Philippine Scouts in the Pacific theater, see Robert Ross Smith, "The Status of Philippine Military Forces During World War II," CMH files.(Back)

Footnote 7-17: Memo, CG, AAF, for ACofS, G-1, 25 Jan 46, sub: Utilization of Negro Manpower in the Postwar Army, WDGAP 291.2.(Back)

Footnote 7-18: Memo, Brig Gen William Metheny, Off, Commitments Div, ACofS Air Staff-3, for ACofS Air Staff-3, 18 Feb 46, WDGOT 291.2.(Back)

Footnote 7-19: DF, DCofAS (Maj Gen C. C. Chauncey) to G-3 25 Feb 46, sub: Utilization of Negro Manpower in the Postwar Army, WDGOT 291.2.(Back)

Footnote 7-20: Memo, Actg ACofS, G-3, for CG, AAF, 14 Mar 46, sub: Utilization of Negro Manpower in the Postwar Army, WDGOT 291.2.(Back)

Footnote 7-21: Memo, ACofS, G-3, for CG, AAF, 21 Mar 46, sub: Authorized Military Personnel as of 31 December 1946 and 30 June 1947, WDGOT 320.2 (21 Mar 46); DF, CG, AAF, to ACofS, G-3, 26 Mar 46, same sub, WDGOT 291.21 (12 Feb 46).(Back)

Footnote 7-22: Memo, Actg Dir, Plans and Policy, ASF, for PMG et al., 23 May 46, sub: Utilization of Negro Manpower in the Postwar Army, AG 291.2 (23 May 46).(Back)

Footnote 7-23: The replies of the individual technical and administrative service chiefs, along with the response of the ASF Personnel Director, are inclosed in Memo, Chief, Plans and Policy Off, Dir of SS&P, for Dir, O&T, 21 Jun 46, sub: Utilization of Negro Manpower in the Postwar Army, WDGSP 291.2 (Negro).(Back)

Footnote 7-24: Under WD Circular 134, 14 May 46, the War Department General Staff was reorganized, and many of its offices, including G-1 and G-3, were redesignated as of 11 June 1946. For an extended discussion of these changes, see James E. Hewes, Jr., *From Root to McNamara: Army Organization and Administration, 1900-1963* (Washington: Government Printing Office, 1975), Chapter IV.(Back)

Footnote 7-25: DF, D/OT to D/PA, 13 Jul 46, sub: Utilization of Negro Manpower in the Postwar Army, WDGOT 291.21 (21 Jun 46); DF, D/PA to D/OT, 30 Jul 46, same sub, WDGAP 291.2 (15 Jul 46).(Back)

Footnote 7-26: Strength of the Army (STM-30), 1 May 46; see also Memo, ACofS, G-1, for Chief, MPD, ASF, 3 Jun 46, sub: Utilization of Negro Personnel, WDGPA 291.2. (12 Jul 46).(Back)

Footnote 7-27: Volunteers for the draft were men classified 1-A by Selective Service who were allowed to sign up for immediate duty often in the service of their choice. The volunteer for the draft was only obliged to serve for the shorter period imposed on the draftee rather than the 36-month enlistment for the Regular Army.(Back)

Footnote 7-28: Report of the Director, Office of Selective Service Review, 31 March 1947, Table 56, copy in CMH.(Back)

Footnote 7-29: Memo, Chief, Manpower Control Gp, D/PA, for TAG, 6 Sep 46, Utilization of Negro Manpower in Postwar Army, WDGPA 291.2; D/PA Memo for Rcd, 1 Sep 46. WDGPA 291.2 (1 Sep 46-31 Dec 46).(Back)

Footnote 7-30: Figures vary for the number actually drafted; those given above are from Selective Service Monograph No. 10, *Special Groups*, Appendix, p. 201. See also "Review of the Month," *A Monthly Summary of Events and Trends in Race Relations* 4 (October 1946):67.(Back)

Footnote 7-31: WD Cir 110, 17 Apr 46.(Back)

Footnote 7-32: Ltr, TAG to CG, AAF, et al., 16 Apr 46, sub: Utilization of Negro Personnel, AGAO-S-A-M 291.2 (12 Apr 46).(Back)

Footnote 7-33: Memo, Actg ACofS, G-3, for CG, AAF, 12 Apr 46, sub: Utilization of Negro Personnel, WDGOT 291.21 (12 Feb 46).(Back)

Footnote 7-34: Memo, ACofS, OPD, for CofS, 13 May 46, sub: Augmentation of the ETO Ceiling Strengths as of 1 Jul 46 (less AAF), WDCSA 320.2 (1946).(Back)

Footnote 7-35: G-1 Memo for Rcd (signed Col E. L. Heyduck, Enl Div), 18 Jun 46, WDGAP 291.2; see also EUCOM Hist Div (prepared by Margaret L. Geis), "Negro Personnel in the European Command, 1 January 1946-30 June 1950," Occupation Forces in Europe Series (Historical Division, European Command, 1952) (hereafter Geis Monograph), pp. 14-18, copy in CMH.(Back)

Footnote 7-36: Ltr, TAG to CG, Each Army, et al., 17 Jul 46, sub: Enlistment of Negroes, AGSE-P342.06 (9 Jul 46); D/PA Summary Sheet to CofS, 9 Jul 46, sub: Enlistment of Negroes in Regular Army, WDGPA 291.2.(Back)

Footnote 7-37: D/OT Memo for Red, 15 Jul 46; DF, D/OT to D/PA, 15 Jul 46, sub: Basic Training of Negro Personnel; both in WDGOT 291.2.(Back)

Footnote 7-38: WD Cir 241, 10 Aug 46.(Back)

Footnote 7-39: WD Cir 93, 9 Apr 47; D/PA Summary Sheet, 1 Sep 49, sub: Method of Reducing Negro Reenlistment Rate, WDGPA 291.2 (6 Apr 49).(Back)

Footnote 7-40: P&A Memo for Red, 30 Sep 46, attached to copy of Ltr, TAG to CG, Each Army, et al., 2 Oct 46, sub: Enlistment of Negroes, AGSE-P342.06, WDGPA 291.2.(Back)

Footnote 7-41: Ltr, TAG to CG, Each Army, et al., 2 Oct 46, sub: Enlistment of Negroes, AGSE-P342.06 (30 Sep 46).(Back)

Footnote 7-42: Ibid., 31 Oct 46, sub: Enlistment of Negroes, AGSE-P342.06 (23 Oct 46); see also WD Cir 103, 1947. An exception to the AGCT 70 minimum for whites was made in the case of enlistment into the AAF which remained at 100 for both races.(Back)

Footnote 7-43: All figures are from STM-30, Strength of the Army. Figures for the Pacific theater were omitted because of the complex reorganization of Army troops in that area in early 1947. On 30 June 1947 the Army element in the Far East Command, the major Army organization in the Pacific, had 18,644 black enlisted troops, 8.56 percent of the command's total.(Back)

Footnote 7-44: Memo, Brig Gen J. J. O'Hare, Dep Dir, P&A, for SA, 9 Mar 48, sub: Implementation of WD Cir 124, CSGPA 291.2.(Back)

Footnote 7-45: G-1 Memo for Rcd, 30 Sep 46, attached to Ltr, TAG to CG, Each Army, et al., 2 Oct 46, sub: Enlistment of Negroes, AGSE-P342.06 (30 Sep 46).(Back)

Footnote 7-46: Ltr, Walter White to SW, 18 Jun 46; Telg, White to SW, 24 Jun 46; both in SW 291.2 (Negro Troops).(Back)

Footnote 7-47: DF, OTIG to D/PA, 23 Jul 46, sub: Assignment of Negro Enlistees Who Have Selected ETO as Choice of Initial Assignment, WDSIG 220.3—Negro Enlistees.(Back)

Footnote 7-48: Pittsburgh *Post Gazette*, December 19, 1946.(Back)

Footnote 7-49: Memo, D/PRD for SW, ASW, and D/P&A, 19 Dec 46, ASW 291.2.(Back)

Footnote 7-50: Ltr, American Veterans Committee, Manhattan Chapter, to SW, 17 Jul 46, SW 291.2 (NT).(Back)

Footnote 7-51: Ltr, LaFollette to SW, 25 Jul 46, SW 291.2.(Back)

Footnote 7-52: Ltr, Reuther and William Oliver to SW, 23 Jul 46, SW 291.2.(Back)

Footnote **7-53:** Ltr, J. H. Holmes to SW, 26 Jul 46; Ltr, Arthur D. Gatz, Nat'l Cmdr, United Negro and Allied Veterans of America, to SW, 20 Jul 46; both in SW 291.2.(Back)

Footnote **7-54:** See Ltrs, SW to Wesley P. Brown, Adjutant, Jesse Clipper American Legion Post No. 430, Buffalo, N.Y., 30 Aug 46, and to Jesse O. Dedmon, Jr., Secy, Veterans Affairs Bureau, NAACP, 18 Nov 46; both in SW 291.2. The quote is from the latter document.(Back)

Footnote **7-55:** Memo, Maj Gen Parks for SW, et al., 19 Dec 46 (with attached note signed "HP"), SW 291.2.(Back)

Footnote **7-56:** DF, D/P&A to D/O&T, 28 Apr 47, sub: Negro Enlisted Strength, WDGPA 291.2 (12 Jul 46); idem for SA, 6 Aug 48, sub: Removing Restrictions on Negro Enlistments, CSGPA 291.2.(Back)

Footnote **7-57:** Memo, ONB (Gen Bradley) for Gen Paul, 9 Aug 48, CSUSA 291.2 Negroes (6 Aug 48). Bradley succeeded Eisenhower as Chief of Staff on 7 February 1948, and Royall succeeded Patterson on 19 July 1947. Royall assumed the title Secretary of the Army on 17 September 1947 under the terms of the National Security Act of 1947.(Back)

Footnote **7-58:** AMP-1 Personnel Annex, 1 Jun 49, P&D 370.0 (25 Apr 49); see also Memo, Chief, Planning Office, P&A, for Brig Gen John E. Dahlquist (Dep P&A), 4 Feb 49, sub: Utilization of Negroes in Mobilization, D/PA 291.2 (4 Feb 49).(Back)

Footnote **7-59:** Ltr, TAG to CG, Each Army, et al., 9 Jul 47, sub: Enlistment of Negroes AGSE-P291.2. (27 Jun 47).(Back)

Footnote **7-60:** T-7286, TAG to CO, Gen Ground, Ft. Monroe (AGF), 27 Aug 47, 291.254 Negroes; Ltr, TAG to CG, Each Army, et al., 3 Sep 47, sub: Enlistment of Negroes, AGSE-P291.2.(Back)

Footnote **7-61:** Msg, TAG to CG's, All ZI Armies, 19 Dec 47, AGSE-P 291.254.(Back)

Footnote **7-62:** Msg, TAG to CG, All Armies (ZI), et al., 17 Mar 49, WCL 22839; D/PA Summary Sheet for VCofS, 1 Sep 49, sub: Method of Reducing the Negro Reenlistment Rate, CSGPA 291.2 (6 Apr 49).(Back)

Footnote **7-63:** DF, D/PA to D/OT, 30 Jul 46, sub: Utilization of Negro Manpower in the Postwar Army, WDGPA 291.2 (15 Jul 46).(Back)

Footnote **7-64:** Cir as Memo, TAG for CG, AAF et al., 10 Jun 46, sub: Organization of Negro Manpower in Postwar Army, AG 291.2 (4 Jun 46).(Back)

Footnote **7-65:** Memo, D/O&T for ASW, 18 Jul 46, sub: Organization of Negro Manpower in Postwar Army, WDGOT 291.2.(Back)

Footnote **7-66:** An attached unit, such as a tank destroyer battalion, is one temporarily included in a larger organization; an assigned unit is one permanently given to a larger organization as part of its organic establishment. On the distinction between attached and assigned status, see Ltr, CSA to CG, CONARC, 21 Jul 55, CSUSA 322.17 (Div), and CMH, "Lineages and Honors: History, Principles, and Preparation," June 1962, in CMH.(Back)

Footnote **7-67:** Memo, Actg, ACofS, G-3, for CG, AGF, 3 Jun 46, sub: Formation of Composite White-Negro Units, with attachment, WDGOT 291.21 (30 Apr 46).(Back)

Footnote **7-68:** Memo, CG, AFG, for CofS, 21 June 46, sub: Formation of Composite White-Negro Units, GNGCT-41 291.2 (Negro) (3 Jun 46).(Back)

Footnote **7-69:** DF, D/O&T to CG, AGF, 24 Jul 46, sub: Formation of Composite White-Negro Units, WDGOT 291.21 (30 Apr 46).(Back)

Footnote **7-70:** Memo, CG, AGF, for D/O&T, 1 Aug 46, sub: Formation of Composite White-Negro Units, CMT 2 to DF, D/O&T to CG, AGF, 24 Jul 46, same sub, WDGOT 291.21 (30 Apr 46).(Back)

Footnote **7-71:** Memo, D/O&T for SW, 19 Sep 46, sub: Request for Memorandum, WDGOT 291.21 (12 Sep 46).(Back)

Footnote **7-72:** DF, CG, AGF, to D/P&A, 15 Sep 47, sub: Utilization of Negro Manpower in the Postwar Army. Policy; AGF DF, 27 Aug 47, same sub; both in GNGAP-M 291.2 (27 Aug 47). The quote is from the former document.(Back)

Footnote **7-73:** DA Cir 32-III, 30 Oct 47. The life of Circular 124 was extended indefinitely by DA Circular 24-II, 17 Oct 47, and DA Ltr AGAO 291.2 (16 Mar 49).(Back)

Footnote **7-74:** Col. H. E. Kessinger, Exec Off, ACofS, G-1, "Utilization of Negro Manpower, 1946," copy in WDGPA 291.2 (1946).(Back)

Footnote **7-75:** DF, ACofS, G-1, to CofS, 3 Jun 46, sub: Implementation of the Gillem Board, WDGAP 291.2 (24 Nov 45); see also Routing Form, ACofS, G-1, same date, subject, and file.(Back)

Footnote **7-76:** For the formation of quartermaster trains in Europe, see Geis Monograph, pp. 89-90.(Back)

Footnote 7-77: Memo, D/P&A for Under SA, 29 Apr 48, sub: Negro Utilization in the Postwar Army, CSGPA 291.2.(Back)

Footnote 7-78: Idem for CofS, 21 Jun 48, CSGPA 291.2.(Back)

Footnote 7-79: DF, D/P&A to CG, AGF, et al., 16 Nov 46, sub: Proposed Directive, Utilization of Negro Military Personnel; see also P&A Memo for Rcd, 14 Nov 46; both in WDGPA 291.2 (12 Jul 46).(Back)

Footnote 7-80: Ltr, Brig Gen B. F. Caffey, CG, 25th RCT (Prov), Ft. Benning Ga., to CG, AGF, 4 Dec 46, AGF 291.2; DF, CG, AGF, to D/P&A, 22 Nov 46, sub: Utilization of Negro Military Personnel, WDGPA 291.2 (Negro) (16 Nov 46).(Back)

Footnote 7-81: DF, CG, AAF, to D/P&A, 27 Nov 45, sub: Utilization of Negro Military Personnel, WDGPA 291.2 (16 Nov 46).(Back)

Footnote 7-82: Memo, D/O&T for D/P&A, 4 Dec 46, sub: Utilization of Negro Military Personnel, WDGOT 291.2 (16 Nov 46).(Back)

Footnote 7-83: Tabs E and F to DF, D/P&A to DCofS, 10 Jan 47, sub: Utilization of Negro Military Personnel in Overhead Installations, WDGPA 291.2 (12 Jul 46).(Back)

Footnote 7-84: DF, D/P&A to DCofS, 10 Jan 47, sub: Utilization of Negro Military Personnel in Overhead Installations, WDGPA 291.2 (12 Jul 46).(Back)

Footnote 7-85: DF, CG, AAF (signed by Dep CG, Lt Gen Ira C. Eaker), to D/P&A, 20 Jan 47, sub: Utilization of Negro Military Personnel in Overhead Installations, WDGPA 291.2 (12 Jul 46).(Back)

Footnote 7-86: Memo, ADCofS for D/P&A, 24 Jan 47, sub: Utilization of Negro Military Personnel in Overhead Installations, WDCSA 291.2 (10 Jan 47).(Back)

Footnote 7-87: Memo, D/P&A for General Hodes, 29 Jan 47, sub: Utilization of Negro Personnel in Overhead Installations, WDGPA 291.2 (12 Jul 46).(Back)

Footnote 7-88: Memo, ADCofS for D/P&A, 4 Feb 47, sub: Utilization of Negro Military Personnel in Overhead Installations, WDCSA 291.2 (10 Jan 47); Ltr, TAG to CG, AAF, et al., 5 Mar 47, same sub, AGAM-PM 291.2 (27 Feb 47).(Back)

Footnote 7-89: Msg, CINCFE to WD for AGPP-P, 3 May 47, C-52352. Although CINCFE was a joint commander, his report concerned Army personnel only.(Back)

Footnote 7-90: Ltr, CG, MTO, to TAG, 16 Apr 47, sub: Utilization of Negro Military Personnel in Overhead Installations; Ltr, CG, Alaskan Dept, to TAG, 14 Apr 47, same sub; Ltr, CG, EUCOM, to TAG, 15 Apr 47, same sub. All in AGPP-P 291.2 (6 Feb 47).(Back)

Footnote 7-91: The reports of all these services are inclosures to DF, TAG to D/P&A, 23 Apr 47, sub: Utilization of Negro Military Personnel in Overhead Installations, AGPP-P 291.2 (6 Feb 47). The quote is from Ltr, Chief of Finance Corps to TAG, 25 Mar 47, same sub.(Back)

Footnote 7-92: WD Cir 118, 9 May 47.(Back)

Footnote 7-93: P&A Memo for Rcd, attached to DF, D/P&A to TAG, 11 Jun 47, sub: Utilization of Negro Manpower in the Postwar Army in Connection With Enlisted Career Guidance Program, WDGPA 291.2 (11 Jun 47).(Back)

Footnote 7-94: Davenport, "Matters Relating to the Participation of Negro Personnel in the Career Program," attached to DF, D/P&A to Brig Gen J. J. O'Hare, Chief, Mil Pers Mgt Gp, P&A Div, 3 Nov 47, WDGPA 291.2 (11 Jul 47).(Back)

Footnote 7-95: For a discussion of the reorganization of the general reserve, see the introduction to John B. Wilson's "U.S. Army Lineage and Honors: The Division," in CMH.(Back)

Footnote 7-96: Ltrs, TAG to CG, Each Army, et al., 18 Dec 47 and 1 Mar 48. sub: Activation and Reorganization of Certain Units of the General Reserve, AGAO-1 322 (28 Nov 47 and 8 Jan 48).(Back)

Footnote 7-97: Army Memo 600-750-26, 17 Dec 47, sub: Enlistment of Negroes for Special Units; DF, D/P&A to TAG, 27 Jan 48, sub: Training Div Assignment Procedures for Negro Pers Enlisting Under Provisions of DA Memo 600-750-26, 17 Dec 47, CSGPA 291.2 (7 Jan 48).(Back)

Footnote 7-98: DF, D/P&A to TAG, 27 Jan 48, sub: Training Div Assignment Procedures for Negro Personnel Enlisting Under Provisions of DA Memo 600-750-26, 17 Dec 47; ibid., 29 Jan 48, sub: Notification to Z1 Armies of Certain Negro School Training; both in CSGPA 291.2 (7 Jan 48).(Back)

Footnote 7-99: Ibid., 1 Mar 48, sub: Utilization of Negro School Trained Personnel, CSGPA 291.2 (7 Jan 48).(Back)

Footnote 7-100: DF D/P&A for Brig Gen Joseph J. O'Hare, Chief Mil Pers Mgt Gp, 3 Nov 47, CSGPA 291.2 (3 Nov 47).(Back)

346

Footnote **7-101:** Memo, Chief, Morale, and Welfare Br, P&A, for Chief, Mil Pers Mgt Gp, P&A, 27 Feb 48, sub: School Input Quotas for Enlisted Personnel From the Replacement Stream (other than Air), CSGPA 291.2.(Back)

Footnote **7-102:** Memo, Brig Gen J. J. O'Hare, Dep Dir, P&A, for SA, 9 Mar 48, sub: Implementation of WD Circular 124, CSGPA 291.2.(Back)

Footnote **7-103:** Ltr, Roy K. Davenport to author, 11 Dec 71, CMH files. Davenport became Deputy Under Secretary of the Army and later Deputy Assistant Secretary of Defense (Manpower Planning and Research) in the Johnson administration.(Back)

Footnote **8-1:** STM-30, Strength of the Army, 1 Jan 47 and 1 Mar 48.(Back)

Footnote **8-2:** Geis Monograph, pp. 138-39 and Chart 4.(Back)

Footnote **8-3:** Ibid., pp. 138-39; Eighth Army (AFPAC) Hist Div, *Occupational Monograph of the Eighth Army in Japan* (hereafter AFPAC Monograph), 3:171.(Back)

Footnote **8-4:** Geis Monograph; AFPAC Monograph, 3:87-88 and charts, 4:91-97 and JAG Illus. No. 3. It should be noted that on occasion individual white units registered disciplinary rates spectacularly higher than these averages. In a nine-month period in 1946-47, for example, a 120-man white unit stationed in Vienna, Austria, had 10 general courts-martial, between 30 and 40 special and summary courts-martial, and 40 of its members separated under the provisions of AR 368-369.(Back)

Footnote **8-5:** "History of MacDill Army Airfield, 326th AAB Unit, October 1946," pp. 10-11, AFCHO files.(Back)

Footnote **8-6:** Florence Murray, ed., *The Negro Handbook, 1949* (New York: Macmillan, 1949), pp. 109-10.(Back)

Footnote **8-7:** Geis Monograph, pp. 145-47.(Back)

Footnote **8-8:** AFPAC Monograph, 2:176.(Back)

Footnote **8-9:** Ltr, Louis R. Lautier to Howard C. Petersen, 28 May 46. ASW 291.2 (NT).(Back)

Footnote **8-10:** Frank L. Stanley, Report of the Negro Newspaper Publishers Association to the Honorable Secretary of War on Troops and Conditions in Europe, 18 Jul 46, copy in CMH.(Back)

Footnote **8-11:** Ray, Rpt of Tour of Pacific Installations to SW Patterson, 7 Aug-6 Sep 46, ASW 291.2.(Back)

Footnote **8-12:** Memo, Ray for ASW Petersen, 1 Nov 46, ASW 291.2.(Back)

Footnote **8-13:** U.S. Congress, Senate Special Committee Investigating National Defense Programs, Part 42, "Military Government in Germany," 80th Cong., 22 November 1946, pp. 26150-89; see also New York *Times*, November 27 and December 4, 1946. The quotation is from the *Times* of November 27th.(Back)

Footnote **8-14:** Senate Special Committee, "Military Government in Germany," 80th Cong., 22 Nov 1946, pp. 26163-64; see also Geis Monograph, pp. 142-43.(Back)

Footnote **8-15:** Geis Monograph, pp. 144-45; EUCOM Hist Div, *Morale and Discipline in the European Command, 1945-1949*, Occupation Forces in Europe Series, pp. 45-46, in CMH.(Back)

Footnote **8-16:** Ray, "Rpt to SecWar, Mr. Robert P. Patterson, of Tour of European Installations," 17 Dec 46, Incl to Memo, SW for DCofS, 7 Jan 47, SW 291.2.(Back)

Footnote **8-17:** WDGPA Summary Sheet, 25 Jan 47, sub: Utilization of Negroes in the European Theater, with Incls, WDGPA 291.2 (7 Jan 47).(Back)

Footnote **8-18:** Interv, author with Lt Gen Clarence R. Huebner (former CG, U.S. Army, Europe), 31 Mar 71, CMH files.(Back)

Footnote **8-19:** Geis Monograph, pp. 143-44.(Back)

Footnote **8-20:** For the use of AR 315-369 to discharge low-scoring soldiers, see Chapter 7.(Back)

Footnote **8-21:** AFPAC Monograph, 4:193.(Back)

Footnote **8-22:** At the suggestion of Secretary Patterson, General Huebner established the position of Negro adviser. After several candidates were considered, the post went to Marcus Ray, who left the secretary's office and went on active duty.(Back)

Footnote **8-23:** Interv, author with Huebner.(Back)

Footnote **8-24:** The 370th and 371st Infantry Battalions (Separate) were organized on 20 June 1947. The men came from EUCOM's inactivated engineer service battalions and construction companies, ambulance companies, and ordnance ammunition, quartermaster railhead, signal heavy construction, and transportation corps car companies; see Geis Monograph, p. 80.(Back)

Footnote **8-25:** Ltr, CG, Ground and Service Forces, Europe, to CG, 1st Inf Div, 1 May 47, sub: Training of Negro Infantry Battalions, quoted in Geis Monograph, pp. 113-14.(Back)

Footnote 8-26: The training center had already moved from Grafenwohr to larger quarters at Mannheim Koafestal, Germany.(Back)

Footnote 8-27: Ltr, D/P&A to Huebner, 15 Oct 47, CSGPA 291.2. This approval did not extend to all civil rights advocates, some of whom objected to the segregated training. Walter White, however, supported the program. See Interv, author with Huebner.(Back)

Footnote 8-28: EUCOM Hist Div, *EUCOM Command Report, 1951*, pp. 128, 251, copy in CMH.(Back)

Footnote 8-29: Ltr, Chief, EUCOM TI&E Div, to EUCOM DCSOPS, 18 Jun 48, cited in Geis Monograph, p. 130.(Back)

Footnote 8-30: Geis Monograph, Charts 3 and 4 and p. 139.(Back)

Footnote 8-31: Not comparable was the brief literacy program reinstituted in the 25th Regimental Combat Team at Fort Benning, Georgia, in 1947.(Back)

Footnote 8-32: Ltr, Huebner to D/P&A, 1 Oct 47, CSGPA 291.2.(Back)

Footnote 8-33: Memo, DCofS for D/P&A, 14 May 48, sub: Report of Visit by Negro Publishers and Editors to the European Theater, CSUSA 291.2 Negroes (14 May 48).(Back)

Footnote 8-34: Ltr, D/P&A to Huebner, 15 Oct 47, CSGPA 291.2.(Back)

Footnote 8-35: Memo, ASW for D/P&A, 23 May 46, sub: Negro Officers in the Regular Establishment; Memo, D/P&A for ASW, 29 May 46, same sub; Memo, "D. R." (Exec Asst to ASW, Lt Col D. J. Rogers) for Petersen, 12 Jun 46. Copies of all in ASW 291.2 (23 May 46).(Back)

Footnote 8-36: Memo, Chief, Manpower Survey Gp, for Paul, 29 Apr 48, sub: Assignment of Officers of Negro T/O&E Units in Compliance with WD Cir 124, 1946, CSGPA 210.31 (29 Apr 48); "Report on Negro Officer Strength in Army," incl w/Memo, D/P&A for DCofS, 21 Jun 48, sub: Report of Negro Publishers and Editors on Tour of European Installations, CSUSA 291.2 Negroes (14 May 48).(Back)

Footnote 8-37: Memo, D/P&A for TAG, 24 May 48, sub: Negro Officers in TO&E Units, CSGPA 291.2 (24 May 48).(Back)

Footnote 8-38: Ibid.; "Report on Negro Officer Strength in Army," incl w/Memo, D/P&A for DCofS, 21 Jun 48, sub: Report of Negro Publishers and Editors..., CSUSA 291.2 Negroes (14 May 48).(Back)

Footnote 8-39: Memo, Asst Secy, GS, for DCofS, 2 Jun 48, sub: Negro ROTC Units, CSUSA 291.2 Negroes (2 Jun 48); see also Department of National Defense, "National Defense Conference on Negro Affairs," 26 Apr 48, morning session, pp. 31-34, copy in CMH.(Back)

Footnote 8-40: "Report on Negro Officer Strength in Army," incl w/Memo, D/P&A for DCofS, 21 Jun 48, sub: Report of Negro Publishers and Editors..., CSUSA 291.2 Negroes (14 May 48).(Back)

Footnote 8-41: Department of National Defense, "National Defense Conference on Negro Affairs," 26 Apr 48, morning session, pp. 20-21. Prior to World War II, an officer held a commission in the Regular Army, in the Army Reserve, or in the National Guard. Another type of commission, one in the Army of the United States (AUS), was added during World War II, and all temporary promotions granted during the war were to AUS rank. For example, a Regular Army captain could become an AUS major but would retain his Regular Army captaincy. Many reservists and some National Guard officers remaining on active duty sought conversion to, or "integration" into, the Regular Army for career security.(Back)

Footnote 8-42: These black officers were converted to Regular Army officers in the following arms and services: Infantry, 13; Chaplain Corps, 9; Medical Service Corps, 1; Army Nurse Corps, 1; Field Artillery, 1; Quartermaster, 7 (4 of whom were transferred later to the Transportation Corps). These figures include the first black doctor and nurse converted to Regular Army officers.(Back)

Footnote 8-43: "Analysis of Negro Officers in the Army," incl w/Memo, D/P&A for DCAS, 21 Jun 48, sub: Report of Negro Publishers and Editors..., CSUSA 291.2 Negroes (14 May 48).(Back)

Footnote 8-44: DF, D/P&A to Chief of Engrs, 25 Jul 47, sub: Appointment of Negro Officers to the Regular Army, w/attached Memo for Rcd, WDGPA 291.2 (23 Jul 47).(Back)

Footnote 8-45: DF, Chief of Engrs to D/P&A, 1 Aug 47, sub: Appointment of Negro Officers to the Regular Army, copy in WPGPA 291.2 (23 Jul 47).(Back)

Footnote 8-46: WD Memo 615-500-4, 21 Nov 46, sub: Flow of Enlisted Personnel From Induction Centers and Central Examining Stations.(Back)

Footnote 8-47: Memo, Marcus Ray for ASW, 23 Jan 47, ASW 291.2.(Back)

Footnote 8-48: Memo, ASW for DCofS, 7 Feb 47, ASW 291.2.(Back)

Footnote 8-49: Ltr, SW Robert P. Patterson to Walter White, 7 Feb 47, SW 291.2.(Back)

Footnote 8-50: Telg, Hugh F. Dormody, Mayor of Monterey, Calif., et al., to Sen. William F. Knowland, 31 Jul 48; Ltr, SA to Sen. Knowland, 16 May 48; both in CSUSA 291.2 Negroes (10 Aug 48).(Back)

Footnote 8-51: AG Memo for Office of SW et al., 10 Jan 47, sub: Designation of Race on Overseas Travel Orders, AGAO-C 291.2 (6 Jan 47), WDGSP; Memo for Rcd attached to Memo, D/SSP for TAG, 6 Jan 47, same sub, AG 291.2 (6 Jan 47).(Back)

Footnote 8-52: Memo, SA for CofSA, 2 Apr 52, sub: Racial Designations on Travel Orders, CS 291.2 (2 Apr 51).(Back)

Footnote 8-53: G-1 Summary Sheet, 26 Apr 52, sub: Racial Designations on Travel Orders; Memo, CofS for SA, 5 May 51, same sub; both in CS 291.2 (2 Apr 51).(Back)

Footnote 8-54: Memo, QMG for DCofS, 15 Apr 47, CSUSA, copy in CMH.(Back)

Footnote 8-55: WDSP Summary Sheet, 22 Jan 47, sub: Staff Study—Segregation of Grave Sites, WDGSP/C3 1894.(Back)

Footnote 8-56: Telg, Secy Veterans Affairs, NAACP, to SW, attached to Memo, SW for DCofS, 11 Apr 47, copy in CMH.(Back)

Footnote 8-57: Memo, Civilian Aide for USW, 15 Mar 47, sub: Segregation in Grave Site Assignment, copy in CMH.(Back)

Footnote 8-58: Memo, SW for DCofS, 15 Apr 47, copy in CMH. The secretary's directive was incorporated in the *National Cemetery Regulations*, August 1947, and Army Regulation 290-5, 2 October 1951.(Back)

Footnote 8-59: Ltr, Royall to Rep. Edward J. Devitt of Minnesota, 4 Sep 47; Ltr, Clifford Rucker to the President, 9 Aug 50; both in SW 291.2.(Back)

Footnote 8-60: Ltr, CG, Atlanta Depot, to DQMG, 19 Mar 56, MGME-P. See also Memo, ASA (M&RF) for CofS, 27 Sep 52, sub: Segregation of National Cemeteries; DF, QMF to G-4, 6 Oct 52, same sub; both in CS 687 (27 Sep 52).(Back)

Footnote 8-61: Memo, D/P&A for CofS, 26 Feb 47, sub: Army Talks on "Utilization of Negro Manpower," WDGPA 291.2 (7 Jan 47).(Back)

Footnote 8-62: WD Cir 76, 22 Mar 47; see also Ltrs, Col David Lane (author of *Army Talk 170*) to Martin Blumenson, 29 Dec 66, and to author, 15 Mar 71, CMH files.(Back)

Footnote 8-63: STM-30, Strength of the Army, 1 Jul 48. For an optimistic report on the execution of Circular 124, see *Annual Report of the Secretary of the Army, 1948*(Washington: Government Printing Office, 1949), pp. 7-8, 83, 94.(Back)

Footnote 8-64: The Air Force became a separate service on 18 September 1947.(Back)

Footnote 8-65: Unless otherwise noted, the following paragraphs are based on Nichols' interviews in 1953 with Generals Eisenhower, Bradley, and Lee and with Lt. Col. Steve Davis (a black officer assigned to the P&A Division during the Gillem Board period); author's interview with General Wade H. Haislip, 18 Mar 71, and with General J. Lawton Collins, 27 Apr 71; all in CMH files; and U.S. Congress, Senate, Hearings Before the U.S. Senate Committee on *Armed Services, Universal Military Training*, 80th Cong., 2d sess., 1948, pp. 995-96. See also Morris Janowitz, *The Professional Soldier: A Social and Political Portrait* (New York: Free Press, 1960), pp. 87ff.(Back)

Footnote 8-66: Ltr, DDE to Gen Bruce Clarke (commander of the 2d Constabulary Brigade when it was integrated in 1950), 29 May 67, copy in CMH.(Back)

Footnote 8-67: The 1946 survey is contained in CINFO, "Supplementary Rpt on Attitudes of Whites Toward Serving With Negro EM," Incl to Memo, Col Charles S. Johnson, Exec Off, CofS, for DCofS, 24 May 49, sub: Segregation in the Army, CSUSA 291.2 Negroes (24 May 48).(Back)

Footnote 8-68: Armed Forces I&E Div, OSD, Rpt No. 101, "Morale Attitudes of Enlisted Men, May-June 1949," pt. II, Attitude Toward Integration of Negro Soldiers in the Army, copy in CMH.(Back)

Footnote 8-69: Memo, Brig Gen B. O. Davis, Sp Asst to SA, for Under SA, 7 Jan 48, sub: Negro Utilization in the Postwar Army, WDGPA 291-2; ibid., 24 Nov 47; both in SA files. The quotations are from the latter document.(Back)

Footnote 8-70: Memo, D/P&A for Under SA, 29 Apr 48, sub: Negro Utilization in the Postwar Army, WDGPA 291.2.(Back)

Footnote 8-71: DF's, CINFO to D/P&A, 9 Feb 48, and Dep D/P&A to CINFO, 12 Feb 48; both in WDGPA 291.2 (9 Feb 48).(Back)

Footnote 8-72: For a detailed discussion of this point, see Mandelbaum, *Soldier Groups and Negro Soldiers*; Stouffer et al., *The American Soldier: Adjustment During Army Life*, ch. XII; Eli Ginzberg, *The Negro Potential* (New York: Columbia University Press, 1956); Ginzberg et al., *The Ineffective Soldier*, vol. III, *Patterns of Performance* (New York: Columbia University Press, 1959); *To*

349

Secure These Rights: The Report of the President's Committee on Civil Rights (Washington: Government Printing Office, 1947); Dollard and Young, "In the Armed Forces."(Back)

Footnote 8-73: Final Rpt, WD Policies and Programs Review Board, 11 Aug 47, CSUSA files.(Back)

Footnote 8-74: Ltr, Howard C. Petersen, ASW, to William M. Taylor, 12 May 47, ASW 291.2.(Back)

Footnote 8-75: Department of National Defense, "National Defense Conference on Negro Affairs," 26 Apr 48, morning session, p. 24.(Back)

Footnote 9-1: Interv, Lee Nichols with Marx Leva, 1953, in Nichols Collection, CMH.(Back)

Footnote 9-2: On the survival of traditional attitudes in the Navy, see Karsten, *Naval Aristocracy*, ch. v; Waldo H. Heinricks, Jr., "The Role of the U.S. Navy," in Dorothy Borg and Shumpei Okamoto, eds., *Pearl Harbor as History* (New York: Columbia University Press, 1973); David Rosenberg, "Arleigh Burke and Officer Development in the Inter-war Navy," *Pacific Historical Review* 44 (November 1975).(Back)

Footnote 9-3: Edward M. Coffman, *The Hilt of the Sword* (Madison: University of Wisconsin Press, 1966), p. 245.(Back)

Footnote 9-4: Quoted in Marriner S. Eccles, *Beckoning Frontiers: Public and Personal Recollections*, ed. Sidney Hyman (New York: Knopf, 1951), p. 336.(Back)

Footnote 9-5: The influence of tradition on naval racial practices was raised during the hearings of the President's Committee on Equality of Treatment and Opportunity in the Armed Services, 13 January 1949, pages 105-08, 111-12.(Back)

Footnote 9-6: SecNav (Josephus Daniels) General Order 90, 1 Jul 14. Alcohol had been outlawed for enlisted men at sea by Secretary John D. Long more than a decade earlier. The 1914 prohibition rule infuriated the officers. One predicted that the ruling would push officers into "the use of cocaine and other dangerous drugs." Quoted in Ronald Spector, *Admiral of the New Empire* (Baton Rouge: University of Louisiana Press, 1974), pp. 191-92.(Back)

Footnote 9-7: Unless otherwise noted the statistical information used in this section was supplied by the Office, Assistant Chief for Management Information, BuPers. See also BuPers, "Enlisted Strength—U.S. Navy," 26 Jul 46, Pers 215-BL, copy in CMH.(Back)

Footnote 9-8: Ltr, SecNav to Harvard Chapter, AVC, 26 Aug 46, P16-3 MM GenRecsNav.(Back)

Footnote 9-9: Interv, Nichols with Secretary John L. Sullivan, Dec 52, in Nichols Collection, CMH. Sullivan succeeded James Forrestal as secretary on 18 September 1947.(Back)

Footnote 9-10: The BuPers Progress Report (Pers 215), the major statistical publication of the department, terminated its statistical breakdown by race in March 1946. The Navy's racial affairs office was closed in June 1946. See BuPers, "Narrative of Bureau of Naval Personnel, 1 September 1945 to 1 October 1946" (hereafter "BuPers Narrative"), 1:73.(Back)

Footnote 9-11: Ibid., p. 143; Selective Service System, *Special Groups* (Monograph 10), 2:200. Between September 1945 and May 1946 the Navy drafted 20,062 men, including 3,394 Negroes.(Back)

Footnote 9-12: "BuPers Narrative," 1:141, 192; see also BuPers Cir Ltr 41-46, 15 Feb 46.(Back)

Footnote 9-13: See Ltr, Chief, NavPers, to CO, Naval Barracks, NAD, Seal Beach, Calif., 8 Oct 45, sub: Eligibility of Negroes for Enlistment in USN, P16 MM, BuPersRecs; Recruiting Dir, BuPers, Directive to Recruiting Officers, 25 Jan 46, quoted in Nelson, "Integration of the Negro," p. 58.(Back)

Footnote 9-14: BuPers, "Enlisted Strength—U.S. Navy," 26 Jul 46, Pers 215-BL.(Back)

Footnote 9-15: Memo, Dir of Planning and Control, BuPers, for Chief, NavPers (ca. Jan 46), sub: Negro Personnel, Pers 21B, BuPersRecs.(Back)

Footnote 9-16: BuPers, Memo on Discrimination of the Negro, 24 Jan 59. filed in BuPers Technical Library.(Back)

Footnote 9-17: Memo, Lt Dennis D. Nelson for Dep Dir. Pub Relations. 26 Mar 48, sub: Problems of the Stewards' Branch, PR 221-5393, GenRecsNav. On mental standards for stewards, sec BuPers Cir Ltr 41-46, 15 Feb 46.(Back)

Footnote 9-18: Ltr, Under SecNav for Congressman Clyde Doyle of California. 24 Aug 49, MM(1), GenRecsNav.(Back)

Footnote 9-19: For examples of the Navy's official explanation of steward duties, see Ltr, Actg SecNav to Lester Granger, 22 Apr 46, QN/MM(2), and Ltr, Under SecNav to Congressman Clyde Doyle of California, 24 Aug 49; both in GenRecsNav. See also Ltr, Chief, NavPers, to Dr. Carl Yaeger, 16 Oct 47, P16-1, BuPersRecs, and Testimony of Capt Fred R. Stickney, BuPers, and Vice Adm William M. Fechteler, Chief of Naval Personnel, before the

President's Committee on Equality of Treatment and Opportunity in the Armed Services (Fahy Cmte), 13 Jan and 28 Mar 49.(Back)

Footnote 9-20: Ltr, Nelson to author, 10 Feb 70.(Back)

Footnote 9-21: Ltr, Dir, Plans and Oper Div, BuPers, to Richard Lueking, Berea College, 6 Dec 46, P16.1, BuPersRecs.(Back)

Footnote 9-22: Department of National Defense, "National Defense Conference on Racial Affairs," 26 Apr 48, morning session, pp. 46-47.(Back)

Footnote 9-23: Memo, Lt D. D. Nelson, office of Public Relations, for Capt E. B. Dexter, Office of Public Relations, 24 Aug 48, sub: Negro Stewards, Petty Officer Ratings, Status of, PR 221-14003, GenRecsNav.(Back)

Footnote 9-24: Ltr, Asst SecNav to Lester Granger, 22 Apr 48, QN-MM (2), GenRecsNav.(Back)

Footnote 9-25: Interv, Nichols with Capt George A. Holderness, Jr., USN, in Nichols Collection, CMH.(Back)

Footnote 9-26: Ltr, Granger to SecNav, 15 Mar 48, SO-3-18-56, SecNav files, GenRecsNav.(Back)

Footnote 9-27: Interv, Nichols with Sullivan; Intervs, author with Lt Cmdr D. D. Nelson, 17 Sep 69, and with James C. Evans, Counselor to the SecDef, 10 Jan 73; Ltr, Nelson to author, 10 Feb 70. All in CMH files.(Back)

Footnote 9-28: Memo, Lt Nelson for Capt Dexter, Pub Rels Office, 24 Aug 48, sub: Negro Stewards, Petty Officer Ratings, Status of, PR 221-14003; idem for Dep Dir, Off of Pub Relations, 26 Mar 48, sub: Problems of the Stewards' Branch, PR 221-5393; both in GenRecsNav. The quotation is from the latter document.(Back)

Footnote 9-29: Ltr, Nelson to SecNav, 7 Jan 49, SecNav files, GenRecsNav. For discussion of the presidential inquiry, see Chapter 14.(Back)

Footnote 9-30: BuPers Cir Ltr, 17 Oct 45.(Back)

Footnote 9-31: Testimony of Capt Fred Stickney at National Defense Conference on Negro Affairs, 26 Apr 48, morning session, p. 47.(Back)

Footnote 9-32: Change 12 to Ankle D-5114, BuPers Manual, 1942.(Back)

Footnote 9-33: "BuPers Hist," pp. 83-85, and Supplement (LN), pp. 4-8, copy in CMH. Unless otherwise noted the data for this section on black officers in World War II are from this source.(Back)

Footnote 9-34: Nelson, "Integration of the Negro," pp. 156-58.(Back)

Footnote 9-35: "BuPers Hist," p. 85. The quotation is from Ltr, Chief, NavPers, to CO, USS *Laramie*, 16 Jul 45, BuPersRecs.(Back)

Footnote 9-36: "BuPers Hist," p. 85.(Back)

Footnote 9-37: Nelson "Integration of the Negro," p. 157.(Back)

Footnote 9-38: ALNAV 252-46, 21 May 46, sub: Transfer to Regular Navy.(Back)

Footnote 9-39: Ltr, Granger to SecNav, 31 Jul 46, 54-1-13, Forrestal file, GenRecsNav. One of these applicants was Nelson, then a lieutenant, who received a promotion upon assignment as commanding officer of a logistic support company in the Marshall Islands. The grade became permanent upon Nelson's assignment to the Public Relations Bureau in Washington in 1946.(Back)

Footnote 9-40: Nelson, "Integration of the Negro," pp. 157-59; Ltr, Nelson to author, 10 Feb 70; Interv, Nichols with Sullivan.(Back)

Footnote 9-41: Ltr. Exec Dir. ACLU, to SecNav, 26 Nov 57, GenRecsNav.(Back)

Footnote 9-42: "BuPers Narrative," 1:295.(Back)

Footnote 9-43: Norfolk *Journal and Guide*, August 20, 1949.(Back)

Footnote 9-44: Ltr, SecNav to William T. Farley, Chmn, Civilian Components Policy Bd, DOD, 4 Mar 50, Q4, GenRecsNav.(Back)

Footnote 9-45: Statement of Dr. Mordecai Johnson at National Defense Conference on Negro Affairs, 26 Apr 48, morning session, p. 42.(Back)

Footnote 9-46: Ltr, Nelson to author, 10 Feb 70; see also "BuPersHist," p. 84.(Back)

Footnote 9-47: Statement of Roy Wilkins at National Defense Conference on Negro Affairs, 26 Apr 48, morning session p. 44.(Back)

Footnote 9-48: Testimony of Stickney at National Defense Conference on Negro Affairs, 26 Apr 48, morning session, p. 43.(Back)

Footnote 9-49: U.S. Congress, House, Committee on Armed Services, Subcommittee No. 3, Organization and Mobilization, *Hearings on S. 1641, To Establish the Women's Army Corps in the Regular Army, To Authorize the Enlistment and Appointment of Women in the Regular Navy and Marine Corps and the Naval and Marine Corps Reserve and for Other Purposes*, 80th Cong., 2d sess., 18 Feb 48, pp. 5603-08, 5657, 5698, 5734-36. The Powell quotation is on page 5734.(Back)

Footnote 9-50: Ltr, SecNav to Congresswoman Margaret Chase Smith (Maine), 24 Jul 47, OG/P14-2, GenRecsNav.(Back)

Footnote 9-51: Memo, Dir, Pol Div, BuPers, for Capt William C. Chapman, Office of Information, Navy Dept, 21 Sep 65; Memo, Chief, NavPers, for Chief, Bur of Public Relations, 16 Dec 48. QR4; both in BuPersRecs.(Back)

Footnote 9-52: See Testimony of Lester Granger and Assistant Secretary Brown at National Defense Conference on Negro Affairs, 26 Apr 48, morning session, pp. 45-46; and Memo, Nelson for Marx Leva, 24 May 48, copy in Nelson Archives.(Back)

Footnote 9-53: Memo, Asst SecNav for Air for Dep CNO, 3 Feb 48, sub: Racial Discrimination, P1-4 (8), GenRecsNav.(Back)

Footnote 9-54: See Memo, Chief, NavPers, for CO, USS *Grand Canyon* (AD 28), 17 Dec 48, sub: Navy Department's Non Discrimination Policy—Alleged Violation of, P14; Ltr, Chief, NavPers, to Cmdt, Twelfth Nav Dist, 27 Feb 46, sub: Officer Screening Procedure and Indoctrination Course in the Supervision of Negro Personnel—Establishment of, Pers 4221; both in BuPersRecs.(Back)

Footnote 9-55: Memo, Nelson for Chief, NavPers, 29 Nov 48, sub: Complaint of Navy Enlisted Man Made to Pittsburgh Courier..., PR221, BuPersRecs.(Back)

Footnote 9-56: Memo, Chief, NavPers, for JAG, 11 Feb 47, sub: HR 279: To Prohibit Race Segregation in the Armed Forces of the United States, GenRecsNav.(Back)

Footnote 9-57: For discussion of the problem of comparative enlistment standards, see Chapter 12.(Back)

Footnote 9-58: Ltr, Lt Cmdr, E. S. Hope to SecDef, 17 May 48, with attached rpt, D54-1-10, GenRecsNav.(Back)

Footnote 9-59: See, for example, Ltr, Granger to SecNav, 10 Jun 47, 54-1-13, Forrestal file, GenRecsNav, and Granger's extensive comments and questions at the National Defense Conference on Negro Affairs, 26 Apr 48.(Back)

Footnote 10-1: Memos, Dir, Div of Plans and Policies, for CMC, 25 Sep and 17 Oct 46, sub: Post War Personnel Requirements, A0-1, MC files. Unless otherwise noted, all the documents cited in this chapter are located in Hist Div, HQMC. The quotation is from the September memo.(Back)

Footnote 10-2: Memo, G. C. Thomas, Div of Plans and Policies, for CMC, 6 Jan 47, sub: Negro Requirements, A0-1.(Back)

Footnote 10-3: USMC Muster Rolls of Officers and Enlisted Men, 1946 and 1948.(Back)

Footnote 10-4: Memo, G. C. Thomas for CMC, 11 Jun 47, sub: Negro Requirements and Assignments, A0-1.(Back)

Footnote 10-5: Memo, Dir, Div of Plans and Policies, for CMC, 28 Aug 47, sub: Requirements for General Duty Negro Marines, A0-1.(Back)

Footnote 10-6: Idem for Div, Pub Info, 10 Nov 48, sub: Information Relating to Negro Marines, A0-1.(Back)

Footnote 10-7: Unless otherwise noted, statistics in this section are from NA Pers, 15658 (A), *Report, Navy and Marine Corps Military Statistics*, 30 Jun 59, BuPers. Official figures on black marines are from reports of the USMC Personnel Accounting Section.(Back)

Footnote 10-8: Memo, Dir, Plans and Policies Div, for CMC, 20 May 48, sub: Procurement and Assignment of Negro Enlisted Personnel, A0-1.(Back)

Footnote 10-9: Ibid., 28 Aug 47, sub: Requirements for General Duty Negro Marines, A0-1.(Back)

Footnote 10-10: Ibid., 14 Nov 49, sub: Designation of Units for Assignment of Negro Marines, A0-1.(Back)

Footnote 10-11: For criticism of assignment restrictions, see comments and questions at the National Defense Conference on Negro Affairs, 26 Apr 48 (afternoon session), pp. 1-10, copy in CMH.(Back)

Footnote 10-12: G-1, Div of Plans and Policies, Operational Diary, Sep 45-Oct 46, 23 Apr 47; Memo, Dir of Personnel (Div of Recruiting) for Off in Charge, Northeastern Recruiting Div, 17 Jan 46, sub: Enlistment of Negro Ex-Marines, MC 706577. See also *Afro-American*, February 16, 1946.(Back)

Footnote 10-13: Msg, CMC to CG, Cp Lejeune, 19 Feb 46, MC 122026; Memo, CG, Cp Lejeune, for CMC, 28 Feb 46, sub: Personnel and Equipment for Antiaircraft Artillery Training Battalion (Colored), Availability of, RPS-1059, MC files.(Back)

Footnote 10-14: Memo, G. C. Thomas for Dir of Personnel, 6 Mar 48, sub: Replacements for Enlisted Personnel (Colored) Assignment of, Request for, A0-3; Msg, CINCPAC/POA PEARL to CNO, 282232Z Apr 46, MC 76735, MC files.(Back)

Footnote **10-15:** Norfolk *Journal and Guide*, May 4, 1946. See also Murray, *Negro Yearbook*, 1949 pp. 272-73. On the general accuracy of the press charges, see Shaw and Donnelly, *Blacks in the Marine Corps*, pp. 47-51.(Back)

Footnote **10-16:** CO, Montford Point, Press Conference (ca. 1 May 47), quoted in Div of Plans and Policies Staff Report, "Rescinding Ltr of Instruction #421," MC files; unsigned, untitled Memo written in the Division of Plans and Policies on black marines and the black press (ca. Aug 55).(Back)

Footnote **10-17:** Memo, Dir, Div of Plans and Policies, for CMC, 3 May 46, sub: Enlisting of Negroes in the Marine Corps From Civilian Sources, A0-1.(Back)

Footnote **10-18:** Ibid., 23 Oct 46, sub: Enlistment of Negroes, 1335-110; Memo, CMC to Off in Charge, Northeastern Recruiting Div, et al., 23 Oct 46, sub: Negro First Enlistments, Quota for Month of November, 1946, AP-1231. There was an attempt to stall first enlistment, see Memo, Dir of Personnel, for Dir, Div of Plans and Policies, 17 May 46, sub: Enlisting of Negroes in the Marine Corps From Civilian Sources; but it was overruled, Memo, Dir, Div of Plans and Policies, for Dir of Personnel, 23 May 46, same sub, A0-1.(Back)

Footnote **10-19:** Memo, Dir, Div of Plans and Policies, for CMC, 28 May 47, sub: Program for Accelerated Attrition of Negro Marines, A0-1; Maj S. M. Adams, "Additional Directives From Plans and Policies—3 June 1947," 3 Jun 47; Speed Ltr, CMC to CG, Marine Corps Air Station, Cherry Point, N.C., et al., 8 May 47, A0-1; Memo, CMC to Depot Quartermaster, Depot of Supplies, 3 Jun 47, sub: Discharge for the Convenience of the Government Certain Enlisted Negro Members of the Marine Corps, 070-15-447.(Back)

Footnote **10-20:** Memo, Dir, Div of Plans and Policies, for CMC, 12 Mar 46, sub: Steward's Branch Personnel, Information Concerning, A0-3, MC files.(Back)

Footnote **10-21:** Ltr, CG, Cp Lejeune, to CMC, 4 Apr 46, sub: Steward's Branch Personnel, 060105.(Back)

Footnote **10-22:** Memo, Dir, Div of Plans and Policies, for CMC, 18 Mar 47, sub: Enlistment of Negro Personnel, 01A7647.(Back)

Footnote **10-23:** Ibid., 16 Apr 47, sub: First Enlistment of Negro Personnel, A0-1, and 9 Oct 47, sub: Procurement and Assignment of Stewards Personnel, Box 1515-30; Ltr, CMC (Div of Recruiting) to Off in Charge, Northeastern Recruiting Div, 29 Apr 47, sub: Negro First Enlistments, 07A11947.(Back)

Footnote **10-24:** Memo, Dir, Div of Plans and Policies, for CMC, 15 Sep 47, sub: Disposition of Negro Personnel Who Enlisted With a View Toward Qualifying for Stewards Duties..., 01A25847.(Back)

Footnote **10-25:** Ibid., 26 Dec 47, sub: Procurement of Steward Personnel, A0-1; see also Ltr, CMC to Chief of Naval Personnel, 6 Jan 48, sub: Discharge of Steward Personnel From Navy to Enlist in the Marine Corps, MC 967879; Memo, Chief of Naval Personnel for CMC, 28 Jan 48, sub: Discharge of Certain Steward Branch Personnel for Purpose of Enlistment in the Marine Corps.(Back)

Footnote **10-26:** Memo, Dir, Div of Plans and Policies, for CMC, 19 Mar 48, sub: Procurement and Distribution of Steward Personnel, A0-1.(Back)

Footnote **10-27:** Ibid., 12 Aug 48, sub: Steward Personnel, Allowances and Procurement, A0-1; Ltr, CMC to CG, Marine Barracks, Cp Lejeune, 16 Aug 48, sub: Negro Recruits, 01A22948.(Back)

Footnote **10-28:** Memo, Dir, Div of Plans and Policies, for CMC, 15 Oct 48, sub: Disposition of Negro Personnel Who Enlist "For Steward Duty Only" and Subsequently Fail to Qualify for Such Duty, Study #169-48; Ltr, QMG of MC to CMC, 17 Sep 48, same sub, CA6.(Back)

Footnote **10-29:** Msg, CG, Cp Lejeune, N.C., to CMC, 31 Dec 48.(Back)

Footnote **10-30:** Memo, Chief of Naval Personnel and CMC for All Ships and Stations, 28 Feb 49, sub: Discharge of Stewards, USN, For the Purpose of Immediate Enlistment in Marine Corps, Pers-66, GenRecsNav; Memo, CMC for Dir of Recruiting, 25 Feb 49, sub: Mental Requirements for Enlistment for "Steward Duty Only," A0-1; Ltr, CMC (Div of Recruiting) to Off in Charge, Northeastern Recruiting Div, 3 Mar 49, sub: Mental Standards for Enlistment for Steward Duty Only, MC1088081; Msg, CMC to Div of Recruiting, 7 Apr 49.(Back)

Footnote **10-31:** Memo, CMC for CG, Marine Barracks, Cp Lejeune, N.C., 8 Dec 47, sub: Negro Recruits, 01A33847.(Back)

Footnote **10-32:** Ltr, CMC to CG, Cp Lejeune, 24 May 48, A0-1; Memo, CMC for Off in Charge of Recruiting Div, 29 Jan 49, sub: Enlistment of Negroes, 07D14848; Msg, CMC to Offs in Charge of Recruiting Divs, 25 Apr 49.(Back)

Footnote 10-33: Ltr, CO, 52d Defense Battalion, to CMC, 15 Jan 46, sub: Employment of Colored Personnel as Antiaircraft Artillery Troops, Recommendations on, 02-46, MC files.(Back)

Footnote 10-34: Memo, Dir of Personnel for Dir, Div of Plans and Policies, 21 Jul 48, sub: General Classification Test Scores of Colored Enlisted Marines, 07DZ0348. The GCT distribution of 991 black marines as of 1 March 1948 was as follows: Group I (130-163), 0%; Group II (110-129), 4.94%; Group III (90-109), 24.7%; Group IV (60-89), 61.45%; and Group V (42-59), 9.54%. Memo, Dir of Personnel to Dir, Div of Plans and Policies, 30 May 48, sub: Marines—Tests and Testing.(Back)

Footnote 10-35: Ltr, CO, MB, NAD, McAlester, Okla., to CMC, 5 Nov 46, sub: Assignment of Colored Marines, 2385.(Back)

Footnote 10-36: Ltr, CO, NAD, McAlester, Okla., to CMC, 5 Nov 46, 1st Ind to Ltr, CO, MB, McAlester, 2385; Memo, Dir, Div of Plans and Policies, for CMC, 3 Dec 46, sub: Assignment of Negro Marines to MB, Naval Magazine, Port Chicago, Calif., in lieu of MB, NAD, McAlester, Okla., A0-1.(Back)

Footnote 10-37: Memo, CMC for CNO, 3 Dec 46, sub: Assignment of Negro Marines to MB, Naval Magazine, Port Chicago, Calif., and MB, NAD, Earle, N.J., A0-1; idem for CO, MB, NAD, Earle, N.J., 9 Jan 47, sub: Assignment of Colored Marines to Marine Barracks, Naval Ammunition Depot, Earle, N.J.; idem for CO, Department of the Pacific, and CO, MB, NAD, McAlester, Okla., A0-1; Memo, CNO for CMC, 6 Jan 47, same sub, OP 30 M.(Back)

Footnote 10-38: Speed Ltr, CMC to Cmdt, Twelfth Naval District, 12 Jun 47; Memo, CMC for CO, MB, Naval Shipyard, Brooklyn, N.Y., 13 Jun 47, sub: Assignment of Negro Marines to Second Guard Company, Marine Barracks Naval Shipyard, Brooklyn, N.Y., A0-1; idem for CO, MB, USNAD, Hingham, Mass., 18 Jun 47, sub: Assignment of Negro Marines, A0-1; Speed Ltr, CMC to Cmdt, Twelfth Naval District, 18 Jun 47, 01A76847; Memo, CMC for CO, MB, NAD, Ft. Mifflin, Pa., 18 Jun 47, sub: Assignment of Negro Marines, A0-1; Memo, Cmdt, Fourth Naval District for CO, MB, NAD, Ft. Mifflin, Pa., 18 Jun 47, same sub.(Back)

Footnote 10-39: Memo, CO, MB, NAD, Hingham, Mass., for CMC, 26 Jun 47, sub: Comments on Assignment of Negro Marines, AB-1; Memo, CO, NAD, Hingham, Mass., for CMC, 26 Jun 47, 1st Ind to AB-1, 26 Jun 47.(Back)

Footnote 10-40: Ltr, Cmdt, First Naval District, to CMC, 30 Jun 47, sub: Assignment of Negro Marines, 2d Ind to AB-1, 26 Jun 47.(Back)

Footnote 10-41: Ltr, CO, Naval Base, New York, to CMC, 10 July 47, sub: Assignment of Negro Marines to Second Guard Company, Marine Barracks, New York Naval Shipyard, Brooklyn, N.Y., NB-139.(Back)

Footnote 10-42: Ltr, Chief, Bur of Ord, to CNO, 11 Aug 47, sub: Naval Ammunition Depot, Earle, N.J.—Assignment of Negro Marine Complement, NTI-34.(Back)

Footnote 10-43: Memo, Dir, Div of Plans and Policies, for CMC, 19 Nov 47, sub: First Enlistments of Negro Personnel, A0-1; Memo, Chief, Bur of Ord, for CNO, 15 Dec 47, sub: Assignment of Negro Marines at Naval Ammunition Depot, Earle, Red Bank, N.J.; Memo, CNO for Chief, Bur of Ord, 6 Jan 48, same sub.(Back)

Footnote 10-44: Memo, Dir, Div of Plans and Policies, 29 Jul 47, sub: Negro Requirements and Assignments, A0-1, MC files.(Back)

Footnote 10-45: Memo, Chief, Bur of Supplies and Accounts, for CNO, 14 Oct 47, sub: Assignment of Negro Marines, P-16-1; Memo, CNO to CMC, 20 Nov 47, same sub, Op 415 D.(Back)

Footnote 10-46: Memo, Gen Vandegrift to SecNav, 25 Aug 47, sub: Assignment of Negro Marines, 54-1-29, GenRecsNav.(Back)

Footnote 10-47: See, for example, the analysis that appeared in the Chicago *Defender*, August 14, 1948.(Back)

Footnote 10-48: Shaw and Donnelly, *Blacks and the Marine Corps*, pp. 47-48; see also Selective Service System, *Special Groups* (Monograph 10), I:105.(Back)

Footnote 10-49: Memo, Dir, Div of Plans and Policies, for CMC, 11 May 48, sub: Appointment to Commissioned Rank in the Regular Marine Corps, Case of Midshipman John Earl Rudder, A0-1; see also Dept of Navy Press Release, 25 Aug 48.(Back)

Footnote 10-50: Memo, Dir of Public Information for CMC, 11 Feb 49, sub: Publicity on Second Lieutenant John Rudder, USMC, AG 1364; see also Ltr, Lt Cmdr Dennis Nelson to James C. Evans, 24 Feb 70, CMH files.(Back)

Footnote 10-51: Memo, Oliver Smith for CMC, 11 Feb 49, with attached CMC note.(Back)

Footnote 10-52: Ltr, A. Philip Randolph to Gen C. B. Cates, 8 Mar 49; Ltr, CMC to Randolph, 10 Mar 49, AW 828.(Back)

354

Footnote 10-53: Memo, Dir, Div of Reserve, for CMC, 6 May 47, sub: General Policy Governing Negro Reservists, AF 1271; Ltr, William Griffin to CMC, 3 Mar 47; Ltr, Col R. McPate to William Griffin, 11 Mar 47.(Back)

Footnote 10-54: Memo, Dir, Div of Plans and Policies, for CMC, 7 May 47, sub: General Policy Governing Negro Reservists, A0-1.(Back)

Footnote 10-55: Memo, Dir of Reserve for CMC, 15 May 47, sub: General Policy Concerning Negro Reservists, AF 394.(Back)

Footnote 10-56: Memo, Dir, Div of Plans and Policies, for CMC, 1 Mar 48, sub: Enlistment of Negro Ex-Marines in Organized Reserve, A0-1.(Back)

Footnote 10-57: USMC Muster Rolls, 1947.(Back)

Footnote 10-58: Interv, Martin Blumenson with 1st Sgt Jerome Pressley, 21 Feb 66, CMH files.(Back)

Footnote 11-1: For a comprehensive and authoritative account of the Negro in the Army Air Forces during World War II, see Osur's *Blacks in the Army Air Forces During World War II*.(Back)

Footnote 11-2: See Memo, CS/AC for G-3, 31 May 40, sub: Employment of Negro Personnel in the Air Corps Units, G-3/6541-Gen 527.(Back)

Footnote 11-3: For the effect on unit morale, see Charles E. Francis, *The Tuskegee Airmen: The Story of the Negro in the U.S. Air Force* (Boston: Bruce Humphries, 1955), p. 164; see also USAF Oral History Program, Interview with Lt Gen B. O. Davis, Jr., Jan 73.(Back)

Footnote 11-4: Lee, *Employment of Negro Troops*, pp. 462-64; see also Interv, author with Lt Gen Benjamin O. Davis, Jr., 12 Jun 70, CMH files.(Back)

Footnote 11-5: A nonrated officer is one not having or requiring a currently effective aeronautical rating; that is, an officer who is not a pilot, navigator, or bombardier.(Back)

Footnote 11-6: Interv, author with Davis; see also Osur's *Blacks in the Army Air Forces During World War II*, ch. V.(Back)

Footnote 11-7: "Summary of AAF Post-War Surveys," prepared by Noel Parrish, copy in NAACP Collection, Library of Congress.(Back)

Footnote 11-8: Noel F. Parrish, "The Segregation of the Negro in the Army Air Forces," thesis submitted to the USAF Air Command and Staff School, Maxwell AFB, Ala., 1947, pp. 50-55.(Back)

Footnote 11-9: Ltr, Hq AAF, to CG, Tactical Training Cmd, 21 Aug 42, sub: Professional Qualities of Officers Assigned to Negro Units, 220.765-3, AFSHRC.(Back)

Footnote 11-10: Parrish, "Segregation of the Negro in the Army Air Forces," pp. 50-55. The many difficulties involved in the assignment of white officers to black units are discussed in Osur's *Blacks in the Army Air Forces During World War II*, ch V.(Back)

Footnote 11-11: AAF Transport Cmd, "History of the Command, 1 July 1946-31 December 1946" pp. 120-26.(Back)

Footnote 11-12: Parrish, "Segregation of the Negro in the Army Air Forces."(Back)

Footnote 11-13: AAF Ltr 35-268, 11 Aug 45.(Back)

Footnote 11-14: Rpt, ACS/AS-1 to WDSS, 17 Sep 45, sub: Participation of Negro Troops in the Post-War Military Establishment, WDSS 291.2.(Back)

Footnote 11-15: Ibid. For an analysis of these recommendations, see Gropman's *The Air Force Integrates*, ch. II.(Back)

Footnote 11-16: WD Bureau of Public Relations, Memo for the Press, 20 Sep 45; Office of Public Relations, Godman Field, Ky., "Col. Davis Issues Report on Godman Field," 10 Oct 45; Memo, Chief, Programs and Manpower Section, Troop Basis Branch, Organization Division, D/T&R, for Dir of Military Personnel, 23 Apr 48, no sub; all in Negro Affairs, SecAF files. See also "History of Godman Field, Ky., 1 Mar—15 Oct 45," AFSHRC.(Back)

Footnote 11-17: "History of the 2143d AAF Base Unit, Pilot School, Basic, Advanced, and Tuskegee Army Air Field, 1 Sep 1945-31 Oct 1945," AFSHRC.(Back)

Footnote 11-18: For an example of black reaction see *Ebony* Magazine V (September 1949).(Back)

Footnote 11-19: Memo, James C. Evans, Adviser to the SecDef, for Capt Robert W. Berry, 10 Feb 48, SecDef 291.2 files.(Back)

Footnote 11-20: "History of the 477th Composite Group," 15 Sep 45-15 Feb 46, Feb-Mar 46, and 1 Mar-15 Jul 46, AFSHRC.(Back)

Footnote 11-21: All figures from STM-30, 1 Sep 45 and 1 Apr 46.(Back)

Footnote 11-22: Memo, TAG for CG's et al., 4 Feb 46, sub: Utilization of Negro Personnel, AG 291.2 (31 Jan 46).(Back)

Footnote 11-23: Under the terms of the National Security Act of 1947 the U.S. Air Force was created as a separate service in a Department of the Air Force on 18 September 1947. The new service included the old Army Air Forces; the Air Corps, U.S. Army; and General Headquarters Air Force. The strictures of WD Circular 124, like those of many other departmental circulars, were adopted by the new service. For convenience' sake the terms *Air Force* and *service* will be employed in the remaining sections of this chapter even where the terms *Army Air Forces* and *component* would be more appropriate.(Back)

Footnote 11-24: "Tactical Air Command (TAC) History, 1 Jan-30 Dec 48," pp. 94-96, AFSHRC; see also Lawrence J. Paszek, "Negroes and the Air Force, 1939-1949," *Military Affairs* (Spring 1967), p. 8.(Back)

Footnote 11-25: Memo, DCofS/Personnel, TAC, for CG, TAC, 18 Mar 48, AFSHRC.(Back)

Footnote 11-26: Memo, DCofS/P&A, USAF, for Asst SecAF, 5 Dec 47, sub: Air Force Negro Troops in the Zone of Interior, Negro Affairs, SecAF files.(Back)

Footnote 11-27: "History of MacDill Army Airfield, Oct 46," pp. 10-11, AFSHRC. For a detailed analysis of the MacDill riot and its aftermath, see Gropman, *The Air Force Integrates*, ch. I; see also ch. 5, above.(Back)

Footnote 11-28: Memo, unsigned (probably DCofS/P&A), for Asst SecAF Zuckert, 22 Apr 48, SecAF files.(Back)

Footnote 11-29: See Air Force Testimony Before the National Defense Conference on Negro Affairs (afternoon session), pp. 29-32, CMH files.(Back)

Footnote 11-30: Memo, DCofS/P&A, TAC, for CG, TAC, 18 Mar 48, sub: Utilization of Negro Manpower, AFSHRC.(Back)

Footnote 11-31: Parrish, "Segregation of the Negro in the Army Air Forces," pp. 72-73.(Back)

Footnote 11-32: Memo, Ray for ASW, 25 Jul 46, ASW 291.2.(Back)
Footnote 11-33: Memo, Petersen for CG, AAF, 29 Jul 46, ASW 291.2.(Back)
Footnote 11-34: Memo, Brig Gen Reuben C. Hood, Jr., Office of CG, AAF, for ASW, 13 Sep 46, ASW 291.2.(Back)

Footnote 11-35: Memo, unsigned, for Asst SecAF Zuckert, 22 Apr 48, SecAF files. The figures cited in this memorandum were slightly at variance with the official strength figures as compiled later in the *Unites States Air Force Statistical Digest I* (1948). The *Digest* put the Air Force's strength (excluding Army personnel still under Air Force control) on 31 March 1948 at 345,827, including 25,404 Negroes (8.9 percent of the total). The 10 percent plus estimate mentioned in the memorandum, however, was right on the mark when statistics for enlisted strength alone are considered.(Back)

Footnote 11-36: Memo, DCofS/P&A, TAC, for CG, TAC, 18 Mar 48, sub: Utilization of Negro Manpower, AFSHRC.(Back)

Footnote 11-37: Memo, Adj, 20th Fighter Wing, for CG, Ninth AF, undated, sub: Transfer of Structural Firefighters; 2d Ind, Hq 332d Fighter Wing, Lockbourne, to CG, Ninth AF, 26 Apr 48, Hist of Ninth AF, AFSHRC.(Back)

Footnote 11-38: Memo, DCofS/P&A, TAC, for CG, TAC, 18 Mar 48, sub: Utilization of Negro Manpower, AFSHRC.(Back)

Footnote 11-39: Memo, Maj Gen Old for CG, TAC, 26 Jan 48, sub: Utilization of Negro Manpower, 9AF 200.3, Hist of Ninth AF, AFSHRC.(Back)

Footnote 11-40: Ltr, Lt Gen Quesada to Maj Gen Old, Ninth AF, 9 Apr 48, Hist of Ninth AF, AFSHRC.(Back)

Footnote 11-41: Ltrs, CG, TAC, to CS/USAF, 1 Sep 48, sub: Reception of Submarginal Enlisted Personnel; VCS/USAF to CG, TAC, 11 Sep 48, sub: Elimination of Undesirable or Substandard Airmen; CG, TAC, to CS/USAF, 24 Sep 48, same sub. All in AFSHRC.(Back)

Footnote 11-42: Ltr, DCofS/P&A, TAC, to CG, Ninth AF, 19 May 48, sub: Submarginal Enlisted Personnel; Record of Dir of Per Staff, TAC, Mtg, 28 Oct 48; both in AFSHRC.(Back)

Footnote 11-43: Ltr, CG, TAC, to CG, Ninth AF, 9 Apr 48, TAC 314 (9 Apr 48), AFSHRC.(Back)

Footnote 11-44: Hq TAC, Record and Routing Sheet, 16 Apr 48, sub: Supervisory Visit 332d Ftr Gp, Lockbourne AFB, AFSHRC.(Back)

Footnote 11-45: Ltr, CG, Ninth AF, to CG, TAC, 10 Feb 48, sub: Assignment of Negro Personnel, Hist of Ninth AF, AFSHRC.(Back)

Footnote 11-46: Hq TAC, Record and Routing Sheet, 16 Apr 48, sub: Supervisory Visit 332d Ftr Gp, Lockbourne AFB, AFSHRC.(Back)

Footnote 11-47: Ltrs, CG, TAC, to CG, Ninth AF, 9 Apr 48, and DCG, TAC, to CG, Ninth AF, 7 May 48, TAC 210.3; both in Hist of Ninth AF, AFSHRC.(Back)

Footnote 11-48: Memo, A-1, Ninth AF, for C/S, Ninth AF, 18 May 48, sub: Manning of 332d Fighter Wing, Hist of Ninth AF; Record of the TAC Staff Conf, 18 May 48; both in AFSHRC.(Back)

Footnote 11-49: Ltr, Brig Gen J. V. Crabb to Maj Gen Robert M. Lee, Hq TAC, 19 May 48, Hist of Ninth AF, AFSHRC.(Back)

Footnote 11-50: Ltr, CG, Ninth AF, to Maj Gen R. M. Lee, TAC, 18 May 48, Hist of Ninth AF, AFSHRC.(Back)

Footnote 11-51: For discussion of these views and their influence on officers, see USAF Oral History Program, Interviews with Brig Gen Noel Parrish, 30 Mar 73, Col Jack Marr, 1 Oct 73, and Eugene Zuckert, Apr 73.(Back)

Footnote 11-52: Ltr, Brig Gen J. V. Crabb to Maj Gen Robert M. Lee, Hq TAC, 19 May 48, Hist of Ninth AF, AFSHRC.(Back)

Footnote 11-53: Interv, author with Davis.(Back)

Footnote 11-54: See history of various aviation air units in "History of the Strategic Air Command, 1948," vols VI and VIII, AFSHRC.(Back)

Footnote 11-55: For discussion of the strength of this outside pressure, see USAF Oral History Program. Interviews with Davis and Brig Gen Lucius Theus, Jan 73.(Back)

Footnote 11-56: Ltr, Lemuel Graves to Gen Carl Spaatz, 26 Mar 48; Ltr, Spaatz to Graves, 19 Apr 48. A copy of the correspondence was also sent to the SecAF. See Col Jack F. Marr, "A Report on the First Year of Implementation of Current Policies Regarding Negro Personnel," n.d., PPB 291.2.(Back)

Footnote 11-57: Department of National Defense, "National Defense Conference on Negro Affairs," 26 Apr 48 (morning session) p. 62. The conference, convened by Secretary of Defense Forrestal, provided an opportunity for a group of black leaders to question major defense officials on the department's racial policies. See ch. 13.(Back)

Footnote 11-58: Department of National Defense, "National Defense Conference on Negro Affairs," 28 Apr 48, (morning session), p. 67.(Back)

Footnote 11-59: Ibid., p. 69.(Back)

Footnote 11-60: Memo, Edwards for SecAF, 29 Apr 48, sub: Conference With Group of Prominent Negroes, Negro Affairs 1948, SecAF files.(Back)

Footnote 11-61: Interv, author with Evans, 7 Apr 70; Note, Evans to Col Marr, 8 Jun 50, SD 291.2.(Back)

Footnote 11-62: Memo, Evans for SecAF, 7 Jun 48, sub: Negro Air Units, D54-1-12. SecDef files.(Back)

Footnote 11-63: DCofS/P Summary Sheet for CofS, 15 Jul 48, sub: Negro Air Units, Negro Affairs 1948, SecAF files.(Back)

Footnote 11-64: During World War II, Edwards served as the Army's Assistant Chief of Staff, G-3. For a discussion of his opposition at that time to the concentration of large groups of men in categories IV and V, see Edwin W. Kenworthy, "The Case Against Army Segregation," *The Annals of the American Academy of Political and Social Science* 275 (May 1951):29. See also Lee's *Employment of Negro Troops*, p. 159. Edward's part in the integration program is based on USAF Oral History Program, Interviews with Zuckert, General William F. McKee, Davis, Senator Stuart Symington, and Marr. See also Interv, author with Lt Gen Idwal H. Edwards, Nov 73, CMH files.(Back)

Footnote 11-65: Ltr, Marr to author, 19 Jun 70, CMH files.(Back)

Footnote 11-66: A group created to review policy and make recommendations to the Chief of Staff when called upon, the Air Board consisted at this time of the Assistant Chiefs of the Air Staff, the Air Inspector, the Air Comptroller, the Director of Information, the Deputy Assistant Chief of Staff for Research and Development, and other officials when appropriate.(Back)

Footnote 11-67: Memo, Maj Leon Bell for Zuckert, 27 Oct 48, SecAF files. Nugent later succeeded Edwards as the chief Air Force personnel officer.(Back)

Footnote 11-68: This attitude is strongly displayed in the USAF Oral History Program, Interviews with Lt Gen Richard E. Nugent, 8 Jun 73, and Marr, 1 Oct 73.(Back)

Footnote 11-69: USAF Oral Hist Interv with Zuckert.(Back)

Footnote 11-70: Colonel Marr recalled a different chronology for the Air Force integration plan. According to Marr, his proposals were forwarded by Edwards to Symington who in turn discussed them at a meeting of the Secretary of Defense's Personnel Policy Board sometime before June 1948. The board rejected the plan at the behest of Secretary of the Army Royall, but later in the year outside pressure caused it to be reconsidered. Nothing is available in the files to corroborate Marr's recollections, nor do the other participants remember that Royall was ever involved in the Air Force's internal affairs. The records do not show when the Air Force study of race policy, which originated in the Air Board in May 1948, evolved into the plan for integration that Marr wrote and the Chief of Staff signed in December 1948, but it seems unlikely that the plan would have been ready before June. See Ltrs, Marr to author, 19 Jun 70, and 28 Jul 70, CMH files; see also USAF Oral Hist Interv with Marr.(Back)

Footnote 11-71: The Air Force integration plan underwent considerable revision and modification before its submission to the Secretary of Defense in January 1949. The quotations in the next paragraphs are taken from the version approved by the Chief of Staff on 29 December 1948.(Back)

Footnote 11-72: Memo, Edwards for SecAF, 29 Apr 48, sub: Conference With Group of Prominent Negroes, Negro Affairs 1948, SecAF files.(Back)

Footnote 11-73: Memo, Zuckert to Evans, 22 Jul 48, sub: Negro Air Units, SecAF files.(Back)

Footnote 12-1: On the development of cold war roles and missions for the services, see Timothy W. Stanley, *American Defense and National Security* (Washington: Public Affairs Press, 1956), Chapter VIII.(Back)

Footnote 12-2: Jonathan Daniels, *The Man of Independence* (Philadelphia: Lippincott, 1950), p. 338. The quotation is from a speech before the National Colored Democratic Convention, Chicago, reprinted in the *Congressional Record*, 76th Cong., 3d sess., vol. 86, 5 Aug 1940, Appendix, pp. 5367-69.(Back)

Footnote 12-3: Quoted in James Peck, *Freedom Ride* (New York: Simon and Schuster, 1962), pp. 154-55.(Back)

Footnote 12-4: Quoted in Daniels, *Man of Independence*, pp. 339-40.(Back)

Footnote 12-5: Msg, HST to NAACP Convention, 29 Jun 47, *Public Papers of the President, 1947* (Washington: Government Printing Office, 1963), pp. 311-13.(Back)

Footnote 12-6: Harry S. Truman, *Memoirs* (New York: Doubleday, 1958), II:180-81; White, *A Man Called White*, pp. 330-31. Truman's concept of civil rights is analyzed in considerable detail in Donald R. McCoy and Richard T. Ruetten, *Quest and Response: Minority Rights and the Truman Administration* (Lawrence, Kansas: University of Kansas Press, 1973), Chapter III.(Back)

Footnote 12-7: White, *A Man Called White*, pp. 330-31.(Back)

Footnote 12-8: Intervs, Nichols with Oscar Ewing, former federal security administrator and senior presidential adviser, and Jonathan Daniels, 1954, in Nichols Collection, CMH; see also McCoy and Ruetten, *Quest and Response*, p. 49.(Back)

Footnote 12-9: White, *A Man Called White*, pp. 330-31.(Back)

Footnote 12-10: Executive Order 9808, 5 Dec 46.(Back)

Footnote 12-11: In addition to Chairman Wilson, the following people served on the committee: Sadie T. M. Alexander, James B. Carey, John S. Dickey, Morris L. Ernst, Roland B. Gittelsohn, Frank P. Graham, Francis J. Haas, Charles Luckman, Francis P. Matthews, Franklin D. Roosevelt, Jr., Henry Knox Sherrill, Boris Shishkin, Dorothy Tilly, and Channing Tobias.(Back)

Footnote 12-12: Parts of the survey of attitudes of participants in the World War II integration of platoons were included in remarks by Congresswoman Helen G. Douglas, published in the *Congressional Record*, 79th Cong., 2d sess., 1 Feb 1946, Appendix, pp. 432-443.(Back)

Footnote 12-13: *To Secure These Rights*, p. 162.(Back)

Footnote 12-14: Ibid., pp. 162-63.(Back)

Footnote 12-15: Ibid., p. 47.(Back)

Footnote 12-16: Truman, Special Message to the Congress on Civil Rights, 2 Feb 48, *Public Papers of the President, 1948*, pp. 121-26.(Back)

Footnote 12-17: Quoted in Walter Millis, ed., *The Forrestal Diaries* (New York: Viking Press, 1951), p. 88.(Back)

Footnote 12-18: Quoted by Granger in the interview he gave Nichols in 1954.(Back)

Footnote 12-19: Quoted in Millis, *Forrestal Diaries*, p. 301.(Back)

Footnote 12-20: Ibid., pp. 117, 147. Timothy Stanley describes the Eberstadt report as the Navy's "constructive alternative" to unification. See Stanley's *American Defense and National Security*, p. 75; see also Hewes, *From Root to McNamara*, pp. 276-77. For a detailed analysis of defense unification, see Lawrence Legere, Jr., "Unification of the Armed Forces," Chapter VI, in CMH.(Back)

Footnote 12-21: Millis, *Forrestal Diaries*, pp. 301, 497.(Back)

Footnote 12-22: Ltr, Forrestal to White, 21 Oct 47, Day file, Forrestal Papers, Princeton University Library.(Back)

Footnote 12-23: Remarks by James Forrestal at Dinner Meeting of the National Urban League, 12 Feb 48, copy in Misc file, Forrestal Papers; see also Ltr, Forrestal to John N. Brown, 27 Oct 47, Day file, ibid.(Back)

Footnote 12-24: In addition to his duties as Civilian Aide to the Secretary of the Army, Evans was made aide to the Secretary of Defense on 29 October 1947. (See Memo, SecDef for SA et al., 29 Oct 47, D70-1-5, files of Historian, OSD.) Evans was subsequently appointed "civilian assistant" to the Secretary of Defense by Secretary Louis Johnson on 28 Apr 49. (See NME Press Release, 17-49-A.)(Back)

Footnote 12-25: Ltr, Gibson to Ohly, 25 Nov 47, D54-1-3, Sec Def files.(Back)

Footnote 12-26: New York Times, November 23, 1947; Herald Tribune, November 23, 1947. See also L. D. Reddick, "The Negro Policy of the American Army Since World War II," Journal of Negro History 38 (April 1953):194-215.(Back)

Footnote 12-27: Ltr, White to Forrestal, 17 Feb 48, D54-1-3, SecDef files.(Back)

Footnote 12-28: Ltr, Forrestal to Rear Adm W. B. Young, 23 Oct 47, quoted in Millis, Forrestal Diaries, p. 334.(Back)

Footnote 12-29: Interv, Blumenson with Marx Leva, Special Assistant to the Secretary of Defense (1947-49) and later Assistant Secretary of Defense (Legal and Legislative Affairs), 4 May 64, CMH files.(Back)

Footnote 12-30: Handwritten Memo, Leva for Forrestal, attached to Ltr, White to Forrestal, 17 Feb 48; Ltr, Leva to Granger, 19 Feb 48; Ltr, Granger to Forrestal, 2 Mar 48. All in D54-1-3, SecDef files. The quotation is from the 2 March letter.(Back)

Footnote 12-31: Memo, Marx Leva for SA et al., 13 Apr 48; idem for Forrestal, 24 Apr 48; ltr, SecDef to All Invited, 10 Apr 48. All in D54-1-3, SecDef files. Those invited were Truman Gibson; Dr. Channing Tobias; Dr. Sadie T. M. Alexander; Mary McLeod Bethune; Dr. John W. Davis of West Virginia State College; Dr. Benjamin E. Mays of Morehouse College; Dr. Mordecai Johnson of Howard University; P. B. Young, Jr., of the Norfolk Journal and Guide; Willard Townsend of the United Transport Service Employees; Rev. John H. Johnson of New York; Walter White; Hobson E. Reynolds of the International Order of Elks; Bishop J. W. Gregg of Kansas City; Loren Miller of Los Angeles; and Charles Houston of Washington, D.C. Unable to attend, White sent his assistant Roy Wilkins, Townsend sent George L. P. Weaver, and Mrs. Bethune was replaced by Ira F. Lewis of the Pittsburgh Courier.(Back)

Footnote 12-32: Representing eight papers, a cross section of the influential black press, the journalists included Ira F. Lewis and William G. Nunn, Pittsburgh Courier; Cliff W. Mackay, Afro-American; Louis Martin and Charles Browning, Chicago Defender; Thomas W. Young and Louis R. Lautier, Norfolk Journal and Guide; Carter Wesley, Houston Defender; Frank L. Stanley, Louisville Defender; Dowdal H. Davis, Kansas City Call; Dan Burley, Amsterdam News. See Evans, list of Publishers and Editors of Negro Newspapers, Pentagon, 18 Mar 48, copy in CMH.(Back)

Footnote 12-33: Sentiments of the meeting were summarized in Ltr, Ira F. Lewis to Forrestal, 24 Mar 48; see also Ltr, Granger to Forrestal, 2 Mar 48; both in D54-1-4, SecDef files.(Back)

Footnote 12-34: WD Ltr, AGAO-S 353 (28 May 47), WDGOT-M, 11 Jun 47.(Back)

Footnote 12-35: A Program for National Security: Report of the President's Advisory Commission on Universal Training, 29 May 1947 (Washington: Government Printing Office, 1947), p. 42.(Back)

Footnote 12-36: Senate, Hearings Before the Committee on Armed Services, Universal Military Training, 80th Cong., 2d sess., 1948, p. 688.(Back)

Footnote 12-37: Ibid., p. 689.(Back)

Footnote 12-38: Ibid., pp. 691-94. The quotation is from page 694.(Back)

Footnote 12-39: Ibid., p. 645.(Back)

Footnote 12-40: The Philadelphia Inquirer, April 11, 1948; PM, April 11, 1948. See also McCloy and Ruetten, Quest and Response, pp. 107-08; "Crisis in the Making: U.S. Negroes Tussle With the Issue," Newsweek, June 7, 1948, pp. 28-29; L. Bennett, Jr., Confrontation Black and White (Chicago: Johnson Press, 1965), pp. 192-94; Grant Reynolds, "A Triumph for Civil Disturbance," Nation 167 (August 28, 1948):228-29.(Back)

Footnote 12-41: New York Times, April 1, 1948.(Back)

Footnote 12-42: Washington Post, April 2, 1948.(Back)

Footnote 12-43: McCoy and Ruetten, Quest and Response, p. 107.(Back)

Footnote 12-44: Department of National Defense, "National Defense Conference on Negro Affairs," 26 Apr 48. This document includes the testimony and transcript of the news conference that followed. Officials appearing before the committee included James Forrestal, Secretary of Defense; Robert P. Patterson, former Secretary of War; Marx Leva, Special Assistant to the Secretary of Defense; James Evans, Adviser to the Secretary of Defense; Kenneth C. Royall, Secretary of the Army; John N. Brown, Assistant Secretary of the Navy; W. Stuart

Symington, Secretary of the Air Force; and personnel officials and consultants from each service.(Back)

Footnote 12-45: NME Press Releases, 26 Apr and 8 Sep 48.(Back)

Footnote 12-46: Memo, Forrestal for Marx Leva, 30 Apr 48; Ltr, Nelson to Leva, 24 May 48; Memo, Leva for SA, 25 May 48. All in D54-1-3, SecDef files.(Back)

Footnote 12-47: Ltr, Grant Reynolds and Randolph to Evans, 3 May 48; Memo, Evans for SecDef, 13 May 48, sub: Commission of Inquiry; both in SecDef files. See also A. Philip Randolph, Statement Before Commission of Inquiry, 8 May 48, copy in USAF Special Files 35, 1948, SecAF files.(Back)

Footnote 12-48: New York *Times*, February 16, 1948.(Back)

Footnote 12-49: Ltr, Sen. Henry C. Lodge, Jr. (Mass.), to SecDef, 19 Apr 48, D54-1-3, SecDef files.(Back)

Footnote 12-50: McCoy and Ruetten, *Quest and Response*, pp. 98-99.(Back)

Footnote 12-51: Ltr, Granger to Leva, 14 May 48, D54-1-3, SecDef files.(Back)

Footnote 12-52: Memo, Leva to Forrestal, 18 May 48, D54-1-3, SecDef files. Forrestal's response, suggesting that Lodge meet with Lester Granger to discuss the matter, was finally sent on 24 Jun 48. See also Memo, Leva for Forrestal, 22 Jun 48, and Ltr, SecDef to Sen. Lodge, 24 Jun 48, both in D51-1-3, SecDef files.(Back)

Footnote 12-53: Memo, James Forrestal for President, 28 May 48, Secretary's File (PSF), Harry S. Truman Library.(Back)

Footnote 12-54: Memo, President for SecDef, 1 Jun 48, Secretary's File (PSF), Truman Library.(Back)

Footnote 12-55: Note, SecDef for President, 31 May 48, sub: Conversation With Senator Taft, Secretary's File (PSF), Truman Library.(Back)

Footnote 12-56: Interv, Nichols with Ewing; Interv, Blumenson with Leva.(Back)

Footnote 12-57: Memo, Clark Clifford for President, 19 Nov 47; ibid., 17 Aug 48, sub: The 1948 Campaign; both in Truman Library. See also Cabell B. Phillips, *The Truman Presidency* (New York: Macmillan, 1966), pp. 198-99, and McCoy and Ruetten, *Quest and Response*, ch. VI.(Back)

Footnote 12-58: Interv, Nichols with Ewing.(Back)

Footnote 12-59: Quoted in Memo, Leva for SecDef, 15 Jul 48, D54-1-3, SecDef files.(Back)

Footnote 12-60: Quoted in Truman, *Memoirs*, II:183; see also Interv, Nichols with Truman, and Millis, *Forrestal Diaries*, p. 458.(Back)

Footnote 12-61: Interv, Nichols with Ewing.(Back)

Footnote 12-62: Memo, Niles for Clifford, 12 May 48; Memo, Clifford for SecDef, 13 May 48, Nash Collection, Truman Library.(Back)

Footnote 12-63: Interv, Nichols with Ewing.(Back)

Footnote 12-64: Nichols, *Breakthrough on the Color Front*, p. 86.(Back)

Footnote 12-65: Ltr, Donald S. Dawson, Admin Asst to the President, to SecDef, 26 Jul 48. The executive order on equal opportunity for federal employees was also issued on 26 July.(Back)

Footnote 12-66: Columbia University Oral Hist Interv with Wilkins.(Back)

Footnote 12-67: Memo, Leva for Forrestal, 26 Jul 48, SecDef files.(Back)

Footnote 12-68: Interv, Nichols with Ewing; Ltr, Atty Gen to President, 26 Jul 48, 1285-0, copy in Eisenhower Library.(Back)

Footnote 12-69: Presidential News Conference, 29 Jul 48, *Public Papers of the President*, 1948, p. 422.(Back)

Footnote 12-70: Ltr, Dawson to Forrestal, 30 Jul 48, SecDef files.(Back)

Footnote 12-71: Memos, Leva for Forrestal, 3 and 12 Aug 48; Ltr, Forrestal to President, 3 Aug 48, D54-1-3, SecDef files.(Back)

Footnote 12-72: Ltr, Royall to President, 17 Sep 48, OSA 291.2 (17 Sep 48).(Back)

Footnote 12-73: Ibid.(Back)

Footnote 12-74: Memo, Royall for Forrestal, 10 Sep 48, OSA 291.2 (10 Sep 48).(Back)

Footnote 12-75: Memo, Leva for Forrestal, 1 Sep 48, and Handwritten Note by Forrestal, D54-1-3, SecDef files.(Back)

Footnote 12-76: Memo, Leva for Forrestal, 18 Sep 48, D54-1-3, SecDef files.(Back)

Footnote 12-77: Interv, Nichols with Ewing; Interv, Blumenson with Leva. Donahue resigned for health reasons shortly after the committee began its work; see Ltr, Donahue to Truman, 23 May 49, Truman Library. Luckman did not participate at all in the committee's work or sign its report. The committee's active members, in addition to its chairman, were Granger, Sengstacke, Palmer, and Stevenson.(Back)

Footnote 13-1: Columbia University Oral Hist Interv with Wilkins.(Back)

Footnote 13-2: Chicago *Defender*, August 7 and August 14, 1948.(Back)

Footnote 13-3: Pittsburgh *Courier*, August 7, August 28, and September 25, 1948.(Back)

Footnote 13-4: Chicago *Defender*, August 21, 1948.(Back)

Footnote 13-5: New York *Times*, September 12, 1948.(Back)

Footnote 13-6: Memo, Donald Dawson for President, 9 Sep 48, Nash Collection, Truman Library; Memo, SecDef for [Clark] Clifford, 2 Aug 48, and Ltr, Bayard Rustin of the Campaign to Resist Military Segregation to James V. Forrestal, 20 Aug 48; both in D54-1-14, SecDef files. It should be noted that Dawson's claim that the black press universally supported the executive order has not been accepted by all commentators; see McCoy and Ruetten, *Quest and Response*, p. 130.(Back)

Footnote 13-7: Bradley succeeded Eisenhower as Chief of Staff on 7 February 1948.(Back)

Footnote 13-8: Washington *Post*, July 28, 1948; Atlanta *Constitution*, July 28, 1948.(Back)

Footnote 13-9: News Conference, 29 Jul 48, *Public Papers of the Presidents: Harry S. Truman, 1948*, p. 165; New York *Times*, July 30, 1948; Chicago *Defender*, August 7, 1948; Pittsburgh *Courier*, August 21, 1948; Washington *Post*, August 23, 1948.(Back)

Footnote 13-10: Interv, Nichols with Bradley.(Back)

Footnote 13-11: Hanson Baldwin, "Segregation in the Army," New York *Times*, August 8, 1948.(Back)

Footnote 13-12: Ltr, A. A. Heist, Dir, American Civil Liberties Union, South California Branch, to Forrestal, 7 Sep 48, D54-1-4, SecDef files.(Back)

Footnote 13-13: Ltrs, Bradley to President Truman, 30 Jul 48, and Truman to Bradley, 4 Aug 48, CSUSA 291.2 (4 Aug 48). See also Ltr, SA to President, 29 Jul 48, OSA 291.2 (Negroes) (7-29-48).(Back)

Footnote 13-14: As provided in various laws since 1920, most notably in Section V of the amendments to the National Defense Act, members of the General Staff's Committee on National Guard Policy and Committee on Reserve Policy were the principal advisers to the Secretary of War on reserve component matters. All questions regarding these organizations were referred to the committees, which usually met in combined session as the Committee on National Guard and Reserve Policy. The combined committee was composed of twenty-one officers, seven each from the Regular Army, the guard, and the reserves. When the business under consideration was restricted exclusively to one of the reserve components, the representatives of the other would absent themselves, the remaining members, along with the Regular Army members, reconstituting themselves as the Committee on National Guard Policy or the Committee on Reserve Policy. These groups, familiarly known as the "Section V Committees," wielded considerable power in the development of the postwar program for the reserves.(Back)

Footnote 13-15: Memo, Chief, Classification and Personnel Actions Br, P&A, for Brig Gen Ira Swift, Chief, Liaison, Planning and Policy Coordination Gp, P&A, 8 Apr 47, sub: Resolution Regarding Employment of Negro Troops in the National Guard; Memo, Dir, P&A, for Dir, Intel, 9 Apr 47, same sub; both in WDGPA 291.2 (3 Apr 47).(Back)

Footnote 13-16: DF, WDGS Cmte on National Guard Policy, to Chief, NGB, 20 May 47, sub: Integration of Negro Troops; idem to Dir, P&A, and Dir, O&T, same date and sub. See also Ltr, Maj Gen Kenneth F. Cramer, CG, 43d Inf Div (Conn. NG) to Col Russell Y. Moore, OCofS, 17 Mar 47. All in Office file, Army Reserve Forces Policy Cmte.(Back)

Footnote 13-17: Memo, Dir, O&T, for WDGS Cmte on National Guard Policy, 23 Jun 47, sub: Integration of Negro Troops, WDGOT 291.2.(Back)

Footnote 13-18: Memo, Exec for Reserve and ROTC Affairs, O&T, for Dir, O&T, 22 Jul 46; O&T Memo for Rcd, 12 Aug 46; both in WDGOT 291.2.(Back)

Footnote 13-19: Memo, Ray for Petersen, 2 Apr 47, sub: Integration of Negro Personnel in the Reserve Components, ASW 291.2.(Back)

Footnote 13-20: Memo, D/O&T for ASW, 17 Apr 47, sub: Integration of Negro Personnel in the Reserve Components, WDGOT 291.2; Memo, D/P&A thru D/O&T for ASW, 10 Apr 47, same sub, WDGPA 291.2; DF, D/P&A to CofS, 20 May 47, sub: Integration of Negro Troops, CSUSA 291.2 Negroes.(Back)

Footnote 13-21: Ltr, Kenneth Royall to Alfred Driscoll, 7 Feb 48; Ltr, W. Stuart Symington to Driscoll, 17 Mar 48; copies of both in CMH.(Back)

Footnote 13-22: Ltrs, SA to Luther Youngdahl and James C. Shannon, 20 May 48, both in OSA 291.2 Negroes (5-28-48); Memos, CofSA for Dir, O&T, 2 Jan and 9 Mar 48, sub: Utilization of Negroes in the National Guard, CSUSA 291.2. Shannon succeeded McConnaughy as governor of Connecticut in March 1948.(Back)

Footnote 13-23: Remarks by Kenneth Royall in the Committee of Four, 9 Mar 48, OSD Historical Office files.(Back)

Footnote 13-24: P&A Summary Sheet, 7 Jul 48, sub: Utilization of Negro Manpower in the National Guard, WDGPA 291.2; O&T Summary Sheet, 8 Apr 48, same sub. See also Memo, Col William Abendroth, Exec, Cmte on NG and Reserve Policy, for CofSA, 30 Jun 48, sub: Utilization of Negro Manpower in the National Guard of the United States, Office file, Army Reserve Forces Policy Cmte. Thirteen of the seventeen committee members concurred with the staff study without reservation; the remaining four concurred with the proviso that states prohibiting segregation be granted the right to integrate.(Back)

Footnote 13-25: Memo, CofSA for SA, 7 Jul 48, CSUSA 291.2 Negroes (1 Jul 48).(Back)

Footnote 13-26: See Ltrs, James Forrestal to A. A. Heist, Dir, American Civil Liberties Union, 13 Sep 48, and Augustus F. Hawkins, 22 Sep 48; both in D54-1-2, SecDef files; DF, Dir, P&A, to CofSA, 2 Nov 49, sub: Executive Order to Permit Integration of Negroes Into Minnesota National Guard, CSUSA 291.2 Negroes (2 Nov 49).(Back)

Footnote 13-27: Ltr, J. Steward McClendon, Secy, Minneapolis Chapter, Am Vets Cmte, to SecDef [*sic*] Royall, 28 May 48, CSUSA 291.2 Negroes (28 May 48).(Back)

Footnote 13-28: Ltr, Maj Gen Jim Dan Hill, Wisconsin National Guard, to Secy, WD Advisory Cmte, 24 Jun 48; see also Ltr, Brig Gen Harry Evans, Maryland National Guard, to Col William Abendroth, Exec, Cmte on NG and Reserve Policy, 22 Jun 48, Office file, Army Reserve Forces Policy Cmte.(Back)

Footnote 13-29: Ltr, Brig Gen A. G. Paxton, Mississippi National Guard, to Col William Abendroth, 13 May 1948, Office file, Army Reserve Forces Policy Cmte.(Back)

Footnote 13-30: Ltr, Marx Leva to author, 24 May 70, CMH files; see also Testimony of Royall at National Defense Conference on Negro Affairs, 26 Apr 48, copy in CMH.(Back)

Footnote 13-31: General Paul's Remarks at Army Commanders Conference, 30 Mar-2 Apr 48, p. 30, CSUSA 337.(Back)

Footnote 13-32: See Testimony of Royall at National Defense Conference on Negro Affairs, 26 Apr 48, pp. 24-26.(Back)

Footnote 13-33: Memo, SA for SecDef, 22 Sep 48, copy in CD30-1-2, SecDef files.(Back)

Footnote 13-34: Ltr, Granger and Conferees to Forrestal, 26 Aug 48, D54-1-3, SecDef files.(Back)

Footnote 13-35: NME Press Release, 8 Sep 48; New York *Times*, September 9, 1948; Memo, Leva for Forrestal, 30 Aug 48; Ltr, Forrestal to Granger, 30 Aug 48. Last two in D54-1-3, SecDef files.(Back)

Footnote 13-36: Memo, SA for SecDef, 22 Sep 48, copy in CD30-1-2, SecDef files.(Back)

Footnote 13-37: Memo (unsigned), Forrestal for Royall, 22 Sep 48. The answer was prepared by Leva and used by Forrestal as the basis for his conversation with Royall. See Memos, Leva for Forrestal, undated, and 30 Sep 48, both in CD30-1-2, SecDef files.(Back)

Footnote 13-38: Memo, SecNav for SecDef, 27 May 48, sub: Liaison With the Selective Service System and Determination of Parity Standards, P14-6; Memo, Actg SecNav for SecDef, 17 Aug 48; sub: Items in Disagreement Between the Services as Listed in SecDef's Memo of 15 Jul 48, P 14-4; both in GenRecsNav. The quotation is from an inclosure to the latter memo.(Back)

Footnote 13-39: CofSA, Rpt of War Council Min, 3 Aug 48, copy in OSD Historical Office files.(Back)

Footnote 13-40: For a detailed analysis of the various service arguments and positions, see Office of the Secretary of Defense, "Proposed Findings and Decisions on Questions of Parity of Mental Standards, Allocation of Inductees According to Physical and Mental Capabilities and Allocation of Negroes" (Noble Report), 29 Oct 48, copy in SecDef files.(Back)

Footnote 13-41: Memo, SecDef for SA et al., 12 Oct 48, with attached Summary of Supplement, copy in CMH.(Back)

Footnote 13-42: DF, Dir, P&A, to CofS, 24 Jan 49, sub: Experimental Unit, GSPGA 291.2 (24 Jan 49).(Back)

Footnote 13-43: Memo, SecDef for President, 29 Feb 48, Secretary's File (PSF), Truman Library.(Back)

Footnote 13-44: Memo, CofS for Dir, O&T, 11 Oct 48, CSUSA 291.2 Negroes (11 Oct 48).(Back)

Footnote 13-45: Lt Col D. M. Oden, Asst Secy, CS, Memo for Rcd, 4 Nov 48, sub: Organization of an Experimental Unit, CSUSA 291.2 (Negroes) (11 Oct 48).(Back)

Footnote 13-46: Memo, Marx Leva for SA, 22 Nov 48; see also idem for Ohly, 16 Nov 48; both in CD 30-1-2, SecDef files.(Back)

362

Footnote 13-47: Interv, author with James C. Evans, 1 Jul 70; Ltr, E. W. Kenworthy, Exec Secy, Presidential Committee, to Lee Nichols, 28 Jul 53; both in CMH files.(Back)

Footnote 13-48: Memo, SA for SecDef, 2 Dec 48, CD 30-1-2, SecDef files.(Back)

Footnote 13-49: Memo, SecAF for SecDef, 22 Dec 48, CD 30-1-2, SecDef files.(Back)

Footnote 13-50: Memo, Actg SecNav for SecDef, 28 Dec 48, CD 30-1-2, SecDef files.(Back)

Footnote 13-51: Memo, Capt H. D. Riley, USN, OSD, for SecDef, 6 Dec 48, sub: Comment on the Secretary of the Army's Proposal Concerning Experimental Non-Segregated Units in the Armed Forces, CD 30-1-2, SecDef files.(Back)

Footnote 13-52: Millis, *Forrestal Diaries*, p. 528.(Back)

Footnote 13-53: DF, Dir, O&T, to DCofS, 14 Jul 48, sub: Report of Visit by Negro Publishers and Editors to the European Theater, CSGOT 291.2 (14 May 48); Memo for Rcd, attached to Memo, Dir, P&A, for DCofS, 21 Jul 48, same sub, CSGPA 291.2 (14 May 48). See also Geis Monograph, pp. 88-89.(Back)

Footnote 13-54: Interv, author with Huebner.(Back)

Footnote 13-55: Ltr, Dir, O&T, to CG, EUCOM, 13 Dec 48, sub: Integration of Negro Units on the Platoon Level Within the Constabulary EUCOM, CSGOT 291.21 (24 Nov 48); DF, Dir, O&T, to CofS, 9 Dec 48, same sub, CSUSA 291.2 (24 Nov 48).(Back)

Footnote 13-56: Interv, author with Huebner.(Back)

Footnote 13-57: Geis Monograph, p. 90. For the reaction of a constabulary brigade commander to the attachment of black infantrymen, see Bruce C. Clarke, "Early Integration,"*Armor* (Nov-Dec 1978):29.(Back)

Footnote 13-58: Ltr, TAG to Distribution, 23 Mar 49, sub: Utilization of Negro Manpower, AGAO 291.2.(Back)

Footnote 13-59: Memo, Actg SecNav for SecDef et al., 28 Dec 48, sub: The Secretary of the Army's Confidential Memorandum of 2 December..., copy in SecAF files.(Back)

Footnote 13-60: Testimony of Stickney Before the President's Committee on Equality of Treatment and Opportunity in the Armed Services, 25 Apr 49, pp. 19-20. See also, Memo, Actg SecNav for SecDef et al., 28 Dec 48, sub: The Secretary of the Army's Confidential Memorandum of 2 December....(Back)

Footnote 13-61: Lt Cmdr G. E. Minor, BuPers, Memo for File, 10 Mar 49, sub: Information for Lt. Nelson-Press Section, Pers 251, BuPersRecs. *Separate* is probably a better term for describing the Steward's Branch, since the branch was never completely segregated. On 31 March 1949, for example, the racial and ethnic breakdown of the branch was as follows:

Negro

Filipino

Chamorro

Chinese

Samoan

Korean

Hawaiian

Puerto Rican

Japanese

American Indian

Caucasian

Total

Source: Figures taken from BuPers, "Steward Group Personnel by Race," 24 May 49, Pers 25, BuPersRecs.(Back)

Footnote 13-62: This dubious assertion on the seagoing interests of races had been most recently expressed by the Chief of Naval Personnel before a meeting of the President's Committee on Equality of Treatment and Opportunity in the Armed Services; see Testimony of Fechteler, 13 Jan 49, pp. 107-08.(Back)

Footnote 13-63: Testimony of Capt J. H. Schultz, Asst Chief of Naval Personnel for Naval Reserve, Before President's Committee on Equality of Treatment and Opportunity in the Armed Services, 26 Apr 49, afternoon session, p. 19.(Back)

Footnote 13-64: Memo, Head, Pers Accounting and Statistical Control Sec, BuPers, for Dir, Fiscal Div (Pers 83), 14 Dec 48, sub: Statistics on Steward Group Personnel in Navy; Memo, W. C. Kincaid, BuPers Fiscal Div, for Cmdr Smith, BuPers, 6 May 48, sub: Negroes, USN—

Transferring From Commissary or Steward Branch to General Service; BuPers, "Steward Group Personnel by Race," 24 May 49. All in Pers 25, BuPersRecs.(Back)

Footnote 13-65: Memo, CMC for CG, MB, Cp Lejeune, N.C., 23 Aug 48, sub: Recruit Training Load at Montford Point Camp, MC 1035238; idem for CG, MCRD, 26 May 49, MC 1091093; Memo, Dir of Recruiting for Off in Charge, Recruit Divs, 13 Jun 49, sub: Enlistment of Negro Personnel. All in Hist Div, HQMC. Unless otherwise noted all documents cited in this section are located in this office.(Back)

Footnote 13-66: Memo, CG, MCRD, Parris Island, for CMC, 15 Sep 49, sub: Negro Recruits, ser. 08355.(Back)

Footnote 13-67: This limited integration program was announced by the Secretary of the Navy on 22 December 1949; see Memo, Under SecNav for Chmn, PPB, 22 Dec 49, PPB files.(Back)

Footnote 13-68: USMC Oral History Interview with Noble, 20-23 May 68.(Back)

Footnote 13-69: Testimony of the Secretary of the Navy Before President's Committee on Equality of Treatment and Opportunity in the Armed Services, 28 Mar 49, afternoon session, p. 15.(Back)

Footnote 13-70: On the closing of Montford Point, see Interv, Blumenson with Sgt Max Rousseau, Admin Chief, G-1 Div, USMC (former member of the Montford Point Camp headquarters), 21 Feb 66, CMH files.(Back)

Footnote 13-71: Memo, CMC for CG, FMF, Pacific, 11 Feb 49, with attached Handwritten Note, Div of Plans and Policies to Asst CMC, 11 Feb 49.(Back)

Footnote 13-72: Memo, Under SecNav for Chmn, PPB, 2 May 49, PPB 291.2.(Back)

Footnote 13-73: Memo, CMC for Asst SecNav for Air, 17 Mar 49, sub: Proposed Directive for the Armed Forces for the Period 1 July 1949 to 1 July 1950, AO-1, MC files.(Back)

Footnote 13-74: Idem for CO, Second Depot Co, Service Cmd, FMF, 2 May 49, sub: Employment of Negroes in the Marine Corps, MC1008783, MC files.(Back)

Footnote 13-75: On 30 June 1949 the Marine Corps had 1,504 Negroes on active duty, 1.9 percent of the total if the one-year enlistees were included or 2.08 percent if the one-year enlistees were excluded. See Office of the Civilian Aide, OSD, *Negro Strength Summary*, 18 Jul 49, copy in CMH. For purposes of comparison, the following gives the percentage of Negroes in the Navy and the Marine Corps for earlier years.

Date	Navy
Dec 43	5.0
Dec 44	5.5
Dec 45	5.9
Dec 46	4.7
Dec 47	5.4
Dec 48	5.05

Source: Officer in Charge, Pers Acctg & Stat Control, Memo for File, 23 Apr 48, Pers 215 BuPersRecs.(Back)

Footnote 13-76: Memo, Dir, Div of Plans and Policies, for CMC, 28 Jul 49, sub: Reassignment of Negro Marines to Existing units (DP&P Study 88-49), MC files.(Back)

Footnote 13-77: Notes on Telecon, author with Zuckert, 28 Apr 70, CMH files.(Back)

Footnote 13-78: Memo, DCofS/P&A, USAF, for SecAF, 29 Apr 48, sub: Conference With Group of Prominent Negroes, Negro Affairs, 1948, SecAF files.(Back)

Footnote 13-79: Telecon, author with Zuckert.(Back)

Footnote 13-80: Ltr, Symington to David K. Niles, 28 Jan 50, SecAF files.(Back)

Footnote 13-81: Memo, SecAF for Zuckert, 5 Jan 48; Penciled Note, signed "Stu," attached to Memo, ASecAF for Symington, 20 Jan 48. All in SecAF files.(Back)

Footnote 13-82: Ltr, W. Stuart Symington to author, 6 May 70, CMH files.(Back)

Footnote 13-83: Telecon, author with Zuckert.(Back)

Footnote 13-84: Ibid.; see also USAF Oral Hist Interv with Zuckert.(Back)

Footnote 13-85: For discussion of the close-held nature of the USAF integration plan, see USAF Oral Hist Intervs with Davis and Marr; see also Ltrs, Marr to author, 19 Jun and 28 Jul 70.(Back)

Footnote 13-86: Memo, Dir, Personnel Planning USAF, for the Fahy Cmte, 15 Jan 49, sub: Air Force Policies Regarding Negro Personnel, SecAF files.(Back)

Footnote 13-87: Summary Sheet DCS/P, USAF, for CS, USAF, and SecAF, 29 Dec 48, sub: Air Force Policies on Negro Personnel, SecAF files.(Back)

Footnote 13-88: Memo, ASecAF for Symington, 5 Jan 49, SecAF files.(Back)

Footnote 13-89: Memo, Maj Gen William F. McKee for Symington, 22 Dec 48, sub: Mr. Royall's Negro Experiment, SecAF files.(Back)

Footnote 13-90: Memo, SecAF for Forrestal, 6 Jan 49, Negro Affairs, 1949, SecAF files.(Back)

Footnote 13-91: Testimony of Lt Col Jack F. Marr Before President's Committee on Equality of Treatment and Opportunity in the Armed Services, 13 Jan 49, afternoon session, p 46.(Back)

Footnote 14-1: Memo, SecDef for SA et al., 21 Oct 48, copy in Fahy Committee file, CMH [hereafter cited as FC file]. The Center of Military History has retained an extensive collection of significant primary materials pertaining to the Fahy Committee and its dealings with the Department of Defense. While most of the original documents are in the Charles Fahy Papers and the Papers of the President's Committee on Equality of Treatment and Opportunity in the Armed Services at the Harry S. Truman Library or in the National Archives, this study will cite the CMH collection when possible.(Back)

Footnote 14-2: Ltrs, James Forrestal to Fahy, 26 Mar 49, and Louis Johnson to Fahy, 18 Apr 49; both in FC file. See also Ltr, Thomas R. Reid to R. M. Dalfiume, 12 Feb 65, copy in CMH.(Back)

Footnote 14-3: Min, Cmte of Four Secretaries Mtg, 26 Oct 48, Office of OSD Historian. The Committee of the Four Secretaries was an informal body composed of the Secretary of Defense or his representative and the secretaries of the three armed services.(Back)

Footnote 14-4: Min, War Council Mtg, 12 Jan 49, Office of OSD Historian; Memo, Secy of War Council for SA et al., 13 Jan 49, sub: Significant Action of the Special Meeting of the War Council on 12 January 1949, OSD 291.2. The War Council, established by Section 210 of the National Security Act of 1947, consisted of the Secretary of Defense as chairman with power of decision, the service secretaries, and the military chiefs of the Army, Navy, Air Force, and Marine Corps.(Back)

Footnote 14-5: Memo, Thomas R. Reid, Chmn, PPB, for Worthington Thompson, OSD, 15 Feb 49, sub: Meeting of Committee of Four, 10 A.M. Tuesday—15 February, FC file.(Back)

Footnote 14-6: Forrestal signed an interim directive appointing members of the board on 22 February 1949. Composed of a civilian chairman and an under secretary or assistant secretary from each service, the board was to have a staff of personnel experts under a director, an officer of flag rank, appointed by the chairman; see NME Press Releases, 28 Dec 48, and 1 Apr 49.(Back)

Footnote 14-7: Min PPB Mtg, 26 Feb 49, FC file.(Back)

Footnote 14-8: Memo, Col J. F. Cassidy, PPB, for Dir, PPB Staff, 25 Feb 49, sub: Policies of the Three Departments With Reference to Negro Personnel, FC file.(Back)

Footnote 14-9: PPB, Draft (Reid and Lanham), Proposed Directive for the Armed Forces for the Period 1 July 1949 to 1 July 1950, 28 Feb 49, FC file.(Back)

Footnote 14-10: Note, Leva thru Ohly to Buck Lanham, attached to Draft of Proposed Directive cited in n. 9.(Back)

Footnote 14-11: Memo, Chmn, PPB, for John Ohly, Assistant to SecDef, 15 Mar 49; Revised Min, PPB Mtg, 18 Mar 49; both in FC file.(Back)

Footnote 14-12: Interv, author with Roy K. Davenport, 7 Oct 71, CMH.(Back)

Footnote 14-13: Memo for Files, Clarence H. Osthagen, Assistant to SecAF, 31 Mar 49, sub: Conference With Thomas Reid, FC file.(Back)

Footnote 14-14: Memo, Thomas Reid for Asst SecNav, 1 Apr 49, sub: Statement on Equality of Treatment and Opportunity, FC file.(Back)

Footnote 14-15: PPB, Draft Memo, SecDef for Svc Secys (prepared by Col J. F. Cassidy for Reid), 31 Mar 49; PPB, Proposed Policy for the National Military Establishment, 4 Apr 49; both in FC file.(Back)

Footnote 14-16: Memo, SecDef for SA et al., 6 Apr 49, sub: Equality of Treatment and Opportunity in the Armed Services; Min, PPB Mtg, 5 Apr 49; both in FC file.(Back)

Footnote 14-17: Min, PPB Mtg, 8 Apr 49, FC file.(Back)

Footnote 14-18: Memo, Reid for SecDef, 14 Apr 49, sub: The President's Committee on Equality of Treatment and Opportunity in the Armed Services, FC file.(Back)

Footnote 14-19: Min, PPB Mtg, 5 May 49; NME Press Release 3-49A, 20 Apr 49; both in FC file.(Back)

Footnote 14-20: This conclusion is based on Interviews, author with Charles Fahy, 8 Feb 68, James C. Evans, 6 Apr 69, and Brig Gen Charles T. Lanham, 10 Jan 71. It is also based on letters to author from John Ohly, 9 Jan 71, and Thomas Reid, 15 Jan 71. All in CMH.(Back)

Footnote 14-21: Memo, Kenworthy for Chief of Military History, 13 Oct 76. CMH.(Back)

Footnote 14-22: Memo, Actg SecNav for Chmn, PPB, 2 May 49, sub: Equality of Treatment and Opportunity in the Navy and Marine Corps; Memo, SA for SecDef, 21 Apr 49, sub: Equality of Treatment and Opportunity in the Armed Services; both in FC file.(Back)

Footnote 14-23: Min, PPB Mtg, 5 May 49, FC file.(Back)

Footnote 14-24: Ibid.; see also Ltr, Thomas Reid to Richard Dalfiume, 1 Apr 65, Incl to Ltr, Reid to author, 15 Jan 71. All in CMH.(Back)

Footnote 14-25: Min, War Council Mtg, 11 Jan 49, FC file; see also Interv, author with W. Stuart Symington, 1974, CMH.(Back)

Footnote 14-26: Memo, SecAF for Chmn, PPB, OSD, 30 Apr 49; Memo, Asst SecAF for SecAF, 20 Apr 49, sub: Department of Air Force Implementation of Department of Defense Policy on Equality of Treatment and Opportunity in the Armed Services; both in SecAF files.(Back)

Footnote 14-27: Min, PPB Mtg, 5 May 49; Memo, Reid for SecDef, 10 May 49, sub: Equality of Treatment and Opportunity in the Armed Forces, FC file.(Back)

Footnote 14-28: Ibid.(Back)

Footnote 14-29: Memo, SA for SecDef, 22 Apr 49, OSA 291.2.(Back)

Footnote 14-30: Memo, SecDef for SA, 13 May 49, sub: Equality of Treatment and Opportunity in the Armed Forces; idem for SecAF and SecNav, 11 May 49, same sub; DOD Press Release 35-49A, 11 May 42. All in FC file.(Back)

Footnote 14-31: Interv, author with Fahy.(Back)

Footnote 14-32: Ibid.; see also Fahy Cmte, "A Progress Report for the President," 7 Jun 49, FC file.(Back)

Footnote 14-33: Memo, Fahy for Brig Gen James L. Collins, Jr. 16 Aug 76, CMH.(Back)

Footnote 14-34: Interv, author with Fahy.(Back)

Footnote 14-35: Interv, Blumenson with Fahy, 7 Apr 66; Interv, author with Davenport, 31 Oct 71; both in CMH.(Back)

Footnote 14-36: Testimony of General Omar N. Bradley, Fahy Cmte Hearings, 28 Mar 49, afternoon session, p. 71.(Back)

Footnote 14-37: Memo, Asst SecAF for Symington, 11 Apr 49, sub: Statement of the Secretary of the Army Before the President's Committee on Equality of Treatment and Opportunity in the Armed Services—March 28, 1949, SecAF files.(Back)

Footnote 14-38: Testimony of Bradley, Fahy Cmte Hearings, 28 Mar 49, afternoon session, pp. 71-72.(Back)

Footnote 14-39: Ibid., p. 83.(Back)

Footnote 14-40: Testimony of the Secretary of the Army, Fahy Cmte Hearings, 28 Mar 49, morning session, p. 28.(Back)

Footnote 14-41: Ltr, Kenworthy to SA, 20 Jul 50, FC file; see also Memo, Kenworthy for Chief of Military History, 13 Oct 76, CMH.(Back)

Footnote 14-42: Ltr, Kenworthy to Fahy, 10 Mar 49, FC file.(Back)

Footnote 14-43: Testimony of the Secretary of the Air Force, Fahy Cmte Hearings, 28 Mar 49, afternoon session, p. 27.(Back)

Footnote 14-44: Fahy Cmte Hearings, 28 Mar 49, afternoon session, pp. 28-29.(Back)

Footnote 14-45: Ibid., p. 29.(Back)

Footnote 14-46: Intervs, Blumenson with Fahy, and author with Fahy.(Back)

Footnote 14-47: This incident is described in detail in Interviews, author with Fahy; Davenport, 17 Oct 71; and E. W. Kenworthy (by telephone), 1 Dec 71. See also Interv, Nichols with Davenport, in Nichols Collection. All in CMH.(Back)

Footnote 14-48: Fahy Cmte Hearings, 28 Apr 49, morning session.(Back)

Footnote 14-49: Interv, Nichols with Fahy, in Nichols Collection, CMH.(Back)

Footnote 14-50: Fahy Cmte, "Second Interim Report to the President," 27 Jul 49, FC file.(Back)

Footnote 14-51: Interv, author with Davenport, 31 Oct 71.(Back)

Footnote 14-52: Fahy Cmte, "Initial Recommendations by the President's Committee on Equality of Treatment and Opportunity in the Armed Services," attached to Fahy Cmte, "A Progress Report for the President", 7 Jun 49, FC file.(Back)

Footnote 14-53: Ltr, Kenworthy to Fahy, 5 May 49, Fahy Papers, Truman Library.(Back)

Footnote 14-54: Fahy Cmte, "A Progress Report for the President," 7 Jun 49, FC file.(Back)

Footnote 14-55: Min, War Council Mtg, 24 May 49; Fahy Cmte, "Initial Recommendations by the President's Committee on Equality of Treatment and Opportunity in the Armed Services," attached to Fahy Cmte, "A Progress Report for the President", 7 Jun 49, FC file. Excerpts from the "Initial Recommendations" were sent to the services via the Personnel

Policy Board, which explains the document in the SecNav's files with the penciled notation "Excerpt from Fahy Recommendation 5/19." See also Ltr, Kenworthy to Fahy, 16 May 49, Fahy Papers, Truman Library.(Back)

Footnote 14-56: Memo, Kenworthy for Chief of Military History, 13 Oct 76, CMH.(Back)

Footnote 14-57: Col J. F. Cassidy, Comments on Initial Recommendations of Fahy Committee (ca. 26 May 49) FC file.(Back)

Footnote 14-58: Min, PPB Mtg, 26 May 49, FC file.(Back)

Footnote 14-59: Memo, Reid for Under SecDef, 23 May 49, sub: Equality of Treatment and Opportunity in the Armed Services; idem for SecDef, 1 Jun 49, sub: Fahy Committee Initial Recommendations—Discussion With Members of the Fahy Committee; both in PPB files. See also Memo, Ohly for Reid, 26 May 49, sub: Equality of Treatment and Opportunity in the Armed Services, FC file.(Back)

Footnote 14-60: Ltr, Kenworthy to Fahy, 24 May 49, FC file.(Back)

Footnote 14-61: Memo, Actg SecNav for SecDef, 23 May 49, sub: Equality of Treatment and Opportunity in the Armed Forces, FC file.(Back)

Footnote 14-62: Draft Memo, Reid for SecNav, 3 Jun 49, and Memo, Reid for SecDef, 1 Jun 49, both in PPB files; Memo, Kenworthy for Fahy, 30 May 49, sub: Replies of Army and Navy to Mr. Johnson's May 11 Memo, FC file.(Back)

Footnote 14-63: NME, Off of Pub Info, Release 78-49A, 7 Jun 49. See Washington *Post*, June 7, 1949, and New York *Times*, June 8, 1949.(Back)

Footnote 14-64: Following the resignation of Secretary Royall, President Truman nominated Gordon Gray as Secretary of the Army. His appointment was confirmed by the Senate on 13 June 1949. A lawyer, Gray had been a newspaper publisher in North Carolina before his appointment as assistant secretary in 1947.(Back)

Footnote 14-65: Memo, Actg SA for SecDef, 26 May 49, sub: Equality of Treatment and Opportunity in the Armed Services; see also P&A Summary Sheet, 19 May 49, same sub, FC file.(Back)

Footnote 14-66: Memo, Kenworthy for Fahy, 30 May 49, sub: Replies of Army and Navy to Mr. Johnson's May 11 Memo, FC file.(Back)

Footnote 14-67: Memo, Reid for SecDef, 1 Jun 49, sub: Army and Navy Replies to Your Memorandum of 6 April on Equality of Treatment and Opportunity in the Army Services; Min, PPB Mtg, 2 Jun 49; both in FC file.(Back)

Footnote 14-68: Min, PPB Mtg, 2 Jun 49; Ltr, Fahy to Johnson, 25 Jul 49, FC file.(Back)

Footnote 14-69: Draft Memo, Lanham for SecDef, 2 Jun 49, FC file.(Back)

Footnote 14-70: Memo, SecDef for SA, 7 Jun 49, sub: Equality of Treatment and Opportunity in the Armed Services; NME, Off of Pub Info, Press Release 78-49A, 7 Jun 49. The secretary gave the Army a new deadline of 20 June, but by mutual agreement of all concerned this date was postponed several times and finally left to the Secretary of the Army to submit his program "at his discretion," although at the earliest possible date. See Memo, T. Reid for Maj Gen Levin Allen, 6 Jul 49, sub: Army Reply to the Secretary of Defense on Equality of Treatment; Min, PPB Mtg, 18 Aug 49. All in FC file.(Back)

Footnote 14-71: Interv, author with Kenworthy.(Back)

Footnote 14-72: Ltr, Kenworthy to Fahy, 20 May 49, Fahy Papers, Truman Library.(Back)

Footnote 14-73: Fahy Cmte, "A Progress Report for the President," 7 Jun 49, FC file.(Back)

Footnote 14-74: Ltr, Fahy to Johnson, 15 Jun 49, FC file.(Back)

Footnote 14-75: Idem to SA, 25 Jul 49, FC file.(Back)

Footnote 14-76: Idem to SecDef, 25 Jul 49, FC file.(Back)

Footnote 14-77: P&A Summary Sheet to DC/S (Adm), 24 Jun 49, sub: Utilization of Negro Manpower, CSUSA 291.2 Negroes. For comments of Army commanders, see the following Memos: Wade H. Haislip (DC/S Adm) for Army Cmdrs, 8 Jun 49, sub: Draft Recommendations of Committee on Equality of Treatment and Opportunity; Lt Gen M. S. Eddy for CofS, 10 Jun 49, same sub; Lt Gen W. B. Smith for CofS, 10 Jun 49, same sub; Lt Gen S. J. Chamberlain, 5th Army Cmdr, for CofS, 13 Jun 49, same sub; Lt Gen John R. Hodge for CofS, 14 Jun 49, same sub; Gen Jacob Devers, 13 Jun 49, same sub; Gen Thomas T. Handy, 4th Army Cmdr, for CofS, 10 Jun 49, sub: Comments on Fahy Committee Draft Recommendations. All in CSUSA 291.2 Negroes.(Back)

Footnote 14-78: An Outline Plan for Utilization of Negro Manpower Submitted by the Army to the President's Committee, 5 Jul 49, Incl to Ltr, Fahy to SecDef, 25 Jul 49, FC file. See also Ltr, Kenworthy to Fahy, 23 Jun 49, Fahy Papers, Truman Library; Fahy Cmte, "Meeting to Discuss the Proposals Made by the Army as Preliminary to the Third Response," 11 Jul 49, FC file.(Back)

Footnote 14-79: Ltrs, Fahy to SecDef and SA, 25 Jul 49; idem to President, 27 Jul 49. All in FC file.(Back)

Footnote 14-80: Memo, Col J. F. Cassidy for Reid, 23 Aug 49, sub: Equality of Treatment and Opportunity in the Department of the Army, FC file.(Back)

Footnote 14-81: New York *Times*, July 16 and 18, 1949.(Back)

Footnote 14-82: Interv, NBC's "Meet the Press" with Gordon Gray, 18 Jul 49; Ltr, SecDef to Charles Fahy, 3 Aug 49, FC file.(Back)

Footnote 14-83: Memo, VCofS for Gray, 29 Aug 49, sub: Equality of Treatment and Opportunity in the Armed Services, CSUSA 291.2 Negroes.(Back)

Footnote 14-84: Interv, Nichols with Gordon Gray, 1953, in Nichols Collection, CMH; Memo, Kenworthy for Cmte, 19 Sep 49, sub: Meeting With Gray, 16 Sep 49, Fahy Papers, Truman Library.(Back)

Footnote 14-85: Ltrs, Fahy to President, 21 Sep and 26 Sep 49, both in FC file.(Back)

Footnote 14-86: Memo, SA for SecDef, 30 Sep 49, sub: Equality of Treatment and Opportunity in the Armed Services, CSGPA 291.2; DOD, Off of Pub Info, Press Release 256-49, 30 Sep 49, FC file.(Back)

Footnote 14-87: Memo, Kenworthy for Cmte, 27 Sep 49, sub: Army's Reply to Secretary Johnson, Fahy Papers, Truman Library; Note, handwritten and signed McCrea, attached to memo, SA for SecDef, 30 Sep 49; Memo, Thompson for Leva, 3 Oct 49, sub: Army Policy of Equality of Treatment and Opportunity, CD 30-1-4; both in SecDef files.(Back)

Footnote 14-88: Ltr, SecDef to Congressman Vinson, 7 Jul 49; Memo, Lanham for Reid, 29 Mar 49; both in PPB files.(Back)

Footnote 14-89: Ltr, Kenworthy to Nichols, 28 Jul 53, in Nichols Collection, CMH.(Back)

Footnote 14-90: Memo, Kenworthy to Cmte, 27 Sep 49, sub: Army's Reply to Secretary Johnson, and Ltr, Kenworthy to Joseph Evans, 30 Sep 49, both in Fahy Papers, Truman Library; Memo, Worthington Thompson for Leva, 3 Oct 49, sub: Army Policy of Equality of Treatment and Opportunity, SecDef files; Ltr, Kenworthy to Nichols, 28 Jul 53, in Nichols Collection, CMH.(Back)

Footnote 14-91: Memo for Rcd, probably written by Philleo Nash, 3 Oct 49, Nash Collection, Truman Library.(Back)

Footnote 14-92: See Los Angeles *Star Review*, October 6, 1949; *Afro-American*, October 8, 1949; Washington *Post*, October 6, 1949; Pittsburgh *Courier*, Octobers, 1949; Norfolk*Journal and Guide*, October 15, 1949; New York *Amsterdam News*, October 15, 1949.(Back)

Footnote 14-93: Ltr, Niles to President, 5 Oct 49, Nash Collection, Truman Library.(Back)

Footnote 14-94: News Conference, 6 Oct 49, as quoted in *Public Papers of the President: Harry S. Truman, 1949*, p. 501.(Back)

Footnote 14-95: Memo, Fahy for President, 11 Oct 49, FC file.(Back)

Footnote 14-96: Penciled Note, signed HST, on Memo, Niles for President, Secretary's File (PSF), Truman Library.(Back)

Footnote 14-97: Memo, Maj Gen Levin C. Allen, Exec Secy, SecDef, for SA, 14 Oct 49; Memo, Vice Adm John McCrea, Dir of Staff, PPB, for Allen, 25 Oct 49; both in CD 30-1-4, SecDef files.(Back)

Footnote 14-98: Memo for Rcd, Karl Bendetsen, Spec Consultant to SA, 28 Nov 49, SA files; Ltr, Kenworthy to Fahy, 22 Nov 49, and Memo, Kenworthy for Fahy Cmte, 29 Oct 49, sub: Background to Proposed Letter to Gray; both in Fahy Papers, Truman Library.(Back)

Footnote 14-99: Ltr, Fahy to Cmte, 17 Nov 49, Fahy Papers, Truman Library.(Back)

Footnote 14-100: Memo, Kenworthy for Cmte, 29 Oct 49, sub: Background to Proposed Letter to Gray, Fahy Papers, Truman Library.(Back)

Footnote 14-101: Msg, TAG to Chief, AFF, et al., WCL 45586, 011900Z Oct 49, copy in AG 220.3.(Back)

Footnote 14-102: Memo, D/PA for TAG, 25 Oct 49, sub: Assignment of Negro Enlisted Personnel, with attached Memo for Rcd, Col John H. Riepe, Chief, Manpower Control Gp, D/PA; Memo, Deputy Dir, PA, for Gen Brooks (Dir of PA), 3 Nov 49, same sub; Msg, TAG to Chief, AFF, et al., WCL 20682, 27 Oct 49. All in CSGPA 291.2 (25 Oct 49).(Back)

Footnote 14-103: Memo, Kenworthy for Chief of Military History, 13 Oct 76, CMH.(Back)

Footnote 14-104: Idem for Cmte, 29 Oct 49, sub: Instructions to Commanding Generals on New Army Policy, Fahy Papers, Truman Library.(Back)

Footnote **14-105:** Lem Graves, Jr. (Washington correspondent of the Pittsburgh *Courier*), "A Colonel Takes the Rap," Pittsburgh *Courier*, October 29, 1949; Washington *Post*, November 3, 1949.(Back)

Footnote **14-106:** DOD, Off of Pub Info, Release 400-49, 3 Nov 49, FC file.(Back)

Footnote **14-107:** Ltr, SA to Fahy, 17 Nov 49, FC file.(Back)

Footnote **14-108:** Ltr, Bendetsen to Fahy, 25 Nov 49; Memo for Rcd, Kenworthy, 28 Nov 49; both in Fahy Papers, Truman Library.(Back)

Footnote **14-109:** Army Draft No. 1 of Revised Circular 124, 16 Nov 49, FC file.(Back)

Footnote **14-110:** Ltr, Fahy to Maj Gen C. E. Byers, 30 Nov 49, FC file.(Back)

Footnote **14-111:** Memo, Kenworthy for President's Cmte, 18 Nov 49, sub: Successor Policy to WD Cir 124; idem for Fahy, 28 Nov 49, sub: Revised WD Cir 124; both in Fahy Papers, Truman Library.(Back)

Footnote **14-112:** Memo for Rcd, Kenworthy, 9 Dec 49, sub: Telephone Conversation With Nash, Fahy Papers, Truman Library.(Back)

Footnote **14-113:** Interv, Nichols with Fahy. J. Lawton Collins became Chief of Staff of the Army on 1 August 1949, succeeding Omar Bradley who stepped up to the chairmanship of the Joint Chiefs of Staff.(Back)

Footnote **14-114:** Intervs, Nichols with Gray and Fahy, and author with Collins.(Back)

Footnote **14-115:** Ltr, Kenworthy to Gray, 20 Jul 50, FC file; Intervs, Nichols with Gray, Davenport, and Fahy.(Back)

Footnote **14-116:** Interv, author with Davenport, 31 Oct 71.(Back)

Footnote **14-117:** Memo, Kenworthy for Chief of Military History, 13 Oct 76, CMH.(Back)

Footnote **14-118:** Memo for Rcd, Karl R. Bendetsen, Spec Asst to SA, 27 Dec 49, sub: Conference With Judge Charles Fahy, SA files. Intervs, Nichols with Gray and Fahy, author with Fahy, and Blumenson with Fahy.(Back)

Footnote **14-119:** Memo for Rcd, Bendetsen, 27 Dec 49, SA files; Ltr, Fahy to Cmte, 27 Dec 49, Fahy papers, Truman Library.(Back)

Footnote **14-120:** Interv, Nichols with Davenport.(Back)

Footnote **14-121:** Ltr, Kenworthy to Nichols, 29 Jul 53, in Nichols Collection, CMH; Interv, Nichols with Davenport.(Back)

Footnote **14-122:** Memo, Fahy for President, 16 Jan 50, FC file; SR 600-629-1, 16 Jan 50; DOD, Off of Pub Info, Release 64-50, 16 Jan 50. The special regulation was circulated worldwide on the day of the issue; see Memo, D/P&A to TAG, 16 Jan 50, WDGPA 291.2.(Back)

Footnote **14-123:** D/PA Summary Sheet for SA, 28 Feb 50, sub: Fahy Committee Proposal re: Numerical Enlistment Quota, CSGPA 291.2 (2 Nov 49); Roy Davenport, "Figures on Reenlistment Rate and Explanation," Document FC XL, FC file; Memo, Fahy for SA, 9 Feb 50, sub: Recapitulation of the Proposal of the President's Committee for the Abolition of the Racial Quota, FC file; Memo, Kenworthy for Dwight Palmer (cmte member), 8 Feb 50, Fahy Papers, Truman Library.(Back)

Footnote **14-124:** Memo, Actg D/PA for Karl R. Bendetsen, Spec Asst to SA, 13 Dec 49, sub: Ten Percent Racial Quota; D/PA Summary Sheet, with Incl, for SA, 28 Feb 50, sub: Fahy Committee Proposals re: Numerical Enlistment Quota; both in CSGPA 291.2 (2 Nov 49). The quotations are from the former document.(Back)

Footnote **14-125:** Memo, Kenworthy for Karl Bendetsen, 19 Oct 49, sub: Manpower Policy, Fahy Papers, Truman Library.(Back)

Footnote **14-126:** Memo for Rcd, Kenworthy, 14 Dec 49, sub: Conference With Maj Lieblich and Col Smith, 14 Dec 49, FC file.(Back)

Footnote **14-127:** Memo, Fahy for President's Cmte, 1 Feb 50, Fahy Papers, Truman Library.(Back)

Footnote **14-128:** Ltr, Niles to President, 7 Feb 50, Secretary's File (PSF), Truman Library.(Back)

Footnote **14-129:** D/PA Summary Sheet for SA, 28 Feb 50, sub: Fahy Committee Proposal re: Numerical Enlistment Quota, CSGPA 291.2 (2 Nov 49).(Back)

Footnote **14-130:** Interv, Nichols with Gray.(Back)

Footnote **14-131:** Ltr, SA to President, 1 Mar 50, Fahy Papers, Truman Library.(Back)

Footnote **14-132:** Memo, President for SA, 27 Mar 50, FC file; Memo, SA for President, 24 Mar 50, sub: Discontinuance of Racial Enlistment Quotas, copy in CSGPA 291.2.(Back)

Footnote **14-133:** Msg, TAG to Chief, AFF, et al., Fort Monroe, Va., WCL 44600, 27 Mar 50, copy in FC file.(Back)

Footnote 14-134: Memo, Clark Clifford for President (ca. Mar 50), Nash Collection, Truman Library.(Back)

Footnote 14-135: Interv, author with Kenworthy.(Back)

Footnote 14-136: Memo, Kenworthy for Fahy, 28 Apr 50, Fahy Papers, Truman Library.(Back)

Footnote 14-137: Ltr, Niles to President, 22 May 50, Nash Collection, Truman Library.(Back)

Footnote 14-138: Memo, Clifford for President, Nash Collection, Truman Library.(Back)

Footnote 14-139: *Freedom to Serve: Equality of Treatment and Opportunity in the Armed Services; A Report by the President's Committee* (Washington: Government Printing Office, 1950).(Back)

Footnote 14-140: Ltr, President to Fahy, 6 Jul 50, Fahy Papers, Truman Library.(Back)

Footnote 14-141: *Freedom to Serve*, p. 27.(Back)

Footnote 14-142: Ltr, SA to President, 1 Mar 50, Fahy Papers, Truman Library.(Back)

Footnote 14-143: Memo, Fahy for SA, 11 May 50, Fahy Papers, Truman Library. Frank Pace, an Arkansas lawyer and former Assistant Director of the Bureau of the Budget, succeeded Gordon Gray as Secretary of the Army on 12 April 1950.(Back)

Footnote 14-144: President Truman appointed Charles Fahy to the U.S. Circuit Court of Appeals for the District of Columbia on 15 October 1949. Fahy did not assume his judicial duties, however, until 15 December after concluding his responsibilities as a member of the American delegation to the United Nations General Assembly.(Back)

Footnote 14-145: Memo, Kenworthy for Fahy, 25 Jul 50, Fahy Papers, Truman Library. In the memorandum the number of additional specialties is erroneously given as six; see DCSPER Summary Sheet, 23 Apr 50, sub: List of Critical Specialties Referred to in SR 600-629-1, G-1 291.2 (25 Oct 49).(Back)

Footnote 14-146: Ltr, Davenport to OSD Historian, 31 Aug 76, copy in CMH. For a discussion of these war-related factors, see Chapters 14 and 17.(Back)

Footnote 14-147: *Freedom to Serve*, pp. 66-67.(Back)

Footnote 14-148: *Ibid.*, p. 67.(Back)

Footnote 15-1: Ltr, Truman to Fahy, 6 Jul 50, FC file.(Back)

Footnote 15-2: Interv, Nichols with Gen Wade H. Haislip, 1953, in Nichols Collection; Telephone Interv, author with Haislip, 18 Mar 71; Interv, author with Martin Blumenson, 8 Jan 68. All in CMH files.(Back)

Footnote 15-3: SR 615-105-1 (AFR 39-9), 15 Apr 49.(Back)

Footnote 15-4: Ltr, Holifield to SecDef, 10 Aug 49, SD 291.2 Negroes.(Back)

Footnote 15-5: Memo, Dep Dir, Personnel Policy Bd Staff, for Chmn, PPB, 13 Sep 49, sub: Project Summary—Change of Nomenclature on Enlistment Forms as Pertains to "Race" Entries (M-63); Memo, Chmn, PPB, for SA et al., 11 Oct 49, sub: Policy Regarding Race Entries on Enlistment Contracts and Shipping Articles; both in PPB 291.2.(Back)

Footnote 15-6: Memo, Evans for Chmn, PPB, 25 Nov 49, sub: Racial Designation and Terminology, SD 291.2; Interv, author with Evans, 22 Jul 71, CMH files.(Back)

Footnote 15-7: Memo, Head, Strength and Statistics Br, BuPers, for Head, Policy Control Br, BuPers, 27 Oct 49, sub: Policy Regarding Race Entries, Pers 25-EL, BuPersRecs; Memo, Under SecNav for Chmn, PPB, 25 Nov 49, sub: Policy Regarding "Race" Entries on Enlistment Contracts and Shipping Articles, GenRecsNav; DF, D/P&A to TAG, 18 Oct 49, same sub, with CMT 2, TAG to D/P&A, 2 Nov 49, copy in AG 291.2 (11 Oct 49).(Back)

Footnote 15-8: Admiral McCrea succeeded General Lanham as director of the board's staff in 1949.(Back)

Footnote 15-9: Memo, Dir, PPB Staff, for Under SecNav, 7 Dec 49, sub: Policy Regarding "Race" Entries on Enlistment Contracts and Shipping Articles, PPB 291.2.(Back)

Footnote 15-10: Idem for Administrative Asst to SA, 8 Dec 49, sub: Policy Regarding "Race" Entries on Enlistment Contracts and Shipping Articles, OSA 291.2.(Back)

Footnote 15-11: Schneider succeeded Thomas Reid as chairman on 2 February 1950.(Back)

Footnote 15-12: Memo, Chmn, PPB, for SA et al., 5 Apr 50, sub: Policy Regarding "Race" on Enlistment Contracts and Shipping Articles, PPB 291.2.(Back)

Footnote 15-13: SR 615-105-1 (AFR 39-9), 6 Sep 50.(Back)

Footnote 15-14: BuPers Cir Ltr 84-50, 1 Jun 50.(Back)

Footnote 15-15: Memo, Dep Asst CS/G-1 for Dep Dir of Staff, Mil Pers, PPB, 7 Aug 50, sub: "Race" Entries on Induction Records, PPB 291.2. The Director, Personnel and Administration, was redesignated the Assistant Chief of Staff, G-1, in the 1950 reorganization of the Army staff; see Hewes, *From Root to McNamara*.(Back)

Footnote 15-16: Memo, Dir, PPB Staff, for Dep ACS, G-1, 29 Aug 50, sub: "Race" Entries on Induction Records, PPB 291.2 (27 Aug 50); Memo, Chief, Class and Standards Br, G-1, for TAG, 6 Sep 50, same sub, G-1 291.2 (11 Oct 49); Ltr, Dir, Selective Service, to Actg Dir of Production Management, Munitions Bd, 27 Nov 50, copy in G-1 291.2; G-1 Memo for Rcd, attached to G-1 DF to TAG, 28 Dec 50, same sub, G-1 291.2 (11 Oct 50).(Back)

Footnote 15-17: Ltr, Clarence Mitchell to SecAF Thomas K. Finletter, 13 Dec 50, SecAF files. Finletter had become secretary on 24 April 1950.(Back)

Footnote 15-18: Ltr, SecAF to Mitchell, Dir, Washington Bureau, NAACP, 3 Jan 51, and Ltr, Mitchell to Asst SecAF, 8 Jan 51, both in SecAF files; Memo, Edward T. Dickinson, Asst to Joint Secys, OSD, for SA et al., 17 Jan 51, OSD files.(Back)

Footnote 15-19: Memo, Dep Asst SecAF (Program Management) for SecAF, 18 Jan 51, SecAF files; Memo, Col Robin B. Pape, Asst to Dir, PPB Staff, for Chmn, PPB, 4 May 51, sub: Racial Entries on Enlistment Records, PPB 291.2.(Back)

Footnote 15-20: Memo, Secy, Cmte on Negro Policies, for ASW, 26 Sep 42, sub: Digest of War Department Policy Pertaining to Negro Military Personnel, ASW 291.2 Negro Troops.(Back)

Footnote 15-21: Msg, CG, China Theater, to War Department, 16 Mar 46, G-1 291.2 (1 Jan-31 Mar 46); Memo Vice CNO for Chief of NavPers, 1 Jul 42, sub: Colored Personnel on Duty in Iceland—Replacement of, P-14, GenRecsNav.(Back)

Footnote 15-22: Memo, Thomas R. Reid for Najeeb Halaby, Dir, Office of Foreign Military Affairs, OSD, 7 Jul 49, sub: Foreign Assignments of Negro Personnel, PPB 291.2 (7 Jul 49).(Back)

Footnote 15-23: Ltr, SecDef to Secy of State, 14 Sep 49, CD 30-1-4, SecDef files.(Back)

Footnote 15-24: Memo, Asst SecAF for Chmn, PPB, 16 Sep 49, sub: Assignment of Negroes to Overseas Areas; Memo, Dir of Staff, PPB, for Asst SecAF, 28 Sep 49, same sub; Memo, Asst SecAF for Chmn, PPB, 12 Oct 49, same sub. All in SecAF files.(Back)

Footnote 15-25: Ltr, James E. Webb to Louis Johnson, 17 Oct 49; Memo, SecDef for SA et al., 27 Oct 49; both in CD 30-1-4, SecDef files.(Back)

Footnote 15-26: DF, D/PA to D/OT, 1 Mar 50, sub: Utilization of Negro Manpower, Ltr, D/PA for Maj Gen Ray E. Porter, CG, USACARIB, 9 Feb 50; both in CSGPA 291.2.(Back)

Footnote 15-27: G-1 Summary Sheet, 12 Apr 50, sub: Utilization of Negro Manpower, CSGPA 291.2.(Back)

Footnote 15-28: Memo, Dir of Personnel, USMC, for Dir, Div of Plans and Policies, 22 Dec 49, Hist Div, HQMC.(Back)

Footnote 15-29: Memo, Dep CS/Pers for SecAF, 28 Dec 49; Memo, Clarence H. Osthagen, Asst to SecAF, for Asst SecAF, 6 Jan 50; Rcd of Telecon, Halaby with Zuckert, 10 Jan 50. All in SecAF files.(Back)

Footnote 15-30: Memo, SecNav for SecDef, 3 Jan 50, sub: Foreign Assignment of Negro Personnel, CD 30-1-4, SecDef files.(Back)

Footnote 15-31: Memo, NEH (Halaby) for Maj Gen J. H. Burns, 10 Feb 50, attached to Ltr, Burns to Rusk, 13 Feb 50, CD 30-1-4, SecDef files.(Back)

Footnote 15-32: Memo, SecDef for SA et al., 5 Apr 50, sub: Foreign Assignment of Negro Personnel; Ltr, Dean Rusk to Maj Gen Burns, 1 Mar 50; Memo, Burns for SecDef, 3 Apr 50. All in CD 30-1-4, SecDef files.(Back)

Footnote 15-33: DF, ACS, G-1, for CSA, 3 Dec 52, sub: Restricted Distribution of Negro Personnel; ibid., 30 Mar 53, sub: Assignment of Negro Personnel to TRUST; both in CS 291.2 Negroes. See also Memo, ACS, G-1, for TAG, 24 Apr 53, sub: Assignment of Negro Personnel, AG 291.2 (13 Apr 53); Memo, ASecAF for SecDef, 28 Apr 50, sub: Foreign Assignment of Negro Personnel, CD 30-1-4, SecDef files.(Back)

Footnote 15-34: G-3 Summary Sheet, 15 Nov 49, sub: Assignment of Negro Personnel, G-3 291.2.(Back)

Footnote 15-35: Msg, Chief, JAMMAT, Ankara, Turkey, to DA, personal for the G-1, 14 Apr 51; Ltr, Brig Gen W. E. Dunkelberg to Maj Gen William H. Arnold, Chief, JAMMAT, 24 Apr 51; idem to Brig Gen John B. Murphy, G-1 Sec, EUCOM, 24 April 51. All in G-1 291.2.(Back)

Footnote 15-36: Jack Greenberg, *Race Relations and American Law* (New York: Columbia University Press, 1959), pp. 359-60.(Back)

Footnote 15-37: Memo, Dep ASA for ASD/ISA, 6 Feb 57, sub: Racial Assignment Restrictions, OSA 291.2 Ethiopia.(Back)

Footnote 15-38: Ltr, Dep Asst Secy of State for Personnel to Dep ASD (MP&R), 24 May 57, OASD (MP&R) 291.2.(Back)

Footnote 15-39: Memo, Dep ASD for ASA (MP&R) et al., 24 Jun 57, ASD (MP&R) 291.2.(Back)

Footnote 15-40: Memo, James C. Evans for Paul Hopper, ISA, 29 Oct 58; Memo for Rcd, Exec to Civilian Asst, OSD, 21 Jan 60, sub: MAAG's and Missions, copies of both in CMH.(Back)

Footnote 15-41: See AFM 35-11L, Appendix M, 14 Dec 60, sub: Assignment Restrictions; Memo, USMC IG for Dir of Pers, MC, 31 Aug 62, sub: Problem Area at Marine Barracks, Argentia, Hist Div, HQMC. See also New York *Times*, December 5, 1959 and November 16, 17, and 18, 1971.(Back)

Footnote 15-42: *Congressional Record*, 81st Cong., 2d sess., vol. 96, p. 8412.(Back)

Footnote 15-43: Ibid., pp. 8973, 9073.(Back)

Footnote 15-44: Ibid., p. 9074; see also Memo, Rear Adm H. A. Houser, OSD Legis Liaison, for ASD Rosenberg, 17 Mar 51, sub: Winstead Anti-nonsegregation Amendment, SD 291.2.(Back)

Footnote 15-45: See Ltrs, Rep. Kenneth B. Keating to Johnson, 19 Dec 49; SecDef to Keating, 20 Jan 50; idem to Hubert H. Humphrey, 24 Mar 50; Humphrey to SecDef, 28 Feb 50; Rep. Jacob Javits to Johnson, 22 Dec 49; Draft Ltr, SecDef to Javits, 16 Jan 50 (not sent); Memos, Leva for Johnson, 12 and 17 Jan 50. All in SD 291.2 Negroes.(Back)

Footnote 15-46: Ltrs, Johnson to Reynolds, 23 Dec 49; Reynolds to Johnson, 13 Jan 50; Reynolds and Randolph to Johnson, 15 Jan 50; Johnson to Reynolds and Randolph, 6 Feb 50. The Committee Against Jim Crow was particularly upset with Johnson's assistants, Leva and Evans; see Ltrs, Reynolds to Johnson, 19 Dec 49; Leva to Niles, 7 Feb 50; Reynolds to Evans, 13 Jan 50. All in SD 291.2.(Back)

Footnote 15-47: Ltr, Javits to Johnson, 22 Dec 49; Press Release, Jacob K. Javits, 12 Jan 50; Ltr, Javits to Johnson, 24 Jan 50. Other legislators expressed interest in the joint commission idea; see Ltrs, Saltonstall to Johnson, 11 Jan 50; Sen. William Langer to Johnson, 29 Oct 49; Henry C. Lodge to Johnson, 30 Nov 49. All in SD 291.2. See also Ltr, Javits to author, with attachments, 28 Oct 71, CMH files.(Back)

Footnote 15-48: Ltr, SecDef to Chmn, Cmte on Rules, 21 Mar 50, SD 291.2 (21 Mar 50).(Back)

Footnote 15-49: *Congressional Record*, 81st Cong., 2d sess., pp. A3267-68; Memo, Leva for Johnson, 9 May 50; Ltr, Johnson to Javits, 18 May 50; both in SecDef files. See also Ltr, Javits to author, 28 Oct 71.(Back)

Footnote 15-50: Carl W. Borklund, *Men of the Pentagon* (New York: Praeger, 1966), pp. 121-24; Ltr, Anna Rosenberg Hoffman to author, 23 Sep 71; Interv, author with James C. Evans, 13 Sep 71; both in CMH files.(Back)

Footnote 15-51: Immediately before her appointment as the manpower assistant, Rosenberg was a public member of the Committee on Mobilization Policy of the National Security Resources Board and a special consultant on manpower problems to the chairman of the board, Stuart Symington.(Back)

Footnote 15-52: Interv, author with Davenport, 17 Oct 71.(Back)

Footnote 15-53: Ltr, Humphrey to Rosenberg, 7 Mar 51, SD 291.2.(Back)

Footnote 15-54: See Memo for Rcd, Maj M. O. Becker, G-1, 13 Mar 51, G-1 291.2; Ltrs, Granger to Leva, 25 Jan 51, Leva to Granger, 13 Feb 51, Clarence Mitchell, NAACP, to Rosenberg, 26 Mar 51, last three in SD 291.2. Legislators attending these briefings included Senators Lehman, William Benton of Connecticut, Humphrey, John Pastore of Rhode Island, and Kilgore.(Back)

Footnote 15-55: See Ltrs, Humphrey to Rosenberg, 10 Mar 51; Rosenberg to Humphrey, 26 Mar 51; Javits to SecDef, 10 Mar 51; Marshall to Javits, 30 Mar 51; Memo, Leva for Rosenberg, 23 Mar 51; Ltrs, Rosenberg to Douglas, Humphrey, Benton, Kilgore, Lehman, and Javits, 26 Jun 51; Memo, Rosenberg for SA, 16 May 51, sub: Private Lionel E. Bolin. All in SD 291.2. See also DF, ACS, G-1, to CSA, 6 Apr 51, sub: Summary of Advances in Utilization of Negro Manpower, CS 291.2 Negroes.(Back)

Footnote 15-56: Ltr, Mitchell to Rosenberg, 26 Mar 51, SD 291.2.(Back)

Footnote 15-57: Telgs, White to Marshall and SA, 9 Jan 51, copy in SD 291.2.(Back)

Footnote 15-58: *Congressional Record*, 81st Cong., 2d sess., vol. 96, p. A888.(Back)

Footnote 15-59: Ibid., p. 904. For the Army's opposition to these proposals, see Memo ACofS, G-1, for CofS, 12 Apr 50, sub: Department of the Army Policies re Segregation and Utilization of Negro Manpower, G-1 291.2 (5 Apr 50).(Back)

Footnote 15-60: Memo for Rcd, Maj M. O. Becker, G-1, 13 Mar 51, G-1 291.2.(Back)

Footnote 15-61: Ltr, SecDef to Havenner, 27 Mar 51, SecDef files.(Back)

Footnote 15-62: Ltr, Mitchell to Rosenberg, 16 Apr 51; Ltr, Rosenberg to Mitchell, 9 May 51; both in SD 291.2.(Back)

Footnote 15-63: Memo, ASD (MP&R) for ASD (Legal and Legis Affairs), 14 Jun 51, SD 291.1; PL 51, 82d Congress.(Back)

Footnote 15-64: Ltr, Mitchell, Dir, Washington Br, NAACP, to Dir of Industrial Relations, DOD, 25 May 51; Ltr, ASD (Legal and Legis Affairs) to Mitchell, 19 Jun 51; Memo, Asst Gen Counsel, OSD, for ASD (Legal and Legis Affairs), 19 Jun 51. All in SD 291.2.(Back)

Footnote 15-65: Ltr, Anna Rosenberg Hoffman to author, 23 Sep 71.(Back)

Footnote 15-66: BuPers Study, Pers A 1224 (probably Jan 59), GenRecsNav.(Back)

Footnote 15-67: Interv, author with Davenport, 17 Oct 71; and Ltr, Anna Rosenberg Hoffman to author, 23 Sep 71.(Back)

Footnote 15-68: G-1 Summary Sheet with incl, 13 Mar 51, sub: Negro Strength in the Army; Memo, ASA for CofS, 13 Apr 51, same sub; both in CS 291.2 Negroes (13 Mar 51).(Back)

Footnote 15-69: Memo, Actg CofS for SA, 31 May 51, sub: Present Overstrength in Segregated Units; G-1 Summary Sheet for CofS, 26 May 51, same sub; Draft Memo, Frank Pace, Jr., for President; Memo, ASA for SA, 1 Jul 51. All in G-1 291.2 (26 May 51).(Back)

Footnote 16-1: Memo, ASecAF for Symington, 25 Mar 49, sub: Salient Factors of Air Force Policy Regarding Negro Personnel, SecAF files.(Back)

Footnote 16-2: Negro strength figures as of 5 April 1949. Ltr, ASecAF to Robert Harper, Chief Clerk, House Armed Services Cmte, 5 Apr 49, SecAF files.(Back)

Footnote 16-3: Memo, Symington for Forrestal, 6 Jan 49, SecAF files.(Back)

Footnote 16-4: Memo, Hoyt S. Vandenberg, CofS, USAF, for SecAF, 12 Jan 49, SecAF files.(Back)

Footnote 16-5: Memo, SecAF for Forrestal, 17 Feb 49; Memo, ASecAF for Symington, 24 Mar 49, sub: Lockbourne AFB; both in SecAF files.(Back)

Footnote 16-6: Memo for Files, Osthagen, Asst to ASecAF, 13 Apr 49, SecAF files.(Back)

Footnote 16-7: Ltr, Joseph H. Evans, Assoc Exec Secy, Fahy Cmte, to Fahy Cmte, 23 Jun 49, FC file. See also "U.S. Armed Forces: 1950," *Our World 5* (June 1950):11-35.(Back)

Footnote 16-8: Draft Memo, Zuckert for Symington, 15 Feb 49, sub: Air Force Policies on Negro Personnel (not sent), SecAF files.(Back)

Footnote 16-9: Washington *Post*, April 4, 1949; USAF Oral History Program, Interview with Lt Col Spann Watson (USAF, Ret.), 3 Apr 73.(Back)

Footnote 16-10: Pittsburgh *Courier*, January 22, 1949.(Back)

Footnote 16-11: Memo, Vandenberg, CofS, USAF, for SecAF, 12 Jan 49, SecAF files.(Back)

Footnote 16-12: Lt Gen I. H. Edwards, "Remarks on Major Personnel Problems Presented to USAF Commanders' Conference Headquarters, USAF," 12 Apr 49, SecAF files. Italics in the original.(Back)

Footnote 16-13: USAF Oral History Program, Interview with Lt Gen Daniel James, Jr., 2 Oct 73. James was to become the first four-star black officer in the armed forces.(Back)

Footnote 16-14: Ltr, Marr to author, 19 Jun 70.(Back)

Footnote 16-15: MATS Hq Ltr No. 9, 1 May 49, SecAF files.(Back)

Footnote 16-16: AF Ltr 35-3, 11 May 49. Effective until 11 May 1950, the order was superseded by a new but similar letter, AF Ltr 35-78, on 14 September 1950.(Back)

Footnote 16-17: Memo, ASecAF for Symington, 12 Jan 49, AF Negro Affairs 49, SecAF files.(Back)

Footnote 16-18: USAF Oral Hist Interv with Zuckert.(Back)

Footnote 16-19: Testimony of Zuckert and Edwards, USAF, Before the Fahy Committee, 28 Mar 49, afternoon session, pp. 7-8.(Back)

Footnote 16-20: Memo, ASecAF for Symington, 29 Apr 49, sub: Department of the Air Force Implementation of the Department of Defense Policy on Equality of Treatment and Opportunity in the Armed Services, SecAF files.(Back)

Footnote 16-21: *Freedom to Serve*, pp. 37-38.(Back)

Footnote 16-22: Memo, SecAF for Chmn, PPB, 30 Apr 49, copy in FC file. McCoy and Ruetten, *Quest and Response*, p. 223, call the deletion a victory for the committee.(Back)

Footnote 16-23: USAF Oral Hist Interv with Davis.(Back)

Footnote 16-24: USAF Oral Hist Interv with Zuckert.(Back)

Footnote 16-25: NME Fact Sheet No. 105-49, 27 Jul 49.(Back)

Footnote 16-26: "Report on the First Year of Implementation of Current Policies Regarding Negro Personnel," Incl to Memo, Maj Gen Richard E. Nugent for ASecAF, 14 Jul 50, sub: Distribution of Negro Personnel, PPB 291.2 (9 Jul 50) (hereafter referred to as Marr Report). See also USAF Oral Hist Interv with Marr.(Back)

Footnote 16-27: USAF Oral Hist Interv with Davis.(Back)

Footnote 16-28: President's Committee on Equality of Treatment and Opportunity in the Armed Forces, "A First Report on the Racial Integration Program of the Air Force," 6 Feb 50, FC file (hereafter cited as Kenworthy Report).(Back)

Footnote 16-29: ATC, "History of ATC, July-December 1949," I:29-31; New York *Times*, September 18, 1949.(Back)

Footnote 16-30: Memo, Actg DCSPER for Zuckert, 14 Jul 50, USAF file No. 3370, SecAF files.(Back)

Footnote 16-31: Memo, ASecAF for Symington, 25 Mar 49, sub: Salient Factors of Air Force Policy Regarding Negro Personnel, SecAF files.(Back)

Footnote 16-32: *Air Force Times*, 10 February 1951. These figures do not take into account the SCARWAF (Army personnel) who continued to serve in segregated units within the Air Force.(Back)

Footnote 16-33: Memo, DepSecAF for Manpower and Organizations for ASD/M, 5 Sep 52, SecAF files.(Back)

Footnote 16-34: Transcript of the Meeting of the President and the Four Service Secretaries With the President's Committee on Equality of Treatment and Opportunity in the Armed Services, 12 Jan 49, FC file, which reports the President's response as being "That's all right."(Back)

Footnote 16-35: Testimony of the Secretary of the Air Force Before the Fahy Committee, 28 Mar 49, afternoon session, p. 33.(Back)

Footnote 16-36: Kenworthy Report, as quoted and commented on in Memo, Worthington Thompson (Personnel Policy Board staff) for Leva, 9 Mar 50, sub: Some Highlights of Fahy Committee Report on Air Force Racial Integration Program, SD 291.2.(Back)

Footnote 16-37: Ltr, Kenworthy to Zuckert, 5 Jan 50, SecAF files.(Back)

Footnote 16-38: See, for example, the Washington *Post*, March 27, 1950.(Back)

Footnote 16-39: Press reaction summarized in Memo, James C. Evans for PPB, 19 Jan 50, PPB 291.2. See also, Ltr, Dowdal Davis, Gen Manager of the Kansas City *Call*, to Evans, 9 Jul 49, SD 291.2; Memo, Evans for SecAF, 5 Jul 49; and Memo, Zuckert for SecAF, 2 Aug 49, both in SecAF files; Chicago *Defender*, June 18, 1949; Minneapolis *Spokesman*, January 13, 1950; *Ebony* Magazine, 4 (September 1949):15; Pittsburgh *Courier*, July 25, 1952; Detroit *Free Press*, May 14, 1953.(Back)

Footnote 16-40: Memo, IG, USAF, for ASecAF, 25 Jul 49, SecAF files.(Back)

Footnote 16-41: Idem for DCSPER, 7 Sep 49, copy in SecAF files; see also ACofS, G-2, Fourth Army, Ft. Sam Houston, Summary of Information, 7 Sep 49, copy in SA 291.2.(Back)

Footnote 16-42: See, for example, Memo, SecAF for SecDef, 17 Feb 49; Ltr, SecAF to Sen. Burnet R. Maybank, 21 Jul 49; both in SecAF files.(Back)

Footnote 16-43: Memo, Evans, OSD, for Worthington Thompson, 18 May 53, sub: Summary of Topics Reviewed in Thompson's office 15 May 53, SD 291.2.(Back)

Footnote 16-44: History Officer, 3202d Installations Groups, "History of the 3202d Installations Group, 1 July-31 October 1950," Eglin AFB, Fla., pp. 8-9.(Back)

Footnote 16-45: This off-the-record comment occurred during the committee hearings in the Pentagon and was related to the author by E. W. Kenworthy in interview on 17 October 1971. See also Memo, Kenworthy to Brig Gen James L. Collins, Jr., 13 Oct 76, copy in CMH.(Back)

Footnote 16-46: Marr Report.(Back)

Footnote 16-47: *Freedom to Serve*, p. 41.(Back)

Footnote 16-48: Ltr, Col Paul H. Prentiss, Cmdr, 1701st AT Wing, to SecAF, 27 Dec 49, SecAF files.(Back)

Footnote 16-49: *Air Force Times*, 10 February 1951.(Back)

Footnote 16-50: Memo for Rcd, ADS(M), 12 Sep 56, sub: Integration Percentages, ADS(M) 291.2. For further discussion of the qualitative distribution program, see Navy section, below.(Back)

Footnote 16-51: "Integration in the Air Force Abroad," *Ebony* 15 (March 1960):27.(Back)

Footnote 16-52: Unless otherwise noted all statistics are from information supplied by the Bureau of Naval Personnel. The exact percentage on 1 July 1949 was 4.7; see Memo for Rcd, ASD(M), 12 Sep 56, sub: Integration Percentages, ASD(M) 291.2.(Back)

Footnote 16-53: Memo, Chief, NavPers, for Under SecNav, 5 Dec 49, sub: Proposed Report to Chairman Personnel Policy Board Regarding the Implementation of Executive Order 9981, Pers 21, GenRecsNav.(Back)

Footnote 16-54: Memo, SecNav for SecDef, 23 May 49, sub: Equality of Treatment and Opportunity in the Armed Forces, copy in FC file.(Back)

Footnote 16-55: ALNAV 447-49, which remained in force until 23 March 1953 when SecNav Instruction 1000.2 superseded it without substantial change.(Back)

Footnote 16-56: Memo, Under SecNav for Chmn, PPB, 22 Dec 49, sub: Implementation of Executive Order 9981, PPB 291.2.(Back)

Footnote 16-57: SecNav, Annual Report to SecDef, FY 1949, p. 230; Memo, Under SecNav Chmn, PPB, 22 Dec 49, sub: Implementation of Executive Order 9981, PPB 291.2.(Back)

Footnote 16-58: Memo, Dir, Recruiting Div, BuPers, for Admin Aide to SecNav, 22 Dec 50, sub: Negro Officer in Recruiting on the West Coast; Ltr, SecNav to Actg Exec Dir, Urban League, Los Angeles, 22 Dec 50; both in Pers B6, GenRecsNav.(Back)

Footnote 16-59: Ltr, Charles W. Washington, Exec Secy, Dayton, Ohio, Urban League, to SecNav, 19 Oct 50, copy in Pers 1376, GenRecsNav.(Back)

Footnote 16-60: Memo, Nelson for Charles Durham, Fahy Committee, sub: Implementation of Proposed Navy Racial Policy, 17 Jun 49, FC file.(Back)

Footnote 16-61: Memo, Under SecNav for Chmn, PPB, 22 Dec 49, sub: Implementation of Executive Order 9981, PPB 291.2.(Back)

Footnote 16-62: Memo, Off in Charge, NROTC Tng, for Chief, Plans & Policy Div, BuPers, 14 Jul 49, sub: NROTC Personnel Problems, Pers 424, BuPersRecs.(Back)

Footnote 16-63: Ltr, Granger to Chief, NavPers, 3 Aug 49, Pers 42, BuPersRecs.(Back)

Footnote 16-64: Memo, Dir of Tng, BuPers, for Chief, NavPers, 1 Jul 49; Ltr, Granger to Cmdr Luther Heinz, 3 Aug 49; Ltr, Heinz to Granger, 18 Aug 49. All in Pers 42, BuPersRecs. See also Interv, author with Nelson, 26 May 69, and Ltr, Nelson to author, 10 Feb 70, both in CMH files.(Back)

Footnote 16-65: Ltr, Chief, NavPers, to Cmdt, All Continental Naval Dists, 17 Mar 50, Pers 42, BuPersRecs; Memo, Under SecNav for Chmn, PPB, 22 Dec 49, PPB 291.2.(Back)

Footnote 16-66: Memo, Under SecNav for Chmn, PPB, 22 Dec 49, PPB 291.2.(Back)

Footnote 16-67: For a public expression of these sentiments see, for example, Ltr, Capt R. B. Ellis, Policy Control Br, BuPers, to President of Birmingham, Ala., Branch, NAACP, 30 Mar 50, Pers 66 MM, GenRecsNav.(Back)

Footnote 16-68: BuPers, "Memo on Discrimination of the Negro," 24 January 1959, Pers A1224, BuPers Tech Library.(Back)

Footnote 16-69: Ltr, Exec Secy, Birmingham, Ala., Branch, NAACP, to Chief, NavPers, 14 Mar 50, Pers A, GenRecsNav.(Back)

Footnote 16-70: Interv, Nichols with Nelson, 1953, in Nichols Collection; Ltr, Nelson to author, 10 Feb 70; both in CMH files.(Back)

Footnote 16-71: Quoted in Memo, Dir of Tng, BuPers, for Chief, NavPers, 1 Jul 49, Pers 42, GenRecsNav.(Back)

Footnote 16-72: Memo for Rcd, Evans, 23 Jun 65, sub: NROTC Boards, ASD/M 291.2.(Back)

Footnote 16-73: Ltr, Exec Dir, ACLU, to SecNav, 26 Nov 57, GenRecsNav.(Back)

Footnote 16-74: Memo, Under SecNav for Chmn, PPB, 22 Dec 49, sub: Implementation of Executive Order 9981, PPB 291.2.(Back)

Footnote 16-75: Memo, Chief, NavPers, for Pers B, 23 Sep 61, copy in Harris Wofford Collection, J. F. Kennedy Library.(Back)

Footnote 16-76: Testimony of Vice Adm William M. Fechteler Before the President's Committee on Equality of Treatment and Opportunity in the Armed Services (the Fahy Cmte), 28 Mar 49, p. 18.(Back)

Footnote 16-77: BuPers Cir Ltr 115-49, 25 Jul 49.(Back)

Footnote 16-78: Memo, Evans for Fahy Cmte, 23 Aug 49, sub: Progress in Navy, Fahy Papers, Truman Library.(Back)

Footnote 16-79: Memo, Under SecNav for Chief, NavPers, 10 Aug 49, MM (1) GenRecsNav.(Back)

Footnote 16-80: BuPers Cir Ltr 141-49, 30 Aug 49. See also Memo, Under SecNav for Chmn, PPB, 22 Dec 49, sub: Implementation of Executive Order 9981, PPB 291.2; Memo, Chief, NavPers, for SecNav, 4 May 50, sub: Equality of Treatment and Opportunity, Pers 42, GenRecsNav.(Back)

Footnote 16-81: Memo, Dir, Plans and Policy, BuPers, for Capt Brooke Schumm, USN, PPB, 17 Jul 50, sub: Secretary of Defense Semi-Annual Report, Negro Enlisted Personnel Data for, Pers 14B; Memo, Head, Strength and Statistics Br, BuPers, for Head, Technical Info Br, BuPers, 25 Aug 53, sub: Information Requested by LCDR D. D. Nelson Concerning Negro Strength, Pers A14; both in BuPersRecs.(Back)

Footnote 16-82: Kimball was sworn in as Secretary of the Navy on 31 July 1951. Ltr, SecNav to Granger, 19 Nov 52, SecNav files, GenRecsNav.(Back)

Footnote 16-83: BuPers, Plans and Policy Div, "Review of Suggestions and Recommendations to Improve Standards, Morale, and Attitudes Toward Stewards Branch of U.S. Navy" (ca. 2 Aug 51), BuPersRecs.(Back)

Footnote 16-84: Ltr, SecNav for Granger, 19 Nov 52, SecNav files, GenRecsNav.(Back)

Footnote 16-85: Ltrs, Chief, NavPers, to James C. Evans, OSD, 19 Jun 53, and Granger, 28 Jul 53, both in P 8 (4), BuPersRecs.(Back)

Footnote 16-86: Memo, Chief, NavPers, for Pers B, 23 Sep 61, Harris Wofford Collection, J. F. Kennedy Library. See also Memo, Chief, NavPers, for ASD/M, 29 Mar 61, sub: Stewards in U.S. Navy, Pers 8 (4), BuPersRecs; Memo, Special Asst to SecDef, Adam Yarmolinsky, for Frederic Dutton, Special Asst to President, 31 Oct 61, sub: Yarmolinsky Memo of October 26, Harris Wofford Collection, J. F. Kennedy Library.(Back)

Footnote 16-87: Ltr, Granger to SecNav, 24 Oct 52, SecNav files, GenRecsNav.(Back)

Footnote 16-88: Secretary Anderson, appointed by President Eisenhower, became Secretary of the Navy on 4 February 1953.(Back)

Footnote 16-89: Ltr, Granger to SecNav, 24 Apr 53, SecNav files, GenRecsNav.(Back)

Footnote 16-90: Detroit *Free Press*, May 16, 1953.(Back)

Footnote 16-91: UP News Release, September 21, 1953, copy in CMH.(Back)

Footnote 16-92: Ltr, Cmdr Durwood W. Gilmore, USNR et al., to Chief, NavPers, Vice Adm J. L. Holloway, Jr., 31 Aug 53, P 8 (4), BuPersRecs.(Back)

Footnote 16-93: Memo, Chief, NavPers, for SecNav, 1 Sep 53, sub: Mr. Granger's Visit and Related Matters, Pers, GenRecsNav.(Back)

Footnote 16-94: Ltr, SecNav to Congressman Adam C. Powell, 19 Mar 54, SecNav files, GenRecsNav.(Back)

Footnote 16-95: See, for example, ASD/M, Thursday Reports, 7 Jan 54 and 12 Apr 56, copies in Dep ASD (Civil Rights) files; see also Memo, Chief, NavPers, for Special Asst to SecDef, 29 Mar 61, sub: Stewards in U.S. Navy, BuPersRecs.(Back)

Footnote 16-96: Memo, Adam Yarmolinsky for Fred Dutton, 31 Oct 61, sub: Yarmolinsky Memo of October 26, Harris Wofford Collection, J. F. Kennedy Library.(Back)

Footnote 16-97: Greenberg, *Race Relations and American Law*, p. 359.(Back)

Footnote 16-98: Memo, Chief, NavPers, for Special Asst to SecDef, 29 Mar 61, sub: Stewards in U.S. Navy, Pers 8 (4), GenRecsNav.(Back)

Footnote 16-99: The Navy commissioned its first black pilot, Ens. Jesse L. Brown, in 1950. He was killed in action in Korea.(Back)

Footnote 16-100: Ltr, Powell to John Floberg, Asst SecNav for Air, 29 Jun 53, SecNav files, GenRecsNav.(Back)

Footnote 16-101: Ltr, Granger to SecNav, 7 Jan 54, SecNav files, GenRecsNav.(Back)

Footnote 16-102: Memo, ASD/M for SA et al., 21 Nov 51, sub: Manuscript on the Negro in the Armed Forces, SecDef 291.2.(Back)

Footnote 16-103: See New York *Herald Tribune*, December 2, 1957, and New York Post, March 14, 1957.(Back)

Footnote 16-104: Gravely would eventually become the first black admiral in the U.S. Navy.(Back)

Footnote 16-105: See, for example, Ltr, Exec Secy, President's Cmte on Equal Treatment and Opportunity in the Armed Services, to CNO, 21 Jun 49, FC file; Memo, Chief, NavPers, for SecNav, BuPersRecs; Memo, ASD/M for SA et al., 21 Nov 51, sub: Manuscript on the Negro in the Armed Forces, SecDef 291.2; Ltr, Exec Secy, ACLU, to SecNav, 26 Nov 57, SecNav files, GenRecsNav.(Back)

Footnote 16-106: Nichols's sampling, presented in the form of approximately a hundred interviews with men and women from all the services, was completely unscientific and informal and was undertaken for the preparation of his book, *Breakthrough on the Color Front*. Considering their timing, the interviews supply an interesting sidelight to the integration period. They are included in the Nichols Collection, CMH.(Back)

Footnote 17-1: Interv, author with Collins.(Back)

Footnote 17-2: Memo, SA for Lt Gen Stephen J. Chamberlin, 30 Nov 49, sub: Utilization of Negro Manpower in the Army, CSGPA 291.2. See also Dir, P&A, Summary Sheet to CofS, 2 Nov 49, sub: Board to Study the Utilization of Negro Manpower in Peacetime Army, CSGPA 291.2, and TAG to Chamberlin, 18 Nov 49, same sub, AG 334 (17 Nov 49). In addition to Chamberlin, the board included Maj. Gen. Withers A. Buress, commanding general of the Infantry Center; Maj. Gen. John M. Divine, commanding general of 9th Infantry Division, Fort

Dix; and Col. M. VanVoorst, Personnel and Administration Division, as recorder without vote.(Back)

Footnote 17-3: Memo, Gen Chamberlin et al. for SA, 9 Feb 50, sub: Report of Board of Officers on Utilization of Negro Manpower in the Army, AG 291.2 (6 Dec 49). A copy of the report and many of the related and supporting documents are in CMH.(Back)

Footnote 17-4: Kenworthy, "The Case Against Army Segregation," p. 32.(Back)

Footnote 17-5: Memo, G-1 for VCofS, sub: Negro Statistics, 16 Jun 50-6 Oct 50, CS 291.2 Negro; idem for G-3, 18 Apr 51, sub: Training Spaces for Negro Personnel, OPS 291.2; Memo, Chief, Mil Opers Management Branch, G-1, for G-1, 1 Feb 51, sub: Distribution of Negro Manpower in the Army, G-1 291.2, and Memo, Chief, Procurement and Distribution Div, G-1, for G-1, 20 Oct 53, same sub and file.(Back)

Footnote 17-6: STM-30, Strength of the Army, Sep 50, Mar 51, and Jul 51.(Back)

Footnote 17-7: IG Summary Sheet for CofS, 7 Dec 50, sub: Policy Regarding Negro Segregation, CS 291.2 (7 Dec 50).(Back)

Footnote 17-8: G-1 Summary Sheet for CofS, 18 Dec 50, sub: Policy Regarding Negro Segregation, G-1 291.2.(Back)

Footnote 17-9: Memo, ASA for SA, 3 Apr 51, sub: Present Overstrength in Segregated Units, G-1 291.2.(Back)

Footnote 17-10: Memo, G-1 for CofS, 26 May 51, sub: Present Overstrength in Segregated Units; DF, G-1 for G-3, 16 Apr 51, sub: Training Spaces for Negro Personnel; both in G-1 291.2.(Back)

Footnote 17-11: Memo, CG, AFF, for G-1, 8 May 51, sub: Negro Strength in the Army, G-1 291.2.(Back)

Footnote 17-12: Memo, ASA for SA, 1 Jul 51, and Draft Memo, SA for President (not sent), both in SA 291.2.(Back)

Footnote 17-13: CMT 2 (Brig Gen D. A. Ogden, Chief, Orgn & Tng Div, G-3), 3 May 51, CMT 3 (Brig Gen W. E. Dunkelberg, Chief, Manpower Control Div, G-1), 21 May 51, and CMT 4 (Ogden), 24 May 51, to G-1 Summary Sheet for CofS, 18 Apr 51, sub: Negro Overstrengths, G-1 291.2.(Back)

Footnote 17-14: The Korean Augmentation to the United States Army, known as KATUSA, a program for integrating Korean soldiers in American units, was substantially different from the integration of black Americans in terms of official authorization and management; see CMH study by David C. Skaggs, "The Katusa Program," in CMH.(Back)

Footnote 17-15: Memo, CO, 9th Inf, for TIG, 29 Oct 50, attached to IG Summary Sheet for CofS, 7 Dec 50, sub: Policy Regarding Negro Segregation, CS 291.2 (7 Dec 50); FEC, "G-1 Command Report, 1 January-31 October 1950."(Back)

Footnote 17-16: S. L. A. Marshall, "Integration," Detroit *News*, May 13, 1956.(Back)

Footnote 17-17: ORO Technical Memorandum T-99, A Preliminary Report on the Utilization of Negro Manpower, 30 Jun 51, p. 34, copy in CMH.(Back)

Footnote 17-18: Ibid., p. 35. For a popular report on the success of this partial integration, see Harold H. Martin, "How Do Our Negro Troops Measure Up?," *Saturday Evening Post* 223 (June 16, 1951):30-31.(Back)

Footnote 17-19: Ltr, Lewis B. Hershey to SA, 21 Sep 50, SA 291.2; Memo, Col W. Preston Corderman, Exec, Office of ASA, for CofS, 8 Sep 50, sub: Racial Complaints, CS 291.2. For an example of complaints by a civil rights organization, see Telg, J. L. LeFore, Mobile, Ala., NAACP, to President, 18 Sep 50, and Ltr, A. Philip Randolph to SecDef, 30 Oct 50, both in SD 291.2 Neg.(Back)

Footnote 17-20: Memo, Evans for Leva, ASD, 5 Oct 50, sub: Racial Complaint From the Mobile Area, SD 291.2 Neg (18 Sep 50).(Back)

Footnote 17-21: Ltrs, Javits to SecDef, 6 Sep and 2 Oct 50; Ltrs, SecDef to Javits, 19 Sep and 10 Oct 50. All in SD 291.2 Neg.(Back)

Footnote 17-22: G-1 Summary Sheet for VCofS, 22 Apr 52, sub: Information for the G-1 Information Book, G-1 291.2; Memo, ASA (M&PR) for ASD (M&PR), 22 Aug 52, sub: Progress Report on Elimination of Segregation in the Army, SD 291.2; Memo, VCofS for SA, 18 Jun 51, sub: Assimilation of Negroes at Ft. Jackson, S.C., SA 291.2. See also Lt Col William M. Nichols, "The DOD Program to Ensure Civil Rights Within the Services and Between the Services and the Community," Rpt 116, 1966, Industrial College of the Armed Forces, p. 24.(Back)

Footnote 17-23: Ltr, Maj Gen W. K. Harrison, CG, 9th Inf Div, Ft. Dix, N.J., to CG, First Army, 19 Jan 51, sub: Request for an Additional Training Regiment, G-1 291.2.(Back)

Footnote 17-24: Memo, DA, G-1 for CGIA, for 9th Inf Div, 28 Feb 51, G-1 291.2; AGAO-I, 3 Mar 51, AG 322.(Back)

377

Footnote 17-25: Memo, ASA for ASD (M&P), 5 Jun 51; Memo, SA for ASD (M&P), 3 Sep 52; both in SD 291.2.(Back)

Footnote 17-26: Roy E. Appleman, *South to the Naktong, North to the Yalu* (Washington: Government Printing Office, 1961), pp. 485-86. For a detailed account of the battlefield performance of the 24th and other segregated units, see ibid., passim.(Back)

Footnote 17-27: Ltr, Maj Gen W. B. Kean to CG, Eighth Army, 9 Sep 50, sub: Combat Effectiveness of the 24th Infantry Regiment, AG 330.1 (A).(Back)

Footnote 17-28: Observer Report, Lt Col J. D. Stevens, Plans Div, G-3, 25 Oct 50, G-3 333 PAC (Sec I-D), Case 18, Tab G.(Back)

Footnote 17-29: FECOM Check Sheet, IG to G-1, FEC, 27 May 51, sub: Report of Investigation; Memo, FEC G-1 for CofS, FEC, 30 Apr 51, sub: G-1 Topics Which CINC May Discuss With Gen Taylor; both are quoted in FECOM Mil Hist Section, "History of the Korean War," III (pt. 2): 151-52, in CMH.(Back)

Footnote 17-30: Ltr, EUSAK IG to CG, EUSAK, 15 Mar 51, sub: Report of Investigation Concerning 24th Infantry Regiment and Negro Soldiers in Combat, EUSAK IG Report.(Back)

Footnote 17-31: Thurgood Marshall, *Report on Korea: The Shameful Story of the Courts Martial of Negro GIs* (New York: NAACP, 1951).(Back)

Footnote 17-32: Ltr, Lt Gen Edward Almond, CofS, FECOM, to TIG, 15 Mar 51, IG 333.9.(Back)

Footnote 17-33: FECOM Check Sheet, IG to G-1, FEC, 27 May 51, sub: Report of Investigation; Memo, FEC G-1 for CofS FEC, 30 Apr 51, sub: G-1 Topics Which CINC May Discuss With Gen Taylor.(Back)

Footnote 17-34: Matthew B. Ridgway, *The Korean War* (New York: Doubleday, 1967), pp. 192-93.(Back)

Footnote 17-35: Memorandum for File, FECOM IG, 2 May 51, copy in AG 330.1.(Back)

Footnote 17-36: Report of Board of Officers on Utilization of Negro Manpower (2d Chamberlin Report), 3 Apr 51, G-1 334 (8 Nov 51).(Back)

Footnote 17-37: Memo, Actg CofS for SA, 31 May 51, sub: Negro Strength in the Army, CS 291.2 Negroes (11 Apr 51); see also Interv, author with Haislip, 14 Feb 71, CMH files.(Back)

Footnote 17-38: Incl to Ltr, Almond to CMH, 1 Apr 72, CMH files.(Back)

Footnote 17-39: Memo, ACofS, G-3, for ACofS, G-1, 22 Feb 51, WDGPA 291.2.(Back)

Footnote 17-40: Memo, Chief, Pers Mgmt Div, G-1, for CofS, G-3, 6 Mar 51, WDGPA 291.2.(Back)

Footnote 17-41: Ltr, Maj Gen Ward Maris, G-4, for Dir, ORO, 29 Mar 51, G-4 291.2. The Operations Research Office, a subsidiary of the Johns Hopkins University, performed qualitative and quantitative analyses of strategy, tactics, and materiel. Some of its assignments were subcontracted to other research institutions; all were assigned by the G-4's Research and Development Division and coordinated with the Department of Defense.(Back)

Footnote 17-42: DA Personnel Research Team, "A Preliminary Report on Personnel Research Data" (ca. 28 Jul 51), AG 333.3.(Back)

Footnote 17-43: ORO-T-99, "A Preliminary Report on the Utilization of Negro Manpower," 30 Jun 51, S4-S6, copy in CMH. A draft version of a more comprehensive study on the same subject was prepared in seven volumes (ORO-R-11) in November 1951. These several documents are usually referred to as Project CLEAR, the code name for the complete version. The declassification and eventual publication of this very important social document had a long and interesting history; see, for example, Memo, Howard Sacks, Office of the General Counsel, SA, for James C. Evans, 3 Nov 55, in CMH. For over a decade a "sanitized" version of Project CLEAR remained For Official Use Only. The study was finally cleared and published under the title *Social Research and the Desegregation of the U.S. Army*, ed. Leo Bogart (Chicago: Markham, 1969).(Back)

Footnote 17-44: ORO, "Utilization of Negro Manpower in the Army: A 1951 Study" (advance draft), pp. viii-ix, copy in CMH.(Back)

Footnote 17-45: Ltr, Dir, ORO, to G-3, 20 Nov 52, G-3 291.2; see also Interv, Nichols with Davis.(Back)

Footnote 17-46: Msg, CINCFE to DA, DA IN 12483, 14 May 51, sub: Utilization of Negro Manpower in the FEC; ibid., DA IN 13036, 15 May 51, same sub. See also Ltrs, CG, Eighth Army, to CINCFE, 7 May 51, sub: Redesignation of Negro Combat Units, and Ridgway to author, 3 Dec 73, both in CMH.(Back)

Footnote 17-47: Ridgway, *The Korean War*, p. 192.(Back)

Footnote 17-48: Section 401, Army Organization Act of 1950 (PL 581, 81st Cong.), published in DA Bull 9, 6 Jul 50. See also Msg, DA to CINCFE, DA 92561, 28 May 51; G-1

378

Summary Sheet for CofS and SA, 14 May 51, sub: Utilization of Negro Manpower; Memo for Rcd, G-1 291.2.(Back)

Footnote 17-49: G-1 Summary Sheets for CofS, 18 and 23 May 51, sub: Utilization of Negro Troops in FECOM, G-1 291.2. See also Elva Stillwaugh's study, "Personnel Problems in the Korean Conflict," pp. 26-29, in CMH.(Back)

Footnote 17-50: See, for example, Msg, DA to CINCFE, DA 92561, 28 May 51; Msg, CINCFE to DA, C6444, 8 Jun 51.(Back)

Footnote 17-51: Memo, Actg CofS for SA, 28 May 51, sub: Utilization of Negro Manpower, CS 291.2.(Back)

Footnote 17-52: Interv, author with Collins.(Back)

Footnote 17-53: Memo for Rcd, Col James F. Collins, Asst to ASD (M&P), 9 Jun 51, SD 291.2.(Back)

Footnote 17-54: Msg, DA to CINCFE, DA 95359, 1 Jul 51.(Back)

Footnote 17-55: Memo, Chief, Public Info Div, CINFO, for Dir, Office of Public Info, DOD, 26 Jul 51; DOD Press Release, 26 Jul 51. For last-minute criticism of the continued segregation see, for example, Ltr, Sens. Herbert Lehman and Hubert Humphrey to SecDef, 25 Jul 51; Memo, ASA for ASD (M&P), 19 Jul 51, sub: Racial Segregation in FECOM; Telg, Elmer W. Henderson, Dir, American Council on Human Rights, to George C. Marshall, SecDef, 31 May 51. All in SecDef 291.2.(Back)

Footnote 17-56: Per Ltr, TAG to CINCFE, 9 Aug 51, AGAO-I 322 (26 Jul 51), implemented by Eighth Army GO 717, 22 Sep 51.(Back)

Footnote 17-57: Msg, DA 81846, 19 Sep 51; Eighth Army GO 774, 16 Oct 51.(Back)

Footnote 17-58: FECOM Mil Hist Section, "History of the Korean War," III (pt. 2):153-57.(Back)

Footnote 17-59: Memo, ASA (M&RF) for ASD (M&P), 22 Aug 52, sub: Integration of Negro Manpower, SD 291.2.(Back)

Footnote 17-60: Ibid.; Stillwaugh, "Personnel Problems in the Korean Conflict," pp. 33-35.(Back)

Footnote 17-61: Msg, CSA to CINCFE, DA 96489, 18 Jul 51.(Back)

Footnote 17-62: Journal Files, G-1, FEC, Oct 51, Annex 2.(Back)

Footnote 17-63: Rad, CINCFE for DA, DA IN 182547, 11 Sep 52, sub: Negro Personnel; Msg, DA to CINCFE, 23 Sep 52, G-1 291.2.(Back)

Footnote 17-64: See, for example, Press Release by Senator Herbert H. Lehman, 27 July 1951, which expressed the praise of nine U.S. senators; Editorial in the Baltimore Sun, December 21, 1951; Ltr, National Cmdr, Amvets, to CINCFE, 5 Dec 51, copies in CMH.(Back)

Footnote 17-65: Semiannual Report of the Secretary of Defense, July 1-December 31, 1951 (Washington: Government Printing Office, 1952), p. 13.(Back)

Footnote 17-66: See, for example, Interv, Nichols with Bradley; Ltr, Ridgway to author, 3 Dec 73; Mark S. Watson, "Most Combat GI's are Unsegregated," datelined 15 Dec 51 (probably prepared for the Baltimore Sun). All in CMH files. See also James C. Evans and David Lane, "Integration in the Armed Services," Annals of the American Academy of Political and Social Sciences 304 (March 1956):78.(Back)

Footnote 17-67: Extracted from a series of interviews conducted by Lee Nichols with a group of wounded soldiers at Walter Reed Army Medical Center, 12 November 1952, in Nichols Collection, CMH.(Back)

Footnote 17-68: In 1951 the European Command was the major Army headquarters in the European theater. It was, at the same time, a combined command with some 20,000 members of the Air Force and Navy serving along with 234,000 Army troops. In August 1952 a separate Army command (U.S. Army, Europe) was created within the European Command. Discussion of the European Command and its commander in the following paragraphs applies only to Army troops.(Back)

Footnote 17-69: Memo, G-1 for DCofS, Admin, 18 Jul 51, G-1 291.2.(Back)

Footnote 17-70: Ltr, Eli Ginzburg to Lt Col Edward J. Barta, Hist Div, USAREUR, attached to Ltr, Ginzberg to Carter Burgess, ASD (M&P), 11 Nov 55, SD 291.2 (11 Nov 55).(Back)

Footnote 17-71: Ltr, Ginzberg to Burgess, 11 Nov 55.(Back)

Footnote 17-72: ORO-R-11, Rpt, Utilization of Negro Manpower in the Army, Project CLEAR, vol. 1; G-1 Summary Sheet for CofSA, 5 Jan 52, sub: Evaluation of ORO-R-11 on Utilization of Negro Manpower in the Army, CS 291.2 Negroes (5 Jan 52).(Back)

Footnote 17-73: G-1 Summary Sheet for CofSA, 5 Jan 52.(Back)

Footnote 17-74: Ibid., 29 Dec 51, sub: Integration of Negro Enlisted Personnel, G-1 291.2 Negroes.(Back)

Footnote 17-75: Ltr, EUCOM to Sub Cmds, 16 Mar 51, sub: Utilization of Negro Personnel, USAREUR SGS 291.2. See also EUCOM Hist Div, "Integration of Negro and White Troops in the U.S. Army, Europe, 1952-1954," p. 4, in CMH. This monograph, prepared by Ronald Sher, will be cited hereafter as Sher Monograph.(Back)

Footnote 17-76: Ltr, Ginzberg to Burgess, 11 Nov 55, CMH files.(Back)

Footnote 17-77: See, for example, *Pathfinder* Magazine 58 (May 7, 1952):11. See also Ltr, Philleo Nash to Donald Dawson, 27 May 52, Nash Collection, Truman Library; Ltr, Brig Gen Charles T. Lanham to Evans, 7 Aug 51, CMH files; CINFO Summary Sheet, 12 Jun 52, sub: Query Washington Bureau, NAACP, CSA 291.2.(Back)

Footnote 17-78: Msg, CofSA to CINCEUR, 4 Dec 51, DA 88688.(Back)

Footnote 17-79: Ltr, AG, EUCOM, to CofSA, 14 Dec 51, sub: Racial Integration in Combat Units; G-1 Summary Sheet, 24 Jan 52, same sub; Ltr, CofSA to Handy, 15 Feb 52; Msg, CINCEUR to CofSA, 22 Mar 52, DA IN 119235; Msg, CofSA to CINCEUR, DA 904459, 24 Mar 52. All in CS 291.2.(Back)

Footnote 17-80: Memo, CINCEUCOM for Commanding Generals et al., 1 Apr 52, sub: Racial Integration of EUCOM Army Units, copy in CS 291.2.(Back)

Footnote 17-81: Sher Monograph, p. 27.(Back)

Footnote 17-82: As of 1 August 1952 the major joint American command in Europe was designated U.S. European Command (USEUCOM). The U.S. Army element in this command was designated U.S. Army, Europe (USAREUR). Gruenther was the commander in chief of the European Command from July 1953 to November 1956. At the same time he occupied the senior position in the NATO Command under the title Supreme Allied Commander, Europe (SACEUR).(Back)

Footnote 17-83: Memo, USCINCEUR for TAG, 30 Sep 53, sub: Racial Integration of USAREUR Units, AG 291.2 (30 Sep 53); see also Sher Monograph, pp. 24-27.(Back)

Footnote 17-84: Memos, G-1 for TAG, 30 Oct 53, sub: Negro Overstrength in USAREUR, and TAG for USCINCEUR, 2 Nov 53, same sub; both in AG 291.2 (30 Oct 53).(Back)

Footnote 17-85: Ltr, USCINCEUR to CG, Seventh Army, 8 Jul 53, sub: Racial Integration of USAREUR Units, USAREUR AG 291.2 (1953).(Back)

Footnote 17-86: Ltr, CINCUSAREUR to SACEUR, 10 Apr 53, USAREUR SGS 291.2 (1953), quoted in Sher Monograph, p. 28.(Back)

Footnote 17-87: Hq USAREUR, "Annual Historical Report, 1 January 1953-30 June 1954," p. 60, in CMH.(Back)

Footnote 17-88: Memo, ASA (M&RF) for J. C. Evans, OASD (M), 26 Nov 52, sub: Negro Integration in Europe, SD 291.2.(Back)

Footnote 17-89: Ltr, Ginzberg to Burgess, 15 Nov 55, CMH files; Ernest Leiser, "For Negroes, It's a New Army Now," *Saturday Evening Post* 225 (December 13, 1952):26-27, 108-12.(Back)

Footnote 17-90: On the integration of these commands, see, for example, G-1 Summary Sheet, 4 Sep 52, sub: Utilization of Negro Personnel; Ltr, CG, USARAL, to DA, 15 Sep 51; Ltr, G-1 to Maj Gen Julian Cunningham, 22 Oct 51. All in G-1 291.2.(Back)

Footnote 17-91: Memo, Chief, Manpower Control Div, G-1, for Gen Taylor, 6 Sep 51, sub: Negro Integration, G-1 291.2.(Back)

Footnote 17-92: Ltr, CG, Sixth Army, to ACofS, G-1, 10 Sep 51, G-1 291.2 Negroes.(Back)

Footnote 17-93: Ltr, G-1 to CG, Sixth Army, 17 Sep 51, G-1 291.2.(Back)

Footnote 17-94: G-1 Summary Sheet for CofS, 21 Sep 51, sub: G-1 Attitude Toward Integration of Negroes Into CONUS Units, CS 291.2 Negroes (21 Sep 51). The staff's decision to halt further integration was announced in Memo, ACofS, G-1, for ACofS, G-3, 18 Jul 51, G-1 291.2.(Back)

Footnote 17-95: *U.S. News and World Report* 35 (October 16, 1953):99-100.(Back)

Footnote 17-96: Hq USAREUR, "Annual Historical Report, 1 July 1954-30 June 1955," p. 83.(Back)

Footnote 17-97: See, for example, *Semiannual Report of the Secretary of Defense, January 1-June 30, 1953*, p. 24; ibid., January 1-June 30, 1954, pp. 21-22; and annual reports of the Secretary of the Army for same period, as well as CINCUSAREUR's response to criticisms by General Mark Clark, *Army Times*, May 19, 1956, and S. L. A. Marshall's devastating rejoinder to General Almond in the Detroit *News*, May 13, 1956. Clark's views are reported in *U.S. News and World Report* 40 (May 11, 1956). See also Ltr, Lt Col Gordon Hill, CINFO, to Joan Rosen, WCBS, 17 Apr 64, CMH files; New York *Herald Tribune*, May 14, 1956; New York *Times* May 6, 1956.(Back)

Footnote 17-98: Ltr, Hannah, ASD (M), to Sen. Lyndon B. Johnson, 27 Feb 53, ASD (M) 291.2.(Back)

Footnote 17-99: One exception was the strong objection in some states to racially mixed marriages contracted by soldiers. Twenty-seven states had some form of miscegenation law. The Army therefore did not assign to stations in those states soldiers who by reason of their mixed marriages might be subject to criminal penalties. See Memo, Chief, Classification and Standards Branch, DCSPER, for Planning Office, 28 Feb 50, sub: Assignment of Personnel; DF, DCSPER to TAG, 4 Jun 54; both in DCSPER 291.2. For further discussion of the matter, see TAGO, Policy Paper, July 1954; New York *Post*, November 13, 1957.(Back)

Footnote 17-100: HUMRRO, Integration of Social Activities on Nine Army Posts, Aug 53. See also Interv, Nichols with Davis. A DCSPER action officer, Davis was intimately involved with the Army's integration program during this period.(Back)

Footnote 17-101: Interv, author with Evans, 4 Dec 73, CMH files.(Back)

Footnote 17-102: Ibid.(Back)

Footnote 17-103: Quoted in John B. Spore and Robert F. Cocklin, "Our Negro Soldiers," *Reporter* 6 (January 22, 1952):6-9.(Back)

Footnote 17-104: Ltr, Dir, ORO, to ACofS, G-3, 20 Nov 52, G-3 291.2.(Back)

Footnote 17-105: Memo for Rcd, G-1, 6 Nov 52, ref: ACofS, G-1, Memo for CofS, sub: Distribution of Negro Personnel, 14 Oct 52, G-1 291.2.(Back)

Footnote 17-106: Hq USAREUR, "Annual Historical Report, 1 July 1954-30 June 1955," pp. 76-80, 92; ibid., 1 July 1955-30 June 1956, pp. 65-67.(Back)

Footnote 18-1: All statistics from official Marine Corps sources, Hist Div, HQMC.(Back)

Footnote 18-2: Memo, CMC for Asst SecNav for Air, 17 Mar 49, MC files.(Back)

Footnote 18-3: MC Memo 119-14, 18 Nov 49, sub: Policy Regarding Negro Marines, Hist Div, HQMC, files. Unless otherwise noted, all documents in this section are located in these files.(Back)

Footnote 18-4: Msg, CMC (signed C. B. Cates) to CG, Dept of Pacific, 18 Nov 49. Aware of the delicate public relations aspects of this subject, the Director of Plans and Policies recommended that this message be classified; see Memo, E. A. Pollock for Asst CMC, 8 Nov 49.(Back)

Footnote 18-5: DP&P Study 119-49, 14 Nov 49, sub: Designation of Units for Assignment of Negro Marines, approved by CMC, 2 Dec 49.(Back)

Footnote 18-6: Memo, CG, 2d Marine Div, for CMC, 18 Feb 50, sub: Assignment of Negro Enlisted Personnel; Memo, CMC to CG, 2d Marine Div, 28 Mar 50, sub: Designation of the Depot Platoon, Support Company, Second Combat Service Group, Service Command, for Assignment of Negro Enlisted Marines; MC Routing Sheet, Enlisted Coordinator, Personnel Department, 27 Mar 50, same sub.(Back)

Footnote 18-7: Ltr, Smith to Franklin S. Williams, Asst Special Counsel, NAACP, 4 Jan 50, AO-1, MC files.(Back)

Footnote 18-8: Ltr, Roy Wilkins to SecDef, 27 Feb 50; Memo, SecNav for SecDef, 17 Apr 50, sub: Activation of Negro Reserve Units in the U.S. Marine Corps; both in SecDef 291.2. See also Ltr, Asst CMC to Franklin Williams, 7 Feb 50.(Back)

Footnote 18-9: Ltr, CMC to Walter White, 2 Jul 51.(Back)

Footnote 18-10: Memo, Div of Plans and Policies for Asst Dir of Public Info, 4 Jun 51, sub: Article in Pittsburgh *Courier* of 26 May 51.(Back)

Footnote 18-11: *Location of Black Marines, 31 March 1951*

Posts and stations inside the United States

Posts and stations outside the United States

Troop training units

Aviation

Fleet Marine Force (Ground)

Ships

En route

Missing in action

Total

Source: Tab 1 to Memo, ACofS, G-1, to Asst Dir of Public Info, 6 Jun 51, sub: Queries Concerning Negro Marines.(Back)

Footnote 18-12: Washington *Post*, February 27, 1951.(Back)

Footnote 18-13: USMC Oral History Interview, Lt Gen Oliver P. Smith, Jun 69.(Back)

Footnote 18-14: MC Policy Memo 109-51, 13 Dec 51, sub: Policy Regarding Negro Marines.(Back)

Footnote 18-15: Memo, CMC for CG, FMF, Pacific, et al., 18 Dec 51, sub: Assignment of Negro Enlisted Personnel.(Back)

Footnote 18-16: Idem for Chief, NavPers (ca. Jun 51), MC files.(Back)

Footnote 18-17: Extract from Thomas L. Faix, "Marines on Tour (An Account of Mediterranean Goodwill Cruise and Naval Occupation Duty), Third Battalion, Sixth Marines (Reinforced), April 17-October 20, 1952," in Essays and Topics of Interest: #4, Race Relations, p. 36.(Back)

Footnote 18-18: The Chief of Staff was quoted in "Integration of the Armed Forces," *Ebony* 13 (July 1958):22.(Back)

Footnote 18-19: Memo, Head of Detail Br, Pers Dept, for Dir of Pers, 10 Jun 52, sub: Policy Regarding Negro Marines, MC files. This method of assigning staff noncommissioned officers still prevailed in 1976.(Back)

Footnote 18-20: Ibid., 4 Aug 52.(Back)

Footnote 18-21: Ibid., 10 Jun 52.(Back)

Footnote 18-22: Ltr, Maj Gen R. O. Bare to CO, 1st Mar Div, 14 Jul 55; Ltr, Dir of Pers to CG, 1st Mar Div (ca. 10 Dec 56). The quotation is from Ltr, CO, Marine Barracks, NAD, Hawthorne, Nev., to Dir of Pers, 15 Dec 62.(Back)

Footnote 18-23: Ltr, Powell to SecDef, 23 Jan 58. See also unsigned Draft Ltr for the commandant's signature to Powell, 12 Feb 58.(Back)

Footnote 18-24: See Ltrs, A. W. Gentleman, Hq MC Cold Weather Tng Cen, Bridgeport, Calif., to Col Hartley, 12 Nov 57; CO, MB, NAS, Jacksonville, Fla., to Personnel Dept, 14 Dec 62; CO, MB, NAD, Hawthorne, Nev., to same, 15 Dec 62.(Back)

Footnote 18-25: Draft Memo, Head of Assignment and Classification Br for Dir, Pers (ca. 1961), sub: Restricted Assignments; Memo, IG for Dir, Pers, 31 Aug 62; Ltr, Lt Col A. W. Snell to Col R. S. Johnson, CO, MB, Port Lyautey, 28 Jun 62. See also Memo, Maj E. W. Snelling, MB, NAD, Charleston, S.C., for Maj Duncan, 27 Nov 62; and the following ltrs: Col S. L. Stephan, CO, MB, Norfolk Nav Shipyard, to Dir, Pers, 7 Dec 62; K. A. Jorgensen, CO, MB, Nav Base, Charleston, S.C., to Duncan, 7 Dec 62; Col R. J. Picardi, CO, MB, Lake Mead Base, to Duncan, 30 Nov 62.(Back)

Footnote 18-26: Shaw and Donnelly, *Blacks in the Marine Corps*, pp. 64-65.(Back)

Footnote 18-27: Speed Ltr, CMC to Distribution List, 22 Jun 50; Routing Sheet, Pers Dept, 21 Jun 50, sub: Enlistment of Stewards.(Back)

Footnote 18-28: Ltrs, CMC to Distribution List, 16 Apr 55 and 18 Nov 55.(Back)

Footnote 18-29: Memo, Head, Enlisted Monitoring Unit, Detail Br, for Lt Col Gordon T. West, 29 Oct 54, Pers A. See also Shaw and Donnelly, *Blacks in the Marine Corps*, pp. 65-66.(Back)

Footnote 18-30: Memo, J. J. Holicky, Detail Br, for Dir of Pers, USMC, 3 Aug 59, sub: Inspection of Occupational Field 36 (Stewards), Pers 1, MC files.(Back)

Footnote 18-31: Memo, Asst Chief for Plans, BuPers (Rear Adm B. J. Semmes, Jr.), for Chief of NavPers, 22 Jun 61.(Back)

Footnote 18-32: USMC Oral History Interview, CWO James E. Johnson, 27 Mar 73.(Back)

Footnote 18-33: Ltr, CMC to Walter White, 2 Jul 51, AO-1, MC files. See also Memo, Div of Plans and Policies (T. J. Colley) for Asst Dir of Public Info, 4 Jun 51, sub: Article in Pittsburgh *Courier* of 26 May 51.(Back)

Footnote 18-34: Memo, Exec Off, ACofS, G-1, for William L. Taylor, Asst Staff Dir, U.S. Commission on Civil Rights, 27 Feb 63, sub: Personnel Information Requested, AO-1C, MC files.(Back)

Footnote 18-35: Shaw and Donnelly, *Blacks in the Marine Corps*, pp. 62-63. 66.(Back)

Footnote 19-1: New York *Times*, October 31, 1954; ibid., Editorial, November 1, 1954.(Back)

Footnote 19-2: C. Vann Woodward, *Strange Career of Jim Crow*, p. 170. This account of the civil rights movement largely follows Woodward's famous study, but the following works have also been consulted: Benjamin Muse, *Ten Years of Prelude: The Story of Integration Since the Supreme Court's 1954 Decision* (New York: Viking Press, 1964); Constance M. Green, *The Secret City: A History of Race Relations in the Nation's Capital* (Princeton: Princeton University Press, 1967); Anthony Lewis and the New York *Times,Portrait of a Decade* (New York: New York *Times*, 1964); Franklin, *From Slavery to Freedom; Freedom to the Free: A Report to the President by the U.S. Commission on Civil Rights* (Washington: Government Printing Office, 1963); *Report of the National Advisory Commission on Civil Disorders*; Interv, Nichols with Clarence Mitchell, 1953, in Nichols Collection, CMH.(Back)

Footnote 19-3: Interv, Nichols with Mitchell.(Back)

Footnote 19-4: Woodward, *Strange Career of Jim Crow*, p. 170.(Back)

Footnote 19-5: 328 U.S. 373 (1946).(Back)

Footnote 19-6: 347 U.S. 483 (1954); see also 349 U.S. 294 (1955).(Back)

Footnote 19-7: Woodward, *Strange Career of Jim Crow*, p. 147.(Back)

Footnote 19-8: 349 U.S. 294 (1955).(Back)

Footnote 19-9: For an outline of the federal and National Guard intervention in these areas, see Robert W. Coakley, Paul J. Scheips, Vincent H. Demma, and M. Warner Stark, "Use of Troops in Civil Disturbances Since World War II" (1945 to 1965 with two supplements through 1967), Center of Military History Study 75.(Back)

Footnote 19-10: 346 U.S. 100 (1953).(Back)

Footnote 19-11: For an authoritative account of Little Rock, see Robert W. Coakley's "Operation Arkansas," Center of Military History Study 158M, 1967. See also Paul J. Scheips, "Enforcement of the Federal Judicial Process by Federal Marshals," in *Bayonets in the Streets; The Use of Troops in Civil Disturbances*, ed. Robin Higham (Lawrence: University Press of Kansas, 1969), pp. 39-42.(Back)

Footnote 19-12: Ltr, Eisenhower to Powell, 6 Jun 53, G 124-A-1, Eisenhower Library. For a later and more comprehensive expression of these sentiments, see "Extemporaneous Remarks by the President at the National Conference on Civil Rights, 9 June 1959," *Public Papers of the Presidents: Dwight D. Eisenhower, 1959*, pp. 447-50.(Back)

Footnote 19-13: For an account of the first major sit-in demonstrations, which occurred at Greensboro, North Carolina, and their influence on civil rights organizations, including the Student Nonviolent Coordinating Committee, see Miles Wolff, *Lunch at the Five and Ten; The Greensboro Sit-in* (New York: Stein and Day, 1970). See also Clark, "The Civil Rights Movement," pp. 255-60.(Back)

Footnote 19-14: *Report of the National Advisory Commission on Civil Disorders*, p. 109.(Back)

Footnote 19-15: Memo, Lt Col Leon Bell, Asst Exec, Off, Asst SecAF, for Col Barnes, Office, SecAF, 9 Jan 51, SecAF files.(Back)

Footnote 19-16: Ltr, CofSA to Ferguson, 7 May 51; see also Ltr, Under SA Earl D. Johnson to Sen. Robert Taft, 19 Jul 51; both in CS 291.2 (27 Apr 51).(Back)

Footnote 19-17: Memo, Dep Chief, NavPers for ASD (M&P), 19 Feb 53, sub: Alleged Race Segregation at U.S. Naval Base, Key West, Florida, P 8 (4)/NB Key West, GenRecs Nav.(Back)

Footnote 19-18: Ltr, ASD (MP&R) Charles C. Finucane to James Roosevelt, 3 Jun 59, ASD (MP&R) files.(Back)

Footnote 19-19: Evans and Lane, "Integration in the Armed Services," p. 83.(Back)

Footnote 19-20: Wilson, former president of General Motors Corporation, became President Eisenhower's first Secretary of Defense on 28 January 1953.(Back)

Footnote 19-21: Memo, CofS, G-1, for ASA, 6 Jan 54, sub: Mass Jailing and Fining of Negro Soldiers in Columbia, S.C.; Memo, ASA for ASD (M&P), same date and sub; Memo, SecDef for President, 7 Jan 54. All in G-1 291.2 (10 Dec 53).(Back)

Footnote 19-22: SecAF statement, 1 May 56, quoted in Address by James P. Goode, Employment Policy Officer for the Air Force, at a meeting called by the President's Committee on Government Employment Policy, 24 May 56, AF File 202-56, Fair Employment Program.(Back)

Footnote 19-23: Memo, CG, 3380th Tactical Training Wing, Keesler AFB, Miss., for (name withheld), Jul 53, sub: Administrative Reprimand; NAACP News Release, 23 Nov 53; copies of both in SecAF files.(Back)

Footnote 19-24: Memo, Cmdr, 3615th Pilot Tng Wing, Craig AFB, Ala., for Cmdr, Flying Dir, Air Tng Cmd, Waco, Tex., 4 Aug 53, sub: Disciplinary Punishment, copy in SecAF files.(Back)

Footnote 19-25: Ltr, Maxwell M. Rabb, President's Assistant for Minority Affairs, to Dr. W. Montague Cobb, as reproduced in Cobb, "The Strait Gate," *Journal of the National Medical Association* 47 (September 1955):349.(Back)

Footnote 19-26: Memo, ACofS, G-1, for TIG, 30 Nov 53, sub: Complaint of Cpl Israel Joshua, G-1 291.2 (3 Nov 53). For an earlier expression of the same sentiments, see ACofS, G-1, Summary Sheet for CofS, 27 Nov 50, sub: Request for Policy Determination, G-1 291.2 (9 Nov 50). Camp Hanford was originally the Hanford Engineer Works, which played a part in the MANHATTAN project that produced the atom bomb.(Back)

Footnote 19-27: Memo, Maj Gen Joe Kelly, Dir, Legis Liaison, USAF, for Lt Col William G. Draper, AF Aide to President, 1 Sep 54, with attachments, sub: Segregation in Gulfport,

383

Mississippi; Memo, Col Draper for Maxwell Rabb, 6 Oct 54; both in GF 124-A-1, Eisenhower Library.(Back)

Footnote 19-28: Career Management Div, TAGO, "Policy Paper," Jul 54, AGAM 291.2 For other pronouncements of this policy, see ibid.; DF, ACS/G-1 to TAG, 4 Jan 54, sub: Assignment of Personnel; and in G-1 291.2 the following: Memo, Chief, Classification and Standards Br, G-1, for Planning Office, G-1, 28 Feb 50, sub: Assignment of Personnel; DF, G-1 to TAG, 8 Mar 50, same sub.(Back)

Footnote 19-29: Ltr, TAGO to Powell, 9 Aug 56, GF 124-A-1, Eisenhower Library.(Back)

Footnote 19-30: Ltrs, C. B. Nichols to President, 28 Mar 55, and Rabb to Nichols, 20 Apr 55; both in G-124-1, Eisenhower Library.(Back)

Footnote 19-31: Ltr, E. Frederic Morrow to Pfc John Washington, 9 Apr 57, in reply to Ltr, Washington to President, 5 Mar 57; both in G-124-A-1, Eisenhower Library.(Back)

Footnote 19-32: UPI News Release, 20 Aug 53, copy in CMH files.(Back)

Footnote 19-33: Executive Order 9980, announcing regulations governing fair employment practices within the federal government, was signed by President Truman on 26 July 1948, the same day and as a companion to his order on equal treatment and opportunity in the services.(Back)

Footnote 19-34: OIR Notice CP75, Chief, Office of Industrial Relations, to Chiefs, Bureaus, et al., 23 Jan 52, sub: Segregation of Facilities for Civil Service Employees; Navy Department Policy.(Back)

Footnote 19-35: Ltr, Actg SecNav Francis Whitehair to Jerry O. Gilliam, Norfolk Branch, NAACP, 19 Mar 52, P 8(4), SecNav files, GenRecsNav.(Back)

Footnote 19-36: Draft Memo, Evans for Rosenberg, SecDef 291.2. Evans delivered the draft memo to Mrs. Rosenberg and discussed the situation with her at length "in the spring of 1952." See Interv, author with Evans, 28 Mar 72, CMH files. On Mrs Rosenberg's request for a survey of the situation, see Memo, ASD (M&P) for Under SecNav, 23 Dec 52. See also Memo, CO, Norfolk Naval Shipyard, for Chief, NavPers, 23 Apr 52, P 8(4), BuPersRecs.(Back)

Footnote 19-37: Memo, Nelson for Aide to Asst SecNav, 20 May 53, P 8(4), GenRecsNav.(Back)

Footnote 19-38: Kimball succeeded Sullivan as Secretary of the Navy on 31 July 1951.(Back)

Footnote 19-39: Ltrs, White to SecNav, 26 May 53; Mitchell to same, 8 Feb 52; Jerry Gilliam to same, 10 Feb 52; Granger to same, 22 May and 27 Jun 52; SecNav to Granger, 16 Jun 52; same to White, 20 Jun 52; Chief, OIR, to Mitchell, 4 Feb 52; Under SecNav to Mitchell, 5 Mar 52. All in P 8(4), GenRecsNav.(Back)

Footnote 19-40: Memo, Actg SecNav for ASD (M&P), 22 Jan 53; Memo, ASD (M&P) for Under SecNav, 23 Dec 52; both in P 8(4), GenRecsNav.(Back)

Footnote 19-41: Ltr, SecNav to Mitchell (ca., Apr 53), OIR 161, GenRecsNav.(Back)

Footnote 19-42: Ltr, Powell to Eisenhower, 17 Apr 53, copy in SecNav files, GenRecsNav.(Back)

Footnote 19-43: Dwight D. Eisenhower, *Mandate for Change 1953-1956* (New York: New American Library, 1963), p. 293.(Back)

Footnote 19-44: Interv, Nichols with Anderson, 18 Sep 53, and Nichols UPI Release, 21 Sep 53; both in Nichols Collection, CMH.(Back)

Footnote 19-45: Ltrs, SecNav to W. Persons, 28 May 53; SecNav to Granger, 28 May and 29 Jul 53; Granger to Anderson, 24 Apr and 2 Jul 53. See also Memo, Chief, NavPers for SecNav, 11 May 53. All in SecNav files, GenRecsNav.(Back)

Footnote 19-46: White, Address Delivered at 44th NAACP Annual Convention, 28 Jun 53, copy in CMH.(Back)

Footnote 19-47: Memo, Under SecNav for President, 23 Jun 53, sub: Segregation in Naval Activities, attached to Ltr, Under SecNav to Sherman Adams, 24 Jun 53, P 8(4), GenRecsNav.(Back)

Footnote 19-48: ALL NAV, 20 Aug 53; Ltr, Chief, Industrial Relations, to Commandant, 6th Naval District, 21 Aug 53, OIR 200, GenRecsNav. For an example of how the new policy was transmitted to the field, see COMFIVE Instruction 5800, 15 Sep 53, A. (2), GenRecsNav.(Back)

Footnote 19-49: Interv, Nichols with Anderson; Nichols News Release, 23 Sep 53, in Nichols Collection, CMH.(Back)

Footnote 19-50: Evans, Weekly Thursday Report to ASD (M&P), 29 Oct 53, SD 291.2. Begun by Evans as a means of informing Rosenberg of activities in his office, the Weekly Thursday Report was adopted by the assistant secretary for use in all parts of the manpower office.(Back)

Footnote 19-51: Memo, Chief, Industrial Relations, for SecNav, 5 Nov 53, sub: Segregation of Facilities for Civil Service Employees; see also Ltr, SecNav to President, 9 Nov 53; both in P 8(4), GenRecsNav.(Back)

Footnote 19-52: Memo, Chief, Industrial Relations, for SecNav, 5 Nov 53, sub: Segregation of Facilities for Civil Service Employees, P 8(4), GenRecsNav.(Back)

Footnote 19-53: PL 815, 23 Sep 50, 64 U.S. 967; PL 874, 30 Sep 50, 64 U.S. 1100.(Back)

Footnote 19-54: Sec. 7a, PL 874, 64 U.S. 1100.(Back)

Footnote 19-55: DA Office of Legislative Liaison Summary Sheet for ASA, 27 Sep 51, sub: Alleged Segregation Practiced at Fort Bliss, Texas, CS 291.2 Negroes (17 Sep 51); Ltr, CG, The Artillery School, to Parents of School Age Children, 2 Sep 52, sub: School Information, AG 352.9 AKPSIGP. For examples of complaints on segregated schools, see Ltrs, Sen. Hubert H. Humphrey to ASD (M&P), 16 Jun 52, and Dir, Washington Bureau, NAACP, to SecDef, 2 Oct 52; both in OASD (M&P) 291.2.(Back)

Footnote 19-56: Draft Ltr, ASA (M&P) to Mitchell. Although he never dispatched it, Korth used this letter as a basis for a discussion of the matter with Mitchell in an October 1952 meeting.(Back)

Footnote 19-57: Ltr, Humphrey to ASD (M&P), 16 Oct 52, OASD (M&P) 291.2.(Back)

Footnote 19-58: Ltr, ASD (M&P) to U.S. Commissioner of Educ, 10 Jan 53, SecDef 291.2.(Back)

Footnote 19-59: Ltr, U.S. Commissioner of Educ to ASD (M&P), 15 Jan 53; Ltr, ASD (M&P) to Humphrey, 10 Jan 53; both in OASD 291.2.(Back)

Footnote 19-60: G-1 Summary Sheet for CofS, 13 Feb 53, sub: Segregation of School Children on Military Installations, G-1 291.2 (15 Jan 53).(Back)

Footnote 19-61: Memo, Exec Off, SA, for ASD (M&P), 20 Feb 53, sub: Proposed Reply to U.S. Commissioner of Education Regarding Segregation in Dependent Schools, copy in G-1 291.2 (15 Jan 53).(Back)

Footnote 19-62: President's News Conference, 19 Mar 53, *Public Papers of the Presidents: Dwight D. Eisenhower, 1953*, p. 108.(Back)

Footnote 19-63: Memo for Rcd, Human Relations and Research Br, G-1 (ca. Mar 53), copy in CMH. See also Memo, Under SecNav for ASD (M&P), 11 Mar 53, sub: Schools Operated by the Department of the Navy Pursuant to Section 6 and 3 of Public Law 874, 81st Congress, A18, GenRecsNav; "List of States and Whether or Not Segregation is Practiced in Schools for Dependents, as Given by Colonel Brody, OPNS Secn, AGO, In Charge of Dependents Schools, 16 Oct 51," OSA 291.2 Negroes.(Back)

Footnote 19-64: Memo, SA for James Hagerty, White House Press Secretary, 20 Mar 53, sub: Segregation in Army Schools, copy in CMH.(Back)

Footnote 19-65: Ibid.(Back)

Footnote 19-66: Memo, Eisenhower for SecDef, 25 Mar 53, sub: Segregation in Schools on Army Posts; Memo, Bernard Shanley (Special Counsel to President) for SA, 25 Mar 53; both in 124A-4 Eisenhower Library.(Back)

Footnote 19-67: Ltr, Secy of HEW, to SecDef, 13 Apr 53, copy in CMH.(Back)

Footnote 19-68: Ltr, SecDef to President, 29 May 53, copy in CMH. On the Army's investigation of the schools, see also G-1 Summary Sheet for CofS, 6 Apr 53, sub: Segregation in Schools on Army Posts, CS 291.2 Negroes (25 Mar 53), and the following: Ltrs, TAG to CG's, Continental Armies et al., 30 Mar 53, and to CG, Fourth Army, 17 Apr 53, sub: Segregation in Schools on Army Posts, AGAO-R 352.9 (17 Apr 53); Memo, Dir of Pers Policy, OSD, for ACS/G-1 and Chief of NavPers, 6 May 53; Statement for Sherman Adams in reply to Telg, Powell to President, as attachment to Memo, ASD (M&P) for SecNav, 5 Jun 53; last two in OASD (M&P) 291.2.(Back)

Footnote 19-69: DOD OPI Release, 1 Feb 54; UPI News Release, 31 Jan 54; Telg, Powell to President, ca. 1 Jun 53; Ltr, President to Powell, 6 Jun 53; Press Release, Congressman Powell, 10 Jun 53; NAACP Press Release, 16 Nov 53; White, Address Delivered at 44th NAACP Annual Convention, 28 Jun 53. Copies of all in Nichols Collection, CMH. See also New York *Times*, February 1, 1954.(Back)

Footnote 19-70: Eisenhower, *Mandate for Change*, p. 293.(Back)

Footnote 19-71: Memo, SecDef for SA et al., 12 Jan 54, sub: Schools on Military Installations for Dependents of Military and Civilian Personnel, SecDef 291.2.(Back)

Footnote 19-72: Telg, Anti-Defamation League of B'nai B'rith to Wilson, 1 Feb 54, SecDef 291.2.(Back)

Footnote 19-73: Telg, Walter White to SecDef, 1 Feb 54; and as an example of a letter from an individual citizen, see Ltr, Mrs. Louis Shearer to SecDef, 1 Feb 54; both in SecDef 291.2.(Back)

Footnote 19-74: Ltr, Winstead to SecDef, 18 Feb 54, SecDef 291.2.(Back)

Footnote 19-75: SecNav Instruction 5700.1, 18 Feb 54, which was renewed by SecNav Instruction 17755.1A, 31 Jul 58. For other services, see Memo, Chief, Pers Ser Div, USAF, for all Major ZI Commands and Alaskan Air Command, 8 Feb 54, sub: Elimination of Segregation in On-Base Schools, AFPMP-12, AF files; Ltr, TAG to CG's, Continental Armies, MDW, 4 Feb 54, sub: Elimination of Segregation in On-Post Public Schools, AGCP 352.9 (4 Feb 54).(Back)

Footnote 19-76: Ltr, SecNav to Clarence Mitchell, 30 Apr 54; Ltr, Jack Cochrane, BuPers Realty Legal Section, to B. Alden Lillywhite, Dept of HEW, 20 Apr 54; both in P 11-1, GenRecsNav. See also Ltr, ASD (M&P) to Commissioner of Educ, 3 May 55; Ltr, ASD (M&P) to Dr. J. W. Edgar, Texas Education Agency, 3 May 55; both in OASD (M&P) 291.2 (3 May 55).(Back)

Footnote 19-77: Ltr, SecAF to Superintendent of Montgomery Public Schools, 12 Jan 55, SecAF files.(Back)

Footnote 19-78: Memo for Rcd, Chief, Morale and Welfare Br, ASD (M&P), 17 Dec 54, sub: Integration of Certain Schools Located on Military Installations, OASD (M&P) 291.2.(Back)

Footnote 19-79: UPI News Release, Incl to Memo, Dir, DOD Office of Public Information, for ASD (M&P), 10 Nov 55, OASD (M&P) 291.2.(Back)

Footnote 19-80: Ltr, Col Staunton Brown, USA, District Engineer, Little Rock District, to Division Engineer, Southwestern Div, 8 Jun 56, sub: Meeting With Representatives of White Hall School District, Pine Bluff Arsenal; Memo, Asst Adjutant, Second Army, for CG, Second Army, 7 Jun 56, sub: Lease for Meade Heights Elementary School; copies of both in OASD (M&P) 291.2.(Back)

Footnote 19-81: Memo, AF General Counsel for Dir of Mil Pers, 29 Mar 55, sub: Lease on Property Occupied by Briggs Air Force Base Dependent's School; Memo, Asst SecAF for ASD (M&P), 24 May 55, sub: Briggs Air Force Base Dependent School; both in SecAF files.(Back)

Footnote 19-82: Memo, ASA for ASD (M&P), 3 May 55, sub: Elimination of Segregation in On-Post Public Schools, OASD (M&P) 291.2.(Back)

Footnote 19-83: Memo, ASD (M&P) for SA et al., 1 Jun 55, sub: Operation of Dependent Schools on Military Installations on an Integrated Basis; idem for SecDef et al., 25 Aug 55, sub: Status of Racial Integration in Schools on Military Installations for Dependents of Military and Civilian Personnel; both in OASD (M&P) 291.2 (25 Aug 55).(Back)

Footnote 19-84: Memo, ASA for ASD (M&P), 16 Jul 56, sub: Status of Racial Integration in Schools at Fort George G. Meade, Maryland, and Pine Bluff Arsenal, Arkansas, OASD (M&P) 291.2.(Back)

Footnote 19-85: Memo, Cmdr Charles B. Reinhardt, OASD (M&P), for Brig Gen John H. Ives, Mil Policy Div, OASD (M&P), 26 Oct 55, sub: School at Patuxent River Naval Air Stations, OASD (M&P) 291.2.(Back)

Footnote 19-86: See the following Memos: ASD (M&P) for SecNav, 18 Nov 55, sub: Integration in Schools on Military Installations for Department of Military and Civilian Personnel; idem for Asst SecNav (P&RF), 23 Jan 56, sub: Segregation in Schools at the New Orleans Naval Base, Algiers, Louisiana; Asst SecNav (P&RF) for ASD (M&P), 7 Apr 56, same sub; ASD (M&P) for Asst SecNav (FM), 15 Aug 58, sub: U.S. Naval Station, New Orleans, Louisiana: One Year Extension of Outlease With Orleans Parish School Board, New Orleans, Louisiana; Ltrs, CO, New Orleans Naval Station, to Rev. Edward Schlick, 24 Feb 56, and Rear Adm John M. Will, OASD (M&P), to Clarence Mitchell, NAACP, 6 Dec 55 and 18 Apr 56. All in OASD (M&P) 291.2. For public interest in the case, see the files of the Chief of Naval Personnel (P 11-1) for the years 1956-59.(Back)

Footnote 19-87: Ltr, Sen. Herbert Lehman to SecDef, 10 Oct 56; Ltr, SecDef to Lehman, 15 Oct 56, both in SD 291.2.(Back)

Footnote 19-88: Memo, Asst Secy of HEW for Secy of HEW, 4 Oct 58, sub: Payments of Segregated Schools Under P.L. 815 and P.L. 874, Incl to Ltr, Asst Secy of HEW to ASD (M&P), 10 Oct 58, OASD (M&P)291.2 (10 Oct 58).(Back)

Footnote 19-89: Memo, Dir of Pers Policy, OSD, for Stephen Jackson, 29 Aug 58, sub: Air Force Segregated School Situation in Pulaski County, Arkansas (San Francisco*Chronicle* article of Aug 26, 58); Memo for Rec, Stephen Jackson, OASD (M&P), 8 Oct 58, sub: Integration of Little Rock Air Force Base School, Jacksonville, Ark., attached to Memo, ASD (M&P) for SA et al., 10 Oct 58. All in OASD (M&P) 291.2.(Back)

Footnote 19-90: See, for example, Ltrs, Dir of Pers Policy, OSD, to Sen. Richard L. Neuberger, 10 Sep 58, and ASD/M to Congressman Charles C. Diggs, Jr., 23 Oct 58. See also Memo, Dep Dir of Mil Pers, USAF, for Asst SecAF (Manpower, Pers, and Res Forces), 9 Oct 58, sub: Dependent Schools. All in OASD (M&P) 291.2.(Back)

Footnote 19-91: Memo, Lt Col Winston P. Anderson, Exec Off, Asst SecAF (M&P), for Asst SecAF (M&P), 24 Nov 58, SecAF files.(Back)

Footnote 19-92: Memo, ASD (MP&R) for SA et al., 10 Oct 58, OASD (MP&R) 291.2; Memo for Rcd, Spec Asst to Asst SecAF, 17 Oct 58, sub: Meeting With Mr. Finucane and Mr. Jackson re Little Rock Air Force Base, SecAF files.(Back)

Footnote 19-93: Memo for Rcd, Dep ASD (MR&P), 8 Oct 58, sub: Integration of Little Rock Air Force Base School, Jacksonville, Ark.; attached to Memo, ASD (MP&R) for SA et al., 10 Oct 58, OASD (MP&R) 291.2.(Back)

Footnote 19-94: Memo for Rcd, Dep Asst SecAF, 24 Nov 58, SecAF files.(Back)

Footnote 19-95: Ibid.; Memo, Lt Col Winston P. Anderson, Exec Off, Asst SecAF (M&P) for Asst SecAF (M&P), 24 Nov 58, SecAF files.(Back)

Footnote 19-96: Memo, Asst SecAF (M&P) for Under SecAF, 26 Nov 58, SecAF files.(Back)

Footnote 19-97: Memo, Dep Asst SecAF (MP&R) for Asst SecAF (MP&R), 26 Nov 58, sub: Little Rock Air Force Base Elementary School, SecAF files.(Back)

Footnote 19-98: Memo, ASD (M) for Chmn, Subcommittee on Education, Cmte on Labor and Pub Welfare, of the U.S. Senate, 25 Apr 61, OASD (M) 291.2.(Back)

Footnote 19-99: Ltr, Rear Adm C. K. Duncan, Asst Chief for Plans, BuPers, to Mrs. Rosetta McCullough, 16 May 63, P 8, GenRecsNav.(Back)

Footnote 19-100: Morton Puner, "What the Armed Forces Taught Us About Integration," *Coronet* (June 1960), reprinted in the *Congressional Record*, vol. 106, pp. 11564-65.(Back)

Footnote 19-101: Press Conference, 21 Jan 59, *Public Papers of the Presidents: Dwight D. Eisenhower, 1959*, p. 122; see also Washington *Post* January 28, 1959.(Back)

Footnote 19-102: See Fred Richard Bahr, "The Expanding Role of the Department of Defense as an Instrument of Social Change" (Ph.D. dissertation, George Washington University, February 1970), ch. III.(Back)

Footnote 19-103: As quoted, ibid., p. 87.(Back)

Footnote 19-104: Morton Puner, "Integration in the Army," *The New Leader* 42 (January 12, 1959).(Back)

Footnote 19-105: Extracted from an interview given by Hannah and published in *U.S. News and World Report* 35 (October 16, 1953):99. See also Ltr, Lt Col L. Hill, Chief, Public Info Div, CINFO, to Joan Rosen, WCBS Eye on New York, 17 Apr 64, CMH Misc 291.2 Negroes.(Back)

Footnote 19-106: *Semiannual Report of the Secretary of Defense, January 1-June 30, 1954* (Washington: Government Printing Office, 1955), pp. 21-22.(Back)

Footnote 19-107: Office of the Assistant Secretary of Defense, Manpower, "Advances in the Utilization of Negro Manpower: Extracts From Official Reports of the Secretary of Defense, 1947-1961." The quotation is from Secretary Wilson's report, 10 Dec 53.(Back)

Footnote 19-108: Bahr, "The Expanding Role of the Department of Defense," pp. 86-87.(Back)

Footnote 19-109: Ginzberg, *The Negro Potential*, p. 90.(Back)

Footnote 20-1: For discussion of charges of discrimination within the services, see Ltrs, ASD (M) to Congressman Charles C. Diggs, Jr., 15 Mar and 5 Sep 61; and the following Memos: Under SecNav for ASD (M), 16 Mar 62, sub: Discrimination in U.S. Military Services; Dep SecAF for Manpower, Personnel, and Organization for ASD (M), 29 Mar 62, sub: Alleged Racial Discrimination With the Air Force; Dep Under SA (M) For ASD (M), 30 Mar 62, sub: Servicemen's Complaints of Discrimination in the U.S. Military. All in ASD (M) 291.2.(Back)

Footnote 20-2: Robert S. McNamara, *The Essence of Security* (New York: Harper & Row, 1972), p. 124.(Back)

Footnote 20-3: James C. Evans, OASD (M), "Suggested List of Military Installations," 9 Jun 61, copy in CMH. Evans's list was based on incomplete data. A great number of military installations were located in Jim Crow areas in 1961. See also Memo, Dep ASD (Military Personnel Policy) for ASD (M), 19 Oct 62, sub: Forthcoming Conference With Representatives From CORE, ASD (M) 291.2.(Back)

Footnote 20-4: Memo, Lee Nichols (UPI reporter) for SecDef, Attn: Adam Yarmolinsky, 13 May 63, sub: Racial Integration in the U.S. Armed Forces, copy in CMH. Nichols had recently toured military bases under Defense Department sponsorship. See also Puner, "Integration in the Army"; news articles in *Overseas Weekly* (Frankfurt), November 18 and 25, 1962, and *Stars and Stripes*, November 15, 1962.(Back)

Footnote 20-5: U.S. Commission on Civil Rights, *Civil Rights '63* (Washington: Government Printing Office, 1963), p. 206.(Back)

Footnote 20-6: Memo, ASD (M) for Asst Legal Counsel to President, 7 Nov 61, sub: Racial Discrimination in the Armed Services, ASD (M) 291.2.(Back)

Footnote 20-7: See transcribed taped interviews conducted by Nichols of the UPI with military and civilian personnel in the Charleston, S.C., area in March 1963, copies in the James C. Evans Collection, AMHRC.(Back)

Footnote 20-8: Ltr, Diggs to President, 27 Jun 62, copy in Gesell Collection, John F. Kennedy Library.(Back)

Footnote 20-9: American Veterans Committee, "Audit of Negro Veterans and Servicemen," 1960, p. 16, copy in CMH.(Back)

Footnote 20-10: Leadership Conference on Civil Rights, "Proposals for Executive Action to End Federally Supported Segregation and Other Forms of Racial Discrimination," August 1961, copy in SD 291.2. See also U.S. Commission on Civil Rights, *Freedom to the Free: A Century of Emancipation* (Washington: Government Printing Office, 1963), pp. 158ff.(Back)

Footnote 20-11: Baltimore *Sun*, August 8, 1962. On the particular problem in the Aberdeen area see Telg, President Kennedy to John Field, President's Cmte on Equal Employment Opportunity, 22 Sep 61, copy in CMH.(Back)

Footnote 20-12: Memo, SecDef for ASD (MP&R) Designate, 27 Jan 61, ASD (M) 291.2.(Back)

Footnote 20-13: This discussion of Kennedy's civil rights position is based on Arthur M. Schlesinger, *A Thousand Days* (Boston: Houghton Mifflin, 1965); Theodore C. Sorensen,*Kennedy* (New York: Harper and Row, 1965); and the following oral history interviews in the J. F. Kennedy Library: Berl Bernhard with Harris Wofford, 29 Nov 65, Roy Wilkins, 13 Aug 64, and Thurgood Marshall, 7 Apr 64; Joseph O'Connor with Theodore Hesburgh, 27 Mar 66. Also consulted were Sorensen's *The Kennedy Legacy* (New York: New American Library, 1970); Victor S. Navasky, *Kennedy Justice* (New York: Atheneum, 1971); William G. Carlton, "Kennedy in History," in *Perspectives on 20th Century America: Readings and Commentary*, ed. Otis L. Graham, Jr. (New York: Dodd, Mead, 1973); Edwin Guthman, *We Band of Brothers: A Memoir of Robert F. Kennedy* (New York: Harper and Row, 1971); Burke Marshall, *Federation and Civil Rights* (New York: Columbia University Press, 1974).(Back)

Footnote 20-14: Quoted from O'Connor's oral history interview with Hesburgh, 27 Mar 66.(Back)

Footnote 20-15: For a critical interpretation of the Kennedy approach to enforcing the Court's decisions, see Navasky's *Kennedy Justice*, pp. 97-98, and Howard Zinn, *Postwar America, 1945-1971* (Indianapolis: Bobbs-Merrill, 1973), ch. iv.(Back)

Footnote 20-16: Press Conference, 1 Mar 61, *Public Papers of the Presidents: John F. Kennedy, 1961*, p. 137.(Back)

Footnote 20-17: 26 *Federal Register* 1977.(Back)

Footnote 20-18: Presidential statement, 7 Mar 61, *Public Papers of the Presidents: Kennedy, 1961*, p. 150. See also "President's Remarks on Meeting of Committee on Equal Employment Opportunity," New York *Times*, April 12, 1961; Memo, President for Heads of All Executive Departments and Agencies, 18 Apr 61, copy in CMH.(Back)

Footnote 20-19: Executive Order 11063, 20 Nov 62, 27 *Federal Register* 11527.(Back)

Footnote 20-20: Memo, Frederick G. Dutton, Spec Asst to President, for Secy of State et al., 31 Mar 61, and Memo, ASD (M) for Dutton (ca. 10 Apr 61), both in ASD (M) 291.2; Memo, Nicholas D. Katzenbach for Vice President Elect, 23 Nov 64, Burke Marshall Papers, and Interv, Bernhard with Wofford, both in J. F. Kennedy Library. According to Wofford there was some discussion over just who would represent the Department of Defense in the group. The department's initial choice seems to have been Evans, but Wofford rejected this selection on the grounds that Evans's position did not place him in the department's power structure. He preferred to have Yarmolinsky or Assistant Secretary Carlisle P. Runge. Yarmolinsky insisted that Runge be included so that it would not appear that racial reform in the Department of Defense was a duty only for the administration's men.(Back)

Footnote 20-21: See Memo, ASD (M) for Under SA et al., 7 Nov 61, sub: Minority Representation in Officer Procurement and Training, ASD (M) 291.2. See also Memos, Wofford for Civil Rights Subcabinet Group, 15 Sep, 20 Oct, and 10 Nov 61, copies in CMH.(Back)

Footnote 20-22: Memo for Rcd, James C. Evans, 21 Jul 61, sub: Meeting, Subcabinet Group on Civil Rights, Friday, July 21, 1961 (Judge Jackson represented Mr. Runge); Ltr, SecDef to Atty Gen, 23 Jun 61; both in ASD (M) 291.2.(Back)

Footnote 20-23: Civil Rights Subcabinet Group, Notes on Meeting of 16 Jun 61; Ltr, Spec Asst to Postmaster Gen to James C. Evans, 26 Jan 62; Memo, Evans for Spec Asst to ASD (M), James W. Platt, 20 Mar 62; Memo, Harris Wofford for Subcabinet Group, 30 Jan 62. Copies of all in CMH.(Back)

Footnote 20-24: Memo for Rcd, James C. Evans, 21 Jul 61, sub: Meeting, Subcabinet Group on Civil Rights, Friday, July 21, 1961 (Judge Jackson represented Mr. Runge), ASD (M&P) 291.2.(Back)

Footnote 20-25: See, for example, Ltr, Chmn, Commission on Civil Rights, to SecDef, 26 Mar 62; Memo, ASD (M) for Under SA et al., 7 May 62, sub: Survey, United States Commission on Civil Rights; Memo, Under SecNav for ASD (M), 25 May 62, sub: United States Commission on Civil Rights Survey of the Department of Defense; Ltr, Yarmolinsky to Berl I. Bernhard, Staff Dir, U.S. Comm on Civil Rights, 14 Nov 62; Memo, ASD (M) for Under SA et al., 31 May 61; Ltr, Bernhard to Runge, 6 Jul 61; Ltr Runge to Bernhard, 17 Jul 61. Copies of all in CMH.(Back)

Footnote 20-26: U.S. Commission on Civil Rights, "The Services and Their Relations With the Community," 17 Jun 63.(Back)

Footnote 20-27: For examples of DOD reports submitted to the White House on this subject, see Memo, ASD (M) for Harris Wofford, 15 Nov 61, and idem for Frank D. Reeves, Spec Asst to President, 29 Jun 61. For examples of White House interest in these reports, see James C. Evans, OASD (M), Notes on Civil Rights Subcabinet Group Meeting, 2 Feb and 2 Mar 62. All in ASD (M) 291.2.(Back)

Footnote 20-28: Memo, Yarmolinsky for Runge, 13 May 61; Memo, ASD (M) for SA et al., 16 Mar 61, sub: Personnel Screening Boards; both in ASD (M) 291.2.(Back)

Footnote 20-29: Memo, Frank D. Reeves, Spec Asst to President, for SecDef, Attn: Adam Yarmolinsky, 19 Apr 61, copy in CMH.(Back)

Footnote 20-30: Ltr, Harris Wofford to ASD (M), 18 Sep 61; Memo for Rcd, James C. Evans, 25 Sep 61, sub: Negro Naval Personnel; Informal Memo, Evans for Runge, 22 Sep 61, same sub. All in ASD (M) 291.2.(Back)

Footnote 20-31: Composed of representatives of some fifty civil rights groups under the chairmanship of Roy Wilkins of the NAACP, the Leadership Conference on Civil Rights presented to President Kennedy a list of proposals for executive action to end federally supported segregation. See U.S. Commission on Civil Rights, *Freedom to the Free*, p. 129.(Back)

Footnote 20-32: Memo, Dutton for Yarmolinsky, 26 Oct 61, copy in ASD (M) 291.2 (22 May 61).(Back)

Footnote 20-33: Memo, SecDef for ASD (M), 13 Mar 61, ASD (M) 291.2.(Back)

Footnote 20-34: Memo, ASD (M) for SecDef, 14 Mac 61, sub: Ceremonial Units and Honor Guard Details, ASD (M) 291.2.(Back)

Footnote 20-35: Informal Memo, Evans for Judge Jackson, 14 Mar 61, sub: Ceremonial Units and Honor Guard Details. Remark repeated by ASD (M) in his Memo for SecDef, 14 Mar 61, same sub. Both in ASD (M) files.(Back)

Footnote 20-36: The Coast Guard incident in particular seems to have impressed Washington. It was cited by Mitchell, Wilkins, and Hesburgh during their oral history interviews at the J. F. Kennedy Library, and it continued to be discussed for some time after the inauguration in official channels. See, for example, Memos, Frederick Dutton for Secy of Treas, 21 Mar 61, sub: Coast Guard Academy, and Theodore Eliot (Spec Asst to Secy of Treas) for Richard N. Goodwin (Asst Spec Counsel to President), 25 Jun 61, sub: Negro in the Coast Guard, with attached note, Dick [Goodwin] to President; Ltr, Asst Secy of Treas to Tim Reardon, 31 Jan 62. All in White House Gen files, J. F. Kennedy Library. The Coast Guard, it should be recalled, was not part of the Department of Defense in 1961.(Back)

Footnote 20-37: Interv, Dennis O'Brien with Roswell L. Gilpatric, 5 May 70, in J. F. Kennedy Library; see also Interv, Bernhard with Wofford.(Back)

Footnote 20-38: Memo, Spec Asst to SecDef for Paul Southwick, White House, 22 Oct 63; James C. Evans, "Equality of Opportunity in the Armed Forces, A Summary Report on Actions and Contributions of the ASD (M), January 1961-July 1962"; copies of both in CMH.(Back)

Footnote 20-39: Although it did not directly affect black servicemen, the contract compliance program deserves mention as a field in which the Department of Defense pioneered for the federal government. During the Kennedy administration the department hired hundreds of contract compliance officers to scrutinize its vast purchasing program, insuring compliance with Executive Order 10925. See Ltr, Adam Yarmolinsky to author, 22 Nov 74, CMH files.(Back)

Footnote 20-40: The Office of the Secretary of Defense also issued several other statements implementing sections of Executive Order 10925; see DOD Dir 1125.4, 2 Jan 62, and OSD Admin Instr No. 31, 13 July 62, both in SD files.(Back)

Footnote 20-41: Memo, SecDef for Secys of Military Departments et al., 28 Apr 61, sub: Military and Civilian Employee Recreational Organizations, copy in ASD (M) 291.2.(Back)

Footnote 20-42: Ltr, Runge to Hill, 14 Jun 61; Memo, Runge for Under SecAF, 28 Jan 61, sub: Military and Civilian Employee Recreational Organizations both in ASD (M) 291.2.(Back)

Footnote 20-43: Ltr, Bernhard to Runge, 6 Jul 61, ASD (M) 291.2.(Back)

Footnote 20-44: Ltr, Runge to Bernhard, 17 Jul 61, with attached Handwritten Note, signed SSJ [Stephen Jackson], 13 Jul 61, ASD (M) 291.2.(Back)

Footnote 20-45: Ltr, Hill to Runge, 26 Jul 61; Memo, ASD (M) for SecAF, 25 Sep 61, sub: Purchase and Sale of Baseball Tickets at Brookley AFB; both in ASD (M) 353.8.(Back)

Footnote 20-46: Memo, R.C. Gilliat for Bartimo, 31 Jul 61, attached to Draft Ltr, Runge to Hill, ASD (M) 353.8.(Back)

Footnote 20-47: Memo, RTA [Robert T. Andrews] for FAB [Frank A. Bartimo], 1 Aug 61, ASD (M) 353.8.(Back)

Footnote 20-48: Memo, Yarmolinsky for Dutton, 4 Aug 61, sub: President's Memorandum of 18 April 1961, ASD (M) 291.2 (22 May 61).(Back)

Footnote 20-49: Note, signed, "MB," 16 Aug 61, sub: Call From Virginia McGuire, attached to Draft Ltr, ASD (M) to Sen. Hill; Memo, ASD (M) for SecAF, 25 Sep 61, sub: Purchase and Sale of Baseball Tickets at Brookley AFB; both in ASD (M) 291.2 (22 May 61).(Back)

Footnote 20-50: Memo, ASD (M) for SecDef, 22 May 61, sub: Availability of Facilities to Military Personnel, ASD (M) 291.2.(Back)

Footnote 20-51: Memo, Dep SecDef for Service Secys, 19 Jun 61, sub: Availability of Facilities to Military Personnel, SD 291.2. For various comments on the draft memo, see the following Memos: Vance and Runge for SecDef, 5 Jun 61; ASD (M) for Dep SecDef, 16 Jun 61, sub: Availability of Facilities to Military Personnel; Dep SecDef for Service Secys, 5 Jun 61, same sub; SecAF for Dep SecDef, 13 Jun 61, same sub. All in ASD (M) 291.2 (22 May 61).(Back)

Footnote 20-52: Interv, author with James C. Evans, 15 Nov 72, CMH files.(Back)

Footnote 20-53: Memo, Maj Gen Albert M. Kuhfeld, USAFJAG (for CofSAF), for ALMAJCOM (SJA), 2 Feb 62, sub: Air Force Policy Statement Concerning Violations of Anti-Discrimination Law, and attached Memo, Dep CofS, Pers, for ALMAJCOM, 30 Jan 62, same sub, SecAF files.(Back)

Footnote 20-54: Memo for Rcd, ASD (P), 23 Mar 60; Memo, Dep Chief, NavPers, for Asst SecNav (Pers and Reserve Forces), 23 Mar 60, sub: Considerations Relative to Department of Defense Policy Concerning Disputes Over Local Laws or Customs; copies of both in ASD (M) 291.2. For the Air Force instructions, see Memo, AF Dep CofS (P) for All Major Cmdrs, 30 Mar 60, sub: Air Force Policy Statement Concerning Involvement of Air Force Personnel in Local Civil Disturbances, SecAF files.(Back)

Footnote 20-55: Memo, ASD (M) for SecDef, 18 Jul 61, sub: Use of Military Police to Halt Sit-ins as Reported by Drew Pearson's Column of July 19 in the Washington Post; Ltr, U.S. Commission on Civil Rights Staff Dir Designate to ASD (M), 26 Jul 61; both in ASD (M) 291.2. The President's office received considerable mail on the subject; see White House Cen files, J. F. Kennedy Library.(Back)

Footnote 20-56: Memo, ASD (M) for SecDef, 18 Jul 61, sub: Use of Military Police..., ASD (M) 291.2.(Back)

Footnote 20-57: Memo, Dep Under SA for Counselor, OASD (M), 12 Jan 62, sub: Off-Base Racial Discrimination in the Fort Hood Area, ASD (M) 291.2.(Back)

Footnote 20-58: Memo, Vance and Runge for SecDef, 5 Jun 61, ASD (M) 291.2.(Back)

Footnote 20-59: Ltr, ASD (M) to John de J. Pemberton, Jr., Exec Dir, American Civil Liberties Union, 31 Jul 63; Memos for Rcd, OSD Counselor, 26 Apr 61 and 9 Jul 63. All in ASD (M) 291.2 (16 Jul 63).(Back)

Footnote 20-60: Memo, General Counsel for ASD (M), 15 Jun 62, sub: Picketing by Members of the Armed Forces, copy in CMH.(Back)

Footnote 20-61: See Memo, James P. Goode, Office of SecAF, for Stephen Jackson and Carlisle Runge, attached to Memo, AF Dep CofS (P) for All Major Cmdrs, 30 Mar 60, sub: Air Force Policy Statement Concerning Involvement of Air Force Personnel in Local Civil Disturbances, SecAF files; Ltr, Under SecNav to Jesse H. Turner, 6 Oct 61, copy in CMH. See also Ltr, Adam Yarmolinsky to Adam C. Powell, 30 Oct 63, SD 291.2 (14 Jul 63).(Back)

Footnote 20-62: Memo, SecDef for Secys of Mil Depts et al., 16 Jul 63, SD files; see also New York *Times*, July 16, 17, 20, 22, 28, and 30, 1963.(Back)

Footnote 20-63: Msg, USCINCEUR to JCS, 201256Z Aug 63; Msg, JCS 2190 to CINSCO et al. (info copies to Service Chiefs of Staff, CINCAL, ASD [M], and ASD [PA]), 221630Z Aug 63.(Back)

Footnote 20-64: Omaha *World Herald*, August 17, 1962; see also Memo, Adam [Yarmolinsky] for L. White, 7 Sep 62, Lee White Collection, J. F. Kennedy Library.(Back)

Footnote 20-65: Memo, ASD (M) for Asst Legal Counsel to President, 7 Nov 61, sub: Racial Discrimination in the Armed Services, ASD (M) 291.2.(Back)

Footnote 20-66: Memo, Jackson for Dep ASD, Family Housing-OASD (I&L), 8 Feb 63, sub: Implementation of EX 11063, Equal Opportunity in Housing, copy in CMH.(Back)

Footnote 20-67: Memo, SecDef for SA et al., 8 Mar 63, sub: Non-Discrimination in Family Housing; Memo, ASD (I&L) for Dep ASD (Family Housing), 8 Mar 63; copies of both in ASD (M) 291.2. The quote is from the latter document.(Back)

Footnote 20-68: See petitions signed by thousands of Negroes to the President demanding redress of grievances against the discriminatory practices of the National Guard, in White House Cen files, 1962, J. F. Kennedy Library.(Back)

Footnote 20-69: Memo for Rcd, James C. Evans, OASD (M), 17 Jul 61, sub: Mr. Runge Receives NAACP Delegation, ASD (M) 291.2.(Back)

Footnote 20-70: Washington *Post*, July 28, 1961.(Back)

Footnote 20-71: Ltr, Murray Gross, Chmn of the AVC, to SecDef, 22 Jun 61, SD 291.2. The report on the integration of the National Guard was inclosed.(Back)

Footnote 20-72: Ltrs, Runge to Murray Gross, 19 Jul and 29 Nov 61, ASD (M) 291.2, and n.d. (ca. Nov 61), copy in Wofford Collection, J. F. Kennedy Library.(Back)

Footnote 20-73: Ltr, SecDef to Rep. Carl Vinson of Georgia, Chmn, House Armed Services Cmte, 5 Aug 61, reprinted in Appendix to *Congressional Record*, 87th Cong., 1st sess., vol. 107, p. A6589.(Back)

Footnote 20-74: ACofS (Reserve Components) Summary Sheet, 11 Feb 57, sub: Race Issue in Armory Debate, copy in DCSPER 291.2.(Back)

Footnote 20-75: DCSPER Summary Sheet, 6 Apr 56, sub: Policy for Reserve Training Assignments of Obligated Non-Caucasian Personnel of the Ready Reserve Who Reside in Segregated Areas, DCSPER 291.2.(Back)

Footnote 20-76: Memo, Dep SecDef for Under Secys, 3 Apr 62, sub: Compliance With E.O. 9981 in the Army, Navy, Air Force, and Marine Corps Reserves, in SD files. The secretary's memo was distributed to the commands; see, for example, Memo, TAG for CINCARPAC et al., 15 May 62 (TAG 291.2/15 May 62).(Back)

Footnote 20-77: Office of the ASD (M), Review of Compliance With E.O. 9981 in the Army, Navy, Air Force, and Marine Corps Reserves, 7 Nov 62, copy in CMH.(Back)

Footnote 20-78: Ltr, Diggs to SecAF, 7 Jul 60; see also Memo, Dir, AF Legis Liaison, for Spec Asst for Manpower, Personnel, and Reserve Forces, USAF, 14 Jul 60, with attached Summary of Findings and Highlights of the Diggs Report Concerning Alleged Discriminatory Practices in the Armed Forces; both in SecAF files.(Back)

Footnote 20-79: U.S. Commission on *Civil Rights*, Civil Rights '63, pp. 173-85. The quotation is from page 185.(Back)

Footnote 20-80: See, for example, Morton Puner, "The Armed Forces: An Integration Success Story," *Anti-Defamation League Bulletin*, Nov 62, pp. 3, 7; and American Veterans Committee, "Audit of Negro Veterans and Servicemen," 1960.(Back)

Footnote 20-81: Memo, DepASD (Special Studies and Requirements) for ASD (M), 16 Jul 63, with attachment, Utilization of Negroes in the Armed Forces, July 1963, copy in CMH. All the tables accompanying this discussion are from the preceding source, with the exception of Table 16, which is from the U.S. Department of Labor, Office of Policy Planning and Research, *The Negro Family: The Case for National Action*, Mar 64, p. 75, where it is reproduced from DOD sources.(Back)

Footnote 20-82: See, for example, the following Memos: Dep Under SA (Manpower) for ASD (M), 30 Mar 62, sub: Servicemen's Complaints of Discrimination in the U.S. Military; AF Dep for Manpower, Pers, and Organization for ASD (M), 29 Mar 62, sub: Alleged Racial Discrimination Within the Air Force; Under SecNav for ASD (M), 16 Mar 62, sub: Discrimination in the U.S. Military Services. All in ASD (M) 291.2 (12 Feb 62).(Back)

Footnote 20-83: Ginzberg, *The Negro Potential*, p. 90.(Back)

Footnote 20-84: U.S. Commission on Civil Rights, *Civil Rights '63*, pp. 210-11.(Back)

Footnote 20-85: Memo, Wofford for Evans, 2 Feb 62, Wofford Collection, J. F. Kennedy Library.(Back)

Footnote 21-1: Interv, author with McNamara, telecon of 11 May 72, CMH files.(Back)

Footnote 21-2: Ltr, Alfred B. Fitt to author, 22 May 72, CMH files.(Back)

Footnote 21-3: The following summary of opinions is based upon (1) Intervs: author with McNamara, 11 May 72, Gerhard A. Gesell, 13 May 72, Robert E. Jordan III, 7 Jun 72, James C. Evans, 4 and 22 Mar 72; O'Brien with Gilpatric, 5 May 70; USAF with Zuckert, Apr 73; (2) Ltrs: Fitt and Yarmolinsky to author, 22 May 72 and 30 May 72, respectively; Rudolph Winnacker, OSD Historian, to James C. Evans, 17 Jul 70; Evans to DASD (CR), 20 Jul 70; ASD (M) to

Congressman Charles C. Diggs, Jr., 15 Mar 61; idem to John Roemer, Vice Chmn, Baltimore CORE, 3 Aug 62; (3) Memos: USAF Dep for Manpower, Pers, and Organization for SecAF, 9 Nov 62, sub: Meeting of President's Committee on Equal Opportunity in the Armed Forces; ASD (M) for Asst Legal Counsel to President, 7 Nov 61, sub: Racial Discrimination in the Armed Services; Evans to Yarmolinsky, 31 Mar 61. Copies of all in CMH. See also Adam Yarmolinsky, *The Military Establishment: Its Impacts in American Society* (New York: Harper & Row, 1971), p. 351.(Back)

Footnote 21-4: Interv, author with Evans, 4 Mar 72.(Back)

Footnote 21-5: USAF Oral Hist Interv with Zuckert, Apr 73; Interv, O'Brien with Gilpatric, 5 May 70.(Back)

Footnote 21-6: Ltr, Yarmolinsky to author, 30 May 72, CMH files.(Back)

Footnote 21-7: Not everyone supporting the idea of an investigatory committee was necessarily an advocate of Yarmolinsky's theories. Roy K. Davenport, soon to be appointed a deputy under secretary of the Army for personnel management, decided that an assessment of the status of black servicemen was timely after a decade of integration. His professional curiosity, like that of some of the other manpower experts in the services, was piqued more by a concern for the fate of current regulations than an interest in the development of new ones. See Interv, author with Davenport, 31 Oct 71.(Back)

Footnote 21-8: Ltr, Diggs to McNamara, 24 Aug 61; Ltr, ASD (M) to Diggs, 5 Sep 61; Memo, ASD (M) for Asst Legal Counsel to President, 7 Nov 61, sub: Racial Discrimination in the Armed Services. All in ASD (M) 291.2.(Back)

Footnote 21-9: Interv, author with McNamara, 11 May 72.(Back)

Footnote 21-10: Ltr, Kennedy to Gesell, 22 Jun 62, as reproduced in White House Press Release, 24 Jun 62, copy in CMH. For an example of the attention the new committee received in the press, see Washington *Post*, June 24, 1962.(Back)

Footnote 21-11: Memo, Yarmolinsky for Lee C. White, 26 Jul 62, sub: Revocation of Executive Order 9981, SD 291.2.(Back)

Footnote 21-12: Interv, author with McNamara, 11 May 72; see also Ltr, Yarmolinsky to author, 30 May 72. Yarmolinsky called the presidential appointment an example of the Defense Department's borrowing the prestige of the White House.(Back)

Footnote 21-13: Memo, ASD (M) for Asst Legal Counsel to President, 7 Nov 61, sub: Racial Discrimination in the Armed Services, ASD (M) 291.2.(Back)

Footnote 21-14: Interv, author with Gesell, 3 Nov 74, CMH files. The Secretary of Defense met with the committee but once for an informal chat.(Back)

Footnote 21-15: Interv, author with Gesell, 13 May 72.(Back)

Footnote 21-16: Memo, Yarmolinsky for Vice President, 13 Mar 62, SD 291.2.(Back)

Footnote 21-17: Memo, ASD (M) for Lee C. White, Asst Spec Counsel to President, 7 Jun 62, sub: Establishment of Committee on Equality of Opportunity in the Armed Forces, ASD (M) 291.2.(Back)

Footnote 21-18: In discussing the Yale connection in the Gesell Committee, it is interesting to note that at least three other officials intimately connected with the question of equal treatment and opportunity, Alfred B. Fitt, the first Deputy Assistant Secretary of Defense (Civil Rights), Cyrus R. Vance, Secretary of the Army, and Deputy Secretary of Defense Gilpatric, were Yale men. Of course, Secretary McNamara was not a Yale graduate; his undergraduate degree is from the University of California at Berkeley, his graduate degree from Harvard.(Back)

Footnote 21-19: Interv, author with Gesell, 13 May 72.(Back)

Footnote 21-20: Ltr, Young to Gesell, 27 Aug 62, Gesell Collection, J. F. Kennedy Library.(Back)

Footnote 21-21: Ltr, Muse to Gesell, 26 Jan 63, Gesell Collection, J. F. Kennedy Library.(Back)

Footnote 21-22: Quoted by Gesell during interview with author, 13 May 72.(Back)

Footnote 21-23: Memo, White for Dep Atty Gen, 23 Jan 63, copy in Lee C. White Collection, J. F. Kennedy Library. (Deputy Attorney General Katzenbach was a member of the White House's civil rights subcabinet.) According to Yarmolinsky, the White suggestion might have originated with Secretary McNamara.(Back)

Footnote 21-24: Ltr, Gesell to SecAF, 25 Oct 62, SecAF files.(Back)

Footnote 21-25: Interv, author with Gesell, 3 Nov 74.(Back)

Footnote 21-26: Memo, Gesell for Cmte Members, 20 Nov 64, Gesell Collection, J. F. Kennedy Library.(Back)

Footnote 21-27: The committee's considerable probings were reflected in the Defense Department's files. See for example, Memo, SecDef for Secys of Mil Depts et al., 28 Sep 62, sub: President's Committee on Equal Opportunity in the Armed Forces, SD 291.2 (12 Feb 62);

Memo, ASD (M) for SA et al., 18 Dec 62, same sub, ASD (M) 291.2; Ltr, SecNav to Gesell, 1 Apr 63; Memo, Under SecNav for SecNav, 9 Apr 63, sub: Meeting With the President's Cmte on Equal Opportunity in the Armed Forces; Ltrs, Under SecNav to Chmn Gesell, 1 Apr and 3 May 63; last four in SecNav file 5350, GenRecsNav, also Marine Corps Bulletin 5050, 28 Jan 63, Hist Div. HQMC. See also Ltrs, Chmn, President's Cmte, to SecAF, 8 Oct 62, USAF, Report for President's Committee on Equal Opportunity in the Armed Forces, 4 Dec 62, and James P. Goode, AF Dep for Manpower, Personnel, & Organization, to Chmn Gesell, 4 Apr 63, both in 2426-62, SecAF files; "Visit of Mr. Nathaniel Colley and Mr. John Sengstacke to 3d Marine Division," copy in CMH. Additionally, see also Ltr, Berl I. Bernhard, U.S. Commission on Civil Rights, to Gesell, 29 Jun 62, Gesell Collection, J. F. Kennedy Library.(Back)

    Footnote 21-28: The President's Committee on Equal Opportunity in the Armed Forces, "Initial Report: Equality of Treatment and Opportunity for Negro Military Personnel Stationed Within the United States, June 13, 1963" (hereafter cited as "Initial Rpt"), p. 10. The following discussion of the committee cannot carry the eloquence or force of the group's report, which was reproduced in the *Congressional Record*, 88th Cong., 1st sess., vol. 109, pp. 14359-69.(Back)

    Footnote 21-29: Ltr, Gesell to Under SecNav, 6 Feb 63, SecNav file 5420 (1179), GenRecsNav.(Back)

    Footnote 21-30: Intervs, author with Gesell, 13 May 72 and 3 Nov 74.(Back)

    Footnote 21-31: Memo, Dep for Manpower, Personnel, & Organization, USAF, for SecAF, 25 Jan 63, sub: Meeting With President's Committee on Equal Opportunity in the Armed Forces, SecAF files.(Back)

    Footnote 21-32: Ltr, Chief of NavPers to CONUS District Cmdrs et al., 22 Apr 63, attached to Memo, Chief of NavPers for Distribution List, 24 Apr 63, sub: President's Committee on Equal Opportunity in the Armed Forces, GenRecsNav 5420.(Back)

    Footnote 21-33: Ltr, Under SecNav to Gesell, 8 Feb 63, SecNav file 5420 (1179), GenRecsNav. For examples of this exchange between the committee and the Navy, see Ltrs, Gesell to Fay, 6 Feb 63, and Fay to Gesell, 3 May and 5 Jun 63, all in SecNav file 5350, GenRecsNav.(Back)

    Footnote 21-34: Interv, author with Gesell, 3 Nov 74.(Back)

    Footnote 21-35: For an example of how an individual service was handling the USO and other on-base social problems, see Memo, Maj Gen John K. Hester, Asst VCofS, USAF, for SecAF, 26 Feb 63, sub: Antidiscrimination Policies, SecAF files. See also "Initial Rpt," pp. 73-74.(Back)

    Footnote 21-36: "Initial Rpt," p. 10.(Back)

    Footnote 21-37: Interv, author with Gesell, 3 Nov 74.(Back)

    Footnote 21-38: "Initial Rpt," pp. 10-11, 30, 51.(Back)

    Footnote 21-39: Memo for Rcd, USAF Dep for Manpower, Personnel, & Organization, 14 Nov 62, sub: Meeting of the President's Committee on Equal Opportunity in the Armed Forces, SecAF file 2426-62.(Back)

    Footnote 21-40: Memo, Dep for Manpower, Personnel, & Organization, USAF, for SecAF, 25 Jan 63, sub: Meeting With President's Committee on Equal Opportunity in the Armed Forces, SecAF files. See also Memo for Rcd, Marine Corps Aide to SecNav, 30 Jan 63, sub: Meeting With Navy-Marine Corps Representatives on Equal Opportunity, SecNav file 5420 (1179), GenRecsNav.(Back)

    Footnote 21-41: "Initial Rpt," p. 61.(Back)

    Footnote 21-42: Interv, author with Gesell, 13 May 72.(Back)

    Footnote 21-43: Idem with Benjamin Muse, 2 Mar 73, CMH files.(Back)

    Footnote 21-44: Memo, Under SecNav for SecNav, 9 Apr 63, sub: Meeting With the President's Cmte on Equal Opportunity in the Armed Forces, SecNav file 5420, GenRecsNav.(Back)

    Footnote 21-45: Ltr, DASD (Family Housing) to Chmn Gesell, 4 Jun 63, Gesell Collection, J. F. Kennedy Library.(Back)

    Footnote 21-46: Ltr, Under SecNav to Chmn Gesell, 5 Jun 63, copy in Gesell Collection, J. F. Kennedy Library; see also Memo, Under SecNav for SecNav, 13 Sep 63, sub: NAS Pensacola, SecNav file 5420 (1179), GenRecsNav.(Back)

    Footnote 21-47: "Initial Rpt," p. 52.(Back)

    Footnote 21-48: Interv, author with Gesell, 3 Nov 74.(Back)

    Footnote 21-49: "Initial Rpt," pp. 68-71.(Back)

    Footnote 21-50: Interv, author with Gesell, 13 May 72.(Back)

    Footnote 21-51: Memo for Rcd, Dep for Manpower, Personnel, & Organization, USAF, 14 Nov 62, sub: Meeting of President's Committee on Equal Opportunity in the Armed Forces,

SecAF files. Deputy Goode's assumptions about the committee's thinking were later confirmed in its "Initial Rpt," pages 68-71, and in author's interview with Gesell on 13 May 1972.(Back)

Footnote 21-52: "Initial Rpt," p. 70.(Back)

Footnote 21-53: Ltr, Gesell to President Kennedy, 13 Jun 63, copy in CMH.(Back)

Footnote 21-54: Interv, author with Gesell, 13 May 72.(Back)

Footnote 21-55: "Initial Rpt," p. 11.(Back)

Footnote 21-56: Ibid., pp. 92-93.(Back)

Footnote 21-57: Ltr, President to SecDef, 21 Jun 63, copy in CMH. The President also sent the committee's report to the Vice President for comment. Indicative of the Pentagon's continuing influence in the committee's work, the Kennedy letter had been drafted by Gesell and Yarmolinsky; see Memo, Yarmolinsky for White, 8 Jun 63, White Collection, J. F. Kennedy Library.(Back)

Footnote 21-58: Memo, SecDef for SA et al., 27 Jun 63, sub: Report of the President's Committee on Equal Opportunity in the Armed Forces; see also Memo, ASD (M) for SecDef, 27 Jun 63; both in ASD (M) 291.2.(Back)

Footnote 21-59: Memo, Dep Under SA (M) for SecDef (ca. 10 Jul 63), with service comments attached, copy in ASD (M) 291.2.(Back)

Footnote 21-60: Memo, SecNav for ASD (M), 10 Jul 63, sub; Report of the President's Committee on Equal Opportunity in the Armed Forces, SecNav file 5410, GenRecsNav.(Back)

Footnote 21-61: Memo, SecAF for ASD (M), 10 Jul 63, sub: Air Force Response to the Gesell Committee Report, SecAF files.(Back)

Footnote 21-62: Interv, author with Gesell, 13 May 72.(Back)

Footnote 21-63: Ibid., and with McNamara, 11 May 72.(Back)

Footnote 21-64: Memo, McNamara for Burke Marshall (ca. 20 Jul 63), Marshall Papers, J. F. Kennedy Library.(Back)

Footnote 21-65: Idem for President, 24 Jul 63, copy in CMH.(Back)

Footnote 21-66: DOD Dir 5120.36, 26 Jul 63.(Back)

Footnote 21-67: Alfred B. Fitt thus characterized the opposition in his Remarks Before Civilian Aides Conference of the Secretary of Army, 6 Mar 64, DASD (CR) files.(Back)

Footnote 21-68: Ltr to SecDef, 29 Jul 63. This letter and the two following are typical of hundreds received by the secretary and filed in the records of ASD (M).(Back)

Footnote 21-69: Ltr, DASD (CR) to James Wilson, Director, National Security Commission, American Legion, 24 Sep 63, written when the legion had the adoption of a resolution against the directive under consideration. See also Ltrs, DASD (CR) to Sen. Frank Moss, 16 Aug 63, and ASD (M) to Congressman George Huddleston, 13 Aug 63; ASD (M), "Straightening Out the Record," 19 Aug 63; Memo, DASD (CR) for General Counsel, 4 Sep 63, sub: Use of the Off-Limits Power. All in DASD (CR) files.(Back)

Footnote 21-70: Ltr, Fitt to author, 22 May 72.(Back)

Footnote 21-71: *Congressional Record*, 88th Cong., 1st sess., vol. 109, p. 14350.(Back)

Footnote 21-72: Ibid., pp. 13778-87, 14349-56.(Back)

Footnote 21-73: Quotes are from ibid., pp. 13778, 13780, 14345-46, 14349, 14351, 14352.(Back)

Footnote 21-74: Ibid., Senate, 31 Jul 63, pp. 13779, 13783.(Back)

Footnote 21-75: Congressional letters critical of the directive can be found in DASD (CR) and SD files, 1963. See, for example, Ltrs, Fulbright to SecDef, 22 Aug 63, R. C. Byrd to SecDef, 13 Aug 63, Goldwater to SecNav, 17 Jul 63, Rivers to ASD (M), 3 Oct 63, Gillis Long to SecDef, 8 Aug 63, Bob Sikes to SecDef, 15 Jul 63. Intense discussion of the constitutionality of the directive and of Vinson's bill took place among department officials during September and October 1963. See the following Memos: DASD (CR) for ASD (M), 25 Oct 63, sub: Vinson Bill Comment With Inclosures; ASD (M) for Under SA et al., 24 Sep 63, sub: H.R. 8460; Asst Gen Counsel (Manpower) for ASD (M), 4 Sep 63. All in ASD (M) 291.2.(Back)

Footnote 21-76: Letters in support of the DOD Directive can be found in ASD (CR) (68A1006) files, 1963.(Back)

Footnote 21-77: A late victim of the anticivil rights forces in Congress was Adam Yarmolinsky. His appointment as deputy director of the Office of Economic Opportunity was withdrawn as a result of criticism in the House. One cause of this criticism was his connection with the Gesell Committee. See Mary McGrory, "A Southern Hatchet Fell," Washington *Star*, August 10, 1964.(Back)

Footnote 21-78: The quote is from author's interview with Gesell on 13 May 1972. See also Ltr, White to Gesell, 8 Jan 64, and Memo, Gesell for Members of the Committee, 26 Feb 64, both in Gesell Collection, J. F. Kennedy Library.(Back)

Footnote 21-79: Memo, Gesell for Members of the Committee, 26 Feb 64.(Back)

Footnote 21-80: The President's Committee on Equal Opportunity in the Armed Forces, "Final Report: Military Personnel Stationed Overseas and Membership and Participation in the National Guard, November 1964" (hereafter cited as "Final Report"), copy in CMH.(Back)

Footnote 21-81: Ltr, Muse to Gesell, 23 Apr 64, Gesell Collection, J. F. Kennedy Library.(Back)

Footnote 21-82: "Final Report," p. 12.(Back)

Footnote 21-83: Interv, author with Gesell, 3 Nov 74.(Back)

Footnote 21-84: The Kennedy quote is from the author's interview with Gesell on 13 May 1972. The Justice Department quote is from Memo, Gordon A. Martin (Dept of Justice) for Burke Marshall, 26 Jul 63, sub: Proposed Gesell Cmte Rpt on the National Guard, Marshall Papers, J. F. Kennedy Library.(Back)

Footnote 21-85: "Final Report," pp. 19-20.(Back)

Footnote 21-86: The National Guard Bureau is a joint agency of the Departments of the Army and Air Force which acts as adviser to the service staffs on National Guard matters and as the channel of communication between the two departments and the state guards. The chief of the bureau is always a National Guard officer.(Back)

Footnote 21-87: The draft was also sent for comment to the National Guard Bureau; see Ltr, Chief, NGB, to Gesell, 13 Nov 64, Gesell Collection, J. F. Kennedy Library.(Back)

Footnote 21-88: Memo, Gesell for Members of the President's Committee on Equal Opportunity in the Armed Forces, 20 Nov 64. The quotation is from Ltr, Young to Gesell, 23 Sep 64. For the reaction of other members see, for example, Ltrs, Sengstacke to Gesell, 9 Oct 64, Muse to Gesell, 16 Sep 64, Fortas to Gesell, 29 Sep 64. All in Gesell Collection, J. F. Kennedy Library.(Back)

Footnote 21-89: Ltr, Gen Wilson, NGB, to Gesell, 13 Nov 64, Gesell Collection, J. F. Kennedy Library.(Back)

Footnote 21-90: Ltr, President to SecDef, 26 Dec 64, copy in CMH.(Back)

Footnote 21-91: Interv, author with Muse, 2 Mar 73.(Back)

Footnote 22-1: Quoted in Ltr, Fitt to author, 22 May 72; see also Interv, author with Jordan, 7 Jun 72.(Back)

Footnote 22-2: See Ltr, J. Francis Pohlhous, Counsel, Washington Bureau, NAACP, to SecDef, 5 Aug 63, ASD (M) 291.2; Telg, NAACP Commanders to SecDef, DA IN 886952, ASD (M) 334 Equal Opportunity in Armed Forces (21 Jul 63); Ltr, Juanita Mitchell, President, Baltimore Branch, NAACP, to SecDef, 11 May 64, copy in CMH. Sec also New York *Times*, July 23, 1963.(Back)

Footnote 22-3: See Ltrs, DASD (CR) to J. Francis Pohlhous, 15 Aug and 6 Sep 63; Albert Fritz, Utah Branch, NAACP, 29 Aug 63; and Juanita Mitchell, 18 Mar 64. See also Ltr, DASD (Civ Pers, Industrial Relations, and Civil Rights) to Moses Newsom, *Afro-American Newspapers*, 2 Feb 65. Copies of all in CMH.(Back)

Footnote 22-4: Charles Moskos, "Findings on American Military Establishment" (Northeastern University, 1967), quoted in Yarmolinsky, *The Military Establishment*, p. 343.(Back)

Footnote 22-5: For many examples of these racial complaints and their disposition, see DASD (CR) files, 1963-64, especially Access Nos. 68-A-1006 and 68-A-1033.(Back)

Footnote 22-6: The Assistant Secretary of Defense (Manpower) prepared a monthly compilation of all discrimination cases in the Department of Defense involving civilian employees. Originally requested by then Vice President Lyndon Johnson in his capacity as chairman of the President's Committee on Equal Opportunity in Employment in June 1962, the reports were continued after the Gesell Committee disbanded. The report for November 1963, for example, listed 144 cases of "Contractor Complaints" investigated and adjudicated and 159 cases of "In-House Complaints" being processed in the Department of Defense. See Memo, ASD (M) for SA et al., 20 Dec 63, ASD (M) 291.2.(Back)

Footnote 22-7: Norman S. Paul succeeded Carlisle Runge as Assistant Secretary of Defense (Manpower) on 8 August 1962.(Back)

Footnote 22-8: DOD Dir 5120.36, 26 Jul 63. For an extended discussion of the functions of the Assistant Secretary of Defense (Manpower) and his civil rights deputy, see Memo, DASD (CR) for Mr. Paul, 21 Sep 65, sub: Policy Formulation, Planning and Action in the Office of the Deputy Assistant Secretary of Defense (Civil Rights), 26 July 1963-26 September 1965, ASD (M) 291.2. This significant document, a progress report on civil rights in the first two years of McNamara's new program, is an important source for much of the following discussion and will be referred to hereafter as Paul Memo.(Back)

Footnote 22-9: DOD News Release 1057-63, 29 Jul 63.(Back)

Footnote 22-10: Memo, ASD (M) for DASD (Education) et al., 23 Jan 63, sub: Coordination of All Matters Related to Racial Problems, ASD (M) 291.2.(Back)

Footnote 22-11: Evans' predecessors included Emmett J. Scott, Special Assistant to the Secretary of War, 1917-19; William H. Hastie, Civilian Aide to the Secretary of War, 1940-43; Truman K. Gibson, 1944-46; and Marcus H. Ray, 1946-47. Evans left Army employ to join the staff of the Secretary of Defense in 1947. See Memo for Rcd, Counselor to ASD (M), 1 Mar 62, ASD (M) 291.2.(Back)

Footnote 22-12: Before assuming the manpower position, Norman Paul was the chief of legislative liaison for the Department of Defense. For a critique of the work of the ASD (M) incumbents in the racial field, see O'Brien's interview with Gilpatric, 5 May 70, J. F. Kennedy Library.(Back)

Footnote 22-13: For a discussion of the effect of the proliferation of assistants in the manpower office, see USAF oral history interview with Evans, 24 Apr 73.(Back)

Footnote 22-14: The incumbents were Alfred B. Fitt, Stephen N. Shulman, Jack Moskowitz, L. Howard Bennett (acting), Frank W. Render II, Donald L. Miller, Curtis R. Smothers (acting), Stuart Broad (acting), and H. Minton Francis.(Back)

Footnote 22-15: This solution was still being recommended a decade later; see Department of Defense, "Report of the Task Force on the Administration of Military Justice in the Armed Forces," 30 Nov 72, vol. I, pp. 51, 112. See also Interv, author with L. Howard Bennett (former DASD [CR]), 13 Dec 73, CMH files.(Back)

Footnote 22-16: Interv, author with Col George R. H. Johnson, Deputy, Plans and Policy, DASD (Equal Opportunity), 9 Aug 73, CMH files.(Back)

Footnote 22-17: Ltr, DASD (CR) to Gesell, 28 Jul 64, Gesell Collection, J. F. Kennedy Library.(Back)

Footnote 22-18: Interv, author with Jordan, 7 Jun 72.(Back)

Footnote 22-19: Memos: Dep to SecAF for Manpower, Personnel, and Organization for ASD (M), 15 Aug 63, sub: Implementation of DOD Directive 5120.36; SA for ASD (M), 15 Aug 63, sub: Equal Opportunity in the Armed Forces; Under SecNav for ASD (M), 15 Aug 63, sub: Outline Plan for Implementing Department of Defense Directive 5120.36, "Equal Opportunity in the Armed Forces," dated 26 Jul 63. All in ASD (M) 291.2.(Back)

Footnote 22-20: Interv, author with Davenport, 2 Aug 73, CMH files.(Back)

Footnote 22-21: Interv, author with Gesell, 13 May 72.(Back)

Footnote 22-22: Memo, Under SecNav for SecNav, 7 Feb 63, sub: Equal Opportunity in the Navy and Marine Corps, SecNav file 5420, GenRecsNav.(Back)

Footnote 22-23: Memo, David M. Clinard, Spec Asst, for SecNav, 11 Oct 63, sub: Interviews With Negro Personnel at Andrews Air Force Base, copy in CMH.(Back)

Footnote 22-24: SecNav Instruction 5350.2A, 6 Mar 63; Personal Ltr, SecNav to All Flag and General Officers et al., 26 Mar 63, copy in CMH; SecNav Notice 5350, 3 Apr 63; AlNav 28, 6 Sep 63. See also Cmdt, USMC, Report of Progress—Equal Opportunity in the United States Marine Corps (ca. 30 Jun 63), Hist Div HQMC; Memo, Chief, NavPers, for Under SecNav, 20 May 63, sub: Interim Progress Report on Navy Measures..., SecNav file 5420, GenRecsNav.(Back)

Footnote 22-25: Ltr, Chief, NavPers, to CONUS District Cmdrs et al., 22 Apr 63, attached to Memo, Chief, NavPers, for Distribution List, 24 Apr 63, sub: President's Committee on Equal Opportunity in the Armed Forces, SecNav file 5420, GenRecsNav.(Back)

Footnote 22-26: Memo, Actg SecAF CofSAF, 8 Dec 62, sub: Anti-Discrimination Policy in the Military Service, SecAF files.(Back)

Footnote 22-27: Memo, SecDef for SA and Navy, 4 Mar 63, sub: Anti-Discrimination Policy in the Military Service, copy in CMH. McNamara received the Air Force document from Charyk through Yarmolinsky. See Memo, Benjamin Fridge, Spec Asst for Manpower and Reserve Forces, for SecAF, 4 Mar 63, sub: Anti-Discrimination Policies; see also Memo, Asst Vice CofS, USAF, for SecAF, 26 Feb 63, same sub, 687-63; both in SecAF files.(Back)

Footnote 22-28: Memo, SecAF for ASD (M), 10 Jul 63, sub: Air Force Response to the Gesell Committee Report, ASD (M) 291.2.(Back)

Footnote 22-29: Memo, ASD (M) for Under SA et al., 13 Sep 63, sub: DOD Directive 5120.36, 26 Jul 63, Equal Opportunity, ASD (M) 291.2.(Back)

Footnote 22-30: Alfred B. Fitt, Deputy Assistant Secretary of Defense (Civil Rights), "Remarks Before Civilian Aides Conference of the Secretary of the Army," 6 Mar 64, copy in CMH.(Back)

Footnote 22-31: Ltr, DASD (Civil Rights) to Gesell, 30 Apr 64, ASD (M) 291.2.(Back)

Footnote 22-32: AR 600-21, 2 Jul 64 (superseded by AR 600-21, 18 Mar 65); AFR 35-78, 19 Aug 64 (superseded in May 71); SecNav Instructions 5350.6, Jan 65, 5350.5A, 16 Dec 65, and 5370.7, 4 Mar 65. See also NAVSO P2483, May 65, "A Commanding Officer's Guide for Establishing Minority Community Relations."(Back)

Footnote 22-33: Memo, DASD (CR) for Paul, 10 Feb 64, sub: Official Attendance at Segregated Meetings, ASD (M) 291.2.(Back)

Footnote 22-34: Memo, Assoc Spec Counsel to President for Heads of Departments and Agencies, 12 Jun 64, sub: Further Participation at Segregated Meetings, copy in CMH.(Back)

Footnote 22-35: Memo, Dep SecDef for Secys of Military Departments et al., 7 Jul 64, sub: Federal Participation at Segregated Meetings, SD 291.2. The Army's regulation, published on 2 July, five days before Secretary Vance's memorandum, was republished on 18 May 1965 to include the prohibition against segregated meetings and other new policies. The Navy prepared a special Secretary of Navy instruction (5720.38, 30 Jul 1964) on the subject.(Back)

Footnote 22-36: Memo, James P. Goode for Dep SecDef, 29 Sep 64, sub: Federal Participation at Segregated Meetings, copy in CMH.(Back)

Footnote 22-37: Draft Memo, DASD (Civ Pers, Indus Rels, and CR) for Dep for Manpower, Personnel, and Organization, USAF, 7 Oct 64, sub: Federal Participation at Segregated Meetings. The memorandum was not actually dispatched, and a note on the original draft discloses that after discussion between the Deputy Assistant Secretary of Defense and the Assistant Secretary of Defense (Manpower) the rejection of the Air Force request was "handled verbally." Copy of the memo in CMH.(Back)

Footnote 22-38: Fitt, "Remarks Before Civilian Aides Conference of the Secretary of the Army," 6 Mar 64.(Back)

Footnote 22-39: Interv, author with Evans, 23 Jul 73, CMH files.(Back)

Footnote 22-40: Paul Memo.(Back)

Footnote 22-41: For accounts of Navy and Marine Corps attempts to attract more Negroes, see Memos: Smedberg for Under SecNav, 20 May 63, sub: Interim Progress Report on Navy Measures in the Area of Equality of Opportunity in the Armed Forces; Under SecNav for SecNav, 15 Jul 63, sub: First Report of Progress in the Area of Equal Opportunity in the Navy Department; E. Hidalgo, Spec Asst to SecNav, for L. Howard Bennett, Principal Asst for Civil Rights, OASD (CR), 1 Oct 65, sub: Summary of Steps Deemed Necessary to Increase Number of Qualified Negro Officers and Enlisted Personnel on the Navy/Marine Corps Team, SecNav file 5420 (1179). All in GenRecsNav. See also Memos, Marine Aide to SecNav for CofS, USMC, 5 Aug 63, sub: Equal Opportunity in the Armed Services, and ACofS, G-1, USMC, for CofS, USMC, 17 Aug 63, same sub, both in MC files. For OSD awareness of the problem, see Stephen N. Shulman, "The Civil Rights Policies of the Department of Defense," 4 May 65, copy in CMH.(Back)

Footnote 22-42: Memo, SecDef for Educators, 6 Oct 65, sub: Equal Opportunity at the Service Academies of the United States Army, Navy, and Air Force, SD 291.2.(Back)

Footnote 22-43: DOD News Release, 13 Aug 64. See the President's Task Force on Manpower Conservation, *One-Third of a Nation: A Report on Young Men Found Unqualified for Military Service* (Washington: Government Printing Office, 1964). Kennedy established the task force in September 1963. Its members included the Secretaries of Labor, Defense, and Health, Education and Welfare and the Director of Selective Service.(Back)

Footnote 22-44: McNamara, *The Essence of Security*, pp. 131-38. See also Bahr, "The Expanding Role of the Department of Defense," ch. V.(Back)

Footnote 22-45: Ltr, Fitt to author, 21 Oct 76, CMH files.(Back)

Footnote 22-46: Fitt left the civil rights office in August 1964 to become the General Counsel of the Army. At his departure the position of Deputy Assistant Secretary of Defense for Civil Rights was consolidated with that of the Deputy for Civilian Personnel and Industrial Relations. The incumbent of the latter position, Stephen Shulman, became Deputy Assistant Secretary of Defense for Civilian Personnel, Industrial Relations, and Civil Rights. Shulman, a graduate of Yale Law School and former Executive Assistant to the Secretary of Labor, had been closely involved in the Defense Department's equal opportunity program in industrial contracts.(Back)

Footnote 22-47: Paul Memo.(Back)

Footnote 22-48: Ibid.(Back)

Footnote 22-49: Shulman, "The Civil Rights Policies of the Department of Defense," 4 May 65.(Back)

Footnote 22-50: Department of Defense, "Report of the Task Force on the Administration of Military Justice in the Armed Forces," 30 Nov 72, vol. I, p. 47.(Back)

Footnote 22-51: Memo, Asst Spec Counsel to President for SecDef, 27 Jun 63, copy in CMH.(Back)

Footnote 22-52: ACSFOR, "Annual Historical Summary, Fiscal Years 1963-64," copy in CMH; Memo, DASD (CR) for Paul, 25 Sep 63, sub: Training Program Keyed Primarily to the Special Problems of Negro Servicemen, ASD (M) files.(Back)

Footnote **22-53:** Memo, Under SA for ASD (M), 14 Sep 63, sub: Training Program Keyed Primarily to the Special Problems of Negro Servicemen; Memo, ASD (M) for Asst Spec Counsel to President, 25 Sep 63; both in ASD (M) files.(Back)

Footnote **22-54:** For a discussion of this argument, see [BuPers] Memo for Rcd, Capt K. J. B. Sanger, USN, 9 Oct 63, Pers 1, BuPersRecs.(Back)

Footnote **22-55:** Interv, author with Davenport, ASA, Manpower (Ret.), 2 Aug 73, CMH files.(Back)

Footnote **22-56:** See, for example, the following Memos: Evans for Judge Jackson, 1 Apr 63, and Mr. Jordan, 3 Sep 64, sub: Racial Designations; Douglas Dahlin for E. E. Moyers, 3 Sep 58, sub: Case History of an OSD Action; James Evans for Philip M. Timpane, 10 Aug 65, sub: Race and Color-Coding. See also Memo for Rcd, Evans, 15 Aug 62, sub: Racial Designations. All in DASD (CR) files.(Back)

Footnote **22-57:** Bureau of the Budget, Circular No. A-46, Transmittal Memorandum No. 8, 8 Aug 69.(Back)

Footnote **22-58:** See Ltr, Clarence Mitchell, NAACP, to ASD (M), 8 Jul 53; Ltr, Congressman Henry S. Reuss of Wisconsin to SecDef, 27 Sep 56; Memo, Yarmolinsky for Fitt, 29 Nov 61; Memo, Dep Under SA for ASD (M), 1 Dec 61, sub: Racial Designation in Special Orders; Ltr, Chmn, Cmte on Gov Operations, House of Representatives, to SA, 9 Jul 62; Memo, ASD (M) for SA, 29 Mar 51, sub: Racial Designations on Travel Orders; Memo, Chief, Mil Personnel Management Div, G-1, for Dir, Personnel Policies, 5 Aug 52, sub: Racial Designations, G-1 291.2; Memo, SecNav for ASD (M), 7 May 54, sub: Deletion of Question Regarding "Race" ... Copies of all in CMH.(Back)

Footnote **22-59:** See Memo, TAG for Distribution, 21 Sep 62, sub: Racial Identification in Army Documents, AGAM (M) 291.2; Memo for Rcd, Evans, 20 Dec 62, sub: Racial Designations—Navy, ASD (M) 291.2; Memo, DASD (CR) for DASD (H&M) et al., 19 Feb 64, sub: Racial Designations on Department of Defense Forms, copy in CMH.(Back)

Footnote **22-60:** See, for example, Ltr, Dir of Personnel Policy (OSD) to J. Francis Pohlhous, Counsel, NAACP, 6 Jul 55, ASD (M) 291.2.(Back)

Footnote **22-61:** Ltr, Director, Civil Service Commission, to Rear Adm Robert L. Moore, Chief of Industrial Relations, USN, 9 Jul 63, copy in CMH.(Back)

Footnote **22-62:** Memo, Spec Asst to ASD (M) for Under SA, 15 Apr 63, sub: Racial Identification on Military Records (similar memorandums were sent to the Secretaries of Navy and Air Force on the same day); Memo, ASD (M) for OASD (Comptroller) (ca. 1 Jun 63); both in ASD (M) 291.2. For service reviews, answers, and exchanges on the subject, see ASD (M) 68A-1006. See also Memo, SSJ [Stephen S. Jackson, Spec Asst to ASD (M)] for Valdes, OASD (M), and James C. Evans, 11 Jun 63, ASD (M) 291.2.(Back)

Footnote **22-63:** Memo, DASD (CR) for DASD (Management), 3 Mar 64, sub: Elimination of Racial Designations on DD Forms (the Army adopted this DOD policy in the form of Change 1 to AR 66-21 in October 1965). See also Memo, DASD (CR) for DASD (H&M) et al., 19 Feb 64, sub: Racial Designations on Department of Defense Forms; idem for Lee C. White, 9 Jul 64. All in ASD (M) files. See also Washington *Evening Star*, June 22, 1964, p. A2.(Back)

Footnote **22-64:** Memo, Philip M. Timpane for DASD (CR), 10 Aug 64, sub: Race on Records, ASD (M) 291.2.(Back)

Footnote **22-65:** Memo, Dep Under SA for DASD (CR), 3 Jun 64, sub: Proposed DOD Instruction Re: Use of Racial Designations in Forms and Records and Annual Racial Distribution Report, copy in CMH.(Back)

Footnote **22-66:** L. Howard Bennett, Untitled Minutes of Equal Opportunity Council Meetings on the Subject of Racial Indicators, 30 Sep 66; Memo, Bennett for Thomas Morris and Jack Moskowitz, 8 Dec 66, sub: Actions to Aid in Assuring Equality of Opportunity During Ratings, Assignment, Selection, and Promotion Processes, copies of both in CMH. Judge Bennett was the executive secretary of the Equal Opportunity Council within the Office of the Secretary of Defense, an interdepartmental working group dealing with racial indicators in September 1966 and consisting of two members from each manpower office of the services and P. M. Timpane of the DASD (Equal Opportunity) office.(Back)

Footnote **22-67:** Memo, Bennett for ASD (M) and DASD (Civ Pers, Indus Rels, and CR), 8 Dec 66, copy in CMH.(Back)

Footnote **22-68:** Interv, author with Johnson, 9 Aug 73.(Back)

Footnote **22-69:** Memo, Exec to DASD (CR) for DASD (CR), 20 Mar 64; see also OASD (CR), Summary of Military Personnel Assignments in Overseas Areas; both in ODASD (CR) files. Negroes were not the only Americans excluded from certain countries for "politically ethnic considerations." Jewish servicemen were barred from certain Middle East countries.(Back)

Footnote 22-70: DOD directive cited in Gesell Committee's "Final Report," p. 7; see also New York *Times*, September 12, 1963.(Back)

Footnote 22-71: New York *Times* and Washington *Post*, December 29, 1964.(Back)

Footnote 22-72: See, for example, New York *Herald Tribune*, January 3, 1965; New York *Times*, March 29, 1964.(Back)

Footnote 22-73: Memo for Rcd, Timpane, 25 Nov 64, ODASD (CR) files.(Back)

Footnote 22-74: Paul Memo.(Back)

Footnote 22-75: For an example of McNamara's extremely self-critical judgments on the subject of equal opportunity, see Brock Brower, "McNamara Seen Now, Full Length," *Life*64 (May 10, 1968): 78.(Back)

Footnote 22-76: Interv, author with McNamara, 11 May 72.(Back)

Footnote 22-77: Memo, William C. Baldes, ODASD (CR), for DASD (CR), 8 Jul 63, ASD (M) 291.2.(Back)

Footnote 22-78: Memo, DASD (CR) for ASD (M), 2 Jul 64, copy in CMH. Emphasis not in original.(Back)

Footnote 22-79: The administration of military justice was not considered by the Civil Rights Commission nor by the Gesell Committee, although it was mentioned once by the NAACP as a cause of numerous complaints and once by the Deputy Assistant Secretary for Civil Rights in regard to black representation on courts-martial. See NAACP, "Proposals for Executive Action to End Federal Supported Segregation and Other Forms of Racial Discrimination," submitted to the White House on 29 Aug 61, White House Central Files, J. F. Kennedy Library; Memo, Philip M. Timpane, ODASD (Civ Pers, Indus Rels, and CR) for DASD (Civ Pers, Indus Rels and CR), 23 Feb 65, sub: Representation by Race on Courts-Martial. ODASD (Civ Pers, Indus Rels, and CR) files.(Back)

Footnote 23-1: Interv, author with McNamara, 11 May 72.(Back)

Footnote 23-2: See Memo, DASD (CR) for ASD (M), 2 Jul 64; Fitt, "Remarks Before the Civilian Aides Conference of the Secretary of the Army," 6 Mar 64; copies of both in CMH. The quoted passage is from the latter document.(Back)

Footnote 23-3: Robert S. McNamara, Testimony Before Senate Armed Services Committee, 3 Oct 63, quoted in New York *Times*, October 4, 1963.(Back)

Footnote 23-4: Memo, William C. Valdes, OASD (M), for Alfred B. Fitt, 8 Jul 63, sub: Case Studies of Minority Group Problems at Keesler AFB, Brookley AFB, Greenville AFB, and Columbus AFB, copy in CMH.(Back)

Footnote 23-5: See Shulman, "The Civil Rights Policies of the Department of Defense," 4 May 65.(Back)

Footnote 23-6: Memos: DASD (CR) for White, Assoc Spec Council to President, 9 Jul 64; Philip M. Timpane. Staff Asst, ODASD (CP, IR, & CR), for DASD (CP, IR, & CR), 11 Feb 65, sub: Service Reports on Equal Rights Activities; DASD (CP, IR, & CR) for John G. Stewart, 23 Dec 64, sub: Civil Rights Responsibilities of the Department of Defense. Copies of all in CMH. For a discussion of the composition and activities of these command-community relations committees and a critical analysis of the command initiatives in the local community in general, see David Sutton, "The Military Mission Against Off-Base Discrimination," *Public Opinion and the Military Establishment*, ed. Charles C. Moskos, Jr. (Beverly Hills, California: Sage Publications, 1971), pp. 149-83.(Back)

Footnote 23-7: See especially UPI Press Release, October 4, 1963; New York *Times*, October 3, 1963; Memo, Robert E. Jordan III, Staff Asst, ODASD (CR), for ASD (M), 2 Oct 63, sub: Status of Defense Department Implementation of DOD Directive 5120.36 ("Equal Opportunity in the Armed Forces," July 26, 1963), ASD (M) 291.2 (14 Jul 63).(Back)

Footnote 23-8: Memo, ASD (M) for Under SA et al., 24 Sep 63, sub: Off-Base Equal Opportunity Inventory, ASD (M) 291.2 (14 Jul 63); DASD (CR) "Summary of Off-Base Equal Opportunity Inventory Responses" (ca. Jan 64), copy inclosed with Ltr, DASD (CR) to Gesell, 2 Apr 64, Gesell Collection, J. F. Kennedy library. For examples of service responses, see BuPers Instruction 5350.3, 3 Oct 63, and Marine Corps Order 5350.2, 1 Oct 63. For details of a service's experiences with conducting an off-base inventory, see the many documents in CS 291.2 (23 Aug 63).(Back)

Footnote 23-9: See, for example, the following Memos: USAF Dep for Manpower, Personnel, and Organization for ASD (M), 6 Feb 64, sub: Off-Base Equal Opportunity Inventory Report, SecAF files; DASD (CR) for Fridge, USAF Manpower Office, 14 May 64; idem for Davenport et al., 3 Aug 64, sub: Off-Base Equal Opportunity Inventory Follow-Up Reports. All in ASD (M) 291.2.(Back)

Footnote 23-10: OASD (CR), Summary of Follow-Up Off-Base Equal Opportunity Inventory (ca. Jun 64), DASD (CR) files.(Back)

Footnote 23-11: Memo, DASD (CP, IR, & CR) for Stewart, 23 Dec 64, sub: Civil Rights Responsibilities of the Department of Defense, copy in CMH.(Back)

Footnote 23-12: Ltr, Fitt to author, 22 May 72.(Back)

Footnote 23-13: Ltr, DASD (CR) to Congressman Charles Diggs, 3 Feb 64, copy in CMH.(Back)

Footnote 23-14: Memo, DASD (CR) for ASD (M), 24 Apr 64, sub: Base Closings; Memo, ASD (M) for ASD (I&L), 29 Apr 64, sub: Base Closing Decisions; both in ASD (M) 291.2.(Back)

Footnote 23-15: Memo, ASD (I&L) for ASD (M), 23 May 64, sub: Base Closing Decisions, copy in CMH.(Back)

Footnote 23-16: Ltr, Principal Asst for CR, DASD (CP, IR, & CR) to Stanley T. Gutman, 18 Dec 64, ASD (M) 291.2.(Back)

Footnote 23-17: Ltr, DASD (CR) to Gesell, 28 Jul 64, copy in CMH.(Back)

Footnote 23-18: Benjamin Muse, *The American Negro Revolution: From Nonviolence to Black Power, 1963-1967* (Bloomington: University of Indiana Press, 1968). The following survey is based on Muse and on Robert D. Marcus and David Burner, eds., *America Since 1945* (New York: St. Martin's, 1972), especially the chapter by James Sundquist, "Building the Great Society: The Case of Equal Rights, From Politics and Policy," and that by Daniel Walker, "Violence in Chicago, 1968: The Walker Report"; *Report of the National Advisory Commission on Civil Disorders*; Otis L. Graham, Jr., ed., *Perspectives on 20th Century America, Readings and Commentary* (New York: Dodd, Mead, 1973); Zinn,*Postwar America, 1945-1971*; Roger Beaumont, "The Embryonic Revolution: Perspectives on the 1967 Riots," in Robin Higham, ed., *Bayonets in the Street: The Use of Troops in Civil Disturbances* (Lawrence: University Press of Kansas, 1969); Woodward's *Strange Career of Jim Crow*.(Back)

Footnote 23-19: Lyndon B. Johnson, "Address Before a Joint Session of the Congress," 27 Nov 63, *Public Papers of the Presidents: Lyndon B. Johnson, 1963-1964* (Washington: Government Printing Office, 1965), I:9.(Back)

Footnote 23-20: Lyndon B. Johnson, *The Vantage Point* (New York: Holt, Rinehart and Winston, 1971), p. 157.(Back)

Footnote 23-21: Interv, Bernhard with Wofford, 29 Nov 65. Special Assistant to Presidents Kennedy and Johnson, Wofford was later appointed to a senior position in the Peace Corps.(Back)

Footnote 23-22: Johnson, *Vantage Point*, p. 160.(Back)

Footnote 23-23: PL 88-352, 78 *U.S. Stat.* 241.(Back)

Footnote 23-24: Muse, *The American Negro Revolution*, p. 183. For a detailed discussion of the provisions of the Civil Rights Act of 1964, see Muse's book, pp. 181-91.(Back)

Footnote 23-25: Woodward, *Strange Career of Jim Crow*, p. 180.(Back)

Footnote 23-26: Johnson, "Remarks at the National Urban League's Community Action Assembly," 10 Dec 64, as reproduced in *Public Papers of the Presidents: Johnson, 1963-1964*, II:1653.(Back)

Footnote 23-27: Lyndon B. Johnson, "Annual Message to Congress on the State of the Union," 4 Jan 65, *Public Papers of the Presidents: Lyndon B. Johnson, 1965* (Washington: Government Printing Office, 1966), I:6.(Back)

Footnote 23-28: Lyndon B. Johnson, "Speech Before Joint Session of Congress," 15 Mar 65, *Public Papers of the Presidents: Johnson, 1965*, I:284.(Back)

Footnote 23-29: 383 U.S. 663 (1966).(Back)

Footnote 23-30: For an account of the Watts riot and its aftermath, see Robert Conot, *Rivers of Blood, Years of Darkness* (New York: Bantam Books, 1967), and Anthony Platt, ed.,*The Politics of Riot Commissions* (New York: Collin Books, 1971), ch. vi.(Back)

Footnote 23-31: Both the Harris and Wilkins remarks are quoted in Sundquist, "Building the Great Society," pp. 205-06.(Back)

Footnote 23-32: Memo, SecDef for SA et al., 10 Jul 64, copy in CMH; see also SecDef News Conference, 15 Jul 64, p. 13, OASD (PA).(Back)

Footnote 23-33: Memo, ASD (M) for Under SA et al., 6 Jul 64, ASD (M) 291.2; see also SecDef News Conference, 15 Jul 64, p. 13.(Back)

Footnote 23-34: Memo, DASD (CR) for Roy Davenport, et al., 5 May 64, sub: Requests for Suit by Military Personnel Under the Civil Rights Bill; idem for ASD (M), 10 Jul 64, sub: DOD Instruction on Processing of Requests by Military Personnel for the Bringing of Civil Rights Suits by the Attorney General; both in ASD (M) 291.2. For an example of a service response, see Memo, Dep Under SA (Pers Management) for DASD (CR), 9 Jul 64, same sub, ASD (M) 291.2.(Back)

400

Footnote 23-35: DOD Instr 5525.2, 24 Jul 64, Processing of Requests by Military Personnel for Action by the Attorney General Under the Civil Rights Act; see also Memo, ASD (M) for Under SA et al., 24 Jul 64, same sub, ASD (M) 291.2.(Back)

Footnote 23-36: DOD Directive 5500.11, 28 Dec 64.(Back)

Footnote 23-37: Memo, ASD (M) for Dir, BOB, 15 Jul 64, sub: Defense Department Regulations to Implement Title VI of the Civil Rights Act; see also Ltr, Spec Asst to DASD (CR), to Gesell, 24 Jul 64; copies of both in Gesell Collection, J. F. Kennedy Library.(Back)

Footnote 23-38: DASD (CP, IR, & CR), The Civil Rights Policies of the Department of Defense, 4 May 65, copy in CMH.(Back)

Footnote 23-39: Ltr, Jordan to William A. Smith, 21 Aug 64, ASD (M) 291.2.(Back)

Footnote 23-40: Memo, DASD (CR) for ASD (M), 10 Jul 64, sub: DOD Instruction on Processing of Requests by Military Personnel for the Bringing of Civil Rights Suits by the Attorney General, ASD (M) 291.2.(Back)

Footnote 23-41: Memo, Timpane (Staff Asst) for Shulman, DASD (CP, IR, & CR), 11 Feb 65, sub: Service Reports on Equal Rights Activities, ASD (M) 291.2.(Back)

Footnote 23-42: For discussion of command initiatives and black morale, see Memo, DASD (CR) for Under SA et al., 25 May 64, sub: Off-Base Equal Opportunity Inventories; Fitt, "Remarks Before Civilian Aides Conference of the Secretary of the Army," 6 Mar 64; Memo, DASD (CR) for Burke Marshall, Dept of Justice, 20 Mar 64, sub: The Civil Rights of Negro Servicemen. Copies of all in CMH.(Back)

Footnote 23-43: For the discussion of McNamara's initial dealings with the National Guard on the subject of race, see Chapter 20.(Back)

Footnote 23-44: "Opinion of the Legal Adviser of the National Guard Bureau, April 1949," reproduced in Special Board to Study Negro Participation in the Army National Guard (ARNG) and the United States Army Reserve (USAR), "Participation of Negroes in the Reserve Components of the Army," 3 vols. (1967) (hereafter cited as Williams Board Rpt), II: 20-21.(Back)

Footnote 23-45: Memo, Asst Gen Counsel (Manpower) for ASD (M), 17 Jul 61, sub: Integration of National Guard, ASD (M) 291.2.(Back)

Footnote 23-46: For a discussion of earlier efforts to integrate the New Jersey National Guard and the attitude of individual states toward Defense Department requests, see Chapter 12.(Back)

Footnote 23-47: Memo, Legal Adviser, NGB, for Bruce Docherty, Office of the General Counsel, DA, 19 Jul 63, sub: Authority to Require Integration in the National Guard, copy in CMH.(Back)

Footnote 23-48: Ltrs, Chief, NGB, to AG's of Alabama et al., 3 Mar 62, 3 Jul 63, and 9 Dec 63; see also Williams Board Rpt, II: 36.(Back)

Footnote 23-49: Ltr, Maj Gen Raymond H. Fleming, Adjutant General, Louisiana National Guard, to Chief, NGB, 16 Jul 63, copy in CMH.(Back)

Footnote 23-50: See Memos: Chief, NGB, for Gen Counsel, DA, 22 Oct 63, sub: Current Status of Integration of National Guard in Ten Southern States; idem for DASD (CR), 30 Dec 63, sub: Year-End Report on Integration of Negroes in the National Guard; idem for Dep Under SA (Manpower and Res Forces), 9 Jan 64, sub: Meeting With National Chairman of the American Veterans Committee. Copies of all in CMH.(Back)

Footnote 23-51: "Statement by Maj. Gen. Winston C. Wilson, Chief, National Guard Bureau Concerning Integration of the National Guard," 28 Dec 64, copy in CMH; see also New York *Times*, December 30, 1964, and Williams Board Rpt, II:38.(Back)

Footnote 23-52: Memo, Dep SecDef for SA and SecAF, 15 Feb 65, sub: Equality of Opportunity in the National Guard, SD 291.2; see also Memo, Chief, NGB, for Chief, Office of Reserve Components, 27 Jan 65. For examples of how Vance's order was transmitted to the individual states, see Texas Air National Guard Regulation 35-1, 17 March 1965, and State of Michigan General Order No. 34, 2 July 1965. In March 1966 the Army and Air Force published a joint regulation outlining procedures to assure compliance with Title VI in the Army and Air National Guard and designating the Chief of the National Guard Bureau as the responsible official to implement departmental directives regarding all federally assisted activities of the National Guard. See National Guard Regulation 24, 30 Mar 66.(Back)

Footnote 23-53: Congressman Multer first introduced such a bill on 13 January 1949 and pressed, unsuccessfully, for similar measures in each succeeding Congress; see Williams Board Rpt, II: 47-48.(Back)

Footnote 23-54: Memo, DASD (CR) for Burke Marshall, 20 Mar 64, sub: The Civil Rights of Negro Servicemen, copy in CMH.(Back)

Footnote 23-55: Ltr, Actg U.S. Comm of Ed to Superintendent of Public Instruction, Fla., et al., 6 Nov 62, with incls; see also Memo for Rcd, Evans, 20 Nov 62, sub: Schools for Dependents, copies of both in CMH.(Back)

Footnote 23-56: AFNS, Release No. 2851, 17 Aug 62.(Back)

Footnote 23-57: Four similar suits were filed in January 1963 regarding segregation in Huntsville and Mobile, Alabama; Gulfport and Biloxi, Mississippi; and Bossier Parish, Louisiana. Ltr, Atty Gen to President, 24 Jan 63 (released by White House on 26 Jan 63), copy in CMH. See New York *Times*, September 18, 1962.(Back)

Footnote 23-58: Washington *Post*, January 17, 1963.(Back)

Footnote 23-59: Both the Marine Corps and the Navy operated installations in the vicinity of Albany, Georgia.(Back)

Footnote 23-60: Memo, ASD (M) for SA et al., 15 Jul 63, sub: Assignment of Dependents of Military Personnel to Public Schools, ASD(M) 291.2.(Back)

Footnote 23-61: Memo, DASD (CR) for Under SecNav, 4 Dec 63, sub: Dependent Schooling in Closed School Districts; Memo, Asst SecNav for DASD (CR), 20 Dec 63, same sub; both in SecNav files, GenRecsNav. See also Memo, DASD (CR) for Burke Marshall et al., 9 Mar 64, sub: Possible September 1964 School Closings Affecting Military Dependents, copy in CMH.(Back)

Footnote 23-62: Memo, DASD (CR) for Under SA et al., 17 Apr 64, sub: Assignment of Dependents of Military Personnel to Public Schools; see also idem for ASD (M), 2 Apr 64, sub: Segregated Schools and Military Dependents. For an example of how this new responsibility was conveyed to local commanders, see BuPers Notice 5350.5, 26 Jul 63, "Assignment of Dependents of Military Personnel to Public Schools." Copies of all in CMH.(Back)

Footnote 23-63: Memo, DASD (CR) for Under SA et al., 25 May 64, sub: Off-Base Equal Opportunity Inventories, copy in CMH.(Back)

Footnote 23-64: For an example of how these contracts for the education of dependents were tied to federal aid, see the case concerning Columbus Air Force Base, Mississippi, as discussed in Ltr, DASD (CR) to J. Francis Pohlhous, NAACP, 5 Nov 63. For the views of the secretary's race counselor on the Fitt assessment, see Ltr, Evans to Mrs. Frank C. Eubanks, 10 Jun 64. Copies of both in CMH.(Back)

Footnote 23-65: Memo, DASD (CR) for Spec Asst to SecAF for Manpower, Personnel, and Reserve Forces, 23 Jun 64, SecAF files. Similar memos were sent to the Army and Navy the same day. For an example of how these reports were used, see Memo, Spec Asst to DASD (CR) for St. John Barrett, Civil Rights Div, Dept of Justice, 20 Aug 64, sub: Desegregation of Schools Serving Children of Shaw AFB, South Carolina, Personnel. Copies of all in CMH.(Back)

Footnote 23-66: Memo, ASD (M) for Under SA et al., 9 Aug 65, sub: Assignment of Dependents of Military Personnel to Public Schools, ASD (M) 291.2.(Back)

Footnote 23-67: Memo, ASD (M) for SA et al., 25 Mar 64, sub: Non-Discrimination in Civil Schooling of Military Personnel; Ltr, DASD (CR) to Congressman John Bell Williams of Mississippi, 18 Mar 64; Ltr, DASD (M) to Sen. Richard Russell of Georgia, 8 Jul 64; Memo, DASD (CR) for Roy Davenport et al., 20 Apr 64. Copies of all in CMH.(Back)

Footnote 23-68: Memo, Timpane for DASD (CP, IR, & CR), 11 Feb 65, sub: Service Reports on Equal Rights Activities. In a related action the department made military facilities available for the use of the College Entrance Examination Board when that body was confronted with segregated facilities in which to administer its tests; see Memos, Dep Chief, Pers Services Div, USAF, for AFLC et al., 8 Mar 63, sub: College Entrance Examinations, and Evans for DASD (M), 15 Jan 63, sub: College Entrance Examination Board Communication. Fitt opposed this policy on the grounds that it removed a wholesome pressure on the segregated private facilities; see Memo, DASD (CR) for ASD (M), 2 Mar 64, sub: College Entrance Examinations at Military Installations. Fitt was overruled, and the military facilities were provided for the college entrance examinations; see Ltr, Regional Dir, College Entrance Examination Bd, to Evans, 13 Apr 64. Copies of all in CMH.(Back)

Footnote 23-69: Memo, ASD (CR) for SecDef, 29 Oct 63, sub: Family Housing and the Negro Serviceman, Civil Rights Commission Staff Report; Memo, ASD (M) for SecDef, 2 Nov 63, sub: Family Housing for Negro Servicemen; both in ASD (M) 291.2.(Back)

Footnote 23-70: Interv, Bernhard with Wofford, 29 Nov 65, p. 60.(Back)

Footnote 23-71: Memo, ASD (M) for SecDef, 2 Nov 63, sub: Family Housing for Negro Servicemen, ASD (M) 291-2.(Back)

Footnote 23-72: Ltr, DASD (CR) to Chmn, President's Cmte on Equal Opportunity in Housing, 19 Sep 63, copy in CMH; see also Paul Memo.(Back)

Footnote 23-73: Ltr, Fitt to author, 22 May 72.(Back)

Footnote **23-74:** Ltr, Dep SecDef to J. Charles Jones, Chairman, ACCESS, 21 Feb 67, copy in CMH; see also the detailed account of the Department of Defense's housing campaign in Bahr, "The Expanding Role of the Department of Defense," p. 105.(Back)

Footnote **23-75:** ACCESS was one of the several local, biracial open-housing groups that sprang up to fight discrimination in housing during the mid-1960's. The center of this particular group's concern was in the Washington, D.C., suburbs.(Back)

Footnote **23-76:** Ltr, Dep SecDef to Jones, 21 Feb 67, copy in CMH.(Back)

Footnote **23-77:** Ltr, Fitt to author, 22 May 72; see also New York *Times* and Washington *Post*, February 2, 1967.(Back)

Footnote **23-78:** Robert E. Jordan, former DASD (CR) assistant, described the secretary's eagerness to support civil rights initiatives: "He would hardly wait for an explanation, but start murmuring, 'Where do I sign, where do I sign?'" Interv, author with Jordan, 7 Jun 72.(Back)

Footnote **23-79:** Quoted by Brower, "McNamara Seen Now, Full Length," p. 78. The TFX mentioned by McNamara was an allusion to the heated and lengthy controversy that arose during his administration over fighter aircraft for the Navy and Air Force.(Back)

Footnote **23-80:** A weakened version of this bill eventually emerged as the Civil Rights Act of 1968.(Back)

Footnote **23-81:** McNamara, *The Essence of Security*, p. 124.(Back)

Footnote **23-82:** Quoted by Brower, "McNamara Seen Now, Full Length," p. 89.(Back)

Footnote **23-83:** Memo, Dep SecDef for Secys of Military Departments, 11 Apr 67, sub: Equal Opportunity for Military Personnel in Rental of Off-Base Housing. Vance's instructions were spelled out in great detail, replete with charts and forms, in Memo, ASD (M) for Dep Under Secys of Military Departments (Manpower), 22 Apr 67, same sub. Copies of both in CMH.(Back)

Footnote **23-84:** Memos, ASD (M) for Dep Under Secys of Military Departments, 22 Apr and 17 Jul 67, sub: Equal Opportunity for Military Personnel in Rental of Off-Base Housing. For the effect of this order on an individual commander, see article by Charles Hunter in Charleston, South Carolina, *Post*, August 30, 1967. See also Interv, author with Bennett, 13 Dec 73.(Back)

Footnote **23-85:** Intervs, author with McNamara, 11 May 72, and Jordan, 7 Jan 72.(Back)

Footnote **23-86:** McNamara, *The Essence of Security*, p. 126.(Back)

Footnote **23-87:** Interv, author with McNamara, 11 May 72.(Back)

Footnote **23-88:** Joint Resolution 47 of the Maryland General Assembly as cited in Memo, SecDef for Secretaries of Military Departments, 22 Jun 67, sub: Unsatisfactory Housing of Negro Military Families Living Off-Post in the Andrews Air Force Base Area, copy in CMH. See also New York *Times*, May 26, 1967, and Yarmolinsky, *The Military Establishment*, p. 352.(Back)

Footnote **23-89:** Interv, author with Gesell, 3 Nov 74.(Back)

Footnote **23-90:** Memo, SecDef for Secretaries of Military Departments, 22 Jun 67, sub: Unsatisfactory Housing of Negro Military Families Living Off-Post in the Andrews Air Force Base Area, SD files. The quotation is from McNamara's News Conference, 22 June 1967, as quoted in the New York *Times*, June 23, 1967.(Back)

Footnote **23-91:** New York *Times*, June 23, 1967. Rivers did criticize later applications of the housing sanctions; see Washington *Post*, December 28, 1977.(Back)

Footnote **23-92:** Actually, McNamara imposed the sanctions in the first two instances, the Secretary of the Army in the other two.(Back)

Footnote **23-93:** DOD News Release No. 1209-67, 26 Dec 67.(Back)

Footnote **23-94:** Memo, SecDef for Service Secys et al., 17 Jul 67, sub: Off-Base Housing Referral Services, SD files.(Back)

Footnote **23-95:** In *Jones* v. *Mayer* (392 U.S. 409, 421 [1968]) the Supreme Court held that the Civil Rights Act of 1968 "bars all racial discrimination, private as well as public, in the sale or rental of property." For Clifford's response, see Memo, SecDef for Secys of Military Departments, et al., 20 Jun 68; Clark Clifford, News Conference, 20 Jun 68; Memo, ASD (M&RA) for Secys of Military Departments, et al., 25 Nov 68. For instructions concerning legal assistance to servicemen and civilian employees of the Department of Defense under the 1968 Civil Rights Act, see DOD Instr 1338.12, 8 Aug 68. Copy of all in CMH.(Back)

Footnote **23-96:** SecDef News Conference, 29 Jun 68, transcript in CMH.(Back)

Footnote **23-97:** McNamara, *The Essence of Security*, p. 127.(Back)

Footnote **23-98:** Bahr, "*The Expanding Role of the Department of Defense*," p. 123.(Back)

Footnote **23-99:** McNamara, *The Essence of Security*, p. 127.(Back)

Footnote **23-100:** This analysis owes much to the author's correspondence with Alfred Fitt and the interviews with McNamara, Gesell, and Jordan. See also Memo, Timpane tor Stephen Schulman, 11 Feb 65, sub: Service Reports of Equal Rights Activities, and Paul Memo. Copies of all in CMH.(Back)

Footnote **23-101:** Interv, author with Bennett, 13 Dec 73.(Back)

Footnote 24-1: Speaking at a later date on this subject, former Army Chief of Staff J. Lawton Collins observed that "when we look about us and see the deleterious effects of military interference in civilian governments throughout ... many other areas of the world, we can be grateful that American military leaders have generally stuck to their proper sphere." See Memo, Collins for OSD Historian, 21 Aug 76, copy in CMH.(Back)

Footnote 24-2: For an extended discussion of the moral basis of racial reform, see O'Connor's interview with Hesburgh, 27 Mar 66.(Back)

Footnote 24-3: For an extended discussion of the law and racial change, see Greenberg, *Race Relations and American Law*; Charles C. Moskos, Jr., "Racial Integration in the Armed Forces," *American Journal of Sociology* 72 (September 1966): 132-48; Ginzberg, *The Negro Potential*, pp. 127-31.(Back)

Footnote 24-4: Interv, author with Muse, 2 Mar 73.(Back)

Footnote 24-5: Portions of the following discussion have been published in somewhat different form under the title "Armed Forces Integration—Forced or Free?" in *The Military and Society, Proceedings of the Fifth Military Symposium* (U.S. Air Force Academy, 1972).(Back)

Footnote 24-6: Quoted in Senate, Hearings Before the U.S. Senate Committee on Armed Services, *Universal Military Training*, 80th Cong., 2d sess., 1948, pp. 995-96.(Back)

Footnote 24-7: For a discussion of this point, see Yarmolinsky's *The Military Establishment*, pp. 346-51.(Back)

Footnote 24-8: Quoted in Ltr, Muse to Chief of Military History, 2 Aug 76, in CMH.(Back)

Footnote 24-9: *Report of the National Advisory Commission on Civil Disorders*, p. 1.(Back)